S0-BRB-909

A COGNITIVE APPROACH
TO LEARNING DISABILITIES

A
COGNITIVE APPROACH
TO
LEARNING DISABILITIES

SECOND EDITION

Edited by
D. Kim Reid
Wayne P. Hresko
H. Lee Swanson

pro·ed
8700 Shoal Creek Boulevard
Austin, Texas 78758

Printed in the United States of America

Library of Congress Cataloging-in-Publication Data

Cognitive approach to learning disabilities / editors, D. Kim Reid,
    Wayne P. Hresko, H. Lee Swanson ; contributors, Arthur J. Baroody
    . . . [et al.]. — 2nd ed.
        p.   cm.
    Rev. ed. of: A cognitive approach to learning disabilities / D.
    Kim Reid, Wayne P. Hresko. c1981.
    Includes bibliographical references (p.   ) and index.
    ISBN 0-89079-421-9
    1. Learning disabilities—United States.   2. Learning disabled
    children—Education—United States.   3. Constructivism (Education)
    4. Cognitive learning—United States.   I. Reid, D. Kim.
    II. Hresko, Wayne P.   III. Swanson, H. Lee, 1947– .   IV. Baroody,
    Arthur J., 1947– .
    LC4705.C64 1990
    371.9—dc20   90-19787
                                                      CIP

pro·ed
8700 Shoal Creek Boulevard
Austin, Texas 78758

1 2 3 4 5 6 7 8 9 10   96 95 94 93 92 91

Contents

Preface

The purpose of this book is to provide an overview of cognitive approaches to learning disabilities, the theoretical and methodological underpinnings that support them, and the body of knowledge that such work has generated. By *cognitive approaches*, we mean those with the goal of specifying the processes that occur in a student's mind before, during, and after performance.

We made no attempt to gloss over significant differences in the way various cognitive scientists approach the study of learning disabilities, because deference to simplicity and clarity in the face of a richly interesting and complex phenomenon often leads to distortion. We had two criteria for determining what to include: that the work be representative of a cognitive approach and that, compiled, it span the entire range of widely applied options. For a textbook, this focus is unique and provides a more readable, more comprehensive alternative to edited volumes containing summaries of research reports.

Like the first edition, this edition is designed for preservice and in-service students of learning disabilities—teachers, psychologists, physicians, speech and language specialists, diagnosticians, and other professionals who have an interest in the evolving nature of this field. Since the study of learning disabilities, like much of human development, is clearly in a period of great flux, readers need information about how specific formulations were arrived at in order to understand apparently contradictory research findings, including conflicting recommendations for intervention.

CONTENTS OF THE BOOK

Part I introduces the reader to the field of learning disabilities by fleshing out three perspectives: those related to definition and demographics, as well as current educational interventions; the somewhat distinct view of learning disorders, including attention deficit disorder, espoused by the medical community; and those theoretical and methodological frameworks that have been instrumental in producing the research findings reported in subsequent sections of the text.

Chapter 1 examines the issues surrounding the current definitions of learning disabilities. Prevalence figures are presented and discussed. Several influences upon the development of the field of learning disabilities are noted, along with the conclusion that students with learning disabilities are best served by educators from a cognitive perspective. General educational characteristics are discussed, providing an introduction to more in-depth analysis in subsequent chapters. Finally, the chapter discusses the issues surrounding the role of attention in learning disabilities.

Chapter 2 focuses on some current trends that are having an impact on the field of learning disabilities. Specifically, the chapter outlines developments in the area of educational technology, the regular education initiative, school-based consultation, and the need for transitional services.

Chapter 3 is concerned with the medical view of learning disabilities. The physician's view of learning disorders is reviewed, as well as such promising techniques as magnetic resonance imaging, positron emission tomography, and brain electrical activity mapping. The chapter concludes with a discussion of the role of the physician as an interdisciplinary team member in the diagnosis of learning disabilities.

Chapter 4 expresses our belief that ultimately all thinking about learning disabilities is either implicitly or explicitly influenced by some framework or theory. It outlines the major tenets of the three most important perspectives: information processing, constructivist, and ecological approaches. Although the distinctions among these approaches are not always clear, there is one significant difference: The first is reductionistic, the latter two holistic. This presentation paves the way for understanding Parts II and III of the text on information processing, and Part IV, which relies more heavily on constructivist and ecological orientations.

Part II provides an overview of research in the field of learning disabilities motivated from an information processing perspective. The chapters in this section provide substantive findings on the psychological aspects of learning disabilities. Chapter 5 provides an overview of information processing theory as it relates to learning disabilities. Several key figures and models are reviewed. Research is reviewed which suggests that learning disabled students differ from their normal achieving counterparts in the encoding, organizing, storing, and retrieving of information. Greatly simplified, their problems are viewed as an interaction between an executive (high-order) system, strategies, and their knowledge base.

Chapter 6 provides an overview of research findings in memory, a critical area known to be deficient in learning disabled individuals. Memory is viewed as an important area of focus because it reflects applied cognition. What we know about learning disabled students' memory problems is consistent with what we know about young and immature children's memory. A number of principles related to memory strategy instruction of learning disabled students are discussed; these principles relate to the purposes and uses of strategies.

Chapter 7 provides a comprehensive review of John Anderson's Adaptive Control of Thought theory of cognition and skill acquisition as a means to tie together research on memory, language, and problem solving. This chapter reviews information on the structure of the learner's knowledge base, the manner in which knowledge is acquired and refined, and the manner in which the learner regulates and uses knowledge. Three dimensions of this model that are discussed are diagnosis, remediation, and theory development.

Part III of the text focuses on assessment practice from a cognitive perspective. Like Part II, this part builds upon some of the earlier concepts presented. Chapter 8 reviews four models that characterize current assessment practice in the field of learning disabilities. The models are assessed along two basic dimensions: attributes versus the situational behaviors that occur in a context, and passive versus active problem solving. These dimensions focus on the extent to which the abilities of the learning disabled student are inferred from test performance and the manner in which social features of the environment are assessed through a problem solving approach.

Within the theoretical and research findings discussed earlier in the text, Chapters 9 and 10 provide a cognitive model of assessment. The model focuses on five conceptual planes: strategy, strategy abstraction, knowledge base, executive functioning, and metacognition. Chapter 9 discusses the assumptions of the assessment model, with particular focus on the executive function, knowledge base, and strategy planes. Chapter 10 extends the discussion by focusing on strategy abstraction and metacognitive functioning. Chapter 10 also illustrates how cognitive assessment occurs, as well as the implications of the proposed cognitive model.

Part IV treats learning disabilities within an educational context. The chapters in this part build on the knowledge of the nature of learning disabilities that has been generated from information processing research. The major breakthroughs in instruction, however, have been based in constructivist and ecological orientations, so this section relies most heavily on them.

Chapter 11 begins with a review of some characteristics that learning disabled students exhibit as a group, and then addresses concerns that dominate the instructional literature. These include a reevaluation of what the teaching–learning interchange should look like, a delineation of the elements of the immediate instructional environment, and emergent changes in expectations for the roles teachers will play. Educator's awareness of and interest in capitalizing on early spontaneous knowledge and internal motivations for learning are also discussed.

Chapter 12 focuses on the oral language characteristics of individuals with learning disabilities. Oral language has been a focal point in understanding learning disabilities. An orientation to a model of language is presented which elaborates on language form, function, and use. The research reviewed interprets studies dealing with semantics, syntax, phonology, and pragmatics.

Chapter 13 is a compilation of new directions in our understanding of the complications of literacy acquisition and of new approaches to literacy. Dyslexic and garden variety readers are characterized as constituting a continuum in which phonological processing attenuates as the disorder becomes more severe. Organizational strategies and techniques that have been demonstrated to be effective for learning to read, as well as reading and writing to learn, are discussed in some detail. Finally, the characteristic writing problems associated with learning disabilities are described. The conclusion derived from these overviews is that the most powerful instructional environments are highly interactive; allow mutual, contingent mediation among students or between teachers and groups of students; and address functionally meaningful, content-specific tasks holistically.

Chapter 14, on mathematics, opens with a review of constructivist principles of mental functioning and applies these to both formal and informal mathematics learning. After caveats are offered with respect to difficulties commonly experienced by so-called mathematically disabled learners, a menu of learning difficulties and instructional interventions is presented.

The final chapter in this text presents something of a futuristic perspective: an argument for holism as a structuring vehicle for the study of learning disabilities. Although holistic influences are obvious in both constructivist and ecological orientations, the position taken in this chapter is a strong one, suggesting that holism is increasingly dominating a wide spectrum of scientific thought and is to be preferred as *the* guiding principle undergirding the understanding of learning problems. When the context is taken into account as an indispensable aspect of behavior, explanations of specific behaviors assume new and different dimensions.

DIFFERENCES BETWEEN THE FIRST AND SECOND EDITIONS

The first edition of this text advocated the use of the definition of learning disabilities embedded in PL 94-142. In the interim, the National Joint Committee on Learning Disabilities issued a new definition that eliminated several of the problems associated with the earlier one. For example, it deleted the phrase "basic psychological processes" in reference to the causative factors of learning problems. This new definition is advocated here.

In keeping with the new definition and the direction the field has taken since 1981, Part II of this edition takes a more integrated and more sophisticated view of the causes and assessment of learning problems. The results of the huge number of research studies that have been conducted during the last decade are synthesized into a meaningful and readable portrait of the nature of learning difficulties.

In the first edition, the recommendations for instructional intervention were theoretically based and in advance of the research that subsequently documented their effectiveness. Although this body of research has enlarged upon, polished, and provided specificity to our theoretical formulations, it does, by and large, support those major principles that we outlined in 1981. The organizational strategies and metascripts that have been developed to accomplish those instructional objectives constitute a significant departure from traditional special education and, although they are gaining widespread attention and acceptance, still represent an approach of limited, although demonstrably powerful, application.

Contributors

We would like to thank those experts who contributed chapters to this text. These authors were selected because they embody the best of the tradition they represent. Although any number of other points of view might have been included, those we selected provide a good sense of the scope of work that is currently being conducted in this field and that is likely to characterize the field's efforts in the future.

Arthur J. Baroody, PhD
College of Education
University of Illinois
Champaign, IL 61820

Nancy M. Bray, EdD
University Affiliated Center
Southwestern Medical School
Dallas, TX 75235

John B. Cooney, PhD
Department of Educational Psychology
University of Northern Colorado
Greeley, CO 80631

Lous Heshusius, PhD
Special Education
York University
North York, Ontario
Canada MEJ 1P3

Wayne P. Hresko, PhD
Programs in Special Education
College of Education
P.O. Box 13857
University of North Texas
Denton, TX 76203-3857

Rene S. Parmar, PhD
State University of New York, Buffalo
Department of Learning and Instruction
593 Baldy Hall
Amherst, NY 14260

D. Kim Reid, PhD
4340 Windhaven
Dallas, TX 75287-2963

H. Lee Swanson, PhD
Faculty of Education
University of British Columbia
Vancouver, British Columbia
Canada V6T 125

Mark Swanson, MD, MPH
University of Affiliated Program
University of Arkansas
Little Rock, AK 72202

PART I

PERSPECTIVES ON LEARNING DISABILITIES

Understanding learning disabilities involves integrating a number of perspectives. This section focuses on the orientations and contributions of the educational and medical community, and the interface with three dominant research orientations: information processing, constructivism, and the ecological approach.

Understanding differences among definitions allows one to become attuned to differing professional opinions. Each individual involved with learning disabled students must solve definitional issues for him- or herself. The definitional orientation a person adopts serves to focus intervention and instructional practices.

The medical profession has had a profound effect on the field of learning disabilities. Some of the seminal research forming the foundation of the learning disabilities field has its basis in the medical profession. To effectively interact with medical personnel, learning disabilities professionals must be aware of their orientation to the field.

This section ends with a discussion of the three most important current theories of learning that are having an impact on the field of learning disabilities: information processing, constructivism, and the ecological approach. Just as definitions focus our individual orientation, an individual's theoretical orientation to learning determines what one accepts as significant and important research.

1

The Educational Perspective

WAYNE P. HRESKO AND

RENE S. PARMAR

The classification *learning disabilities* is the only category of exceptionality that is defined as an educational phenomenon, necessarily based in the context of school learning. Although causes and dimensions of learning disabilities have been researched and treated by physicians, psychologists, optometrists, speech therapists, and so forth, *classification as a person with learning disabilities requires that the student evidence difficulties in school subjects.* Central nervous system (CNS) dysfunction is often cited as the presumed cause of learning disabilities; however, no policy regulating identification procedures requires a diagnosis of brain damage for an individual to be classified as learning disabled. Since the passage of Public Law (PL) 94-142, learning disabilities have been defined as delays in acquiring or using knowledge in the areas of reading, writing, mathematics, or oral language. Consequently, the major responsibility for the identification, classification, and remediation of learning disabilities rests with the educational community.

State and local education agencies are given considerable latitude in determining criteria to be used in classifying a student as having learning disabilities. As a result, there is a serious lack of consensus at both govern-

3

mental and professional levels (Algozzine & Ysseldyke, 1987). Current definitions allow students to be served in special education settings without determination of the exact *nature* (McKinney, 1987) or *degree of severity* of the learning handicap. Students whose low achievement may be attributed to any of a number of factors, such as limited English proficiency, poor motivation, social disadvantage, or environmental disadvantage, find themselves in classrooms for the learning disabled. For example, learning disability programs have become primary placement programs for minority children who are low achievers. In Texas, Hispanic students are overrepresented by a factor of 300% (Ortiz & Yates, 1983). Upper–middle-class low-achieving children whose parents cannot accept diagnoses of emotional disturbance or mental retardation choose learning disabilities as an acceptable alternative. Disproportionately high numbers of children identified as learning disabled are common in high-income school districts. Other children who are having learning "problems" but who do not clearly exhibit specific learning disabilities are often classified as such so that they can qualify for services.

The learning disabilities field, rather than being guided by professionally developed direction, is buffeted by social, economic, and political factors. A number of authors have chosen to examine the field of learning disabilities from the viewpoint of societal control; that is, learning disability exists as a result of the need to subjugate a portion of society in order that the remainder may feel superior. Sleeter (1986) suggested that the learning disabilities field grew out of the school reform movement of the 1950s. As standards were increased, school officials were in need of a method of dealing with the middle-class children for whom parents did not want the stigma of the existing handicapping conditions. This view is not widely held, however, and has caused considerable controversy (Kavale & Forness, 1987). For an in-depth analysis of the social and political aspects of the learning disability classification, the interested reader is referred to Franklin (1987) for a series of essays and to Coles (1987) for a scathing critique.

Clearly, numerous factors impinge upon the diagnosis of learning disability. Many of these factors relate to social or political reasons, whereas others relate to the components of the definitions used. Reasons for this lack of consensus and conformity become apparent when current definitions in usage are examined.

The Definition of Learning Disability

Definitions of learning disabilities are numerous. Hammill (1990) has identified 11 definitions that are in various stages of acceptance by the profession, with each stressing different elements. However, two theoretical definitions prevail: (a) the federal definition as provided in PL 94-142 and modified by the United States Office of Education (1977), and (b) the National Joint Committee on Learning Disabilities' (NJCLD) (1983) definition.[1] A third definition was proposed by the Interagency Committee on Learning Disabilities (1987). These three definitions, along with the definition from the 1968 National Advisory Committee on Handicapped Children and that from the Learning Disabilities Association of America (formerly Association for Children and Adults with Learning Disabilities [ACLD]), are presented in Table 1–1. Table 1–2 presents the commonality of elements across the 11 definitions identified by Hammill.

Definition of Learning Disability in PL 94-142

The federal definition of learning disability is the outgrowth of a series of meetings held during the developmental phase of PL 94-142. As with all definitions of learning disabilities, it is a definition by consensus. The implications of the consensus method for reaching agreement are that (a) no organization or agency necessarily supports *all* aspects of the definition, and (b) operational procedures are left vague to avoid philosophical conflict. Thus, the definition has come under criticism from a variety of perspectives, as listed in Table 1–3.

This definition is used by over half of the states, whereas a modified definition is used in the remaining states, except Kansas. Since the federal definition lacks specificity, there is much room for inter- and intrastate variance. The differences in prevalence and incidence figures are reported elsewhere in this chapter.

Definition of Learning Disability by the NJCLD

NJCLD developed a consensus definition to clarify some ambiguities fostered by PL 94-142. This definition is endorsed by all of the major organizations involved with the education of the learning disabled, but as of January 1989, only one state, Kentucky, had adopted it. While it does provide a more concrete statement regarding etiology, it also raises some unanswered questions. Table 1–4 contains a critique of this definition.

---

1. The member organizations of the NJCLD are the Council for Learning Disabilities, Division for Learning Disabilities, International Reading Association, Orton Dyslexia Society, American Speech–Language–Hearing Association, Learning Disabilities Association of America (formerly the Association for Children and Adults with Learning Disabilities), National Association of School Psychologists, and Division for Children with Communication Disorders.

TABLE 1-1
Current Definitions of Learning Disabilities

The term "specific learning disability" means a disorder in one or more of the basic psychological processes involved in understanding or in using language, spoken or written, which may manifest itself in an imperfect ability to listen, speak, read, write, spell, or do mathematical calculations. The term includes such conditions as perceptual handicaps, brain injury, minimal brain dysfunction, dyslexia, and developmental aphasia. The term does not include children who have learning disabilities which are primarily the result of visual, hearing, or motor handicaps; of mental retardation; of emotional disturbance; or of environmental, cultural, or economic disadvantage. (PL 94-142 as modified, USOE, 1977, p. 65083)

"Learning disabilities" is a general term that refers to a heterogeneous group of disorders manifested by significant difficulties in the acquisition and use of listening, speaking, reading, writing, reasoning, or mathematical abilities. These disorders are intrinsic to the individual, presumed to be due to central nervous system dysfunction, and may occur across the life span. Problems in self-regulatory behaviors, social perception, and social interaction may exist with learning disabilities but do not by themselves constitute a learning disability. Although learning disabilities may occur concomitantly with other handicapping conditions (e.g., sensory impairment, mental retardation, serious emotional disturbance) or with extrinsic influences (e.g., cultural differences, insufficient or inappropriate instruction), they are not the result of those conditions or influences. (National Joint Committee on Learning Disabilities, 1988, p. 1)

"Learning disabilities" is a generic term that refers to a heterogeneous group of disorders manifested by significant difficulties in the acquisition and use of listening, speaking, reading, writing, reasoning, or mathematical abilities, *or of social skills*. These disorders are intrinsic to the individual and presumed to be due to central nervous system dysfunction. Even though a learning disability may occur concomitantly with other handicapping conditions (e.g., sensory impairment, mental retardation, social and emotional disturbance), *with* socioenvironmental influences (e.g., cultural differences, insufficient or inappropriate instruction, psychogenic factors), *and especially with attention deficit disorder, all of which may cause learning problems, a learning disability* is not the direct result of those conditions or influences. (National Institute of Child Health and Human Development, Interagency Committee on Learning Disabilities, 1987)

Children with special learning disabilities exhibit a disorder in one or more of the basic psychological processes involved in understanding or in using spoken or written languages. These may be manifested in disorders of listening, thinking, talking, reading, writing, spelling, or arithmetic. They include

---

TABLE 1-1 (continued)

---

conditions which have been referred to as perceptual handicaps, brain injury, minimal brain dysfunction, dyslexia, developmental aphasia, etc. They do not include learning problems which are due primarily to visual, hearing, or motor handicaps; to mental retardation or emotional disturbance; or to environmental disadvantage. (National Advisory Committee on Handicapped Children, 1968)

Specific learning disabilities is a chronic condition of presumed neurological origin which selectively interferes with the development, integration, and/or demonstration of verbal and/or nonverbal abilities. Specific learning disabilities exist as a distinct handicapping condition and vary in manifestations and degree of severity. Throughout life, the condition can affect self-esteem, education, vocation, socialization, and/or daily living activities. (Association for Children with Learning Disabilities, 1986, p. 15)

Definition of Learning Disability by the Interagency Committee

In the 1987 document, *Learning Disabilities: A Report to the U.S. Congress* (Interagency Committee on Learning Disabilities, 1987), the usefulness of the NJCLD definition was acknowledged, but two significant changes were proposed (see Table 1-1; the changes are noted in italic). Research projects currently under consideration for funding by the National Institute of Neurological and Communicative Disorders and Stroke must use this definition *instead of* the PL 94-142 of the NJCLD definition, but it has not been adopted by any state or federal agency. The Interagency Committee on Learning Disabilities (ICLD) (1987, p. 222) acknowledges the problems that changes in the federal definition would create. The changes would (a) have the potential for increasing prevalence figures at a time when the government is attempting to reduce them, (b) necessitate a revision of the Education of All Handicapped Children Act, and (c) raise legal questions regarding the wording of the NJCLD definition. Since this definition is an extension of the NJCLD, all of the criticisms that apply to the NJCLD definition also apply to the committee. Additional criticisms from the National Institute of Child Health and Human Development are in Table 1-5.

Problems Common to All Definitions

There are significant problems with all definitions currently in use in the field of learning disabilities. They *describe* characteristics of learning disability but

TABLE 1-2
Elements of Learning Disabilities Definitions

Definition	Underachievement determination	CNS dysfunction	Process clause	Life span	Language	Academic	Thinking	Other	Allows for multihandicap
Kirk (1962)	Intraindividual	Yes	Yes	Yes	Yes	Yes	No	No	Yes
Bateman (1965)	Aptitude–Achievement	No	Yes	No	No	No	No	No	Yes
NACHC (1968)	Intraindividual	Yes	Yes	No	Yes	Yes	Yes	No	Yes
Northwestern (1969)	Aptitude–Achievement	No	Yes	No	Yes	Yes	No	Spatial Orientation	Yes
CEC/DCLD (1967, 1971)	Intraindividual	Yes	Yes	No	No	No	No	No	No
Wepman et al. (1975)	Intraindividual	No	Yes	No	No	Yes	No	No	—[a]
USOE (1976)	Aptitude–Achievement	No	Yes	No	Yes	Yes	No	No	Yes
USOE (1977)	Intraindividual	Yes	Yes	Yes	Yes	Yes	No	No	Yes
NJCLD (1988)	Intraindividual	Yes	No	Yes	Yes	Yes	Yes	No	Yes
ACLD (1986)	Intraindividual	Yes	No	Yes	Yes	Yes	Yes	Integration; Motor	—[a]
ICLD (1987)	Intraindividual	Yes	No	Yes	Yes	Yes	Yes	Social Skills	Yes

[a]Definitions silent on this element.

From "On Defining Learning Disabilities: An Emerging Consensus" by D. D. Hammill, 1990, *Journal of Learning Disabilities*, 23(2), p. 81. Copyright 1990 by PRO-ED. Reprinted with permission.

TABLE 1–3
Critique of the PL 94-142 Definition

---

1. The term *children* is restrictive because learning disabilities continue into adolescence and adulthood.

2. *Basic psychological processes* are defined differently by persons supporting different theoretical positions.

3. "Spelling" has been eliminated because it is subsumed under other areas of functioning (i.e., written expression) (U.S. Office of Education, 1977).

4. Inclusion of *specifically referenced conditions* (i.e., perceptual handicap, dyslexia, minimal brain dysfunction) produces confusion by equating learning disabilities with other ill-defined conditions.

5. The *exclusion* clause suggests that learning disabilities cannot occur in conjunction with other handicapping conditions. It is, however, possible for learning disabilities to be either secondary to or combined with other conditions.

6. *Imperfect ability* does not specify the degree of severity needed for classification.

7. The *exclusion of environmental, cultural, or economic disadvantage* precludes interactive factors and fails to acknowledge the contextual nature of learning.

---

do not specify underlying cause. All of the definitions refer to a condition that is intrinsic to the individual and related to either basic psychological problems or CNS dysfunction. In daily practice, however, these conditions are neither diagnosed nor inferred.

Reference is made to "significant" problems in all definitions, but what constitutes "significant" is elaborated only in state and local operational definitions. Consequently, considerable latitude exists from state to state. Table 1–6 indicates what the various components are of learning disabilities definitions, how often the components occur in definitions, and whether the components are used as diagnostic criteria (McNutt, 1986).

In conclusion, limitations exist within each of the current definitions. The most recent revision of the NJCLD definition offers the most promise. With the recognition that social disabilities and environmental influences may interact with and therefore compound learning disabilities, the NJCLD definition more comprehensively addresses the concerns of many professionals. In addition, CNS dysfunction must be interpreted to include not only structural anomalies, but also information processing difficulties. Finally, the

---

TABLE 1–4
Critique of the NJCLD Definition

---

1. Individuals can be labeled without a clear specification of the nature or severity of the learning problem.

2. Problems in defining "significant" lead to many of the inconsistencies across the states regarding definition and prevalence.

3. *Intrinsic* may imply a structural deficit, neither correctable by nor amenable to educational methods.

4. The definition fails to address specific versus global disabilities. Specificity changes as the individual grows older. With young children, disabilities are usually specific. As the child grows older, however, disabilities appear to transcend specific academic areas and become more diffuse.

5. The definition does not give sufficient consideration to the interaction of environment and individual abilities; thus, children from minority cultures are overrepresented in learning disabilities classes.

TABLE 1–5
Critique of the National Institute of Child Health
and Human Development Definition

---

1. The potential impact of environmental conditions is acknowledged as affecting the manifestation of learning disabilities.

2. Socioemotional factors are recognized as contributing to learning disabilities.

3. Undue prominence is given to attention deficit disorders as a major cause of learning disabilities. There is no evidence to support such a claim. On the other hand, there is some indication that learning difficulties may be the precipitating factor in attentional problems.

---

question of specificity of learning disabilities must be addressed. As some have suggested, the concept of specific disabilities (Stanovich, 1987) and the concept of homogeneous grouping based on the given disabilities (Siegel, 1988) are both probably ineffective. Learning disabilities are manifest across domains of cognitive functioning (Siegel, 1988; Siegel & Heaven, 1986; Siegel & Ryan, 1984; Siegel & Ryan, 1988), and educational approaches must

TABLE 1–6
Amount of Agreement in Learning Disabilities Definitions and Criteria

Component	Definition	Criteria	Amount of agreement
Process disorder	97.9%*	13.0%	Low
Language	87.2%*	100.0%ª†	High
Academic	100.0%*	100.0%ª†	High
Neurology	76.6%*	—	Low
Exclusion	91.5%*	95.7%†	High
Discrepancy	19.1%	100.0%†	Low
Failure to achieve	19.1%	84.4%†	Low
Minimum IQ	6.4%	26.1%	Medium

ªThe language and academic components within the criteria were satisfied through the discrepancy component where the seven (or more) areas were listed.

*Component is in the federal definition. †Component is in the federal criteria.

From "The Status of Learning Disabilities in the States: Consensus or Controversy?" by G. McNutt, 1986, *Journal of Learning Disabilities, 19*, p. 13. Copyright 1986 by PRO-ED. Reprinted by permission.

address all aspects of the individual's utilization of the information processing system.

The Prevalence of Learning Disability

The PL 94-142 definition of learning disabilities provided the impetus for widespread growth in the number of available educational programs. In 1968, only 13 states offered programs for students with learning disabilities. One year later, learning disabilities was added to the official list of handicapping conditions by Congress, and 43 states offered programs. By 1970, a survey of elementary and secondary public schools conducted by the federal government, revealed that *over 1 million children* had been diagnosed as having learning disabilities, more students than had been labeled mentally retarded, and second only to the number with speech impairments. The U.S. Office of Education (USOE) in 1974–1975 reported that approximately 2 million children were learning disabled, compared with 1.5 million who were mentally retarded. Only 250,000 of the learning disabled population were being served, however, compared with the 1.25 million mentally retarded children enrolled in public schools. By 1978–1979, 1.15 million children were reported to be receiving services as learning disabled, whereas only 920,000 mentally retarded children were receiving special education. Clearly, some powerful social and political factors were influencing special education service delivery (Anderson, Martinez, & Rich, 1980; Carrier, 1986; Chandler, 1980).

Prevalence figures are subject to fluctuations, due to such factors as the definition employed, the type of discrepancy formula used (if any), the academic areas tested, and the characteristics of the population to which the individual child belongs (e.g., age group, intelligence level, level of basal performance and cutoff scores required on given evaluation devices, and sociocultural factors). As a result, estimates of the number of learning disabled can vary from 1% to 30% of the school-aged population.

PL 94-142 in 1975 included a provision that no more than 2% of the school-aged population in a state could be classified as learning disabled. As a result of public and professional pressures, in December 1977, the USOE removed this 2% limit. As reasons, the USOE cited (a) the nebulous nature of the disorder, (b) the fact that other conditions had no comparable limitation, and (c) the fact that the limit might hinder future research.

Although imposing a limit would have required professionals to take a serious look at definitional issues, removing the limit allowed considerable variation. For example, prevalence declines when the definition becomes more exclusive. Conversely, prevalence increases when the definition becomes more liberal (i.e., "learning problems found in children who have traditionally been classified as mildly handicapped, whether it be emotionally disturbed, mentally retarded, or learning disabled" [Hallahan & Kauffman, 1976, p. 28]). Liberalizing the definition results in a diluted conceptualization of learning disabilities, which may more accurately be referred to as learning problems.

The argument for collapsing across groups of children with learning problems (i.e., learning disabled, mild behavior disordered, and mildly retarded), often referred to as generic classification, is both a practical and a theoretical one. Some argue that little data exist that either support or challenge the efficacy of subgrouping mildly handicapped children for instruction. Although Becker (1978) demonstrated that performance differences exist which discriminate among the groups, nobody has yet shown that the heterogeneity of a combined group increases instructional complexity or reduces effectiveness.

If we disregard the issue of generic learning problems, and focus on accepted definitions of learning disabilities, the question arises as to what constitutes an *acceptable* prevalence figure for learning disabilities. When a concerted effort is made to exclude those children whose problems are not really handicapping, as well as those who are more appropriately subsumed under other categories of handicapping conditions, the 1% to 3% prevalence estimate seems quite satisfactory.

A number of researchers have concluded that the prevalence of learning disabilities exceeds the preferred 3% figure (Bruinincks & Weatherman,

1970; Hallahan, Keller, & Ball, 1986; Meier, 1971; Myklebust & Boshes, 1969; Shepard & Smith, 1983). Table 1–7 presents the prevalence of learning disabilities for the United States as of 1987. First, note that the number of children served exceeds 1.9 million students, which represents an increase of over 1 million children in the past 10 years. Second, note that this figure represents in excess of 40% of all children served in special education.

Keogh (1987) recently concluded an extensive review of prevalence figures. Her conclusions indicate that prevalence figures generally exceed all conservative estimates, *but are relatively stable across states*. Keogh compared the prevalence figures from states having over 200,000 handicapped individuals and those having fewer than 50,000. She found that the prevalence of learning disabilities is quite similar (46% vs. 42%). Furthermore, the prevalence of learning disabilities in the rural state of South Dakota is 30% of the handicapped population, whereas the prevalence in the generally suburban state of Massachusetts is 35%. This relative consistency across large and small, rural and urban states suggests that whatever definitions are being used, the numbers of children being identified are virtually the same. Whether the *learning and academic characteristics* of the various groups are comparable is unknown, however.

The Effect of Discrepancy Formulas on Prevalence Figures

Current practice leans toward the use of discrepancy formulas to determine standard score differences between aptitude and achievement (i.e., the difference between an IQ score and a reading score). The use of discrepancy formulas, however, is controversial (Algozzine, Forgone, Mercer, & Trifiletti, 1979; Hanna, Dyck, & Holen, 1979; Reynolds, 1984–1985). In a recent position paper, the Council for Learning Disabilities (CLD) (1987) called for phasing out the use of discrepancy formulas. CLD argued that such formulas are inadequate because they focus on single aspects of learning, are based on inadequate or inappropriate assessment instruments, fail to take into account correlations between IQ and academic areas, and do not discriminate between the learning disabled and underachievers. They suggest that examiners perform more comprehensive diagnostic evaluations, that agencies devise alternative service delivery systems, and, when necessary, that the graduated regressed standard score be used for quantification of discrepancy.[2]

The most prevalent type of discrepancy formula sets a difference of a specific number of standard score points as a critical discrepancy (e.g., 15

---

2. The graduated regressed standard score is determined by taking into account the correlation between the measured IQ and the measured achievement.

TABLE 1-7
Number of Children 3-21 Years Old Served Under EHA-B
By Handicapping Condition During the School Year 1986-1987

State	All conditions	Learning disabled	Mentally retarded	Emotionally disturbed
Alabama	90,419	28,889	31,374	6,213
Alaska	9,095	5,356	334	343
Arizona	51,989	27,983	5,251	3,950
Arkansas	44,792	22,870	11,071	461
California	388,713	219,961	26,733	9,772
Colorado	45,198	22,455	2,999	8,351
Connecticut	61,392	28,446	3,973	12,635
Delaware	11,419	6,660	751	1,818
District of Columbia	2,527	980	192	72
Florida	173,277	70,063	20,660	19,134
Georgia	90,270	25,742	24,106	16,042
Hawaii	11,171	6,558	1,065	475
Idaho	18,323	9,614	2,967	479
Illinois	210,415	94,525	20,685	19,612
Indiana	97,425	34,806	17,777	3,588
Iowa	55,738	22,069	11,858	6,104
Kansas	40,351	16,757	5,883	4,083
Kentucky	70,352	21,450	18,019	2,557
Louisiana	69,500	31,501	9,614	3,320
Maine	25,503	10,043	3,541	3,664
Maryland	88,530	49,891	5,976	3,539
Massachusetts	128,106	44,510	27,317	17,557
Michigan	149,384	64,841	15,335	18,965
Minnesota	81,986	36,919	12,410	9,571
Mississippi	54,626	24,533	10,059	290
Missouri	97,218	41,950	14,541	8,070
Montana	14,755	7,532	1,195	634
Nebraska	29,899	12,068	4,831	2,170
Nevada	14,026	8,142	927	908
New Hampshire	15,354	9,241	799	1,399
New Jersey	166,196	75,807	6,132	14,216
New Mexico	29,413	13,083	2,298	2,927
New York	250,318	149,800	22,527	38,461
North Carolina	105,945	44,667	21,455	7,143
North Dakota	11,664	5,248	1,520	467
Ohio	191,445	74,723	43,740	7,335
Oklahoma	63,986	28,041	11,388	1,142

TABLE 1-7 (continued)

State	All conditions	Learning disabled	Mentally retarded	Emotionally disturbed
Oregon	41,784	25,360	1,704	2,104
Pennsylvania	181,625	74,092	32,854	13,902
Puerto Rico	38,686	8,126	19,450	1,559
Rhode Island	18,705	12,358	1,045	1,264
South Carolina	72,338	24,616	17,343	6,345
South Dakota	13,534	5,317	1,526	510
Tennessee	95,169	44,571	14,268	2,045
Texas	290,185	156,760	25,928	21,869
Utah	40,882	15,958	3,302	10,720
Vermont	8,855	4,398	788	476
Virginia	101,874	47,306	14,275	7,428
Washington	66,436	33,567	7,798	3,159
West Virginia	45,857	19,394	9,365	2,317
Wisconsin	73,351	22,710	5,250	9,367
Wyoming	9,564	4,786	504	489
American Samoa	114	0	50	0
Guam	1,463	732	518	0
Northern Marianas	184	100	20	0
Trust Territories	—	—	—	—
Virgin Islands	—	—	—	—
Bureau of Indian Affairs	5,366	2,864	458	273
U.S. & Insular Areas	4,166,692	1,900,739	577,749	341,294
50 States, District of Columbia, & Puerto Rico	4,159,565	1,897,043	576,703	341,021

Note. Data as of October 1, 1987.

From *Tenth Annual Report to Congress on the Implementation of the Education of the Handicapped Act*, p. B-4, by the U.S. Office of Education, 1988, Washington, DC.

points, 1 *SD*, etc.; Reynolds, 1984–1985). Unfortunately, such formulas have deficiencies, most noticeably their failure to adjust discrepancy figures as a function of IQ or other relevant factors (Mercer, Hughes, & Mercer, 1985). Thanks to the work of Cone and Wilson (1981), the use of more comprehensive and more appropriate statistical techniques, such as regression, are beginning to gain acceptance. More complex analyses take into account the correlations between aptitude and achievement, statistical properties of the tests used, and intelligence level of the students.

The Current and Future State of Affairs

Prevalence figures have been climbing rather dramatically over the past 20 years. During this time, many professionals have suggested that inadequate assessment instruments and poor assessment practices are primarily responsible. Hallahan et al. (1986), however, argued that assessment practices have become better defined and more consistent. Although they did not suggest that definitional issues have been resolved, they argued "that the definition and identification criteria for learning disabilities are at least as well articulated, and perhaps more so, than those for other categories in special education" (p. 13). Similar conclusions have been reached by others (Cone, Wilson, Bradley, & Reese, 1985; Mercer et al., 1985).

Even with better definitions and criteria, many inadequate assessment instruments and inappropriate assessment practices remain in use. More technically adequate measures and better trained teachers and assessment personnel alone, however, will not reduce prevalence figures. Theoretical and operational definitions must be refined if decreases in prevalence figures are to be attained. As Kavale (1987) noted, "the lack of theory is . . . a primary reason why we seldom, if ever, experience any dramatic breakthroughs in LD" (p. 23).

Rising prevalence rates can be attributed more to changes in the provision of services than to the characteristics of appraisal instruments. More services are being provided today than at any other time. Emphasis on providing services to secondary and transition (vocationally oriented) students has increased the prevalence figures and will probably continue to do so. As the provisions of PL 99-457 are implemented, services will be provided to growing numbers of preschool children, and the prevalence figures will most assuredly rise further.

Trends Influencing the Learning Disabilities Field

Explanations of and interventions for learning disabilities have been based upon several models, including the perceptual or perceptual–motor process deficit model, the brain dysfunction or medical model, and the behavioral model. These three models form the mainstream historical legacy of the field (Carnine & Woodward, 1988; Poplin, 1988).

There are, of course, other orientations to both the understanding and treatment of learning disabilities, many of which are controversial. These controversial treatments include, but are not limited to, neurophysiological retraining (patterning and optometric visual training, use of Dramamine for vestibular dysfunction, applied kinesiology (cranial faults, cloacal reflexes, and ocular lock), and orthomolecular medicine (megavitamins, trace elements, hypoglycemia, food additives, and refined sugars). In a review of these controversial approaches, Silver (1987) concluded that for most of them, the research base is either nonexistent or severely lacking. Because these approaches are not considered mainstream, they are not reviewed here. Instead, the focus is on the three major models.

Tenets of the Perceptual and Perceptual-Motor Models

The perceptual, perceptual–motor, or basic psychological process model is associated with the work of outstanding figures in the development of the field of learning disabilities, such as Strauss and Werner, Lehtinen, Cruickshank, Frostig, and Kirk. Strauss and Lehtinen's work focused on basic perceptual tasks effective in differentiating mentally retarded persons who were brain injured from those who were not. It was subsequently discovered that people with normal intelligence who had learning problems exhibited performances and characteristics similar to those of brain-damaged mentally retarded individuals. The assumption was made that brain injury could be inferred from the overt characteristics. The explanation was that learning disabilities were manifestations of the brain's inability to process information adequately. Basic psychological processes, namely, perception, attention, and memory, were thought to be affected. Thus, learning disabilities were viewed as deficits or deficiencies in hardware that affected the way an individual interpreted or represented information. For an in-depth historical perspective, through 1974, the reader is referred to Wiederholt (1974) and Myers and Hammill (1990).

As with any seminal contribution to science, this view has come under criticism. During the last 20 years, researchers have been generally unable to support the view that perceptual or perceptual–motor disabilities are the cause of most learning disabilities (see Hammill & Larsen, 1974; Kavale & Mattison, 1983; Larsen & Hammill, 1975; Spear & Sternberg, 1987).

Recently, Kavale and Forness' (1986) meta-analysis suggested that the differences reported by Strauss and Werner were minute and did not reflect meaningful differences. (Meta-analysis is a statistical technique used to summarize scores from different research studies.) Although some people may have impaired abilities to process the physical attributes of information, they represent an extremely small percentage of all learning disabled individuals (see Liberman, 1985; Vellutino, 1986). According to Spear and Sternberg (1987), "The bulk of available evidence indicates that the deficits of disabled readers are verbal rather than nonverbal and cognitive rather than perceptual in nature" (p. 21).

Furthermore, there is little evidence to suggest that significant organic (structural or hardware) problems form the basis of attentional or memory problems. Fewer than 1 of 10 individuals referred for neurological evaluations are actually diagnosed as having organic brain damage.

The Medical Perspective

The medical perspective views learning disabilities as a function of neurological, neurobiological, genetic, or hormonal dysfunction related to the biological functioning of the brain. It is not surprising that the medical profession would have an impact on the field of learning disabilities. As Wiederholt (1974) and Kavale and Forness (1986) noted, the field grew out of the research on the oral and written language characteristics of individuals with acquired brain injury. Beginning in the early 1800s, several physicians began investigating the phenomenon of aphasia. Eventually, various models of aphasia were developed which implicated different areas of the brain. Later in the 1800s and early 1900s, others began expanding this study to reading and writing.

The medical influence in learning disabilities was further extended by the work of Ernest Duyere in 1925 (Koupernik, MacKeith, & Francis-Williams, 1975). Duyere attempted to establish a link between overt behavior and brain lesions. He reasoned that if a particular brain lesion could be associated with an overt behavior, then the reverse diagnosis could be made (i.e., an overt behavior could be used as indicator of a specific lesion). This *inferred* brain damage, the basis of the work by Strauss and Lehtinen (1947) and Strauss and Kephart (1955), established the tentative association between hyperactivity and minimal brain damage.

Throughout the 1960s, a continued interest in finding medical answers to the problems of the learning disabled was kept alive. During this time period, considerable energy was spent determining the appropriateness of such terms as *central nervous system dysfunction, minimal brain damage, minimal brain injury,* and *minimal brain dysfunction,* and in investigating the medical basis for learning differences (see Chalfant & Scheffelin, 1969; Clements, 1966; Clements & Peters, 1962). As a result of this medical orientation, several lines of investigation were opened. These included the search for such problems as biochemical disorders (Wender, 1971, 1972), maturational lag (Kinsbourne, 1973), and genetic factors (Cantwell, 1976). Many of these lines of investigation continue today.

Current investigations into the medical basis for learning differences are significantly different from those of the 1960s and 1970s. Previously, the medical emphasis suggested that only a medical, pharmacological treatment would be the appropriate intervention. Currently, it is recognized that, although a problem may be medically based or require some medical treatment, the treatment of choice is most often educational.

As the ability of the scientific community to determine individual structural deficits has increased, there also has been gradual increased determination to locate specific neurological, neurophysiological, and neurobiological determinants of learning disabilities. This research has produced a number of important findings. For example, Smith and Pennington (1987) listed over 14 different genetic syndromes related to learning disabilities (see Table 1–8). Howard-Peebles (1982, 1988) has investigated the *fragile X syndrome* suggesting a linkage to a wide range of cognitively related problems. Neurometrics (Johns, 1977) and neuroscience (Duffy, Denckla, Bartels, & Sandini, 1980) have emerged as potentially useful ways to examine neurologically based learning difficulties. Using hybrid computer techniques, such as positron emission tomography (PET), brain electrical activity mapping (BEAM), and topological brain mapping, researchers have begun to document differences between normally achieving and learning disabled individuals.

Since the original edition of this text, a new disability emphasis has emerged, that of closed head trauma, or acquired cerebral trauma. Individuals with acquired cerebral trauma often exhibit the characteristics of learning disabled individuals. There is, however, one essential difference: There is no doubt as to the existence of structural damage in individuals with acquired cerebral trauma. Due to the extensive damage and resultant acquired loss of abilities, these individuals are not usually served in traditional educational settings. In addition, the interested reader is referred to the *Journal of Learning Disabilities*, Volume 21, Issues 8, 9, and 10, published in 1988, for a special series on acquired cerebral trauma.

The Behavioral Model

A third model, behaviorism, currently dominates educational practices, but remains too simplistic to explain learning disabilities. The behavioral approach focuses on the way information is presented to the learner. Tasks are analyzed into subcomponents in an effort to define small pieces for easy instruction. The basis of intervention rests upon accurate delineation of the material to be learned and the way in which responses are elicited from the learner. The use of this model, therefore, focuses on what is to be learned, almost to the exclusion of how the learner should go about learning. Although a significant number of proponents support this position, there has been a continuing movement away from behaviorism. For a review of the arguments surrounding behaviorism, see Chapter 4 of this text, as well as recent work by Poplin (1988).

What We Can Learn from These Models

The "models" presented above do not focus directly on the problems of learning disabled individuals (i.e., difficulties in learning), but were borrowed from

TABLE 1-8
Genetic Syndromes with Associated Learning Disabilities

Syndrome	Transmission	Characteristics
Noonan	Autosomal dominant	Verbal disability Performance apraxia
Neurofibromatosis	Autosomal dominant	Learning disabilities
Dysmorphic facies, laryngeal and pharyngeal hypoplasia, spinal abnormalities, learning disabilities	Autosomal dominant	Verbal disabilities
Velo–cardial–facial	Autosomal dominant	Abstraction Visual motor deficits
Tourette	Possible autosomal dominant	Reading disability Learning Disabilities
Phenylketonuria (treated)	Autosomal recessive	Learning disabilities Neuropsychological deficits
Aarskog	X-linked recessive	Learning disabilities Dyslexia
Lesch–Nyhan	X-linked recessive	Expressive language deficits Dysarthria
Cleft lip and palate	Multifactorial	Sensory-integration deficits
Fragile X, x-linked mental retardation	X-linked recessive	Verbal apraxia in some
45 X (Turner syndrome)	Chromosomal	Spatial, numerical, subtle language, and attention deficits
47,XYY	Chromosomal	Slight depression of verbal IQ
47,XXY	Chromosomal	Language delay, depressed verbal IQ, dysphasia, dyslexia

TABLE 1–8 (continued)

Syndrome	Transmission	Characteristics
Trisomy 9p	Chromosomal	Disproportionate language delays
18p –	Chromosomal	Disproportionate expressive language delays

From "Genetic Influences" by S. D. Smith, and B. F. Pennington, 1987, in *Handbook of Learning Disabilities: Volume I. Dimensions and Diagnosis* (p. 57) by K. A. Kavale, S. R. Forness, and M. Bender, 1987, Austin, TX: PRO-ED. Copyright 1987 by PRO-ED. Reprinted by permission.

other disciplines and adapted to the learning disabled population. Learning disabilities, by definition, involve the lack or impairment of the ability to learn. What is needed is not another "borrowed" model, but a unified "theory" of learning disabilities. This theory must focus not only on the *material* to be learned, but also on the *learner* and the *context* of learning. Other models may be adopted, but, as Bonet (1989) noted, *academic learning disabilities remain the domain of the educator.* Gallagher (1986) wrote,

> Discovering the etiology of mental retardation or speech pathology or emotional disturbance would provide no more help in educational planning than would discovering the causes of learning disabilities. The truth of the matter is that knowledge of the cause of the condition does not lead to specific educational treatment, *nor should it be expected to.* (p. 598)

What is important is the way the individual constructs a knowledge base, interacts with that knowledge base during the acquisition of new knowledge, and applies that knowledge and associated strategies in differing educational environments. The cognitive approach takes into account the active participation of the learner, views learning disabilities from a cognitive psychology perspective, and uses information processing and other cognitive theories to answer the question of how learning disabled children learn. Although all cognitive psychology determines the parameters of the questions to be answered, information processing theory had most often determined the type of data accepted for verifying theories.

For many years, researchers in learning disabilities have been calling for information related to actual school-related tasks. The cognitive approach attempts to maintain rigorous research standards using tasks related directly to real world situations (Palincsar & Brown, 1986). The cognitive approach has received widespread support and generated significant research on both the theory and practice of instruction (see Dillon & Sternberg, 1986; Gagné, 1985; Reid, 1988a, 1988b; Schmeck, 1988). This view is explained in Chapter 7 and further delineated in subsequent chapters. The following section briefly reviews some of the basic components as they relate to learning and the learning disabled.

WHY IS A COGNITIVE APPROACH PREFERRED?

A cognitive psychology approach to understanding the learning disabled has several advantages. First, it directly focuses on the acquisition of knowledge. Second, it places the learner at the focus of the problem. Third, it looks at the interaction of the learner and the learning situation. Learning, defined as long-term cognitive change, depends upon the individual's ability to construct meaning from experience. The learner is an active participant in this learning process (Gallagher & Reid, 1981; Reid, 1988b). The learner controls not only what is learned, but how meaning is constructed. To do this, the learner engages in active learning to code information so that it can be utilized to expand all three aspects of the knowledge base: declarative, procedural, and conditional.

Active Learning

Learning is an active process. The ability of a learner to learn is dependent upon his or her ability to activate the correct information necessary to complete a given learning problem or situation. Do learning disabled individuals have problems in this area? The research indicates that a significant number of learning disabled individuals do not spontaneously activate either learning strategies or previously learned information. Learning in learning disabled individuals is closely aligned with the concept of *welding*, a phenomenon that occurs when a particular strategy is applied only in settings replicating the original learning context. (The strategy becomes "welded" to the content.) Only after considerable experience is the strategy dissociated with the initially learned material and adapted to other situations. For example, a child's ability to summarize information is apparent when the child is in specific settings, but not when the child is in a situation only tangentially related to the original setting. In most individuals, welding is a transient phenomenon. Normally achieving individuals begin to generalize usable strategies. For learning disabled individuals, however, successful strategies remain tied to the original context for considerably longer periods.

Coding

When information is received and determined to be relevant, it must be acted upon. To be useful in the future, the information must be linked to prior knowledge, elaborated upon, and encoded in a manner that provides timely and appropriate access and activation. In the learning disabled, there is some question about whether these processes occur at optimal levels.

Several studies suggest that learning disabled and normally achieving individuals process and encode information similarly. A majority of learning disabled individuals, however, do not appear to elaborate spontaneously. Wong (1978) and Torgesen and Licht (1983) established that learning disabled individuals neither spontaneously engage in elaborative strategies for context remembrance nor engage in developing short definitional information. Optimal encoding suggests that an individual elaborates upon information in order to link the new information with existing knowledge structures.

How One Utilizes Knowledge

Having information stored and being able to access information do not guarantee that an individual will be able to *utilize* that information appropriately. Using knowledge depends on being able to select not only the appropriate knowledge to use, but also the appropriate and flexible strategies and procedures. Furthermore, an individual must be able to evaluate the effectiveness of selected strategies, and switch from one strategy to another based upon an evaluation of the success of the strategy employed. This process also requires that an individual determine whether a strategy utilized in one setting is appropriate for use in another setting.

Knowledge Systems

From a cognitive perspective, learning further involves the development and coordination of three knowledge systems: declarative, procedural, and conditional.

Declarative knowledge. Knowledge that consists mainly of shared factual information is referred to as declarative. Declarative knowledge is regarded as shared since the information is available to all individuals. The information contained in declarative knowledge represents the attributes or characteristics of objects or events without coloration from individual emotions.

The exact nature of the structure of declarative knowledge is unknown, and debate among researchers is strong. One accepted structure is a hierarchically arranged network, in which a classification system is developed that moves from specific modes and characteristics to more general (global), more inclusive, characteristics.

Research regarding the structure and extent of declarative knowledge in learning disabled individuals suggests that they have a knowledge structure similar to normally achieving individuals. The extent of that knowledge, however, is different.

Procedural knowledge. Procedural knowledge differs from declarative knowledge in that it represents "how to" rather than "what is." For example, think of the information required to add several two-digit numbers which require carrying. To solve the problem, one needs knowledge of the sum of separate digits (declarative knowledge), basic knowledge of the manner in which the number system is structured (ones, tens, hundreds, etc.), and the way in which numbers are combined (procedures to be used).

Procedural knowledge, based upon pattern recognition and action sequences, requires several different types of actions for development. Pattern recognition requires that strategies of generalization (the selection and sequencing of examples) and discrimination (the selection and sequencing of nonexamples) be invoked if accurate pattern recognition (and subsequent selection of procedures) is to be attained. Action sequences differ from procedural knowledge in that they (a) are based upon information derived from declarative knowledge, (b) are originally guided by declarative knowledge, (c) require the determination of knowledge sequences, and (d) are the result of knowledge compilation that results in either proceduralization, composition, or automatization.

As information becomes more complex, learners begin to decrease their reliance on the declarative aspects of learning and transform their knowledge into series of propositions or procedures. What originally had the form of discrete steps changes into a procedural unit. Composition takes the concept of combinations one step further. The results of proceduralization (taking declarative knowledge and developing procedures) are relatively small productions. Composition is the process by which several products (procedures) are collapsed into one larger procedure. The development of procedural knowledge is vastly important. Since individuals appear to have limited cognitive capacity (working memory), there need to be ways in which information can be dealt with quickly and efficiently, thus freeing up our limited capacity to deal with other more important aspects.

Conditional knowledge. Having a knowledge base and knowing how to use that knowledge base are important; however, knowing what and how solves only part of the problem. One also must understand when to use the information. Conditional knowledge refers to knowing when a particular strategy or knowledge is needed to solve a problem successfully.

Educational Treatment

The goals of educational intervention for learning disabled children have lacked clarity in the past. Instructional provisions for learning disabled students have included only a restricted set of options. Students may have been placed in contained classes, given tutors, or placed in regular classes with tutorial or other supplemental help.

Educational philosophers since Plato have emphasized the active participation of learners in the learning process, the concept of self-motivation (e.g., Forebel, Rousseau, Montessori, Piaget, and Dewey), and the view of education as an ongoing process concerned with individual growth, fostering self-determination and autonomy (Wood & Shears, 1986). Yet, current practices in learning disabilities are at odds with what these educators claim education is about (Wilson & Cowell, 1984).

Educational goals for learning disabled individuals include several dimensions. Learning disabled individuals must (a) be able to develop strategies for encoding and elaborating new information, (b) develop the abilities needed to retrieve information from long-term memory, (c) be able to engage in planning approaches to information acquisition and learning, and (d) access and use prior-learned information and engage in new learning activities *independently and successfully.*

Important Concepts of Learning

In this text, the orientation toward learning is from a cognitive psychology perspective. Therefore, learning is defined through several characteristics (Gallagher & Reid, 1981). Learning involves the active participation of the learner, is dependent upon the learner, results in long-term changes in the individual's knowledge base, and is internal to the learner. Furthermore, a cognitive perspective includes a consideration of the multidimensional nature of learning, including not only the above, but also a consideration of the nature of the task and materials and the type of instruction or intervention (Griswold, Gelzheiser, & Sheperd, 1987; Sheperd, Gelzheiser, & Solar, 1985; Turnure, 1986). This orientation toward education is not unique to this text. For example, Foster (1986) has redefined a list of 10 principles of learning developed by Blair in 1965 in terms of current cognitive psychology principles. An expansion of Foster's outline is presented in Table 1–9. These principles, which are global in nature, reflect the assumptions of the cognitive community.

WHAT ARE THE ACADEMIC CHARACTERISTICS OF THE LEARNING DISABLED?

Learning disabled individuals are both identified and categorized by the nature of their disabilities. Some researchers suggest that behavioral problems

---

TABLE 1–9
Ten Principles of Learning from a Cognitive Perspective

---

1. Learners learn by demonstrations, observations, and engagement.

2. The learners' previous actions indicate future behavior. However, learner reflections may lead to alternative actions.

3. Reinforcement, in and of itself, is not sufficient for learning. "Reinforcement effects are often subtle, nonobvious, covert, and relative to the individual and the situation" (Foster, 1986, p. 237).

4. As individuals become older, the concepts of readiness become less applicable.

5. An individual's understanding of him- or herself and the surrounding context has a direct bearing on learning.

6. What learners are observed doing in overt rehearsal may not be what they are doing internally. Learners often use many different strategies during rehearsal.

7. Strategies successful in one task are transferred more or less easily depending on the similarities of the tasks.

8. Learning occurs intentionally as well as incidentally and at different levels of meaning.

9. External influences on learning are effective only to the extent that they interact with the learner's perception of self and the environment.

10. Learning depends on the learner's interpretation of the pertinence of the information and the learner's ability to engage in the learning task as well as the material to be learned.

Adapted from "Ten Principles of Learning Revised in Accordance with Cognitive Psychology: With Implications for Teaching" by S. F. Foster, *Educational Psychologist*, *21*(3), p. 237.

are the primary source of referral; however, classification is determined by educational achievement. Although the definition of learning disabilities includes reference to reasoning skills, most individuals are referred and classified on the basis of their reading, mathematics, writing, and oral language skills.

Difficulties Encountered in Reading

One of the most pervasive characteristics of learning disabled children is the high prevalence of reading disabilities. Although it is widely agreed that there are different manifestations of reading disorders, one recurrent problem is the lack of ability to recognize words quickly and accurately. Learning disabled students with reading problems frequently are inhibited by slow lexical access, thereby decreasing attentional capacity and comprehension (Snider & Tarver, 1987). As they grow older, they exhibit cumulative deficits in language and knowledge acquisition, which further complicate reading (Snider & Tarver, 1987; Stanovich, 1987). Learning disabled students, due to the typical types of instruction, usually do not increase their reading levels beyond the fourth or fifth grade (Miller, 1983, as cited in Deshler, Schumaker, Lenz, & Ellis, 1984).

Difficulties Encountered in Writing

Like reading, writing is a prominent problem area for learning disabled students. Writing difficulties are pervasive, and these disabilities last well into adulthood. Learning disabled children tend to produce short sentences of five or fewer words because (a) they experience anxiety regarding their writing competency; (b) they often demonstrate lower levels of knowledge, since advanced information may not be presented in remedial or resource classrooms; and (c) their efforts to produce written work puts such a strain on cognitive processes that complex planning and writing cannot occur concurrently (Hayes & Flower, 1987; Roit & McKenzie, 1985).

Learning disabled students typically view writing as a task of error avoidance (Gagné, 1985) rather than as a process of production (Hayes & Flower, 1987). For them, surface structure is more important than meaning. They are more likely to edit for the conventions of writing rather than for content, and they generally fail to edit with cohesion or coherence as considerations.

Difficulties Encountered in Oral Language

Language disabilities have long been recognized as a pervasive source of problems for the learning disabled (Gerber & Bryen, 1981; Hresko, 1979; McGrady, 1967; Myers & Hammill, 1969; Vogel, 1975; Wiig & Semel, 1980). In fact, pervasive language disorders are cited in even the earliest learning disability research.

One recent study attempted to determine the prevalence of language disorders among a population of learning disabled students (Gibbs & Cooper, 1989). In a sample of 242 children aged 8 through 12, 96.2% of the population exhibited some type of communication disorder, with 90.5% exhibiting general difficulties in oral language. Despite the high prevalence of oral language disorders in this sample, only 6% were receiving language/

communication intervention. Thus, the major responsibility for remediation of language/communication deficits fell to the child's special education teacher.

In a related vein, several researchers have addressed the question of the communicative competence of learning disabled individuals (Donahue & Bryan, 1983; Friel-Patti & Conti-Ramsden, 1984; McCord & Haynes, 1988). Findings consistently suggest that learning disabled individuals do not have the overall level of communicative competence that normally achieving individuals possess. Although the communicative competence disability is often very observable, sometimes it is subtle. In a representative study, Mathinos (1988) reported that on gross measures of communicative competence, no differences appeared between the learning disabled individuals and other children. When more subtle aspects, such as strategy usage, were examined, however, definitive differences were noted. Because these differences affect the quality and success of the learning disabled individual's communicative interactions, they are of particular import to teachers. It is within the educational setting that problems in communication occur, both between students and with teachers and other adults. Similar findings have been evidenced by McCord and Haynes (1988). For a more detailed discussion of oral language, see Chapter 12 in this text.

Difficulties Encountered in Mathematics

Both mathematical reasoning and arithmetic computation are problems for the learning disabled. A child is deemed to have a learning disability in the area of mathematics if he or she demonstrates average or above average levels of general aptitude, but significantly lower performance in mathematics as measured by a standardized mathematics test or a curriculum-based assessment device. Mathematics learning disabilities have been observed in children with and without concurrent reading disabilities.

Mathematics disabilities can be divided into two areas: computational disabilities and problem solving disabilities. Computational disabilities are more clearly linked to neurological dysfunction and perceptual problems, whereas problem solving disabilities are influenced by a variety of factors, such as inadequate development of basic concepts, poor or incorrect conceptualization, insufficient use of developed skills, and lack of opportunity to learn (Romberg, 1976). How much is due to poor teaching of mathematics is unclear.

Computational disabilities are characterized by the inability to manipulate arithmetic symbols and perform mathematical calculations. Computational disabilities have been termed *dyscalculia* and *acalculia* (partial or complete absence of the ability to do the above) (Bush & Andrews, 1973). In current literature, the deficit is linked to a deficient capability for internal data manipulation and memory (Houck, Todd, Barnes, & Engldhard, 1980).

The child who experiences difficulty in reading and interpreting mathematical symbols may make errors in applying the operations of addition, subtraction, multiplication, and division, or in applying mathematical computation skills to problems presented in practical contexts (Houck et al., 1980). Children who may be able to solve a problem such as $20 \div 5$ on paper may not recognize the need to apply the same strategy in the following problem: Jack has 20 apples. He divided them equally among his 5 friends. How many did each one get?

The disability becomes more apparent as the reading level of word problems becomes more complex, extraneous information and distractors are incorporated, key words are not evident, and more steps are required to terminal solution. Furthermore, higher performance levels result when students are already familiar with the context (Greeno, Riley, & Gelman, 1984). Difficulties in problem solving have been linked most closely to inappropriate teaching strategies (Cawley, 1970; see also Chapter 14 in this text). Teachers may present mathematical skills in isolation, with little opportunity for practical applications. Additionally, the types of learning promoted in schools (e.g., paper-and-pencil work, lecture format instruction, working in isolation, emphasis on skill practice) are seldom directly related to the way in which people must deal with problems in the real world. Shared cognition, contextualized reasoning, and situation-specific competencies need to receive more emphasis, in contrast to individual cognition, abstract reasoning, and generalized competencies, which are currently reinforced in schools (Resnick, 1987).

The effects of a mathematics learning disability may be exacerbated through continuous exposure to traditional teaching modes. Intervention for the learning disabled must focus on alternative approaches—extensive use of manipulatives, presentation of alternative algorithms, and production-oriented activities once the concepts have been mastered—and alternative curricula—teaching operations in order of learner choice, use of aids such as calculators to overcome computational obstacles, and focus on functional mathematics. The indications of average to above-average aptitude in much of the learning disabled population points to their ability to grasp concepts presented to nondisabled learners. The approach, however, needs to be reconceptualized to meet their unique and special needs.

The Effect of Curriculum Matches and Mismatches on the Student

Public school systems generally do not teach to individual abilities or differences. Traditional public school settings are developed to meet the average needs of large groups of children. Thus, they are designed to teach to the average child, not to the gifted or the learning disabled child. The curriculum for the learning disabled is seldom clearly defined or matched to the curriculum of the regular class. Both teachers and appraisal specialists lack the training in the design and use of ongoing assessment techniques.

The Effect of Instructional Presentations on the Student

From an educational perspective, the instructional presentations for learning disabled students must be different from those for the regular class student. First, alternatives to instruction can be used. Sometimes referred to as *bypass* techniques, these include calculators, taped books, word processors, automatic outliners, and so forth. Second, production of information by active students needs to be encouraged. Techniques such as reciprocal teaching, requiring cooperative learning, and so on, are needed. Third, curriculum must be designed so that instructional materials reflect real-world situations and activities. Finally, students must be given the opportunity to transfer new knowledge to a variety of settings.

HOW IMPORTANT ARE DEFICITS IN ATTENTION AND ATTENTIONAL DEFICIT DISORDERS?

Since the early literature in learning disabilities, distractibility and attentional deficits have often been viewed as defining characteristics of learning disabilities (see Chalfant & Scheffelin, 1969; Cruickshank & Hallahan, 1973; Myklebust & Johnson, 1967). Although attention is not mentioned in current definitions, several authors include attentional deficits or inattentive behavior as defining characteristics of learning disabilities (Hallahan & Kauffman, 1988; Hallahan & Reeve, 1980; Lerner, 1989).

In the original edition of this book, considerable text was devoted to explicating the research surrounding attention. At that time, the possibility was broached that attentional problems per se were not a defining characteristic of learning disabled individuals, and perhaps other factors led learning disabled individuals to exhibit attentional characteristics that differ from those of normal individuals. Because the early research showed that attentional problems are characteristic of minimal brain dysfunction, brain injury, hyperactivity, and other syndromes, it is no wonder that the attentional deficit label also was associated with learning disabilities (Douglas & Peters, 1979; Lambert, Windmiller, Sandoval, & Moore, 1976). However, Douglas and Peters (1979), Krupski (1986), and McNellis (1987) noted, although different groups may exhibit similar attentional deficits, the sources of these deficits are different. Douglas and Peters (1979) suggested that the hyperactive individual has a "constitutional predisposition involving poor impulse control, an inability to sustain attention, and poorly modulated arousal levels, which result in a tendency to seek stimulation and salience" (p. 233). In the learning disabled individual, frustration due to problems in basic learning processes often result in overt behaviors resembling the attentional problems of the hyperactive child. Hyperactive individuals and those with learning disabilities often have problems with cognitive control variables viewed as critical to learning (Cotugno, 1987; Santostefano, 1985).

Several questions can be raised regarding research concerning learning disabilities and attention. First, is there a research base suggesting that learning disabled individuals do in fact have attentional deficits? Second, are attentional problems structural (related to neurophysiological deficits) or functional (resulting from an interaction of the individual with the environment)? Third, what are the educational implications of attentional problems? Fourth, is there a well-documented rationale for the DSM-III classification of attention deficit hyperactivity disorder (American Psychiatric Association, 1980, 1986)?

Attention, like many other terms used in the field of learning disabilities, has many different manifestations and connotations, depending upon the writer or researcher in question (Kahneman, 1973; Treisman, 1964). Moray (1969) argued that a minimum of seven different types of attention must be delineated, whereas Neisser (1976) suggested that attention is an unnecessary concept and does not even exist.

Krupski (1986) and McNellis (1987) each reviewed the existing research regarding learning disabilities and attention. Krupski (1986) referenced two types of attention research: sustained attention and selective attention. McNellis (1987) suggested that three types of attention have been studied in the learning disabled population: arousal, vigilance (sustained attention), and selective attention.

Arousal

Throughout the development of the field, researchers have attempted to link learning disabilities to attentional problems that are due to low levels of arousal. The results have been equivocal at best. Although some support is found in the literature, McNellis (1987) pointed to several confounding factors. First, the research populations usually are derived from clinical populations (i.e., individuals who have been referred to psychiatric clinics or neurology clinics in medical centers). Thus, the population probably does not represent the general learning disabled population. Second, the populations studied are not clearly differentiated with respect to hyperactivity. Usually in the clinical population, children are referred not only for learning difficulties, but also for more severe behavioral manifestations (e.g., acting out behavior, hyperactivity). Third, learning disabled children usually show significant increases in performance on tasks measuring arousal when given sustained practice, thus suggesting other factors at work. McNellis (1987), however, noted that most tasks in this area are both monotonous and boring: "One cannot help but wonder whether a very interesting reward . . . would eliminate possible group differences in reaction time, in these failure-oriented . . . youngsters" (p. 66).

An additional point to ponder is the relationship among IQ, learning disabilities, and clinical populations. Although most definitions of learning disabilities suggest that IQ is in the normal range for learning disabled individuals, research suggests that the mean IQ of this population ranges from the low to middle 80s to the middle 90s. For example, across several studies involving a sample of 3,000 learning disabled children, Kirk and Elkins (1975) reported 83 to be the average IQ for 35% of the research population (Keogh, 1987). Unfortunately, measures of attention (whether those of arousal, sustained attention, or selective attention) are known to be inversely but highly correlated with IQ (see Witkin, Oltman, Raskin, & Karp, 1971), with attentional problems increasing as IQ decreases.

Sustained Attention

Sustained attention (vigilance) refers to the individual's ability to monitor incoming information over an extended period of time. In general, learning disabled individuals consistently score below their nonhandicapped peers on a variety of vigilance measures (see Danier et al., 1981; Swanson, 1980, 1983). However, several questions arise. For example, Keogh and MacMillan (1983) and others (Keogh, Major-Kingsley, Omori-Gordon, & Reid, 1982) suggested that sustained attention studies in general are not based on well-defined populations.

According to Krupski (1986), although the results of the preponderance of relevant attention studies support the hypothesis that learning disabled and hyperactive individuals perform more poorly than nonhandicapped peers, these results *do not* support the position that learning disabled and hyperactive individuals perform differentially on vigilance tasks, using reaction time data and physiological measures.

Vigilance on a task is a function of several factors. Prior knowledge of the material, individual motivation, and task difficulty and interest level all interact to determine performance. Thus, according to McNellis (1987), "clinical LD populations and tedious vigilance tasks with unmotivated, atypical youngsters cannot be taken as very strong support for the notion of attentional [vigilance] deficits in LD children" (p. 66).

Selective Attention

Selective attention refers to an individual's ability to attend to *relevant* information. This aspect of attention is usually measured by examining an individual's ability to direct attention to a particular task or by measuring an individual's distractibility during task presentation.

In the 1970s, a task designed by Hagen (1967) was frequently used to ascertain abilities in central versus incidental learning. Hallahan and his associates (Hallahan, Gajar, Cohen, & Tarver, 1978; Tarver & Hallahan, 1974) applied this task to learning disabled subjects and suggested that these subjects exhibited a deficit in central versus incidental learning. According to the findings, learning disabled subjects were less able to focus on the central tasks and more likely to engage in less focused (incidental) learning. The researchers concluded that learning disabled subjects did not have sufficient control of their attentional processes to learn relevant tasks. Subsequent research by these individuals indicated that the attentional capabilities of the learning disabled could be altered by the demands of the task and the rewards provided.

In recent years, the Hagen task has come under criticism by many researchers who view the task more as a measure of memory and verbal abilities than of attention (see Bryan & Bryan, 1980; Copeland & Wisniewski, 1981; Douglas & Peters, 1979; Fleisher, Soodak, & Jelin, 1984). At best, the task is now thought to provide minimal understanding of selective attention.

Selective attention has also been investigated using tasks designed to indicate the effects of similarity between tasks and distractors. Traditionally, these tasks have been referred to as distal, proximal, and embedded distractors. Research findings consistently indicate that learning disabled individuals are not hampered by distal distractors, that is, those that are physically distant and distinguishable from the task to be accomplished. Conversely, learning disabled individuals appear to be negatively affected by proximal distractors, that is, distractors that are close to the task (Krupski, 1986). For example, in one study (Radosh & Gittelman, 1981), the proximal distractor was the appeal and complexity of the border surrounding a page of arithmetic problems. As the border became more appealing, the hyperactive students' performances deteriorated. An even more proximal task, embedded distractors, produces consistent errors in the hyperactive population. Specifically, when irrelevant stimuli of high salience (see Rosenthal & Allen, 1978) are included in tasks that have high cognitive demands, most studies indicate that both learning disabled and hyperactive individuals perform differently from nonhandicapped individuals. At least some researchers (Copeland & Weissbrod, 1983; Pelham, 1979), however, have come to different conclusions. When nonhyperactive learning disabled individuals were compared with nonhandicapped individuals on speeded classification tasks, no indications of differential distractor effects were found. In general, however, the overwhelming findings have indicated "that a variety of visual and auditory embedded distractors had a greater effect on the performance of hyperactive and learning-disabled youngsters than on normal control groups" (Krupski, 1986, p. 183).

The selective attention research is indeed interesting. One of the most important findings is that only when the cognitive demands of the task increase do significant increases in selective attention occur. This correlation leads to a very important question. As Krupski (1986) asked,

> If neither incidental learning nor distractibility are appropriate literatures from which to draw conclusions about selective attention, what, one might ask, is? One answer to this question is that, given the difficulties in operationalizing the concept of selective attention, it may best be discarded as well. (p. 187)

McNellis (1984, 1987) reported findings that fail to corroborate *any* of the existing research regarding selective attention deficits in learning disabled individuals. Using a series of selective attention tasks with a well-defined population, McNellis concluded that (a) low intercorrelations among selective attention tasks suggest that each measures a separate factor or ability; (b) general selective attention differences between learning disabled and non–learning disabled individuals do not appear; and (c) when strategy variables are eliminated from central versus incidental learning tasks, learning disabled and non–learning disabled differences disappear. Her careful findings, along with those of Pelham (1979), indicate that the suggested attention and learning disabilities relationship is not viable: "Psychologists and educators are going to have to look somewhere other than at 'attention' to find a single syndrome that may typify learning-disabled children" (McNellis, 1987, p. 78).

As indicated in several of the above sections pertaining to attention, research findings often depend upon the characteristics used to determine the learning disabled and control groups. One potentially fruitful endeavor for clarifying the characteristics of the learning disabled population is the use of marker variables in learning disabilities research (Keogh, Major, Reid, Gandara, & Omori, 1978; Keogh et al., 1982). The use of marker variables establishes "a set of core variables which are collected in common by those conducting research" (Keogh et al., 1978, p. 6). As background characteristics, marker variables allow comparisons of research findings across studies. Two potential problems, however, must be noted: marker variables can be described only for preexisting populations, and they are likely to lead to lists of correlates that may or may not constitute defining characteristics of learning disabilities.

Unfortunately, since the call for the use of marker variables, little change has occurred in the manner in which learning disabilities research is conducted. Several current authors have lamented the fact that learning disabilities research occurs on existing populations that (a) are varied in the manner in which they have been diagnosed, (b) have significant variability in intelligence levels, (c) have variable academic problems, and (d) have various academic difficulty levels.

Although attentional problems of learning disabled individuals have received considerable attention throughout the years, interest was enhanced during the early 1980s. In 1980, the DSM-III classification system (American Psychiatric Association, 1980) acknowledged that some individuals could be classified as having attentional deficit disorders (ADDs), and that ADD exists both with and without hyperactivity. Although slightly modified, the DSM-III-R classification (American Psychological Association, 1987) continues to acknowledge this classification. Considerable attention has been given to the coordinated effects of learning disabilities and ADD. The term "ADD" has been widely adopted by both parents and the medical profession. Unfortunately, no objective, standard method exists for diagnosing ADD. Parents and educational personnel are often quick to label a child as having ADD and to substitute medication for the need to adapt the curriculum to the needs of the child. The relation of ADD to learning disabilities is vague and not presently well understood. The 1980 DSM-III classification provided for ADD both with and without hyperactivity. Although most learning disabled individuals are not hyperactive, this allowed for any child who had learning difficulties and was distracted to be labeled ADD. Subsequently, the DSM-III-R classifications no longer include ADD without hyperactivity. The current classification is attention deficit hyperactivity disorder (ADHD). The DSM-III-R manual notes that additional research is needed to clarify the classification and determine its validity. Table 1–10 contains the diagnostic criteria for ADHD. Sufficient research has not been conducted into the classification of ADHD or the educational or pharmacological approaches to treatment (Henker & Whalen, 1989; Shaywitz & Shaywitz, 1988). A more complete discussion of the relations between ADD and learning disability is provided in Chapter 3.

SUMMARY

This chapter has provided an overview of learning disabilities within an educational perspective. Although the lack of an adequate definition generates considerable controversy and results in tremendous service variability, the definition of the National Advisory Committee on Handicapped Children, revised and used as the basis of PL 94-142, has provided a framework from which many professionals have worked. Other definitions include those of the National Joint Committee on Learning Disabilities and the Interagency Committee on Learning Disabilities.

Prevalence issues have been of great concern in the learning disabilities field. Although many professionals suggest that the prevalence of learning disabilities ranges between 1% and 3%, current figures suggest that the prevalence of learning disabilities varies between 3% and 7% of the school-aged population. These figures change according to the operational and theoretical definitions employed.

TABLE 1-10
Diagnostic Criteria for Attention Deficit Hyperactivity Disorder

---

Note: Consider a criterion met only if the behavior is considerably more frequent than that of most people of the same mental age.

A. A disturbance of at least 6 months during which at least eight of the following are present:
   1. Often fidgets with hands or feet or squirms in seat (in adolescents, may be limited to subjective feelings of restlessness)
   2. Has difficulty remaining seated when required to
   3. Is easily distracted by extraneous stimuli
   4. Has difficulty awaiting turn in games or group situations
   5. Often blurts out answers to questions before they have been completed
   6. Has difficulty following through on instructions from others (not due to oppositional behavior or failure of comprehension) (e.g., fails to finish chores)
   7. Has difficulty sustaining attention in tasks or play activities
   8. Often shifts from one uncompleted activity to another
   9. Has difficulty playing quietly
   10. Often talks excessively
   11. Often interrupts or intrudes on others (e.g., butts into other children's games)
   12. Often does not seem to listen to what is being said to him or her
   13. Often loses things necessary for tasks or activities at school or at home (e.g., toys, pencils, books, assignments)
   14. Often engages in physically dangerous activities without considering possible consequences (not for the purpose of thrill-seeking) (e.g., runs into street without looking)

Note: The above items are listed in descending order of discriminating power based on data from a national field trial of the DSM-III-R criteria for disruptive behavior disorders.

B. Onset before the age of 9.

C. Does not meet the criteria for pervasive developmental disorder.

Criteria for severity of attention deficit hyperactivity disorder:
   Mild: Few, if any, symptoms in excess of those required to make the diagnosis and only minimal or no impairment in school and social functioning.
   Moderate: Symptoms or functional impairment intermediate between "mild" and "severe."
   Severe: Many symptoms in excess of those required to make the diagnosis and significant and pervasive impairment in functioning at home and school and with peers.

From *Diagnostic and Statistical Manual of Mental Disorders* (3rd ed. revised, pp. 52–53) by American Psychiatric Association, 1987, Washington, DC: Author. Copyright 1987 by American Psychiatric Association. Reprinted by permission.

A brief historical overview of the learning disabilities field was provided. Some orientations used in developing explanations of learning disabilities were discussed, including those based on perceptual and perceptual–motor abilities, medical orientations, and behavioral theories. The possible contributions and the inherent difficulties of each were introduced. As noted, in the final analysis, learning disabilities interventions are best accomplished by educators from a cognitive-based approach.

Significant components of the cognitive approach were presented. The concepts of activation, coding, utilization, and knowledge systems were briefly examined. Examples of problems in reading, writing, oral language, and mathematics were given. Also provided were considerations related to curriculum mismatches and differing instructional presentations.

Once thought to be a central issue in learning disabilities, the dimensions of attention have come under considerable controversy. The issues surrounding attention were examined, with the conclusion that traditional attribution of learning disabilities to attentional problems may be inaccurate. Also, difficulties with the concepts of attention deficit disorders were addressed.

REFERENCES

Algozzine, B., Forgone, C., Mercer, C., & Trifiletti, J. (1979). Toward defining discrepancies for specific learning disabilities: An analysis and alternatives. *Learning Disability Quarterly, 2,* 25–31.

Algozzine, B., & Ysseldyke, J. E. (1987). Questioning discrepancies: Retaking the first step 20 years later. *Learning Disability Quarterly, 10,* 301–313.

American Psychiatric Association. (1980). *Diagnostic and statistical manual of mental disorders* (2nd ed.). Washington, DC: Author.

American Psychiatric Association. (1987). *Diagnostic and statistical manual of mental disorders* (3rd ed. rev.). Washington, DC: Author.

Anderson, R., Martinez, D., & Rich, L. (1980). Perspectives for change. In J. Schifani, R. Anderson, & S. Odle (Eds.), *Implementing learning in the least restrictive environment* (pp. 3–45). Baltimore: University Park Press.

Association for Children with Learning Disabilities. (1986). ACLD description: Specific learning disabilities. *ACLD Newsbriefs,* pp. 15–16.

Becker, L. D. (1978). Learning characteristics of educationally handicapped and retarded children. *Exceptional Children, 44,* 502–511.

Bonet, K. (1989). Learning disabilities: A neurobiological perspective in humans. *Remedial and Special Education, 10*(3), 8–19.

Bruinincks, R. H., & Weatherman, R. F. (1970). *Handicapped children and special education program needs in northeast Minnesota.* Minneapolis: University of Minnesota, Department of Special Education.

Bryan, T. H., & Bryan, J. H. (1980). Learning disorder. In H. E. Rie & E. D. Rie (Eds.), *Handbook of minimal brain dysfunction: A critical view* (pp. 456–482). New York: Wiley.

Bush, C. L., & Andrews, R. C. (1973). *Dictionary reading and learning disabilities terms.* Matawan, NJ: Educational and Psychological Associates Press.

Cantwell, D. P. (1976). Genetic factors in the hyperkinetic syndrome. *Journal of Child Psychiatry, 15,* 214–223.

Carnine, D. W., & Woodward, J. (1988). Paradigms lost: Learning disabilities and the new ghost in the old machine. *Journal of Learning Disabilities, 21,* 233–236.

Carrier, J. G. (1986). *Learning disability: Social class and the construction of inequality in American education.* New York: Greenwood Press.

Cawley, J. R. (1970). Teaching arithmetic to mentally handicapped children. *Focus on Exceptional Children, 2,* 1–8.

Chalfant, J., & Scheffelin, M. (1969). *Central processing dysfunctions in children. A review of research.* Washington, DC: U.S. Department of Health, Education, and Welfare.

Chandler, B. (Ed.). (1980). *Standard education almanac 1980–1981.* Chicago: Marquis.

Clements, S. D. (1966). *Minimal brain dysfunction in children: Terminology and identification.* Washington, DC: Cosponsored by the Easter Seal Research Foundation of the National Society for Crippled Children and Adults and the National Institute of Neurological Diseases and Blindness Public Health Service.

Clements, S. D., & Peters, J. E. (1962). Minimal brain dysfunctions in school-age children. *Archives of General Psychiatry, 6,* 185–197.

Coles, G. (1987). *The learning mystique: A critical look at learning disabilities.* New York: Pantheon.

Cone, T. E., & Wilson, L. R. (1981). Quantifying a severe discrepancy: A critical analysis. *Learning Disability Quarterly, 4,* 359–371.

Cone, T. E., Wilson, L. R., Bradley, C. M., & Reese, J. H. (1985). Characteristics of LD students in Iowa: An empirical investigation. *Learning Disability Quarterly, 8,* 211–220.

Copeland, A. P., & Weissbrod, C. S. (1983). Cognitive strategies used by learning disabled children: Does hyperactivity always make things worse? *Journal of Learning Disabilities, 16,* 473–477.

Copeland, A. P., & Wisniewski, N. M. (1981). Learning disability and hyperactivity: Deficits in selective attention. *Journal of Experimental Child Psychology, 32,* 88–101.

Cotugno, A. J. (1987). Cognitive control functioning in hyperactive and non-hyperactive learning disabled children. *Journal of Learning Disabilities, 20,* 563–567.

Council for Learning Disabilities. (1987). The CLD position papers: Use of discrepancy formulas in the identification of learning disabled individuals. *Journal of Learning Disabilities, 20,* 349–350.

Cruickshank, W., & Hallahan, D. (1973). *Psychoeducational foundations of learning disabilities.* Englewood Cliffs, NJ: Prentice-Hall.

Danier, K. B., Klorman, T., Salzman, L. F., Hess, D. W., Davidson, P. W., & Michael, R. L. (1981). Learning-disordered children's evoked potentials during sustained attention. *Journal of Abnormal Child Psychology, 9,* 79–94.

Deshler, D. D., Schumaker, J. B., Lenz, B. K., & Ellis, E. (1984). Academic and cognitive intervention for LD adolescents: Part II. *Annual Review of Learning Disabilities, 2,* 67–76.

Dillon, R. F., & Sternberg, R. J. (1986). *Cognition and instruction.* New York: Academic Press.

Donahue, M., & Bryan, T. (1983). Conversational skills and modeling in learning disabled boys. *Applied Psycholinguistics, 2,* 213–234.

Douglas, V. I., & Peters, K. G. (1979). Toward a clearer definition of the attentional deficit of hyperactive children. In G. A. Hale & M. Lewis (Eds.), *Attention and cognitive development* (pp. 173–247). New York: Plenum Press.

Duffy, F. H., Denckla, M. B., Bartels, P. H., & Sandini, G. (1980). Dyslexia: Regional differences in brain electrical activity by topographic mapping. *Annals of Neurology, 7,* 412–420.

Fleisher, L. S., Soodak, L. C., & Jelin, M. A. (1984). Selective attention deficits in learning disabled children: Analysis of the data base. *Exceptional Children, 51,* 136–141.

Foster, S. F. (1986). Ten principles of learning revised in accordance with cognitive psychology: With implications for teaching. *Educational Psychologist, 21,* 235–243.

Franklin, B. M. (Ed.). (1987). *Learning disability: Dissenting essays.* New York: Falmer Press.

Friel-Patti, S., & Conti-Ramsden, G. (1984). Discourse development in atypical language learners. In S. Kuczaj (Ed.), *Discourse development* (pp. 167–194). New York: Springer-Verlag.

Gagné, E. D. (1985). *The cognitive psychology of school learning.* Boston: Little, Brown.

Gallagher, J. J. (1986). Learning disabilities and special education: A critique. *Journal of Learning Disabilities, 19,* 595–601.

Gallagher, J. M., & Reid, D. K. (1981). *The learning theory of Piaget and Inhelder.* Monterey, CA: Brooks/Cole.

Gerber, A., & Bryen, D. N. (1981). *Language and learning disabilities.* Baltimore, MD: University Park Press.

Gibbs, D. P., & Cooper, E. B. (1989). Prevalence of communication disorders in students with learning disabilities. *Journal of Learning Disabilities, 22,* 60–63.

Greeno, J. G., Riley, M. S., & Gelman, R. (1984). Conceptual competence and children's counting. *Cognitive Psychology, 16,* 94–143.

Griswold, P. C., Gelzheiser, L. M., & Sheperd, M. J. (1987). Does a production deficiency hypothesis account for vocabulary learning among adolescents with learning disabilities? *Journal of Learning Disabilities, 20,* 620–626.

Hagen, J. W. (1967). The effect of distraction on selective attention. *Child Development, 38,* 685–694.

Hallahan, D. P., Gajar, A. H., Cohen, S. B., & Tarver, S. G. (1978). Selective attention and locus of control in learning disabled and normal children. *Journal of Learning Disabilities, 11,* 231–236.

Hallahan, D. P., & Kauffman, J. M. (1976). *Introduction to learning disabilities: A psycho-behavioral approach.* Englewood Cliffs, NJ: Prentice-Hall.

Hallahan, D. P., & Kauffman, J. M. (1988). *Exceptional children: Introduction to special education.* Englewood Cliffs, NJ: Prentice-Hall.

Hallahan, D. P., Keller, C. E., & Ball, D. W. (1986). A comparison of prevalence rate variability from state to state for each of the categories of special education. *Remedial and Special Education, 7*(2), 8–14.

Hallahan, D. P., & Reeve, R. E. (1980). Selective attention and distractibility. In B. K. Keogh (Ed.), *Advances in special education* (Vol. 1, pp. 141–181). Greenwich, CT: JAI Press.

Hammill, D. D. (1990). On defining learning disabilities: An emerging consensus. *Journal of Learning Disabilities, 23*(2), 74–84.

Hammill, D. D., & Larsen, S. (1974). The effectiveness of psycholinguistic training. *Exceptional Children, 41,* 3–15.

Hanna, G. S., Dyck, N. J., & Holen, M. C. (1979). Objective analysis of achievement–aptitude discrepancies in LD classification. *Learning Disability Quarterly, 2,* 32–38.

Hayes, J. R., & Flower, L. S. (1987). On the structure of the writing process. *Topics in Language Disorders, 7*(4), 42–54.

Henker, B., & Whalen, C. K. (1989). Hyperactivity and attention deficits. *American Psychologist, 44,* 216–223.

Houck, C., Todd, R., Barnes, D., & Engldhard, J. (1980). LD and math: Is it the math or the child? *Academic Therapy, 15,* 557–570.

Howard-Peebles, P. N. (1982). Nonspecific X-linked mental retardation: Background, diagnosis and prevalence. *Journal of Mental Deficiency Research, 26,* 205.

Howard-Peebles, P. N. (1988). Cytogenetic and historical aspects of fragile X syndrome. *Early Childhood Update, 4*(4), 5.

Hresko, W. P. (1979). Elicited imitation ability of children from learning disabled and regular classes. *Journal of Learning Disabilities, 12,* 456–461.

Interagency Committee on Learning Disabilities (1987). *Learning disabilities: A report to the U.S. Congress* (Report No. 222). Washington, DC: National Institute of Child Health and Human Development.

Johns, E. R. (1977). Neurometrics: Numerical taxonomy identifies different profiles of brain function within groups of behaviorally similar people. *Science, 196,* 1393–1410.

Kahneman, D. (1973). *Attention and effort.* Englewood Cliffs, NJ: Prentice-Hall.

Kavale, K. A. (1987). Theoretical quandaries in learning disabilities. In S. Vaughn & C. S. Bos (Eds.), *Research in learning disabilities: Issues and future directions* (pp. 19–29). Boston: Little, Brown.

Kavale, K. A., & Forness, S. R. (1986). *The science of learning disabilities.* San Diego, CA: College-Hill.

Kavale, K. A., & Forness, S. R. (1987). History, politics, and the general education initiative: Sleeter's reinterpretation of learning disabilities as a case study. *Remedial and Special Education, 8*(5), 6–12.

Kavale, K. A., Forness, S. R., & Bender, M. (1987). *Handbook of learning disabilities: Vol. 1. Dimensions and Diagnosis.* Austin, TX: PRO-ED.

Kavale, K. A., & Mattison, P. (1983). "One jumped off the balance beam": Meta-analysis of perceptual–motor training. *Journal of Learning Disabilities, 16,* 165–173.

Keogh, B. K. (1987). Learning disabilities: Diversity in search of order. In M. C. Wang, H. J. Walberg, & M. C. Reynolds (Eds.), *The handbook of special education: Research and practice* (pp. 225–251). Oxford, England: Pergamon Press.

Keogh, B. K., & MacMillan, D. L. (1983). The logic of sample selection: Who represents what? *Exceptional Education Quarterly, 4,* 84–96.

Keogh, B. K., Major, S. M., Reid, H. P., Gandara, P., & Omori, H. (1978). Marker variables: A search for comparability and generalizability in the field of learning disabilities. *Learning Disability Quarterly, 1,* 5–11.

Keogh, B. K., Major-Kingsley, S. M., Omori-Gordon, H., & Reid, H. P. (1982). *A system of marker variables for the field of learning disabilities.* Syracuse, NY: Syracuse University Press.

Kinsbourne, M. (1973). Minimal brain dysfunction as a neurodevelopmental lag. *Annals of the New York Academy of Sciences, 205,* 268–273.

Kirk, S. A., & Elkins, J. (1975). Characteristics of children enrolled in the child service demonstration centers. *Journal of Learning Disabilities, 8,* 630–637.

Koupernik, C., MacKeith, R., & Francis-Williams, J. (1975). Neurological correlates of motor and perceptual development. In W. Cruickshank & D. P. Hallahan (Eds.), *Perceptual and learning disabilities in children* (Vol. 2, pp. 105–135). Syracuse, NY: Syracuse University Press.

Krupski, A. (1986). *Psychological and educational perspectives on learning disabilities.* New York: Academic Press.

Lambert, N. M., Windmiller, M., Sandoval, J., & Moore, B. (1976). Hyperactive children and the efficacy of psychoactive drugs as a treatment intervention. *American Journal of Orthopsychiatry, 46,* 335–352.

Larsen, S., & Hammill, D. (1975). The relationship of selected visual perceptual abilities to learning. *Journal of Special Education, 9,* 281–291.

Lerner, J. W. (1989). *Learning disabilities: Theories, diagnosis, and teaching strategies* (5th ed.), Boston: Houghton Mifflin.

Liberman, I. Y. (1985). Should so-called modality preferences determine the nature of instruction for children with reading disabilities. In F. H. Duffy & N. Gershwind (Eds.), *Dyslexia: A neuroscientific approach to clinical evaluation* (pp. 93–103). Boston, MA: Little, Brown.

Mathinos, D. A. (1988). Communicative competence of children with learning disabilities. *Journal of Learning Disabilities, 21,* 437–443.

McCord, J. S., & Haynes, W. O. (1988). Discourse errors in students with learning disabilities and their normally achieving peers: Molar versus molecular views. *Journal of Learning Disabilities, 21*(4), 237–243.

McGrady, H. J. (1967). Language pathology and learning disabilities. In H. Myklebust (Ed.), *Progress in learning disabilities* (Vol. 1). New York: Grune and Stratton.

McKinney, J. D. (1987). Perspectives on changes in educational policy. In S. Vaughn & C. S. Bos (Eds.), *Research in learning disabilities: Issues and future directions* (pp. 215–237). Austin, TX: PRO-ED.

McNellis, K. L. (1984). *The selective attention deficit in learning disabled children.* Unpublished doctoral dissertation, Cornell University, Ithaca, NY.

McNellis, K. L. (1987). In search of attentional deficit. In S. J. Ceci (Ed.), *Handbook of cognitive, social, and neuropsychological aspects of learning disabilities* (Vol. 2, pp. 63–81). Hillsdale, NJ: Erlbaum.

McNutt, G. (1986). The status of learning disabilities in the states: Consensus or controversy? *Journal of Learning Disabilities, 19,* 12–16.

Meier, J. H. (1971). Prevalence and characteristics of learning disabilities found in second grade children. *Journal of Learning Disabilities, 4,* 1–16.

Mercer, C. D., Hughes, C., & Mercer, A. R. (1985). Learning disabilities definitions used by State Education Departments. *Learning Disability Quarterly, 8,* 45–55.

Moray, N. (1969). *Attention: Selective processes in vision and hearing.* London: Hutchison.

Myers, P., & Hammill, D. D. (1969). *Methods for learning disorders.* New York: Wiley.

Myers, P. L., & Hammill, D. D. (1990). *Learning disabilities: Basic concepts, assessment practices, and instructional strategies.* Austin, TX: PRO-ED.

Myklebust, H. R., & Boshes, B. (1969). *Minimal brain damage in children.* (Final report; U.S. Public Health

Service Contract 108-65-142. U.S. Department of Health, Education, and Welfare.) Evanston, IL: Northwestern University Publication.

Myklebust, H. R., & Johnson, D. J. (1967). *Learning disabilities: Educational principles and practices.* New York: Grune and Stratton.

National Advisory Committee on Handicapped Children. (1968). Special education for handicapped children. (First Annual Report). Washington, DC: Department of Health, Education & Welfare.

National Joint Committee on Learning Disabilities. (1983). Learning disabilities definition. *Learning Disability Quarterly, 6,* 42–44.

National Joint Committee on Learning Disabilities. (1988). [Letter to NJCLD member organizations.]

Neisser, U. (1976). *Cognition and reality.* San Francisco: W. H. Freeman.

Ortiz, A. A. & Yates, J. R. (1983). Incidence of exceptionality among Hispanics: Implications for manpower planning. *NABE Journal, 7,* 41–54.

Palincsar, A. S., & Brown, A. L. (1986). Interactive teaching to promote independent reading. *Reading Teacher, 39,* 771–777.

Pelham, W. E. (1979). Selective attention deficits in poor readers? Dichotic listening, speeded classification, and auditory and visual central and incidental learning tasks. *Child Development, 50,* 1050–1061.

PL 94-142. Education for All Handicapped Children Act (November 29, 1975).

PL 99-457. 1986 Amendments to the Education for All Handicapped Children Act.

Poplin, M. S. (1988). Holistic/constructivist principles of the teaching/learning process: Implications for the field

of learning disabilities. *Journal of Learning Disabilities, 21*(7), 401–416.

Radosh, A., & Gittelman, R. (1981). The effect of appealing distractors on the performance of hyperactive children. *Journal of Abnormal Child Psychology, 9,* 179–189.

Reid, D. K. (1988a). Reflections on the pragmatics of a paradigm shift. *Journal of Learning Disabilities, 21,* 417–421.

Reid, D. K. (1988b). *Teaching the learning disabled: A cognitive developmental approach.* Boston: Allyn and Bacon.

Resnick, L. (1987). Learning in school and out. *Educational Researcher, 16*(9), 13–20.

Reynolds, C. R. (1984–1985). Measurement issues in learning disabilities. *Journal of Special Education, 18,* 445–471.

Roit, M. L., & McKenzie, R. G. (1985). Disorders of written communication: An instructional priority for learning disabled students. *Journal of Learning Disabilities, 18,* 258–260.

Romberg, T. (1976). The diagnostic process in mathematics instruction. In J. Higgins & J. Heddens (Eds.), *Remedial mathematics: Diagnostic and prescriptive approaches.* Mathematics Education Reports. Columbus: Ohio State University.

Rosenthal, R. H., & Allen, T. W. (1978). An examination of attention, arousal, and learning dysfunctions of hyperkinetic children. *Psychological Bulletin, 85,* 689–715.

Santostefano, S. (1985). *Cognitive control therapy with children and adolescents.* New York: Pergamon Press.

Schmeck, R. R. (Ed.). (1988). *Learning strategies and learning styles.* New York: Plenum Press.

Shaywitz, S. E., & Shaywitz, B. A. (1988). Attention deficit disorder: Current perspectives. In J. F. Kavanagh & T. J. Truss (Eds.), *Learning disabilities:*

Proceedings of the national conference. Parkton, MD: York Press.

Shepard, L. A., & Smith, M. L. (1983). An evaluation of the identification of learning disabled students in Colorado. *Learning Disability Quarterly, 6,* 115–127.

Sheperd, M. J., Gelzheiser, L. M., & Solar, R. A. (1985). How good is the evidence for a production deficiency among learning disabled students? *Journal of Educational Psychology, 77,* 553–561.

Siegel, L. S. (1988). Definitional and theoretical issues and research on learning disabilities. *Journal of Learning Disabilities, 21,* 264–266.

Siegel, L. S., & Heaven, R. (1986). Defining and categorizing learning disabilities. In S. Ceci (Ed.), *Handbook of cognitive, social, and neuropsychological aspects of learning disabilities* (Vol. 1, pp. 95–121). Hillsdale, NJ: Erlbaum.

Siegel, L. S., & Ryan, E. B. (1984). Reading disability as a language disorder. *Remedial and Special Education, 5,* 28–33.

Siegel, L. S., & Ryan, E. B. (1988). Development of grammatical sensitivity, phonological, and short-term memory skills in normally achieving and learning disabled children. *Developmental Psychology, 24,* 28–37.

Silver, L. A. (1987). The "Magic Cure": A review of the current controversial approaches for treating learning disabilities. *Journal of Learning Disabilities, 20,* 498–504, 512.

Sleeter, C. E. (1986). Learning disabilities: The social construction of a special education category. *Exceptional Children, 53*(1), 46–64.

Smith, S. D., & Pennington, B. F. (1987). Genetic influences. In K. A. Kavale, S. R. Forness, & Bender, M. (Eds.), *Handbook of learning disabilities* (Vol. 1, pp. 49–75). Boston: Little, Brown.

Snider, V. E., & Tarver, S. G. (1987). The effect of early reading failure on acquisition of knowledge among students with learning disabilities. *Journal of Learning Disabilities, 20*(6), 351–357.

Spear, L. C., & Sternberg, R. J. (1987). An information-processing framework for understanding reading disability. In S. J. Ceci (Ed.), *Handbook of cognitive, social, and neuropsychological aspects of learning disabilities* (Vol. 2, pp. 3–32). Hillsdale, NJ: Erlbaum.

Stanovich, K. E. (1987). Cognitive processes and the reading problems of learning-disabled children: Evaluating the assumption of specificity. In J. K. Torgesen & B. Y. L. Wong (Eds.), *Psychological and educational perspectives on learning disabilities* (pp. 85–116). New York: Academic Press.

Strauss, A. A., & Kephart, N. C. (1955). *Psychopathology and education of the brain injured child* (Vol. II). New York: Grune and Stratton.

Strauss, A. A., & Lehtinen, N. C. (1947). *Psychopathology and education of the brain injured child* (Vol. 1.). New York: Grune and Stratton.

Swanson, H. L. (1983). Relations among metamemory, rehearsal activity and word recall in learning disabled and nondisabled readers. *British Journal of Educational Psychology, 53,* 186–194.

Swanson, H. L. (1980). Conceptual rule learning in normal and learning disabled children. *Journal of General Psychology, 102,* 255–263.

Tarver, S. G., & Hallahan, D. P. (1974). Attentional deficits in children with learning disabilities: A review. *Journal of Learning Disabilities, 7,* 560–569.

Torgesen, J. K. & Licht, B. G. (1983). The learning disabled child as an inactive learner: Retrospects and prospects. In J. D. McKinney & L. Feagans (Eds.), *Current topics in learning disabilities* (Vol. 1, pp. 3–31). Norwood, NJ: Ablex.

Treisman, A. M. (1964). Monitoring and storage of irrelevant messages in selective attention. *Journal of Verbal Learning and Verbal Behavior, 3*, 449–459.

Turnure, J. E. (1986). Instruction and cognitive development: Coordinating communication and cues. *Exceptional Children, 53*, 109–111.

United States Office of Education. (1977). Definition and criteria for defining students as learning disabled. *Federal Register, 42:250*, p. 65083. Washington, DC: U.S. Government Printing Office.

United States Office of Education. (1988). *Tenth annual report to Congress on the implementation of the Education of the Handicapped Act.* Washington, DC: Author.

Vellutino, F. R. (1986). Linguistic and cognitive correlates of learning disability: Reactions to three reviews. In S. J. Ceci (Ed.), *Handbook of cognitive, social and neuropsychological aspects of learning disabilities* (Vol. 1, pp. 317–335). Hillsdale, NJ: Erlbaum.

Vogel, S. A. (1975). *Syntactic abilities of normal and dyslexic children.* Baltimore, MD: University Park Press.

Wender, P. H. (1971). *Minimal brain dysfunction in children.* New York: Wiley.

Wender, P. H. (1972). The minimal brain dysfunction syndrome in children. *Journal of Nervous and Mental Disease, 165*, 55–71.

Wiederholt, J. L. (1974). Historical perspectives on the education of the learning disabled. In L. Mann & D. Sabatino (Eds.), *The second review of special education* (pp. 103–152). Philadelphia, PA: JSE Press.

Wiig, E. H., & Semel, E. M. (1980). *Intervention for the learning disabled.* Columbus, OH: Merrill.

Wilson, J., & Cowell, B. (1984). How should we define handicap? *Special Education: Forward Trends, 11*(2), 33–35.

Witkin, H., Oltman, P., Raskin, E., & Karp, J. (1971). *A manual for the embedded figures test.* Palo Alto, CA: Consulting Psychologists Press.

Wong, B. Y. L. (1978). The effects of directive cues on the organization of memory and recall in good and poor readers. *Journal of Educational Research, 72*(1), 32–38.

Wood, S., & Shears, B. (1986). *Teaching children with severe learning difficulties: A radical reappraisal.* London: Croom Helm.

2

Educational Trends in Learning Disabilities

WAYNE P. HRESKO AND

RENE S. PARMAR

Several educational trends appear to be gaining support and are having an effect on the field of learning disabilities. These trends include use of computers and other high technology for instruction, assessment, and curriculum management; integrative education approaches; school consultation models; and transitioning.

HOW ARE ADVANCES IN COMPUTERS AND HIGH TECHNOLOGY AFFECTING THE LEARNING DISABILITIES FIELD?

During the last decade, no area has grown as significantly as high technology. High technology has affected the education of the learning disabled by altering methods of instruction, assessment, and curriculum management. Ten years ago, computers were rarely found in schools. Today, schools without computers are rarely found. Mokros and Russell (1986) reported that 88% of the schools they surveyed were using microcomputers with learning disabled students. This increased reliance on the use of high technology is a direct result of evolution in the learning disabilities field.

Evolution of Computers

The original computers used in schools were slow, had little memory capacity, and were barely more than workbooks on video monitors. The new generation of computers and computer software provides students with fast computation, expanded memory, extremely good video resolution, and advanced graphics capability. Today's computers rarely contain less than 256 kilobytes, and often several megabytes of memory. This increase in memory has allowed educators to bring to each school software applications usually restricted to large, costly computers. Furthermore, the original computers had less attractive displays (monitors), usually presenting information in green, amber, black and white, or low-resolution color. New computer displays are bright, have high resolution, and often have excellent color. No longer relegated to floppy disks of limited capacity, current computers have high-density floppy disk storage, and can easily be fitted for hard disks with even greater capacity. This increased capacity is significant for software applications. Today's computers also have become much faster, typically running at least eight times faster than the original school computers. Finally, the price of computers has decreased over the years, making it possible for schools to obtain fast computers, with good resolution and large storage capacity, at a reasonable price.

Use of Computers to Help Learning Disabled Students

Computers and high technology have several applications in the education of learning disabled students. Computer use in the schools has traditionally been limited to drill and practice (Cartwright, Cartwright, & Ward, 1989). Advances in technology have increased applications to include problem solving simulations, curriculum-oriented adaptive testing, interactive video disk instruction, computer data management, computer-assisted test scoring, and computer-based testing.

Computers are excellent for problem solving simulations in that they provide learning situations in which students' responses can be almost instantaneously evaluated and the outcomes of the choices presented. For example, for the student studying global political situations, the computer can indicate on a global level the effects of a given response to a problem.

In curriculum-oriented adaptive testing, the presentation of the items changes based upon the responses of each student. The testing is thus "adapted" to the abilities of the student. Computers keep track of the responses and present the questions or stop the testing as appropriate.

Interactive video disk instruction involves the presentation of concepts, using high-quality video presentation that is guided by computer-based information. Again, the presentation is modified based on each student's responses.

Current information on student achievement, placement, and so forth, is required for compliance in most states. Computer-based data management allows educational personnel to attain almost instant data for individual students, classes, classification categories, schools, or districts. Education has adapted the techniques of data handling in business to the management of student data. Computers are best used when they enhance human abilities and decrease the potential for errors.

Computer-assisted test scoring is another excellent computer application. Several varieties of scoring systems are available. In one type, school personnel enter a student's raw data, and the computer calculates the test's standard scores, quotients, comparisons, and so on. A second variety goes one step further by providing a narrative report. A third variety uses the standard scores from the test and develops narrative information either from the standard score information or from research literature. Caution should be used in selecting scoring systems, especially those that provide narrative reports. Computer-based narrative reports often are not complete with respect to background information, influence of extraneous variables, and, most importantly, the clinical impressions and observations of the person performing the assessment.

Some individuals have attempted to administer standardized tests through computer presentation, utilizing both on-screen presentation of instructions and synthesized voice instructions. Although this type of administration has potential, caution should be maintained. Some research suggests that norms based on pencil-and-paper presentations may not be appropriate for computer-based administrations (Varnhagen & Gerber, 1984). Thus, tests adapted for computer administration may need to be renormed prior to assessing children.

As computer sophistication and high technology capabilities continue to evolve, the field of education will be affected by increasing reliance on computer use. Microcomputer use is beneficial not only for the academic and management applications (Carnine, 1989), but also for the personal gains encountered. High technology has the potential to increase student motivation to learn as well as to enhance self-concepts and feelings of empowerment (Ellis & Sabornie, 1988). These personal attributes often perpetuate and confound the learning disabled student's achievement in school. Thus, computers may provide a useful avenue for remediation.

Although much has been expected of computers in the education of the exceptional child, those expectations have not been realized. Research to date has failed to substantiate significant or even moderate gains in the academic areas. Furthermore, although some researchers have focused on the potential effects of computers on thinking and reasoning ability, research has failed to show significant effects. Thus, widespread high hopes for educational uses of the computer remain to be realized.

HOW WILL THE REGULAR EDUCATION INITIATIVE AND OTHER INTEGRATIVE EDUCATION APPROACHES IMPACT THE FIELD?

PL 94-142 has made a tremendous impact on the range of educational and related services offered to students with disabilities since it was signed into law in 1975. PL 94-142 has modified the face of education by changing the structural relationship of regular and special education and by guarantying handicapped students and their parents certain constitutional rights and procedural safeguards (Skrtic, 1986).

A growing number of people are now questioning the wisdom of such a separation and demarcation. Issues such as flawed classification systems, effectiveness of current categorical programs, validity of pullout programs, and an incomplete research base, have prompted authors to postulate the need for a critical look at current educational practice (Hagerty & Abramson, 1987; Lilly, 1987; Stainback & Stainback, 1984; Wang & Walberg, 1988). Madeline Will, then assistant secretary for the Office of Special Education and Rehabilitative Services, U.S. Department of Education, captured the interest of the education field when she recommended that special education and regular programs be allowed to collectively contribute skills and resources to better serve all students (Will, 1986). This concept of shared responsibility has come to be known as the Regular or General Education Initiative (REI or GEI) and has created considerable controversy, mainly because of those who interpret REI as mandating the abandonment or radical restructuring of special education (Council for Children with Behavioral Disorders [CCBD], 1989). Proponents of the REI are questioning the justification for separate educational programs. Even before the passage of PL 94-142, some were questioning the efficacy of separate programs for disabled individuals for remediating educational difficulties, and more recent research indicates that the practice may, in fact, be less beneficial (Haynes & Jenkins, 1986). Anti-REI professionals maintain that disabled learners need highly trained instructors, whereas pro-REI advocates insist that all students require only teachers who demonstrate "good teaching" techniques (Jenkins, Pious, & Peterson, 1988; Kindsvatter, Wilen, & Ishler, 1988).

Evolution of Mainstreaming

Whether one sides with or against those advocating for a single system of education, the underlying goal of all special services is ultimate affiliation with the mainstream of society. Reynolds (1988) summarizes the history of special education in two words: *progressive inclusion*. Historically treated with neglect and abuse, individuals with disabilities were finally recognized enough to be placed into residential facilities. As time passed, the handicapped population was given a place in segregated day schools and classes. With increasing magnitude, the trend in the past decade has been to move previously excluded students into resource rooms and the mainstream of regular classes. The PL 94-142 guarantee of a free and appropriate public education with nonhandicapped peers in the least restrictive environment possible has come to mean "mainstreaming" to many people. Mainstreaming implies the gradual movement of a disabled student from special to regular classroom settings, until total integration is accomplished. Although regular class placement would seem to be the ultimate goal of special education, caution must be exercised to prevent the focus on the student's physical integration from over-looking true social integration (Honig & McCarron, 1987; Jenkins, Odom, & Speltz, 1989; Raab, Nordquist, Cunningham, & Bliem, 1986).

Model Programs Developed for Integrated Education

The mainstreaming movement has led to the development of model programs utilizing an integrative education approach (Brophy, 1986; Epps & Tindall, 1987; Heller, Holtzman, & Messick, 1982; Nevin & Thousand, 1987). One such program, the Adaptive Learning Environments Model (ALEM), had its inception at the University of Pittsburgh's Learning Research and Development Center as an individualized instructional program (Wang & Stiles, 1976). These model programs were created as a part of the National Follow-Through effort designed to facilitate continuation of the gains made by children enrolled in Head Start (Wang & Birch, 1984). The underlying assumptions were the forerunners of ALEM's broader foundation. Basically, the assumptions are stated as a recognition that children display a wide range of entry-level abili-ties in the educational setting, and instructional experiences must be provided to accommodate the individual needs. These early models, as with the later ALEM, rely heavily on concepts suggested by Glaser (1972). Guidelines for the pre-ALEM programs focused on assessing observable student performance and providing educational alternatives. Each class required two adults, a teacher and an aide. The adults' duties were defined as "traveling" and "test-ing and tutoring" (Wang & Stiles, 1976, p. 173).

ALEM's creators added the term "adaptive instruction" in 1980. Wang (1980) defined adaptive instruction as the use of alternative instructional strategies and resources to meet the needs of the individual student. Advocat-ing for "label-less" education, the major characteristics of the program were (a) the use of criterion assessments and efficient record keeping to diagnose and monitor learning progress, (b) the view of student responsibility as an outcome of adaptive instruction and the consequent teaching of self-management skills, (c) the organizational modification of multi-age grouping and team teaching, and (d) a heightened degree of family involvement. The school was described as a social system for the development of socialization, and the basics of education were defined as being the development of personal discipline, self-efficacy, and adaptability (Wang, 1980; Wang & Baker, 1985–1986). Wang (1981) gave a broad overview of the mainstreaming program describing the approach as "a diagnostic–prescriptive approach to individualized programming, built-in systems of continuous monitoring of student progress, the teaching of self-management skills, the expectation of student self-responsibility and family involvement" (p. 203).

Components of other innovative approaches promoting integrative education include (a) peer-tutoring or the buddy system, (b) heterogeneous grouping, and (c) cooperative learning. Peer-tutoring or the buddy system involves the matching of nonhandicapped students to their disabled peers. The matching provides an avenue for the less able student to receive individualized instruction or encouragement and promotes social integration. It is important for the teacher to remember that assistance can be provided from both directions; in some instances, the disabled child will be able to take the lead.

Heterogeneous grouping facilitates an atmosphere of interdependence and integration. In a nonstigmatizing manner, students of different ages and abilities are grouped according to their needs at a given moment. Group membership fluctuates with the variance of the objective, and students have ample access to peers for guidance. The existence of individual differences diminishes in importance as the student is not in constant comparison to an established norm.

Cooperative learning is the "instructional use of small groups so that students work together to maximize their own and each other's learning" (D. W. Johnson & R. T. Johnson, 1989, p. 6). Cooperative learning approaches are receiving widespread recognition and merit (D. W. Johnson & R. Johnson, 1987; Slavin, 1986). As opposed to traditional competitive or individualistic approaches, cooperative learning situations provide the opportunity for all group members to develop and use leadership skills (McElroy, 1989). The basic elements of cooperative learning include the following (D. W. Johnson & R. T. Johnson, 1989):

• Positive interdependence

• Promotive interaction

• Individual accountability

• Social skills development

• Group processing

The cooperative learning approach has been applied specifically to learning disabled adolescents (Taymans, 1989).

The Future of REI and Integrative Education

Anyone working with a handicapped child must identify integration as one of the goals for that individual. Unfortunately, more extremist writers have capitalized on REI's concept of integration and, by using volatile language that calls for the abandonment or radical restructuring of special education, have generated emotional controversy regarding the issue (Hagerty & Abramson, 1987; Reynolds, Wang, & Walberg, 1987; Skrtic, 1986; Wang & Walberg, 1988). Because of some of the derogatory terms used and implied accusations, those involved in education are facing a dilemma; a territorial battle threatens to cause increased dissension before a resolution is found. The October 1988 issue of *Exceptional Children* unintentionally provided excellent examples of the conflict (Fuchs & Fuchs, 1988a, 1988b; Wang & Walberg, 1988). The original concept may have been presented in an attempt to improve educational standards, but the theory has created opinionated followers.

The emotionality of the proposed REI emanates from very valid concerns regarding the initiative. One of the main concerns of those involved with special education is that the proposed educational reform will jeopardize the gains achieved thus far for handicapped students (Hagerty & Abramson, 1987; National Association of School Psychologists, 1985). The provision of an equal opportunity to an appropriate education, the recognized need for extended-year services, and the use of medical and technological interventions that allow students to attend school are only a few of the many gains that may disappear in a unitary system. REI threatens to undo much of the unfinished advocacy for disabled students (Clark & Astuto, 1988; Verstegen, 1987; Verstegen & Clark, 1988). Professionals in the field continue to advocate for the existence of a continuum of services that match the needs of disabled students (Braaten, J. Kauffman, Braaten, Polsgrove, & Nelson, 1988; McCarthy, 1987). To the chagrin of many, a full continuum of services is available only as a result of funding patterns that are reliant upon categorical identification. REI would abolish the use of categorical identification, which would serve to totally eliminate any guarantee that the students most in need of the services would be the ones who receive them. REI influence can be viewed as being detrimental to the provision of quality services. Under the Reagan–Bush administration, the practice of combining funding for various programs into block grants has yielded a dismal picture for handicapped children (Clark & Astuto, 1988; CCBD, 1989; Verstegen, 1987; Verstegen & Clark, 1988). Acceptance of REI may further and more seriously reduce services to disabled children.

Proponents of REI seemingly ignore the reasons for the establishment of special education. PL 94-142 was created because handicapped students were being inadequately served in regular education, or excluded altogether (Association for Children and Adults with Learning Disabilities, 1986; Braaten et al., 1988; CCBD, 1989; Sapon-Shevin, 1987; Sizer, 1984). Problems still exist in the regular education service delivery system (National Commission on Excellence in Education, 1983; Pugach & Sapon-Shevin, 1987; Skrtic, 1986; Teacher Education Division, 1986). If special education is absorbed into the regular education programming, it may be necessary to rediscover it at a later date.

Central to the issue of REI are the teachers (Davis, 1989). Apparently unbeknownst to REI proponents, current research indicates that regular education teachers feel incompetent and, almost more importantly, unmotivated to work with special needs students (Aloia & Aloia, 1983; Cruickshank, 1981; Horvath, Hitchings, & Sinder, 1983; Talebian, 1984). As Lieberman (1985) so graphically stated, "We cannot drag regular educators kicking and screaming into a merger with special education" (p. 513). The most effective teachers have been found to be the least tolerant of behavioral and learning differences (Gersten, Walker, & Darch, 1988). This attitude is extremely resistant to change (Gersten, Carnine, & Woodward, 1987) and actually worsens after a teacher has worked with a handicapped student (L. N. Kauffman, 1981). Teachers are also subject to periodic evaluations by administrators, which often influence the salaries they will receive. Teachers have been rated higher when they show relatively more concern about higher achieving students and less concern about lower achieving students (Mitman, 1985). The effect of a teacher's attitude on the performance of a student has long been recognized (Harris & Rosenthal, 1985; Rosenthal & Jacobson, 1968). From this data, it easily can be inferred that the full-time placement of disabled learners into regular classes will unfairly affect their learning because of the inflexibility and unwillingness of regular teachers (Alves & Gottlieb, 1986).

The extreme concept of REI coupled with the excellence movement will serve to make school even more challenging for disabled students (Torch, 1984). Students who have difficulty in the mainstream would be put into situations in which competency testing and higher standards are a major focus. Teachers would be forced to choose between directing instruction toward maximizing the mean achievement of the class or remediating difficulties of the lower achieving students (Boyer, 1983; Gerber, 1988; J. M. Kauffman, Gerber, & Semmel, 1988). Many barriers are still preventing the provision of effective integrative educational services (Gersten et al., 1988). Two of the most critical barriers relate to the way teachers are trained (Grissmer & Kirby, 1987; National Education Association, 1983; Pugach & Lilly, 1984) and the way education is currently funded (Keogh, 1988; Lynn, 1983; Shepard, 1987).

WHAT IS SCHOOL-BASED CONSULTATION IN LEARNING DISABILITIES?

As special education seeks alternative ways of servicing students, one proposed option is school-based consultation. Consultation has the potential of providing services to exceptional students in the regular classroom (West & Brown, 1987). Although some say that consultation has been a part of special and regular education for years, others note that consultation is only recently emerging as a viable method of providing services (West & Idol, 1987).

Consultation has three basic connotations (Kurpius & Robinson, 1978). In medical literature, consultation refers to the process by which a physician requests the expert counsel of another physician (Bindman, 1966; Caplan, 1964). From an organizational background, consultation implies effort toward a planned social change at a system level (Argyris, 1962; Bennis, 1969a, 1969b; Lippitt, 1969; Schein, 1969). Within the mental health profession, consultation describes the process whereby a consultant assists another professional (consultee) in regard to a client for whom the consultee retains responsibility (Caplan, 1964). From these frameworks, several models of consultation have been proposed (Conoley & Conoley, 1982; West & Idol, 1987). In education, consultation refers to the provision of services to teachers and/or students for the solving of classroom-related behavioral or instructional problems. Of the consultation models applicable to education, three will be discussed: the mental health model, the collaborative model, and the corporate model.

The mental health model of consultation has perhaps the longest history. It is based upon traditional psychological understandings and approaches to modifying behavior. This model was developed in the 1960s by Caplan (1964, 1970), who proposed that case discussion and problem solving with a consultant will enhance service provider effectiveness. The consultant was admonished to focus on individuals' relationships rather than on intrapsychic conflicts. Mental health consultation is used by those who perceive merit in analyzing the motives and psychological construction of consultees (Conoley & Conoley, 1988). Mental health consultants most commonly focus on teacher perceptions, skills, and emotions in the course of the consultation. Direct work with children is done only to model desired behaviors. This adult-focused service is typically hierarchical in nature, although the potential exists for it to become more egalitarian (Gallessich, 1985).

The collaborative consultation model being used in education has been described by Idol, Paolucci-Whitcomb, and Nevin (1986) as a team approach to the generation of creative solutions to mutually defined problems which provides for comprehensive and effective programs for students with special needs within most integrated environments. Collaborative consultation is a teaching and troubleshooting approach to student support which relies on an interdependence between the consultant and consultee from which both can benefit. This model regards all individuals involved in the consultation as possessing parity and equality in the pursuit of cooperative problem solving. The following underlying assumptions are critical to a collaborative consultation model (Pryzwansky, 1974):

1. Mutual consent on the part of two or more professionals

2. Mutual commitment to the objectives of and the resolution of the problems

3. Joint development of the intervention plan

4. Mutual responsibility for implementation and evaluation of the plan

The organizational consultation model is based on a combination of human relations theories (Bennis, 1969a, 1969b; Lippitt, 1969), organizational dimensions (Schmuck & Runkel, 1972), and advocacy approaches (Conoley & Conoley, 1982). This model focuses on how individuals influence one another within organizational structures, how that influence is impacted by the physical and mental environments, and how these considerations shape personal growth (Rogers, 1959). In the organizational model, the consultant assumes a facilitative role in which he or she serves as an assistant to the consultee in the process of reactive and proactive problem solving.

The Advantages of Consultation

The consultation models appear to have several advantages. First, because services are provided in the classroom, even if only indirectly, no student is required to leave his or her usual placement. Second, by directly employing the usual classroom teacher to provide services, no additional personnel are needed. Third, consultation requires that problems be solved rather than temporary bandages being applied. Fourth, since experts are enlisted to aid teachers, the skills developed with teachers remain in the classroom.

In a study of the preferences of education professionals, Babcock and Pryzwansky (1983) found that the collaborative consultation model was rated over the other approaches. Subsequent research indicates that the preference of one model or style over another may vary depending upon the stage of the consultation, but that collaborative consultation remains the model of overall choice (West, 1985). Given the advantages and clear indication of preference, concern is generated over the low incidence of consultation occurrences. West (1985) indicated that resource teachers average only 46 consultation contacts with regular class colleagues during the entire school year. As the resource and regular class teachers, in essence, "share" the students, their given rate of little more than one contact per week creates concern regarding the amount of consultation initiated (or more aptly *not* initiated) by teachers of self-contained and less integrated students. Certain obstacles must be hindering the acceptance of consultation.

The Barriers to Implementation of Consultation

Proponents of integrated programs are advocating for an increased reliance on consultation services instead of special services. Certain obstacles must be resolved, however, before consultation will be assimilated as a component of education in this sense. These barriers include (a) philosophical variations, (b) professional preparation of consultants, (c) fiscal limitations, (d) issues of accountability, and (e) the hierarchical nature of consultation.

As mentioned, the concept of consultation has evolved from a variety of philosophical bases. Continued reliance on isolated points of reference will prohibit the application of consultation to situations other than the one directly related to the individual theory. Consultation must be approached by avoiding adherence to a particular set of theoretical premises, and accepted for its attempts to combine strengths of differing models. Thus, the interaction of people and environments in which the consultation is occurring will be enhanced (Friend, 1988).

Professional preparation of consultants is typically relegated to the specific field from which the consultant is emerging. As a result, consultants are trained in isolated programs, which diminishes the ability for the consultation to reflect an integrated approach. Consultation has been described as an "artful science" (Idol & West, 1987, p. 474) which encompasses skills from many theoretical approaches. A transdisciplinary approach would increase the capabilities of the consultant (Golightly, 1987).

The fiscal limitations of initiating consultation services can be a cause for concern. New consultants must be hired to provide the full-time services prescribed in the models. Consultation has been recognized, however, as being extremely cost-effective in the long run. By allowing the provision of support services to larger caseloads (Heron & Kimball, 1988) and by providing teachers with skills that reduce special education referrals (Idol, 1986), the use of consultation will actually diminish the current costs of education for handicapped learners.

The issue of accountability must be resolved before consultation can be broadly implemented. If a student's needs remain unmet in the classroom, who is ultimately responsible? Some argue that the teacher must implement the consultant's recommended interventions, no matter how unappealing they might appear, whereas others argue that the consultant is accountable for expanding his or her repertoire of interventions to match the teacher's style. Research indicates that classroom teachers may be unwilling to implement the consultant's recommendations (Reisberg & Wolf, 1986). Solutions to this dilemma include matching the style and feasibility of the collaboration to the specific situation (Gans, 1986), and having the consultant work with teachers within the context of the classroom during daily school operations (McGill & Robinson, 1989).

Another barrier to widespread acceptance of the consultation model is the attitude that consultation is hierarchical in nature (L. J. Johnson, Pugach, & Hammitte, 1988). Because consultation is an outgrowth of the need to share expert opinions, a relationship is shaped in which a "less competent" individual receives assistance from a "more capable" specialist (Pryzwansky, 1974). Not only does this attitude create hesitancy on the part of a teacher to ask for and receive consultation, but it can also cause resistance toward the implementation of any suggestions. As L. J. Johnson et al. (1988) wrote, "Although classroom teachers may be receptive during consultation sessions, systematic change on the part of the teacher will be less well received and less attainable as long as the consultative relationship is conceptualized hierarchically" (p. 45). Favored models of consultation promote a reciprocal relationship in which each member maintains equal status. Changing the traditional view of the hierarchical nature of consultation will require underlying attitudinal adjustment.

Ecological Consultation

Ecological consultation (Conoley & Conoley, 1988) refers to attempts to incorporate the strengths of consultation and circumvent the barriers by relying on the integration of the various models. Consultants having this combined ecological viewpoint provide a myriad of services. They directly teach and counsel students, indirectly affect the youth by offering inservice training and consultation to teachers, and serve key roles in performing case management duties and parent consultation. Figure 2–1 indicates the main aspects of the ecological model of consultation. Activities inherent to the consultation process that must be conducted in an ecological manner include written communication, interpersonal communication, noninteractive observation, interactive testing, record review and materials preparation, and modeling and demonstrating (Tindal & Taylor-Pendergast, 1989).

To perform in an ecological manner, consultants must be able to analyze teacher variables (Rosenshine & Stevens, 1986) and instructional variables (Bauwens & Ehlert, 1987), as well as individual student and peer variables. As Reisberg and Wolf (1988) wrote,

> The consultant needs more than a laundry list of effective interventions. An understanding of the variables that may affect student performance, matched with a knowledge of the assessment tools and interventions effective with each variable, can provide the consultant with a model for joint problem solving. (p. 37)

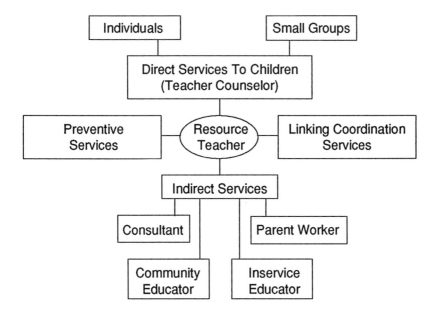

Figure 2-1. Components of the Ecological Model of Consultation. From "Useful Theories in School-Based Consultation" by J. C. Conoley and C. W. Conoley, 1988, *Remedial and Special Education, 9*(6), p. 19.

In the education of learning disabled students, the advantages of consultation may help eliminate some of the obstacles to implementing current trends. Because of the growing emphasis on prereferral interventions, the Regular Education Initiative (REI), and the demand for integrated education (Tindal & Taylor-Pendergast, 1989), consultation may become a focus in many programs in both public schools and educational training programs (Idol & West, 1987). To date, the majority of literature in special education consultation is accurately described as being used to justify and promote the maintenance of students in regular classrooms. With this objective in mind, West and Idol (1987) stated, "Working collaboratively, we can pool our diverse expertise and experiences toward the common goal of developing consultation as a viable, effective service delivery option for learning disabled and other exceptional students in the mainstream, as well as for low achieving students" (p. 406).

WHY IS TRANSITION AN IMPORTANT ISSUE FOR THE LEARNING DISABLED?

As demonstrated by traditional policy and structured by public mandate, public education is restricted by a finite time frame. Typically, students are encouraged to attend school from kindergarten to 12th grade. Exceptions have been defined in PL 94-142 so that students with handicaps may receive school instruction until they are 21 years of age. Yet, even with an age extension, all students must exit the educational system at a specified point in time.

For most individuals, the bestowal of a diploma indicates that it is time to enter the work force or to secure further education at a monetary expense so that they will be better prepared to find and maintain employment. Serious concern has been raised as to the effectiveness of special and regular education in preparing the disabled student population for these postschool endeavors. These concerns are supported by research studies. It is estimated that 67% of Americans with handicaps between the ages of 16 and 64 are not working (Rusch & Phelps, 1987). Unemployment is often equated with failure to complete a public school program, and one reason that so many handicapped people are unable to secure employment is the high dropout rate for students with disabilities. It is estimated that 39% of the population with disabilities do not graduate from high school, compared with 15% of the nonhandicapped population (Transition Services Task Force, 1989). This dropout rate is even higher when considering only the learning disabled population. It is estimated that 54% of students with learning disabilities will not complete high school (Zigmond & Thornton, 1985). Of those who do graduate and obtain employment, less than 15% earn above minimum wage (Edgar, 1987).

A solution to this horrifying dilemma lies in establishing transitional programs for disabled youth. Transition is defined as "a purposeful, organized, and outcome-oriented process designed to help 'at risk' students move from school to employment and a quality adult life" (Dougan & Kaney, 1988, p. 14). It has been hypothesized that quality secondary programs, ongoing employment services, and employment alternatives will be the "bridges" that will enable disabled youth to successfully move from the educational realm to the work force (Will, 1984). Some skeptics describe the use of the word "transition" as the terminology of choice for trendy professionals, a word promising a concept that lacks validity and providing only better means to document school failure (Ferguson & Ferguson, 1989).

Skeptics aside, there appears to be general agreement that successful transitioning consists of effective school instruction, collaborative transitional planning, and placement into meaningful employment (Malouf, 1982; Rusch & Chadsey-Rusch, 1985; Wehman, Kregel, & Barcus, 1985). Despite the general consensus and plentiful literature addressing each of these elements, however, 95% of graduates with disabilities are not competitively employed 3 years after graduation (Winget, 1989). At which point does the transitional effort become dysfunctional?

Improving the Curriculum

The curricula encountered by nonhandicapped secondary students are inappropriate for successful postschool endeavors of the handicapped population

(Edgar, 1987). Instead of the traditional curricula, a specialized instructional focus needs to be established (Brolin, 1987). Wehman et al. (1985) and Peters, Templeman, and Brostrom (1987) advocated a functional, integrated, and community-based curriculum. Rather than providing clear direction, however, this curricular description is open to numerous interpretations and great variability. "Functional" denotes different approaches to different interpreters. Some define a functional curriculum as emphasizing practice in daily living skills (Brown, Halpern, Hasazi, & Wehman, 1987), others suggest an increased emphasis on social skill development (Brown et al., 1987), and still others recommend development of independent problem solving skills and information processing strategies (Mithaug, Martin, & Agran, 1987). Most recognize that the severely disabled require a functional curricula instigated early in the school career (Wehman, 1983; Wehman et al., 1985), but that idea contradicts current educational reforms which place a heavy emphasis on academics (McDill, Natriello, & Pallas, 1985). Brolin (1987) and Edgar (1987) suggested that the obvious resolution is to compromise the integration aspect of mainstreaming and provide the functional training in a segregated environment, recognizing that disabled students will require differential training in skills that will transition them into postschool life. If the curricula are to be presented in a community-based fashion, the disabled students will necessarily be segregated from their nondisabled peers; for example, nonhandicapped learners are limited in the number of "field trips" in which they are allowed to participate. Although research supports functional, integrated, and community-based curricular approaches as promoting successful transition, current school practices discourage their implementation.

Transitional Planning

Although interagency collaboration is vital for successful transitional planning (Kiernan & Conley, 1989; McDonnel & Hardman, 1985), a survey of school administrators indicates that 33% do not consider interfacing to be a priority in their schools (Benz & Halpern, 1987). The administrators who do believe interagency coordination is important do not share the same focus as the parents of the students with disabilities. These administrators network with employers, whereas the parents would like to see more postschool educational opportunities for their children (Benz & Halpern, 1987). Dougan and Kaney (1988) suggested softening this difference by making the families responsible for interagency cooperation during the last 2 years of handicapped students' school careers. Whether this responsibility falls upon the schools or the families, it is agreed that local autonomy of the transitional process results in more successful postschool experiencies (Peters et al., 1987). A comprehensive implementation of interagency cooperation is yet to be realized.

Meaningful Employment of Disabled Individuals

Transition implies more than the movement from school environments to work settings. Transition also entails economic self-sufficiency (Neubert, Tilson, & Ianacone, 1989). Successful transitioning cannot be measured by job retention for 60 days; transitioning must be evaluated in terms of a life-style. Within this element of meaningful employment, there are some optimistic trends. A higher percentage of disabled graduates are working on regular job sites (as opposed to sheltered workshop settings) now than a few years ago (Brown et al., 1987; Kerachsky & Thornton, 1987; Whitehead, 1986). Unfortunately, because this shift often involves a better salary, disabled individuals find themselves facing the loss of other benefits when they "move up" in the job market (Brown et al., 1987). Also, the number of job openings for disabled employees outside of sheltered workshops is limited (Edgar, 1987). Handicapped individuals who attempt to secure employment often find themselves limited to the stereotypic "food, flowers, and filth" opportunities. Meaningful employment options are increasing, but many potential employees with disabilities find themselves limited by what is available (Kiernan & Conley, 1989). Underemployment is as serious an issue as unemployment. Although some propose that an interagency council should commit itself to making sure that sufficient options are available (e.g., Winget, 1989), this is often difficult in practice.

The Future of the Transition Movement

The transition of disabled young adults from the school environment to meaningful postschool endeavors is one of the nation's priorities (Rusch & Phelps, 1987), especially for the mildly handicapped population (Benz & Halpern, 1987; Neubert et al., 1989). Most people involved can agree that successful transitioning involves appropriate school preparation, shared responsibility among agencies, and maintenance in gainful employment, but transitioning efforts have not been effective on a large scale. Other aspects, such as the integrative educational movement and the increased use of high technology will have impacts upon the focus of transitional efforts. The debate over the usefulness of supported employment, as defined by the 1986 amendments to the Rehabilitation Act (Transition Services Task Force, 1989), will also affect the outcome of the transition movement. Undeniably vital, transitioning is one of the critical issues for the 1990s (Knowlton & Clark, 1987).

SUMMARY

This chapter has provided an overview of some of the major trends having an effect on the educational considerations for students with learning disabilities. Advances in computers and high technology were discussed as potential opportunities for instructional as well as management uses of computers in education. After a short historical overview of computers in education, potential applications for the use of computers with learning disabled students were indicated.

The influence of the Regular Education Initiative (REI) and Integrated Education approaches on educational service provision for learning disabled students was considered. This section presented the evolution of the mainstreaming concept, as well as overviews of mainstreaming models and strategies. Reasons for apprehension were cited. Proponents and opponents are forming opinionated alliances, and the outcome of REI efforts remains to be seen.

School-based consultation was presented in the context of varying theoretical bases. The three models most applicable to education were presented: the mental health, collaborative, and corporate models. The advantages and the barriers to implementation of effective consultation were discussed. An ecological consultation format was presented as demonstrating potential widespread acceptance.

Finally, the need for transition services was mentioned as one of the most critical challenges facing the next decade of educators in working with learning disabled students. The recognition of the need for such activities and the actual demand for the services are growing at such a rapid rate that transitioning has become one of the nation's priorities. Although there is some agreement regarding the necessary components for an effective transitioning program, such programs have not been entirely successful. The chapter concluded with a discussion of the problems inherent in transitioning efforts and speculated on future developments of such efforts.

REFERENCES

Aloia, G. F., & Aloia, S. D. (1983). Teacher expectation questionnaire: A scale to help determine the most appropriate placement for mainstreamed handicapped students. *Journal for Special Educators, 19,* 11–20.

Alves, A. J., & Gottlieb, J. (1986). Teacher interactions with mainstreamed handicapped students and their nonhandicapped peers. *Learning Disabilities Quarterly, 9*(1), 77–80.

Argyris, C. (1962). *Interpersonal competence and organizational effectiveness.* Homewood, IL: Dorsey.

Association for Children and Adults with Learning Disabilities (1986). Regular education/special education initiative: A position paper by the ACLD. *Exceptional Parent, 16*(5), 59–64.

Babcock, N. L., & Pryzwansky, W. B. (1983). Models of consultation: Preferences of educational professionals at five steps of service. *Journal of School Psychology, 21,* 359–366.

Bauwens, J., & Ehlert, B. J. (1987). Systematic classroom variable analysis. *Collaborative Endeavors, 4*(6), 4–5.

Bennis, W. G. (1969a). *Changing organizations.* New York: McGraw-Hill.

Bennis, W. G. (1969b). *Organizational development: Its nature, origin and prospects.* Reading, MA: Addison-Wesley.

Benz, M. R., & Halpern, A. S. (1987). Transition services for secondary students with mild disabilities: A statewide perspective. *Exceptional Children, 53,* 507–514.

Bindman, A. J. (1966). The clinical psychologist as a mental health consultant. In L. E. Abt & B. J. Reiss (Eds.), *Progress in clinical psychology.* New York: Grune and Stratton.

Boyer, E. L. (1983). *High school: A report on secondary education in America.* New York: Harper and Row.

Braaten, S., Kauffman, J., Braaten, B., Polsgrove, L., & Nelson, C. M. (1988). The regular education initiative: Patent medicine for behavioral disorders. *Exceptional Children, 55,* 21–27.

Brolin, D. E. (1987). Career education: A continuing high priority for educating exceptional students. *Journal of Career Development, 13,* 50–56.

Brophy, J. B. (1986). Research linking teacher behavior to student achievement: Potential implications for instruction of Chapter 1 students. In B. I. Williams, P. A. Richmaond, & B. J. Mason (Eds.), *Decisions for compensatory education: Conference proceedings and papers* (IV, pp. 121–179). Washington, DC: Research and Evaluation Associates.

Brown, L., Halpern, A. S., Hasazi, S. B., & Wehman, P. (1987). From school to adult living: A forum on issues and trends. *Exceptional Children, 53,* 546–554.

Caplan, G. (1964). *Principles of preventative psychiatry.* New York: Basic Books.

Caplan, G. (1970). *The theory and practice of mental health consultation.* New York: Basic Books.

Carnine, D. (1989). Teaching complex content to learning disabled students: The role of technology. *Exceptional Children, 55,* 524–533.

Cartwright, G. P., Cartwright, C. A., & Ward, M. E. (1989). *Educating special learners* (3rd ed.). Belmont, CA: Wadsworth.

Clark, D. L., & Astuto, T. A. (1988). *Education policy after Reagan—What next?* Occasional paper No. 6, Policy Student Center of the University Council for Educational Administration, University of Virginia, Charlottesville.

Conoley, J. C., & Conoley, C. W. (1982). *School consultation: A guide to practice and training.* New York: Pergamon Press.

Conoley, J. C., & Conoley, C. W. (1988). Useful theories in school-based consultation. *Remedial and Special Education, 9*(6), 14–20.

Council for Children with Behavioral Disorders (CCBD). (1989). Position statement on the regular education initiative. *Behavioral Disorders, 14*(3), 201–207.

Cruickshank, W. M. (1981). A new perspective in teacher education: The neuroeducator. *Journal of Learning Disabilities, 10,* 193–194.

Davis, W. E. (1989). The regular education initiative debate: Its promises and problems. *Exceptional Children, 55,* 440–446.

Dougan, P., & Kaney, H. (1988). *California transition: Resources and information for special education.* Sacramento, CA: Resources in Special Education.

Edgar, E. (1987). Secondary programs in special education: Are many of them justifiable? *Exceptional Children, 53,* 555–561.

Ellis, E. S., & Sabornie, E. J. (1988). Effective instruction with microcomputers: Promises, practices and preliminary findings. In E. L. Meyer, G. A.

Vergason, & R. J. Whelan (Eds.), *Effective instructional strategies for exceptional children* (pp. 355–379). Denver: Love.

Epps, S., & Tindall, G. (1987). The effectiveness of differential programming in serving mildly handicapped students: Placement options and instructional programming. In M. C. Wang, M. C. Reynolds, & H. J. Walberg *(Eds.), Handbook of special education: Research and practice: Vol. 1. Learner characteristics and adaptive education* (pp. 213–218). Oxford, England: Pergamon Press.

Ferguson, D., & Ferguson, D. (1989, April). *The interpretivist view of special education and disability: Stories of special education and disability told from the other side.* Paper presented at the Convention of the Council for Exceptional Children, San Francisco.

Friend, M. (1988). Putting consultation into context: Historical and contemporary perspectives. *Remedial and Special Education, 9*(6), 7–13.

Fuchs, D., & Fuchs, L. (1988a). Evaluation of the adapative learning environments model. *Exceptional Children, 55,* 115–127.

Fuchs, D., & Fuchs, L. (1988b). Response to Wang and Walberg. *Exceptional Children, 55,* 133–146.

Gallessich, J. (1985). Toward a meta-theory of consultation. *The Counseling Psychologist, 13,* 336–354.

Gans, K. D. (1986). Life values, regular education and special educators. *Teacher Education and Special Education, 9,* 74–76.

Gerber, M. M. (1988). Tolerance and technology of instruction: Implications for special education reform. *Exceptional Children, 54,* 309–314.

Gersten, R., Carnine, D., & Woodward, J. (1987). Direct instruction research: The third decade. *Remedial and Special Education, 8*(6), 48–56.

Gersten, R., Walker, H., & Darch, C. (1988). Relationship between teachers' effectiveness and their tolerance for handicapped students. *Exceptional Children, 54,* 433–438.

Glaser, R. (1972). Individuals and learning: The new aptitudes. *Educational Researcher, 1,* 5–13.

Golightly, C. J. (1987). Transdisciplinary training: A step forward in special education teacher preparation. *Teacher Education and Special Education, 10,* 126–130.

Grissmer, D. W., & Kirby, S. N. (1987). *Teacher attrition: The uphill climb to staff the nation's schools.* Santa Monica, CA: RAND Corp.

Hagerty, G. J., & Abramson, M. (1987). Impediments to implementing national policy change for mildly handicapped students. *Exceptional Children, 51,* 315–323.

Harris, M. J., & Rosenthal, R. (1985). Mediation of interpersonal expectancy effects: 31 meta-analyses. *Psychological Bulletin, 97,* 363–386.

Haynes, M. C., & Jenkins, J. R. (1986). Reading instruction in special education resource rooms. *American Educational Research Journal, 23*(23), 161–190.

Heller, K., Holtzman, W., & Messick, S. (Eds.). (1982). *Placing children in special education: A strategy for equity.* Washington, DC: National Academy of Sciences.

Heron, T. E., & Kimball, W. H. (1988). Gaining perspective with the educational consultation research base: Ecological considerations and future recommendations. *Remedial and Special Education, 9*(6), 21–28, 47.

Honig, A. S., & McCarron, P. A. (1987, April). *Prosocial behaviors of handicapped and typical peers in an integrated preschool.* Paper presented at the Biennial Meeting of the Society for

Research and Child Development, Baltimore, MD.

Horvath, M. J., Hitchings, W. E., & Sinder, W. (1983). A study of educators' perceptions of the least restrictive environment. *The Journal for Special Educators, 20,* 1–8.

Idol, L. (1986). *Collaborative school consultation: Recommendations for state departments of education.* Reston, VA: National Task Force on Collaborative School Consultations, Teacher Education Division, Council for Exceptional Children.

Idol, L., Paolucci-Whitcomb, P., & Nevin, A. (1986). *Collaborative consultation.* Austin, TX: PRO-ED.

Idol, L., & West, J. F. (1987). Consultation in special education (Part II): Training and practice. *Journal of Learning Disabilities, 20*(8), 474–494.

Jenkins, J. R., Odom, S. L., & Speltz, M. L. (1989). Effects of social integration on preschool children with handicaps. *Exceptional Children, 55,* 420–428.

Jenkins, J. R., Pious, C. G., & Peterson, D. L. (1988). Categorical programs for remedial and handicapped students: Issues of validity. *Exceptional Children, 55,* 147–158.

Johnson, D. W., & Johnson, R. (1987). *Learning together and alone: Cooperative, competitive, and individualistic learning.* Englewood Cliffs, NJ: Prentice-Hall.

Johnson, D. W., & Johnson, R. T. (1989). Cooperative learning: What special education teachers need to know. *Pointer, 33*(2), 5–10.

Johnson, L. J., Pugach, M. C., & Hammitte, D. J. (1988). Barriers to effective special education consultation. *Remedial and Special Education, 9*(6), 41–47.

Kauffman, J. M., Gerber, M. M., & Semmel, M. I. (1988). Arguable assumptions underlying the regular education initiative. *Journal of Learning Disabilities, 21,* 6–11.

Kauffman, L. N. (1981). *The impact of P.L. 94-142 on elementary teacher attitudes and needs for personnel resources, and staff preparation in a typical New Jersey school district.* Unpublished manuscript.

Kerachsky, S., & Thornton, C. (1987). Findings from the STETS transitional employment demonstration. *Exceptional Children, 53,* 515–523.

Keogh, B. K. (1988). Improving services for problem learners: Rethinking and restructuring. *Journal of Learning Disabilities, 21,* 19–22.

Kiernan, W. E., & Conley, R. W. (1989). Issues, outcomes and barriers to employment for adults with developmental disabilities. *Journal of Rehabilitation Administration, 13,* 5–11.

Kindsvatter, R., Wilen, W., & Ishler, M. (1988). *Dynamics of effective teaching.* New York: Longman.

Knowlton, H. E., & Clark, G. M. (1987). Transition issues for the 1990s. *Exceptional Children, 53,* 562–563.

Kurpius, D., & Robinson, S. E. (1978). Overview of consultation. *Personal and Guidance Journal, 56,* 321–323.

Lieberman, L. M. (1985). Special education and regular education: A merger made in heaven? *Exceptional Children, 51,* 513–576.

Lilly, M. S. (1987). Lack of focus on special education in literature on educational reform. *Exceptional Children, 53,* 325–326.

Lippitt, G. L. (1969). *Organizational renewal.* New York: Appleton-Century-Crofts.

Lynn, L. E. (1983). The emerging system for educating handicapped children. *Policy Studies Review, 2*(1), 21–58.

Malouf, D. (1982). Is your school helping or hindering the career/vocational development of handicapped students? *Pointer, 26,* 18–20.

McCarthy, J. M. (1987). A response to the regular education initiative: A position paper of the Division for Learning Disabilities (DLD). *Learning Disabilities Focus, 2*(2), 75–77.

McDill, E., Natriello, G., & Pallas, A. (1985). Raising standards and retaining students: The impact of the reform recommendations on potential dropouts. *Review of Educational Research, 55,* 415–433.

McDonnel, J., & Hardman, M. (1985). Planning the transition of severely handicapped youth from school to adult services: A framework for high school programs. *Education and Training of the Mentally Retarded, 20,* 275–286.

McElroy, K. B. (1989). A taste of cooperativeness within an elementary school. *Pointer, 33*(2), 34–38.

McGill, N. B., & Robinson, L. (1989). Regular education teacher consultant. *Teaching Exceptional Children, 21*(2), 71–73.

Mithaug, D. E., Martin, J. E., & Agran, M. (1987). Adaptability instruction: The goal of transitional programming. *Exceptional Children, 53,* 500–505.

Mitman, A. L. (1985). Teachers' differential behavior toward higher and lower achieving students and its relation to selected teacher characteristics. *Journal of Educational Psychology, 77,* 149–161.

Mokros, J. R., & Russell, S. J. (1986). Learner-centered software: A survey of microcomputer use with special needs students. *Journal of Learning Disabilities, 19*(3), 185–190.

National Association of School Psychologists (NASP). (1985, April 19). Advocacy for appropriate educational services for all children: A position statement. *SpecialNet.* To: Federal, From NASP.CTASP.

National Commission on Excellence in Education. (1983). *A nation at risk: The imperative for educational reform.* Washington, DC: U.S. Department of Education.

National Education Association (NEA). (1983). *Teacher supply and demand in public schools, 1981–1982.* Washington, DC: Author.

Neubert, D. A., Tilson, G. P., & Ianacone, R. N. (1989). Postsecondary transition needs and employment patterns of individuals with mild disabilities. *Exceptional Children, 55,* 494–500.

Nevin, A., & Thousand, J. (1987). What research says about limiting or avoiding referrals to special education. *Teacher Education and Special Education, 9,* 149–161.

Peters, J. M., Templeman, T. P., & Brostrom, G. (1987). The school and community partnership: Planning transition for students with severe handicaps. *Exceptional Children, 53,* 531–536.

Pryzwansky, W. B. (1974). A reconsideration of the consultation model for delivery of school-based psychological services. *Journal of Orthopsychiatry, 44,* 579–583.

Pugach, M., & Lilly, M. S. (1984). Reconceptualizing support services for classroom teachers: Implications for teacher education. *Journal of Teacher Education, 35,* 48–55.

Pugach, M., & Sapon-Shevin, M. (1987). New agendas for special education policy: What the national reports haven't said. *Exceptional Children, 53,* 295–299.

Raab, M. M., Nordquist, V. M., Cunningham, J. L., & Bliem, C. D. (1986). Promoting peer regard of an autistic child in a mainstreamed preschool using preenrollment activities. *Child Study Journal, 16,* 265–283.

Reisberg, L., & Wolf, R. (1986). Developing a consulting program in special education: Implementation and interventions. *Focus on Exceptional Children, 19*(3), 1–15.

Reisberg, L., & Wolf, R. (1988). Instructional strategies for special education consultants. *Remedial and Special Education, 9*(6), 29–40, 47.

Reynolds, M. C. (1988). Past, present and future of school integration. *Impact, 1*(2), 2.

Reynolds, M. C., Wang, M. C., & Walberg, H. J. (1987). The necessary restructuring of special and regular education. *Exceptional Children, 53*, 391–398.

Rogers, C. R. (1959). A theory of therapy personality and interpersonal relationships, as developed in the client-centered framework. In S. Koch (Ed.), *Psychology: A study of science: Vol. II. Formulations of the personal and social concept.* New York: McGraw-Hill.

Rosenshine, B., & Stevens, R. (1986). Teaching functions. In M. C. Wittrock (Ed.), *Handbook of research on teaching* (3rd ed., pp. 376–391). New York: Macmillan.

Rosenthal, R., & Jacobson, L. (1968). *Pygmalion in the classroom.* New York: Holt, Rinehart and Winston.

Rusch, F. R., & Chadsey-Rusch, J. (1985). Employment for persons with severe handicaps: Curriculum development and coordination of services. *Focus on Exceptional Children, 17*, 1–8.

Rusch, F. R., & Phelps, L. A. (1987). Secondary special education and transition from school to work: A national priority. *Exceptional Children, 53*, 487–492.

Sapon-Shevin, M. (1987). The national education reports and special education: Implications for students. *Exceptional Children, 53*, 300–306.

Schein, E. H. (1969). *Process consultation: Its role in organizational development.* Reading, MA: Addison-Wesley.

Schmuck, R. A., & Runkel, P. J. (1972). Organizational training. In R. A. Schmuck & P. J. Runkel (Eds.), *Handbook of organizational development in schools* (pp. 14–30). Palo Alto, CA: Mayfield.

Shepard, L. A. (1987). The new push for excellence: Widening the schism between regular and special education. *Exceptional Children, 53*, 327–329.

Sizer, T. F. (1984). *Horace's compromise: The dilemma of the American high school.* Boston: Houghton-Mifflin.

Skrtic, T. M. (1986). The crisis in special education knowledge: A perspective on perspective. *Focus on Exceptional Children, 18*(7), 2–15.

Slavin, R. E. (1986). *Using student team learning* (3rd ed.). Baltimore, MD: Johns Hopkins University, Center for Research on Elementary and Middle Schools.

Stainback, W., & Stainback, S. (1984). A rationale for the merger of special and regular education. *Exceptional Children, 51*, 102–111.

Talebian, S. (1984). *Analysis of opinions of educators regarding mainstreaming handicapped students.* Unpublished doctoral dissertation, University of Southern California, Los Angeles.

Taymans, J. M. (1989). Cooperative learning for learning disabled adolescents. *Pointer, 33*(2), 28–32.

Teacher Education Division (TED). (1986, October). *A message to all TED members concerning the national inquiry into the future of education for students with special needs.* (Available from Immediate Past President, CEC Teacher Education Division, 2150 Brisbane Avenue, Reno, NV 89503.)

Tindal, G. A., & Taylor-Pendergast, S. J. (1989). A taxonomy for objectively analyzing the consultation process. *Remedial and Special Education, 10*(2), 6–16.

Torch, T. (1984). The dark side of the excellence movement. *Phi Delta Kappan, 66,* 173–176.

Transition Services Task Force. (1989). *Meeting the challenge: Transition planning in Texas for people with disabilities, report to the 71st legislature.* Austin, TX: Texas Planning Council for Developmental Disabilities.

Varnhagen, S., & Gerber, M. M. (1984). Use of microcomputers for spelling assessment: Reasons to be cautious. *Learning Disabilities Quarterly, 7,* 266–270.

Verstegen, D. A. (1987). Two hundred years of federalism: A perspective on national fiscal policy in education. *Journal of Educational Finance, 12,* 516–548.

Verstegen, D. A., & Clark, D. L. (1988). The diminution in federal expenditures for education during the Reagan administration. *Phi Delta Kappan, 70,* 134–138.

Wang, M. C. (1980). Adaptive instruction: Building on diversity. *Theory into Practice, 19*(2), 122–128.

Wang, M. C. (1981). Mainstreaming exceptional children: Some instructional design and implementation considerations. *The Elementary School Journal, 81*(4), 195–221.

Wang, M. C., & Baker, E. T. (1985–1986). Mainstreaming programs: Design features and effects. *Journal of Special Education, 19*(4), 503–521.

Wang, M. C., & Birch, J. W. (1984). Effective special education in regular class. *Exceptional Children, 50,* 391–398.

Wang, M. C., & Stiles, B. (1976). An investigation of children's concepts of self-responsibility from their school learning. *American Educational Research Journal, 13*(3), 159–179.

Wang, M. C., & Walberg, H. J. (1988). Four fallacies of segregationism. *Exceptional Children, 55,* 128–137.

Wehman, P. (1983). Toward the employability of severely handicapped children and youth. *Teaching Exceptional Children, 15,* 219–225.

Wehman, P., Kregel, J., & Barcus, J. M. (1985). From school to work: A vocational transition model for handicapped students. *Exceptional Children, 52,* 25–37.

West, J. F. (1985). Regular and special educators' preferences for school-based consultation models. (Doctoral dissertation, The University of Texas at Austin.) *Dissertation Abstracts International, 47*(2), 504A.

West, J. F., & Brown, P. (1987). State departments of education policies on consultation in special education: The state of the states. *Remedial and Special Education, 8*(3), 45–51.

West, J. F., & Idol, L. (1987). School consultation (Part I): An interdisciplinary perspective on theory, models, and research. *Journal of Learning Disabilities, 20*(7), 388–407.

Whitehead, C. W. (1986). The sheltered workshop dilemma: Reform or replacement. *Remedial and Special Education, 7,* 18–24.

Will, M. (1984). *OSERS programming for the transition of youth with disabilities: Bridges from school to working life.* Washington, DC: U.S. Department of Education.

Will, M. (1986). Educating children with learning problems: A shared responsibility. *Exceptional Children, 52,* 411–416.

Winget, P. (Ed.). (1989). Transition bridges school to work. *The Special EDge, 3,* 1, 10.

Zigmond, N., & Thornton, H. (1985). Follow-up of post secondary age learning disabled graduates and drop-outs. *Learning Disabilities Research, 1,* 50–66.

3

Learning Disabilities: The Medical View

MARK E. SWANSON AND

NANCY M. BRAY

Physicians were among the first professionals to address the needs of the handicapped. Not surprisingly, perhaps, the earliest diagnostic and treatment efforts were directed on behalf of individuals demonstrating the more visible and severe conditions, such as sensorial impairment, mental retardation, and emotional disturbance. Only in the past two decades has attention turned toward more subtle conditions, such as learning disabilities. Despite the comparatively recent recognition of the problems posed by learning disabilities, there is no doubt that the condition has always affected a portion of the population.

Initial methods of diagnosis and treatment were developed by medical professionals, usually neurologists or ophthalmologists. European physicians who made numerous contributions to our early knowledge base about cognitive disorders included Gall (1807), who noted the loss of linguistic ability in patients with head injuries; Jackson, whose early theoretical framework about cerebral functioning was described in Taylor (1932); Head (1926), whose interest was in aphasia; and Hinshelwood (1917), who provided observations about congenital word blindness. In America, Orton's (1937) cerebral dominance theory to explain learning disorders and Strauss and Lehtinen's

(1947) work with brain-injured children contributed significantly to the understanding of learning problems. Despite early work with children who would later be described as "learning disabled," little was initially accomplished in the development of services.

Not until the middle of the twentieth century did poor academic achievement become the focus of concern by educators as well as health professionals. These low-achieving children appeared to have average or above-average intellectual ability and a history of quality instruction, yet they seemed to have difficulty mastering basic academic skills, most often reading. A behavioral pattern of short attention span, distractibility, impulsiveness, excess motor activity, clumsiness, and poor small muscle skills often coexisted with the lack of achievement. Upon medical examination, these children did not appear to have gross brain dysfunction or "hard signs," as measured by standard neurological examinations or tests, but did evidence some of the "soft signs" or behavioral indices of central nervous system (CNS) immaturity or dysfunction. As a result, such diagnoses as minimal brain injury, minimal brain dysfunction, central processing dysfunction, or perceptual handicaps were common.

Eventually, more careful delineation of specific disorders led to the use of medical terms to describe academic problems, including *dyslexia* (reading disability), *dyscalculia* (arithmetic disability), or *dysgraphia* (impaired handwriting). The diagnostic label tended to reflect one of two orientations about the nature of learning disorders, either characterizing them as involving CNS dysfunction or emphasizing the behavior without reference to the etiology. Because the primary manifestation involved difficulties in learning, the term *learning disabilities* offered by Samuel Kirk in the early 1960s gained widespread acceptance.

Although the majority of initial diagnostic and treatment efforts were rooted in work conducted by physicians, the responsibility to a large extent has shifted to the schools. This shift is appropriate, since the schools provide the primary treatment milieu for learning disorders. It should be noted, however, that children with learning disabilities experience a multiplicity of problems which extend to medicine and the allied health professions. Furthermore, as children with learning disabilities grow into adults, they face additional challenges; their problems do not magically disappear when they leave school.

Physicians are concerned with all factors affecting a patient's life. Although in the past, primary-care physicians addressed health management issues almost exclusively, the scope of their responsibilities has now broadened to include prevention efforts, such as monitoring progress in all areas of development (including school performance), providing anticipatory counseling to parents, and consulting with families on a wide variety of issues related to their children's well-being. Since the passage of PL 94-142 in 1975 (now amended in PL 99-457), physicians have been called upon to serve as consultants, interdisciplinary team members, and case managers on behalf of patients with special learning needs. The need for expert physician input in the management of the learning and other developmental disabilities has led to the emergence of "developmental pediatrics" as a subspecialty area of pediatrics. To train for that specialty, physicians complete their 3 years of pediatric residency and then receive intensive medical and interdisciplinary training in developmental disabilities for an additional 2 or 3 years.

In addition to pediatricians and family practitioners, the primary-care physicians who assume the most active role with patients who have learning disabilities, other medical specialists often act as consultants. Table 3–1 provides examples of various medical and allied health professionals who may serve in a consultation role.

HOW DO PHYSICIANS AND OTHER PROFESSIONALS DEFINE LEARNING DISORDERS?

A lack of agreement among experts in medicine, education, and psychology tends to cloud the complex area of learning disorders with ambiguity. Even definitions of particular kinds of learning disorders lack precision and concurrence.

Primary care physicians, often the first professionals consulted when a child is achieving poorly in school, must separate the varied and interwoven strands that may cause a child's academic problems. Children fail to achieve for many reasons. Two conditions—specific learning disabilities and attention deficit disorders—comprise the physician's classification of learning disorders.[1]

In evaluating a child's trouble in school, these two conditions demand the physician's consideration. The first, *specific learning disabilities*, involve difficulties in processing information. Physicians define specific learning disabilities as problems in memory, temporal sequential organization, visual–spatial processing, receptive language, expressive language, and voluntary motor function (Levine, Brooks, & Shonkoff, 1980), whereas educators define them as problems in reading, mathematics, and written language. The second, *attention deficit disorders* (currently termed the attention deficit hyperactivity disorder), relate to difficulties with sustained attention. Physicians define them as involving distractibility, impulsivity, repetitive modulation of activity, insa-

---

1. For purposes of discussion in this chapter, both specific learning disabilities and attention deficit disorders are considered to be "learning disorders." Both conditions are brain based, exist on a continuum, are clinically (rather than physiologically) defined and diagnosed, and are lifelong conditions whose courses are influenced by life events.

TABLE 3-1
The Role of Allied Health and Medical Specialists
in Learning Disorders Consultation

Specialist	Area assessed
Allied Health	
Audiologist	Hearing acuity
Occupational therapist	Fine motor (small muscles) and sensory motor functioning
Physical therapist	Ambulation and posture (large muscles)
Psychologist	Intellectual and emotional functioning
Speech pathologist	Speech and language functioning
Medical	
Geneticist	Heritability of conditions and risk to future offspring
Neurologist	Presence of anatomical and functional deficits of the brain
Ophthalmologist	Visual function
Psychiatrist	Emotional disorders

tiability, and task impersistence (Levine et al., 1980). Figure 3-1 illustrates the relationship between learning disabilities and attention deficit disorders, which can occur independently or concurrently.

On the surface, specific learning disabilities and attention deficit disorders may seem quite different. From a medical perspective, however, they bear many similarities in terms of the underlying brain process, measurement of severity, functional definition, time of onset and diagnosis, and other factors. The following lists eight ways in which learning disabilities and attention deficit disorders are similar:

1. Both are explained by a presumed, if not precisely identified, abnormal anatomical or physiological brain process.

2. Both are disorders on a continuum, from mild to severe, leading to a certain arbitrariness about who "has" the condition.

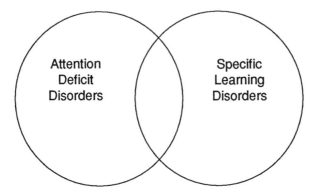

Figure 3-1. Relationship between specific learning disabilities and attention deficit disorders.

3. Both have been functionally, or operationally, defined as a series of clinical behaviors.

4. Both are clinically diagnosed, with no unequivocal physiological tests available to the physician to aid in diagnosis.

5. Both are likely present but unexpressed at birth (i.e., often children with these conditions are not identified until school age, and only retrospectively are some subtle indicators apparent in the preschool development).

6. Both have clinical manifestations that vary greatly with environmental factors, especially those at home and in school.

7. Both require input and assessment from nonmedical professionals.

8. Both have interventions that are largely derived from collective wisdom and experience, rather than from unequivocal scientific studies.

Any discussion of medical diagnosis requires an explanation of two frequently used classification systems. Most primary care physicians tend to rely on the World Health Organization's (1978) *Clinical Modification of the World Health Organization's International Classification of Diseases* (ICD-9-CM). An expanded version of ICD-9-CM, the revised *Diagnostic and Statistical Manual of Mental Disorders* (DSM-III-R), is often used by psychiatrists or psychologists (American Psychiatric Association, 1987).

The medical perspective presented in this chapter will concentrate on both specific learning disabilities and attention deficit disorders. Although, to the scientific purist, imprecision in defining these conditions on a pathophysiological basis may be frustrating, it may actually benefit the patient by minimizing the use of powerful labels. The popularization of specific learning disabilities and attention deficit disorders by the media in recent years has led to greater public acceptance of people with these conditions, but it has also led to a confusing body of misinformation and much more frequent "diagnosis" by a variety of professionals.

HOW IS STUDY OF THE BRAIN CONTRIBUTING TO KNOWLEDGE ABOUT LEARNING DISABILITIES?

Physicians interested in defining learning problems have drawn upon those medical specialties involved in unraveling the mysteries of the human brain. Developmental pediatrics, neurology, psychiatry, genetics, radiology, and pathology have made and continue to make valuable contributions. Scientific work in anatomy, physiology, and pharmacology has also proven valuable.

Limitations

Compared with our knowledge about other human organ systems, our current understanding of the brain remains quite primitive. There are three major reasons for this. First, the living human brain is inaccessible to direct investigations (such as tissue samples) which have been useful in studying the function of other organs, because of risks inherent in such studies. A second reason is the incredible complexity of brain structure and function. The unavailability of animal models that adequately parallel the human brain and its functioning has been a third barrier.

Despite these limitations, steady advancement in knowledge of brain functions continues, much of it spurred by emerging technologies in clinical medicine and the basic sciences. Autopsy studies of people with learning disabilities, for example, have demonstrated an absence of standard brain symmetry, an excessive number of neurons in specified regions of the brain, and microdysgenesis (small areas of abnormally placed neurons and focally distorted cortical architecture). Although these findings suggest that at least certain subtypes of reading disabilities may have anatomical correlates (Galaburda, 1988), additional research is needed to verify this association.

Current Medical Technological Advances in the Study of the Brain

In recent years, an explosion of new technologies has advanced the study of the brain. Until 1970, to observe the living brain, physicians were dependent on simple X-rays, measures of brain electrical activity, and invasive techniques (where contrast substances, such as dye, are injected into blood vessels and the cerebrospinal fluid). Designed specifically for the detection and delineation of severe clinical brain conditions, such as brain tumors, strokes, and epilepsy, these techniques have not proven to be sensitive to the vast majority of less severe brain conditions, such as learning disorders. The advent of computed tomography (CT; previously called computerized axial tomography) scanning in the early 1970s allowed noninvasive, safe detection of the anatomical lesions in the brain associated with pathological conditions. Unfortunately, this technology has not detected the minor brain differences believed to be present with the learning disorders.

The most promising recent advances in our scientific knowledge about learning disorders have resulted from more detailed anatomical studies, including investigations of brain metabolic activity; more sophisticated studies of brain electrical activity; and indirect measures of neurotransmitter activity. Among these techniques are magnetic resonance imaging, positron emission tomography, and brain electrical activity mapping.

Magnetic resonance imaging (MRI) is a noninvasive technique which can define anatomical variations in the brain in greater detail than the CT scan. The second technique, positron emission tomography (PET), investigates brain function by quantifying glucose metabolism in various brain regions. In conjunction with genetic and neuropsychological investigations, MRI and PET studies of reading disabled adults are being conducted in a number of research centers in attempts to establish the physiological and anatomical correlates of reading disability subtypes (Lubs et al., 1988). This promising study has yet to yield any significant findings. The PET technology has also been applied to studies of expressive and receptive language. Researchers are finding that processing of information in the brain probably follows multiple routes through different brain areas on its course from input to output (Montgomery, 1989).

The third method, brain electrical activity mapping (BEAM), combines the techniques of electroencephalography (EEG) and sensory-evoked potentials (i.e., brain response to visual stimuli) to provide computer-generated pictures of the brain. Using BEAM technology, a small study of reading disabled subjects was able to document an expected brain dysfunction in the language-associated left posterior of the brain, but also found other unexpected brain differences in the frontal lobe when compared with normal individuals (Duffy, Denckla, McAnulty, & Holmes, 1988). Proponents of this technology suggest that BEAM may measure pathological as well as compensatory brain activity, thus holding promise for diagnosis *and* documentation of specific learning disabilities.

Although innovative technologies for the investigation of attention deficit disorders have not been as numerous as those for other learning disabilities, new approaches are encouraging. One investigative thrust has focused on neurotransmitters, the biochemical substances that allow individual brain cells (neurons) to connect with each other. Deficits in neurotransmitter function and quantity have been postulated as a potential cause of attention deficit disorders. Although neurotransmitter activity cannot be quantified directly, measurement of metabolites in the urine serves as an indirect indication of brain neurotransmitter activity. Significant differences between normal children and those with attention deficit disorders have been found in urinary neurotransmitter metabolites. In those children who had experienced clinical improvement after administration of stimulants, changes in urinary metabolite values were found (Shekim, Dekirmenjian, & Chapel, 1979), suggesting that neurotransmitter function may be a chemical marker for attention deficit disorders.

The study of the human brain is progressing on multiple fronts. One can reasonably anticipate that scientists will continue their quest for greater knowledge about the neuroanatomical and neurochemical bases of learning disorders. Ultimately, complete understanding awaits the knowledge of brain function at its most fundamental levels.

WHAT GENETIC, PRENATAL, PERINATAL, AND POSTNATAL FACTORS INFLUENCE THE PREVALENCE AND SEVERITY OF THE LEARNING DISORDERS?

Investigation into learning disorders has naturally led physicians to explore etiological factors that may account for a person's difficulties. It has long been observed that learning disorders seem to occur in families, suggesting a genetic component. In addition, certain "high-risk" factors during the prenatal, perinatal, and postnatal periods may result in subtle forms of neurological dysfunction, including the learning disorders.

Genetic Factors

Several researchers have documented an increased incidence of learning disabilities, hyperactivity, and minor neurodevelopmental disorders (essentially soft signs) in the biological relatives of affected children, in contrast to adoptive relatives. This higher incidence within families suggests genetic transmission of these disorders (Morrison & Stewart, 1971, 1973; Rasmussen, Gustavson, & Bille, 1984; Smith, Kimberling, Pennington, & Lubs, 1983). Although research to establish the precise genetic mechanism is only in the formative stages, the approaches used to date (adoption studies, twin studies, gene mapping, pedigree analysis) are all quite promising.

Other inherited conditions are known to involve brain dysfunction. Those associated with learning disorders include neurofibromatosis, a condition that has great clinical variability and is associated with visual–perceptual disability and language deficits (Eliason, 1986), and Fragile X syndrome, a chromosomal disorder associated with mild mental retardation and learning disorders, including auditory processing problems and attention deficits (Hagerman, Kemper, & Hudson, 1985). Thus, it appears that various types of learning disorders may be inherited in a relatively "pure" form or as part of a condition that involves brain dysfunction.

Prenatal Period

The worldwide emphasis on the health of mothers from early pregnancy to birth attests to the importance of optimizing conditions for the developing fetus during the prenatal period. In fact, the mother's nutritional status even prior to the pregnancy can adversely affect the growth of the fetal organs, including the brain (Frank, 1984).

The infants of adolescent, poor, or older mothers are often at risk. Teenage mothers and socioeconomically disadvantaged mothers may receive minimal or no prenatal care or may have substandard nutrition, thus increasing the risk for prematurity, low birth weight, and other problems. Older mothers (over 35 years of age) have a higher chance of developing conditions such as toxemia (high blood pressure, edema, and protein in the urine), which may compromise oxygen flow to the fetus and result in brain injury or stillbirth.

The prenatal period is divided into three overlapping stages. During the first trimester of pregnancy, major organs of the fetus, including the brain, are being formed. The second trimester sees continued growth of major organs. The third trimester is a time of not only rapid brain growth, but also completion of the intricate architecture of the brain. During any of these periods, the subtle anatomical and/or biochemical changes associated with the learning disorders may be caused by chronic maternal conditions, acute maternal infections, or fetal exposures to toxic substances.

Autoimmune disorders in the mother, for example, have been directly linked to learning disorders; such diseases as systemic lupus erythematosus (a chronic multiorgan disease affecting young women), myasthenia gravis (a disorder characterized by muscle fatigue), and erythroblastosis fetalis (a disease in which the baby's blood cells are destroyed) involve production of maternal antibodies that directly damage fetal organs. It is speculated that occurrence of this antibody-mediated process, particularly during the second and third trimesters of pregnancy, could cause focal damage to the rapidly developing fetal brain that is similar to that associated with reading disabilities (Galaburda, 1988).

Occurring more commonly are maternal chronic illnesses that threaten the developing fetal brain by depriving it, intermittently or chronically, of the substances necessary for normal growth and development. Illnesses such as asthma, sickle-cell disease, or epilepsy can be associated with intermittent hypoxia (lack of oxygen) to both mother and fetus. The placenta controls the flow of oxygen and nutrients to the baby. As a vascular organ, it can be adversely affected by chronic illness that involves the cardiovascular system (e.g., diabetes, kidney disease, and heart diseases) and, thus, threaten brain growth.

All of these chronic maternal conditions, including the earlier discussed materal malnutrition, produce a higher incidence of malformations of fetal structures, including those of the brain. That chronic maternal illnesses and conditions are frequently risk factors for the development of the learning disorders was clearly demonstrated in a large study of children diagnosed as having minimal brain dysfunction or hyperactivity (Hartsough & Lambert, 1985).

In addition to chronic conditions, certain acute maternal viral infections, such as rubella, have long been known to cause pronounced effects on the developing brain. Less well documented, but still suspect, are the subtle effects of other viruses, such as cytomegalovirus (CMV), a ubiquitous agent that causes only mild maternal symptoms and is not preventable by current medical practice. It is known that CMV has had devastating effects on the fetal brain in a small percentage of cases. Clinical suspicion remains about the apparent increased occurrence of the learning disorders following maternal infection, suggesting that CMV or other viruses may have a less severe effect on the developing brain (Conboy et al., 1987).

Evidence of fetal brain damage from exposure to toxic substances is well established. The most frequently implicated substance is alcohol. Although the full-blown fetal alcohol syndrome (microcephaly, short stature, and mental retardation) is well recognized, there is increasing evidence that a "fetal alcohol effect" in certain children may appear in the form of specific learning disabilities and attention deficits (Marino, Scholl, Karp, Yanoff, & Hetherington, 1987). Maternal use of tobacco and "street" drugs, such as cocaine or marijuana, should also be considered a risk factor for brain dysfunction (Butler & Goldstein, 1973; Naeye & Peters, 1984).

Even prescribed, therapeutic drug use in pregnancy may pose a potential threat to fetal development. Antiepileptic medications have undergone the most study in this respect; certain identifiable syndromes have been linked to specific drugs (e.g., hydantoin and valproate). Other drugs such as phenobarbital and carbarmazepine may produce more subtle effects on the brain. Additional therapeutic drugs might well be implicated in the future. Scientific study should attempt to separate the effects of the underlying maternal disease on the fetus from those of the prescribed drugs.

Perinatal Period

The perinatal period, from the onset of labor to 30 days after birth, presents still another time of risk for the infant and his or her brain. The newborn, especially if premature, can experience interruption of the flow to the brain of vital substances, such as oxygen and glucose, on an intermittent basis, with possible deleterious effects. The risks of intracranial bleeding and infection, particularly in premature infants, compound the dangers.

Even more pervasive and worrisome is the problem of a less than optimal supply of the nutritional elements (e.g., vitamins, amino acids, and essential fatty acids) to the growing premature brain. Medical complications may cause a state of inadequate nutrition to last for days, weeks, or even months, thereby jeopardizing normal brain growth and development. Long-term follow-up of premature infants is confirming the increased prevalence of both specific learning disabilities and attention deficit disorders, even for those children born without major medical complications (Hunt, Cooper, & Tooley, 1988; Klein, Hack, Gallagher, & Fanaroff, 1985).

Postnatal Period

Rapid brain growth continues for the first 2 years after birth. During this time, the brain can undergo sufficient damage to cause a range of clinical outcomes, from learning disorders to mental retardation, with obvious implications for school performance.

For example, acute central nervous system infections, especially bacterial meningitis from *Hemophilus influenzae*, can cause cognitive impairment, specific learning disabilities, and attention deficits, both through direct effects on the brain and through associated hearing loss (Sell, 1987). Encephalitis, which is usually viral, has not yet been found to have such dramatic effects, although further study is needed.

Two other conditions should be viewed as likely causes of learning disorders. Children who experience hypoxia, as a result of acute respiratory illness, suffocation, or near drowning (Pearn, 1977), may have relatively subtle but lasting brain dysfunction. Some young children also suffer severe, acute, or repeated, mild brain trauma. The latter is particularly troubling since it represents the growing number of infants and toddlers who are identified as victims of child abuse. Prospective studies and follow-up of this high-risk group are difficult but vital to further understanding of the full implications of child maltreatment.

In addition to CNS infections, hypoxia, and trauma, chronic illness can adversely affect the child's brain and subsequent school performance. The brain may be directly damaged by diseases such as Duchenne muscular dystrophy (Dorman, Hurley, & D'Avignon, 1988) and immune deficiencies (Gabel, Winsten, Hegedus, Tarter, & Fireman, 1985) or by the treatment of diseases such as leukemia and cancer for which the chemotherapeutic agents and radiation used may damage the brain (Peckham, Meadows, Bartel, & Marrero, 1988). School performance in such chronically ill children is further threatened by secondary factors, such as malaise, lethargy, and frequent absence.

Chronic malnutrition is another insidious contributor to the prevalence of learning disorders. Children who suffered moderate to severe protein–energy malnutrition (deficiency of both protein and calories) in the first year of life have demonstrated significantly lower academic achievement in mathematics, language, and science than children with adequate nutritional intake. These children are also reported to have problems with classroom behavior (Galler, Ramsey, & Solimano, 1984).

Iron deficiency anemia, long suspected of causing low school performance, was the focus of a recent study. After receiving a course of iron supplementation, anemic Indonesian children achieved significant academic improvement compared with nontreated children, when overall nutritional status and pretreatment performance on intelligence testing were controlled. It was also found that the anemic children did not fully catch up to the level of nonanemic children in 3 months, suggesting that the effects of iron depletion and replenishment may be quite insidious (Soemantri, Pollitt, & Kim, 1985).

In addition to the problems associated with chronic malnutrition, acute hunger (in economically disadvantaged children) and the ingestion of substances such as lead (from lead-based paint or car exhaust) may also contribute to low academic performance. Acute ingestion of lead in large amounts can cause organ damage and death. More recently, lead has been demonstrated to have adverse behavioral effects (in the form of inattention or lethargy) at levels considered to be raised but not "toxic" (David, Clark, & Voeller, 1972; David, Hoffman, Sverd, & Clark, 1977).

Prescribed use of therapeutic drugs may also directly hamper school performance or behavior through side effects on the CNS. Phenobarbital, for example, a medication commonly used for seizure control, has been linked with lower performance on neuropsychological tests and with higher ratings of hyperactivity in studies of cognitively normal children with mild epilepsy (Vining et al., 1987). The effects of theophylline and other asthma medications on learning and behavior are more equivocal; consistent reporting of school difficulties following prescription of these drugs points out the need for further study. Physicians and pharmaceutical companies continue to investigate side effects of the many therapeutic drugs which affect the brain.

This review of the current state of knowledge of medical disorders and treatments associated with the learning disorders has indicated that almost all areas require more study to further delineate the actual pathophysiological mechanisms as well as the clinical effects. As discussed, many factors play a role in brain development from conception through early childhood (see Figure 3–2). Although most specific learning disabilities and attention deficit disorders cannot be cured, these difficulties can be prevented or ameliorated through better health care practices, such as adequate nutrition of mother

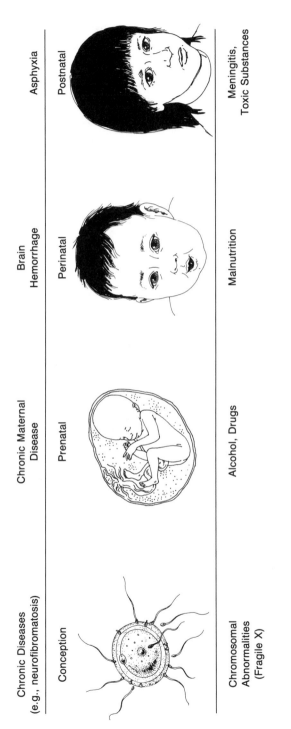

Chronic Diseases (e.g., neurofibromatosis)	Chronic Maternal Disease	Brain Hemorrhage	Asphyxia
Conception	Prenatal	Perinatal	Postnatal
Chromosomal Abnormalities (Fragile X)	Alcohol, Drugs	Malnutrition	Meningitis, Toxic Substances

Figure 3–2. Examples of timed effects of various factors on brain development.

and child and avoidance of substances known to have harmful effects. Changes in current medical practice (e.g., treatment of prematurity, meningitis, and leukemia) will likely result in amelioration of learning disorders in some children.

WHAT SCREENING AND DIAGNOSTIC TOOLS ARE AVAILABLE TO HEALTH PROFESSIONALS?

Because of their expense and experimental nature, most cutting-edge processes (such as CT, MRI, and BEAM) are not generally available or necessarily appropriate for the large number of children with known or suspected learning disorders. Most often, parents turn to physicians for a *clinical* diagnosis. Following are some of the diagnostic methods used by health professionals to aid in the evaluation of children with poor school achievement.

The Early Years

Early identification of learning disorders in children has garnered increasing attention in recent years. Ideally, timely recognition of a child's problems followed by implementation of an effective intervention program will maximize chances for school success, thus avoiding the educational and psychological costs of delayed remediation to the child, family, and school.

Among those attempting to formulate tools for early diagnosis was a team of British researchers who devised a battery of tests to assess cognitive, motor, and social development of 5-year-old children at school entry as a means of predicting subsequent school difficulties. Of the 351 children, 60% who were diagnosed as having a significant neurodevelopmental disorder at age 5 later demonstrated considerable difficulty in school by age 10. Fewer than 5% of the children scoring in the accelerated ranges on this assessment battery needed referral for specialized testing (Bax & Whitmore, 1973). Repetition of this study with an ethnically mixed group, using a similar neurodevelopmental battery, confirmed the initial results. In this second study, 77% of 230 children scoring in the lowest 10% needed referral to the school assessment personnel because of learning or behavioral problems by age 10 (Bax & Whitmore, 1987). Of particular interest was the higher incidence of learning difficulties by age 10 of those children with low motor skills at age 5, independent of cognitive ability. Notably, the clinical impressions of well-trained school physicians (i.e., physicians with special training in school and developmental problems) were found to be about as predictive as the more formal neurodevelopmental scores. American pediatricians have also pointed out the underutilized potential of screening instruments for early identification of specific learning disabilities (Shapiro, Palmer, Wachtel, & Capute, 1983).

The early detection of primary attention deficits that will persist into the school years is very difficult. A recent longitudinal follow-up of 224 normal children showed that only 12% of preschool children suspected of having attention deficit disorders actually continued to manifest these symptoms in kindergarten (Palfrey, Levine, Walker, & Sullivan, 1985). The results of this investigation, coupled with the recognition of the ambiguous definitions currently available and the developmental nature of the disorders, encourage a cautious approach to the diagnosis of attention deficit disorders in preschool children.

Early childhood education programs for the handicapped, ages 3 to 5, are generally aimed at those children with more easily recognized problems, such as mental retardation, motor handicap, and language delay. Particular criteria for determining learning disabilities in preschoolers are not as well specified as they are for older children, where formulaic approaches, such as the discrepancy between expectations based on intellectual performance and actual school achievement, are utilized. Experts are only now focusing attention on diagnosing specific learning disabilities in preschool children who may require developmental or early educational intervention (see Chapter 1).

The School Years

Physicians are more likely to be called upon to evaluate a child after school problems have developed. At this point, a physician's goal is to determine systematically a *differential diagnosis* for poor school achievement. The process involves ruling out conditions that appear not to be impeding the learning process while ascertaining all the factors that may be contributing to low school achievement and/or problem behaviors. Possible contributing conditions include specific learning disabilities, attention deficit disorders, cognitive limitations, psychiatric disturbances, and a wide spectrum of learned behaviors (including noncompliance, resistance, and withdrawal). Since many of these factors occur simultaneously, the physician must explore all realms that directly affect a child's functioning. Hearing and vision are usually screened. In addition to the physical examination and physician's first-hand observations, the child's medical, developmental, behavioral, family, social, and school history should be elicited. Important sources of information include teacher observations, psychoeducational test data, and behavior ratings provided by parents and teachers. Table 3–2 summarizes information that should be collected by the physician.

The physician's most active role is in obtaining the multifaceted history and conducting the physical examination. The latter traditionally involves determination of the presence or absence of neurological soft signs (fine and gross motor clumsiness), which are believed to reflect maturational delay or

TABLE 3–2
Information Needed by Physician for Differential Diagnosis
of Learning Disorders

Areas of concern	Information source
Sustained attention	Medical history
	Family history
	Behavioral history
	Teacher observations
	Behavior rating scales
	Physician observation
Academic achievement	Medical history
	Developmental history
	Family history
	Social history
	School history
	Psychoeducational testing
Motor coordination	Medical history
	Developmental history
	Family history
	Physical examination
Behavior	Developmental history
	Behavioral history
	Social history
	Teacher observations
	Behavior rating scales

minor neurological dysfunction. Although careful study has generally failed to demonstrate a strong relationship between *individual* soft signs and specific learning disabilities, an association between a composite group of neuro-maturational tasks and learning disabilities may exist (Shaywitz, Shaywitz, McGraw, & Groll, 1984). *Developmental output failures* (a term physicians use to refer to problems in written language), for example, have been associated with delayed fine motor skills, memory, expressive language, finger agnosia (inability to perceive finger tip position), and inattention (Levine, Oberklaid, & Meltzer, 1981).

Levine et al. (1988) developed a series of standardized, extended neuro-developmental examinations intended for use by pediatricians who wish to evaluate a child's functioning in the areas of memory, attention, language, and motor coordination. Items on these examinations reflect tasks from traditional neuropsychological, motor, and language tests, as well as signs of minor neurological dysfunction. Delayed or disordered performance on these measures often can be classified within specific "clusters of dysfunction" that have been shown to be statistically associated with school problems (Levine et at., 1988). The increased popularity of this series of examinations is at least partly a reflection of the scarcity of useful tools. The examinations are best used as part of a multidisciplinary evaluation, leading to *descriptions* (rather than *labeling*) of children.

It should be clear that the physician has limited capacity to diagnose specific learning disabilities through a physical examination (even one that seeks out neurological soft signs), but that he or she may have strong suspicions based on a history of academic problems associated with language, memory, motor, and organizational deficits. Psychoeducational testing (including testing of intelligence, language, and academic achievement), interpreted in the context of all available information, is needed to convert the physician's hypothesis into an educational diagnosis that will facilitate intervention.

Responsibility for the final diagnosis of attention deficit disorders, on the other hand, clearly rests with the physician, using the sum of information listed in Table 3–2. No single behavioral or laboratory test diagnoses this condition. The diagnosis must be made clinically, based on the presence of four important features: the pervasiveness of symptoms (i.e., they must occur in various situations), the persistence of symptoms since the preschool years, their significant interference with school performance, and the absence of environmental factors (i.e., family instability, violence, abuse, or neglect) that might be the exclusive cause of similar behavioral patterns.

The current DSM-III-R classification of attention deficit hyperactivity disorder acknowledges variations from mild to severe. In mild to moderate cases, a child has a greater chance of compensating successfully for attention deficits with environmental and behavioral interventions. Children with severe attention deficits are likely to require a multimodal approach, which includes sophisticated behavior management, school and environmental manipulation, and medication (discussed in the next section). Physicians cannot use a "diagnostic trial" of stimulant medication as a shortcut to the proper diagnosis of attention deficit disorders for three reasons. First, "normal" individuals tend to respond to stimulants in many of the same ways as patients with attention deficit disorders; that is, they have improved attention, lessened distractibility, and decreased motor activity (Rapoport et al., 1978). Second, as with most drugs, there is a large placebo effect (Conners & Taylor, 1980). Third, what appears to be a positive response to medication may reflect observer bias, if the observer is aware of the treatment status.

Although diagnosis of learning disorders during the preschool years is an attractive possibility, it is generally not reliable. Once a child experiences school problems, the physician assumes a role as a member of an inter-disciplinary team constituted for purposes of evaluation. The physician has the primary role in diagnosing attention deficit disorders, but a lessened responsibility for diagnosing specific learning disabilities. Because these conditions exist on a continuum and are developmentally related, physicians are more frequently using descriptions rather than labels in their evaluations of children with school problems.

WHAT IS THE TYPICAL COURSE OF LEARNING DISORDERS? HOW PREVALENT ARE THEY?

As defined earlier, learning disorders are viewed medically as disorders of brain structure or function. Their typical natural history, or lifelong course from infancy to adulthood, reflects a continuous, dynamic interaction between a developing organ (the brain) with certain biological tendencies and a change-able, psychosocial environment. The result of this interaction is a pattern of observable behavior. Table 3–3 summarizes the similarities and differences between specific learning disabilities and attention deficit disorders in their natural presentation and lifelong course.

Early indications of both conditions begin in the preschool years, although not in a sufficiently consistent manner to allow definitive diagnosis. The full manifestations of both become apparent during the early school years. Their impact on overall performance, however, is determined only in part by the presence and severity of the learning disorder. Other determinants include intelligence, temperament, and special skills that allow for compensation and promote self-esteem, as well as environmental factors such as parental capacity for nurturing, the family's educational expectations, the student–teacher match, and the school milieu. In general, the effects of specific learning disabilities and attention deficit disorders can be ameliorated if the child possesses other strengths and has positive environmental influences.

The natural histories of the specific learning disabilities have significant differences from those of the attention deficit disorders. Specific learning disabilities appear as language delays and disorders or as organizational problems in the preschool years, but only when the child faces academic material in an organized educational setting do these deficiencies manifest themselves in low academic achievement. When the long-term outcome of one group of 114 students with learning disabilities was compared with that of 144 unaffected siblings, the former experienced significantly less success in academic pursuits, social relationships, and educational attainment. Better long-term outcomes were associated with higher intellectual abilities, less severe learning disabilities, strong family support and function, and parents who themselves experienced educational and work success. The presence of more

TABLE 3–3
**Similarities and Differences Between Specific Learning Disabilities
and Attention Deficit Disorders**

	Specific learning disabilities	Attention deficit disorders
Time of presentation	Manifested in preschool years in inconsistent fashion; effect on academic performance begins in early school years	Manifested in preschool years in inconsistent fashion; effect on academic performance begins in early school years
Manner of presentation	May present as language delays/disorders, organizational problems in preschool years, but not in a way that permits definitive diagnosis	Disorders emerge in preschool years manifested as behavior problems; almost impossible to distinguish from other behavioral variants
Other factors affecting academic performance	Innate and environmental factors affect clinical manifestations of conditions	Innate and environmental factors affect clinical manifestations of conditions
Prevalence	Difficult to determine because of definitional problems; estimates range from 3% to 20%	Difficult to determine because of definitional problems; estimates range from 1% to 6%
Intervention	Educational	Behavioral and environmental; medication
Lifelong course into adulthood	Better outcomes may be associated with positive family support, good intellectual abilities, and absence of attention deficit disorders	Outcomes range from marked social maladaptation to adequate, productive adjustment

severe learning disabilities, hyperactivity, and mathematics difficulties correlated negatively with ultimate success (Hartzell & Compton, 1984).

Similar to learning disabilities, attention deficit disorders emerge during the preschool years. Since they manifest themselves as behavioral variants, they must be separated from (a) unsocialized behavior (resulting from a child's being raised in an unstructured setting with inconsistent limits); (b) oppositional, resistive behavior (a persistence of the 2-year-old's struggles for autonomy); and (c) aggressive, acting-out behavior (resulting from unresolved childhood anger and frustration, often associated with family violence and chaos). Distinguishing these behaviors from each other during the school years is difficult enough; it can be next to impossible during the preschool years. In one study, parents, psychologists, and health professionals evaluated 224 children at eight checkpoints between birth and kindergarten for *definite* or *possible concern* regarding primary attention deficits. Overall, 13% of the children met criteria for *definite concern* at one or more checkpoints; 41% met criteria when *possible* or *definite concern* categories were merged. Notably, only 5% of the group evidenced *definite* symptoms which persisted into kindergarten. The peak age of onset of identifiable symptoms was 3½ years (Palfrey et al., 1985). These findings suggest that caution should be exercised in the diagnosis of attention deficit disorders in the preschool years: Young children may demonstrate behaviors associated with this condition that are in actuality normal developmental phenomena. A premature or inaccurate diagnosis may promote significant negative consequences in the form of labeling and care-giver bias. The preferred interventions for virtually all problem behaviors in this age group are behavioral and environmental, since medication is not approved by the Federal Food and Drug Administration for children under the age of 6 years. School achievement appears to be positively correlated with intelligence, supportive and functional families, and the absence of learning disabilities (Palfrey et al., 1985).

A prevalence study of attention deficit disorders in an elementary school population of 5,000 in northern California found agreement among three defining groups—parents, school staff, and physician—on the presence of hyperactivity in only 1% of the population. Hyperactive ratings were given to 5% of these children by at least one of the defining groups. The fact that prevalence rates did not increase with time suggests that children move in and out of the hyperactive group (Lambert, Sandoval, & Sassone, 1978). This finding is consistent with observations by Palfrey and her colleagues (1985) that confirm this shifting in preschool populations. The prevalence rates of attention deficit disorders vary dramatically according to the definition, the professional performing the assessment, and the age at which the child is diagnosed.

Because they are disorders of brain function (with biological and environmental components) and because their effects are manifested during the school years, specific learning disabilities and attention deficit disorders bear many similarities in their histories. Professionals are limited in their ability to predict the lifelong course for a single child affected by specific learning disabilities or attention deficit disorders, because of ambiguity about definition, cooccurrence with other brain conditions (including each other), and the wide variability of interaction between the child's individual characteristics and the psychosocial enviroment. As shown in Figure 3–3, however, as time progresses, psychosocial (environmental) factors play a larger role in an individual's performance than do learning disorders.

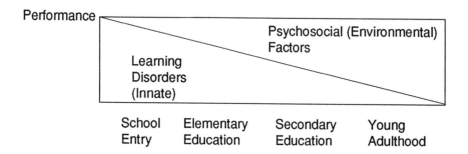

Figure 3–3. Relative contribution of learning disorders (specific learning disabilities and attention deficit disorders) to school and postschool performance.

WHICH MEDICALLY BASED INTERVENTIONS HAVE SHOWN PROMISE IN TREATING CHILDREN WITH LEARNING DISORDERS?

A physician may be consulted to evaluate a child with school difficulties for two reasons. First, the school or parent desires the performance of a physical exam to "rule out" medical problems. As previously discussed, children with learning disabilities may have more specific soft signs of minor neurological dysfunction than other children, but the discovery of such soft signs does not constitute a diagnosis of a specific learning disorder. Second, the physician may be requested to evaluate specifically for attention deficit disorders and the advisability of a trial of stimulant medication.

Alarmingly, prescription of stimulant medication for patients with attention deficit disorders has reached epidemic proportions in certain areas of the country. The Drug Enforcement Agency nearly doubled production quotas for manufacture of methylphenidate (Ritalin), the most commonly prescribed stimulant, between 1985 and 1987 (Viadero, 1987). Researchers who have monitored prescriptions of medication for attention deficits in Baltimore County (Maryland) have reported that nearly 6% (i.e., from 1 to 2 students per class) of elementary school children were on medication in 1987, compared with 1% in 1971. Stimulants were prescribed in 99% of cases diagnosed as attention deficit disorders. Interestingly, this increase in medications seems to have coincided with the establishment of a county-wide network of clinics for evaluation of school problems (Safer & Krager, 1988).

Although one would hope that the increase in prescriptions of stimulant medication would be based on an emerging body of information about the effectiveness of this treatment, such is not the case. In the face of intense public debate about the attention deficit disorders, the professional community remains dependent on a knowledge base that has changed little since the late 1970s.

In children with attention deficit disorders, stimulants have been shown to improve certain aspects of behavior, such as speed and accuracy in arithmetic (Douglas, Barr, O'Neill, & Britton, 1986). The benefits of stimulant medication on short-term academic achievement, however, have been demonstrated only inconsistently, if at all. In one example, a crossover study of medication and placebo in hyperactive, non–learning disabled children failed to detect any differences in academic achievement (Rie, Rie, Stewart, & Ambuel, 1976). Another study concluded that improved reading ability was at least partially mediated through stimulant-induced behavior improvement in combination with reading therapy for a group of hyperactive, reading disabled children (Richardson, Kupietz, Winsberg, Maitinsky, & Mendell, 1988). At the same time, studies have consistently shown that parents and teachers perceive improved academic performance, presumably because of the child's improved classroom behavior while on medication. It bears repeating that the research has consistently shown that the majority of children on stimulant medication, both with and without attention deficit disorders, will show more consistent on-task behaviors.

The prescription of unwarranted medication may adversely affect a child's development of self-control and self-esteem if great care is not taken to attribute improved behavior to the *child*, not the medication. While awaiting research to clarify medication-mediated academic achievement, professionals need to be aware that a child's improved on-task behavior while on stimulant medication may mask ongoing learning disabilities or emotional disturbances. Thus, for these types of problems, other interventions would be more appropriate.

Table 3–4 lists medications prescribed for the attention deficit disorders, with a summary of advantages and disadvantages of each. The most frequently prescribed is methylphenidate (Ritalin). Other stimulants used for treatment of attention deficit disorders are dextroamphetamine (Dexedrine) and pemoline (Cylert). The increased side effects of dextroamphetamine make it less acceptable than methylphenidate for most children. Pemoline may take 5 weeks to demonstrate effect and, because of possible toxic effects, requires monitoring of liver function. Two other classes of medications are also used for attention deficit disorders. Many psychiatrists prescribe the tricyclic antidepressants (such as imipramine), especially when depressive symptoms are noted. The major tranquilizers (such as thioridazine) are not typically prescribed for treatment of attention deficit disorders.

The American Academy of Pediatrics (1987) stated its position on the use of stimulant medication as follows:

> Medication for Attention Deficit Disorder should never be used as an isolated treatment. Proper classroom placement, physical education programs, behavior modification, counseling, and provisions of structure should be employed before a trial of pharmacotherapy is attempted. This integrated approach should continue once the medication has begun.

TABLE 3–4
Medications for the Attention Deficit Disorders

Drug (dose)	Indications/advantages	Disadvantages
Stimulants		
Methylphenidate (Ritalin) (0.3–0.7 mg/kg/dose)	Short acting; well studied; minimal, short-lived side effects; drug holidays easy to arrange	Overprescription threatens valid use; sustained release may not be reliably absorbed
Dextroamphetamine (Dexedrine) (best estimate is ½ of methylphenidate dose)	Can be used in children over 3	Insomnia and anorexia more common than with methylphenidate
Pemoline (Cylert) (18.75–75 mg/day)	Once a day administration	Up to 5 weeks before effect seen; blood tests for liver function must be followed
Tricyclic Antidepressants		
Imipramine (Tofranil) (25–75 mg/day, but no more than 2.5 mg/kg/day)	May treat depressive symptoms; still occasionally used for enuresis	Less effective than stimulants; more serious and frequent side effects; large placebo effect in depression studies; overdose may be fatal
Amitryptiline (Elavil) (75–150 mg/day)	May treat depressive symptoms	Not recommended for children under 12; not well studied
Desipramine (Pertrofrane) (75–150 mg/day)	May treat depressive symptoms	Not well studied
Antipsychotic Drugs		
Thioridazine (Mellaril) (3–6 mg/kg)	Useful for brain-injured, aggressive children; best tolerated in most children	Sluggishness, depressed cognitive functioning; blurred vision; increased appetite
Haloperidol (Haldol) (0.1–0.3 mg/kg)	Useful in Tourette's syndrome	Sluggishness, depressed cognitive functioning; may develop extrapyramidal side effects

TABLE 3-4 (continued)

Drug (dose)	Indications/advantages	Disadvantages
Chlorpromazine (Thorazine) (50–100 mg/kg/day)	Useful for brain-injured, aggressive children	Sluggishness, depressed cognitive functioning; may develop extrapyramidal side effects

It is an interesting commentary that the American Academy of Pediatrics prompts consideration of a variety of nonpharmacological strategies as the first approach to the management of attention deficit disorders. This position clearly stands in contrast to the approach of many nonmedical professionals who view evaluation for medication as the initial step.

For specific learning disabilities, several recent studies have suggested that piracetam, a drug whose structure resembles that of the neurotransmitter gamma-aminobutyric acid (GABA), was superior to a placebo in improving and sustaining reading ability and comprehension in a study of 225 reading disabled children (Wilsher et al., 1987).

Nonpharmacologial interventions have also been evaluated recently. Self-instruction, progressive muscle relaxation, and aerobic exercise have all been proposed as strategies to improve academic performance in learning disabled children. In one study of 30 volunteer children, self-instruction and muscle relaxation were shown to produce similar positive effects on cognitive tasks requiring deliberation and concentration, with both strategies being superior to no treatment (Zieffle & Romney, 1985). In another research project, 54 learning disabled boys were randomly assigned to either an aerobic exercise or less vigorous exercise program for 20 weeks. Although improved self-esteem and physical fitness resulted, academic achievement was unaffected during the period of study (MacMahon & Gross, 1987).

Although research has not been conclusive, it would seem that non-pharmacological intervention methods warrant further study in light of the liability issues associated with traditional pharmacological therapies and the growing concern over the effects of drug therapy on children. These effects include the child's rationalization (to self and others) for being on medication, the response of significant adults (parents and teachers) to the child on medication, the impact on the child's perception of his or her ability to internalize control (Whalen & Henker, 1976), and the physical consequences of long-term use.

Increasingly, parents ask physicians to prescribe medication for their children who are achieving poorly at school. Stimulants have proven effective in improving some behaviors related to learning in carefully selected children with primary attention deficit disorders. The recent widespread increase in stimulant prescriptions, however, is more likely due to overdiagnosis of attention deficit disorders and fascination with Ritalin as a "wonder drug" than to an actual increase in prevalence of the condition or newly demonstrated effectiveness of the medication. Other nonpharmacological interventions of some promise have been noted.

WHAT POPULAR INTERVENTIONS HAVE FAILED TO DEMONSTRATE EFFECTIVENESS?

Ambiguity about pathophysiology, etiology, natural history, prevalence, diagnosis, and treatment of the learning disorders has created a situation ripe for eager entrepreneurs and quasi-scientific professionals to bombard the public with a variety of theories. America's free market system and willingness to embrace new ideas makes this country the most active arena for debates about interventions for the learning disorders. What has resulted is a large number of unproven and disproved approaches, called the "fad therapies" (Golden, 1987).

Approaches Based on Neuromotor Theories of Learning Disorders

Patterning has been advocated as a method to remediate learning disabilities by promoting neurological reorganization and cerebral dominance through retracing basic motor sequences in a systematic way. This approach is based upon the largely unsubstantiated view that lack of cerebral dominance is a prominent feature of learning disabilities. Virtually all relevant professional organizations have expressed at least skepticism about the use of patterning, and many prominent professionals from the medical and educational communities have roundly condemned it as not only ineffective for children but possibly harmful to the parents, because of the major stress placed on family members to comply with every detail of the strategy (American Academy of Pediatrics, 1982).

Another technique, sensory integration (SI) therapy, has received wide acclaim, particularly from occupational therapists, the health professionals who traditionally have attempted to improve fine motor skill functioning. SI therapy is based on the theory that the learning disabilities are due to suboptimal organization of the midbrain and brain stem. Therapy is therefore directed to stimulate the vestibular (balance, in the inner ear) and somatosensory (sense of body position) systems, rather than to improve higher cortical functions. A recent study typified the research findings when it showed no improvement in the academic performance of 45 children with learning disabilities; this group demonstrated markedly depressed postrotary nystagmus (a severe form of sensory integration dysfunction) and were provided 9 months of individual SI therapy (Carte, Morrison, Sublett, Uemura, & Setrakian, 1984).

Anti–motion-sickness medication has been promoted for the vestibular and vestibular–cerebellar dysfunction claimed to be associated with reading disability. However, a recent study concluding that no relationship exists between academic achievement and vestibular dysfunction seriously undermines the theoretical basis of this approach (Polatajko, 1985).

Optometric visual training programs continue to be widely used despite the lack of evidence that reading disabilities are in any way related to problems in the visual system. Not only have visual training programs failed to demonstrate improvement in academic achievement, but a risk of these programs is that "such training . . . may delay or prevent proper instruction or remediation" (American Academy of Pediatrics, 1984).

In a twist on the visual system interventions, tinted glasses have been touted as an effective therapy for reading disabilities. Proponents of the system claim that up to 50% of learning disabilities are associated with "scotopic sensitivity syndrome," a condition for which tinted glasses are recommended as an adjunct to instruction. Again, it should be remembered that no evidence links learning disabilities and visual system problems.

Approaches Based on Biochemical Theories of Learning Disorders

The rationale for biochemically based therapies for the learning disorders is derived from questionable theory stemming from studies on adults and from anecdotal evidence of positive effect. One approach much acclaimed in the popular literature has been the use of megavitamin therapy. The use of large doses of vitamins for brain dysfunction originated from work with schizophrenic adults and children. There is no convincing evidence that mild vitamin deficiencies play a role in any type of brain dysfunction. Several clinical trials of large vitamin doses have also shown no positive effect. In one study, 20 children with learning disorders were divided into matched groups of 10, with one group receiving the vitamins ascorbic acid, niacin, and pyridoxine for 6 months and the other receiving a placebo. Although 18 children were perceived by parents as showing behavioral improvement, objective tests of intellectual and academic achievement measured no group differences (Kershner & Hawke, 1979). When large doses of the same vitamins were administered to 41 children with attention deficits in a crossover study, no significant differences appeared in most behavior scores. The vitamin-treated children actually showed a higher incidence of more disruptive behavior, and 42% of the children showed early signs of liver toxicity while on vitamins (Haslam, Dalby, & Rademaker, 1985). Thus, evidence to date suggests that vitamin therapy leads to no academic improvement, to risk of liver toxicity, and to possibly less desirable behavior.

The notion that deficiencies of certain minerals (e.g., copper, zinc, magnesium, manganese, or chromium) might be associated with learning difficulties still persists, despite lack of any credible evidence to support it. A single, unreplicated, methodologically flawed paper (Pihl & Parkes, 1977) suggested a relationship between learning problems and trace mineral content in hair. Evidence of a connection between brain content and nutritional status is still lacking, as is evidence that mineral therapy improves learning. Administration of large doses of minerals suggested by some has not been established as a safe practice.

A question commonly asked by both parents and teachers is whether excess sugar causes or exacerbates hyperactive behavior in children with attention deficit disorders. Two recent studies reached the same conclusion: There is no objective evidence of deterioration of behavior or learning in children with attention deficit disorders when they ingest large amounts of sugar (Gross, 1984; Wolraich, Milich, Stumbo, & Schultz, 1985). The hypothesis that children with learning disorders may be suffering from hypoglycemia (low blood sugar) has also failed to be established. Although excessive carbohydrates may cause dental caries or contribute to poor nutrition in any child, their dietary restriction in the hope of improving the child's academic abilities cannot be supported on the basis of research conducted thus far.

The most controversial dietary regime proposed in recent years has been the additive-free (Feingold) diet. Proponents suggest that many children with attention deficit disorders are experiencing a toxic reaction to naturally occurring salicylates (e.g., aspirin) and to various food additives and colorings. The proposed treatment is an extremely restrictive, additive-free diet, ideally followed by the entire family. Years of study by a number of respected researchers led to a Consensus Development Conference convened by the National Institutes of Health (1982). This conference concluded that, at most, a small subgroup of children with attention deficits may improve on the special diet. When 13 placebo-controlled studies were reviewed recently, Wender (1986) concluded that only 2 or 3 (1%) of the 240 subjects in the combined groups showed "consistent behavioral change in the expected direction." Although families may report improved behavior while the child is on a restrictive diet, and the improvement may be real, it is probably due to a placebo effect and enhancement of environmental factors (e.g., increased family interaction and support) rather than to the diet itself. In fact, families rarely adhere to the diet strictly. As long as the child's diet is nutritionally sound, physicians and nutritionists need not feel compelled to dissuade families who believe in the diet. On the other hand, in light of the low chance of any improvement and the daily inconvenience, there is no reason to recommend the diet to a family to improve a child's behavior or learning.

TABLE 3–5
Regarding "Fad Therapies"

1. Investigate the newest approaches, within and outside of your discipline.

2. Insist upon proof of rigorous scientific validation before endorsing an approach.

3. Assist parents in evaluating any approach, including advantages and disadvantages to the child and the family.

4. Adopt a nonjudgmental stance with parents if a controversial approach causes no harm and does not pose a barrier to the child receiving valid intervention services.

Parents and professionals often ask about the role of allergies in learning and behavioral problems. That allergies may be a contributing factor has been supported anecdotally, but not confirmed by scientific studies. A survey of 316 allergic and 84 nonallergic children found no significant differences in academic performance and behavioral problems, except for the possible negative effects of upper respiratory congestion and eustachian tube dysfunction, which are not unique to allergies (McLoughlin et al., 1983). Although allergies and their treatment do not directly affect school performance, the impact of upper respiratory symptoms and certain medications on learning and behavior cannot be completely discounted.

Common fad therapies for the treatment of learning disorders are still in vogue in certain parts of this country. Although scientific proof in support of these therapies is scant or nonexistent, some parents (and professionals) will likely continue to advocate their usage. Table 3–5 provides suggestions to professionals faced with queries about questionable or unproven therapies. Many of the therapies entail a risk of physical and emotional harm to children and families. A nonjudgmental approach may be justified if the therapy is totally harmless and does not interfere with the use of appropriate interventions.

SUMMARY AND CONCLUSIONS

Since the brain is difficult to study directly, scientists have had to utilize indirect measures to study brain function. New technologies such as MRI, BEAM, and PET are moderately promising in their potential to help scientists unlock the mystery of how the brain works, especially in the area of learning.

The etiology of learning disorders is varied. Heredity probably plays a major role in the "purest" form of specific learning disabilities and attention deficit disorders, that is, those conditions unassociated with other brain problems. Many inherited diseases have adverse effects on learning and attention span, through direct disease effects on the brain, medication effects on the brain, and psychosocial effects of chronic illness. During the time of maximal brain growth (the third trimester of pregnancy through 2 years of age), medical problems may occur that interfere with brain development and lead to learning disorders that are often unexpressed until school age. Substance abuse by pregnant mothers and prematurity with all its medical complications may be major contributors to learning disorders. In the postnatal period, infections of the brain (e.g., meningitis), acute oxygen deprivation (e.g., from near drowning), malnutrition, and the disease processes or treatment associated with chronic illnesses (e.g., leukemia) can lead to learning disorders by disturbing normal growth and development of the brain.

Early detection of specific learning disabilities and attention deficit disorders remains difficult, mostly because of the clinical ambiguity of these disorders in the preschool years. Medical and educational professionals have a better chance of detecting these conditions at school entry or in the early school years, although no single instrument or test is very valuable. A child with a suspected attention deficit disorder is likely to be referred to a physician for definitive diagnosis, whereas a physician usually refers a child to the educational system or a psychologist for identification of specific learning disabilities. In either case, the child and family are best served when the professionals involved in diagnosis and treatment share information and communicate well with each other.

Because specific learning disabilities and attention deficit disorders are not well-defined pathological conditions, intervention for these disorders focuses on remediation and bypass strategies, rather than curative strategies. How well a child learns to compensate for the learning disorder is a function not only of the severity of the learning disorder, but also of the helpfulness of the psychosocial environment, including family and school. Even the most highly touted medically based interventions (e.g., stimulant medication) have been found to yield equivocal long-term benefits. Other biochemical and sensorimotor-based interventions remain unproven in terms of short-term benefits, and a few popular interventions are frankly fraudulent and irresponsible. Multimodal approaches, including well-accepted behavior modification techniques and creative environmental manipulation, probably hold more promise than any single intervention. Especially to be avoided is an intervention plan that advocates stimulant medication alone for attention deficit disorders, because it will probably be ineffective and may tend to mask other treatable conditions (e.g., specific learning disabilities and behavioral problems).

Since the learning disorders cannot be defined in terms of traditional pathophysiology, the physician must share his or her traditional role of diagnostician with the other professionals, whose skills aid in diagnosis. This role as interdisciplinary team member is new for many physicians, a role for which tradition and training may not have prepared them. Physicians must also deal with time constraints. The care of children with learning disorders is very labor intensive. Parents must be interviewed extensively, and school personnel must be contacted by phone. The physician, whose income is directly related to patient volume, tackles patients' school problems with justified uncertainty about the ability to be cost-effective. A role as team member and child advocate may be taken on with ambivalence by the physician because of these financial constraints and inadequate training. There appears to be, however, a growing role for "developmental pediatricians," who are specially trained to work with children with learning disorders and their families.

REFERENCES

American Academy of Pediatrics. (1982). The Doman–Delacato treatment of neurologically handicapped children. *Pediatrics, 70,* 810–812.

American Academy of Pediatrics. (1984). Learning disabilities, dyslexia, and vision. *Pediatrics, 74,* 150–152.

American Academy of Pediatrics, Committee on Children with Disabilities and Committee on Drugs. (1987). Medication for children with an attention deficit disorder. *Pediatrics, 80,* 758–760.

American Psychiatric Association. (1987). *Diagnostic and statistical manual of mental disorders* (3rd ed.). Washington, DC: Author.

Bax, M., & Whitmore, K. (1973). Neurodevelopmental screening in the school entrant medical examination. *Lancet, 2,* 368–370.

Bax, M., & Whitmore, K. (1987). The medical examination of children on entry to school: The results and use of neurodevelopmental assessment. *Developmental Medicine and Child Neurology, 29,* 40–55.

Butler, N. R., & Goldstein, H. (1973). Smoking in pregnancy and subsequent child development. *British Medical Journal, 4,* 573–575.

Carte, E., Morrison, D., Sublett, J., Uemura, A., & Setrakian, W. (1984). Sensory integration therapy: A trial of a specific neurodevelopmental therapy for the remediation of learning disabilities. *Developmental and Behavioral Pediatrics, 5,* 189–194.

Conboy, T. J., Pass, R. F., Stagno, S., Alford, C. A., Myers, G. J., Britt, W. J., McCollister, F. P., Summers, M. N., McFarland, C. E., & Boll, T. J. (1987). Early clinical manifestations and intellectual outcome in children with congenital cytomegalovirus infection. *Journal of Pediatrics, 111,* 343–348.

Conners, C. K., & Taylor, E. (1980). Pemoline, methylphenidate, and placebo in children with minimal brain dysfunction. *Archives of General Psychiatry, 37,* 922–930.

David, O., Clark, J., & Voeller, K. (1972). Lead and hyperactivity. *Lancet, 2,* 900–903.

David, O. J., Hoffman, S. P., Sverd, J., & Clark, J. (1977). Lead and hyperactivity: Lead levels among hyperactive children. *Journal of Abnormal Child Psychology, 5,* 405–416.

Dorman, C., Hurley, A. D., & D'Avignon, J. (1988). Language and learning disorders of older boys with Duchenne muscular dystrophy. *Developmental Medicine and Child Neurology, 30,* 316–327.

Douglas, V. I., Barr, R. G., O'Neill, M. E., & Britton, B. G. (1986). Short term effects of melthylphenidate on the cognitive, learning and academic performance of children with attention deficit disorder in the laboratory and the classroom. *Journal of Child Psychology and Psychiatry, 27,* 191–211.

Duffy, F. H., Denckla, M. B., McAnulty, G. B., & Holmes, J. A. (1988). Neurological studies in dyslexia. In F. Blum (Ed.), *Language, communication, and the brain* (pp. 149–162). New York: Raven Press.

Eliason, M. J. (1986). Neurofibromatosis: Implications for learning and behavior. *Developmental and Behavioral Pediatrics, 7*(3), 175–179.

Frank, D. A. (1984). Malnutrition and child behavior: A view from the bedside. In J. Brozek and B. Schurch (Eds.), *Malnutrition and behavior: Critical assessment of key issues* (pp. 307–327). Lausanne, Switzerland: Nestle Foundation.

Gabel, S., Winsten, N., Hegedus, A. M., Tarter, R. E., & Fireman, P. (1985). Neuropsychological functioning in children with immunodeficiency disorders. *Developmental and Behavioral Pediatrics, 6*(3), 154–156.

Galaburda, F. (1988). The pathogenesis of childhood dyslexia. In F. Blum (Ed.), *Language, communication, and the brain* (pp. 127–138). New York: Raven Press.

Gall, F. J. (1807). Craniologie our decouvertes nouvelles concernant le cerveau. *le Crane et les Organes, 4,* 1813.

Galler, J. R., Ramsey, F., & Solimano, G. (1984). The influence of early malnutrition on subsequent behavioral development: III. Learning disabilities as a sequel to malnutrition. *Pediatric Research, 18,* 309–313.

Golden, G. S. (1987, October). A hard look at fad therapies for developmental disorders. *Contemporary Pediatrics,* pp. 40–60.

Gross, M. D. (1984). Effect of sucrose on hyperkinetic children. *Pediatrics, 74,* 876–878.

Hagerman, R., Kemper, M., & Hudson, M. (1985). Learning disabilities and attentional problems in boys with the Fragile X syndrome. *American Journal of Diseases in Children, 139,* 674–678.

Hartsough, C. S., & Lambert, N. (1985). Medical factors in hyperactive and normal children: Prenatal, developmental, and health history findings. *American Journal of Orthopsychiatry, 55,* 190–201.

Hartzell, H. E., & Compton, C. (1984). Learning disability: 10-year follow-up. *Pediatrics, 74,* 1058–1064.

Haslam, R. H. A., Dalby, J. T., & Rademaker, A. W. (1985). Effects of megavitamin therapy on children with attention deficit disorders. *Pediatrics, 74,* 103.

Head, H. (1926). *Aphasia and kindred disorders of speech.* Cambridge, England: Cambridge University Press.

Hinshelwood, J. (1917). *Congenital word blindness.* London: H. K. Lewis.

Hunt, J. V., Cooper, A. B., & Tooley, W. H. (1988). Very low birth weight infants at 8 and 11 years of age: Role of neonatal illness and family status. *Pediatrics, 82,* 596–602.

Kershner, J., & Hawke, W. (1979). Megavitamins and learning disorders: A controlled double-blind experiment. *Journal of Nutrition, 109,* 819–826.

Klein, N., Hack, M., Gallagher, J., & Fanaroff, A. A. (1985). Preschool performance of children with normal intelligence who were very low-birthweight infants. *Pediatrics, 75*, 531–538.

Lambert, N. M., Sandoval, J., & Sassone, D. (1978). Prevalence of hyperactivity in elementary school children as a function of social system definers. *American Journal of Orthopsychiatry, 48*, 446–463.

Levine, M. D., Brooks, R., & Shonkoff, J. P. (1980). *A pediatric approach to learning disorders.* New York: Wiley.

Levine, M. D., Oberklaid, F., & Meltzer, L. J. (1981). Developmental output failure—A study of low productivity in school age children. *Pediatrics, 67*, 18.

Levine, M. D., Rappaport, L., Fenton, T., Coleman, W., Hathaway, T. J., Kent, W. L., Meltzer, L. J., & Zallen, B. G. (1988). Neurodevelopmental readiness for adolescence: Studies of an assessment instrument for 9–14 year-old children. *Developmental and Behavioral Pediatrics, 9*, 181–188.

Lubs, H. A., Smith, S., Kimberling, W., Pennington, B., Glenn, K. G., & Duara, R. (1988). Dyslexia subtypes: Genetics, behavior, and brain imaging. In F. Blum (Ed.), *Language, communication, and the brain* (pp. 139–148). New York: Raven Press.

MacMahon, J. R., & Gross, R. T. (1987). Physical and psychological effects of aerobic exercise in boys with learning disabilities. *Developmental and Behavioral Pediatrics, 8*, 274–277.

Marino, R. V., Scholl, T. O., Karp, R. J., Yanoff, J. M., & Hetherington, J. (1987). Minor physical abnomalies and learning disability: What is the prenatal component? *Journal of the National Medical Association, 79*(1), 37–39.

McLoughlin, J., Nall, M., Isaacs, B., Petrosko, J., Karibo, J., & Lindsey, B. (1983). The relationship of allergies and allergy treatment to school performance and student behavior. *Annals of Allergy, 51*, 506–510.

Montgomery, G. (1989). The mind in motion. *Discover, 10*, 58–68.

Morrison, J. R., & Stewart, M. A. (1971). A family study of the hyperactive child syndrome. *Psychological Psychiatry, 3*, 189–195.

Morrison, J. R., & Stewart, M. A. (1973). The psychiatric status of the legal families of adopted hyperactive children. *Archives of General Psychiatry, 28*, 888–891.

Naeye, R. L., & Peters, E. C. (1984). Mental development of children whose mothers smoked during pregnancy. *Journal of The American College of Obstetricians and Gynecologists, 64*, 601-607.

National Institutes of Health. (1982). Defined diets and childhood hyperactivity. *Journal of the American Medical Association, 248*, 290–292.

Orton, S. T. (1937). *Reading, writing, and speech problems in children.* New York: Norton.

Palfrey, J. S., Levine, M. D., Walker, D. K., & Sullivan, M. (1985). The emergence of attention deficits in early childhood: A prospective study. *Developmental and Behavioral Pediatrics, 6*, 339–348.

Pearn, J. H. (1977). Neurologic and psychometric studies in children surviving fresh water immersion accidents. *Lancet, 1*, 7–9.

Peckham, V. C., Meadows, A. T., Bartel, N., & Marrero, O. (1988). Educational late effects in long-term survivors of childhood acute lymphocytic leukemia. *Pediatrics, 81*, 127–133.

Pihl, R. O., & Parkes, M. (1977). Hair element content in learning disabled children. *Science, 198*, 204–206.

Polatajko, H. J. (1985). A critical look at vestibular dysfunction in learning-disabled children. *Developmental Medicine and Child Neurology, 27,* 283–292.

Rapoport, J. L., Buchshaum, M. S., Zahn, T. P., Weingartner, H., Ludlow, C., & Mikkelsen, E. J. (1978). Dextroamphetamine: Cognitive and behavioral effects in normal prepubertal boys. *Science, 199,* 560–563.

Rasmussen, F., Gustavson, K. H., & Bille, B. (1984). Familial minor neurodevelopmental disorders. *Clinical Genetics, 25,* 148–154.

Richardson, E., Kupietz, S., Winsberg, B. G., Maitinsky, S., & Mendell, N. (1988). Effects of methylphenidate dosage in hyperactive reading-disabled children: II. Reading achievement. *Journal of American Academy of Child and Adolescent Psychiatry, 27*(1), 78–87.

Rie, H. E., Rie, E. D., Stewart, S., & Ambuel, P. (1976). Effects of Ritalin on underachieving children: A replication. *American Journal of Orthopsychiatry, 46,* 313–322.

Safer, D. J., & Krager, J. M. (1988). A survey of medication treatment for hyperactive/inattentive students. *Journal of American Medical Association, 260,* 2256–2272.

Sell, S. H. (1987). Haemophilus influenzae type b meningitis: Manifestations and long term sequelae. *Pediatric Infectious Disease Journal, 6,* 775–778.

Shapiro, B. K., Palmer, F. B., Wachtel, R. C., & Capute, A. J. (1983). Issues in the early identification of specific learning disability. *Developmental and Behavioral Pediatrics, 5*(1), 15–20.

Shaywitz, S. E., Shaywitz, B. A., McGraw, K., & Groll, S. (1984). Current status of the neuromaturational examination as an index of learning disability. *Journal of Pediatrics, 104,* 819–825.

Shekim, W. O., Dekirmenjian, H., & Chapel, J. L. (1979). Urinary MHPG excretion in minimal brain dysfunction

and its modification by d-amphetamine. *American Journal of Psychiatry, 136,* 667.

Smith, S. D., Kimberling, W. J., Pennington, B. F., & Lubs, H. A. (1983). Specific reading disability: Identification of an inherited form through linkage analysis. *Science, 219,* 1345–1347.

Soemantri, A. G., Pollitt, E., & Kim, I. (1985). Iron deficiency anemia and educational achievement. *American Journal of Clinical Nutrition, 42,* 1221–1228.

Strauss, A. A., & Lehtinen, L. E. (1947). *Psychopathology and education of the brain-injured child.* New York: Grune and Stratton.

Taylor J. (Ed.). (1932). *Selected writings of Hughlings Jackson.* London: Hudden and Stroughton.

Viadero, D. (1987). Debate grows on classroom's "Magic Pill." *American Education's Newspaper of Record, 7*(7), 1, 19.

Vining, E. P. G., Mellits, D. E., Dorsen, M. M., Cataldo, M. F., Quaskey, S. A., Spielberg, S. P., & Freeman, J. M. (1987). Psychologic and behavioral effects of antiepileptic drugs in children: A double-blind comparison between phenobarbital and valproic acid. *Pediatrics, 80,* 165–174.

Wender, E. H. (1986). The food additive-free diet in the treatment of behavior disorders: A review. *Developmental and Behavioral Pediatrics, 7*(1), 35–41.

Whalen, C. K., & Henker, B. (1979). Psychostimulants and children: A review and analysis. *Psychological Bulletin, 83,* 1113–1130.

Wilsher, C. R., Bennett, D., Chase, C. J., Conners, K., DiIanni, M., Feagans, L., Hanvik, L., Helfgott, K., Koplewicz, H., Overby, P., Reader, M., Rudel, R., & Tallal, P. (1987). Piracetam and dyslexia: Effects on reading tests. *Journal* of *Clinical Psychopharmacology, 7,* 230–237.

Wolraich, M., Milich, R., Stumbo, P., & Schultz, F. (1985). Effects of sucrose ingestion on the behavior of hyperactive boys. *Pediatrics, 106,* 675–682.

World Health Organization. (1978). *Clinical modification of the World Health Organization's international classification of diseases* (9th ed. rev.). Ann Arbor, MI: Author.

Zieffle, T. H., Romney, D. M. (1985). Comparison of self-instruction and relaxation training in reducing impulsive and inattentive behavior of learning disabled children on cognitive tasks. *Psychological Reports, 57,* 271–274.

4

Learning Disorders:
Theoretical and Research Perspectives

D. KIM REID

The previous chapters have provided overviews of definitions, explanations, treatments, and assessment practices from the educational and medical perspectives on learning disabilities. The purpose of this chapter is to sort out some of the dominant theoretical perspectives and the research frameworks that support those explanations and practices.

WHY DO WE NEED TO BE CONCERNED WITH THEORY AND RESEARCH?

Although we are frequently unaware of it, all of us with an interest in learning disabilities (regardless of type of training) bring a (frequently implicit) system of ideas to our understanding of what learning is and why and how learning problems occur. We refer to these explanations, which are independent of the phenomena themselves, as *theories*. A variety of theories have been popular as explanations for learning disabilities (e.g., distortions in the perception of visual and auditory stimuli, allergic reactions to chemicals ingested in certain foods, and failures related to short-term memory). The learning problems themselves have not changed, but our understanding of what they are and what causes them has altered.

Individuals with learning problems, their parents, and the professionals who treat them often find this variety of theories baffling and frustrating. Because we are concerned about helping specific people, we want to know what causes problems and how to correct them; however, in science, observations must be made, hypotheses generated and tested, and results replicated again and again. Substantiated hypotheses must then be tested against other equally plausible hypotheses, before we have any assurance that we might have a useful idea. Furthermore, fashions change in science (Bruner, 1986), as they do in every other field of endeavor. Sweeping changes in criteria for what are acceptable data never fail to render some time-honored ideas less "true" or even null.

Ironically, this decade has been one of both great change and great tenacity. Although our approaches to the study of learning and learning disabilities have evolved rapidly and significantly, many of our assessment and treatment practices, mostly through bureaucratic institutionalization, have remained remarkably stable in light of the dynamic research activity that has dramatically altered so many previous conceptions.

We titled this book *A Cognitive Approach to Learning Disabilities* to indicate that we do not subscribe to the underlying abilities and behavioral models mentioned in the previous chapters. This title, however, does not lend so much clarity to our perspective as one might wish. The word *cognitive* when used to describe psychoeducational approaches has a wide array of meanings. There is no single cognitive perspective, but rather a rich and subtle blend of perspectives that often makes the meaning of disagreements, discrepant findings or treatments, and even apparent consensus difficult to interpret. What we know and think about these various cognitive perspectives influences how we approach learning disabilities and the types of interventions we recommend.

WHAT IS THE NATURE OF THE THEORIES AND FRAMEWORKS THAT ARE IMPORTANT TO THE STUDY OF LEARNING DISABILITIES?

As professionals in the field, we must understand the ways proponents of the various positions structure their data collection and interpret their findings if we are to understand how these positions are used to motivate and articulate treatment approaches. This text represents a compilation of at least three varieties of widely used (across the fields of scientific endeavor) cognitive approaches, each of which has influenced the others: (a) information processing, (b) constructivism, and (c) the ecological approach (sometimes referred to as the contextual or comparative psychology approach). These approaches collectively affect the work that is being done in the field of learning disabilities. (The following descriptions draw heavily from Reid, in press.)

Information Processing

Because information processing has become the dominant perspective in research and the development of theory in the field of learning disabilities, the second and third parts of this text are devoted to it. Only a brief overview will be given here, just enough to enable us to compare information processing with the other perspectives that are currently influencing cognitively oriented explanations and practices.

Information processing is not a theory, but rather a framework to guide our thinking, a way of looking at the world (Mandler, 1985). Before the 1950s, most people, including scientists, thought of learning (in humans and in other animals) as a process of acquiring *associations* (in Chapter 1, this approach was described as *behaviorism*). A mother, for example, who hugged her infant son each time his facial muscles relaxed into a smile was thought to be teaching him to smile socially, because the baby would "associate" the smile with her warmth, be "reinforced" for his smiling behavior, and therefore repeat that behavior increasingly often. A chicken who received a food pellet each time she pecked a bar would associate bar-pecking with the food reinforcement and would, therefore, peck the bar whenever hungry.

Most scientists believed that one could produce desirable, or "target," behavior (smiling, bar-pecking) by preceding or following the learner's activity with pleasant consequences or "reinforcers." The animal, human or not, was considered to be passively responsive to these simple interactions. Hypothetically, one could teach anything to anybody if it were taught (if behaviors were elicited and reinforced) in small enough pieces, in hierarchical order, and with enough practice. Although our educational system recognizes that there needs to be some "readiness" on the part of the student for what is being learned, our conception of instruction is still largely based on behavioral ideas: students learn the individual skills that are components of a target behavior, practice them, and eventually master that behavior.

Information processing emerged during the 1950s and has become widely accepted as better than behaviorism as a perspective for learning and learning problems. Instead of assuming that associations produce learning, the information processing community is interested in what *the learner does* while potential associations are occurring. These researchers want to know how a person collects, interprets, stores, and modifies information that is available in the environment or is already in one's head. They believe that a set of activities (e.g., perception and memory) operate together in a *process of cognition*. These mental activities are often described in flow charts, such as that presented in Figure 4-1, using a computerlike metaphor.

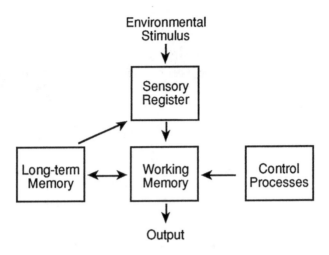

Figure 4–1. Process of cognition flowchart.

Information is first registered by the senses. That information is stored temporarily in the sensory register, until the brain has enough time to interpret what is there and, in so doing, screen out irrelevant information (called noise). Interpretation of the incoming stimuli must be sought from the brain's long-term storehouse of knowledge, the long-term memory. Of course, how any given stimulus is interpreted is also a function of the real-world context or of what one has on one's mind at a particular time (i.e., what is going on in working memory). In Figure 4–2, for example, the symbol in Lines A and B is interpreted as a "B" in the letter context in Line A, and as a "13" in the number sequence in Line B. "Does" is an auxiliary verb in Line C and a plural noun in Line D. Finally, to interpret Diagram E, one must know that the cat got loose near the elevator!

How we act on the information that has entered the sensory register and what and how much of it is processed in working memory or even added to long-term memory depend on our purpose. We carry out one set of mental acts, for example, if we want to remember a phone number only long enough to dial the phone. Our mental operations are very different, however, if we are trying to acquire information that will later be used to write a comprehensive discussion of a topic under study. In the first case, we would probably rehearse the number by repeating it to ourselves. In the second, we would think about how the new information is related to what we already knew, whether we believe it, and so forth. Because we make implicit choices about how we want to deal with information, scientists hypothesize that the human mind stores more than simply information.

A. A   I3   C   D   E   F

B. I0   I I   I2   I3   I4   I5

C. Does Mary want to go with us?

D. The buck chased the does.

E.

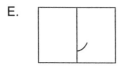

Figure 4–2. Working memory's effect on interpreting information.

People also need to develop and remember a series of control processes to manipulate that information. These processes include planning, monitoring, evaluating results, and so forth. As mentioned in Chapter 1, *declarative knowledge* refers to the information per se, *procedural knowledge* refers to our ability to carry out various activities, and *conditional knowledge* refers to our knowing when and if a particular procedure needs to be performed.

This way of looking at human cognition is analogous to the computer that takes in information, stores it temporarily in memory, performs certain functions with it, and then stores (or not) the result. The emphasis is not on what the information is, how salient it is, or how often it is repeated, but on what the learner selects out of the information available and what he or she does with that information. This framework most frequently leads to studies that test a hypothesis against competing hypotheses in an experimental setting.

Parts II and III of this book provide an in-depth description of one approach to information processing (Adaptive Control of Thought [ACT✱]) and report much of the information about learning disabilities that has been generated by a wide array of information processing studies. The sections also suggest how assessment based on an information processing framework might be conceived and carried out.

The information processing framework has been less successful in education than in describing the nature of learning problems and the characteristics of learning disabled persons. Few studies using an information processing framework have demonstrated the effectiveness of interventions that do not suffer from problems of generalizability. The main difficulty seems to be that information processing studies, in many ways fundamentally continuous with the previous behavioral point of view (Glaser, 1990), treat both information and control processes as discrete entities that can be dissected into subskills for instruction. These skills then tend to be taught in isolation and for their own sake (e.g., a child's task might be to learn to paraphrase, because the ability to paraphrase is an important component of studying). What happens most often, however, is that students who learn strategies as isolated behaviors seldom apply them in situations in which they would be useful. Thus, this body of literature has had minimum impact on pedagogical practice. Many instructional programs based on information processing are, in fact, seldom used beyond the laboratories where they were invented (see, e.g., tutorial programs based on ACT* theory, and the GUIDON project described in Glaser's [1990] overview of the reemergence of learning theory within instructional research).

Constructivism

The final section of this book, Part IV, is about research findings in instructional content areas, such as oral language, reading and writing, mathematics, and so forth. In Part IV, we describe intervention formats that have been both highly successful and widely tested. Most derive from constructivist (and/or ecological) approaches to the investigation of human functioning. Constructivism has exerted considerable influence on the fields of psycholinguistics and mathematics in particular.

The two major authors of this framework, Piaget and Vygotsky, developed different theories in opposition to behaviorism. Each asked the implicit question of how knowledge was *constructed by the child*, focusing on the role the child plays in his or her own development. Piaget's answer to that question— *biological constructivism*—benefited from over 50 years of continual study; Vygotsky's genius, however, survived only a few years. Ironically, it is Vygotsky's *social constructivism* that is predominant today. Vygotsky's prominence has resulted in part because many aspects of Piaget's theory have been either adopted by mainstream psychology or questioned by subsequent researchers, and in part because theories positing that interactions between the learner and the environment sustain a mutual, interdependent influence are becoming increasingly fashionable (see also "Ecological Approaches" below). For a more in-depth discussion of Piaget's learning theory and the research that supports it, see Gallagher and Reid (1983).

Biological constructivism.   For Piaget, a person's development (i.e., learning in its broadest sense) begins with responses to environmental stimuli experienced while in the uterus. For example, evidence indicates that, as they approach the time of their birth, many babies attend more carefully (i.e., exhibit reduced heart rate) to human voices than to random noises (e.g., doors closing, car engines starting) that penetrate the uterine environment. Since they respond differently to the two groups of stimuli, these babies may be said to have "learned" to distinguish voices from other environmental sounds, to have established (still quite primitive) functional *voice* versus *nonvoice* categories.

After birth, the baby continues to parlay its few instinctive behaviors and reflexes into a continuously expanding number of possibilities for interpreting, structuring, and responding to its environment. These increases occur through two major processes: differentiation and integration.

Differentiation was described above in the discussion of voice–nonvoice categorization: Even before birth, the baby has enough experience with sounds to distinguish (in a purely functional way) human voices from background noise. Examples that occur within a few days after birth include making distinctive cries for attention, food, and discomfort; discriminating additional functional categories, such as "things that provide food when sucked"; and so forth. Where there were once general phenomena (e.g., noise, crying, sucking), these phenomena have become functionally separate (e.g., two sets of noise, human and environmental; three cries that communicate different needs/states; and two groups of objects for sucking, pleasure objects and nourishment objects).

As the baby matures, new abilities are generated through the *integration* of capacities and reflexes. For example, the baby begins to reach toward what it sees, grasp what it touches, pull what it grasps, physically search for an object, walk to an object or person, and so forth. Eventually, these integrated behaviors are integrated with still other behaviors, ultimately becoming so complex that they enable the performance of very complicated tasks, such as those required for sports and driving. Although these integrated behaviors are often apparently physical, a pervasive intellectual component guides and controls them.

Piaget schematized development as a spiral (see Figure 4–3). Old behaviors are continuously differentiated and integrated into more and more possibilities for responding. It is important to understand that new behaviors (e.g., the ability to throw a ball in a smooth and coordinated way) are added, but the older more primitive behaviors (e.g., the ability to grasp the ball, pull the arm back, release the ball, etc.) are not lost; they are simply combined and recombined in an increasing variety of ways.

Although Piaget recognized that new abilities were generated from those already acquired, he did not advocate teaching learners primitive behaviors in order to have them acquire more complex ones. Unlike the behaviorists, who believed that stimulation would lead to a response, Piaget argued that the response had to be available *before* the learner could be sensitive to the stimulus—something like the phenomenon that occurs when a joke goes "over your head."

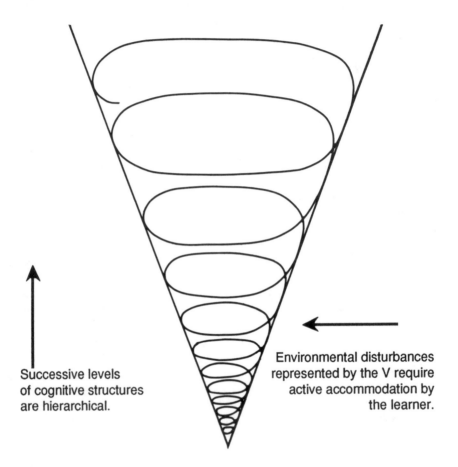

Mental constructions become enriched as experiences are filtered and modified by prior knowledge.

Successive levels of cognitive structures are hierarchical.

Environmental disturbances represented by the V require active accommodation by the learner.

Figure 4–3. Spiral of knowing.

Piaget described the ability to be aware of and interpret a stimulus as *assimilation.* Its complementary process is *accommodation,* the ability to adjust to reality and, on some occasions, to add new options to the assimilation scheme by adjusting the knowledge base to take previously unlearned options into account. Assimilation and accommodation may be quite specific (recognizing that new two-lip sandwich on a sesame-seed bun as the McJagger) or may occur between and among large systems of knowledge.

An example of the latter is the coordination of understandings derived from what is known about number and what is known about length. Inhelder, Sinclair, and Bovet (1974), for example, asked young children to decide who had walked further when "streets" were aligned in two different configurations (see Figure 4–4). When directed to look at Set A, the children agreed that Bill and Bob had walked the same distance, since the endpoints of the roads matched (equality based on what they knew about length) and they both passed the same number of houses (equality based on what they knew

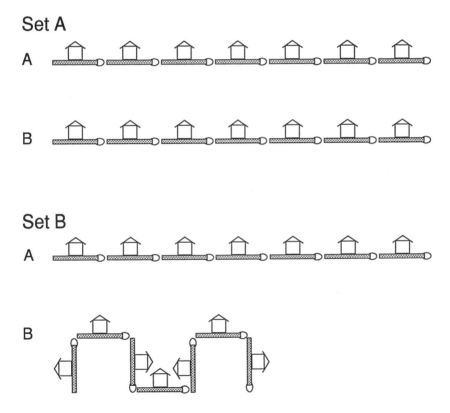

Figure 4–4. Matchstick roads. Adapted from *Learning and the Development of Knowledge* (p. 138) by B. Inhelder, H. Sinclair, and M. Bovet, 1974, Cambridge, MA: Harvard University Press. Adapted by permission.

about number). But, when confronted with Set B (even though they had watched the examiner shift the position of the matches), many of the children became confused. Even though Bob and Bill walked past the same number of houses, it appeared that Bob walked further than Bill. The answer they derived from their knowledge of number conflicted with what they knew from their knowledge of length.

Some of the children who were initially confused resolved their conflict by realizing that one of the roads in Set B zigzagged and that, although the distance traveled down the road was unchanged (the same number of houses was passed), the endpoints looked different because of the zigzags. In this case, a new option was added (learned) to their knowledge (assimilation base) of length: Not only are things the same length when their endpoints converge, but they can also be the same length if one of the items zigzags; that is, as long as nothing is added or subtracted from the zigzagged road, if the zigzags are straightened out, the endpoints of the two roads will meet. These students then had two ideas for assessing equality of length.

There is no way to teach children about length and then to teach them about number and expect them to be able to solve the problem above. Not only must they have the knowledge, but they must be able to coordinate new knowledge with old knowledge and one system of knowing with another. Human understanding is always ruled by the system as a whole. Piaget believed that the learner *constructed* his or her own knowledge through both maturation and experience: His emphasis was on the *self-regulation* of the learner.

Social constructivism. Vygotsky (1987), on the other hand, emphasized the way learners' social interactions effect their learning. Instead of picturing learners as scientists who are trying to make sense of the world, Vygotsky argued that children learn through participating in social (and consequently culturally determined) experiences.

Ninio and Bruner's (1978) investigations of how children acquire language, for example, indicate that care givers, most often mothers, treat their children as if they were social beings from the moment of birth. They talk to their babies as if the infants understand, allow pauses between vocalizations that are typical of conversational turn-taking, and treat the baby's actions and vocalizations as if they had meaningful intent.

A mother also performs nearly all of every task by herself at first, while the baby has few skills, but, as the child acquires more and more ability, he or she participates to a greater extent. Rituals such as bathing, feeding, and reading are examples of this supported, joint participation. In feeding, for example, the mother initially performs the entire task; the child responds only by sucking. Gradually, however, especially as the child begins using a bottle, the mother might encourage the child to grasp it as she holds it. As the baby's muscles strengthen, the mother provides less and less support, until finally the baby holds the bottle unaided. The conversion to solid foods and the utilization of utensils follows a similar path, with the mother providing only the help the child really needs.

Vygotsky also argued that learners, as their thinking matures, depend more and more on socially constructed systems, such as mathematics and language. For example, scientific concepts are usually taught verbally and are most often poorly understood initially. Because language is the primary vehicle for internalizing thought, however, verbally taught scientific concepts are part of a higher level of conscious awareness, a system of organized thought that is gradually applied to the context of everyday concepts and rapidly improves the understanding of them. Vygotsky believed that *instruction leads development,* that is, that higher levels of formal knowledge lead to enhanced scientific thinking, which, in turn, enriches spontaneous, everyday behavior.

Since instruction leads development, Vygotsky argued against using the products of knowledge as a measure of what a person is able to learn. Instead, he advocated exploration of the *zone of proximal development,* that is, what learners can do when they are engaged in meaningful activity with adults or others who are competent at performing the task of interest. Learners' levels of participation demonstrate not only what they know formally, but also what they are able to learn, a much more important index for educators.

Stone (1985; Stone & Wertsch, 1984) noted that the higher functions Vygotsky defined require reflective awareness and deliberate control, and that they amount to what we now refer to as strategic, or metacognitive, behaviors. Of course, Piaget's preoccupation with self-regulation (1977) and the differences between success (being able to do something) and understanding (knowing why it works) (1978) also focused on metacognitive behaviors. Brown (1975) and Flavell (1985), the American writers who popularized concerns with strategic behaviors, are also progeny of the constructivist tradition.

Ecological Approaches

Ecological approaches emphasize the study of the organism *within* its environment. Although Vygotsky's constructivism is to some extent ecological in nature, it is not one of the most fundamental ecological movements affecting theoretical and research perspectives in the field of learning disabilities. Vygotsky highlighted the importance of context in learning, but he put relatively little emphasis on the adaptive significance of behavior. The ecological approach, like information processing, is a framework to guide the way we think about learning, rather than a theory per se.

Ecologists (and also contextualists and comparative psychologists) disagree with the behavioral assumption that general learning principles apply across species. Striking differences exist in the learning disabilities of different species, of the same animal in different situations, and of the same animal at different points in its life span. Because many natural learning behaviors do not surface in carefully controlled laboratory studies, ecologists prefer studies conducted in natural environments, a significant departure from information processing studies. Furthermore, unlike the information processing tradition, which tries to formulate and simulate models of human performance (see Figure 4–1), ecologists try to *describe* human behavior in detail as it occurs.

> The ecological approach . . . [takes] the environment seriously, focusing on cognition in ordinary settings. To study concept formation, one begins with an analysis of everyday concepts; to study perception, one begins with visual control of action in cluttered environments; to study memory, one begins with the kinds of things people ordinarily remember. Such an approach usually forces the researcher to look at . . . variables that occur over time, rather than at brief flashes and momentary responses popular in information processing research. It also implies a concern with cognitive development and cognitive change, including both the changes due to age and those that come with the acquisition of skill—i.e., with learning itself. Most important, perhaps, is that [ecologists] . . . are generally reluctant to construct models or to postulate hypothetical mental events. Too often, they believe, those hypotheses have substituted for careful analysis of the real environment and the real events that occur in it. (Neisser, 1985, p. 21)

WHAT SPECIFIC CONTRIBUTIONS DOES EACH OF THESE APPROACHES MAKE TO THE STUDY AND TREATMENT OF LEARNING DISABILITIES?

No one perspective is *the* answer to our need for theoretical grounding in the field of learning disabilities, but each makes an important contribution. Much of the existing research has examined processes that occur within the individual—the research task for which information processing is best suited. Relatively few studies have investigated the performances of learning disabled persons in groups and/or natural contexts—the types of settings in which education takes place. Current trends suggest that scientific fashions are changing in our field and that *in situ* investigations are likely to be more frequent in the near future.

Information Processing

As Parts II and III will demonstrate, information processing has been highly successful in describing how people deal with information in real time and the types of processing difficulties that constitute the nature of learning disorders. Persons with such disorders tend to experience difficulties with representation, elaboration, strategic behaviors, and mnemonic processes. Not only has information processing proven to be a significant vehicle for examining what learning disabled persons do vis-à-vis information, but it also has the capability to elucidate and enrich the interpretation of studies carried out within an ecological tradition (Gelfand, 1985).

Several criticisms must be raised, however, in considering the utility of information processing studies for the design of instructional intervention. The first, and probably most severe, criticism is that, in this framework, complex processes are analyzed and reduced to their component parts for purposes of instruction, yet there is no indication that such reductions are necessary for learning. Indeed, there is widespread concern that fragmentation of complex processes such as reading and writing can impede learning. Human learners are highly adaptive. Although two activities may share many skills, learning disabled students are often able to perform one but not the other. There is no evidence that level of success in a particular subskill affects overall task performance. Some children, for example, are competent readers, but lack sophisticated knowledge of phonics. Conversely, our schools are replete with children who can perform well on phonics exercises but are unable to read.

Gavelek and Palincsar (1988) raised two other important criticisms of the information processing approach. First, it sets the locus of disability within the individual's mental processes and knowledge structures, ignoring whatever effects the social environment might have. Second, the view of learning is essentially and fundamentally nondevelopmental. As Brown (1979) pointed out, in the computer model that the information processing perspective employs, "The principal structures of the system are fixed; they do not grow, neither do they function in a dynamic interaction with a meaningful environment" (p. 226). A system that neither grows nor accounts easily for adaptation has limited potential for explaining human learning processes that change constantly throughout both individual life spans and the evolution of the species.

Constructivism

Recent research conducted within a constructivist framework has focused on changes in a person's understanding as it is revealed through changes in actions and behaviors as they develop and evolve over time. A researcher basing an investigation on biological constructivism (see, e.g., Moses, Klein, & Altman, 1990; Reid & Knight-Arest, 1981; Wansart, 1990a, 1990b) might ask a student to perform a rather difficult task in a laboratory setting (or observe a student performing tasks, such as classroom assignments, in a natural environment) and observe how the student's actions change from trial to trial as he or she figures out how to solve the task. (For overviews of this research tradition in learning disabilities, see Reid, 1991; Reid, Knight-Arest, & Hresko, 1981). Researchers who utilize a social constructivist orientation (e.g., Brown, Palincsar, and Stone) observe the changes that occur in task comprehension and task-solution strategies as learners participate in group problem solving sessions.

Although biological constructivism emphasizes the learner's interpretation and regulation of knowledge and social constructivism examines the impact of social interaction and social institutions on development, both focus specifically on the dynamics of change. Interest is in how human babies evolve into highly intelligent, highly competent adults. Both constructivist perspectives have the potential to provide valuable information for educators, because they treat learners as dynamic systems interacting with other dynamic systems, which comes rather close to examining an essential characteristic of classroom functioning.

Biological constructivism.   The discussion of the cognitive approach to instruction that was provided in the first edition of this book follows both constructivist and, to the degree that they overlap, information processing principles (see Table 4–1). A brief review of that discussion is provided before more recent work is addressed.

In contrast to the then-prevailing behaviorist assumptions, early cognitive approaches utilized principles derived from research and theorizing which demonstrated that complex processes (e.g., oral and written language, mathematical reasoning) require more than hierarchically organized associations: They also require control processes. The view of the human organism shifted from that of a passive respondent who is at the mercy of environmental influences to one who *selectively* engages in constant, dynamic interchanges with the environment. What is learned during any interaction was thought to be dependent on what the learner already knows—that is, the learner's *interpretation* (or assimilation) of potential, environmental information—rather than on stimulus saliency or consequences or antecedents for behavior. Also in contrast to behaviorism, knowledge was not viewed as a copy of reality, but rather as an entity transformed and enriched by each learner's mental constructions (reasoning, imaging, inferring, drawing of inferences, etc.).[1] To this point, our first edition conformed to both constructivist and information processing principles.

In discussing educational implications, however, we parted company with information processing. To some extent, that decision was motivated by the

---

1. Piaget (1978), for example, described an experiment in which children were asked why an "R" appeared to turn around when viewed in a mirror, while an "A" did not. Some of the children simply reported that it was magic or that the "Rs" *actually* turned around while the "As" did not. There was no problem for them to solve!

TABLE 4-1
Theoretical and Educational Principles

Theoretical Grounding

Complex behavior requires control processes.

Inherently active learners select and interpret information from the environment.

What learners know determines what they will learn.

Knowledge is a personally meaningful construction.

Educational Implications

Effective instruction must be child centered, holistic, and higher order.

Learning takes place covertly.

Errors promote growth.

Teaching is a process of providing the learner with activities that encourage the construction of meaning.

Holistic presentation of academic content allows organization and compensation.

Instructional goals change momentarily as learners gain knowledge and acquire skill.

Learners must be active in their own learning.

The purpose of education is *long-term* maintenance.

scarcity (in 1979–1980, when we were writing) of information processing research that addressed educational issues. Beyond that, however, our conviction was that constructivist principles were both better suited to educational intervention and represented a more significant break with behaviorism. (As mentioned above, information processing tends to be continuous with the behavioral tradition that spawned it.) Consequently, we concluded that instruction needed to be (a) child centered rather than curriculum centered, (b) holistic rather than skills/components oriented, and (c) focused on the role of higher order rather than lower level functions.

Furthermore, we (Reid & Hresko, 1981, pp. 49–50) argued that it is important to do the following:

1. Consider what is accomplished *internally* (or *covertly*) by the learner. People learn not only by doing, but also by observing others; imitating

models; watching films, TV, and the like; seeing a demonstration; discussing issues; and listening to a lecture. Sometimes they learn without practice, without reinforcement, and without any overt action. *Cognitive elaborations*, such as inferencing, imaging, remembering, and drawing analogies, influence learning.

2. Regard learning as a personal *construction*. Learners create their own mental realities, rather than responding predictably to the sensory qualities of their environments. Furthermore, errors are a natural and important part of the learning process.

3. Recognize that the learner is the most important element in the teaching–learning situation, not the materials, lessons, teaching techniques, or other factors external to the learner.

4. Provide activities to facilitate the learner's ability to construct meaning from experience. Such activities must be contextually embedded and relevant to the learner. Presentation of the material must be holistic (rather than reductionistic), so that learners understand the purpose and function of new knowledge. Without a meaningful framework, learners will not know how to organize new information. Instructional plans must be regarded as tentative guidelines, because the learner's immediate goals will change as new information, skill, or interests are acquired.

5. Inform learners that they must be active in their own learning. Learners come closer and closer to what is considered "objective reality" by consistently enriching and elaborating past knowledge.

6. Focus on maintenance of information in long-term store. Most procedures employed in education, especially in special education (e.g., explanation, demonstration, rehearsal, drill, and practice), are effective in ensuring that information will be understood. To ensure that it will be *maintained*, it is important to help children transform or elaborate on new information. The instructional techniques that have been demonstrated to be most effective in facilitating these types of activity are still seldom used in classrooms for the learning disabled. They include participating in discussions, constructing summaries, generating topic sentences, recalling previous experiences, drawing inferences, composing pictures or illustrations, and deriving analogies, metaphors, and rule statements—all activities that enable learners to construct personal meanings.

Poplin (1988a, 1988b) recently offered very similar arguments. Building on Piaget's schematization of the growth of human knowledge as a spiral, she advocated an approach to instruction that also departs significantly from the behavioral and information processing models. Rather than viewing the goals of education as enabling learners to perform a variety of tasks, Poplin follows the constructivist bent of regarding learning as the construction of meaning. The principles she espouses are presented in Table 4–2. Poplin's very important additions to the principles noted by Reid and Hresko (Table 4–1) included (a) more explicit descriptions of the structuralist values (1 and 2) that are related to considering the human organism as a unified system, (b) greater elaboration of the constructivist assumptions (4 and 7) that humans are inherently active and that learning proceeds from whole to part to whole, and (c) delineation of the holistic premises (9 and 10) that learning is enhanced by interest and trust.

Social constructivism. Those educational studies that have been based on social constructivism also respect the principles of biological constructivism outlined above. Rather than examine the behaviors of learners as if they operate in isolation, however, these studies are designed to reveal the effects that social processes have on an individual's learning. The reader is directed to Chapter 11 for a detailed description of a very powerful, highly flexible, and widely researched teaching technique, *reciprocal teaching* (also see Palincsar & Brown, 1984), which conforms to social constructivist principles.

Strengths and weaknesses of constructivist studies. Both biological and social constructivist studies have been important to education of the learning disabled, because they have frequently addressed educational performance directly and because they tend to demonstrate generalizable results, probably because of their emphasis on meaningfulness: knowing not only what to do, but why it works and when to use it (Brown & Campione, 1986).

Because the emphasis is on change, whether self or socially regulated, the basic model of learning is considerably more dynamic and complex than that derived from concepts of instruction that were built on views of the learner as a passive respondent. Brown, Bransford, Ferrara, and Campione (1983) used the tetrahedral model of learning presented in Figure 4–5 to explicate some of the important aspects of this and other theoretical positions that emphasize the integrity and activity that characterize the individual learner. This model was originally developed separately by Bransford (1979) and Jenkins (1979).

This rather popular model of learning highlights the important influences in any situation in which learning takes place. First, there is a learner, say Kerry, who brings a complex of characteristics and knowledge that are already in place: Kerry might be bright or not, have a specific learning problem or not, have an interest in mathematics or not, know about horses or not, know how to read more or less well, know how to organize a long division problem or not, and so forth. Kerry will respond to whatever task we give her by selecting certain activities from her unique repertoire of abilities and information. If she is very familiar with the content to be learned, she will most likely be able to do a lot of "reading between the lines," supplying information

---

TABLE 4–2
Principles of the Structuralist/Constructivist/Holistic
Teaching/Learning Process

Structuralist Values

1. The whole of the learned experience is greater than the sum of its parts.

2. The interaction of the learned experience transforms both the individual's spiral (whole) and the single experience (part).

3. The learner's spiral of knowledge is self-regulating and self-preserving.

Constructivist Beliefs

4. All people are learners, always actively searching for and constructing new meanings, always learning.

5. The best predictor of what and how someone will learn is what they already know.

6. The development of accurate forms follows the emergence of function and meaning.

7. Learning often proceeds from whole to part to whole.

8. Errors are critical to learning.

Holistic Thought

9. Learners learn best from experiences about which they are passionately interested and involved.

10. Learners learn best from people they trust.

11. Experiences connected to the learner's present knowledge and interest are learned best.

12. Integrity is a primary characteristic of the human (learner's) mind.

WHOLE > SUM OF PARTS (Structuralism)

From "Holistic/Constructivist Principles of the Teaching/Learning Process: Implications for the Field of Learning Disabilities" by M. S. Poplin, 1988, *Journal of Learning Disabilities, 21*, p. 405. Copyright 1988 by PRO-ED. Reprinted by permission.

that the author or the problem does not. If she is an expert, she may have ready-made solutions for the problem. If the task is new to her, she may struggle through trial and error toward a solution. In some cases, she may not have enough background information to recognize that there is a problem at all.

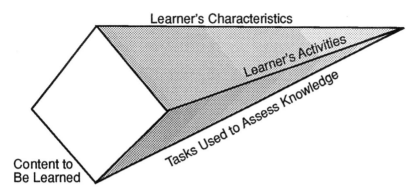

Figure 4-5. Tetrahedral model of learning. Adapted from *Human Cognition: Learning, Understanding, and Remembering* (p. 8) by J. D. Bransford, 1979, Belmont, CA: Wadsworth. Adapted by permission of Wadsworth Publishing.

Furthermore, the mental activities that Kerry uses will depend on the nature of the task to be accomplished. If she is asked to learn Latin, she might memorize declensions or translate Latin text into English. If she is asked to learn French, she may do some memorizing, but she will not translate into English. The task will impose a different set of demands: Her job will be to think in French, not to think in English.

Finally, how we ask Kerry to demonstrate that she has learned and what her own purpose is for learning both will have a major impact on what processes she engages in. If she is to use her French to write an essay, she might spend much of her study time practicing reading and writing. If she is planning a trip to Paris, she would be more likely to spend the bulk of her study time in conversation with people who speak French. All four aspects of the tetrahedral model come into play in a dynamically integrated way when a learner is in the process of constructing knowledge.

Although they have had a significant impact on current understandings of how oral and written language is acquired and how students learn mathematics (see Part IV), constructivist models do have some failings. Biological constructivism tends to view the learner as a virtually independent (although interactive) system, thereby overlooking the certain and enormous impact of sociocultural factors. Social constructivism treats the learner as a social being who learns through interactions with others (particularly competent adults), but tends to minimize the importance of individual and species-wide adaptation. It pays short shrift to the interactions that occur between the macroenvironment (interpersonal and situational variables, social position, and the beliefs, values, and norms associated with societal order [Doise, 1987]) and the microlevel interdependencies among organismic, functional, and environmental effects that occur with respect to the accomplishment of specific tasks (Schlechter & Toglia, 1985). These shortcomings explain the current increased interest in ecologically based studies.

Ecological Perspectives

Brown (1979) was among the first to note the potential usefulness of studies that treat "human learning as an adaptation to a natural environment with significant properties of its own" (p. 107). Relatively few educational studies based on an ecological framework have been conducted, however, because they are both time and labor intensive and, since variables are observed rather than controlled, such studies are messier and harder to interpret. An extremely small subset of ecologically based studies has addressed issues related to persons with learning disabilities. Those that exist (see Chapter 15 for an overview), however, are especially instructive to educators, because they were carried out in natural settings, most often classrooms, and address issues that extend beyond the confines of school-determined academic goals. Consequently, unlike in laboratory studies, the need to make intelligent guesses about how the findings might relate to the real world of teaching and learning is negligible. (Many studies based on constructivist principles have also been conducted *in situ*, but, with very few exceptions [see, e.g., Wansart, 1990b], they have been more tightly controlled.)

Guba (1978) described researchers' goals in naturalistic inquiry in education as alternating between discovery and verification (see Figure 4-6). During the initial period of discovery, the observer places very few constraints on the situation being observed. Unlike in laboratory studies, variables and explanations are not formulated in advance. Hence, the parameters of the observation are very broad. Over time, observers begin to discover the meaning of what they have observed and to propose categories within which the observed behaviors can be assimilated and accounted for. The purpose of observation then changes. Verification, rather than discovery, becomes the goal. As the researcher tries to elicit the response categories of interest to test their utility and validity, the scope of observation narrows. Most researchers cycle repeatedly through periods of discovery and verification. Such studies painstakingly describe and interpret behavior as it unfolds to control and respond to real environmental events.

Studies that have treated learning disorders as adaptations to significant environmental influences have frequently been associated with and reported in arguments for a paradigm shift to holism. Briefly, holism is a broad movement that is occurring across many sciences. One might view it as a fundamental change of fashion in science, one that renders the knowledge generated by reductionist models as banal and uninteresting. In opposition

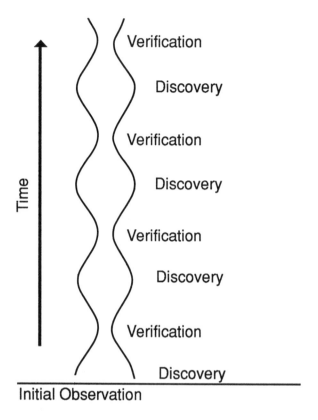

Figure 4-6. Strategy for observation in naturalistic inquiry. Adapted from *Toward a Methodology of Naturalistic Inquiry in Educational Evaluation* (p. 7) by E. G. Guba, Los Angeles: Center for the Study of Evaluation, University of California. Adapted by permission.

to the reductionist and mechanistic assumptions of behaviorism and information processing, its most distinguishing characteristic is that it views humans as organized, whole systems with their own integrity, and, consequently, as inherently dynamically active and self-regulated. Holists are opposed both to the separation of academic content into subskills that are to be acquired by learners in hierarchical order and to tight controls exerted by teachers and schools over what, when, where, why, and how learning takes place. They encourage teachers to actively attempt to both respect and nurture individual differences by granting students a very significant role in planning and directing their own learning. In Chapter 15, Heshusius describes in detail these and other tenants of holism, along with the whole-language interventions that are compatible with them.

SUMMARY AND CONCLUSIONS

We have seen that the cognitive approach in learning disabilities actually represents an amalgam of perspectives with different research traditions and fundamentally different criteria for what constitutes acceptable, scientific data. The three most prominent perspectives are the information processing, constructivist, and ecological frameworks.

The information processing approach emerged from early learning theory and is still largely compatible with that tradition. Most important to professionals interested in learning disabilities are its concerns with model building and simulation, its computer metaphors, and its reductionist stance. It has been highly successful in clarifying the nature of learning disorders, but has been considerably less effective in spawning educational and other treatment-related interventions that have generalizability. It also is poorly suited for explanations of growth and adaptation.

Biological and social constructivism share a preoccupation with developmental processes. The former views intellectual development as an extension of biological development and, consequently, focuses on the self-regulatory and adaptive aspects of behavior change. Social constructivism, on the other hand, posits that humans are inextricably and fundamentally social. Consequently, it isolates sociocultural factors—social interaction per se, language, and mathematics—as the driving forces behind development. Constructivism has not enjoyed the wide popularity of information processing in the field of learning disabilities, but it has fostered the generation of such important concepts as metacognition and has engendered such highly effective educational interventions as collaborative learning.

The ecological (contextual, comparative psychology) approach has exerted the most recent impact on the field of learning disabilities and, like most new ideas, is undergoing a period of controversy. It shares the nonreductionist stance of the constructivist approaches, but subscribes to an even more fundamentally holistic conception in which human learning is viewed as adaptation within a macroenvironmental niche. Ecological studies are conducted in natural settings without preconceived hypotheses: Observers alternate between periods of discovery and verification. Such studies are costly with respect to time and labor. Obviously, ecologists favor the holistic orientations to instruction (e.g., the whole language approach to reading and writing).

Although there is clear evidence that all three of these research traditions have influenced research and instructional design in our field, their individual impact has not always been apparent. Many professionals lump all this work together under the rubric "information processing," without any awareness that constructivism and the ecological perspective have been exerting increasingly more authority on the direction the field is taking.

Part of the reason for this confusion comes from the significant overlaps among these perspectives. All three perspectives share a view of the learner as an inherently active organism who assimilates (rather than associates) information. It is not true, however, that all differences among these perspectives are reconcilable, that a rapprochement can be achieved by "broadening the information processing variables influencing the learning process" (Swanson, 1988, p. 290). This faulty assumption fails to appreciate that reductionism and holism are fundamentally conflicting premises.

It has not been our purpose in this text to advocate one position over the others. Rather, we have chosen to present an overview that respects the field's diversity and complexity. Although I have made no attempt to camouflage my personal sympathies for the constructivist and ecological positions, I have attempted to point out the achievements and shortcomings of each perspective. More space is devoted to the discussion of biological constructivism because it played an important role in the formulation of educational principles for the first edition of this book and because, unlike information processing, social constructivism, and the ecological perspective, it is not treated elsewhere in this book.

Each remaining chapter of this book has been authored by a person who is a prominent advocate of one or more of these three perspectives. Although we do not share a common framework, each of us respects the integrity and achievements of those who pursue other lines of inquiry. It is too soon to know how the future will judge our respective contributions.

REFERENCES

Bransford, J. D. (1979). *Human cognition: Learning, understanding, and remembering.* Belmont, CA: Wadsworth.

Brown, A. L. (1975). The development of memory: Knowing, knowing about knowing, and knowing how to know. In H. Reese (Ed.), *Advances in child development and behavior* (Vol. 10, pp. 104–152). New York: Academic Press.

Brown, A. L. (1979). Learning and development: The problems of compatibility, access and induction. *Human Development, 25,* 89–115.

Brown, A. L., Bransford, J. D., Ferrara, R. A., & Campione, J. C. (1983). Learning, remembering, and understanding. In J. H. Flavell & E. M. Markman (Eds.), *Handbook of child psychology* (Vol. 3, pp. 77–166). New York: Wiley.

Brown, A. L., & Campione, J. C. (1986). Psychological theory and the study of learning disabilities. *American Psychologist, 41,* 1059–1068.

Bruner, J. (1986). *Actual minds, possible worlds.* Cambridge, MA: Harvard University Press.

Doise, W. (1987). *Levels of explanation in social psychology.* Cambridge, England: Cambridge University Press.

Flavell, J. H. (1985). *Cognitive development.* Englewood Cliffs, NJ: Prentice-Hall.

Gallagher, J. M., & Reid, D. K. (1983). *The learning theory of Piaget and Inhelder.* Austin, TX: PRO-ED.

Gavelek, J. R., & Palincsar, A. S. (1988). Contextualism as an alternative worldview of learning disabilities: A response to Swanson's "Toward a metatheory of learning disabilities." *Journal of Learning Disabilities, 21,* 278–281.

Gelfand, H. (1985). The interface between laboratory and naturalistic cognition. In T. M. Shlechter & M. P. Toglia (Eds.), *New directions in cognitive science* (pp. 276–293). Norwood, NJ: Ablex.

Glaser, R. (1990). The reemergence of learning theory within instructional research. *American Psychologist, 45,* 29–39.

Guba, E. G. (1978). *Toward a methodology of naturalistic inquiry in educational evaluation.* Los Angeles: Center for the Study of Evaluation, University of California.

Inhelder, B., Sinclair, H., & Bovet, M. (1974). *Learning and the development of cognition.* Cambridge, MA: Harvard University Press.

Jenkins, J. J. (1979). Four points to remember: A tetrahedral model and memory experiments. In L. S. Cermak & F. I. M. Craik (Eds.), *Levels of processing in human memory* (pp. 429–446). Hillsdale, NJ: Erlbaum.

Mandler, G. (1985). *Cognitive psychology: An essay in cognitive science.* Hillsdale, NJ: Erlbaum.

Moses, N., Klein, H. B., & Altman, E. (1990). An approach to assessing and facilitating causal language in learning disabled adults based on Piagetian theory. *Journal of Learning Disabilities, 23,* 220–227.

Neisser, U. (1985). Toward an ecologically oriented cognitive science. In T. M. Shlechter & M. P. Toglia (Eds.), *New directions in cognitive science* (pp. 17–32). Norwood, NJ: Ablex.

Ninio, A., & Bruner, J. (1978). The achievement of antecedents of labelling. *Journal of Child Language, 5,* 1–15.

Palincsar, A. S., & Brown, A. L. (1984). Reciprocal teaching of comprehension-fostering and comprehension monitoring activities. *Cognition and Instruction, 1,* 117–175.

Piaget, J. (1974). *Adaptation vitale et psychologie de l'intelligence: Selection organique et phénocopie.* Paris: Hermann.

Piaget, J. (1977). *The development of thought: Equilibration of cognitive structures.* New York: Viking Penguin.

Piaget, J. (1978). *Success and understanding.* Cambridge, MA: Harvard University Press. (Original French edition published 1975)

Poplin, M. S. (1988a). Holistic/constructivist principles of the teaching/learning process: Implications for the field of learning disabilities. *Journal of Learning Disabilities, 21,* 401–416.

Poplin, M. S. (1988b). The reductionist fallacy in learning disabilities: Replicating the past by reducing the present. *Journal of Learning Disabilities, 21,* 389–400.

Reid, D. K. (1991). Assessment strategies inspired by genetic epistemology. In H. L. Swanson (Ed.), *Handbook on the assessment of learning disabilities: Theory, research, and practice* (pp. 249–263). Austin, TX: PRO-ED.

Reid, D. K. (in press). Learning disorders and the flavors of cognitive science. In L. Meltzer (Ed.), *Cognitive, linguistic, and developmental perspectives in learning disabilities.* Austin, TX: PRO-ED.

Reid, D. K., & Hresko, W. P. (1981). *A cognitive approach to learning disabilities.* Austin, TX: PRO-ED.

Reid, D. K., & Knight-Arest, I. (1981). Cognitive processing in learning disabled and normally achieving boys in a goal-oriented task. In M. Friedman (Ed.), *Intelligence and learning* (pp. 503–508). New York: Plenum Press.

Reid, D. K., Knight-Arest, I., & Hresko, W. P. (1981). Cognitive development in learning disabled children. In J. Gottlieb & S. S. Strichart (Eds.), *Developmental theories and research in learning disabilities* (pp. 104–154). Baltimore: University Park Press.

Schlechter, T. M., & Toglia, M. P. (1985). Ecological directions in the study of cognition. In T. M. Schlechter & M. P. Toglia (Eds.), *New directions in cognitive science* (pp. 1–16). Norwood, NJ: Ablex.

Stone, C. A. (1985). Vygotsky's developmental model and the concept of proleptic instruction: Some implications for theory and research in the field of learning disabilities. *Research Communications in Psychology, Psychiatry, and Behavior, 10*, 129–152.

Stone, C. A., & Wertsch, J. V. (1984). A social interactional analysis of learning disabilities remediation. *Journal of Learning Disabilities, 17*, 194–199.

Swanson, H. L. (1988). Comments, countercomments, and new thoughts. *Journal of Learning Disabilities, 21*, 289–298.

Vygotsky, L. S. (1987). Thinking and Speech. In R. W. Rieber & A. S. Carton (Eds.), *The collected works of L. S. Vygotsky: Vol. 1. Problems of general psychology* (pp. 39–288). New York: Plenum Press.

Wansart, W. L. (1990a). Learning to solve a problem: A micro-analysis of the solution strategies of learning disabled children. *Journal of Learning Disabled Children, 23*, 164–170, 184.

Wansart, W. L. (1990b). *Learning disabled or learning enabled? Writing in a collaborative classroom context.* Manuscript submitted for publication.

PART II

UNDERSTANDING THE NATURE OF LEARNING DISABILITIES: INFORMATION PROCESSING

To adequately represent what goes on in a "student's head" as he or she attempts to read, compute, spell, problem solve, or communicate is critical if one is to understand learning disabilities. The importance of this point is supported in many definitions of learning disabilities, which attempt to focus on the intrinsic nature of learning, as well as the voluminous number of studies on learning disabilities that attempt to "map out" what goes on in a student's mind. One way to represent what goes on in a learning disabled student's mind is provided in information processing theory. This theory has provided one of the major frameworks of psychological research on learning disabilities to date.

Part II provides a historical foundation to our understanding of information processing theory. Major contributors and various models of information processing are presented. The reader will soon discover that the majority of models covered in this section use memory skill as a foundation of learning. Thus, this section provides a separate chapter on the study of memory. Research on memory is the study of applied cognition. Without memory, learning does not take place. Part II concludes with what we know about information processing in the learning disabled student, and then makes application to instruction.

5

Information Processing: An Introduction

H. LEE SWANSON

The purpose of this chapter is to provide an overview of information processing theory as it applies to learning disabilities. Helping learning disabled students to become better processors of information is an important educational goal. This goal is based upon several studies suggesting that the information processing approaches used by learning disabled students do not appear to exhaust, or even to tap, their intellectual capabilities (e.g., Barclay & Hagen, 1982; Kolligian & Sternberg, 1987; Palincsar & Brown, 1984; Swanson, 1988). For example, their lack of success in the classroom—in academic tasks or in social interactions—has been demonstrated on skills that are modifiable or teachable, such as their inability to shift from one strategy to another, to abandon inappropriate strategies, to process information with one strategy and then select another, or even to consider several processing approaches in rapid succession in order to arrive at a solution to a problem. In the spirit of this broad educational goal, the objective of this chapter is to provide a foundation for understanding the learning disabled student's information processing abilities.

WHAT ARE THE COMPONENTS AND STAGES
OF INFORMATION PROCESSING?

To understand how learners act on sensory information, the processing of information conceptualized in terms of components and stages of processing is studied. Greatly simplified, the *information processing* approach is conceptualized as the study of how sensory input is transformed, reduced, elaborated, stored, retrieved, and used (Neisser, 1976; Newell, 1980). To understand how each of these processes plays a part in the flow of information, three general components that typically underlie information processing models must be identified: (a) a constraint or structural component, akin to the hardware of a computer, which defines the parameters within which information can be processed at a particular stage (e.g., sensory storage, short-term memory, long-term memory); (b) a control or strategy component, akin to the software of a computer system, which describes the operations of the various stages; and (c) an executive process, by which learners' activities (e.g., strategies) are overseen and monitored (see Figure 5–1). Each of these components is discussed in detail later in the chapter.

It also is important to note that the flow of information occurs in a sequence of stages (see Table 5–1). Each stage operates on the information available to it. Operations at each stage transform information in some manner such that the output of each stage represents transformed information, and this transformed information is the input for the succeeding stage. The analysis of these succeeding stages is often given in flowchart form.

WHAT IS THE THEORETICAL CONTEXT?

Let us now consider why such a theory is important for our understanding of learning and learning disabilities. Traditionally, when one assesses the processing difficulties of learning disabled people, it is in terms of right or wrong responses on some task. These responses take place in the classroom context, and the student is viewed as being unsuccessful in achieving some activity (e.g., reading) that is related to that context. From an information processing perspective, the student's response is *distinct* from the learning activity; that is, instead of focusing on right or wrong responses, the focus is on the student's search for patterns, discovery of information, and strategy changes. To understand this alternative view, it is necessary to provide a historical foundation. Within the information processing orientation, perhaps the most influential expositions are those of Bruner, Goodnow, and Austin (1956), Newell and Simon (Newell, Shaw, & Simon, 1958; Newell & Simon, 1972), Atkinson and Shiffrin (1968), Craik and Lockhart (1972), Neisser (1967), Baddeley and Hitch (Baddeley, 1981; Baddeley & Hitch, 1974), and

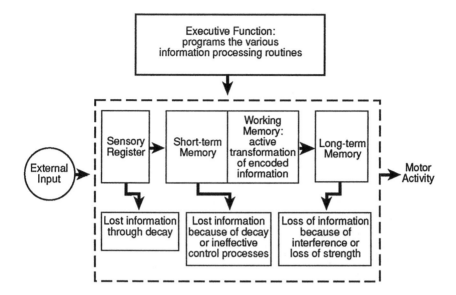

Figure 5–1.   A simplified model of information processing.

Brown (1975). (See comments in Chapter 3 suggesting that Brown's work does not belong to this tradition.) Each theorist's contribution is outlined in Table 5–2 and discussed more thoroughly in the following sections.

Strategy Development

The organized sequence of responses a person makes in a deliberate effort to achieve the solution to a problem is called a *strategy*. It is a plan representing stages of information gathering (what information the person chooses as important) and information processing (how the gathered information is processed). The pioneer work in strategy development was done by Bruner et al. (1956). In their study, children were presented a series of cards that had pictures of objects that varied on the dimensions color, size, and shape. The child's task was to figure out whether each picture was or was not an example of a rule. Specifically, Bruner et al. studied how children come to learn a conjunctive rule (red and square). They noted that children use several distinct strategies in their conceptual learning (see Table 5–3).

This early research laid a foundation for the notion that children's problem solving behavior is highly organized and consciously planned. Two aspects of Bruner et al.'s findings have implications for the field of learning

---

TABLE 5-1
Stages of Information Processing Activity

---

1. *Encoding:* The process of analyzing input information. The child matches the input against past learning. This process also involves extracting different types of information from a stimulus. For example, a child who is presented a series of words to be remembered for a spelling test, may process the words by their orthographic features, the phonological features represented by the printed word, and/or the semantic features represented by the meaning of the word.

2. *Elaboration:* The process of making connections between the material to be learned and information previously stored. For example, a child who is presented spelling words to remember, forms associations to those words by using extra ways of mediating the information (e.g., using the process of imagery to visualize the word *boy*), proposing or answering questions about the word (e.g., asking "Is a boy the same as a man?"), categorizing information (e.g., thinking that the word *boy* represents one of the two genders), or associating the word with a context (e.g., recalling that the teacher used the word *boy* in several sentences).

3. *Transformation:* The process of applying rules to incoming information (e.g., the word *perceive* follows the "I before E except after C" rule). In contrast to encoding and elaboration, this process requires the application of previously stored rules about information processing.

4. *Storage:* The process of adding input information to the existing information within the mental system. This process forms a memory trace. Forgetting this memory trace can be attributed to an interference from other learning (e.g., the child has difficulty remembering how to spell the word "perceived" for the present spelling test because the previous week's spelling test included the word "received," i.e., proactive interference). The effects of interference can be controlled by the degree to which the child has overlearned and reviewed the material.

5. *Retrieval:* The process of making available information that was previously stored. The process generally requires the reproduction of information with minimal aids (i.e., free recall, serial recall). For example, the child is asked to spell a word with all letters in their correct order.

6. *Searching:* The process of accessing information by determining the presence or absence of additional properties. For example, a child is asked if any of the word spellings that were forgotten rhyme with the word "receive" (i.e., cued recall). The child may develop an aid to remembering the word internally, or the aid may be external (e.g., teacher induced).

TABLE 5-1 (continued)

---

7. *Comparing:* The process by which information is compared with previously stored information and recognized to be either old or new, same or different, and so on. For example, a student recognizes that he or she has already learned 10 words on the list of 20 words to be given on a spelling test.

8. *Reconstruction:* The process by which the recalled information is modified from the original presentation. It is generally assumed that information recall is not a duplicate of the information encoded (Neisser, 1981).

TABLE 5-2
Contributions of Theorists to an Information Processing Model
of Learning Disabilities

Person	Contribution
Bruner et al.	Delineation of strategies during problem solving
Newell and Simon	A. General problem solving model B. Differentiation of heuristics (general problem solving approaches that do not always lead to a solution) and algorithms (approaches that always lead to a solution)
Atkinson and Shiffrin	A. Multiple store model of memory B. Focus on the structure and strategies of memory
Craik and Lockhart	A. Level of processing B. Variations occur in the depth of processing for certain information
Neisser	Clarifies role of the executive function
Baddeley and Hitch	Concept of memory as a dynamic working memory system
Brown	Clarifies the role of metacognition in performance

TABLE 5-3
Conceptual Learning Strategies Identified
by Bruner, Goodnow, and Austin (1956)

Conservative focusing: Conservative focusing yields relevant pieces of information about a concept by a *process of elimination.* Conservative focus begins when the child accepts the first positive instance of a concept. When the concept is encountered in another instance, the child varies his or her idea of the concept by only one attribute. For example, if the first card were red and not square and an example of the concept, and the next card were green and square, the child would focus on the attribute square since red has already been established as part of the conjunctive concept.

Focus gambling: Focus gambling involves varying one's choices of relevant attributes (shape, color, size) to more than one value at a time.

Simultaneous scanning: Instead of adopting a single attribute or two attributes as a basis for elimination of irrelevant pieces of information, some children form a simple hypothesis about the solution (e.g., all red and square forms are an example of the rule). Simultaneous scanning involves generating all possible hypotheses on the basis of the first positive instance of the concept and using each following instance to eliminate untenable hypotheses.

Successive scanning: Successive scanning involves a "trial-and-error" approach (test one hypothesis at a time). The child must remember which hypothesis has been tried to avoid redundant stimulus selections.

---

disabilities. First, the strategies that are available to children for forming concepts vary. Second, some strategies may be more effective than others, but children might find effective strategies difficult to discover. Consequently, it cannot be assumed that all children (especially learning disabled children) come equipped with the best strategies or will be able to discover the best strategies during learning activities.

To extend some of the observations of Bruner et al., Swanson (1981, 1982) sought to understand how learning disabled children problem solve. In two experiments, learning disabled and nondisabled children solved problems that required the use of disjunctive (either–or) and conditional (if–then) rules. An array of stimulus cards was arranged in front of each child. Each card included three dimensions with three attributes (or values): number—1, 2, 3; color—red, yellow, green; and shape—circle, triangle, star. Children were told that they were going to play a game in which they had to solve a problem. They were to tell the experimenter if a card was or was not an example of a rule. The experimenter then showed a stimulus card that provided a positive example of the rule. Every response by the child was followed by information feedback indicating whether the rule chosen by the child was or was not an example of the concept. The results suggested that on the difficult rules, learning disabled children were deficient compared with nondisabled children. These results generally coincide with the earlier findings of Bruner et al. that not all children come equipped with the best strategies for problem solving.

Problem Solving

Unquestionably, a major contribution to the general theory of problem solving behavior is the research of Newell et al. (1958). Their theory has taken the form of discovering proofs for theorems in symbolic logic through a complex computer program. This program, called "Logic Theorist," follows certain patterns of human processing. For example, insight to or solution of a problem is based on the logical elimination and selection of alternative hypotheses. Effective learning is not done through simple trial and error, but is determined by the extent to which behavior is governed by understanding of a rule. Furthermore, learning is accomplished by using a sequence of operations, generating problems, and remembering them in an ordered fashion.

Newell and Simon (1972) studied how a problem solver would evaluate the properties of alternative solutions in making a choice and the difficulties imposed by evaluation. They considered the chess player whose problem is to choose moves at certain points in the game that may determine the outcome of the game. The evaluation of alternatives is extremely complex because of the number of alternatives available to the player as well as to the opponent. Alternatives in moves lead to a multitude of possibilities, eventually leading to a tie, loss, or win. To understand these difficulties, Newell and Simon required subjects to "think aloud" while problem solving. Their use of think-aloud protocols to understand problem solving rests on two assumptions. First, thinking aloud does not interfere with the subject's performance on the problem solving task, and second, verbalization provides a complete record of the basic processes that are being executed. Available evidence supports these assumptions (Ericsson & Simon, 1984).

Based upon think-aloud protocols, Newell and Simon (1972) suggested that the essence of human problem solving is to be understood through a description of three major determinants: (a) space (problem space) the solver uses to represent the problem, (b) task demands, and (c) the environment in which the task takes place. The task environment describes a general class of problems to which a problem belongs (e.g., logic). Therefore, the task environment is objective and external to the subject's perceived definition of the task. The problem solver, on the other hand, defines the problem space or constraints (decisions, moves, strategies, logical relationships) incorporated into task solution. When presented with a problem, the problem solver strives to reduce the problem space. When each decision eliminates a number of available alternatives, the task becomes easier.

Newell and Simon's (1972) research has two major implications for understanding learning disabilities. First, what students say (based on an analysis of think-aloud protocols) verifies whether effective problem solving, via the use of strategies, is occurring. Students' verbalizations about how they problem solve allow knowledgeable observers to identify appropriate or inappropriate strategies. For example, possible strategies include generating unusual or new ideas (divergent thinking), breaking a mental set to look at a problem differently, avoiding premature judgments, clarifying the essentials of a problem, and attending to relevant facts and conditions of the problem. Second, and of more importance, Newell and Simon's research suggests that human thinking is analogous to an information processing system.

The usefulness of Newell and Simon's model for studying intellectual functioning of learning disabled children is apparent in a study by Swanson (1988). Because this study has a number of implications for understanding learning disabilities, we will look at this study in some detail. It was assumed that the intellectual performance of learning disabled children could be clarified by an analysis of the various mental processes they used during tasks on which they performed at levels comparable to nondisabled children. This perspective is *unique*, because research in the field of learning disabilities focuses primarily on specific processing deficits on tasks in which learning disabled children do poorly, and thus provides an incomplete account of such children's information processing limitations. The framework for conceptualizing ability group differences in mental processing is presented in terms of Newell and Simon's information processing model of problem solving. As previously stated, the theory emphasizes two important processes: problem space and a solution process that involves a search through the problem space. Problem space is a mental representation that contains partial information about a problem and its solution (Newell, 1980; Newell & Simon, 1972). Because a subject's problem space contains only partial knowledge, it is necessary to initiate a *general search* (heuristic) for information, as well as to discover a state that contains a solution to the problem (an algorithm). The processes used in this search for information and problem solution are referred to as problem-space operators.

The purpose of Swanson's (1988) study was to test the hypothesis that learning disabled and nondisabled children access qualitatively different mental processes when arriving at a correct solution. For the problem, children were presented with an item from the Picture Arrangement subtest of the Wechsler Intelligence Scale for Children–Revised. Five cards, which tell a story when correctly arranged, were placed in the following incorrect order, from the child's left to right: (a) a female child running in the rain and getting wet, (b) the female child walking in the rain with an umbrella, (c) the female child inside a house and a female adult pointing out the window to clouds while holding onto an umbrella, (d) the female child walking outside with a few raindrops falling, and (e) the female child, wet, inside a house with the adult female looking over her shoulder at her. The correct sequence is c, d, a, e, b. The child was asked to think aloud while solving the problem. All verbal responses were transcribed from audiotapes.

The mental components (coded verbal responses) were organized into heuristics. As stated, a heuristic is a general approach to problem solving that may or may not lead to a correct response. The heuristics noted included (a) a representation, understanding, or definition of the problem; (b) a means or plan for acquiring information; and (c) a means of interpreting and evaluating information for problem solution. Heuristics provide, at best, a general constellation of the mental components involved in problem solving. Thus, an alternative regrouping of components into strategies was done to better specify the interplay between problem solving components. This regrouping was based on the assumptions that heuristics do not always guarantee problem solution and that some subjects use strategies that are more likely to guarantee solutions.

The clustering of these mental components into certain strategies was based upon extensive literature. For example, the strategies that have been identified in the problem solving literature (e.g., Hayes, 1981) include means–ends analysis, systematic use of feedback, pattern extraction, if–then logic, prioritizing strategies, and systematic trial-and-error search. The means–ends analysis or general problem solver subroutine (e.g., Newell & Simon, 1972) is assumed to assess a subject's attempt to reach a goal state by taking a sequence of steps, each of which reduces the distance to the goal. The feedback strategy represents the subject's use of new information as it becomes available during the picture arrangement process. It was assumed that when children pay attention to feedback, they can generate and test relevant hypotheses toward problem solution (e.g., Gholson, 1980). Pattern extraction represents an interpretation of information based upon details in the picture sequences. This interpretation reflects one of two types of mediation: verbal analytic or visual spatial (Hunt, 1974). It is assumed that the type of mediation used to guide a problem solving search reflects the amount of verbal information stored in the problem solver's memory (i.e., less verbally efficient subjects tend to use spatiovisual processing patterns, whereas more verbally efficient problem solvers rely on verbal analytic reasoning). The hypothetico–deductive category reflects if–then thinking in which predictions are confirmed or disconfirmed. It is assumed that a subject generates a tentative hypothesis based on a partial understanding of the problem and then "tests out" his or her solution. The evaluation subroutine represents a "check" on the adequacy of the hypothesis. In addition, when a strategy has been evaluated as inadequate, the subject makes a transition from the previous strategy to another. This routine reflects a prioritizing and reprioritizing of strategies. The final strategy subroutine is assumed to reflect systematic problem solving that goes beyond blind trial and error (Hayes, 1981). In a blind trial-and-error search, the problem solver picks directions in problem solution, without considering whether they have already been explored. In a system trial-and-error search, it is assumed that the problem solver keeps track of the directions that have been chosen and utilizes only unexplored directions.

The results of Swanson's (1988) study indicated that both learning disabled and nondisabled groups were comparable in overall mental processing (i.e., total number of mental components used). Ability groups were different, however, in the coordination of problem-space operators (i.e., heuristics and strategies). The findings also suggest that nondisabled children's performance was best predicted by strategies, whereas disabled children's performance was best predicted by a heuristic. For example, nondisabled children were more likely than disabled children to use a strategy subroutine that involved systematic problem solving, evaluation, pattern extraction, and feedback.

Three implications related to this study appear important to our understanding of learning disabilities. First, our ultimate goal in focusing on the problem solving of learning disabled subjects is to understand the means by which different processing routes can be used to access information for correct problem solution. From an information processing perspective, it is generally acknowledged that individuals have a number of alternative means for achieving successful performance. The findings suggest that mental processing in learning disabled children is more likely to be influenced by heuristics than by strategies. Such general methods of problem solving allow them to perform in the normal range of intelligence. Unfortunately, although these general problem solving methods have greater generality than explicit strategies (or algorithms), they also have relatively less power. The findings suggest that learning disabled children may not understand how explicit strategies or algorithms can be used in task performance. Thus, instruction that helps such children organize certain mental processes into algorithms is an important focus for intervention for classroom tasks.

Second, Swanson's (1988) findings are in contrast to some models that view learning disabled children as passive or "inactive" learners (e.g., Hagen, Barclay, & Newman, 1982; Torgesen, 1982). Rather, children with learning disabilities in that study were able to tag new information and abandon inappropriate strategies throughout different phases of the task. Likewise, they had relatively little difficulty in accessing various pieces of information in order to solve a problem. Thus, when compared with nondisabled children, it appears that learning disabled children "actively" develop strategic thought patterns, although *inefficiently*. These inefficiencies appear to be related to their use of heuristic subroutines and suggest that such learning disabled children may be constrained in their ability to use strategies.

Finally, the think-aloud protocols for both ability groups reflect thinking that is "multidirectional" or opportunistic. (This concept is further discussed in Chapter 9.) This kind of thinking is in contrast to the step-by-step or linear thinking that traditionally captures most school curriculum and materials. More specifically, when children problem solve, their think-aloud protocols reflect the "picking and choosing" of *multiple* pieces of information (i.e., components) rather than a step-by-step or component-by-component process; that is, children make decisions related to task performance that do not meet the requirement that each component of their thinking fits into a completely integrated or hierarchical plan. As children make decisions, their problem solving approach may develop by processes that may not be coherently integrated. Thus, in terms of intervention, a possible goal may become one of helping learning disabled students better integrate various mental components so that a *smooth coordination* of information processing occurs during task performance.

Multiple Stores

Atkinson and Shiffrin (1968) provided a categorization of an information processing system (memory) along two major dimensions: structural features of memory that are fixed or unvarying from one situation to another and control processes that vary from task to task. As with Newell and Simon (1972), a computer analogy is used to illustrate the distinction between memory structure and control process. Each component is reviewed briefly.

Sensory register.   Figure 5–2 illustrates three basic structural components of information processing: sensory register, short-term store, and long-term store. Environmental information is assumed first to enter the appropriate sensory register (e.g., visual, auditory). Information in this initial store is thought to be a relatively complete copy of the physical stimulus that is available for further processing for a maximum of 3 to 5 sec. An example of sensory registration for the visual modality is an image or icon. For example, in a reading task, if an array of letters is presented tachistoscopically and the child is asked to write those letters after a 30-sec delay between instructions, the child will be able to reproduce about six or seven letters. As shown in Figure 5–2, incoming information from other modalities (auditory, kinesthetic) receives sensory registration, but less is known about their representation. For example, students who are presented a letter of the alphabet may produce a photographic trace that decays quickly, or they may physically scan the letter and transfer the information into an auditory (e.g., echo of sound), visual, or linguistic (meaning) representation. In other words, information presented

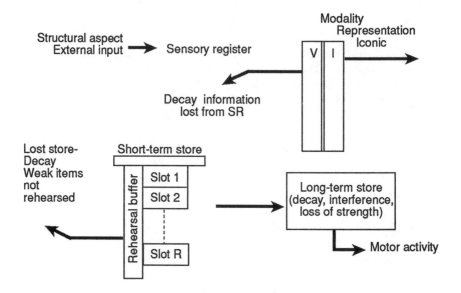

Figure 5-2. Atkinson and Shiffrin's three structural components of information processing. Adapted from "Human Memory" by R. Atkinson and R. Shiffrin in *The Psychology of Learning and Motivation* (p. 11) by K. Spence and J. Spence (Eds.), 1968, New York: Academic Press.

visually may be recorded into other modalities (e.g., auditory). The transfer of a visual image to the auditory–visual–linguistic store, is made at the discretion of the person. In the reading process, each letter or word is scanned against information in long-term memory and the verbal name. Certainly, this representation will facilitate transfer of information from the sensory register to a higher level of information processing.

Short-term memory.   From the sensory register, information is transferred into the limited-capacity short-term memory. Information lost in this memory is assumed to decay or disappear, but actually time of decay is longer than time available in the sensory register. Exact rate of decay of information cannot be estimated, since this component is greatly controlled by the subject. The short-term memory retains information in terms of auditory–verbal–linguistic representations. Atkinson and Shiffrin found it difficult to separate verbal and linguistic aspects from an auditory representation. For example, a child recalling letters may subvocally rehearse a letter by voicing the quality of the letter as well as the place of articulation in the mouth. These kinesthetic activities are difficult to separate from the actual linguistic aspects of recall.

Variation in short-term memory capacity is explained again by the control processes (to be discussed in the following section) and the meaningfulness of the material. The crucial factor in capacity is the person's ability to encode units or sequence the items so that they can be recorded into smaller units. Other factors that affect capacity include (a) information load, (b) similarity of items, (c) number of items processed during subsequent activities, and (d) passage of time. The exact nature of problems with the capacity of short-term memory is somewhat obscure in learning disabled students (Cooney & Swanson, 1987). Research has been unclear as to whether the limitation is one of processing capacity, storage capacity, or some interaction between the two.

Long-term memory.   The amount of information, as well as the form of information, transferred to long-term memory is primarily a function of control processes (e.g., rehearsal). Long-term memory is a permanent storage of information and has unlimited capacity. How information is stored is determined by the uses of links, associations, and general organization plans. Information stored in long-term memory is primarily semantic. Forgetting occurs because of item decay (loss of information) or interference.

Control processes.   Control processes that work within and between structural components are referred to as coding techniques or mnemonics and are used by subjects in an effort to remember information. The variety of these techniques is unlimited, but classification is rather difficult. In the sensory register, sample strategies may include scanning information and generating names for information, matching features or differences among stimuli, or focusing on one distinct feature.

Control processes in short-term memory include a choice as to which information to scan and a choice of what and how to rehearse. Rehearsal refers to the conscious repetition of information, either subvocally or orally, to recall information (e.g., a phone number or street address) at a later time. Additional control processes involve organization (ordering, classifying, or tagging information to facilitate retrieval) and mediation (comparing new items with items already in memory). Organization strategies may include the following:

1. Chunking: Grouping items so that each one brings to mind a complete series of items (e.g., grouping words into a sentence).

2. Clustering: Organizing items in categories (e.g., animals, furniture).

3. Mnemonics: Using idiosyncratic methods for organizing materials.

4. Coding: Varying the qualitative form of information (e.g., using images rather than verbal labels or substituting pictures for words).

Mediation may be facilitated by the following:

1. Making use of preexisting associations, eliminating the necessity for new ones.

2. Utilizing verbal instructions or asking the child to imagine, to aid in retrieval and organization.

3. Cuing at recall by using verbal and imaginary information to facilitate mediation.

Short-term memory also uses a rehearsal buffer (as shown in Figure 5–2), giving the subject some control over which items to eliminate from rehearsal and which items to include.

Control processes in long-term memory generally involve some type of "search" strategy. The search of long-term memory varies in degrees of order, such as a letter-by-letter search or use of conceptual categories or temporal events.

Summary and implications.   The multistore model views information as flowing through component stores in a well-regulated fashion, progressing from the sensory register, to short-term memory, and finally to long-term memory. These stores can be differentiated in children's functioning by realizing that (a) short-term memory has a limited capacity, and thus makes effective use of rehearsal and organizing mechanisms; (b) storage in long-term memory is mostly semantic; and (c) two critical determinants of forgetting in long-term memory are item displacement and interference as a result of a lack of retrieval strategy. Because a great deal of research has focused on learning disabled children's memory problems from a multistore approach, let us briefly review some relevant studies.

A major source of difficulty that learning disabled children experience during their attempts to memorize material has been highlighted by Gelzheiser, Solar, Sheperd, and Wozniak (1983). These authors recorded a brief statement made by a learning disabled student following an attempt to retain a passage containing four paragraphs about diamonds. The student reported that she could identify major themes of the story, but could not categorize the various pieces of information under these major topics. She was able to abstract the essence of the story, but was unable to use this as a framework to organize the retention of the specific passage. This suggests that learning disabled students may be capable of abstracting categories of words from serially presented lists of words, but they may not be able to chunk (i.e., categorize together) these words for use at later retrieval.

Cermak (1983) presented evidence to support this thesis in a study in which learning disabled and nondisabled children were asked to learn a list of 20 common nouns in five trials. The children were told to rehearse the words aloud during each trial. At the conclusion of each trial, they were asked to recall as many of the words as they could. Three types of word lists were used: a random list of unrelated words , a list containing 5 words from each of four categories randomly distributed within the list, and a list containing 5 words from each of four categories with the words presented in category blocks. The learning disabled students recalled fewer words than did non-disabled students following all types of presentation.

Swanson (1983) arrived at a similar conclusion when he found that learning disabled children rarely reported the use of an organizational strategy when they were required to rehearse several items. He reasoned that, because these children were capable of rehearsal, the problem was not a production deficiency in rehearsal, but instead a failure to perform elaborative processing of each word. Elaborative processing was defined as the processing that goes beyond the initial level of analysis to include more sophisticated features of the words and ultimately the comparison of these features with others in the list.

Automaticity

Before leaving our discussion of the multistore model, there is one important construct to consider in relation to the model. In revision of the multistore model (Shiffrin & Schneider, 1977), the term *automaticity* has come into play. It is assumed that if some processes are automatic, fewer demands are placed on short-term memory capacity. Automaticity has been used to describe several sorts of mental operations. Sometimes the term represents preattentive involuntary processing, initiated by stimulus events (e.g., Neisser, 1967), and at other times it represents processes independent of capacity demands (e.g., Hasher & Zacks, 1979; Samuels, 1987). Shiffrin and Schneider (1977), for example, characterized automaticity as involving rapid, involuntary, parallel processing, as opposed to slow, sequential, and controlled processing.

Since this term occurs frequently in the learning disabilities literature (e.g., Samuels, 1987; Spear & Sternberg, 1987), some clarification is necessary. Some studies assume that cognitive processes place space and/or time demands upon a limited capacity system (e.g., short-term memory). Processing that becomes more and more independent of this capacity system, because of practice and experience, is assumed to be automatic. For example, learning to read is initially a laborious activity and proceeds on a letter-by-letter basis, requiring much attention on the part of the child. After considerable practice and experience, reading becomes faster, letters are processed in parallel, and words are activated with little attentional load (Samuels, 1987). This conceptualization, however, is in contrast to other accounts which view automaticity as an unlearned process (e.g., Neisser, 1967). Furthermore, some authors (e.g., Cheng, 1985) have suggested that automatic processing may not represent an activity that becomes capacity free, but rather reflects an efficient restructuring, reordering, and/or reorganizing of tasks.

My point is that only when a theoretical model can demonstrate the various *learnable* and *nonlearnable* characteristics of automaticity will one have an explanatory sense of the academic problems of learning disabled children. Thus, studies that describe the various cognitive activities of learning disabled students as reflecting poor automaticity are further enhanced if their description is embodied in a theoretical framework that accounts for what is learnable and what is not.

Levels of Processing

Craik and Lockhart (1972) suggested that multistore models of information processing are inadequate in explaining the various characteristics of memory stores. For example, they cite literature (Cermak, 1972) suggesting that information in short-term store is both visual and semantic rather than being coded in an auditory–verbal–linguistic manner. They provide a description of various structural features of multistore models (Table 5–4). The Craik and Lockhart model deemphasizes the structures of a memory system and proposes that control processes should be a central focus.

The memory system of Craik and Lockhart focuses on the processing of incoming information. Processing is considered in a series of analyses. For example, a child is presented with several words. The child may remember the words very shallowly or in terms of the visual features, giving rise to a short-lived memory trace; the child may process the words into sound features represented by the printed word, giving a somewhat more stable memory trace; or the child may process the word into semantic terms, giving a much more durable memory trace. A shallow analysis is concerned with perceptual or sensory features of information (e.g., angles, brightness). The child merely matches the input against past learning. A deeper analysis is concerned with stimulus enrichment and elaboration through a semantic analysis. The child may put words into a sentence, free associate other comparable words, or make a story with the word. The focus at this level is on the extraction of meaning.

Another emphasis of this model is the differentiation between two rehearsal processes. One type of rehearsal involves the recycling of items in memory while the depth of encoding remains unchanged. The second type of rehearsal involves the processes that increase the depth of encoding. In these terms, simple repetition of words represents the first type of rehearsal, whereas a word elaboration technique is an example of the second type. Implicit in this assumption is that simple repetitions of items to be remembered serve to maintain information in consciousness, whereas stimulus enrichment and elaborations are required for deeper encoding.

Although the level of processing model is plagued with criticism (Baddeley, 1978), it can be applied in several ways to help in understanding learn-

TABLE 5–4
Multistore Models

Feature	Sensory registers	Short-term memory	Long-term memory
Entry of information	Preattentive; before awareness	Requires attention	Rehearsal
Maintenance of information	Not possible	Continued attention; rehearsal	Repetition; organization
Format of information	Literal copy of input	Auditory-semantic; visual	Semantic; auditory and visual
Capacity information loss	Large decay	Small (7 ± 2) Displacement; possible decay	No known limit; possibly no loss; loss of accessibility
Trace duration	¼ to 2 sec	Up to 30 sec	Minutes to years
Retrieval	Readout	Automatic chunking; conscious awareness	Retrieval cues; search process; executive function

ing disabled children's information processing abilities. First, a focus is placed on the type of control processes used by subjects rather than on structural differences (e.g., short-term memory vs. long-term memory) in information processing. Second, the model implies a continuum (depth) of processing rather than a series of stores (e.g., short-term memory). Third, what a person does with material to be processed is more important than what is recalled. Mere repetition of material enhances recall and recognition, but factors such as the student's imposing meaningfulness give greater coherence and integration of information.

The "Executive" Function

Memory for information is made up of *reconstructions* of events. As stated by Neisser (1967),

> We store traces of earlier cognitive acts, not the product of those acts. The traces are not simply "revived" or "reactivated" in recall; instead, the stored fragments are used as information to support a new construction. It is as if the bone fragments used by the paleontologist did not appear in the model he builds at all—as indeed they need not, if it is to represent a fully fleshed-out, skin-covered dinosaur. The bones can be thought of somewhat loosely, as remnants of the structure which created and supported the original dinosaur, and thus as sources of information about how to reconstruct it. (p. 285)

The information recalled is based on key pieces of information that have been salvaged. Relying on Bartlett's earlier work (1932), Neisser (1967) suggested that we rely only on cues or fragments of information for retrieval, and that the information we retrieve reflects a reconstruction. For example, if a child thought that a letter of the alphabet looked something like a human figure and then tried to remember that item based on encoding, recall may not include an actual representation of the letter.

The reconstruction processes that lead to the retrieval of information are governed by *executive routines*, that is, programs *that determine the order* in which mental activities will be performed. In other words , they are the organization directives for various retrieval strategies. The executive function does not perform the searching task, or organize and sort out material. Instead, it programs the various mental activities. Computers have a built-in executive function; humans have the ability to modify and develop overall routines for information retrieval.

Neisser sums up his model in six points:

1. Information stored in memory does not have a one-to-one relationship to what subjects originally perceived. Information exists as fragments of overt and covert activity.

2. Retrieval of information consists of many programmed searches simultaneously or independently undertaken (parallel search or multiple search).

3. A general search strategy, separate from the executive function, seeks actively to organize and reconstruct retrieval information step by step (sequential analysis). The search strategy lays out all information to be organized and sorted.

4. Control of parallel and sequential processes is directed by the executive routine.

5. Executive function and search processes are learned and based on earlier processing, the implication being that:
   a. We learn to organize and retrieve.
   b. There are individual styles of organization.

6. Failure to recall is failure to perceive, the implication being that:
    a. We are attending to wrong stimuli.
    b. There is a misguided search strategy.

In terms of application, one might focus on the student's executive processing ability. Research of the notion that learning disabilities represent executive function deficits may be summarized as follows: learning disabled students experience difficulty with such self-regulatory mechanisms as checking, planning, monitoring, testing, revising, and evaluating during an attempt to learn or solve problems (e.g., Borkowski, Weyhing, & Carr, 1988; Bos & Filip, 1982; Brown & Palincsar, 1982, 1988; Butkowsky & Willows, 1980; Palincsar & Brown, 1984; Wong, 1978, 1979; Wong & Jones, 1982; Wong, Wong, Perry, & Sawatsky, 1986). They also perform poorly on a variety of tasks that require the use of general control processes or strategies for solution (e.g., Dallago & Moely, 1980; Deshler, Alley, Warner, & Schumaker, 1981; Englert et al., in press; Garner & Reis, 1981). Under some conditions, well-designed strategy training that influences monitoring improves performance (e.g., Borkowski et al., 1988; Duffy, Roehler, Meloth, et al., 1986; Duffy, Roehler, Sivan, et al., 1987; Gelzheiser, 1984; Graham, 1985; Graves, 1986; Hallahan, Lloyd, Kosiewica, Kaufman, & Graves, 1979; Hasselborn & Korkel, 1986; Leon & Pepe, 1983; Malamoth, 1979; Short & Ryan, 1984; Torgesen, Murphy, & Ivey, 1979; Wong, 1982), whereas at other times some general cognitive constraints prevent the effective use of monitoring processes (e.g., Baker, Ceci, & Hermann, 1987; Shankweiler, Liberman, Mark, Fowler, & Fisher, 1979; Swanson, 1984; Wong, Wong, & Foth, 1977; see Cooney & Swanson, 1987, for a review). However, when training of information processing components includes self-evaluation (e.g., predicting outcomes, organizing strategies, using various forms of trial and error), and attributions (attitudes or beliefs) related to effective strategy use are appropriate (Licht, 1983; Licht, Kistner, Ozkarogoz, Shapiro, & Claussen, 1985), and subskills are automatized (see Kolligian & Sternberg, 1987; Pellegrino & Goldman, 1987; Samuels, 1987; however, see Cheng, 1985), training attempts are successful (e.g., Borkowski et al., 1988; Englert et al., in press; Graves, 1986; McLoone, Scruggs, Mastropieri, & Zucker, 1986; Meichenbaum,1982; Palincsar & Brown, 1984; Schumaker, Deshler, Alley, Warner, & Denton, 1982; Scruggs, Mastropieri, & Levin, 1987; Short & Ryan, 1984; Torgesen et al., 1979; Wong & Sawatsky, 1984; Worden & Nakamura, 1983).

Thus, research that focuses primarily on isolated processing deficiencies may not adequately capture the executive or higher order nature of intellectual and academic functioning of students with learning disabilities (cf. Stanovich, 1986). That is, learning disabilities may be the result of a unique coordination of multiple processes that include high order activities (executive functioning), rather than merely a specific type of processing deficiency isolated to a particular academic domain. It is not the intent of the above comment to suggest that deficit models of learning disabilities be abandoned, but rather that they be put into perspective. While the notion of a "specific deficit" is a critical assumption to the field of learning disabilities (Stanovich, 1986; e.g., a localized deficiency can be treated effectively if diagnosed properly), this orientation has generated a number of competing hypotheses. Furthermore, even if a specific deficit is isolated, the problem is pervasive over time in its influence on cognition and the acquisition of knowledge.

Working Memory

Baddeley and Hitch (1974) suggested that the multistore model proposed by Atkinson and Shiffrin (1968) has several limitations. In particular, they suggested that short-term store should be replaced with the concept of working memory. Working memory is viewed as a more *dynamic* and active system because it simultaneously focuses on processing and storage demands, whereas short-term memory focuses primarily on the storage of information and is considered a more passive system.

The prevailing opinion is that short-term memory is a proper subset of processes of which working memory is capable. As stated by Ellis and Hunt (1983), "Working memory shares some of the characteristics of short-term memory . . . [Working memory] describes the active processes involved in retention, rehearsal, chunking. . . ." (p. 78). Short-term memory is partly understood as a component of a limited capacity system from accumulating and holding segments of information (e.g., speech or orthographic units) as they arrive during a listening or reading task. Material in short-term memory is retained if it is rehearsed.

In contrast to the opinion that working memory and short-term memory are interconnected, Brainerd and Kingman (1984) suggested that "short-term memory and working memory do not overlap and develop independently of each other" (p. 210). Evidence suggesting that short-term and working memory may be independent systems comes from correlational studies.

For example, the correlations between working memory tasks and reading are higher than those found between short-term memory tasks and reading. Evidence in support of this assumption suggests that measures of short-term memory, such as digit- or word-span tasks, are weakly correlated with reading (Daneman & Carpenter, 1980; Perfetti & Lesgold, 1977), whereas working memory tasks, such as Daneman and Carpenter's sentence-span task (1980), are highly correlated with reading comprehension.

Unfortunately, a key weakness in understanding the relationship between learning disabilities and achievement (e.g., reading) is the lack of specificity as to which components of working memory are involved (e.g., Baddeley, Logie, Nimmo-Smith, & Brereton, 1985). Thus, it is necessary to specify which components of working memory are most related to fluent, as well as dysfluent, reading performance. The multiple component model proposed by Baddeley and colleagues may shed some light on this issue.

Their working memory system consists of a model control center that selects and operates various processes: the articulatory loop which specializes in rehearsal and verbal storage, and the visual–spatial "scratch pad" which specializes in imagery and spatial memory. The articulatory loop and the visual–spatial scratch pad are *slave* systems that can be used by the central executive for specific purposes. An important assumption of this model is that the slave systems and the central executive occupy separate but interrelated capacity pools. Provided that the storage demands of the slave systems can be met, the central executive uses its capacity for separate activities. When storage demands exceed storage capacity in the slave systems, however, some central executive capacity must be devoted to storage, with the result that fewer resources will be available for alternative activities.

How does working memory formulation help us understand learning disabilities better than the concept of short-term store? First, it suggests that verbal rehearsal plays a *smaller* role in learning and memory. This is an important point because some studies do show that performance deficits of learning disabled children are not related to rehearsal, per se (e.g., see Swanson, 1983). Second, the idea of a working memory system is useful because it is viewed as an active memory system directed by a central executive. Third, the assumption that there are several different processing systems is more realistic than Atkinson and Shiffrin's (1968) notion of a unitary short-term store.

A recent study (Swanson, Cochran, & Ewers, 1989) sought to determine the *extent* to which less skilled readers suffer from working memory deficiencies. A sentence-span task (Daneman & Carpenter, 1980; also see Baddeley et al., 1985) was used to measure the efficiency of storage and processing operations combined. The task required children to recall the last word of several sentences, as well as to answer a comprehension question about a sentence. Materials for the sentence-span task were unrelated declarative sentences, 7 to 10 words in length. The sentences were randomly arranged into sets of two, three, four, or five. The following are three examples of sentences for which the child was to recall the last words:

1. We waited in line for a *ticket.*

2. Sally thinks we should give the bird its *food.*

3. My mother said she would write a *letter.*

To ensure that children comprehended the sentences (i.e., processed their meaning) and did not merely try to remember the target word (i.e., treat the task as one of short-term memory), they were required to answer a question after each group of sentences was presented. Questions were related to a randomly selected (but never the last) sentence in the set. For the above three-sentence set, for example, they were asked, "Where did we wait?" The results of this study suggest that learning disabled readers' working memory deficits were inferior to those of nondisabled readers. Thus, studies that suggest that learning disabled children's memory deficiencies are localized to a short-term store system must be reevaluated within the context of a model that incorporates the operations of working memory.

Knowing, Knowing About Knowing, and Knowing How to Know

Brown (1975) viewed memory development as integrated with cognitive development. Consequently, it is affected by such skills as language, problem solving, and comprehension. Brown proposed that memory can be described as three knowledge systems: (a) knowing—development of a knowledge system, especially semantic memory; (b) knowing about knowing—awareness of knowledge about one memory system (metacognition); and (c) knowing how to know—strategies and skills a child possesses for deliberate memorization.

In her model, Brown distinguished between semantic and episodic memory. Semantic memory refers to storing information about concepts and words (Tulving, 1983); such a memory is embedded within the structure of language. Episodic memory, on the other hand, refers to remembered biographical events ("you visited me") or repetitive experiences or events.

Another distinction in Brown's model is between the concepts of production and mediational deficiencies. *Mediational deficiencies* refer to the fact that children are unable to utilize a strategy efficiently. For example, young children may not spontaneously produce a potential mediator to process task requirements, but even if they did, they would fail to direct their performance. *Production deficiencies* suggest that children can be taught efficient strategies that they fail to produce spontaneously and that these taught strategies will direct and improve their performance.

A third distinction in Brown's model results from the concept that the more strategic information is needed for effective performance, the more likely the task will be affected by growth and change in the child. Therefore, Brown recognized that (a) tasks have semantic or episodic requirements, (b) failure to use a strategy is related to mediation and production deficiencies, and (c) tasks that require strategies are sensitive to developmental changes in the child. Brown's developmental model is represented in Figure 5–3.

Perhaps the most unique focus of Brown's model is the child's metacognitive functioning (to be further discussed in Chapter 10). As might be expected, metacognition, or knowledge and awareness of cognitive operations, changes with age (see Pressley, Johnson, & Symons, 1987, for a review). Metavariables refer to the child's concept of behavior, and the relation of

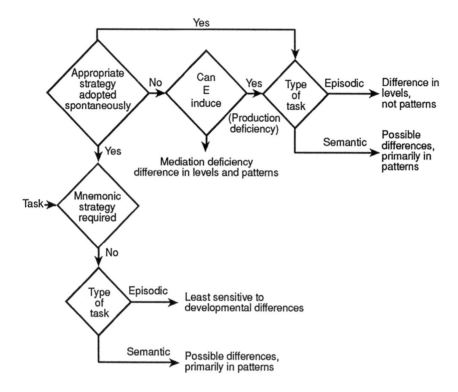

Figure 5-3. Brown's developmental model of information processing. Adapted from "The Development of Memory: Knowing, Knowing About Knowing, and Knowing How to Know" by A. L. Brown in *Advances in Child Development and Behavior* (Vol. 10, p. 139) by H. W. Reese (Ed.), 1975, New York: Academic Press.

these variables to their actual memory performance (sample questions for assessment are proposed in Chapter 10).

As suggested by Brown and others, special attention should be given to knowing, knowing about knowing, and knowing about how to know when assessing the information processing abilities of learning disabled children. Such an assessment should be sensitive enough to (a) differentiate strategic from nonstrategic qualities, (b) differentiate semantic from episodic sequences, and (c) identify tasks most susceptible to developmental changes.

SUMMARY

In summary, perhaps no theoretical base currently adds to our understanding of learning disabilities more than that of information processing. Within this framework, learning disabled students, as well as their nondisabled counterparts, are perceived as learning through various intervening stages of cognition, such as encoding, organizing, storing, retrieving, comparing, and generating (reconstructing) information. These stages also include higher and lower order processes (e.g., mechanisms that regulate and deploy relevant skills versus elementary processing components). Greatly simplified, learning disabled children's task performance is seen as an interaction between *executive routines, control processes, and their knowledge base.* This interaction will be clarified in Chapter 10. Gradually, it has become apparent that the learning disabled student controls much, and in some cases all, of what is learned relatively independently of the teacher.

REFERENCES

Atkinson, R., & Shiffrin, R. (1968). Human memory, a proposed system and its control processes. In K. Spence & J. Spence (Eds.), *The psychology of learning and motivation: Advances in research and theory* (Vol. 2, pp. 85–195). New York: Academic Press.

Baddeley, A. (1978). The trouble with levels: A reexamination of Craik and Lockhart's framework for memory research. *Psychological Review, 85,* 139–152.

Baddeley, A. D. (1981). The concept of working memory: A view of its current state and probable future development. *Cognition, 10,* 17–23.

Baddeley, A. D., & Hitch, G. (1974). Working memory. In G. H. Bower (Ed.), *The psychology of learning and motivation* (Vol. 8, pp. 199–239). New York: Academic Press.

Baddeley, A., Logie, R., Nimmo-Smith, T., & Brereton, N. (1985). Components of fluent reading. *Journal of Memory and Language, 24,* 119–131.

Baker, J. G., Ceci, S. J., & Hermann, N. D. (1987). Semantic structure and processing: Implications for the learning disabled child. In H. L. Swanson (Ed.), *Memory and learning disabilities*

(pp. 83–110). Greenwich, CT: JAI Press.

Barclay, C. R., & Hagen, J. W. (1982). The development of mediated behavior in children: An alternative view of learning disabilities. In J. P. Das, R. F. Mulcahy, & A. E. Wall (Eds.), *Theory and research in learning disabilities* (pp. 61–84). New York: Plenum Press.

Bartlett, F. (1932). *Remembering.* London: Cambridge University Press.

Borkowski, J. G., Weyhing, R. S., & Carr, M. (1988). Effects of attributional retraining on strategy-based reading comprehension in learning-disabled students. *Journal of Educational Psychology, 80,* 46–53.

Bos, C., & Filip, D. (1982). Comprehension monitoring skills in learning disabled and average students. *Topics in Learning and Learning Disabilities, 2,* 79–85.

Brainerd, C. J., & Kingman, J. (1984). On the independence of short-term memory and working memory in cognitive development. *Cognitive Psychology, 17,* 210–247.

Brown, A. (1975). The development of memory: Knowing, knowing about knowing, and knowing how to know.

In H. Reese (Ed.), *Advances in child development and behavior* (Vol. 10). New York: Academic Press.

Brown, A., & Palincsar, A. (1982). Inducing strategic learning from texts by means of informed, self-control training. *Topics in Learning and Learning Disabilities, 2,* 1–18.

Brown, A. L., & Palincsar, A. S. (1988). Reciprocal teaching of comprehension strategies: A natural history of one program for enhancing learning. In J. Borkowski & J. P. Das (Eds.), *Intelligence and cognition in special children: Comparative studies of giftedness, mental retardation, and learning disabilities* (pp. 139–155). New York: Ablex.

Bruner, J., Goodnow, J., & Austin, G. (1956). *A study of thinking.* New York: Wiley.

Butkowsky, I S., & Willows, D. M. (1980). Cognitive-motivational characteristics of children varying in reading ability: Evidence for learned helplessness in poor readers. *Journal of Educational Psychology, 72,* 408–422.

Cermak, L. (1972). *Human memory.* New York: Ronald Press.

Cermak, L. (1983). Information processing deficits in learning disabled children. *Journal of Learning Disabilities, 16,* 599–605.

Cheng, P. W. (1985). Restructuring versus automaticity: Alternative accounts of skill acquisition. *Psychological Review, 92,* 414–423.

Cooney, J. B., & Swanson, H. L. (1987). Memory and learning disabilities: An overview. In H. L. Swanson (Ed.), *Memory and learning disabilities: Advances in learning and behavioral disabilities* (pp. 1–40). Greenwich, CT: JAI Press.

Craik, F., & Lockhart, R. (1972). Level of processing: A framework for memory research. *Journal of Verbal Learning and Verbal Behavior, 11,* 671–684.

Dallago, M. L. P. & Moely, B. E. (1980). Free recall in boys of normal and poor reading levels as a function of task manipulation. *Journal of Experimental Child Psychology, 30,* 62–78.

Daneman, M., & Carpenter, P. A. (1980). Individual differences in working memory and reading. *Journal of Verbal Learning and Verbal Behavior, 19,* 450–466.

Deshler, D. D., Alley, G. R., Warner, M M., & Schumaker, J. B. (1981). Instructional practices for promoting skill acquisition and generalization in severely learning-disabled adolescents. *Learning Disability Quarterly, 4,* 415–421.

Duffy, G. G., Roehler, L. R., Meloth, M., Vavrus, L., Book, C., Putnam, J., & Wesselman, R. (1986). The relationship between explicit verbal explanation during reading skill instruction and student awareness and achievement: A study of reading teacher effects. *Reading Research Quarterly, 21,* 237–252.

Duffy, G. G., Roehler, L. R., Sivan, E., Racliffe, G., Book, C., Meloth, M., Vavrus, L., Wessleman, R., Putnam, J., & Bassiri, D. (1987). The effects of explaining the reasoning associated with using reading strategies. *Reading Research Quarterly, 22,* 347–368.

Ellis, H. C., & Hunt, R. (1983). *Fundamentals of human memory and cognition.* Dubuque, IA: W. C. Brown.

Englert, C. S., Raphael, T. E., Anderson, L. M., Anthony, H., Fear, K., & Gregg, S. (in press). A case for writing instruction: Strategies for writing informational text. *Learning Disabilities Focus.*

Ericsson, K. A., & Simon, H. A. (1984). *Protocol analysis: Verbal reports as data.* Cambridge, CA: MIT Press.

Garner, R., & Reis, R. (1981). Monitoring and resolving comprehension obstacles: An investigation of spontaneous look backs among upper-grade good and poor comprehenders. *Reading Research Quarterly, 16*, 569–582.

Gelzheiser, L. M. (1984). Generalization from categorical memory tasks to prose in learning disabled adolescents. *Journal of Educational Psychology, 76*, 1128–1138.

Gelzheiser, L. M., Solar, R. A., Sheperd, M. J., & Wozniak, R. H. (1983). Teaching learning disabled children to memorize: Rationale for plans and practice. *Journal of Learning Disabilities, 16*, 421–425.

Gholson, B. (1980). *The cognitive-developmental basis of human learning: Studies in hypothesis testing.* New York: Academic Press.

Graham, S. (1985). Effects of direct instruction and metacomprehension on finding main ideas. *Learning Disability Research, 1*, 90–100.

Graves, A. (1986). Effects of direct instruction and metacomprehension on finding main ideas. *Learning Disability Research, 2*, 78–83.

Hagen, J. W., Barclay, C. R., & Newman, R. S. (1982). Metacognition, self-knowledge, and learning disabilities: Some thoughts on knowing and doing. *Topics in Learning and Learning Disabilities, 2*, 19–26.

Hallahan, D. P., Lloyd, J., Kosiewica, M., Kaufman, J., & Graves, J. (1979). A self monitoring of attention as a treatment for learning disabled boys' off task behavior. *Learning Disability Quarterly, 2*, 24–32.

Hasher, L., & Zacks, R. T. (1979). *Decision-making during the planning process.* Santa Monica, CA: Rand Corp.

Hasselborn, M., & Korkel, J. (1986). Metacognitive versus traditional reading instructions: The mediating role of domain-specific knowledge on children's text processing. *Human Learning, 5*, 75–90.

Hayes, J. R. (1981). *The complete problem solver.* Philadelphia: Franklin Institute Press.

Hunt, E. (1974). Quote the raven? Nevermore! In. L. E. Gregg (Ed.), *Knowledge and cognition.* Potomac, MD: Erlbaum.

Kolligian, J., & Sternberg, R. J. (1987). Intelligence, information processing, and specific learning disabilities: A triarchic synthesis. *Journal of Learning Disabilities, 20*, 8–17.

Leon, J. A., & Pepe, H. J. (1983). Self-instruction training: Cognitive behavioral modifications for remediating arithmetic deficits. *Exceptional Children, 50*, 54–60.

Licht, B. G. (1983). Cognitive–motivational factors that contribute to the achievement of learning disabled children. *Journal of Learning Disabilities, 16*, 483–490.

Licht, B. G., Kistner, J. A., Ozkarogoz, T., Shapiro, S., & Claussen, L. (1985). Causal attributions of learning disabled children: Individual differences and their implications for persistence. *Journal of Educational Psychology, 77*, 208–216.

Malamoth, Z. N. (1979). Self-management training for children with reading problems. Effects on reading performance and sustained attention. *Cognition Therapy and Research, 3*, 279–290.

McLoone, B. B., Scruggs, T. E., Mastropieri, M. A., & Zucker, S. F. (1986). Memory strategy instruction and training with learning-disabled adolescents. *Learning Disability Research, 2*, 45–53.

Meichenbaum, D. (1982). *Teaching thinking: A cognitive behavioral approach.* Austin, TX: Society for Learning Disabilities and Remedial Education.

Neisser, U. (1967). *Cognitive psychology.* New York: Appleton-Century-Crofts.

Neisser, U. (1976). *Cognition and reality.* San Francisco: Freeman.

Neisser, U. (1981). John Dean's memory: A case study. *Cognition, 9*, 1–22.

Newell, A. (1980). Reasoning, problem solving and decision processes: The problem space as a fundamental category. In R. Nickerson (Ed.), *Attention and performance VIII*. Hillsdale, NJ: Erlbaum.

Newell, A., Shaw, F., & Simon, H. (1958). Elements of a theory of human problem solving. *Psychological Review, 65*, 151–166.

Newell, A., & Simon, H. (1972). *Human problem solving*. Englewood Cliffs, NJ: Prentice-Hall.

Palincsar, A. S., & Brown, A. L. (1984). Reciprocal teaching of comprehension-fostering and comprehension monitoring activities. *Cognition and Instruction, 1*, 117–175.

Pellegrino, J., & Goldman, S. (1987). Information processing and math. *Journal of Learning Disabilities, 20*, 23–34.

Perfetti, C. A., & Lesgold, A. N. (1977). Discourse comprehension and sources of individual differences. In M. A. Just & P. A. Carpenter (Eds.), *Cognitive processes in comprehension* (pp. 141–183). Hillsdale, NJ: Erlbaum.

Pressley, M., Johnson, C. J., & Symons, S. (1987). Elaborating to learn and learning to elaborate. *Journal of Learning Disabilities, 20*, 76–91.

Pressley, M., & Levin, J. R. (1987). Elaborative learning strategies for the inefficient learner. In S. J. Ceci (Ed.), *Handbook of cognitive, social and neuropsychological aspects of learning disabilities* (pp. 175–212). Hillsdale, NJ: Erlbaum.

Samuels, S. J. (1987). Information processing and reading. *Journal of Learning Disabilities, 20*, 18–22.

Schumaker, J. B., Deshler, D. D., Alley, G. R., Warner, M. M., & Denton, P. H. (1982). Multipass: A learning strategy for improving reading comprehension. *Learning Disability Quarterly, 5*, 295–304.

Scruggs, T. E., Mastropieri, M. A., & Levin, J. R. (1987). Transformational mnemonic strategies for learning disabled students. In H. L. Swanson (Ed.), *Memory and learning disabilities: Advances in learning and behavioral disabilities* (pp. 225–244). Greenwich, CT: JAI Press.

Shankweiler, D., Liberman, I. Y., Mark, S. L., Fowler, L. A., & Fisher, F. W. (1979). The speech code and learning to read. *Journal of Experimental Psychology: Human Learning and Memory, 5*, 531–545.

Shiffrin, R. M., & Schneider, W. (1977). Controlled and automatic human information processing: II. Perceptual learning, automatic attending, and a general theory. *Psychological Review, 84*, 127–190.

Short, E. J., & Ryan, E. B. (1984). Metacognitive differences between skilled and less skilled readers: Remediating deficits through story grammar and attribution training. *Journal of Educational Psychology, 76*, 225–235.

Spear, L. C., & Sternberg, R. J. (1987). An information-processing framework for understanding reading disability. In S. Ceci (Ed.), *Handbook of cognitive, social and neuropsychological aspects of learning disabilities* (pp. 3–32). Hillsdale, NJ: Erlbaum.

Stanovich, K. (1986). Matthew effects in reading. Some consequences of individual differences in the acquisition of literacy. *Reading Research Quarterly, 21*, 360–387.

Swanson, H. L. (1981). Encoding of logical connective rules in learning disabled children. *Journal of Abnormal Child Psychology, 9*, 507–516.

Swanson, H. L. (1982). Conceptual processes as a function of age and enforced attention in learning disabled children:

Evidence for deficient rule learning. *Contemporary Educational Psychology, 7*, 152–160.

Swanson, H. L. (1983). Relations among metamemory, rehearsal activity and word recall in learning disabled and nondisabled readers. *British Journal of Educational Psychology, 53*, 186–194.

Swanson, H. L. (1984). Semantic and visual memory codes in learning disabled readers. *Journal of Experimental Child Psychology, 37*, 124–140.

Swanson, H. L. (1988). Learning disabled children's problem solving: Identifying mental processes underlying intelligent performance. *Intelligence, 12*, 261–278.

Swanson, H. L. Cochran, K., & Ewers, C. (1989). Working memory and reading disabilities. *Journal of Abnormal Child Psychology, 17*, 745–756.

Torgesen, J. (1982). The learning disabled child as an inactive learner: Educational implications. *Topics in Learning and Learning Disabilities, 2*, 45–53.

Torgesen, J. K., Murphy, H. A., & Ivey, C. (1979). The effects of an orienting task on the memory performance of reading disabled children. *Journal of Learning Disabilities, 12*, 396–401.

Tulving, E. (1983). *Elements of episodic memory.* New York: Oxford.

Wong, B. Y. L. (1978). The effects of directive cues on the organization of memory and recall in good and poor readers. *Journal of Educational Research, 72*, 179–223.

Wong, B. Y. L. (1979). Increasing retention of main ideas through questioning strategies. *Learning Disability Quarterly, 2*, 42–47.

Wong, B. Y. L. (1982). Strategic behaviors in selecting retrieval cues in gifted, normal achieving and learning disabled children. *Journal of Learning Disabilities, 15*, 33–37.

Wong, B. Y. L., & Jones, W. (1982). Increasing metacomprehension in learning-disabled and normally-achieving students through self-questioning training. *Learning Disability Quarterly, 5*, 228–240.

Wong, B. Y. L., & Sawatsky, D. (1984). Sentence elaboration and retention of good, average and poor readers. *Learning Disability Quarterly, 6*, 229–236.

Wong, B. Y. L., Wong, R., & Foth, D. (1977). Recall and clustering of verbal materials among normal and poor readers. *Bulletin of the Psychonomic Society, 10*, 375–378.

Wong, B. Y. L., Wong, R., Perry, N., & Sawatsky, D. (1986). The efficacy of a self-questioning summarization strategy for use by underachievers and learning-disabled adolescents. *Learning Disability Focus, 2*, 20–35.

Worden, P. E., & Nakamura, G. V. (1983). Story comprehension and recall in learning-disabled vs. normal college students. *Journal of Educational Psychology, 74*, 633–641.

6

Learning Disabilities and Memory

H. LEE SWANSON

The purpose of this chapter is to provide an overview of the research in memory, a critical area known to be deficient in learning disabled individuals. Memory is probably one of the most important areas of focus in learning disabilities because it reflects applied cognition; that is, memory functioning reflects all aspects of learning. Memory is also important because many intervention programs that attempt to enhance the overall cognition of learning disabled persons rely on principles related to memory research. This chapter provides an overview of research that characterizes the learning disabled student's memory function and ends with instructional principles derived primarily from memory research.

WHAT IS THE HISTORICAL PERSPECTIVE?

Prior to 1976, few studies investigated learning disabled students' memory processes; however, a survey of learning disabilities journals between 1976 and 1979 revealed that 18% of the reports were concerned with memory processes (Torgesen & Dice, 1980). A majority of the research published prior to 1976 was concerned with perceptual–motor behavior of brain-injured and/or reading disabled children, and little if any experimental research dealt directly with memory difficulties (Hallahan & Cruickshank, 1973). Prior to 1970, most studies merely stated that learning disabled children perform poorly on certain tasks (e.g., digit span). Few, if any, attempts were made to isolate the nature of learning disabled students' memory deficits. Most studies focused on children with reading difficulties. For example, one early experimental study (Rizzo, 1939) compared retarded and nonretarded readers on three different short-term memory tasks. In one task, children were presented letter strings simultaneously; in another, letters were presented visually but in succession; and in a third, letters were presented auditorially but in a sequential fashion. In all three tasks, retarded readers were inferior to normal readers. Unfortunately, Rizzo did not adequately discuss the mental processing mechanisms that might account for retarded readers' poor memory performance.

Another characteristic of the early research concerned with the memory processes of learning disabled children was that constructs such as perception, attention, memory, and cognition were conceptualized as independent of one another. Several founders of the field argued, for example, that word perception must be adequately developed and/or remediated before subsequent learning or memory can take place (e.g., Strauss & Kephart, 1955). Thus, the reciprocal interaction among various processes was not taken into consideration.

Some contributors to our understanding of learning disabilities and memory are listed in Table 6–1. The earliest link between learning disabilities and memory was established in the early literature on reading disabilities by Kussmaul. In 1877, Kussmaul called attention to a disorder he called word blindness, which was characterized as an inability to read, although vision, intellect, and speech were normal. Following Kussmaul's contribution, several cases of reading difficulties acquired by adults due to cerebral lesions, mostly involving the angular gyri of the left hemisphere, were reported (see Hinshelwood, 1917, for a review). In one important case study, published by Morgan (1896), a 14-year-old boy of normal intelligence had difficulty recalling letters of the alphabet. He also had difficulty recalling written words, which seemed to convey "no impression to this mind." Interestingly, the child appeared to have good memory for oral information. This case study was important because word blindness did not appear to occur as a result of a cerebral lesion. After Morgan's description of this condition, designated as a specific reading disability, research was expanded to include children of normal intelligence who exhibited difficulties in reading. Hinshelwood's (1917) classic monograph presents a number of case studies describing reading disabilities in children of normal intelligence. On the basis of these observations, Hinshelwood inferred that reading problems of these children were related to a "pathological condition of the visual memory center" (p. 21).

TABLE 6–1
Earlier Views on Memory in the Learning Disabled

Person	Source of Deficit	Manifestation
Kussmaul	Cerebral lesion	Word blindness
Hinshelwood	Structural damage to brain that supports visual memory	Problems in visual memory
Orton	Delayed lateral cerebral dominance for language	Strephosymbolia; Problems in visual and auditory memory
Strauss and Kephart	Perception	Poor retention of visual designs

At the same time Hinshelwood's monograph appeared, a little known text by Bronner (1917) reviewed case studies linking mental processing difficulties to children of normal intelligence. For example, consider Case 21:

> Henry J., 16 years old, was seen after he had been in court on several occasions. The mental examination showed that the boy was quite intelligent and in general capable, but had a very specialized defect. The striking feature of all the test work with this boy was the finding that he was far below his age in the matter of rote memory. When a series of numerals was presented to him auditorially he could remember no more than four. His memory span for numerals presented visually was not much better . . . he succeeded here with five. Memory span for syllables was likewise poor . . . On the other hand when ideas were to be recalled, that is, where memory dealt with logical material, the results were good. (p. 120)

A majority of case studies reviewed in the text suggested that disabled children's immediate (short-term) memory was deficient and that remote (long-term) memory was somewhat intact. Bronner also noted that little about memory and its application to complex learning activities was known. (This point is also made in current reviews; see, e.g., Cooney & Swanson, 1987.) For example, the author stated,

> Very many practically important laws of memory have not yet been determined; those most firmly established concern themselves mainly with nonsense or other

type of material quite unlike the activities of everyday life. In a common sense way we are aware that both immediate and remote memory are essential, that we need to remember what we see and hear . . . that to remember an idea is probably more useful in general, than to have a good memory for rote material, but a defect for the latter may be of great significance in some kinds of school work. (p. 110)

Researchers from the 1900s to the 1940s generally viewed reading difficulties as being associated with structural damage to portions of the brain that support visual memory (e.g., see Geschwind, 1962, for a review; also see Monroe, 1932). A contrasting position was provided by Orton (1925, 1937), who suggested that reading disorders were reflective of a neurological–maturational lag resulting from a delayed lateral cerebral dominance for language. Orton described the phenomenon of a selective loss or diminished capacity to remember words as strephosymbolia (twisted symbols). Orton (1937) noted that although

these children show many more errors of a wide variety of kinds it is clear that their difficulty is not in hearing and not in speech mechanism . . . but in recalling words previously heard again or used in speech, and that one of the outstanding obstacles to such recall is remembering all of the sounds in their proper order. (p. 147)

In cases of visual memory, Orton stated that such children with reading disabilities have major difficulties in "recalling the printed word in terms of its spatial sequence of proper order in space" (p. 148). Thus, for Orton, reading disabled children's memory difficulties were seen as reflecting spatial sequences in visual memory or temporal sequences in auditory memory. Although the conceptual foundation of much of Orton's research has been challenged (see Vellutino, 1979), much of the evidence for linking learning disabilities and memory processes has been established from the earlier clinical studies of Morgan, Hinshelwood, and Orton. To date, reading difficulties are viewed primarily as related to language skills (e.g., Vellutino & Scanlon, 1985), and memory difficulties are popularly conceptualized in terms of language processes (see Baddeley, 1984; Jorm, 1983).

Unfortunately for the field of learning disabilities, theories accounting for reading difficulties were not as influential in shaping the historical understanding of cognitive processes in learning disabled children as was the work of Strauss and Werner and their colleagues (Strauss & Kephart, 1955; Strauss & Lehtinen, 1947; Werner, 1948). Many recent commentaries have questioned the earlier paradigms and conclusions of Strauss and Werner (see Kavale & Forness, 1985a, 1985b, for reviews). Their work with exogenous brain-injured mentally retarded children has been a foundation for many of the concepts in the field to date (see Hallahan & Cruickshank, 1973). Strauss and Werner viewed learning disabilities as a process disturbance that occurred most notably in the areas of perceptual–motor functioning. Such processing disturbances were assumed to be caused by neurological dysfunctions, which in turn were assumed to produce discrepancies in academic performance (high and low achievement scatters).

Unfortunately, the relationship between memory and learning disabilities was somewhat obscured by the work of Strauss and Werner. In their classic test, the *Psychopathology and Education of the Brain-Injured Child*, Strauss and Lehtinen (1947) suggested that memory skills of brain-injured children were intact or at least normal. For example, in a case report of a brain-injured female child, they noted that her most outstanding capacity was her excellent auditory memory, which they reported as consistently good with respect to digits, sentences, and meaningful material. Also, her vocabulary development was adequate for abstract words, and word naming was fluent. Based on several case studies, the authors further stated that "the characteristic excellent verbal memory and tendency to automatization has a profound significance for the teaching methods of brain injured children" (p. 142). The authors suggested that educational remediation should not focus on automatization (i.e., repeated practice), but rather on "insight and analysis." No doubt, such conclusions reflected the authors' theoretical orientation (Gestalt psychology).

Strauss and Kephart (1955), in a revision of Strauss and Lehtinen's (1947) earlier text, provided little empirical research (although emerging clinical support) that related memory processes to learning disabled children's functioning. Some case histories (e.g., those on p. 229) began to report an adequate memory for remote information (long-term memory), but not of immediate information (short-term memory). In addition, a chapter by Goldberg (pp. 144–164) in Strauss and Kephart's text suggested that brain-injured children of normal intelligence have poor retention for visual designs. More recent research has not supported the notion that learning disabled children have difficulties remembering designs (e.g., see Vellutino & Scanlon, 1985, for a review) or that recall deficiencies are related to problems in perceptual processes (e.g., Vellutino, 1979).

It was not until the late 1960s and early 1970s that systematic studies appeared comparing learning disabled and nondisabled children's performance on memory tasks. These studies focused on modality-specific memory processes (i.e., auditory or visual memory) and cross-modality instructional conditions, but they provided conflicting evidence. For example, two studies on auditory memory were found that focused on children labeled learning disabled. (Several other studies were available on brain-damaged, mentally retarded, or aphasic children.) Conners, Kramer, and Guerra (1969) compared learning disabled and normally achieving children on their abilities to remember numbers presented to them on a dichotic listening task. The results of their study were that learning disabled children did not differ from

their nondisabled peers in short-term recall. In contrast, Bryan (1972) compared learning disabled and normally achieving children on a task that
required subjects to recall a list of words presented by tape recorder and
words presented by slide projector. Learning disabled and comparison samples performed better with the visual than with the auditory stimuli, but learning disabled children performed more poorly than the nondisabled children
under both conditions.

Conflicting results were also found among studies investigating visual
memory information processing abilities of reading disabled children. Goyen
and Lyle (1971, 1973) investigated young reading disabled student's (children under 8.5 years) recall of critical details of visual stimuli presented
tachistoscopically for various exposure duration intervals. Their results showed
that the reading disabled students did not recall as well as younger and older
normal readers. In another study, Guthrie and Goldberg (1972) compared
disabled and skilled readers on several tests designed to measure visual short-
term memory. In contrast to Goyen and Lyle, they found that childrens' scores
on memory subtests from the Illinois Test of Psycholinguistic Abilities did
not clearly differentiate the ability groups. In view of the conflicting results,
it was not possible to develop any definitive conclusions regarding the visual
memory processes of learning disabled children.

Cross-modality research with learning disabled students also began to
appear during this time period. For example, Senf and Feshbach (1970) found
differences between good and poor readers' memory on cross-modality
presentation conditions. Samples included culturally deprived, learning disabled, and normal control readers of elementary and junior high school age.
Subjects were compared on their recall of digits presented auditorially,
visually, and audiovisually. The learning disabled sample exhibited poor recall
of stimuli organized into audiovisual pairs, which was attributed to problems
of cross-modality matching. Older culturally deprived and normal children
recalled the digits in paired order more accurately than their younger counterparts, whereas older learning disabled children recalled no better than
the younger learning disabled. The learning disabled sample also exhibited
a higher prevalence of visual encoding errors. The implication of this research
was that some prerequisite skills of pairing stimuli had not developed in the
learning disabled children, and the possession of these skills was essential
for reading. In contrast to this study, Denckla and Rudel (1974) found that
learning disabled children's poor recall was not related to encoding errors,
but rather to temporal sequencing. Their results suggested that subjects who
had difficulties in temporal sequencing would have difficulty recalling information from spatial tasks or tasks that required matching of serial and spatial
stimuli (as in the Senf & Feshbach, 1970, study). To date, research on cross-
modality matching is equivocal (e.g., see Koppitz, 1971; then see Torgesen,
Bowen, & Ivey, 1978).

To summarize, the studies in the late 1960s and early 1970s, although contradictory, did establish a foundation for the study of learning disabilities in the context of memory. We now turn to a discussion of the more recent conceptualizations related to learning disabled children's memory.

Parallels to Memory Development

Researchers agree that what we know about learning disabled children's memory is somewhat paralleled by what we know about the differences between older and younger children's memory (e.g., Cooney & Swanson, 1987). That is, in most cases, memory performance of learning disabled children has been likened to that of younger children. The parallels between learning disabled versus nondisabled memory research and younger versus older student memory research are apparent in that performance differences (a) appear in effortful memory tasks, but not for tasks requiring automatic processing; (b) emerge on tasks that require the use of cognitive strategies (e.g., rehearsal and organization); (c) are influenced by the individual's knowledge base; and (d) are influenced by the individual's awareness of his or her own memory processes (metacognition). We briefly review each of these parallels.

A large body of research suggests that remembering becomes easier with age because mental operations become more automatic through repeated use (e.g., Dempster, 1985; Hasher & Zacks, 1979). Research in memory suggests, however, that a distinction can be made between the development of memory processes that are dependent upon overt conscious "effort" and those that are not (e.g., Ceci, 1982; Hasher & Zacks, 1979). Memory that results only after some conscious intent to remember is said to be effortful; that which occurs without intent or effort is considered to be automatic (e.g., Hasher & Zacks, 1979). Effortful memory is assumed to be dependent upon the development of an available store of "cognitive resources." Thus, differences in memory performance between ability groups (learning disabled vs. nondisabled) and children of various ages are presumed to be dependent upon effortful memory due to individual differences in the amount of cognitive resources available (e.g., Howe, Brainerd, & Kingman, 1985; Swanson, 1984a, 1986a). In contrast, automatic memory is assumed to be comparable between ability groups (e.g., Ceci, 1982, 1984). The empirical evidence for this effortful–automatic distinction is emerging with respect to the presence or absence of individual differences across ages in measures of memory functioning (e.g., Dempster, 1985; Spear & Sternberg, 1987; Worden, 1986).

To date, the research on learning disabled children's memory directly parallels memory development in the area of effortful processing. For example, it has been shown that normally achieving children below the age of 9 years and learning disabled children perform quite poorly relative to older children or age-related counterparts, respectively, on tasks such as free recall (e.g., Guttentag, 1984). Older children and nondisabled age-related counterparts have been found to utilize deliberate mnemonic strategies to remember information (e.g., see Cohen, 1978, 1981; Dawson, Hallahan, Reeves, & Ball, 1980; Hallahan, Gajar, Cohen, & Tarver, 1978; Koorland & Wolking, 1982; Swanson, 1978; Swanson & Rathgeber, 1986; Tarver, Hallahan, Kauffman, & Ball, 1976; Torgesen, 1978; Wong, 1978, for a review).

An excellent example of research on mnemonic strategies is provided in a series of studies conducted by Bauer (1977) involving the primacy effect in free recall. Learning disabled and nondisabled children were required to free-recall as many words as possible from lists of monosyllabic nouns. Recall for each serial position showed that learning disabled children were deficient in the recall of items early in the list (primacy). Primacy performance has traditionally been associated with rehearsal (Ornstein & Naus, 1978), as well as elaborative encoding (e.g., Bauer & Embert, 1984). In contrast to research on primacy performance, studies that examined the recency effect have found that learning disabled are not unlike nondisabled youngsters, and that younger and older children are comparable in performance (e.g., Bauer, 1977; Swanson, 1977a; Tarver et al., 1976). It is assumed that recall of the most recently presented items represents the encoding of information in an automatic fashion (i.e., without the benefit of using deliberate mnemonic strategies; Swanson, 1983a, 1983b, 1983c). Thus, the trend found with free-recall tasks suggests that ability-group and age-related differences tend to be limited to items that occur at the beginning and middle serial positions and thus reflect strategy deficits, such as rehearsal (Swanson, 1983a).

In addition to the ability-group and age-related differences in the use of rehearsal, differences in the use of organizational strategies have been investigated. Ability-group and age-related differences (e.g., see Ornstein & Corsale, 1979; Torgesen, 1978; Worden, 1986, for a review) have suggested that learning disabled and younger children are less likely to organize or take advantage of the organizational structure of items (Swanson, 1986b, 1986c, 1987a; Swanson & Rathgeber, 1986). Intervention strategies (i.e., directing children to sort or cluster items prior to recall) have in many cases lessened or eliminated ability-group differences (e.g., Dallago & Moely, 1980; Torgesen, Murphy, & Ivey, 1979; Wong, Wong, & Foth, 1977). Although learning disabled and younger children tend to make less use of semantic relationships inherent in the free-recall material, when organizational instructions are provided, both learning disabled and younger children are capable of using a semantic organization strategy with some degree of effectiveness (e.g., Dallago & Moely, 1980).

Another important parallel between learning disabilities research and age-related memory development comes from studies that focus on children's knowledge about the world (e.g., Bjorklund, 1985; Chi, 1981; Swanson,

1986b). For example, familiarity with words, objects, and events permits subjects to integrate new information with what they already know (e.g., see Bjorklund, 1985, for a review). One way in which a knowledge base may affect memory performance is through its influence on the efficiency of mental operations performed upon the to-be-memorized items. Several authors (e.g., Chi, 1981; Ornstein & Naus, 1978) have suggested that, in some situations, an individual's knowledge base may mediate strategy use; that is, organizational and rehearsal strategies may be executed more spontaneously and efficiently contingent upon an individual's knowledge base. Indirect support for this view was provided by Torgesen and Houck (1980). Learning disabled students with severe short-term memory problems, learning disabled youngsters with normal short-term memory, and normal children were compared for their recall of material scaled for familiarity. Their results indicate that children who learn normally and learning disabled children who have no short-term memory problems gained an advantage in recall as their familiarity with the items increased; that is, recall differences were reduced with less familiar material. This finding suggests that an individual's knowledge base (i.e., an individual's familiarity with material) influences the development or utilization of memory processes.

Another important link between learning disabilities memory research and age-related research is the focus on children's thinking about cognitive strategies and executive functions. Brown (1975) summarized this development as "knowing how to know" and "knowing about knowing." Developmental improvement in remembering and the advantage accrued by nondisabled children is associated with the use of rehearsal, organization, and elaboration strategies to facilitate encoding and retrieval. Recent research (e.g., see Forrest-Pressley & Gillies, 1983; Pressley, Borkowski, & O'Sullivan, 1984; Swanson, 1987c) has focused on how and to what degree the effective use of effortful processes (e.g., cognitive strategies) relates to metacognition. Metacognition refers to knowledge of general cognitive strategies (e.g., rehearsal); awareness of one's own cognitive processes; the monitoring, evaluating, and regulating of those processes; and beliefs about factors that affect cognitive activities (see, e.g., Brown & Campione, 1981; Flavell, 1979). Differences in metacognition have been proposed as one source of individual differences in intelligence (e.g., Borkowski & Cavanaugh, 1981). Comparisons of various groups of children (e.g., normal, mentally retarded, disabled) have revealed substantial differences in metacognitive knowledge, at least about memory and the memorial processes (see Campione, Brown, & Ferrara, 1982, for a review). At present, what we know from the literature is that children between 4 and 12 years of age become progressively more aware of the person, task, and strategy variables that influence remembering (e.g., Pressley et al., 1984). For example, Wong (1982) compared learning disabled, normally achieving, and gifted children in their recall of prose. Her results indicated that when compared with the normal and gifted children, learning disabled children lacked self-checking skills and were less exhaustive in their selective search of retrieval cues. These results suggest that learning disabled children were less aware of efficient strategies related to prose recall.

Categorizing Learning Disabilities Memory Research

Learning disabilities memory research may be categorized in terms of the orientation of existing research programs. As shown in Figure 6–1, three categorizations are apparent. First, many of the studies of learning disabled persons' memory processes are descriptive in that they report how learning disabled students of various ages compare with nondisabled students in their ability to remember a stimulus array. The ages vary from elementary school children to adults (e.g., Gelzheiser, 1984; Golden, McCutcheon, Delay, & Issac, 1982; Worden, Malmgren, & Gabourie, 1982; Worden & Nakamura, 1983); tasks may require recognition, recall, or reconstruction (i.e., story recall) of information; and the stimuli might include words, digits, visual patterns, or prose. A sample study of ability-group comparison is provided by Swanson (1977b). Ten-year-old learning disabled and mentally retarded children were compared on a probe-memory task for their recall of pictorial or three-dimensional representations (concrete objects). The results of the study indicated that both groups were better able to recall concrete than pictorial material, although ability-group differences in favor of the learning disabled children were found only on the concrete representations. Similar recall strategies occurred for both ability groups (e.g., primacy effects) in both conditions, suggesting that similar information processing algorithms were used.

A second group of studies in the learning disabilities field focuses on memory instruction. The emphasis in these studies is on teaching learning disabled children under various conditions or with different types of memory devices how to remember presented material (e.g., Gelzheiser, 1984). These studies have generally shown that learning disabled children can be taught through instructions (e.g., Gelzheiser, 1984), modeling (e.g., Dawson et al., 1980), and reinforcement (e.g., Torgesen & Houck, 1980) to use some simple strategies that they do not produce spontaneously (e.g., Dallago & Moely, 1980). In a sample study, Mastropieri, Scruggs, Levin, Gaffney, and McLoone (1985) conducted two experiments in which learning disabled adolescents recalled the definitions of 14 vocabulary words according to either a pictorial mnemonic strategy (the "keyword" method) or a traditional instructional approach. The keyword method involved constructing an interactive visual image of the to-be-associated items. For example, to remember that the English word *carlin* means old woman via the keyword method, the learner is directed to the fact that the first part of *carlin* sounds like the familiar word *car*. Then the learner constructs an interactive image that relates a car and an old woman, such as an elderly woman driving an old car. The results of

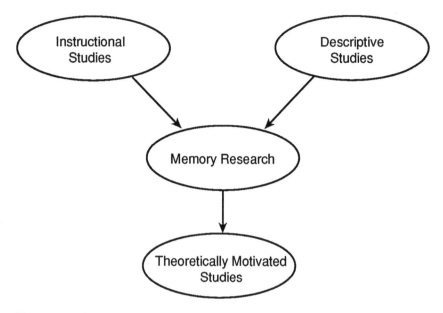

Figure 6–1.   Categories of memory research on learning disabilities.

the first experiment (experimenter-generated mnemonic illustrations) and the second experiment (student-generated mnemonic images) indicated that the keyword strategy was substantially more effective than the traditional approach.

A third group of studies could be regarded as theoretical pieces in which a focus is placed upon individual differences and methodological issues in the study of memory (e.g., Ceci, Ringstrom, & Lea, 1980; Shankweiler, Liberman, Mark, Fowler, & Fischer, 1979). The purpose of this work is to relate various dimensions of memory to specific performance deficits. These studies have been relatively rare compared with the preponderance of descriptive and instructional studies. As a consequence, much of what we know about learning disabilities is derived from description at a clinical or instructional level rather than a comprehensive theoretical framework.

WHAT ARE THE APPLICATIONS OF MEMORY RESEARCH TO PRACTICE?

Strategy Deficit Model

Currently, a number of memory researchers in the field of learning disabilities have converged on the notion that learning disabled students' ability to access knowledge remains inert, unless they are explicitly prompted to use certain cognitive strategies (e.g., see Swanson, 1988b, for a review). For example, learning disabled students may be taught to (a) organize lists of pictures and words into common categories, (b) rehearse the category names during learning, and (c) use the names and retrieval cues at the time of the test (e.g., see Cooney & Swanson, 1987, for a review). The data suggest that when learning disabled children are explicitly encouraged to use such strategies on some tasks, their performance improves, and thus the discrepancy between general intellectual ability and contextually related deficits is lessened.

Based on these findings, the disabled learner has been viewed as having poor strategies for approaching the complex requirements of academic tasks, and so is unable to meet his or her academic potential. Thus, the learning disabled student is described as an inefficient learner, one who either lacks certain strategies or chooses inappropriate strategies and/or generally fails to engage in self-monitoring behavior. Critical to the strategy deficit model is the concept of *access*, the notion that the information necessary for task performance resides within the child. Some children are able to access this information flexibly; that is, a particular behavior is not delimited to a constrained set of circumstances (Campione, Brown, Ferrara, Jones, & Sternberg, 1985). In addition, some children are "aware" of these processes and are able to consciously describe and discuss their own cognitive activities that allow them to access information.

Advantages to Conceptualizing Learning Disabilities in Terms of Strategy Deficiencies

There are five advantages to conceptualizing learning disabilities in terms of strategy deficiencies:

1. *The focus is placed on what is modifiable.* Differences between ability groups are conceptualized in terms of cognitive processes that are susceptible to instruction, rather than fundamental or general differences in ability. Thus, rather than focusing on isolated elementary memory processing deficiencies, the types of questions that are addressed by strategy research are more educationally relevant. For example, a focus is placed on what learning disabled students can do without strategy instruction, what they can do with strategy instruction, what can be done to modify existing strategy instruction, and what can be done to modify existing classroom materials to improve instruction.

2. *It allows for conscious and active rule creation and rule following.* Cognition involves planful activities, and a focus on strategies allows one to search for underlying "plans" that influence behavior. Also, a strategy approach

allows for a counterperspective of learning disabled students' instructional needs when contrasted with simplistic stimulus response, direct instruction, and/or rote drill and practice approaches to instruction.

3. *It incorporates the notion that environmental factors might be seen to operate differentially on the students' declarative and procedural knowledge.* That is, certain strategies might be seen to operate differentially on students with different declarative and procedural knowledge. There is a small but significant body of research suggesting that when explicit information processing models are used to study task performance, it is possible to demonstrate aptitude by strategy interactions. Thus, the efficacy of a strategy for learning depends upon a person's pattern of cognitive abilities (e.g., Chi, 1981).

4. *It allows for the child to be actively involved in the instruction.* Students can participate in the analysis of which cognitive strategies work best for them.

5. *It allows for theorizing and instructional development.* For example, materials can be developed that maximize strategy use.

As discussed in Chapter 5 (also see Chapter 8), effective strategy instruction must entail information (a) about a number of strategies, (b) about how to control and implement those procedures, and (c) about how to gain recognition of the importance of effort and personal causality in producing successful performance. Furthermore, any of these components taught in isolation is likely to have rather diminished value in the classroom context. The following section describes eight major principles that must be considered if strategy instruction is to be successful.

Principles of Strategy Instruction

Strategies serve different purposes. One analysis of the cognitive strategy research suggests that no single best strategy works for learning disabled students within or across particular domains (Swanson, 1989). As can be seen in a number of studies, research is in pursuit of the best strategy to teach learning disabled students (see Cooney & Swanson, 1987, for a review). A number of studies, for example, have looked at enhancing learning disabled children's performance through the use of advanced organizers, skimming, asking, questioning, taking notes, summarizing, and so on. Although learning disabled students have been exposed to various types of strategies, it is not known which strategies are the most effective. In some situations, such as remembering facts, the keyword approach appears to be more effective than direct instruction models, but of course the rank ordering of different strategies changes in reference to the different types of learning outcomes expected. For example, certain strategies are better suited to enhancing students' understanding of what they previously read, whereas other strategies are better suited to enhancing students' memory of words or facts. The point is that different strategies can affect different cognitive outcomes in a number of ways.

Strategy instruction must operate on the law of parsimony. A number of "multiple component packages" of strategy instruction have been suggested for improving learning disabled children's functioning. These components have usually encompassed some of the following: skimming, imaging, drawing, elaborating, paraphrasing, mnemonics, accessing prior knowledge, reviewing, orienting to critical features, and so on. No doubt there are some positive aspects to these strategy packages in that (1) these programs are advanced over some of the studies in the learning disabilities literature that focus on rather simple or "quick fix" strategies (e.g., rehearsal or categorization to improve performance); (2) these programs promote a domain skill, and have a certain metacognitive embellishment about them; and (3) the best of these programs involve (a) teaching a few strategies well rather than superficially, (b) teaching students to monitor their performance, (c) teaching students when and where to use the strategy in order to enhance generalization, (d) teaching strategies as an integrated part of an existing curriculum, and (e) teaching that includes a great deal of supervised student feedback and practice.

The difficulty of such packages, however, at least in terms of instructional intervention, is that little is known about which components best predict student performance, and they do not readily permit one to determine why the strategy worked. The multiple component approaches that are typically found in a number of learning disabilities strategy intervention studies must be carefully contrasted with a component analysis approach that involves the systematic combination of instructional components known to have an additive effect on performance. Good strategies are composed of the sufficient and necessary processes for accomplishing their intended goal, consuming as few intellectual processes as necessary to do so.

Good strategies for students without learning disabilities are not necessarily good strategies for learning disabled students. Strategies that enhance access to procedural and/or declarative knowledge for normal students, will not be well suited for all learning disabled children. For example, Cooney and Swanson (1987) discovered that students who do well in math benefited from strategies that enhanced the access of procedural knowledge, whereas children who are poor in mathematics benefited by strategies that enhanced declarative knowledge. To further illustrate, Wong and Jones (1982) trained learning disabled and nondisabled adolescents in a self-questioning strategy to monitor reading comprehension. Results indicated that although the strategy training benefited the adolescents with learning disabilities, it actually lowered the performance of nondisabled adolescents. This concept is also illustrated in a study by Dansereau et al. (1979) in which college students were presented a networking strategy for transforming text material into nodes and links. Control subjects, who were not taught the strategy, showed a typical positive correlation between their grade-point average (GPA) and achievement; for the experimental subjects, however, the GPA and achievement scores were negatively correlated. Not only were the strategy instructions ineffective, they were actually damaging to the high-GPA subjects.

To illustrate this point further with learning disabled children, Swanson (1988b) presented learning disabled, mentally retarded, gifted, and average achieving students a series of tasks that involved base and elaborative sentences. Their task was to recall words embedded in a sentence. The results of the first experiment suggested that learning disabled children differ from the other groups in their ability to benefit from elaboration. It was assumed that the elaboration requirement placed excessive demands on learning disabled children's central processing strategies when compared with the other ability groups. This finding was qualified in the next experiment and suggested that encoding difficulty must be taken into consideration when determining strategy effects, but the results suggested that disabled children may require additional strategies for their performance to become comparable with that of their cohorts. In another study (Swanson, Cooney, & Overholser, 1988), learning disabled college students were asked to recall words in a sentence under semantic and imagery instructional conditions. The results suggested, contrary to the extant literature, that disabled readers were better able to remember words in a sentence during instructional conditions that induced semantic processing. In contrast, nondisabled readers favored imagery processing over semantic processing conditions. In sum, these results suggest that strategies that are effective for nondisabled students may be less effective for learning disabled students.

The use of effective strategies does not necessarily eliminate processing differences. It is commonly assumed that if learning disabled children are presented a strategy that allows for the efficient processing of information, then improvement in performance is due to the fact that the strategies are affecting the same processes as they do in nondisabled students (e.g., Torgesen et al., 1979). This assumption has emanated primarily from studies that have imposed organization on seemingly unorganized material. For example, considerable evidence indicates that learning disabled readers do not initially take advantage of the organizational features of material (e.g., Dallago & Moely, 1980). When learning disabled children are instructed to organize information into semantic or related categories, some of these studies (e.g., Torgesen et al., 1979) suggest that their performance is comparable to that of nondisabled students. However, the notion that disabled readers process the organizational features of information in the same manner as nondisabled students is questionable (Swanson, 1987a). For example, Swanson and Rathgeber (1986) found in categorization tasks that disabled readers can retrieve information without interrelating superordinate, subordinate, and coordinate classes of information, as the nondisabled children do. Thus, learning disabled children can learn to process information in an organizational sense without knowing the meaning of the material. The point is that simply because learning disabled children are sensitized to internal structure of material via some strategy (e.g., by cognitive strategies that require the sorting of material), it does not mean they will make use of the material in a manner consistent with what was intended from the instructional strategy.

To further illustrate this problem, let us consider a pilot study recently completed in a learning disabilities classroom (Swanson, Kozleski, & Stegick, 1987). Two learning disabled adolescents, who had serious memory and reading (i.e., comprehension) problems, were given two tasks. One task required remembering critical details of various stories read daily from a newspaper column. The second task, which assessed any possible generalization of training effect from the primary task, required the retrieval of critical information on a social studies assignment. Intervention on the primary task required the child to use a visual mnemonic strategy to organize main ideas and to link the main ideas in terms of an outline. Mental processes were assessed by asking the children to verbally report the "ways" they were remembering the information. Student responses during task performance were tape recorded, and the verbal protocols were coded and categorized in terms of the information processing strategies used. The results suggested that the students used a number of strategies (e.g., rehearsal) to sustain and/or direct their prose recall. A majority of these strategies emerged over training sessions and, in many cases, were sustaining the imagery or visual mnemonics.

Comparable performance does not mean comparable strategies. The previous principle suggests that *during* intervention different processes may be activated that are not necessarily the intent of the instructional intervention. It is also likely that disabled subjects use different strategies on tasks in which they seem to have little difficulty, and these tasks will likely be overlooked by the teacher for possible intervention. It is commonly assumed that although learning disabled children have isolated processing deficits and require general learning strategies to compensate for these processing deficits, their processing of information is comparable with that of their normal counterparts on tasks with which they have little trouble. Several authors suggest, however, that there are a number of alternative ways for achieving successful performance (Newell, 1980), and some indirect evidence indicates that the learning disabled may use qualitatively different mental operations (Shankweiler et al., 1979) and processing routes (e.g., Swanson, 1986a) from their nondisabled counterparts. For example, results of a recent study (Swanson, 1988a), reviewed in Chapter 5, suggest that disabled children may use qualitatively different processes on tasks with which they have little difficulty.

Strategies must be considered in relation to a student's knowledge base and capacity. Levin (1986) suggested that there must be a match between strategy and learner characteristics. One important variable that has been overlooked in the learning disabilities intervention literature is the notion of processing constraints (Swanson, 1982, 1987b, 1987c; Swanson, Cochran, & Ewers, 1989). Most learning disabilities strategy research, either implicitly or explicitly, has considered cognitive capacity to be a confounding variable and has made very little attempt to measure its influence. Swanson (1984a) conducted three experiments related to learning disabled students' performance on a word recall task, and found that recall is related to cognitive effort or the mental input that a limited capacity system expends to produce a response. He found that learning disabled readers were inferior to non-disabled readers in their recall of materials that made high effort demands. Furthermore, skilled readers accessed more usable information from semantic memory for enhancing recall than did disabled readers. In a subsequent study, Swanson (1986a) found that disabled children were inferior in the quantity and internal coherence of information stored in semantic memory, as well as the means by which it is accessed. The implication of this finding is also noted in the study (Swanson, 1988b) discussed earlier, comparing use of elaborative encoding strategies by learning disabled, mentally retarded, gifted, and average achieving students. The results suggested that slow learners, average, and gifted children improved in performance using elaborative strategies when compared with nonelaborative strategies. In contrast, disabled children were less positively influenced by elaborative strategies, possibly due to excessive demands placed on central processing capacity.

Comparable strategy use may not eliminate performance differences. In a *production deficiency* view of learning disabilities (see Chapter 5), it is commonly assumed that, without instruction, learning disabled students are less likely to produce strategies than are their normal counterparts. Several studies have indicated that residual differences remain between ability groups even when ability groups are instructed and/or prevented from strategy use (Gelzheiser, 1984; Swanson, 1983b, 1987a; Wong et al., 1977). For example, in a study by Gelzheiser, Cort, and Sheperd (1987), learning disabled and nondisabled children were compared on their ability to use organizational strategies. After instruction in organizational strategies, the disabled and nondisabled children were compared on their abilities to recall information on a posttest. The results indicated that disabled children were comparable in strategy use to nondisabled children, but were deficient in overall performance. In another study, Swanson (1983b) found that the recall of a learning disabled group did not improve from baseline level when trained with rehearsal strategies. They recalled less than normally achieving peers, although the groups were comparable in the various types of strategy used. The results basically support the notion that groups of children with different learning histories may continue to learn differently, even when the groups are equated in terms of strategy use. Thus, although a learning disability may include difficulties in learning to use a strategy, some of these learning disabled students will require intervention to equate performance differences with their counterparts.

Strategies taught do not necessarily become transformed into expert strategies. One mechanism that promotes expert performance is related to strategy transformation (e.g., Chi, Glaser, & Farr, 1988). It often appears that children who become experts at certain tasks have learned simple strategies and, through practice, discover ways to modify them into more efficient and powerful procedures. In particular, the proficient learner uses higher order rules to eliminate unnecessary or redundant steps in order to hold increasing amounts of information. The learning disabled child, in contrast, may learn most of the skills related to performing an academic task and perform appropriately on that task by carefully and systematically following prescribed rules or strategies. Although learning disabled children can be taught strategies, recent evidence suggests that the difference between learning disabled and nondisabled children (experts in this case) is that the latter have modified such strategies to become more efficient (Swanson & Cooney, 1985; Swanson & Rhine, 1985). Possible strategy transformation difficulties of learning disabled students are outlined in Chapter 9. It is plausible that the learning disabled child remains a novice because he or she fails to transform simple strategies into more efficient forms (see Swanson & Cooney, 1985).

SUMMARY

In summary, we have briefly characterized research on memory and learning disabilities. What we know about a learning disabled individual's memory is somewhat paralleled by what we know about the differences between older and younger children's memory. The parallel relates to effortful processing, focus on cognitive strategies, development of a knowledge base, and awareness of one's own memory processes. A number of principles related to memory strategy instruction apply to learning disabilities. These principles relate to the purposes of strategies, the use of a few processes as necessary, individual differences in strategy use and performance, learner constraints, and the transfer of strategies into more efficient processes.

REFERENCES

Baddeley, A. (1984). Reading and working memory. *Visible Language, 18,* 311–322.

Bauer, R. H. (1977). Memory processes in children with learning disabilities: Evidence for deficient rehearsal. *Journal of Experimental Child Psychology, 24,* 415–430.

Bauer, R. H., & Embert, J. (1984). Information processing in reading-disabled and nondisabled children. *Journal of Experimental Child Psychology, 37,* 271–281.

Bjorklund, D. F. (1985). The role of conceptual knowledge in the development of organization in children's memory. In C. J. Brainerd (Ed.), *Basic processes in memory development* (pp. 103–134). New York: Springer-Verlag.

Borkowski, J. G., & Cavanaugh, J. C. (1981). Metacognition and intelligence theory. In M. Friedman, J. P. Das, & N. O'Connor (Eds.), *Intelligence and learning* (pp. 253–258). New York: Plenum Press.

Bronner, A. F. (1917). *The psychology of special abilities and disabilities.* Boston: Little, Brown.

Brown, A. L. (1975). The development of memory: Knowing, knowing about knowing, and knowing how to know. In H. Reese (Ed.), *Advances in child development and behavior* (Vol. 10). New York: Academic Press.

Brown, A. L., & Campione, J. C. (1981). Inducing flexible thinking: The problem of access. In M. Friedman, J. P. Das, & N. O'Connor (Eds.), *Intelligence and learning* (pp. 515–530). New York: Plenum Press.

Bryan, T. (1972). The effect of forced mediation upon short-term memory of children with learning disabilities. *Journal of Learning Disabilities, 5,* 605–609.

Campione, J. L., Brown, A. L., & Ferrara, R. A. (1982). Mental retardation and intelligence. In R. J. Sternberg (Ed.), *Handbook of human intelligence.* New York: Cambridge University Press.

Campione, J. C., Brown, A. L., Ferrara, R. A., Jones, R. S., & Sternberg, E. (1985). Breakdown in flexible use of information: Intelligence-related differences in transfer following equivalent learning performance. *Intelligence, 9,* 297–315.

Ceci, S. J. (1982). Extracting meaning from stimuli: Automatic and purposive processing of the language-based learning disabled. *Topics in Learning and Learning Disabilities, 2,* 46–53.

Ceci, S. J. (1984). Developmental study of learning disabilities and memory. *Journal of Experimental Child Psychology, 38,* 352–371.

Ceci, S. J., Ringstrom, M. D., & Lea, S. E. G. (1980). Coding characteristics of normal and learning-disabled 10-year-olds: Evidence for dual pathways to the cognitive system. *Journal of Experimental Psychology: Human Learning and Memory, 6,* 785–797.

Chi, M. T. H. (1981). Knowledge development and memory performance. In M. P. Friedman, J. P. Das, & N. O'Connor (Eds.), *Intelligence and learning* (pp. 221–230). New York: Plenum Press.

Chi, M. T. H., Glaser, R., & Farr, M. (1988). *The nature of expertise.* Hillsdale, NJ: Erlbaum.

Cohen, R. L. (1978). Cognitive deficits, learning disabilities, and WISC verbal–performance consistency. *Developmental Psychology, 14,* 624–634.

Cohen, R. L. (1981). Short-term memory deficits in reading disabled children, in the absence of opportunity for rehearsal strategies. *Intelligence, 5,* 69–76.

Conners, C. K., Kramer, K., & Guerra, F. (1969). Auditory synthesis and dichotic listening in children with learning disabilities. *Journal of Special Education, 3,* 163–170.

Cooney, J. B., & Swanson, H. L. (1987). Memory and learning disabilities: An overview. In H. L. Swanson (Ed.), *Memory and learning disabilities* (pp. 2–40). Greenwich, CT: JAI Press.

Dallago, M. L. P., & Moely, B. E. (1980). Free recall in boys of normal and poor reading levels as a function of task manipulation. *Journal of Experimental Child Psychology, 30,* 62–78.

Dansereau, D. F., McDonald, B. A., Collins, D. W., Garland, J., Holley, C. D., Diekhoff, G., & Evans, S. H. (1979). Evaluation of a teaching strategy system. In H. F. O'Neil & C. D. Spielberger (Eds.), *Cognitive and affective learning strategies* (pp. 3–43). New York: Academic Press.

Dawson, M. H., Hallahan, D. P., Reeves, R. E., & Ball, D. W. (1980). The effect of reinforcement and verbal rehearsal on selective attention in learning-disabled children. *Journal of Abnormal Child Psychology, 8,* 133–144.

Dempster, F. N. (1985). Short-term memory development in childhood and adolescence. In C. J. Brainerd & M. Pressley (Eds.), *Basic processes in memory development: Progress in cognitive development research* (pp. 209–248). New York: Springer-Verlag.

Denckla, M. B., & Rudel, R. G. (1974). Rapid "automatized" naming of pictured objects, colors, letters, and numbers by normal children. *Cortex, 10,* 186–202.

Flavell, J. (1979). Metacognition and cognitive monitoring. *American Psychologist, 34,* 906–911.

Forrest-Pressley, D. D. L., & Gillies, L. A. (1983). Children's flexible use of strategies during reading. In M. Pressley & J. R. Levin (Eds.), *Cognitive strategy research: Educational applications.* New York: Springer-Verlag.

Gelzheiser, L. M. (1984). Generalization from categorical memory tasks to prose by learning disabled adolescents. *Journal of Educational Psychology, 76,* 1128–1138.

Gelzheiser, L. M., Cort, R., & Sheperd, M. J. (1987). Is minimal strategy instruction sufficient for LD children? Testing the production deficiency

hypothesis. *Learning Disability Quarterly, 10,* 267–276.

Geschwind, N. (1962). The anatomy of acquired disorders of reading. In J. Money (Ed.), *Reading disability: Progress and research needs in dyslexia* (pp. 115–129). Baltimore: Johns Hopkins Press.

Golden, A. J., McCutcheon, B. A., Delay, E. R., & Issac, W. (1982). Perceptual speed and short-term retention of visual stimuli in preschool children. *Journal of Applied Developmental Psychology, 3,* 329–335.

Goyen, J. D., & Lyle, J. (1971). Effect of incentives upon retarded and normal readers on a visual-associate learning task. *Journal of Experimental Child Psychology, 11,* 274–280.

Goyen, J. D., & Lyle, J. (1973). Short-term memory and visual discrimination in retarded readers. *Perceptual and Motor Skills, 36,* 403–408.

Guthrie, J. T., & Goldberg, H. K. (1972). Visual sequential memory in reading disability. *Journal of Learning Disabilities, 5,* 41–46.

Guttentag, R. E. (1984). The mental effort requirement of cumulative rehearsal: A developmental study. *Journal of Experimental Child Psychology, 37,* 92–106.

Hallahan, D. P., & Cruickshank, W. M. (1973). *Psychoeducational foundations of learning disabilities.* Englewood Cliffs, NJ: Prentice-Hall.

Hallahan, D. P., Gajar, A. H., Cohen, S. B., & Tarver, S. G. (1978). Selective attention and focus of control in learning disabled and normal children. *Journal of Learning Disabilities, 11,* 231–236.

Hasher, L., & Zacks, R. T. (1979). Automatic and effortful processes in memory. *Journal of Experimental Psychology: General, 108,* 356–388.

Hinshelwood, J. (1917). *Congenital word blindness*. London: Lewis.

Howe, M. L., Brainerd, C. J., & Kingman, J. (1985). Storage–retrieval processes of normal and learning disabled children: A stages-of-learning analysis of picture–word effects. *Child Development, 56,* 1120–1133.

Jorm, A. F. (1983). Specific reading retardation and word memory: A review. *British Journal of Psychology, 74,* 311–342.

Kavale, K. A., & Forness, S. R. (1985a). The historical foundation of learning disabilities: A quantitative synthesis assessing the validity of Strauss and Werner's exogenous versus endogenous distinction of mental retardation. *Remedial and Special Education, 6,* 18–25.

Kavale, K. A., & Forness, S. R. (1985b). *The science of learning disabilities*. San Diego: College-Hill Press.

Koorland, M. A., & Wolking, W. D. (1982). Effect of reinforcement on modality of stimulus control in learning. *Learning Disability Quarterly, 5,* 264–273.

Koppitz, E. M. (1971). *Children with learning disabilities: A five year follow-up study*. Orlando, FL: Grune and Stratton.

Kussmaul, A. (1877). Disturbances of speech. *Cyclopedia of practical medicine, 14,* 581–875.

Levin, J. R. (1986). Four cognitive principles of learning strategy instruction. *Educational Psychologist, 21,* 3–17.

Mastropieri, M. A., Scruggs, T. E., Levin, J. R., Gaffney, J., & McLoone, B. (1985). Mnemonic vocabulary instruction for learning disabled students. *Learning Disability Quarterly, 8,* 57–63.

Monroe, M. (1932). *Children who cannot read*. Chicago: University of Chicago Press.

Morgan, W. P. (1896). A case of congenital word blindness. *British Medical Journal, 2,* 1378–1379.

Newell, A. (1980). Reasoning, problem solving and decision processes: The problem space as a fundamental category. In R. Nickerson, (Ed.), *Attention and performance VIII*. Hillsdale, NJ: Erlbaum.

Ornstein, P., & Corsale, C. (1979). Organizational factors in children's memory. In C. R. Puff (Ed.), *Memory organization and structure* (pp. 219–258). Orlando, FL: Academic Press.

Ornstein, P. A., & Naus, M. J. (1978). Rehearsal processes in children's memory. In P. A. Ornstein (Ed.), *Memory development in children*. Hillsdale, NJ: Erlbaum.

Orton, S. T. (1925). "Word-blindness" in school children. *Archives of Neurology and Psychiatry, 14,* 581–615.

Orton, S. T. (1937). *Reading, writing, and speech problems in children*. New York: Norton.

Pressley, M., Borkowski, J. G., & O'Sullivan, J. T. (1984). Memory strategy instruction is made of this: Metamemory and durable strategy use. *Educational Psychologist, 10,* 94–107.

Rizzo, N. D. (1939). Studies in visual and auditory memory span with reference to reading disability. *Journal of Experimental Education, 8,* 208–244.

Scruggs, T. E., Mastropieri, M. A., Levin, J. R., & Gaffney, J. S. (1987). Facilitating the acquisition of science facts in learning disabled students. *American Educational Research Journal, 22,* 575–586.

Senf, G. M., & Feshbach, S. (1970). Development of bisensory memory in culturally deprived, dyslexic and normal readers. *Journal of Educational Psychology, 61,* 461–470.

Shankweiler, D., Liberman, I. Y., Mark, S. L., Fowler, L. A., & Fischer, F. W.

(1979). The speech code and learning to read. *Journal of Experimental Psychology: Human Learning and Memory, 5,* 531–545.

Spear, L. C., & Sternberg, R. J. (1987). An information-processing framework for understanding reading disability. In S. Ceci (Ed.), *Handbook of cognitive, social and neuropsychological aspects of learning disabilities* (pp. 3–32). Hillsdale, NJ: Erlbaum.

Strauss, A. A., & Kephart, N. C. (1955). *Psychopathology and education of the brain-injured child: Vol. 2. Progress in theory and clinic.* Orlando, FL: Grune and Stratton.

Strauss, A. A., & Lehtinen, L. E. (1947). *Psychopathology and education of the brain-injured child.* Orlando, FL: Grune and Stratton.

Swanson, H. L. (1977a). Nonverbal visual short-term memory as a function of age and dimensionality in learning disabled children. *Child Development, 45,* 51–55.

Swanson, H. L. (1977b). Response strategies and dimensional salience with learning disabled and mentally retarded children on a short-term memory task. *Journal of Learning Disabilities, 10,* 635–642.

Swanson, H. L. (1978). Verbal encoding effects on the visual short-term memory of learning-disabled and normal readers. *Journal of Educational Psychology, 70,* 539–544.

Swanson, H. L. (1982). Verbal short-term memory coding of learning disabled in relation to normal and deaf readers. *Learning Disability Quarterly, 5,* 21–28.

Swanson, H. L. (1983a). A developmental study of vigilance in learning disabled and non-disabled children. *Journal of Abnormal Child Psychology, 11,* 415–429.

Swanson, H. L. (1983b). Relations among metamemory, rehearsal activity and word recall in learning disabled and nondisabled readers. *British Journal of Educational Psychology, 53,* 186–194.

Swanson, H. L. (1983c). A study of nonstrategic linguistic coding on visual recall of learning disabled and normal readers. *Journal of Learning Disabilities, 16,* 209–216.

Swanson, H. L. (1984a). Effects of cognitive effort and word distinctiveness on learning disabled and nondisabled readers' recall. *Journal of Educational Psychology, 76,* 894–908.

Swanson, H. L. (1984b). Semantic and visual memory codes in learning disabled readers. *Journal of Experimental Child Psychology, 37,* 124–140.

Swanson, H. L. (1986a). Do semantic memory deficiencies underlie disabled readers' encoding processes? *Journal of Experimental Child Psychology, 41,* 461–488.

Swanson, H. L. (1986b). Learning disabled readers' verbal coding difficulties: A problem of storage or retrieval? *Learning Disability Research, 1,* 73–82.

Swanson, H. L. (1986c). Verbal coding deficits in learning disabled readers. In S. Ceci (Ed.), *Handbook of cognitive, social and neuropsychological aspects of learning disabilities* (Vol. 1, pp. 203–228). Hillsdale, NJ: Erlbaum.

Swanson, H. L. (1987a). The combining of multiple hemispheric resources in learning disabled and skilled readers' recall of words: A test of three information processing models. *Brain and Cognition, 6,* 41–54.

Swanson, H. L. (1987b). Organization training and developmental changes in learning disabled children's encoding preferences. *Learning Disability Quarterly, 8,* 8–18.

Swanson, H. L. (1987c). The validity of metamemory—Memory links with children of high and low verbal ability. *British Journal of Educational Psychology, 57,* 179–190.

Swanson, H. L. (1988a). Learning disabled children's problem solving: Identifying mental processes underlying intelligent performance. *Intelligence, 12,* 261–278.

Swanson, H. L. (1988b). Memory subtypes of learning disabled readers. *Learning Disability Quarterly, 14,* 342–357.

Swanson, H. L. (1989). Central processing strategy differences in gifted, average, learning disabled and mentally retarded children. *Journal of Experimental Child Psychology, 47,* 370–397.

Swanson, H. L., Cochran, K., & Ewers, C. (1989). Working memory and reading disabilities. *Journal of Abnormal Child Psychology, 17,* 745–756.

Swanson, H. L., & Cooney, J. (1985). Strategy transformations in learning disabled children. *Learning Disability Quarterly, 8,* 221–231.

Swanson, H. L., Cooney, J. D., & Overholser, J. D. (1988). The effects of self-generated visual mnemonics on adult learning disabled readers' word recall. *Learning Disabilities Research, 4,* 26–35.

Swanson, H. L., Kozleski, E., & Stegick, P. (1987). Effects of cognitive training on disabled readers' prose recall: Do cognitive processes change during intervention. *Psychology in the Schools, 24,* 378–384.

Swanson, H. L., & Rathgeber, A. (1986). The effects of organizational dimensions on learning disabled readers' recall. *Journal of Educational Research, 79,* 155–162.

Swanson, H. L., & Rhine, B. (1985). Strategy transformations in learning disabled children's math performance: Clues to the development of expertise. *Journal of Learning Disabilities, 18,* 596–603.

Tarver, S. G., Hallahan, D. P., Kauffman, J. M., & Ball, D. W. (1976). Verbal rehearsal and selective attention in children with learning disabilities: A developmental lag. *Journal of Experimental Child Psychology, 22,* 375–385.

Torgesen, J. K. (1978). Memorization process in reading-disabled children. *Journal of Educational Psychology, 69,* 571–578.

Torgesen, J. K., Bowen, C., & Ivey, C. (1978). Task structure vs. modality of the Visual–Oral Digit Span test. *Journal of Educational Psychology, 70,* 451–456.

Torgesen, J. K., & Dice, C. (1980). Characteristics of research on learning disabilities. *Journal of Learning Disabilities, 13,* 531–535.

Torgesen, J. K., & Houck, D. G. (1980). Processing deficiencies of learning disabled children who perform poorly on the digit span subtest. *Journal of Educational Psychology, 72,* 141–160.

Torgesen, J. K., Murphy, H. A., & Ivey, C. (1979). The effects of an orienting task on the memory performance of reading disabled children. *Journal of Learning Disabilities, 12,* 396–401.

Vellutino, F. R. (1979). *Dyslexia: Theory and research.* Cambridge, MA: MIT Press.

Vellutino, F. R., & Scanlon, D. M. (1985). Linguistic coding and reading ability. In S. Rosenberg (Ed.), *Advances in applied psycholinguistics* (Vol. 2, pp. 71–96). New York: Cambridge University Press.

Werner, H. (1948). *Comparative psychology of mental development.* New York: International Universities Press.

Wong, B. Y. L. (1978). The effects of directive cues on the organization of memory and recall in good and poor readers. *Journal of Educational Research, 72,* 179–223.

Wong, B. Y. L. (1982). Strategic behaviors in selecting retrieval cues in gifted, normal achieving and learning disabled children. *Journal of Learning Disabilities, 15,* 33–37.

Wong, B. Y. L., & Jones, W. (1982). Increasing metacomprehension in learning disabled and normally-achieving students through self-questioning training. *Learning Disability Quarterly, 5,* 228–240.

Wong, B. Y. L., Wong, R., & Foth, D. (1977). Recall and clustering of verbal materials among normal and poor readers. *Bulletin of the Psychonomic Society, 10,* 375–378.

Worden, P. E. (1986). Comprehension and memory for prose in the learning disabled. In S. J. Ceci (Ed.), *Handbook of cognitive, social and neuropsychological aspects of learning disabilities* (Vol. 1, pp. 241–262). Hillsdale, NJ: Erlbaum.

Worden, P. E. Malmgren, I., & Gabourie, P. (1982). Memory for stories in learning disabled adults. *Journal of Learning Disabilities, 15,* 145–152.

Worden, P. E., & Nakamura, G. V. (1983). Story comprehension and recall in learning-disabled vs. normal college students. *Journal of Educational Psychology, 74,* 633–641.

7

A Cognitive Theory of Learning:
Implications for Learning Disabilities

JOHN B. COONEY

In Chapter 1, Hresko advanced the view that learning disabilities are an educational problem, and that the treatment of choice is educational. Thus, a thorough understanding of the learning process is necessary to establish the solid foundation upon which to develop sound interventions. The purpose of this chapter is to explicate a theory of learning and skill performance that is consistent with the cognitive theme of the text.

For the first half of this century, the psychology of learning served as the cornerstone of scientific psychology. Once the source of great intellectual debates between behavioral and cognitive theorists (e.g., Hull, 1935, 1943; Koffka, 1935; Skinner, 1938, 1950, 1953; Tolman, 1932, 1942), interest in learning began to wane during the late 1950s (Anderson, 1981; Greeno, 1980; Shuell, 1986). Cognitive psychology appeared to have won the debate by marshaling compelling evidence against the metapostulates of stimulus–response (S-R) learning theory (see Bower & Hilgard, 1984, pp. 416–421). Proponents of the cognitive approach were quick to point out the inadequacies of S-R

The writing of this chapter was supported in part by a fellowship from the Center for Research on Teaching and Learning, University of Northern Colorado.

learning theories, yet extent cognitive theories of learning were also inadequate (Estes, 1975; Langley & Simon, 1981).

For almost two decades, cognitive psychology remained silent about the issue of learning. When cognitive psychology finally returned to the issue of learning, it was in a language and context much different from that of the earlier generation of learning theories. Interest had shifted to computer simulations (Newell & Simon, 1956; Simon & Feigenbaum, 1964) and artificial intelligence (Feigenbaum & Feldman, 1963; Shortliffe, 1976; Winston, 1977). Another distinguishing feature of this work was the focus on learning and performance in specific domains, such as reading comprehension (Perfetti & Lesgold, 1977), composition (Gregg & Steinberg, 1980), mathematics (Resnick & Ford, 1981), physics (Chi, Feltovich, & Glaser, 1981; Heller & Reif, 1984), and computer programming (Adelson, 1981; Jeffries, Turner, Polson, & Atwood, 1981), to name a few. The emphasis on learning and performance in specific domains of knowledge should not be taken to mean that all of cognitive psychology was advocating the development of separate theories of learning for various mental faculties. Although there are proponents to this approach (e.g., Chomsky, 1980), the approach explicated in this chapter is of a more general nature: a theory of learning developed to account for learning across domains.

WHAT IS A MODEL OF THE LEARNING PROCESS?

The work of John Anderson (1976, 1982, 1983, 1987) represents the most explicit formulation of a comprehensive cognitive theory of learning. It is not, however, the only cognitive view of learning (e.g., Bandura, 1977, 1986; R. M. Gagné, 1985; Norman, 1982; Rumelhart & Norman, 1978, 1981; Sternberg, 1984). Anderson's (1983) theory goes by the acronym ACT, which stands for *Adaptive Control of Thought*. The final reformulation of his framework, referred to as ACT* (pronounced "act star"), is based on the assumption of a unitary cognitive system. On this issue, Anderson (1983) wrote:

> The most deeply rooted preconception guiding my theorizing is a belief in the unity of human cognition, that is, that all the higher cognitive processes, such as memory, language, problem solving, imagery, deduction, and induction, are different manifestations of the same underlying system. This is not to deny that there are many powerful special-purpose peripheral systems for processing perceptual information and coordinating motor performance. However, behind these lies a common cognitive system for higher level processing. (p. 1)

Anderson's intention clearly was to develop an account of learning and performance that is not domain specific. Examine the general framework of

ACT✳ depicted graphically in Figure 7–1. Note that three distinct memory systems are postulated: *working memory, declarative memory,* and *production memory.* The declarative memory system functions as a repository of the factual information we have about the environment (i.e., knowledge about things), whereas production memory functions as a repository of knowledge about how to do things (i.e., procedural knowledge). Both of these memory systems are viewed as relatively permanent, with no apparent storage limitations. In contrast, working memory is a temporary storage system with limited capacity. Essentially, working memory is used as a temporary repository for (a) information resulting from encoding operations, (b) information retrieved from declarative memory, (c) actions resulting from the execution of productions, and (d) instructions for generating performances. As discussed in Chapter 6 mental operations performed in working memory may also add information to or modify the long-term memory systems. To understand the learning process within this framework, it is necessary to explore the way that declarative knowledge and procedural knowledge are represented.

Declarative Memory

One important characteristic of memory is that we remember the *meaning* of our experiences (Anderson, 1974; Bartlett, 1932; Bransford, Barclay, & Franks, 1972; Bransford & Franks, 1971; Posner, 1969). This does not mean

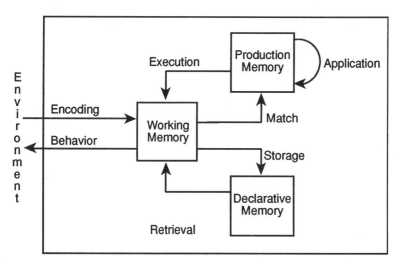

Figure 7–1. Interrelationships among the structural components of the ACT✳ production system framework. Adapted and reprinted by permission of the publishers from *The Architecture of Cognition* (p. 19) by J. R. Anderson, 1983, Cambridge, MA: Harvard University Press. Copyright 1983 by the President and Fellows of Harvard College.

that we are unable to remember verbatim passages. Rather, surface features or the exact details of events are lost more rapidly than memory for meaning (Baggett, 1975; Keenan & Kintsch, 1974; McKoon & Keenan, 1974). This phenomenon occurs even when we intend to remember surface features (Wanner, 1968). Thus, a central problem for any cognitive theory is to describe the representation of meaning in memory. To solve this problem, the ACT✳ framework uses the formalism of a *proposition*, a unit developed by linguists to represent the meaning of events. In earlier formulations of the ACT framework, propositional representations were used exclusively to describe declarative memory codes; however, in the ACT✳ formulation, three types of memory codes were postulated: temporal strings (one, two, three), spatial images (a circle within a square), and propositions. Due to space limitations, only the propositional representation will be discussed here.

Propositional representations.   Propositions are the smallest units of information that can be judged to be true or false. Simply stated, propositions are idea units that represent relationships among objects and events (i.e., concepts). Consider the following sentence:

Chris solved the most difficult algebra problem on the
weekly test.   (1)

This complex sentence can be decomposed to a set of simple sentences, each expressing a primitive unit of meaning.

Chris solved a problem.   (2)

The problem was on a test.   (3)

The test was a weekly event.   (4)

The problem was an algebra problem.   (5)

The problem was the most difficult.   (6)

Each of these sentences roughly corresponds to the set of abstract propositions that represents the meaning of the complex sentence. One method for expressing these primitive units of meaning is the linear propositional notation developed by Kintsch (1977), illustrated below:

(SOLVE, CHRIS, PROBLEM)   (7)

(ON-TEST, PROBLEM)   (8)

(WEEKLY, TEST)   (9)

(ALGEBRAIC, PROBLEM)   (10)

(MOST-DIFFICULT, (ALGEBRAIC, PROBLEM))   (11)

    or

(MOST-DIFFICULT, 10)

Each proposition (7 through 11) is expressed as an ordered list of terms enclosed by parentheses, and each contains one *relational* term and one or more *arguments*. The relational term is always written first and asserts a connection among the arguments. Relations correspond to verbs, verb forms, and adjectives. Arguments of the proposition refer to the nouns (agents, objects, subjects, recipients, etc.). For example, the relation SOLVE in Proposition 7 takes at least two arguments: the agent of the solution (CHRIS) and the object of the solution (PROBLEM). Proposition 8 asserts that the location of the problem was on a test, and Proposition 9 asserts that the test is one that is administered weekly. Note that propositions may be embedded in other propositions as arguments. Proposition 10, which represents the assertion that the problem is algebraic, is embedded as an argument in Proposition 11 to represent the fact that the algebra problem is the most difficult.

It is important to understand that propositional notation is arbitrary. It does not imply that we remember information in the form of the lists given above. Such lists are only one convention for representing meaning. Other propositional notation systems exist. For example, Sentence 1 can be expressed as a propositional network. Charts a through e of Figure 7–2 depict network representations that correspond to the propositions expressed as lists in Propositions 7 through 11, respectively. Notice that each proposition is designated by a numbered ellipse that is connected to relations and arguments by labeled arrows. The relations, arguments, and propositions are called the *nodes* of the network. The labeled arrows are called *links*, and they function to connect the nodes of the network. The integration of the individual propositions into a larger hierarchical network, based on common nodes, is shown in Figure 7–2f.

The propositional network depicted in Figure 7–2 can also be extended to more complex systems of knowledge, such as mathematics, history, biology, physics, and geography. In general, predictions derived from the propositional network structures are consistent with many aspects of human behavior in these domains. For example, recent work on simple arithmetic indicates that addition, subtraction, and multiplication facts are stored in separate, but interrelated propositional networks (Ashcraft & Fierman, 1982; Campbell, 1987; Cooney, Swanson, & Ladd, 1988; Goldman, Pellegrino, & Mertz, 1988; K. Miller, Perlmutter, & Keating, 1984). According to Campbell (1987), the nodes of the multiplication network correspond to the operands and the products.

Another example of a network representing some aspects of knowledge about animals is presented in Figure 7–3, a propositional version of the associative network proposed by Collins and Quillian (1969). Notice the hierarchical structure of the network. Concepts such as bird and fish are subordinate to the concept of animal. In turn, canary and ostrich are subordinate to bird. Also notice that each concept in the hierarchy is linked to one or more propositions that are properties of the concept. The number of propositions linked

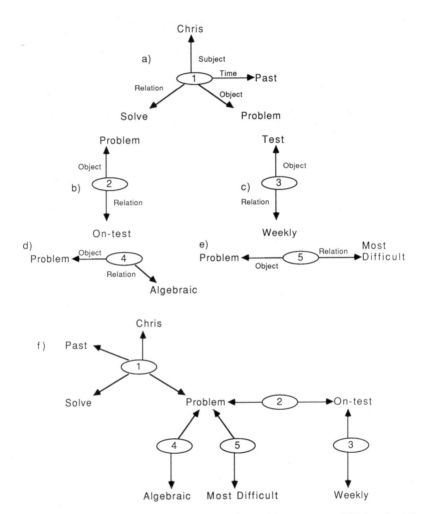

Figure 7–2. Propositional network representations of the sentence, "Chris solved the most difficult algebra problem on the weekly test."

to a concept varies, as does the length of the link. Both of these features are important to understanding retrieval of information. In the scheme used here, the length of the link indicates the strength of association between concepts and between concepts and their properties (Collins & Loftus, 1975). A primary factor determining the strength of these associations is their frequency of occurrence. Finally, notice that the properties of any concept are stored at the highest possible node. Although this arrangement is economical, there are exceptions to this principle (Conrad, 1972). If a property is frequently paired with a concept, the property will be stored directly with the concept even if it could be stored at a higher level in the network (Anderson, 1985).

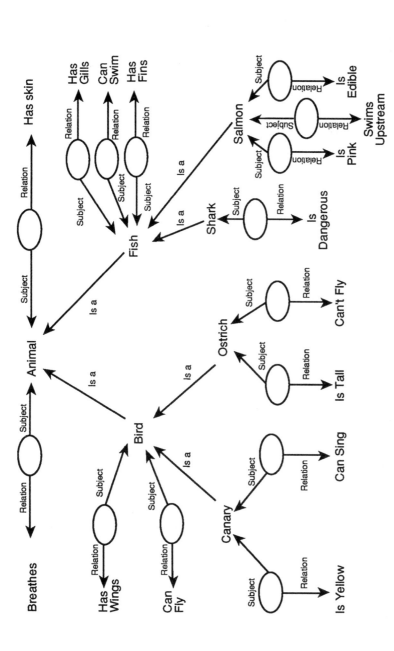

Figure 7–3. A propositional network representing knowledge about animals. Adapted from "Retrieval Time from Semantic Memory" by A. M. Collins and M. R. Quillian, 1969, *Journal of Verbal Learning and Verbal Behavior, 8*, p. 241. Reprinted with permission of the author.

An important assumption made by ACT* is that propositions are stored and retrieved as units in an all-or-none fashion. Although there is some controversy about this postulate (Anderson, 1976; Anderson & Bower, 1972; Foss & Harwood, 1975), it is accepted for its functional value within production memory. The basic argument is whether propositions constitute the basic elements of memory (holistic view) or the basic elements are the nodes of the network (the elementaristic view; Kintsch, 1977). Interestingly, Anderson has taken both sides of this controversy. In ACT*, however, the partial recall of a proposition has no functional value. Consider Proposition 7 given above. Intuitively, it does not make sense to encode or retrieve (SOLVE, CHRIS). The finding that memory is influenced by the number of propositions rather than the number of words in a sentence is evidence in favor of the holistic view. For example, Kintsch and Glass (1974) found that memory was better for sentences that contain only one proposition (e.g., "Sam sells vegetables to Guido") than for sentences that contain three propositions (e.g., "The crowded passengers squirmed uncomfortably"), even though both sentences contain the same number of words. Furthermore, partial recall of a sentence was more likely when it contained multiple propositions, and the partial recall of sentences corresponded to propositions contained in a sentence.

Spreading activation. Retrieval of declarative information is described in terms of the process of *spreading activation*. Moreover, spreading activation defines working memory, the process of making information available for processing. Specifically, activation is energy that spreads through the declarative network. Beginning with a source node, activation spreads along the links of the network to the most closely associated concepts and their properties. What ideas come to mind when you read the word *canary*? If your knowledge is structured similarly to the propositional network given in Figure 7–3, you are likely to remember that canaries are yellow and sing. Information about other specific birds and about animals may also become available (active) after a few seconds. Thus, activation spreads along the links of the network, and retrieval speed is proportional to the distance between the source node and related nodes in the network.

Evidence supporting this view was provided in the now classic experiment conducted by Collins and Quillian (1969). These investigators asked subjects to indicate whether the following statements were true or false by pressing one of two buttons:

A. A canary can sing.

B. A canary can fly.

C. A canary has skin.

Assume that the word *canary* serves as a source of activation (i.e., source node) in each of these sentences. Now, examine Figure 7–3 and notice where the information needed to verify these statements is located in the network. In the case of Sentence A, activation need only spread to propositions directly associated with canary. To verify Sentence B, activation must spread from the canary node and associated propositions to the bird node and associated propositions. Verification of Sentence C requires activation to spread from the canary node and associated propositions, to the bird node and associated propositions, and then to the animal node and associated propositions. Thus, the time to verify these sentences should vary in proportion to the distance (the number of intervening propositions) that activation must spread in the network. This is exactly what Collins and Quillian (1969) found.

The depth that activation can spread in the network is dependent on several factors. First, there is the strength of the links between the source node and related nodes in the network. ACT✳ assumes that the strength of links between nodes increases with frequency of repetition and that the speed of retrieval increases with strength. Thus, practice (repetition) should have an effect on the speed of retrieval. Several experimental results are consistent with this notion (Anderson, 1976, 1983). Note that in Figure 7–3, the strength of the link between bird and canary is stronger than that between bird and ostrich. Under these circumstances, judgments about a canary being an instance of a bird will take less time than judgments about an ostrich being an instance of a bird. Second, the number of links between a source node and related propositions affects the spread of activation in the network. Activation from a given node is divided among the attached links proportional to their strength of connection. Thus, holding constant the strength of the links between a source node and related nodes, the source node with fewer links will deliver higher levels of activation to related nodes. Inspection of Figure 7–3 shows that the salmon node has three links, whereas canary has two links. According to ACT✳, information about canaries will be retrieved faster than information about salmon. This is the so-called *fan effect*, which has been demonstrated in several experiments (Anderson, 1974; Lewis & Anderson, 1976; Peterson & Potts, 1982). A third factor to consider in describing the spread of activation through the network structure is the strength of the coupling factor, which describes the strength between a node in the network and its input (e.g., external stimulus). Finally, ACT✳ postulates that the level of activation varies with increases or decreases in input; however, a limit is placed on the total activation of a node by a decay process. Specifically, the current level of activation for any node in the network decays exponentially in proportion to its level of activation. Mathematically, the level of activation for a node in the network can be described by the following differential equation:

$$\frac{da_i(t)}{dt} = Bn_i(t) - p*a_i(t).$$

In this equation, $a_i(t)$ is the activation of node $_i$ at time t, $n_i(t)$ is the input to node i at time t, B is the coupling factor, and $p*$ is the decay factor. Simply stated, this equation predicts that the change in activation is positively proportional (as a function of B) to the amount of input and negatively proportional to the current level of activation. The level of input to a given node is expressed in ACT$*$ as the following equation:

$$n_i(t) = c_i^*(t) + \sum_j r_{ji}\, a_j(t - \delta t).$$

In this equation, the total activation input to node i at time t, $n_i(t)$, is determined by the amount of source activation for node i at time t, $c_i^*(t)$, and the activation received from the j nodes that are attached to node i (a_j). If i is not a source node at time t, then $c_i^*(t) = 0$; otherwise $c_i^*(t) = c_i^*$. Also note that the activation input to $n_i(t)$ from a_j is proportional to the strength of the link (r_{ji}) between node i and node j. Finally, note that the total activation input to node i at time t is influenced by a delay in the rate of transmission between node i and node j.

It is also possible to describe the spread of activation throughout the propositional network. To describe the change in the level of activation of several nodes in the propositional network, the first equation can be rewritten to represent the activation of more than one node by considering an n-element vector $A(t)$ to represent the n nodes in the network. Accordingly, the first equation given above becomes:

$$\frac{dA(t)}{dt} = BN(t) - p^*A(t).$$

To describe the total activation input to several nodes at time t, the second equation can be rewritten as follows:

$$N(t) = C^*(t) + RA(t - \delta t),$$

where all terms in uppercase letters represent n-element vectors that contain their lowercase counterparts as the elements. For a more thorough mathematical analysis of the spreading activation concept, see Anderson (1983, pp. 86–96, 121–125).

In summary, ACT$*$ describes declarative memory as a network of interrelated propositions. Propositions describe the relationship of one thing to another and are considered to be the smallest units of meaning that are stored in declarative memory. The organization of propositions is hierarchical; however, exceptions to this phenomenon have been noted. Information is retrieved from a propositional network according to the principles of spreading activation. The active portion of this propositional network at any moment in time defines working memory, but working memory may also consist of temporary knowledge structures that are not yet a part of declarative memory. Finally, declarative knowledge is not responsible for generating behavior;

this generation of behavior is governed by the information contained in production memory.

Production Memory

Turn back to Figure 7–1 and examine the processes related to production memory. Note that a *matching* process and an *execution* process are involved in working memory. Also, note the loop labeled *application*. The contents of production memory are referred to as *productions*. According to ACT✻, all productions are represented as condition–action pairs. The condition specifies a specific pattern of information. If the pattern of information stored with a production (i.e., the condition) matches the pattern of information active in working memory, then the action component of the production is executed. The execution of the production results in the action's becoming part of working memory. This process of pattern matching and execution is referred to as *production application*. Finally, the process of *application* illustrated by the loop in Figure 7–1 is included to indicate that new productions are learned by studying what has happened from the application of existing productions.

At this point, some examples of productions might be helpful. A normal reader makes many inferences without giving much thought to the process of making the inference. Suppose you read a passage from a mystery novel that contained the facts (propositions) that Mrs. Mabry is Elaine's mother and that Paul is married to Elaine. You are very likely to infer that Mrs. Mabry is Paul's mother-in-law. An informal production that makes this type of thought possible is given below:

IF person 1 is mother of person 2
    and person 2 is married to person 3,
THEN person 1 is mother-in-law of person 3.

Notice that the condition (the IF portion of the production) specifies a conjunction of features: (*mother-of*, person 1, person 2) and (*married-to*, person 2, person 3). The propositions currently active in working memory are (*mother-of*, Mrs. Mabry, Elaine) and (*married-to*, Elaine, Paul). When there is a match between an active portion of working memory and the conditions of a production stored in long-term memory, the production applies and the action specified by the production (the THEN component of the production) becomes part of working memory. Thus, the inference that Mrs. Mabry is Paul's mother-in-law is made, and that fact becomes active (part of working memory). Productions such as this one accrue strength as a function of their successful application. Also, the speed of pattern matching varies in proportion to the strength of the production. Thus, ACT✻ would predict that readers who have used this production frequently will make the inference more rapidly.

The production underlying the mother-in-law inference is quite simple; however, it is possible to represent more complex forms of cognition with the same concepts. Table 7-1 contains a production system developed by Anderson (1982) for performing addition problems. This production system is capable of performing addition of integers greater than 9 and assumes that the sums for addition problems consisting of the positive integers 0–9 exist in declarative memory. Notice that this system is composed of 12 productions, labeled P1 through P12. It is important to note that the production numbers do not indicate the order in which they are executed.

The flow of control can be illustrated by example. Consider the following problem and the flowchart in Figure 7–4a:

$$\begin{array}{r} 76 \\ + 27 \\ \hline \end{array}$$

If the goal to perform this problem is active in working memory, then P1 is the first production to apply. The action of P1 is to set a subgoal of iterating through the columns of the addition problem. The application of the next production depends upon what actions have already occurred. Because we are just beginning the problem, the rightmost column has not been summed. Thus, the conditions of P2 are matched and executed. The action of P2 is to set the subgoal of iterating through the rightmost column of the problem and set the running total to zero. The next condition that matches the contents of working memory is P6. The action of P6 is to create the subgoal of adding the digit of the top row (6) into the running total. Notice that the only action performed by the three productions (P1, P2, and P6) is to set subgoals. That is to say, attention was shifted from doing the addition problem to locating the rightmost column of the problem, to locating the digit in the first row of the rightmost column, and finally to adding the identified digit to the running total. With attention focused on the goal of adding a digit to the running total, a match can be found with the condition stated in P10. Thus, P10 activates 6 in working memory as the value of the running total, marks the digit as processed, and POPs the goal of adding a digit to the running total. POPing a goal means that attention is directed from the current goal to the goal that was established immediately before it. Thus, POPing the goal of adding a digit to the running total returns attention to the goal of iterating through the rows of the rightmost column.

With attention focused on the goal of iterating through the rows of a column, having processed one row, and having another row below it, a match with P7 can be found. The action of P7 is to set the subgoal of adding the digit from the next row (7) to the running total (6). Under these conditions, P10 applies and 7 is added to the running total. That is to say, the fact, 6 + 7 = 13 is retrieved from declarative memory. Also, the digit 7 is marked as processed, and control is returned to the subgoal of iterating through the

TABLE 7-1
A Production System Representation for Performing Arithmetic

P1.　　IF　the goal is to do an addition problem,
　　THEN　the subgoal is to iterate through the columns of the problem.

P2.　　IF　the goal is to iterate through the columns of an addition
　　　　　problem
　　　　　and the rightmost column has not been processed,
　　THEN　the subgoal is to iterate through the rows of that rightmost
　　　　　column
　　　　　and set the running total to zero.

P3.　　IF　the goal is to iterate through the columns of an addition
　　　　　problem
　　　　　and a column has just been processed
　　　　　and another column is to the left of this column,
　　THEN　the subgoal is to iterate through the rows of this column to the
　　　　　left
　　　　　and set the running total to the carry.

P4.　　IF　the goal is to iterate through the columns of an addition
　　　　　problem
　　　　　and the last column has been processed
　　　　　and there is a carry,
　　THEN　write out the carry
　　　　　and POP the goal.

P5.　　IF　the goal is to iterate through the columns of an addition
　　　　　problem
　　　　　and the last column has been processed
　　　　　and there is no carry,
　　THEN　POP the goal.

P6.　　IF　the goal is to iterate through the rows of a column
　　　　　and the top row has not been processed,
　　THEN　the subgoal is to add the digit of the top row into the running
　　　　　total.

P7.　　IF　the goal is to iterate through the rows of a column
　　　　　and a row has just been processed
　　　　　and another row is below it,
　　THEN　the subgoal is to add the digit of the lower row to the running
　　　　　total.

TABLE 7–1 (continued)

P8.   IF   the goal is to iterate through the rows of a column
and the last row has been processed
and the running total is a digit,
THEN   write the digit
and delete the carry
and mark the column as processed
and POP the goal.

P9.   IF   the goal is to iterate through the rows of a column
and the last row has been processed
and the running total is of the form "string + digit,"
THEN   write the digit
and set carry to the string
and mark the column as processed
and POP the goal.

P10.   IF   the goal is to add a digit to a number
and the number is a digit
and a sum is the sum of the two digits,
THEN   the result is the sum
and mark the digit as processed
and POP the goal.

P11.   IF   the goal is to add a digit to a number and the number is of
the form "string + digit"
and a sum is the sum of the two digits
and the sum is less than 10,
THEN   the result is "string + sum"
and mark the digit as processed
and POP the goal.

P12.   IF   the goal is to add a digit to a number
and the number is of the form "string + digit"
and a sum is the sum of the two digits
and the sum is of the form "1 + digit*"
and another number sum* is the sum of 1 plus string,
THEN   the result is "sum* + digit*"
and mark the digit as processed
and POP the goal.

From "Acquisition of Cognitive Skill" by J. R. Anderson, 1982, *Psychological Review, 89,* p. 376. Copyright 1982 by the American Psychological Association. Reprinted with permission.

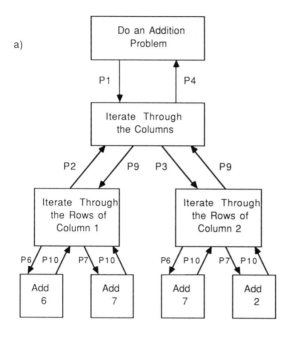

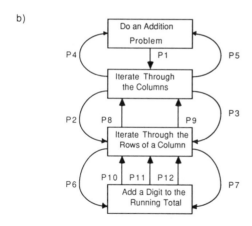

Figure 7-4. (a) A representation of the flow of control among the various productions in Table 7-1 for the problem 76 + 27. The rectangles represent goal states, and the arrows represent productions that can change the goal states. Control begins with the top goal. Adapted and reprinted by permission of the publishers from *The Architecture of Cognition* (p. 10) by J. R. Anderson, 1983, Cambridge, MA: Harvard University Press. Copyright 1983 by the President and Fellows of Harvard College. (b) A representation of the flow of control among the productions in Table 7-1 for any addition problem. From "Acquisition of Cognitive Skill" by J. R. Anderson, 1982, *Psychological Review, 89*, p. 370. Copyright 1982 by the American Psychological Association.

rows of Column 1 (the rightmost column). This time, the last row of Column 1 has been processed. Under this condition, P9 applies. The action resulting from the execution of P9 is to write down the 3 in 13, set the carry to 1, and POP the goal. POPing the subgoal of iterating through the rows of a column, directs attention to the next highest subgoal in the hierarchy, that is, iterating through the columns. Because a column has just been processed and there is another column to the left, P2 does not apply as it did before. The conditions of P3, however, do provide a match with the contents of working memory. As a result, the running total is set to the value of the carry (1) and attention is focused on iterating through the rows of the second column. The sequence of production execution is the same as before. P6 applies, which sets the subgoal of adding the digit of the top row (7) to the running total. P10 applies next: to add 7 + 1 by retrieving 8 from declarative memory. The running total was set to 1 by the previous execution of P9. P10 also marks 7 as processed and POPs the goal of adding a digit to the running total. The next digit (2) is processed by the matching and execution of P7 and P10, respectively. At this point, all rows of the column have been processed. This condition matches P9, which executes the procedure for writing the digit 0, setting the carry to 1, marking the column as processed, and shifting attention to the goal of iterating through the columns. Thus, working memory contains the facts that the last column has been processed and that the carry was set to 1. These two results match the conditions of P4. The execution of P4 results in writing the digit 1 to the left of the 0 and shifting attention to the highest goal in the hierarchy: to do the addition problem.

Figure 7–4b presents the flow of control among productions for performing any addition problem. Notice the way that the productions are grouped to form levels in a hierarchy. At the top of the hierarchy is Production P1. At the next level of the hierarchy, Productions P2–P5 set the goal of iterating through the columns of an addition problem. Before one can iterate through the columns, it is necessary to process each column. Thus, Productions P6–P9 establish the goal of iterating through the rows of a specified column. Before one can process the rows of a specified column, it is necessary to add the digits of a specified row of a specified column to a running total. Productions P10–P12 accomplish the goal of adding a digit to the running total.

In sum, ACT✳ uses the formalism of a production system as a way of representing cognitive skills. Each production consists of a condition or a set of conditions and an action or a series of actions. The productions are goal oriented in that each production asserts a goal as part of its condition. Furthermore, productions underlying cognitive skills are believed to be hierarchically organized. Although the idea that human cognition is goal oriented and hierarchical in structure is not unique to ACT✳ (see G. A. Miller, Galanter, & Pribram, 1960), Anderson (1982) stated that it is difficult to prove this hypothesis directly. There is, however, evidence that instructions organized into hierarchically grouped and goal-oriented steps result in better performance than the serial or linear instructions typical of most teaching (Smith & Goodman, 1984). Just because our behavior occurs in a serial fashion does not mean that our knowledge about skills is organized in a linear fashion. ACT✻ accounts for the serial nature of behavior by postulating that only one goal can be active in working memory at a given moment in time. Accordingly, only one production can be executed at any given moment in time.

Two other features of productions in ACT✻ are essential to the following discussion of learning. First, it is important to realize that productions contain slots for variables. Consider Production P4 from Table 7–1 written in a form that reveals the implied variable slots:

> IF the goal is to iterate through the LVcolumns of an addition problem
> and LVcolumn has been processed
> and there is an LVcarry,
> THEN write the LVcarry
> and POP the goal.

Terms with the prefix of LV are referred to as local variables. Each time the production applies, the local variables take on new values. For the problem given above, 76 + 27, P4 would apply when the contents of working memory correspond to (a) the goal is to iterate through the two columns of the addition problem, and (b) Column 2 has been processed. After the production is executed, the local variables lose their values. Thus, the local variables are assigned values for the purpose of matching the condition of a production.

Second, pattern matching is the basic mechanism that determines which productions will apply, and there are many occasions when the contents of working memory match the conditions of two or more productions. ACT✻ includes a set of principles for resolving such conflicts. The principle of *refractoriness* states that the same production cannot apply to a set of propositions in working memory twice in the same way. This is similar to the refractory periods that apply to neural firing. In the context of productions, the refractory period ends when a different production is executed to change the contents of working memory. Refractoriness prevents the endless repetition of a production. The *specificity* of a production is a second principle of conflict resolution. Given two productions that match the contents of working memory, the production that is most specific takes precedence. Thus, if the condition term of Production PY is more specific than the condition term of Production PX, PY will apply before PX. Consider the following productions:

> PX.   IF the goal is to generate the plural of a noun,
> THEN say "noun + s."

> PY.   IF the goal is to generate the plural of knife,
> THEN say "KNIVES."

If the word *knife* is active in working memory and the goal is to generate a plural, both productions match. Production PY, however, is more specific and would be executed before PX.

A third principle of conflict resolution is the *strength* of the production, where strength is a function of the frequency of successful application of the production. A production takes a unit of time t_1 to be selected and another unit of time t_2 for testing and application. According to ACT*, t_2 is constant across productions, whereas t_1 varies with the strength of the production. Specifically, t_1 varies randomly from selection to selection with an expected value of a/s, where $s = strength$ and a is a constant. Furthermore, it is assumed that the distribution of t_1 is exponential. Thus, a specific production will take precedence over a general production (assuming both match) if and only if the selection time of the specific production is less than the selection time plus application time of the general production. Let t_{x1} and t_{x2} be the selection time and application time, respectively, for the general Production PX. Similarly, let t_{y1} and t_{y2} be the selection and application times for Production PY. Then PY will be selected if $t_{y1} < (t_{x1} + t_{x2})$.

The power of a production system is considerable. With such a system, it is possible to explain and simulate a wide range of cognitive phenomena. For example, it is possible to simulate the processes of letter and word recognition (Anderson, 1983), language processing (Anderson, Kline, & Lewis, 1977), and language acquisition (Anderson, 1983). Anderson (1983, pp. 56–69) also presented a production system underlying the manipulation of visual images, such as the mental rotation task used by Shepard and Metzler (1971). Additionally, phenomenon associated with lexical decision tasks (e.g., priming and the time course of priming) have been successfully modeled in ACT*. Another important cognitive phenomenon explained by ACT* is that of controlled and automatic processing (Schneider & Shiffrin, 1977; Shiffrin & Schneider, 1977). Performance on a variety of school-related tasks such as geometry (Anderson, 1982) and algebra (Lewis, 1981) is also predicted by ACT*.

Having established the basis for representing knowledge in declarative and production memory and the processes that operate on these knowledge structures, we now focus our attention on the processes regulating the formation of productions: the processes of learning cognitive skills.

Learning Processes

Widespread acceptance of any one definition of learning is unlikely in the near future. Nevertheless, it is helpful to begin this part of the discussion with some sort of working definition of learning. Bower and Hilgard (1984) offered the following definition:

Learning refers to the change in a subject's behavior or behavior potential to a given situation brought about by the subject's repeated experiences in that situation, provided that the behavior change cannot be explained on the basis of the subject's native response tendencies, maturation, or temporary states. (p.11)

The key operative components of this definition include (a) a change in behavior or behavior potential, (b) repeated experience, and (c) the exclusion of certain classes of behavior.

The first component of this definition allows that learning may be viewed either as the acquisition of behavior or as the acquisition of knowledge structures that can affect the potential of the learner to behave differently. The former view is acceptable to behavioristic theories, whereas the latter is consistent with cognitive theories. As a cognitive theory, ACT✱ emphasizes changes in knowledge (declarative and productions) as the basis of learning.

The exclusion of certain changes in behavior (or behavior potentiality) serves to further narrow our meaning of learning. Exclusion of maturation, native response tendencies, and temporary physical states (e.g., illness, fatigue, drugs, motivation) is a major component of this definition. These are the major competing explanations for changes in an organism's behavior and are typically ruled out before describing a change in performance as a result of learning. In many instances, however, experience interacts with these factors (e.g., imprinting and language acquisition).

The inclusion of the assertion that learning arises from repeated experience, whether direct, vicarious, or symbolic, is a component common to all theories of learning. Estimates on the amount of repeated practice necessary to learn vary, however. Simon (1980) estimated that the addition of a single chunk of information to declarative memory requires about 8 sec of processing. In contrast, Anderson (1982) estimated that at least 100 hr of practice is required to acquire a cognitive skill to a "reasonable degree of proficiency." To acquire expertise in the use of a cognitive skill, Norman (1982) estimated the lower bound at about "two and a half years of study, eight hours a day, five days a week, 50 weeks a year," approximately 5,000 hr. Most children acquire some degree of expertise in comprehending and speaking a language, reading, performing arithmetic, writing, and so on, in as much time. Hayes (1985) found that among recognized masters of music, art, and literature, 10 years of practice often preceded the masters' most productive years. As both Anderson (1982) and Norman (1982) noted, very little is known about what happens to skills over such periods of time. Repeated experience does not specify the sufficient conditions for learning (Bower & Hilgard, 1984). Recently, Dempster (1988) attempted to focus the attention of educational practitioners and researchers on the importance of the nature of practice.

As a general theory of learning, ACT✱ attempts to fill the gap in our understanding about what happens to cognitive skills practiced over long periods of time and to describe the basic processes that are responsible for learning. According to ACT*, the learning of a cognitive skill is a matter of transforming declarative knowledge into procedural knowledge. At a descriptive level, ACT* corresponds to the three stages of learning motor skills that were explicated by Fitts (1964). Following some initial instruction or observation of a skill, the learner is usually capable of generating a crude approximation of the target skill. Performance is usually accompanied by verbal mediation and many errors. In ACT*, this phase of the learning process is referred to as the *declarative stage*. With continued practice, errors are gradually eliminated, and the verbal mediation once needed to guide performance begins to fade. Additionally, there is a significant speedup of performance. This marked change in performance is referred to as the *knowledge compilation stage*. To an untrained observer, it might appear that learning is complete at this point. Nothing could be further from the truth. As we will see, performance of the skill continues to improve with practice. This latter stage of learning, referred to as the *procedural stage*, may continue throughout an individual's life. Execution of the skill continues to speed up, albeit gradually, and the skill continues to be applied in a much more appropriate fashion with greater precision. In sum, learning is the process of converting declarative knowledge into productions and the tuning of those productions over time.

Although there would be little disagreement that the acquisition of most skills follows this pattern, these phenomena of skill acquisition have defied theoretical analysis (Anderson, 1982; Norman, 1980). The remainder of this chapter describes the way in which ACT* accounts for these phenomena and concludes with a discussion of how we might begin to view learning disabilities in the context of a theory of learning.

Declarative stage.   ACT* asserts that the learning of a skill begins with encoding facts (propositions) about the skill. Consider the first few steps of the instructions adapted from E. D. Gagné (1985) for adding fractions:

1. Find the least common denominator.

2. Divide the denominator of the first fraction into the least common denominator.

3. Multiply the quotient from Step 2 by the numerator of the first fraction.

4. Write the product from Step 3 above a line and the least common denominator below that line.

5. Repeat Steps 2–4 for the second fraction.

The learner cannot acquire productions from these instructions in a direct fashion. Rather, the instructions must first be encoded as a set of declarative facts. A propositional network for these instructions is presented in Figure 7–5.

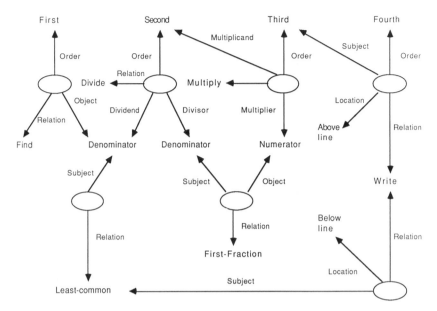

Figure 7–5. A propositional network for adding fractions. Adapted from *The Cognitive Psychology of School Learning* (p. 120) by E. D. Gagné. Copyright 1985 by Ellen D. Gagné. Reprinted by permission of HarperCollins Publishers.

Furthermore, the propositional network is not capable of generating behavior. Rather, the student must *translate* each proposition into an action sequence using existing domain-specific and general-purpose productions. Examples of the action sequences that might be translated from the first four instructions are presented in Table 7–2.

Suppose the problem presented for practice was ½ + ⅓. To begin solving this problem, the student must activate the first proposition. Rehearsing or rereading the instruction will maintain the proposition in working memory. As long as the proposition is active in working memory, existing domain-specific and general-purpose productions are matched to the elements of the proposition. Examples of domain-specific productions include productions for recognizing patterns that represent fractions, productions for adding and multiplying more than two digits, and productions for finding a least common denominator. Equally important is the domain-specific declarative knowledge about number facts ($2 \times 3 = 6$, $⁶\!/_3 = 2$, $2 + 4 = 6$) and mathematical concepts (e.g., part–whole, numerator, denominator, factors). Examples of some general-purpose productions that are used to guide performance during the first attempts to perform the skill might include productions for tagging propositions according to a temporal sequence, rehearsal productions for keeping a proposition active in working memory, and productions for writing digits. Knowledge of the concepts above and below are also required.

TABLE 7–2
Interpretation of the Declarative Network
for Adding Fractions Into Productions

P1.　　IF　the goal is to add fractions
　　　　　　and there are two fractions,
　　　THEN　the subgoal is to find the least common denominator.

P2.　　IF　the goal is to add fractions
　　　　　　and there are two fractions
　　　　　　and the least common denominator is known,
　　　THEN　divide the denominator of the first fraction into the least
　　　　　　common denominator.

P3.　　IF　the goal is to add fractions
　　　　　　and there are two fractions
　　　　　　and the quotient of Step 2 is known,
　　　THEN　multiply the numerator of the first fraction by the quotient from
　　　　　　Step 2.

P4.　　IF　the goal is to add fractions
　　　　　　and there are two fractions
　　　　　　and the product from Step 3 is known
　　　　　　and the least common denominator is known,
　　　THEN　write Result 2 above a line
　　　　　　and write the least common denominator below that line.

Adapted from *The Cognitive Psychology of School Learning* (p. 121) by E. D. Gagné. Copyright 1985 by Ellen D. Gagné. Adapted by permission of HarperCollins Publishers.

The first statement instructs the student to find a least common denominator. For this example, assume that this production already exists in long-term memory as Production P5 (not shown). Accordingly, the production applies and is executed. The application of P5 would result in assigning the value of 6 to the common denominator. Assuming that the value of the least common denominator is active in working memory, the second statement will be encoded as divide 2 into 6. If the least common denominator is not active in working memory, the value must be recalculated before the second step can be successfully completed. Successful completion of the second step depends on the accurate retrieval of a number fact from declarative memory. Assuming correct retrieval, the value 3 is added to working memory. Successful performance of the third step requires the student to maintain the result obtained in Step 2 active in working memory, activate a representation of the numerator of the first fraction, and then multiply the two values. This new variable created in working memory has a value of 3. Finally, the proposition encoded as Step 4 activates a general-purpose writing production that places the result of Step 3 above a line and the result of Step 1 below a line. Of course, if these results were not maintained in an active state, each must be recalculated.

After reading this description, it should be clear that the declarative stage of learning resembles the performance of a novice. Part of the difficulty of learning in this stage arises from the considerable burden imposed on the working memory system. Propositions must be encoded, maintained in an active state via rehearsal, and translated into an action sequence. Part of the difficulty may also be attributed to the inadequacy of the instructions themselves. For example, the instructions do not inform the student to write down or remember certain intermediate results. Thus, when the results are called for, they may have to be recalculated. Then, the student must remember what step he or she was working on when the result was called for. As a result, additional demands are placed on the working memory system. Now, imagine trying to follow these instructions if the prerequisite knowledge (e.g., finding a common denominator) was not available. Prerequisite declarative networks and production systems that are weak in strength will also cause difficulties during the initial stages of skill acquisition.

Knowledge compilation.   Knowledge compilation is a transitional stage in the learning process that results in the transformation of declarative knowledge into productions that apply the knowledge directly. In other words, knowledge about the skill can be applied without first having to translate it. The analogy of running a computer program is often used to describe the difference between the application of declarative and procedural knowledge. When high-level computer languages (e.g., FORTRAN, PASCAL) are used to write a program, the instructions in the program must first be translated into a form (machine language) that can be acted upon by the central processing unit. In other words, each time the program is executed, it must first be translated. The process of translating from a high-level language to machine language is called compilation. Once the program is running as intended by the programmer, it is possible to store the program in compiled form. Now, when the program is executed, it bypasses the interpretive or translation stage. Program execution requires less time and fewer resources. In human learning, unlike computer programming, knowledge compilation is a gradual process that occurs as a result of practice. In ACT*, the two subprocesses responsible for knowledge compilation are *composition* and *proceduralization*.

Composition is the process by which a sequence of productions that follow each other are collapsed into a single production that has the same effect. Thus, composition reduces the number of productions that must be matched and executed to carry out a task. Notice that Productions P2 and P3 always occur in sequence. ACT* predicts that these productions, with practice, will be collapsed into fewer productions. For example, Productions 2 and 3 in Table 7–2 could be composed into the following production:

P6.   IF the goal is to add fractions
         and there are two fractions to add
         and the least common denominator is known,
    THEN write the least common denominator below a line
         and divide the denominator of the first fraction
         into the least common denominator to get Result 1
         and write the product of Result 1 and the numerator
         of the first fraction above a line.

The effects of this composition would be a reduction in the amount of time required to perform these operations and a reduction of the demands placed on working memory. Composition is responsible for the speedup and elimination of piecemeal application of the skill.

Proceduralization is the process responsible for reducing the number of clauses in the condition of a production. Again, there is a reduction in demands placed on the working memory that is necessary to match the conditions of a production. This economy can be accomplished by creating a hierarchy of subgoals. Consider Productions P7 and P8 given below:

P7.   IF the goal is to iterate through the fractions
         and the last fraction has not been processed,
    THEN the subgoal is to convert a fraction.

P8.   IF the goal is to convert a fraction,
    THEN write the least common denominator below that line
         and divide the denominator of the first fraction into
         the least common denominator to get Result 1.
         and write the product of Result 1 and the numerator of
         the first fraction above the line
         and mark the fraction as processed
         and POP the goal.

Compare Production P8 with Production P6. The action sequence is essentially identical for both productions; however, the conditions of each production are substantially different. For Production P6 to apply, three propositions must be active in working memory. In contrast, P8 requires that only one proposition be active in working memory for the production to apply. The reduction in the number of conditions that must be matched for P8 to apply is accomplished by creating other productions, such as P7, that has the goal of iterating through the fractions of a problem and testing for the presence of another fraction to process. Production P7, of course, was triggered by a production that calculates a least common denominator and sets the subgoal of iterating through a series of fractions. The reduction in the demands placed on working memory is accompanied by a reduction and eventual elimination of verbal rehearsal during the performance of a skill. Thus, the fading of verbal rehearsal during practice is evidence that proceduralization is under way.

Procedural stage.   Observations of learning a complex skill indicate that learning continues even after a skill has been compiled into a task-specific procedure. An experiment by Neves and Anderson (1981) on the learning of a complex reasoning task provides an example of this phenomenon. The reasoning task involved a novel artificial proof system with nine postulates. Each proof consisted of 10 lines, and the student's task was to justify each line of the proof. Each line could be justified by information that was given or by information that was derived from previous lines by application of one of the postulates. The interesting twist to this investigation was that only the current line of the proof could be seen on a computer monitor; however, the subject could request to see previous lines, givens, or postulates. Thus, the experimenters were able to trace the number of requests for information, the interval of time between each request, and the total time taken for each proof. The number of requests provides a rough index of the number of productions that were applied, and the interval of time between each request provides an index of the speed of the individual productions.

The results of Neves and Anderson's (1981) experiment are presented in Figure 7–6. Note that there were reductions in the total amount of time required to solve the problems, the number of steps (productions) that were required to solve the problems, and the time per step. Furthermore, all three of these performance variables were found to exhibit the same lawful relationship with the amount of practice—a *power law*. That is, when plotted on a log–log scale, the relationship between performance and practice approximates a straight line that changes as a function of practice. Performance on a wide variety of tasks in other domains such as addition (Blackburn, cited in Crossman, 1959), reading (Kolers, 1975), perceptual–motor skills (Snoddy, cited in Newell & Rosenbloom, 1981), pattern recognition (Neisser, Novick, & Lazar, 1963), memory (Anderson, cited in Newell & Rosenbloom, 1981), and the use of computer interfaces (Card, English, & Burr, cited in Newell & Rosenbloom, 1981) also exhibit the same lawful relationship with practice.

The implication of this law is that performance will always improve with practice, no matter how much prior practice one has received. The amount of improvement, however, is gradual. ACT✳ postulates three different learning mechanisms that account for the continued gradual improvement of performance following compilation: *generalization, discrimination,* and *strengthening.*

Generalization is a process that modifies the conditions of a production in such a way that the production applies in a broader range of situations. Generalization accounts for the ability to perform successfully in novel situations. For example, suppose that a child has compiled the following productions to form the plurals of objects:

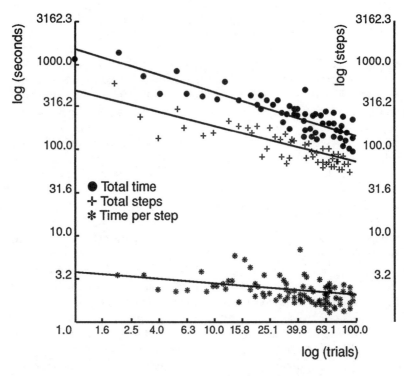

Figure 7-6. Results of Neves and Anderson's (1981) experiment showing the power law of practice. From "Knowledge Compilation: Mechanisms for the Automatization of Cognitive Skills" by D. M. Neves and J. R. Anderson in *Cognitive Skills and Their Acquisition* (p. 76) by J. R. Anderson (ed.), 1981, Hillsdale, NJ: Erlbaum.

P1.   IF the goal is to generate the plural of *marble,*
          THEN say "marbles."

P2.   IF the goal is to generate the plural of *boat,*
          THEN say "boats."

Generalization is itself the result of a production that produces a metasearch of the conditions of other productions. When overlap in the conditions of two productions is detected, a new production is formed. In the case of P1 and P2, generalization is accomplished by creating the following production:

P3.   IF the goal is to generate the plural of LVobject,
          THEN say "LVobject + s."

Notice that generalization was accomplished by creating a local variable (LVobject) in place of a specific object. The new production, P3, is a generalization of P1 and P2 in the sense that it applies to a greater range of situations than does either P1 or P2. Interestingly, ACT✳ postulates that generalization does not eliminate P1 and P2; rather, they coexist in production memory with P3.

Discrimination is a process that modifies the conditions of a production in such a way that the production is restricted to a more limited range of situations. Under certain conditions, discrimination may also result in learning a new action (response). Like generalization, the discrimination process arises from the application of a production that compares the values of the variables in the correct and incorrect application of the production.

Suppose that after forming the generalization of P3, a child generates "knifes" as the plural of *knife*. Subsequently, the child is informed that his or her response is incorrect. The student is informed that *knives* is the plural of *knife*. The discrimination production compares the values of the variable, LVobject, from the correct and incorrect applications. These two values are examined for features that occur in only one of the values of the variable. The result of the comparison process is the addition of another test to the condition of Production P3. The condition of the production now tests for the presence of the suspected feature. In addition to a restrictive condition, the discriminated production will require the creation of a new response. If successful, the new production will be strengthened. For the sake of brevity, let us assume that the word ending is suspected as a critical feature and a test is constructed and added to the condition of P3 to create P4:

P4.   IF the goal is to generate the plural of LVobject, and
        LVobject = LVstring + fe
      THEN say "LVstring + ves."

Also, notice that it was necessary to create a new response for this production. The creation of the new response (say "LVstring + ves") is called an *action discrimination*, whereas the addition of a more restrictive condition ("and LVobject = LVstring + fe") is called a *condition discrimination*. The condition discrimination will restrict the misapplication of P3. Production P4 is certainly a refinement over P3, and it will handle other nouns such as *wife*, but what about *thief* and *wolf*? It is obvious that the condition of P4 is still too general and that further condition discrimination is necessary. One interesting implication of ACT✳ is that action discriminations are formed only when feedback is obtained about the correct action. When feedback is limited to information that an action is incorrect, the response is not altered. Only condition discriminations can be formed with this type of feedback. As with productions arising from the generalization process, productions arising from the discrimination process coexist with the productions from which they were constructed.

Strengthening processes, as the name implies, are responsible for increasing the strength of productions, but they are also responsible for reducing the strength of productions. According to ACT✳, when a production applies successfully, the strength of that production increases in an additive fashion. In contrast, the unsuccessful application of a production reduces the strength of that production in a multiplicative fashion. For example, assume that the strength of a production is 1 when it is created. Each successful application strengthens that production by 1; however, if the production fails, its strength is reduced by 25%. This relationship implies that the failure of a production has a stronger effect on production strength than does the success of a production. Furthermore, ACT* assumes that these strength adjustments (increases and decreases) apply to all generalizations of the production that was executed. This means that each time P1 and P2 are successfully applied, P3 is strengthened. Accordingly, the generalized production, P3, will eventually accrue greater strength than P1 or P2. In this way, generalized productions eventually gain control over behavior.

In sum, ACT* postulates that the acquisition of a novel skill begins with encoding action sequences as propositions (i.e., in declarative form). To perform the skill, the individual must translate the actions described by the propositions. With practice, the declarative representation of the skill is compiled into a procedural form that does not require interpretation. The processes of composition and proceduralization are postulated as the mechanisms underlying compilation. Once a skill has been compiled into a production, learning continues indefinitely. Procedures are tuned according to the principles of generalization, discrimination, and strengthening.

WHAT ARE THE IMPLICATIONS OF THE MODEL FOR LEARNING DISABILITIES?

One primary advantage of ACT* is that it offers the researcher and the practitioner a precise language for talking about (a) the structure of the learner's knowledge, (b) the manner in which knowledge is acquired and refined, and (c) the manner in which the learner regulates the use of knowledge. The benefits of this precise lexicon are manifold. Three of these dimensions are relevant to the field of learning disabilities: (a) diagnosis of learning disabilities, (b) remediation of learning disabilities, and (c) theory development.

Diagnosis

Given the specificity of the language in ACT*, a description of a child's learning disability should be equally precise. Labels and generalizations about a particular child are to be avoided. Rather, the diagnosis is based on the identification of missing, weak, or erroneous knowledge structures in the declarative and/or production memory system. Attention should also be focused on the working memory system as it is directly involved in the process of composition, generalization, and discrimination.

Analysis of a learner's declarative knowledge structure is critical for the design of effective instruction. This problem is appropriately described by the iceberg metaphor of learning and teaching used by Norman (1982). According to this metaphor, all that the teacher may observe is the student's behavior (the tip of the iceberg). The tip of the iceberg, however, does not reflect what is under the surface of the water. Effective instruction is determined by what is below the surface. Thus, the teacher must ascertain the knowledge structures underlying the student's performance. All the student can observe is the materials and events of the instructional episode (the tip of the iceberg). The student, however, must activate some underlying structure to understand the instructional episode. A major problem, of course, is that many possible knowledge structures can be constructed to fit the constraints of the material the student observes, providing ample opportunity for the formation of incorrect hypotheses.

Unfortunately, methods used to evaluate the structure of a learner's knowledge are not standardized. Furthermore, a detailed analysis of that learner's knowledge structure related to a specific task may require many hours, more time than that afforded to standardized testing. Such an analysis requires asking many who, what, when, where, and why questions about the topics related to instruction (Norman, 1982). One promising approach to this analysis is the procedure of concept mapping described by Novak and Gowin (1984). Concept mapping is a procedure that requires the student to construct a diagram of his or her knowledge about concepts, a diagram that closely resembles the propositional networks described earlier. If desired, a scoring procedure may be applied to each student's concept map. An important result of this procedure is that it provides the teacher with a glimpse of the iceberg beneath the surface.

We also need to rethink our criteria for successful performance. Consider the following definition of mastery for learning the basic addition facts: The learner will respond with a probability of a correct response greater than or equal to .98 and median solution latency less than or equal to 2 sec. The first component of this definition, proportion correct, is a traditional criteria for mastery. It is also the dimension of performance measured by standardized tests. When a student performs poorly on such tests, it is important to determine which operations the student cannot perform and the efficiency of operations that are performed correctly. Standardized testing does not separate these two factors. One solution to this problem is a chronometric (time-based) evaluation of a student's performance. Chronometric data of this nature can be useful for identifying the strength of the information in declarative memory. Other uses of mental chronometry in the study of learning disabilities have been discussed by Jensen (1987).

Many of the comments above also apply to the analysis of procedural knowledge. Instruction is usually sequenced with the assumption that certain prerequisite skills exist and will be used at the appropriate time. In the case of children identified as learning disabled, this assumption is not always tenable. As noted earlier, skill acquisition depends on the existence of many domain-specific and general-purpose productions. Tuning skills through generalization and discrimination also depends on the existence of certain productions. Techniques for assessing procedural knowledge are in the early stage of development (Card, Moran, & Newell, 1983; Kieras & Polson, 1985). Part of the problem is that few tasks have been analyzed into production systems. In the absence of more formal methods, verbal protocols serve a useful purpose for understanding the flow of control within the student as he or she learns the skill. In the think-aloud procedure, the student is presented with a specific task and instructed to speak his or her thoughts while performing the task. Recording students' protocols on video- or audiotape provides a permanent record and permits a fine-grained analysis of the qualitative nature of the steps taken to perform the task.

Given the evidence that learning continues after declarative knowledge has been compiled into a production system, some set of criteria should also be established to ensure that procedural learning is occurring. As with addition facts, systematic practice of cognitive skills is rarely provided past the point of correct responding. Again, some criteria for the automaticity of cognitive skills needs to be developed. Indeed, Sternberg and Wagner (1982) presented a compelling case that the failure to automatize certain skills is a distinguishing feature of learning disabilities. Computer-based tasks, similar to the one used by Neves and Anderson (1981), could be developed in other skill domains to assess the automaticity of skill performance. Variables such as number of steps, time per step, total time, and number and nature of errors, are of central importance in the analysis of procedural learning. Without these kinds of data, we deprive ourselves of a glimpse of the iceberg under the surface that is necessary to design effective interventions and the baseline that is needed to evaluate the effects of those interventions.

Assessment of the working memory system is also of central importance in the diagnosis of learning problems. Recall that ACT* defines working memory as a temporary memory system for holding information retrieved from long-term memory, the results of encoding operations, and the actions of productions in an accessible state (i.e., usable form). Additionally, the processes of composition, generalization, and discrimination are carried by the working memory system.

It is well known that there are individual differences in the capacity of working memory (Case, Kurland, & Goldberg, 1982; Dempster, 1985) that account for a substantial portion of the variance in the performance of many intellectual tasks such as reading (Daneman & Carpenter, 1980; Perfetti & Lesgold, 1977) and mathematics (Brainerd, 1983; Cooney & Swanson, in press). Case et al., (1982) argued that the total capacity of working memory is constant and invariant with age. The capacity for storage of information is viewed as a function of the efficiency of processing operations. For example, a student who attempts to perform a task with weak or inefficient productions will devote more of his or her total capacity for processing than a student who has acquired more finely tuned productions. Accordingly, the student with the more finely tuned (automatized) productions will have greater capacity available for the storage of information. This advantage would be evident in the speed of composing productions and the processes of generalization and discrimination. It follows that educational interventions would have to be designed with this limitation in mind.

Tasks designed to measure the capacity of the working memory system have undergone considerable refinement over the last decade. The simplest measure of working memory capacity, the digit span, is already a component on standardized tests of intelligence (e.g., the Wechsler Intelligence Scale for Children–Revised). Other measures have been designed to measure the capacity of the system with respect to the trade-off between storage and processing operations (see Baddeley, 1986; Case et al., 1982). In one variant of the working memory task (see Daneman, 1982), students are asked to read a series of unrelated sentences, which increase in number from trial to trial, and to remember the final word of each sentence. Subsequently, students are asked a question about one of the sentences to ensure that comprehension has occurred, and then to recall the final words of each sentence. A measure of working memory is obtained by counting the maximum number of final words correctly recalled, in order, conditional upon giving a correct response to the comprehension question. The importance of this measure in the diagnosis of learning disabilities was emphasized in a recent experiment by Swanson, Cochran, and Ewers (1990), who found that learning disabled children may be distinguished by their performance on tasks designed to measure working memory processes. Moreover, their findings indicated that learning disabled children's performance on the working memory task was related to achievement in reading, mathematics, and spelling. At the present time, it is not known if instruction can be designed to accommodate individual differences in working memory. Evidence concerning the effects of training on working memory capacity is equivocal (Dempster, 1985). Thus, insofar as the measure provides a means for identifying children who are likely to experience difficulty learning, it would be prudent in the meantime to identify any working memory capacity limitations.

Remediation

If we are to be faithful to our model of learning, techniques for remediating a learning disability must be derived from procedures that are known to influence the acquisition and refinement of declarative and procedural knowledge and the processes regulating the use of procedural and declarative knowledge. Viewing intellectual skills in terms of production systems encourages the specification of a skill in terms of very precise action sequences and the conditions in which such sequences are appropriate. The success of strategies such as the mnemonic keyword method (Scruggs, Mastropieri, & Levin, 1987), self-questioning techniques (Wong & Sawatsky, 1984), self-instructional skills (Meichenbaum, 1984), and comprehension monitoring (Palincsar & Brown, 1984) with low-achieving students is due in part to the precise specification of the action sequences (the skills) and in part to a set of conditions that specify the goal of the skill and the situations in which it is appropriate to use the skill. All too often, it is the precise specification of the condition element of the skill that is the missing ingredient of instruction. In fact, the failures of strategy instruction are directly attributed to the lack of this kind of information (Pressley, Goodchild, Fleet, Zajchowski, & Evans, 1986).

Another reason that instruction is often inadequate is that the teacher does not have a good understanding of the student's flow of control (Anderson, 1982). The instructions for adding fractions discussed earlier implicity assume that the learner can and will maintain all of the intermediate results in working memory; however, the learner has no way of knowing when and how the intermediate results will be used. The instructions are poor because they do not convey the goal of each step or the flow of control among the steps. Although this seems to be conventional wisdom, the data suggest otherwise. In one text that I examined, the total instruction on reducing fractions was the expression, $\frac{4}{6} = \frac{2}{3}$. Anderson (1983) noted a similar problem with geometry instruction. In short, much improvement may be gained by paying more attention to the declarative stage of learning mathematics. The action sequences and the conditions for those action sequences must be clearly specified. Alternatives to the linear form of instruction should also be examined. One promising approach was reported by Smith and Goodman (1984). As mentioned earlier, these investigators compared performance of subjects using instructions that were arranged in a linear format with that of subjects using the same set of instructions that were arranged in a hierarchical format and embellished with explanatory information. Subjects who received the hierarchical instructions exhibited better comprehension of the instructions and performance on the electronic circuit assembly task than their counterparts who received linear instructions.

It is also important to design practice materials that ensure the strengthening of all declarative and procedural knowledge related to a particular skill. Basic research on children's arithmetic has clearly demonstrated that basic arithmetic facts vary in their strength: some facts are retrieved faster and are less susceptible to interference than others (Campbell, 1987; Campbell & Graham, 1985). The culprit, in my view, is inadequate practice. Some facts get more repetition than others. Similarly, practice of mathematical skills that involve many different productions does not always ensure that all productions receive adequate practice. Upon careful inspection of the production system for adding multidigit numbers in Table 7–1, it is clear that some productions will be used more frequently that others, depending on the nature of the problems that are presented for practice. Practice must take into consideration all of the productions in the system and ensure that they are adequately strengthened.

Evidence concerning the effects of practice designed to automatize skills related to reading is equally encouraging. For example, Beck, Perfetti, and McKeown (1982) examined the effects of an intensive long-term (5-month) vocabulary training program on reading processes. The results of their investigation indicated that the instructional program accounted for significant decreases in the response latencies on lexical decision and sentence verification tasks and a significant increase in scores on a standardized vocabulary test. There was also evidence that the vocabulary practice program increased reading comprehension when the passage contained the practiced words.

The virtue of practicing productions and the retrieval of declarative information after they have been learned should not be underestimated. Although evidence is clear that performance continues to improve past this point, many educators are content to move on to new skills once successful performance occurs. The primary arguments against extended practice I have heard from classroom teachers are that it is an overworked theme in education, a boring activity that children find aversive, and that the number of topics that must be presented in a given unit of instructional time preclude allocating the time necessary for extended practice.

The argument that practice is an overworked theme or a simplified solution is not supported by the literature. Dempster's (1988) review of this literature indicated that the most important manipulations of the practice variable (spaced presentations) is not well understood by practitioners and researchers. Moreover, recommendations contrary to the experimental literature on practice are being disseminated. This revelation is all the more reason for concern about designing instruction with appropriate conditions for practice.

Although I have never found evidence that practice, in the form of drills, for example, is more boring or aversive than other forms of instruction, it is a common complaint that arises in my discussions with teachers about the issue. Our views of practice, however, need not be confined to drills. Indeed, we must explore more creative avenues for practice that mitigate boredom and at the same time encourage the strengthening of important declarative and procedural knowledge. Dempster (1988) suggested that judiciously spaced practice trials may be one solution to this problem. In general, two spaced presentations of the same material is about twice as effective as two massed presentations. Spaced presentation of the same material has also been found to have a stronger effect on learning than variable encoding (e.g., presenting the to-be-learned item in two different contexts; Dempster, 1987).

Unfortunately, this powerful principle is rarely exploited in the classroom. The third argument, that there are too many topics to cover, may be one reason that spaced presentation of material is not a part of the classroom routine. With these constraints imposed on the teacher, it would indeed be difficult to achieve the conditions of spaced practice. Accordingly, curriculum developers and administrators must become aware of this important aspect of the learning process and work with teachers to remove the barriers to spaced practice. Where the barrier may not exist (e.g., the resource classroom), we must act quickly to implement this important principle.

Theory Construction

The role of theory in the field of learning disabilities is controversial. Researchers and practitioners are often characterized as being at opposite ends of the continuum concerning the role of theory. A special issue of the *Journal of Learning Disabilities* (Swanson, 1988a, 1988b) reflects these extreme positions and the many other viewpoints in between. The distinction between theoretically driven and atheoretically driven approaches in research and practice, however, is unnecessary and untenable. At a global level of analysis, the activities of the various factions in the field are more similar than dissimilar. The primary concern is to find solutions to problems of the learning disabled child. Observations are made, and a solution to the problem is proposed. According to Popper (1963), a noted philosopher of science, observation is always selective: "It [observation] needs a chosen object, a definite task, an interest, a point of view, a problem" (p. 46). Thus, problems determine what observations are made. Furthermore, Popper asserted that a proposed solution to a problem is in fact a theory, and that what distinguishes a scientific theory from a nonscientific theory is the *principle of refutability*. This means that a prediction derived from theory must be capable of being falsified, and thus refute the theory that generated the prediction. Thus, the value of our proposed solutions to (theories about) problems of the learning disabled is determined by passing the test of refutability.

ACT* is a solution proposed to answer the "epistemological question: How does structured cognition emerge?" (Anderson, 1987, p. 206). As a theory, it passes the test of refutability. For example, ACT* makes many potentially refutable predictions concerning generalization and discrimination (Anderson, 1983), the transfer (both positive and negative) of cognitive skills between two situations (Singley & Anderson, 1985), and the nature of the errors made during the process of learning a skill (Anderson & Jeffries, 1985). If ACT* is an accurate description of the learning process and of the regulation of cognitive activity, then predictions concerning the diagnosis and prescription for remediations generated from the theory should improve the learning disabled child's performance of cognitive skills. If learning disabled children's performance is at variance with the predictions of ACT*, then we have much to gain in refining a theory of the learning process and the regulation of cognition, in other words, in finding solutions to the learning problems of our children.

REFERENCES

Adelson, B. (1981). Problem solving and the development of abstract categories in programming. *Memory and Cognition, 9*, 422–433.

Anderson, J. R. (1974). Retrieval of propositional information from long-term memory. *Cognitive Psychology, 6*, 451–474.

Anderson, J. R. (1976). *Language memory and thought*. Hillsdale, NJ: Erlbaum.

Anderson, J. R. (1981). *Cognitive skills and their acquisition* (pp. xi–xiii). Hillsdale, NJ: Erlbaum.

Anderson, J. R. (1982). Acquisition of cognitive skill. *Psychological Review, 89*, 369–406.

Anderson, J. R. (1983). *The architecture of cognition*. Cambridge, MA: Harvard University Press.

Anderson, J. R. (1985). *Cognitive psychology and its implications* (2nd ed.). San Francisco: W. H. Freeman.

Anderson, J. R. (1987). Skill acquisition: Compilation of weak-method problem solutions. *Psychological Review, 94*, 192–210.

Anderson, J. R., & Bower, G. H. (1972). Configural properties in sentence memory. *Journal of Verbal Learning and Verbal Behavior, 11*, 594–605.

Anderson, J. R., & Jeffries, R. (1985). Novice LISP errors: Undetected losses of information from working memory. *International Journal of Man–Machine Studies, 22*, 403–423.

Anderson, J. R., Kline, P., & Lewis, C. (1977). A production system model for language processing. In P. Carpenter & M. Just (Eds.), *Cognitive processes in comprehension* (pp. 271–311). Hillsdale, NJ: Erlbaum.

Ashcraft, M. H., & Fierman, B. A. (1982). Mental addition in third, fourth, and sixth graders. *Journal of Experimental Child Psychology, 33*, 216–234.

Baddeley, A. (1986). *Working memory*. Oxford, England: Clarendon Press.

Baggett, P. (1975). Memory for explicit and implicit information in picture stories. *Journal of Verbal Learning and Verbal Behavior, 14*, 538–548.

Bandura, A. (1977). *Social learning theory*. New York: Prentice-Hall.

Bandura, A. (1986). *Social foundations of thought and action: A social cognitive theory*. New York: Prentice-Hall.

Bartlett, F. C. (1932). *Remembering*. Cambridge, England: Cambridge University Press.

Beck, I. L., Perfetti, C. A., & McKeown, M. G. (1982). Effects of long-term vocabulary instruction on lexical access and reading comprehension. *Journal of Educational Psychology, 74*, 506–521.

Bower, G. H., & Hilgard, E. R. (1984). *Theories of learning* (5th ed.). New York: Prentice-Hall.

Brainerd, C. J. (1983). Young children's arithmetic errors: A working memory analysis. *Child Development, 54*, 812–830.

Bransford, J. D., Barclay, J. R., & Franks, J. J. (1972). Sentence memory: A constructive versus interpretive approach. *Cognitive Psychology, 3*, 193–209.

Bransford, J. D., & Franks, J. J. (1971). The abstraction of linguistic ideas. *Cognitive Psychology, 2,* 331–350.

Campbell, J. I. D. (1987). Network interference and mental multiplication. *Journal of Experimental Psychology: Learning, Memory, and Cognition, 13,* 109–123.

Campbell, J. I. D., & Graham, D. J. (1985). Mental multiplication skill: Structure, process, and acquisition. *Canadian Journal of Psychology, 39,* 338–366.

Card, S. K., Moran, T. P., & Newell, A. (1983). *The psychology of human–computer interaction.* Hillsdale, NJ: Erlbaum.

Case, R., Kurland, D. M., & Goldberg, J. (1982). Operational efficiency and the growth of short-term memory span. *Journal of Experimental Child Psychology, 33,* 386–404.

Chi, M. T. H., Feltovich, P. J., & Glaser, R. (1981). Categorization and representation of physics problems by experts and novices. *Cognitive Science, 5,* 121–152.

Chomsky, N. (1980). Rules and representations. *Behavioral and Brain Sciences, 3,* 1–62.

Collins, A. M., & Loftus, E. F. (1975). A spreading activation theory of semantic processing. *Psychological Review, 82,* 407–428.

Collins, A. M., & Quillian, M. R. (1969). Retrieval time from semantic memory. *Journal of Verbal Learning and Verbal Behavior, 8,* 240–247.

Conrad, C. (1972). Cognitive economy in semantic memory. *Journal of Experimental Psychology, 92,* 149–154.

Cooney, J. B., & Swanson, H. L. (in press). Individual differences in memory for mathematical story problems: Memory span and problem perception. *Journal of Educational Psychology.*

Cooney, J. B., Swanson, H. L., & Ladd, S. F. (1988). Acquisition of mental multiplication skill: Evidence for the transition between retrieval and counting strategies. *Cognition and Instruction, 5,* 323–345.

Crossman, E. R. F. W. (1959). A theory of the acquisition of speed-skill. *Ergonomics, 2,* 153–166.

Daneman, M. (1982). The measurement of reading comprehension: How not to trade construct validity for predictive power. *Intelligence, 6,* 331–345.

Daneman, M., & Carpenter, P. A. (1980). Individual differences in working memory and reading. *Journal of Verbal Learning and Verbal Behavior, 19,* 450–466.

Dempster, F. N. (1985). Short-term memory development in childhood and adolescence. In C. J. Brainerd & M. Pressley (Eds.), *Basic processes in memory development: Progress in cognitive development research* (pp. 209–248). New York: Springer-Verlag.

Dempster, F. N. (1987). Effects of variable encoding and spaced presentation on vocabulary learning. *Journal of Educational Psychology, 79,* 162–170.

Dempster, F. N. (1988). The spacing effect: A case study in the failure to apply the results of psychological research. *American Psychologist, 43,* 627–634.

Estes, W. K. (1975). The state of the field: General problems and issues of theory and metatheory. In W. K. Estes (Ed.), *Handbook of learning and cognitive processes* (Vol. 1, pp. 1–24). Hillsdale, NJ: Erlbaum.

Feigenbaum, E. A., & Feldman, J. (1963). *Computers and thought.* New York: McGraw-Hill.

Fitts, P. M. (1964). Perceptual–motor skill learning. In A. W. Melton (Ed.), *Categories of human learning* (pp. 243–285). New York: Academic Press.

Foss, D. J., & Harwood, D. A. (1975). Memory for sentences: Implications for human associative memory. *Journal of*

Verbal Learning and Verbal Behavior, *14*, 1–16.

Gagné, E. D. (1985). *The cognitive psychology of school learning*. Boston, MA: Little Brown.

Gagné, R. M. (1985). *The conditions of learning and theory of instruction* (4th ed.). New York: Holt, Rinehart and Winston.

Goldman, S. R., Pellegrino, J. W., & Mertz, D. L. (1988). Extended practice of basic addition facts: Strategy changes in learning-disabled students. *Cognition and Instruction, 5,* 223–265.

Greeno, J. G. (1980). Psychology of learning, 1960–1980: One participant's observations. *American Psychologist, 35,* 713–728.

Gregg, L. W., & Steinberg, E. R. (Eds.). (1980). *Cognitive processes in writing*. Hillsdale, NJ: Erlbaum.

Hayes, J. R. (1985). Three general problems in teaching general skills. In S. F. Chipman, J. W. Segal, & R. Glaser (Eds.), *Thinking and learning skills: Vol. 2. Research and open questions* (pp. 391–405). Hillsdale, NJ: Erlbaum.

Heller, J. I., & Reif, F. (1984). Prescribing effective human problem-solving processes: Problem description in physics. *Cognition and Instruction, 1,* 177–216.

Hull, C. L. (1935). The conflicting psychologies of learning—A way out. *Psychological Review, 42,* 491–516.

Hull, C. L. (1943). *Principles of behavior*. New York: Appleton-Century-Crofts.

Jeffries, R., Turner, A. A., Polson, P. G., & Atwood, M. E. (1981). The processes involved in designing software. In J. R. Anderson (Ed.), *Cognitive skills and their acquisition* (pp. 255–283). Hillsdale, NJ: Erlbaum.

Jensen, A. R. (1987). Mental chronometry in the study of learning disabilities. *Mental Retardation and Learning Disability Bulletin, 15*(2), 67–88.

Keenan, J. M., & Kintsch, W. (1974). The identification of explicitly and implicitly presented information. In W. Kintsch (Ed.), *The representation of meaning in memory* (pp. 153–176). Hillsdale, NJ: Erlbaum.

Kieras, D. E., & Polson, P. G. (1985). An approach to the formal analysis of user complexity. *International Journal of Man–Machine Studies, 22,* 365–394.

Kintsch, W. (1977). *Memory and cognition*. New York: Wiley.

Kintsch, W., & Glass, G. (1974). Effects of propositional structure on sentence recall. *The representation of meaning in memory* (pp. 140–151). Hillsdale, NJ: Erlbaum.

Koffka, K. (1935). *Principles of Gestalt psychology*. New York: Harcourt, Brace and World.

Kolers, P. A. (1975). Memorial consequences of automatized encoding. *Journal of Experimental Psychology: Human Learning and Memory, 1,* 689–701.

Langley, P., & Simon, H. A. (1981). The central role of learning in cognition. In J. R. Anderson (Ed.), *Cognitive skills and their acquisition* (pp. 361–380). Hillsdale, NJ: Erlbaum.

Lewis, C. (1981). Skill in algebra. In J. R. Anderson (Ed.), *Cognitive skills and their acquisition* (pp. 85–110). Hillsdale, NJ: Erlbaum.

Lewis, C. H., & Anderson, J. R. (1976). Interference with real knowledge. *Cognitive Psychology, 8,* 311–335.

McKoon, G., & Keenan, J. M. (1974). Response latencies to explicit and implicit statements as a function of the delay between reading and test. *The representation of meaning in memory* (pp. 166–176). Hillsdale, NJ: Erlbaum.

Meichenbaum, D. (1984). Teaching thinking: A cognitive behavioral perspective. In S. Chipman, J. Segal, & R. Glaser (Eds.), *Thinking and learning skills:*

Vol. 2. *Research and open questions* (pp. 407–426). Hillsdale, NJ: Erlbaum.

Miller, G. A., Galanter, E., & Pribram, K. H. (1960). *Plans and the structure of behavior.* New York: Holt, Rinehart and Winston.

Miller, K., Perlmutter, M., & Keating, D. (1984). Cognitive arithmetic: Comparison of operations. *Journal of Experimental Psychology: Learning, Memory and Cognition, 10,* 46–60.

Neisser, U., Novick, R., & Lazar, R. (1963). Searching for ten targets simultaneously. *Perceptual and Motor Skills, 17,* 955–961.

Neves, D. M., & Anderson, J. R. (1981). Knowledge compilation: Mechanisms for the automatization of cognitive skills. In J. R. Anderson (Ed.), *Cognitive skills and their acquisition* (pp. 57–84). Hillsdale, NJ: Erlbaum.

Newell, A., & Rosenbloom, P. S. (1981). Mechanism of skill acquisition and the law of practice. In J. R. Anderson (Ed.), *Cognitive skills and their acquisition* (pp. 1–55). Hillsdale, NJ: Erlbaum.

Newell, A., & Simon, H. A. (1956). The logic theory machine. *IRE Transactions on Information Theory, IT-2,* 61–69.

Norman, D. A. (1980). Twelve issues for cognitive science. *Cognitive Science, 4,* 1–32.

Norman, D. A. (1982). *Learning and memory.* San Francisco: W. H. Freeman.

Novak, J. D., & Gowin, D. B. (1984). *Learning how to learn.* New York: Cambridge University Press.

Palincsar, A. S., & Brown, A. L. (1984). Reciprocal teaching of comprehension-fostering and comprehension monitoring activities. *Cognition and Instruction, 1,* 117–175.

Perfetti, C. A., & Lesgold, A. M. (1977). Discourse comprehension and sources of individual differences. In M. A. Just & P. A. Carpenter (Eds.), *Cognitive*

processes in comprehension (pp. 141–183). Hillsdale, NJ: Erlbaum.

Peterson, L. R., & Potts, G. R. (1982). Global and specific components of information integration. *Journal of Verbal Learning and Verbal Behavior, 21,* 403–420.

Popper, K. (1963). *Conjectures and refutations.* New York: Basic Books.

Posner, M. I. (1969). Abstraction and the process of recognition. In G. H. Bower (Ed.), *The psychology of learning and motivation* (Vol. 3, pp. 43–100). New York: Academic Press.

Pressley, M., Goodchild, F., Fleet, J., Zajchowski, R., & Evans, E. D. (1987, April). *What is good strategy use and why is it hard to teach? An optimistic appraisal of the challenges associated with strategy instruction.* Paper presented at the American Educational Research Association, Washington, DC.

Resnick, L. B., & Ford, W. (1981). *The psychology of mathematics for instruction.* Hillsdale, NJ: Erlbaum.

Rumelhart, D. E., & Norman, D. A. (1978). Accretion, tuning and restructuring: Three modes of learning. In J. W. Cotton & R. L. Klatzky (Eds.), *Semantic factors in cognition* (pp. 37–53). Hillsdale, NJ: Erlbaum.

Rumelhart, D. E., & Norman, D. A. (1981). Analogical processes in learning. In J. R. Anderson (Ed.), *Cognitive skills and their acquisition* (pp. 335–359). Hillsdale, NJ: Erlbaum.

Schneider, W., & Shiffrin, R. M. (1977). Controlled and automatic human information processing: I. Detection, search, and attention. *Psychological Review, 84,* 1–66.

Scruggs, T. E., Mastropieri, M., & Levin, J. R. (1987). Implications of mnemonic-strategy research for theories of learning disabilities. In H. L. Swanson (Ed.), *Memory and learning disabilities: Advances in learning and behavioral* disabilities (pp. 225–244). Greenwich, CT: JAI Press.

Shepard, R. N., & Metzler, J. (1971). Mental rotation of three-dimensional objects. *Science, 171,* 701–703.

Shiffrin, R. M., & Schneider, W. (1977). Controlled and automatic human information processing: II. Perceptual learning, automatic attending, and a general theory. *Psychological Review, 84,* 127–190.

Shortliffe, E. (1976). *Computer-based medical consultation: MYCIN.* New York: Elsevier.

Shuell, T. J. (1986). Cognitive conceptions of learning. *Review of Educational Research, 56,* 411–436.

Simon, H. A. (1980). Problem solving and education. In D. T. Tuma & F. Reif (Eds.), *Problem solving and education* (pp. 81–96). Hillsdale, NJ: Erlbaum.

Simon, H. A., & Feigenbaum, E. A. (1964). An information-processing theory of some effects of similarity, familiarization, and meaningfulness in verbal learning. *Journal of Verbal Learning and Verbal Behavior, 3,* 385–396.

Singley, M. K., & Anderson, J. R. (1985). The transfer of text-editing skill. *Journal of Man–Machine Studies, 22,* 403–423.

Skinner, B. F. (1938). *The behavior of organisms: An experimental analysis.* Englewood Cliffs, NJ: Prentice-Hall.

Skinner, B. F. (1950). Are theories of learning necessary? *Psychological Review, 57,* 193–216.

Skinner, B. F. (1953). *Science and human behavior.* New York: Macmillan.

Smith, E. E., & Goodman, L. (1984). Understanding written instructions: The role of an explanatory schema. *Cognition and Instruction, 1,* 359–396.

Sternberg, R. J. (1984). A theory of knowledge acquisition in the development of verbal concepts. *Developmental Review, 4,* 113–138.

Sternberg, R. J., & Wagner, R. K. (1982). Automatization failure in learning disabilities. *Topics in Learning and Learning Disabilities, 2,* 1–11.

Swanson, H. L. (1988a). Comments, countercomments and new thoughts. *Journal of Learning Disabilities, 21*(5), 289–298.

Swanson, H. L. (1988b). Toward a metatheory of learning disabilities. *Journal of Learning Disabilities, 21*(4), 196–209.

Swanson, H. L., Cochran, K. F., & Ewers, C. A. (1990). Can learning disabilities be determined from working memory performance? *Journal of Learning Disabilities, 28,* 59–68.

Tolman, E. C. (1932). *Purposive behavior in animals and men.* New York: Appleton-Century-Crofts.

Tolman, E. C. (1942). *Drives toward war.* New York: Appleton-Century-Crofts.

Wanner, H. E. (1968). *On remembering, forgetting, and understanding sentences. A study of the deep structure hypothesis.* Unpublished doctoral dissertation, Harvard University.

Winston, P. H. (1977). *Artificial intelligence.* Reading, MA: Addison-Wesley.

Wong, B. Y. L., & Sawatsky, D. (1984). Sentence elaboration and retention of good, average, and poor readers. *Learning Disability Quarterly, 6,* 229–236.

PART III

AN INFORMATION PROCESSING APPROACH TO ASSESSMENT

Assessment is a process of discerning individual characteristics that are important in establishing an intervention program in relation to a student's needs. An immense frustration exists in the field of learning disabilities in that most assessment procedures exist in a theoretical vacuum. Although a number of tests are available to administer to learning disabled students, there seems to be a lack of conceptual models for assessing learning disabilities from a cognitive perspective. This separation from cognitive theory and measurement is apparent in most diagnostic and case study workups on students with learning disabilities in the public schools. The purpose of Part III is to provide an overview of testing procedures and concepts and various testing approaches. Four models of assessment are synthesized, and the various limitations of each model are described. This section also provides an assessment approach of learning disabilities that encapsulates some of the areas of cognition that influence academic performance. The proposed assessment model includes five cognitive areas, and the validity of the model rests on experimental findings and test observation. The various areas of concern have been gleaned from the information processing models discussed in the previous chapters.

8

Assessment Practices

H. LEE SWANSON

Τhe assessment of learning disabled students is "a variable process depending on the questions asked, the child involved, the classroom context, and myriad of environmental, social and developmental factors" (Swanson, 1988, p. 97). One traditionally thinks of assessment in terms of test administration, scoring, and interpretation. It is important, therefore, to understand how the concept of assessment is separate from testing practice. Assessment, in contrast to testing, aims at discerning individual characteristics that are important for establishing an individual intervention program in relation to a child's educational needs. In addition to testing and systematically compiling a sampling of a child's behavior, assessment also includes such things as observation, interviewing, experimental teaching, and the administration of informal tests across multiple contexts. Various other methods, however, may be combined and utilized to communicate information about the child. Although it is helpful and important to share some ideas and impressions about the nature and assessment of learning disabled individuals, it is not wise to define and limit the meaning of assessment in a manner that would be too precise and perhaps even inflexible.

Given this distinction between assessment and testing, the purpose of the present chapter is to review assessment models that characterize many of the current practices in the field of learning disabilities. Not only does this chapter provide the reader with an overview of various assessment approaches, it also provides a point of contrast with Chapters 9 and 10. A perusal of the literature suggests that there are a number of approaches to assessment, each of which requires a different set of assumptions and testing procedures. To provide as inclusive a representation as possible, we have delineated these approaches in terms of the attribute, behavioral, ecological, and decision making models.

WHAT IS THE ATTRIBUTE MODEL?

Traditionally, psychological and educational assessment of children with learning disabilities (or of all exceptional children, for that matter) has been conceptualized by the classic works of Galton (1892), Cattell (1908), Binet (1902), Goddard (1910), and Terman (1921), which are discussed in textbooks on the assessment of exceptional children (e.g., Sattler, 1988). These earlier works provide a foundation for the attribute model, sometimes referred to as the construct model. Historically, the attribute model is based on the assumptions that (a) individuals can be characterized by attributes that can be placed at some point on a continuum, (b) individuals differ among themselves with respect to attributes, and (c) there is true placement (score) on the continuum of attributes that may be approximated by test data. Implicit in this model, at least as carried out in the field of learning disabilities, is an assumption that learning is determined by inherent factors—constructs or traits (i.e., attributes). Contemporary application of the attribute model is illustrated through what is popularly called "diagnostic–prescriptive teaching." Because this model has been influential in the field of learning disabilities, a brief review of the approach is necessary.

Diagnostic–Prescriptive Teaching

Assessment, from a diagnostic–prescriptive approach, focuses on the identification of effective instructional strategies for any number of variables related to academic learning (see Deno, 1986, for a review). Procedures of diagnostic–prescriptive assessment include (a) selecting a construct (e.g., language, perception) for consideration; (b) dividing the construct into sequential, quantifiable, and measurable categories; (c) administering tests to evaluate performance in these categories; and (d) developing a program to remediate the deficit on the test-related skills. The objective of assessment from this approach includes a determination of (a) the cause of the learning handicap for purposes of classification, (b) diagnostic information about a child's style of learning and psychological processes, and (c) academic content needs for instruction. This assessment process generally utilizes a standardized instrument to identify a child's strengths and weaknesses. Testing is followed by extrapolation of that information to provide a plan for instruction. Within the last few years, the diagnostic–prescriptive process has been waning in its influence. Several authors (e.g., Coles, 1978, 1988; Newcomer, 1977) have raised some questions as to whether this procedure can be used to determine what a child does or does not know and under what conditions a child learns best within the context in which the problem behavior was manifested. Some additional criticisms emanate from traditional test construction theory (Anastasi, 1984; Sternberg, 1979), whereas others stem from the social ramifications of the misuse of tests (Mercer & Lewis, 1978; Messick, 1984; Reynolds, 1984). Let us briefly consider two of these concerns.

First, for some children, test instruments may not be totally appropriate for providing information about learning problems or for prescribing instructional activities (e.g., D. Fuchs, Fuchs, Benowitz, & Barringer, 1987). For example, the model of learning reflected in the Illinois Test of Psycholinguistic Abilities, which had considerable influence in the field of learning disabilities during the late 1960s and early 1970s, has been criticized (Hammill, 1972; Hammill & Larsen, 1974a, 1974b). This model assumed that learning problems were a failure within the child, and that strengthening the weak areas noted on the test would improve learning. Hammill and Larsen's (1974a) review of studies on the efficacy of psycholinguistic training concluded that such procedures were not effective. Some tests simply are not related closely enough to classroom activities to be used as designators of specific teaching activities for learning disabled students.

Second, some test information does not readily transfer to instruction (Deno, 1986). One major problem related to diagnostic–prescriptive teaching is the assumption that the classroom teacher will be able to translate testing information into effective individual programming. The teacher receives statements that reveal, for example, that the child has auditory memory difficulties, along with results from other tests on the child's visual discrimination, oral reading, comprehension, and phonetic abilities. These statements seem at least one step removed from the direct programming task of the regular or special education teacher because behavior is situation specific (Deno, 1985, 1986; Ysseldyke & Mirlain, 1982); that is, behaviors generated in a testing situation may not be similar to the behavior generated in the classroom. Even within a classroom, behavior varies as the situation varies. Behavior that is appropriate during seat work may not be appropriate during instruction. Because test constructs describe a contextual behavior, removed from the setting in which the learning problem occurred as the basis for referral, it is highly possible that teacher judgments may be in conflict with those of the test (for further discussion, see Ellis, 1980; L. S. Fuchs & Fuchs, 1986; Lentz & Shapiro, 1986).

In summary, the primary limitation of using tests within a diagnostic–prescriptive framework is that it reduces opportunities for interaction of other extraneous variables that might be affecting the child's performance (Dillon, 1980). This is true when tests are seen as a basis for learning disabilities evaluation. If tests are used for administration purposes (e.g., ability assessment), they must (a) outline strategies that contribute to verifiable educational recommendations, (b) outline the populations that can best be served by these procedures, (c) indicate how diagnostic information will generalize across different task situations, and (d) relate to a theoretical orientation through which further systematic assessment can be directed. On the other hand, there is much to commend in the diagnostic–prescriptive approach, including its emphasis on test validity and reliability, and its focus on individual variations in responses. Based on our discussion related to diagnostic–prescriptive teaching, selection of a test plays a critical role in how instruction is directed. Thus, one must answer a number of questions when selecting a test. Some of these questions are provided in Table 8–1.

When selecting a test (as shown in Table 8–1), several technical aspects of a test should be taken into account. The test, as a measurement device, must be consistent in the value or number achieved when administered on successive occasions (reliability), and it must measure what it is supposed to measure (validity). Reliability and validity are briefly discussed below.

Reliability

A standardized test instrument provides a score that consists of two components: a *true score*, which represents an obtained score uncontaminated by chance events or conditions, and an *error component* (error of measurement), which represents the extent to which scores are attributable to chance. An *obtained* or *raw score* is the measure the child received on a test. The relationship between obtained score, true score, and error component is represented by the formula: Obtained score = True score + Error component. The variations in a child's obtained score represent the degree to which the measurement instrument is reliable. An obtained score would be unsatisfactory if most of the variability were a reflection of chance. A highly unreliable test reflects many variations in obtained scores that are caused by chance. Therefore, in a broad sense, the reliability of a child's obtained score is the extent to which that score is attributable to "true" score difference and chance errors.

Although reliability can be defined as the consistency of a child's obtained score on the same test or equivalent items on different occasions, it more technically relates to the ratio of true to obtained scores. We know that if an individual takes the same test more than once, the same score will probably not be obtained on each administration. Repeating the measurement

---

TABLE 8-1
Questions Related to Test Selection

---

1. What questions do we wish to answer about the individual?
   a. What norm-referenced instrument is needed for a decision to be made?
   b. What possible deficits (e.g., emotional, intellectual) does the individual have?
   c. What developmental levels are present in the individual?
   d. What is the possible cause of the problem?
   e. What learning approach is necessary?
   f. What referral or recommendations are needed?

2. Is this test valid enough (i.e., does the test measure what it is supposed to measure) to provide answers to the preceding questions?

3. How practical is the test?
   a. What training is needed by the examiner?
   b. How long does it take to administer?
   c. What is the cost of the test?

4. Is the test suitable for the individual's age and gender?

5. What other handicapping conditions (e.g., sensory, language, cognitive, besides a learning disability) may affect test selection?

6. What type of evaluation is necessary?
   a. Placement evaluation (identify entry behavior)
   b. Formative evaluation (identify learning progress)
   c. Diagnostic evaluation (identify end-of-year or unit achievement)
   d. Summative evaluation (identify end-of-year or unit achievement)

7. What type of decision is necessary?
   a. Selection of individuals for placement in special education programs
   b. Placement—Determine appropriate category or instructional setting
   c. Remediation
   d. Feedback—Inform student's parents and other involved persons about progress
   e. Program improvement—Determine whether linguistic or basal reading approach would be more effective

---

permits an estimate of the true score, as well as of the error of measurement of a single score. Therefore, reliability may be defined as the portion of score variance that results from the true score, or the subject's performance that will remain constant. As shown in Table 8–2, various types of reliability are reported in tests that are used to assess individuals with learning disabilities. The most common types are described below.

TABLE 8–2
Types of Reliability

Reliability	Description
Parallel form	Relationship between scores on two or more forms of the same test
Split-half method	Relationship of the entire test to two halves of the test
Test–retest	Same test given at two different points in time

Parallel forms. Parallel test forms are two or more tests of some construct(s) that are administered to the same person. Errors of measurement occur because the two tests most likely differ on item sampling. The reasons for this are apparent. The content of the test may include items from a large array of objectives. These items are pretested with an appropriate norm group in which some objectives are screened out. A cross-sectional sample of test items that represent the same level of difficulty or the same level of importance as the original pool of objectives is modified. Thus, the chance error involved in the equivalent forms is high. In addition, the time interval between testings may cause variations to occur in the test measurement, as may variations in the child's behavior.

Split-half method. The split-half method consists of dividing a test into two shorter forms for the purpose of estimating reliability. The division of items provides two tests that have the properties of parallel forms. One method of dividing items is an odd–even procedure (forming half-tests by placing odd-numbered items in one test and even-numbered items in the other test).

Several limitations are apparent in the split-half method. First, split-half reliability cannot be used when items are timed, for example, when a test includes a comprehension question but also includes a 5-min time limit. Wide differences will occur in the test, but the differences will most likely reflect how quickly the child can read. Second, scores obtained on a single testing are not sensitive to individual variation from day to day. In other words, the test score is precise only during a specific testing period. In addition, items on the test may not be experimentally independent. If tests are divided on an odd–even basis, items may overlap in content rather than reflect an equivalent sample of a construct.

Standard Error of Measurement

If a student were to take the same test on several occasions, the student's scores would almost certainly vary from occasion to occasion. This outcome in the variability of scores occurs because the test is not perfectly reliable. This variability represents what is called the standard error of measurement, a measurement of how close an individual's score is to his or her true score. Because it is impractical to administer the same test to a single child without inducing carryover effects (e.g., practice, memory), an estimate must be made of the student's true score. This estimate is called the standard error of measurement.

Validity

Another factor that determines the usefulness of a test is its validity, the extent to which the tests are serving their stated purposes. Several types of validity are important, depending on the intended use of a test. The types of validity are outlined in Table 8–3.

Content validity.   Content validity refers to how well a test samples a particular domain, trait, or characteristic. In establishing content validity, the test items should reflect the curriculum instruction and/or the desired cognitive and/or affective behaviors. The adequacy with which items reflect curricular activities can be evaluated on the basis of textbooks, teacher objectives, opinions of educators, and the degree to which these items are an adequate sample.

TABLE 8–3
Types of Validity

Type	Description
Content	Adequacy of the items
Construct	Theory underlying the test
Congruent	Relationship of one test to an earlier test
Concurrent	Relationship of the test to a current measure
Predictive	Relationship of the test to a later point in time

Construct validity. The theory underlying the test must be assessed on both logical (reasonable) and empirical grounds. Construct validity refers to the psychological or educational constructs of a test. This type of validity asks the following questions: To what extent does the test represent the theoretical trait (e.g., intelligence, abstract reasoning) under study? How does the measurement instrument fit into an organized body of knowledge?

Congruent validity. The process of validating one test with an earlier test is called congruent validity. The new test is validated against another test through a correlational analysis. Difficulties arise when a new measure is correlated with another test of doubtful construct validity and, therefore, can be no better than the original measure. One example of congruent validity is the extent to which Test X correlates with the Stanford–Binet.

Concurrent validity. Concurrent validity is defined as how well test scores match measures of contemporary criterion performance. Stated another way, concurrent validity refers to statements about the prediction of events that occur at roughly the same time the test instrument is applied. Contemporary measures may include, for example, current school marks, criterion-referenced measures, or counseling interviews. Procedures for developing an accurate estimate of concurrent validity include detailing classroom performance and its relative contribution to predictive success, analyzing the extent to which the test in question measures proficiency in performing each school task, and determining the validity of each test for a given academic (or related) task.

Predictive validity. As the name suggests, predictive validity attempts to forecast some measurement based on a current test or observation. A typical example in education is the prediction of success (e.g., in reading or math) in school. The basic evidence in support of predictive validity is the relationship between two variables, the criterion (construct of interest) and prediction (construct of the test). A test is said to have predictive validity for reading performance, for example, if the scores on a test correlate with grades or other measures that are given at some future time (e.g., L. S. Fuchs, Fuchs, & Deno, 1982). A test cannot have predictive validity if the construct of concern has not been empirically investigated. The predictive function of a test is important because it is the only way in which the appropriateness of its construct(s) can be empirically assessed. For a theoretical base of a test to be empirically testable, it must yield predictions that can be directly evaluated in the classroom.

Summary

Without validity, a test is of little value. Validity and reliability are related: If a test is demonstrated to have content, construct, congruent, concurrent, or predictive validity, it must have some degree of reliability; however, it is important to remember that tests can be reliable and have little or no validity. Validity is best conceptualized as having both a reasonable and an empirical base. Special emphasis should be given to the theoretical base from which the test is derived, as well as its value in predicting classroom functioning.

WHAT IS THE BEHAVIORAL APPROACH?

The behavioral approach to assessment of learning disabled children is quite broad in scope (Lloyd & Blandford, 1989; Lovitt, 1989). An important characteristic of a behavioral model is that it attempts to consider attributes or constructs, stated in observable terms (e.g., attention, amount of eye contact to task), and the situational (environmental) determinants of behavior (Craighead, Kazdin, & Mahoney, 1981; Greenwood, Delquardi, & Hall, 1984; Gresham, 1984; Lentz & Shapiro, 1986; Nelson & Hayes, 1979).

Within the behavioral model, no general class of learning disabled children's behavior is likely to be sufficient for describing their behavior. Classifications of learning disabled children are described functionally, not in terms of attributes or underlying deficiencies.

The following are four aspects of the behavioral model, as conceptualized for assessment:

1. Identification and description of behaviors and behavioral settings. This aspect focuses on applying reliable techniques for given behaviors (e.g., problem solving, memory, disruptive behavior) delineated in the environmental context in which they occur.

2. Assessment of incidence and generalization of the behavior. This aspect focuses on obtaining answers to questions such as the following: Does the behavior occur in situations other than the regular or special classroom? To what environmental events is the behavior related? What event and what context set the occasion for the behavior? What is the rate or frequency of this behavior?

3. Assessment of behavior determinants. This aspect focuses on the relationship between behaviors or behavioral settings and their long-term consequences (e.g., the relationship between special education placement and later regular classroom functioning).

4. Assessment of the consequences of behavior. A behavior is assessed by the degree to which it is under the control of consequences.

Differences Between the Attribute and Behavioral Model

Although the behavioral and attribute assessment models share some of the main concerns in their desire to produce reliable, valid, and useful data, they vary considerably in their assumptions of how children learn. Goldfried and Kent (1972) provided three major differences between the assumptions of behavioral and traditional attribute assessments. First, the attribute model views test behavior as a sign of a hypothetical construct that accounts for the consistency in an individual's behavior, whereas the behavioral model is less inferential in postulating underlying factors as accounting for problem behaviors. Regarding the latter approach Mischel (1968) wrote, "Emphasis is on what a person does in situations rather than inferences about what attributes he has" (p. 10). The behavioral approach is more likely to look at test results as the relationship between behavior and specific environmental factors (Ollendick & Hersen, 1984).

Second, the selection of test items or situations differs for the two approaches. The attribute model assumes that behavior will be quite stable, regardless of the specific situational context. Therefore, minimal efforts are made to depart from standardized instructions or test items. In certain cases, attempts are made to gather peripheral information using informal testing procedures. The behavioral model is concerned with the relationship between behavior and specific environmental contexts and, therefore, attempts to sample these situations thoroughly.

The third assumption relates to the sign versus sample interpretation of test responses. The sign approach, characteristic of the attribute model, assumes that a test response is an indirect manifestation of some underlying educational or psychological construct. The sample approach, characteristic of a behavioral model, assumes that test responses constitute only a subset of actual behaviors that occur in the classroom.

Establishment of Content Validity

In a discussion of the behavioral model, several authors have outlined a procedure for establishing content validity of child functioning (Goldfried & D'Zurilla, 1969; Lentz & Shapiro, 1986; Lloyd & Blandford, 1989; Lovitt, 1989; Meichenbaum, 1977). Goldfried and D'Zurilla viewed the first step as situational analysis, or the sampling of typical situations in which a given behavior of interest is likely to occur (e.g., classroom, home). The second phase consists of response enumeration, which suggests a sampling of typical responses to each relevant situation generated during the situational analysis. Both phases are carried out through direct measurement of behaviors as they occur within these natural settings. The final phase, criterion analysis, includes a response evaluation with regard to competency level. These competency judgments may be made by significant individuals who would typically label the behavior as inappropriate or maladaptive. These judgments can be made in relation to standardized test performance or generally to how well the child fits the definition of capability. Each situation may have associated with it a variety of different responses that can be grouped functionally according to the demand of the context (e.g., classroom). Perhaps the most well-known application of a behavioral model to instruction of learning disabled children is task analysis.

Task Analysis

Task analysis focuses on a child's level of skills in relation to a particular task. Assuming that successful learning outcomes are based on having prerequisite skills, one can assess the skills the child can demonstrate at various points along the way toward achieving learning objectives (Powers, 1984). Through the use of a variety of formal and informal assessment techniques, the teacher determines at what point the child will enter the continuum. Task analysis identifies the component or prerequisite tasks a student must ultimately be able to do to perform a desired behavior. The following are important questions for assessment using this approach: What specific educational tasks are important for the child to learn? What are the sequential steps in learning this task? What specific behaviors does the child need to perform this task?

Task analysis logically follows the writing of performance objectives, which describe what is being learned. Task analysis then suggests the sequential learning steps involved in developing the skill to perform a particular objective. Because task analysis is learner oriented, the following components are necessary:

1. Stating the task in behavioral or performance terms. For example,

   Math: The learner will write the correct response to multiplication problems given in the form of mathematical sentences or story problems in which each of the two factors is less than 10.

   Reading: Given words containing the /e/ sound, represented by –e in the CV pattern, in lists of other words, the child will circle the known –e pattern words as rhyming words.

2. Testing the prerequisite skills. The teacher evaluates the prospective learner to see if he or she possesses the required skill. After the component of readiness has been assessed through tasks that determine prerequisite skills, the task is analyzed for its sequential learning steps.

3. Following a general scope and sequence for test development. Analyzing the skills means listing the steps necessary to complete a long-range task.

Limitations

The behavioral approach, which places little emphasis on standardized tests, focuses on the enabling objectives or skill level of the child. A task analysis assumes that, because certain tests are structurally unsound, as related to the classroom context, many standardized tests are useless in developing educational objectives. Such an argument, according to Eaves and McLaughlin (1977), obscures the point of standardized testing in that the value of testing is not the specification of objectives, but is "in deciding whether or not the objective needs to be specified at all" (p. 100). The behavioral model ensures situational generalizability to the classroom, but special arrangements are needed to measure the variety of setting characteristics that may relate to task achievement. Although task analysis provides measures from which learning outcomes can be achieved as related to the classroom context, it does not provide a scheme for conceptualizing and choosing which independent variables (e.g., teacher characteristics, peer interactions) relate to classroom objectives.

WHAT IS THE ECOLOGICAL MODEL?

The ecological model incorporates behavioral and ability assessment measures, although most of its literature focuses on social interaction (see Gresham & Elliott, 1984, 1987; Scott, 1980). Assessment data are gathered, for example, pertaining to academic needs, school–community intervention, family environmental intervention, and architectural intervention (e.g., residential and home living centers built for therapeutic purposes). The focus of the ecological approach is on socializing, or teaching the child to perform socially competent or adaptable behavior. A systematic comparison between ecological and nonecological assessment models is provided in Table 8–4. Because of its focus on socially acceptable behaviors, the ecological model has only a sparse representation in the learning disabilities literature (in contrast to such fields as child behavior/emotional disorders).

Points of Evaluation

The goal of ecological assessment is to determine the adaptation of individuals to the demands of their environment. The role of assessment is not merely to identify elements in the school system that impair or are incongruent for child functioning. Assessment should identify elements in the child's ecosystems, as well as the demands from program elements in the school context. The following are focal points for evaluation:

TABLE 8–4
Comparison of Ecological with Traditional Assessment

Nonecological strategies	Ecological strategies
Responsive only to child crisis	Responsive to child, adaptive class-room context
Deals in specific assessment measures	Concern with comprehensive assess-ment and individually adapted measures
Requires consent from social system for assessment and intervention	Requires participation from child's social system for assessment and intervention
Assesses conflict in classroom	Assesses conflict of child in all natural settings
Assessment information provides short-range classroom planning	Assessment information provides long-range community planning
Standardized and formalized class-room assessment	Innovative classroom assessment
Separate ancillary assessment for child and community	Coordinated assessment services for child and parent

1. Accountability—To determine if information from the child's evaluation is directed to each individual or group concerned with the child's school-related performance.

2. General needs assessment—To determine if the child arrives at goals and objectives for the classroom/community.

3. Individual needs assessment—To determine how the child's instructional needs can be met.

4. Strategies for providing instruction—To determine the most advantageous way to facilitate school learning.
   a. Curriculum—To assess the quality of program planning and organiza-tion for classroom/community.
   b. Classroom—To assess the extent to which educational programs are being appropriately implemented.
   c. In-class evaluation—To assess the extent to which criterion-referenced or formative evaluations have occurred.

    d. Learning locus of control—To assess the extent to which the student perceives his or her own efforts as necesary for academic success.

    e. Materials—To assess whether specific material or stimulus improves student performance.

    f. Teacher—To assess the ability of the personnel within the educational context to achieve the goals of the community and objectives of the school.

    g. Environment—To assess the extent to which the classroom contingencies encourage the learning disabled child to meet educational/community objectives.

    h. Staff training—To assess the extent to which training is being provided to teachers to meet learning disabled children's needs.

    i. Administrative support—To assess the extent to which school staff make decisions that result in successful child performance.

5. Instructional outcome—To assess the extent to which a child is becoming competent in the goals and objectives provided.

6. Resources—To assess the extent to which adequate funding is available to meet all individual needs.

Steps in Assessment

Ecological assessment begins with identifying congruence within the family, and gradually progresses toward community. Primarily, the assessment goal is established by finding a goodness-of-fit between students and each of their ecosystems. Once the student's ecosystem has been defined by the student or parents, assessment categories are determined and parameters are selected. The teacher then selects relevant measurement instruments. A "valid" instrument may be totally irrelevant for a given learning disabled child's ecological system. It is important to find and develop instruments sufficiently sensitive to record child and community changes.

    Whatever the focus in the community and child interaction process, the measurement of educational outcomes involves two basic issues: the selection of outcome variables for ecological adaptation and the appropriate points of measurement. Outcome variables can include such aspects as adaptive school performance data as measured by standardized and informal tests, behavior ratings, and systematic classroom observations by teachers; behavior at home (e.g., parent evaluation forms, adaptive behavior ratings); behavior in the community as measured by social services, mental health, and other relevant community organization services; and attitude changes as measured from inventories or sociometric questionnaires directed to all significant individuals in the child's ecosystem. The appropriate point of measurement refers to the information that is meaningful to the teacher, parents, and salient members of the community. One method of measurement is attitude assessment. A wide range of attitude assessments has been described in several texts and is beyond the scope of this chapter.

Summary

The assessment of ecological competence includes a number of social responsibilities. Among those obtained from several reviews (e.g., Scott, 1980) are (a) development of a child–context framework in which labels that arise from intelligence testing or other tests are avoided, (b) recognition of pluralism of cultural background, (c) determination of appropriate opportunities for the whole range of measured competencies, and (d) assessment of the child without assessment of past and present environments. An ecological perspective implies a greater emphasis on adaptation than on selection.

WHAT IS A DECISION MAKING MODEL?

Several authors (Adelman & Taylor, 1989; Cronbach & Gleser, 1965; Cummings, Huebner, & McLeskey, 1986; Haertel, 1985; Wedell, 1970) have suggested that the attribute, behavioral, and ecological models are all inadequate for the assessment of exceptional (e.g., learning disabled) children because they lack a basis for decision making. A premise of the decision making model is that assessment involves not only gathering information and summarizing results, but also systematically using the data obtained to arrive at decisions. This model is concerned with strategies for making decisions. In contrast to the attribute model, which focuses on a static procedure (i.e., administering a series of tests), the decision making model is a problem solving approach.

Cronbach and Gleser (1965) viewed decision theory as a "general model for stating any particular testing problem" (p. 139). Problems characteristically lead to either a terminal decision or an investigatory decision. The investigatory process, information gathering, and decision making continue until a terminal decision is made. A function of the model is to provide a rule or strategy for utilizing test information. When utilizing a strategy, Cronbach and Gleser suggested that the following questions be answered:

1. Would additional information (e.g., test data) permit better decisions?

2. Does this strategy provide the best remediation possible with this body of information?

3. Does the existing data conform to an evaluation and prediction of possible outcomes?

Decision Making Principles

Four heuristic principles are applicable to this assessment model. First, the child should be given the opportunity to operate in various learning environments. The child should not be viewed simply as a passive recipient of information from the school environment, but as an active problem solver adapting to all aspects of the environment. Second, test information should represent diverse goals and sources of information, not simply the means to an end (e.g., placement into special education). Therefore, assessment is seen as autotelic; that is, the best way to assess a child is to place that child in an environment in which different tasks can be tried with no consequences for performance outcomes. Third, the child should be assessed under a general theory of probability inference. Realizing that children can learn the same information in several ways, the most productive method must be determined for each child, as well as the problem strategy that will lead to greatest independence from special programs. Finally, assessment should be responsive to learning activities and provide a structure for the child to learn whatever is to be learned, but also to learn about himself or herself as a learner; that is, responsive assessment observes the child spelling "cup" and allows him or her to spell it "kup." There is no rule or consequence for this performance; rather, it provides strategies for succeeding in the environment (obtaining a satisfactory response from the environment) and insight into how the information in the environment was devised to help the child learn.

From the above perspective, conventional psychometric testing is to some degree inefficient. One distinct advantage of decision making theory is that it indicates the precise level of difficulty that is optimal for testing a child of any given competence. This is in sharp contrast to the attribute model that treats precision of measurement as if it were independent of a child's given level of functioning.

Applications

Decision making theory raises the possibility of making tests more efficient in choosing items that are optimal at the child's level of functioning, as estimated from his or her response to previous test items (Skaggs & Lissitz, 1986). This procedure of adapting a test to an individual has been called "tailored testing" (Lord, 1969). Two notions in tailored testing within a decision theory framework are possible. First, a system of rules governing the testing strategy is mapped out in which branching (inefficiencies on certain tests lead to assessment on others) and step sizes (how test items vary in difficulty) are delineated. An example of this approach, provided by Wedell (1970), is discussed later in this chapter. A second approach to tailored testing is not to use static test frameworks (e.g., intelligence test, followed by achievement test, followed by personality test), but to perform a selection of tests during the interview period. Such a procedure requires extended time for interaction between the tester and the child. A Bayesian procedure may provide a basis for test selection.

Bayesian Estimation

Several articles (e.g., Haney, 1984) have called attention to the weak conceptualization of what constitutes referral for testing, what variables yield poor academic performance, and whether a test score is a true evaluation based on observations in the classroom and other settings. In the context of decision making, no inference about a child's true functioning can be made from observed performance without specifying the distribution of performance by other children with *similar* difficulties. Thus, the problem becomes one of estimating a distribution of ability among a population of children from a random sample of learning disabled subjects. This would be considered an empirical Bayesian estimation problem. Because Bayesian theory is rather technical and there are so many different applications, the discussion here is restricted to a few general remarks.

Bayesian theorists believe that attribute assessment (e.g., diagnostic–prescriptive testing) fails because it neglects information about deficient child performance *between* similar children. Accordingly, improving the understanding of a learning disabled child's performance involves the use of relevant information gathered about diagnosed comparable children. Test performance of children is taken to be a random sample. The degree of confidence one places in the child's score as related to the general population is not an issue, but the score should be in the range of the distribution suggested by assumptions of learning disabled children's functioning. Thus, the test items that are chosen for assessing learning disabled children will maximize their disability. Bayesian formation, as applied to assessment of learning disabled children, is best in the fetal stage, but it may provide a basis for the termination or redirection of certain test data, with the aim of maximizing overall prediction of who is learning disabled and who is not (see Wissink, Kass, & Ferrell, 1975, for discussion).

Sequential Strategy

Wedell (1970) viewed assessment as a strategy that reflects continuous decision making. Such a strategy incorporates decisions related to factors that contribute to successful educational performance. Factors contributing to a child's level of functioning are sensorimotor functions (physical condition), acquisition of cognitive concepts (e.g., conservation of volume, reversibility, socialized speech), acquisition of cognitive skills (e.g., language), application of concepts and skills to educational tasks, motivational base, and differential opportunities in acquiring the preceding factors.

Wedell's proposed strategy of four successive stages is provided in Table 8–5. Stage 1 focuses on screening to isolate factors that seem to be contributing to the child's problem. Mechanical skills of the child are gathered by abbreviated tests, observation checklists, anecdotal records, and surveys of information. After the screening information has been collected, the diagnostician evaluates the information (Stage 2). If the diagnostician can formulate a tentative hypothesis, Stage 3 provides an immediate check on the assumptions, the main focus of educational assessment, and, in particular, makes use of standardized assessment procedures. Several outcomes are possible, as shown in Stage 4. Assessment at Stage 4 is an ongoing process of hypothesis verification. Wedell's model is concerned not only with gathering certain kinds of data, but also with using these data systematically to arrive at a decision.

SYNTHESIS AND SUMMARY

As shown in Table 8–6, the four models previously reviewed provide a framework for understanding how learning disabilities can be assessed along two basic dimensions: (a) attributes (e.g., memory, metacognition) and the situational behaviors that occur in context, and (b) *passive* (static) versus *active* problem solving or decision making. These dimensions focus on the extent to which abilities of the learning disabled child are inferred from test and behavioral performances (passive) and how social features of the environment are assessed through a problem solving test battery. As shown in Table 8–6, the first model involves an attributional approach (e.g., the administration of a battery of tests). The second model involves a behavioral analysis orientation against predefined objectives of the classroom. The third model involves decision making related to possible explanations of learning disabled children's behavior. The fourth model involves the extent to which behaviors occur outside the school context. These models may be characterized as assessing interactions between the learning disabled child and the environment in terms of interpretative (*passive* construct), operative (*passive* behavioral), decision making (*active* interpretative), and context generalizing (*active* behavioral) variables.

An obvious implication of the representation in Table 8–6 is that the majority of assessments of learning disabilities have focused on a single model of child–environment interchange (in some cases two [e.g., behavioral–attitude], but rarely all four models). Consequently, most models of assessment tend to overemphasize particular aspects of learning disabled children's

TABLE 8-5
Wedell's Sequential Strategy

Stages	Number for areas of further investigation
Stage 1: Screening assessment	
Observation and conversation	
Attention, responsiveness, educational motivation	44
Social adjustment—classroom	37–39
Adjustment beyond educational context	35–38, 41, 42
History	
Personal	40
Medical	42
Educational	41
Sensorimotor state	24–27, 29–31
Health	
Speech (primarily expressive language)	28
Testing	
General abilities (abbreviated individual intelligence test)	
Verbal	10–13, 22, 23
Nonverbal	18–23
Educational achievement	
Reading (e.g., word recognition)	1, 4–6
Spelling (e.g., word spelling)	2, 4, 6, 7
Math (oral problem with explanation of method)	3, 8, 9
Stage 2: Evaluation of screening assessment	
Possible outcomes	
Rapport too poor for reliable evaluation	44
Discontinue testing and observe	
Build rapport for subsequent testing	
Formulate hypothesis	
No problem: Discontinue assessment	
Problem not psychoeducational: Rerefer	
Screening indicates areas for further investigation	
No hypothesis possible	
Stage 3: Hypothesis testing	
Testing	
Educational skills (assessment leading to 44, 45 where required)	
Adaptive skills:	
1 Reading (comprehension)	10–13
2 Spelling (composition)	10–13
3 Math (problems)	12–14, 1

TABLE 8–5 (continued)

Stages	Number for areas of further investigation
Basic skills:	
4 Reading: knowledge of letter sounds	14–16, 18, 19
5 Blending	14, 18, 19
6 Knowledge of spelling patterns	14–17 and rules, 22
7 Handwriting	19, 20
Math:	
8 Written sums	20
9 Basic operations	22, 31
Cognitive skills (assessment leading to 44, 45 where required)	
Language:	
Expressive:	
10 Vocabulary	14, 18, 26, 28
11 Syntax	14, 15, 18
Receptive:	
12 Vocabulary	14, 15, 18
13 Syntax	14, 15, 18
Memory:	
14 Auditory: Verbal	18
15 Nonverbal: Rhythm	18
Visual:	
16 Simple	19
17 Sequential	19
Perceptual	
18 Auditory	26, 27
19 Visual	24, 25, 31
Perceptual–motor:	
20 Pencil copying	19, 29, 31, 21
21 Three-dimensional copying	19, 29, 31
Concept development and reasoning	
22 e.g., Piagetian analysis (seriation, conservation, and reasoning)	12, 13, 19, 44
23 e.g., cognitive style	44
Sensory screening	
Vision:	
24 Acuity	42
25 Eye movement	42
Hearing:	
26 Speech sounds	42

TABLE 8–5 (continued)

Stages	Number for areas of further investigation
27 Pure tone	42
Motor function screening	
28 Articulation	43
29 Fine motor skills	39, 40–42
30 Gross motor skills	39, 40, 42
31 Awareness of body coordinates	41
Lateral preference	
32 Eye	40–42
33 Hand	40–42
34 Foot	40–42
Adjustment	
35 Personality	40–42
36 Attitudes	40–42
37 Family relations	40
38 Peer group relations	40, 41
39 Social adequacy	40, 41

Consultation
  40 Family and personal history (e.g., social worker)
  41 School behavior: Peer and teacher–pupil relations, study habits
      (class teacher, counselor)
  42 Medical information
  43 Speech (speech pathologist)
Experimental investigation (cognitive and behavioral)
  44 e.g., Response to graded clues; brief instruction and rewards in
      free-field or structured situations
Stage 4: Diagnostic formulation
Provisional diagnosis
  45 Recommend experimental action (e.g., in classroom), retesting,
      serial testing
  Problem not primarily psychoeducational; transfer case as appropriate
Full diagnostic formulation and recommendation for action, including provision
for report back on adequacy of diagnosis.

functions, while ignoring or downplaying the possibility that the form, situations, and direction of child–environment relationships vary. Thus, an important goal in assessment is to unify the various models in order to have a comprehensive understanding of learning disabilities.

TABLE 8-6
Information Transaction

	Attributes	Context
Passive	*Interpretative*[a] Standardized and informal Representation of intellectual, perceptual, language, emotional, academic performance Static battery (Attribute Model)	*Operative*[b] Functional assessment Behavioral observations of class- relevant behaviors (Behavioral Model)
Active	*Decision making* Problem-solving battery in natural and simulated settings (Decision Making Model)	*Context generalizing* Ecological variables Generalization of behavior (Ecological Model)

[a]*Interpretative* refers to intermediate variables involved in explaining test performance (e.g., attention, memory). [b]*Operative* refers to situational variables (e.g., behavior in the classroom) that contribute to the interpretation of test performance.

The present chapter has presented some alternative conceptualizations of assessment. Readers are encouraged to seek additional sources to elaborate on these alternatives. The next two chapters provide an orientation to assessment that is consistent with the orientation of this text.

REFERENCES

Adelman, H. S., & Taylor, L. (1991). Issues and problems related to the assessment of learning disabilities. In H. L. Swanson (Ed.), *Handbook on the assessment of learning disabilities: Theory, research, and practice* (pp. 21–44). Austin, TX: PRO-ED.

Anastasi, A. (1984). *Psychological testing* (5th ed). New York: Macmillan

Binet, A. (1902). *L'Étude experimentale de l'intelligence*. Paris: Ancienne Librairie Schleicher.

Cattell, J. M. (1908). Mental tests and measurements. *Mind, 14*, 373–381.

Coles, G. (1978). The learning disabilities test battery: Empirical and social issues: *Harvard Educational Review, 48*, 313–340.

Coles G. (1988). *The learning mystique: A critical look at learning disabilities*. New York: Panthenon Books.

Craighead, W., Kazdin, A., & Mahoney, M. (1981). Assessment and treatment strategies. In W. Craighead, A. Kazdin,

& M. Mahoney (Eds.), *Behavior modification.* Boston: Houghton Mifflin.

Cronbach, L., & Gleser, B. (1965). *Psychological tests and personnel decisions* (2nd ed.). Urbana: University of Illinois Press.

Cummings, J. A., Huebner, E. S., & McLeskey, J. (1986). Psychoeducational decision making: Reason for referral versus test data. *Professional School Psychology, 2,* 249–256.

Deno, S. L. (1985). Curriculum-based assessment: The emerging alternative. *Exceptional Children, 52,* 219–232.

Deno, S. L. (1986). Formative evaluation of individual programs: A new role for school psychologists. *School Psychology Review, 16,* 290–305.

Dillon, R. (1980). Matching students to their preferred testing conditions: Improving the validity of cognitive assessment. *Educational and Psychological Measurement, 40,* 999–1004.

Eaves, R., & McLaughlin, P. (1977). A systems approach for the assessment of the child and his environment: Getting back to basics. *Journal of Special Education, 11,* 99–111.

Ellis, R. (1980). Analysis of social skills: The behavior analysis approach. In W. Singleton, P. Spurgeon, & R. Stamers (Eds.), *The analysis of social skill.* New York: Plenum Press.

Fuchs, D., & Fuchs, L. S. (1986). Test procedure bias: A meta-analysis of examiner familiarity effects. *Review of Educational Research, 56,* 243–262.

Fuchs, D., Fuchs, L. S., Benowitz, S., & Barringer, K. (1987). Norm-referenced tests: Are they valid for use with handicapped students? *Exceptional Children, 54,* 263–271.

Fuchs, L. S., & Fuchs, D. (Eds.). (1986). Linking assessment to instructional interventions: An overview. *School Psychology Review, 15,* 318–323.

Fuchs, L. S., Fuchs, D., & Deno, S. L. (1982). Reliability and validity of curriculum-based informal reading inventories. *Reading Research Quarterly, 18,* 6–26.

Galton, F. (1892). *Hereditary genius* (2nd ed.). New York: Macmillan.

Goddard, H. (1910). Four hundred feebleminded children classified by the Binet method. *Pedagogical Seminary, 17,* 387–399.

Goldfried, M. (1977). Behavioral assessment. In N. Sundberg (Ed.), *Assessment of persons* (pp. 66–75). Englewood Cliffs, NJ: Prentice-Hall.

Goldfried, M., & D'Zurilla, T. (1969). A behavioral–analytic model for assessing competence. In C. D. Spielberger (Ed.), *Current topics in clinical and community psychology.* New York: Academic Press.

Goldfried, M., & Kent, R. (1972). Traditional versus behavioral assessment of personality assessment. *Psychological Bulletin, 77,* 409–420.

Greenwood, C., Delquardi, J., & Hall, R. (1984). Opportunity to respond and student academic performance. In W. Heward, T. Heron, D. Hill, & J. Trap-Porter (Eds.), *Focus on behavior analysis in education* (pp. 58–88). Columbus, OH: Merrill.

Gresham, F. (1984). Behavioral interviews in school psychology: Issues in psychometric adequacy and research. *School Psychology Review, 13,* 17–25.

Gresham, F. M., & Elliott, T. N. (1984). Assessment and classification of children's social skills: A review of methods and issues. *School Psychology Review, 13,* 292–301.

Gresham, F., & Elliott, T. N. (1987). The relationship between adaptive behavior and social skills. *Journal of Special Education, 21,* 149–166.

Haertel, E. (1985). Construct validity and criterion-referenced testing. *Review of Educational Research, 55,* 23–46.

Hammill, D. (1972). Training visual perceptual processes. *Journal of Learning Disabilities, 5,* 552–559.

Hammill, D. D., & Larsen, S. C. (1974a). The effectiveness of psycholinguistic training. *Exceptional Children, 41,* 5–14.

Hammill, D. D., & Larsen, S. C. (1974b). The relationship of selected auditory perceptual skills and reading ability. *Journal of Learning Disabilities, 7,* 429–435.

Haney, W. (1984). Testing reasoning and reasoning about testing. *Review of Educational Research, 54,* 597–654.

Lentz, F. E., & Shapiro, E. S. (1986). Functional assessment of the academic environment. *School Psychology Review, 15,* 346–355.

Lloyd, J. W., & Blandford, B. J. (1991). Assessment for instruction. In H. L. Swanson (Ed.), *Handbook on the assessment of learning disabilities: Theory, research, and practice* (pp. 45–58). Austin, TX: PRO-ED.

Lord, F. M. (1969). A study of item bias using item characteristic curve theory. In N. H. Poortinga (Ed.), *Basic problems in cross-cultural psychology.* Amsterdam: Swits and Vitlinger.

Lovitt, T. (1991). Behavioral assessment of learning disabilities. In H. L. Swanson (Ed.), *Handbook on the assessment of learning disabilities: Theory, research, and practice* (pp. 95–120). Austin, TX: PRO-ED.

Meichenbaum, D. (1977). *Cognitive-behavior modification: An integrative approach.* New York: Plenum Press.

Mercer, J R., & Lewis, J. (1978). *SOMPA: System of Multicultural Pluralistic Assessment.* New York: Psychological Corporation.

Messick, S. (1984). The psychology of educational measurement. *Journal of Educational Measurement, 21,* 215–237.

Mischel, W. (1968). *Personality and assessment.* New York: Wiley.

Nelson, R., & Hayes, S. (1979). The nature of behavioral assessment: A commentary. *Journal of Applied Behavior Analysis, 12,* 49–50.

Newcomer, P. (1977). Special education services for the mildly handicapped: Beyond a diagnostic and remedial model. *Journal of Special Education, 11,* 153–165.

Ollendick, T. H., & Hersen, M. (1984). An overview of child behavioral assessment. In T. H. Ollendick & M. Hersen (Eds.), *Child behavioral assessment: Principles and procedures.* Elmsford, NY: Pergamon.

Powers, M. D. (1984). Behavioral assessment and the planning and evaluation of interventions for developmentally disabled children. *School Psychology Review, 14,* 155–161.

Reynolds, C. R. (1984). Perspectives on bias in mental testing. In C. R. Reynolds & R. T. Brown (Eds.), *Perspectives on individual differences.* New York: Plenum Press.

Sattler, J. (1988). *Assessment of children* (3rd ed.). San Diego: Author.

Scott, M. (1980). Ecological theory and methods for research in special education. *Journal of Special Education, 14,* 279–294.

Skaggs, G., & Lissitz, R. (1986). IRT test equating: Relevant issues and a review of recent research. *Review of Educational Research, 56,* 495–529.

Sternberg, R. (1979). The nature of mental abilities. *American Psychologist, 34,* 214–230.

Swanson, H. L. (1988). Assessment practices in learning disabilities. In K. Kavale (Ed.), *Learning disabilities: State of the art and practice* (Vol. 1, pp. 77–97). Austin, TX: PRO-ED.

Terman, L. (1921). Intelligence and its measurement. *Journal of Educational Psychology, 12,* 127–133.

Wedell, K. (1970). Diagnosing learning difficulties: A sequential strategy. *Journal of Learning Disabilities, 3,* 311–317.

Wissink, J., Kass, C., & Ferrell, W. (1975). A Bayesian approach to the identification of children with learning disabilities. *Journal of Learning Disabilities, 8,* 158–160.

Ysseldyke, J., & Mirlain, P. (1982). Assessment information to plan instructional interventions: A review of the research. In C. Reynolds & T. Gutkins (Eds.), *The handbook of school psychology* (pp. 395–409). New York: Wiley.

9

A Cognitive Assessment Approach I

H. LEE SWANSON

A tremendous surge has occurred in research on the cognitive abilities of learning disabled children from an information processing orientation (see Chapters 5 and 6). Despite the growing focus on cognitive processes, as in this book, as of yet, there has been no adequate models from a cognitive orientation to understand and assess the learning disabled student's functioning. In this chapter, a "multidirectional" model is presented to begin readdressing some of the imbalance between experimental findings and practical assessment needs. Consistent with many of the concepts discussed in Chapter 5, assessment of learning disabled students is directed to five cognitive areas: strategy, strategy abstractions, knowledge base, executive function, and metacognition. Each of these areas, or *cognitive planes*, is defined and described. In the present chapter, discussion related to assumptions of the model and descriptions of the executive function, knowledge base, and strategy planes are provided. In Chapter 10, we continue our discussion of the model by discussing the strategy abstraction and metacognitive planes. We complete our discussion by illustrating how assessment occurs and providing some of the implications of the proposed cognitive model. Some new information is presented in both chapters, but the majority of the information is consistent with the information processing approaches discussed in Chapter 5.

WHAT ARE THE ASSUMPTIONS OF THIS MODEL?

A major assumption of the multidirectional model is that intelligent task performance requires the student to integrate several kinds of capabilities. He or she must select from a repertoire of strategies (executive function) a plan of action (strategy) relevant to the problem. The student also must have the necessary information (knowledge base) and knowledge of his or her cognitive resources (metacognition) to be able to transfer and efficiently refine (strategy abstraction) his or her learning processes (Swanson, 1984, 1985). By inference, learning disabled children need to integrate all cognitive planes into one complex act for successful task performance (i.e., reading). Therefore, efficient cognitive functioning is not simply that certain cognitive planes become enhanced or accessible, but that a smooth coordination of all cognitive components occurs.

To accomplish the goal of assessing learning disabled students from a cognitive orientation, cognitive planes that produce individual differences in learning need to be identified and explained. These planes must be broad enough to capture the complexity of learning, as well as to provide a framework for how instruction should occur. The cognitive planes in Figure 9–1 have been gleaned from several information processing models that focus on problem solving and individual differences (e.g., Borkowski, Johnston, & Reid, 1987; Brown & Campione, 1986; Rumelhart, 1978; Sternberg, 1987). In essence, what learning disabled children bring to a task is reflected in the knowledge base plane, and the remainder of the cognitive planes focus on how the children access and apply that knowledge. It is important to keep in mind that the cognitive planes are *not* exclusive or independent of one another. All the cognitive planes in Figure 9–1 are important, and it seems likely that, in many cases, three or even all five planes should be assessed in order to develop a comprehensive instructional program. Let us briefly review some of the assumptions related to the model in Figure 9–1.

Opportunistic Thinking

In contrast with traditional views of learning, which assume that certain skills are acquired through a linear or step-by-step fashion, a cognitive model assumes that, during problem solving tasks, individuals use cognitive processes that do not fit into a completely integrated or hierarchical plan (see Hayes-Roth & Thorndyke, 1979). As people make decisions, their cognitive processes are not coherently integrated. For example, their thinking may make use of isolated processes within or between cognitive planes. In the case of the learning disabled student, however, the processes within and between the cognitive planes are more poorly coordinated than in the case of nondisabled students. The educational goal becomes one of helping the learning disabled student

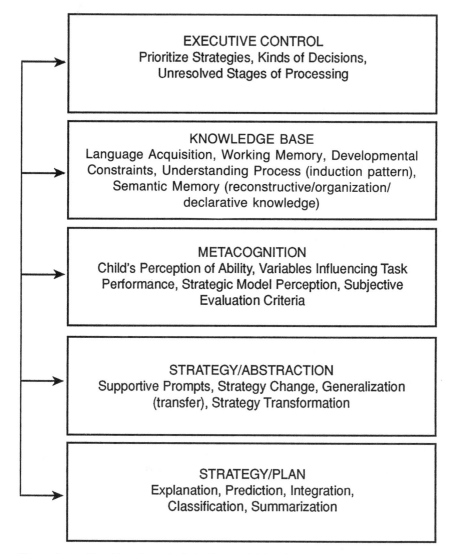

Figure 9–1. Cognitive planes included in a multidirectional assessment model.

integrate various mental components so that a smooth coordination of information processing occurs during task performance.

Availability Versus Accessibility

The selection of the cognitive planes is also based on the assumption that learning reflects an interaction between the accessibility and the availability of knowledge. In the context of learning, *accessibility* refers to the notion that the information necessary for task performance resides within the child. Some children are able to access this information with flexibility; that is, a particular behavior is not delimited to a constrained set of circumstances (Brown & Campione, 1986). In addition, some children are aware of or are able to verbally describe and discuss the cognitive activities that allow them to access information (Brown & Campione, 1981, refer to this as "reflective access"). Numerous researchers in learning disabilities have accepted the notion that learning disabled children's ability to access knowledge remains inert unless they are explicitly prompted to use certain cognitive strategies (e.g., Torgesen, Murphy, & Ivey, 1979; Wong, 1978; Worden, 1986). For example, learning disabled children may be taught to (a) organize lists of pictures and words in common categories, (b) rehearse the category names during learning, and (c) use the names as retrieval cues at the time of the test. Data indicate that when learning disabled children are explicitly encouraged to use such strategies, their performance improves.

Availability, on the other hand, refers to the fact that the knowledge required for successful task performance is represented in the child's conceptual knowledge system. This knowledge is often described in terms of a specific representational system (Anderson, 1983, refers to this as a "spreading activation memory system"). Research fairly clearly shows that a highly organized knowledge base influences task performance in children (e.g., Chi, 1978). Unfortunately, the learning disabilities field is deficient in basic research related to understanding the learning disabled child's knowledge base (see Swanson, 1986), and the research that is available considers the learning disabled child's knowledge base in an all-or-none fashion. A distinction is usually made between knowledge that is available and knowledge that is unavailable. Unfortunately, this dichotomy does not appear to capture task performance, since knowledge access and availability interact; that is, processes of access interact with conceptual knowledge (e.g., see Anderson's, 1983, descriptions of declarative and procedural knowledge).

Thinking Aloud

Based upon the preceding discussion, we broadly defined *process assessment* as a systematic approach to identifying underlying cognitive operations that direct numerous aspects of task performance. Of course, the major problem in proposing such a model is determining how one goes about identifying internally organized strategic skills that influence task performance. We reason that directing children's "thinking aloud" through a process of inquiry during problem solving is one means of understanding and identifying information processing components (e.g., Ericsson & Simon, 1984). The usefulness of a subject's verbalization, directed through an inquiry or questioning procedure, rests on the assumption that such verbalization provides a record of the basic processes being executed (e.g., Ericsson & Simon, 1984).

Based upon the above assumptions, consider the think-aloud protocol in Table 9–1. The reader should keep in mind, however, that the protocol is only illustrative and that theoretical support for the various cognitive planes is neither supported nor weakened by such a methodology. This protocol represents a 15-year-old learning disabled student who has difficulty "knowing" the meaning of certain words in a reading passage. The teacher asks several questions to assess what the adolescent knows about the words. The student's strategy for determining word meaning is summarized somewhat in Statement 44. Two problems arise, however, in the interpretation of such a protocol. First, how does one place the student's verbal statements within a comprehensive information processing framework? Second, the complexity and variability in the adolescent's verbal behaviors prohibit viewing him as simply a step-by-step learner; that is, some of his verbalized strategies are less than orderly and reflect such information processing handicaps as poor interim decisions and word knowledge constraints. To provide an assessment framework that incorporates the components of information processing known to influence task performance and to help the reader analyze some important components in learning, the five major planes shown in Figure 9–1 are discussed and related to the think-aloud sequence. We consider how to isolate important components of the protocol in terms of cognitive processes.

TABLE 9–1
Think-Aloud Sequences

---

1. T: What are you going to do when you find a word you don't know the meaning of?
2. S: I'm going to try to figure it out.
3. T: How do you try to figure it out?
4. S: I try to get the meaning from the paragraph or title of the SRA reader.
5. T: What do you do when the word is by itself?
6. S: Go look it up in the dictionary. Try to spell it first . . . (pause) because I can't look it up if I can't spell it.
7. T: What is the quickest way to find out the meaning of a word?
8. S: Figure it out from how it's used in the paragraph.
9. T: If I gave this problem to two people and one of them was a linguist and one of them was an engineer, which one would have an easier time finding the answer?
10. S: The linguist.
11. T: Why?
12. S: I guess because he works with words.

TABLE 9-1 (continued)

13. T: Do you think it is easier to find the meaning of a word when you see it in reading material or when you see the word just by itself?
14. S: When it is in reading material.
15. T: Why?
16. S: Because you can use the rest of the material to help figure out the meaning. You can also break the word up into syllables.
17. T: What is important about the syllables of words when you are trying to figure out the meaning?
18. S: If you can find the meanings of some of the syllables, it could tell you the meaning of the word.
19. T: Is there anything important about beginnings and endings of a word?
20. S: Yes, they can help you understand the whole word, or at least give you some ideas.
21. T: When you've done this in the past, has it been successful?
22. S: I think so . . . but I still missed a lot of answers on my social studies assignment.
23. T: If I gave Susan a paragraph to read in which there was an unfamiliar word and I gave Sally only the word, which one would have an easier time figuring out the meaning?
24. S: It depends on the word, but probably the first girl because she can make a better guess.
25. T: If you come across several words in what you are reading and you don't know what they mean, what are you doing to do?
26. S: I try to figure it out from the paragraph.
27. T: How do you do that?
28. S: I read the whole paragraph, then I go back to the word and read it in the sentence and see if I understand it. I keep doing this until I understand the word or until I decide to give up.
29. T: How do you decide that you understand the word?
30. S: If my idea makes sense in the paragraph, then I decide I understand it.
31. T: Is there any other way to check your answer to see if it is correct?
32. S: I can look it up in the dictionary.
33. T: How do you usually do? Are you usually correct?
34. S: No, not always.
35. T: What would you do if your science teacher gave you a list of words you didn't know and told you that you can't go home until you write the meanings for all of them?
36. S: I would look them up in the dictionary. If they aren't there, I would go to an encyclopedia, since they could have more scientific words. I might break the word down into syllables and analyze it. If I still can't get it, I would call my friend Jerry who gets good grades in science.

TABLE 9-1 (continued)

37. T: Is this problem of understanding words similar to something you've done before?
38. S: Sort of.
39. T: How is it similar?
40. S: Sometimes people will be talking to me and say something I don't understand. Then I have to ask them to explain what they mean.
41. T: Now could you summarize for me what you need to know and how to find the meaning of the word "pythoness"?
42. S: I have to be able to sound the word out or at least the first part so I could look it up in the dictionary or "break the word up." I need to know how to divide it into syllables and what the syllables mean . . . I have to know how to use a dictionary . . . I guess I need to know how to read. I have to know how to go about learning new words.
43. T: Let's try this all out on the word "pythoness." Tell me exactly what you plan to do first, second, third, and so on to find the meaning.
44. S: Get a piece of paper and a pen. Spell the word phonetically and divide it into syllables. Guess what the word means. Look it up in the dictionary under the letter p. If I can't find it spelled the way I thought, I will try other phonetic spellings.
45. T: OK, let's try it. What does the word "pythoness" mean?
46. S: (He writes it down and divides it into syllables: py/thon/ess.) It might have something to do with a snake, a python.
47. T: What does the suffix "ess" mean?
48. S: I don't know.
49. T: "ess" means woman.
50. S: A woman? Well, I think the word means a woman . . . female snake.
51. T: How do you know you're right about what the word means?
52. S: If it makes sense to me (child reads sentence). Yeah, the sentence makes sense.
53. T: If you look the word up in the dictionary, do you think it will have the same meaning as yours?
54. S: Yeah! I know I'm right. (Gets the dictionary and looks up the word.) "A pythoness is a woman who tells the future."
55. T: How did you do?
56. S: Only half right—only right about the woman part.
57. T: Now try another word using your "way of figuring" out new words. (Teacher points to the word "laundress.")
58. S: A woman who does the laundry. I already know that.
59. T: One more. What does the word "generate" mean?
60. S: Mainly to do something, to get something going, electricity.
Sequence continues.

WHAT COMPONENTS MAKE UP A COGNITIVE MODEL?

Executive Function

Executive functioning has been explained (see Chapter 5) with respect to its importance and application to mental retardation (Campione, Brown, & Ferrara, 1982), but rarely with respect to learning disabilities (Brown & Palincsar, 1982; Pressley, Johnson, & Symons, 1987; Swanson, 1987a). Various terms have been used to refer to executive function (self-regulation of cognition, homunculus, central processor). Its major functions, as shown in Figure 9–2, include planning activities prior to undertaking a problem, monitoring behavior in action, reorganizing strategies, and evaluating the outcomes of any strategic action. Strategy deficits in inefficient learners have been noted in terms of failure to monitor cognitive progress or failure to notice important task differences in learning problems (Brown, Armbruster, & Baker, 1985; Borkowski, Carr, & Pressley, 1987; Pressley & Levin, 1987, for a review).

Executive functions can be inferred from several statements in the protocol (Table 9–1). For example, in Statement 4, the student suggests a strategy to determine word meaning. He then comes up with another strategy if the first one fails (e.g., Statement 6) and suggests giving up if his alternative strategy fails (28). This protocol suggests that the student may have a strategy for selecting strategies. Therefore, the important assessment question becomes whether the student can review his or her own cognitive strategies, select and reject them appropriately, and persist in searching for the most suitable task strategies at various stages of performance (Palincsar & Brown, 1987; Pressley et al., 1987).

To answer such a question, three components (as shown in Table 9–2) are proposed for assessing such executive decision making. Support for these components can be found in studies in which learning disabled students had difficulty checking, planning, and monitoring control processes (Brown & Palincsar, 1988; Palincsar & Brown, 1984; Swanson, 1983; Torgesen et al., 1979). First, a determination is made of how decisions or strategies are prioritized. For example, learning disabled students are assessed on their ability to generate several alternative responses to the question, "What is the best way to find out what a word means?" The order of their decisions indicates preferences for possible processing activities. Second, an assessment is made of the kinds of decisions children with learning disabilities make at a specific point in implementing strategy. For example, on a reading comprehension test, the students must decide if a rough understanding of a word is necessary (e.g., guessing the word meaning from context) or if a more precise understanding is needed. Finally, it is necessary to determine how learn-

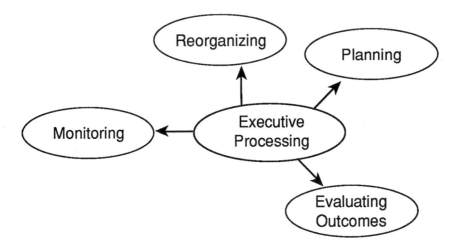

Figure 9-2. Components of executive processing.

ing disabled students make decisions related to an unresolved processing stage (e.g., dictionary not available, cannot understand gist of passage). It is assumed that this information assesses the limits of the learning disabled students' available strategies.

When a learning disabled student is presented a task, whether it is a problem solving situation or a reverbalization of information content, where does the processing begin? Neisser (1967) viewed the human organism as somewhat analogous to a computer: The person must determine the order in which his or her problem solving strategies or schemes of recall will be performed. Based on the task, stimulus input, and expected outcome or response desired, the child must organize his or her skills into some efficient scheme. At the highest part of the intended hierarchy, the child's decisions or strategies must be prioritized. For example, the child may form several responses to the questions, "Who discovered America?" and "What is the best way to solve a math problem mentally?" (e.g., "What is the answer to 567 divided by 12.13?"). These decisions indicate preferences for possible processing activity. For example, responses to the first question may include native Americans, Leif Eriksson, Christopher Columbus, and lost tribes of Israel. By approaching the question from a secular, parochial, ethnic, or traditional knowledge standpoint, decisions would include prioritizing what response to provide before going to the next question. Possible strategies for solving the math problem might include moving the decimal point, multiplying

---

TABLE 9–2
Procedures for Determining Activities Related to Executive Processing

---

1. Determine how decisions are prioritized.
   Activity: Have the student generate several alternatives to a problem and have the student prioritize decisions.

2. Determine the kinds of decisions made when implementing a strategy as related to the outcome.
   Activity: Have the student assess the kinds of decisions that must be made when reading a passage as related to literal comprehension, inferential comprehension.

3. Determine the kinds of decisions that occur when performance is not successful.
   Activity: Have the student explain how he or she plans to answer a particular math problem that the student got wrong on a class assignment.

---

by another digit, subtracting the product. The student basically plans what to do before working out the details of the solution.

A lower step of the executive function would consider what kinds of decisions must be made at a specific point in implementing the strategy. For example, in solving the math problem, the student must decide if an approximate answer is sufficient (estimates are acceptable if the response is in multiple-choice format), if exact answers are required (the answer includes a remainder), or if the product of the first multiplication must be provided then subtracted.

A final assessment of the executive function might include decisions relating to any unresolved stages of processing. Assessment of this situation requires key questions on the examiner's part. These questions might include the following:

1. Can you tell me what your choices are?

2. What steps are you going to follow?

3. If that works, what will you do next?

4. If your overall plan fails, what alternatives do you have?

5. Where would you search for the answer if yours is incorrect?

6. If your answer is correct, what else may be a correct approach or answer?

7. On the outcome of the step you mentioned, what will be carried out simultaneously? Next? Last?

In summary, the focus of the executive function is to detail the student's coordination, direction, and organization of search strategies and problem solving routines. The kinds of decisions that will be made and how decisions will be directed when a sequence of operations may provide unresolved steps is related to the child's metacognitive knowledge (discussed later).

Knowledge Base

The majority of information processing research on learning disabilities has focused on processing and ignored the information part of information processing theory. Recent studies, however, have suggested that differences between learning disabled and nondisabled children reflect not only strategic or control processing functions, but also differences in the basic information stored in long-term memory (Baker, Ceci, & Herrmann, 1987; Scott, Greenfield, & Sterental, 1986; Swanson, 1986). This concept is an important dimension in information processing models (Chi, 1978; Chi & Koeske, 1984; Waldrop, 1984). For example, Chi (1978) demonstrated that very young children proficient in chess or dinosaur classification can show adultlike strategies, whereas adult novices show childlike strategies. The implication is that dramatic differences observed in the performance of mature (e.g., nondisabled) and immature (e.g., learning disabled) problem solvers are consequences of differences in the underlying knowledge base (e.g., cognitive structures prior to learning) rather than of differences in strategies. A knowledge base places formal restrictions on the class of logically possible strategies within a given academic domain. It is assumed that students with learning disabilities bring to a learning task a set "structure" that limits the class of strategies they are likely to use. To accommodate this perspective, five components for assessment of knowledge base (as shown in Figure 9–3) are reviewed; language competence, working memory, developmental constraints, understanding ability, and semantic memory.

Language competence. An assessment of learning disabled children's knowledge base is influenced by their language competence (see Donahue, 1986, for a review). Earlier studies (Vellutino, Steger, DeSetto, & Phillips, 1975; also see Vellutino, 1979, for a review) comparing learning disabled and nondisabled children noted that learning disabled children demonstrate language skill difficulties in such areas as vocabulary comprehension, productive vocabulary, morphology, syntactic–semantic ability, and general social communication development (Bryan, Donahue, Pearl, & Herzog, 1984; Donahue, 1986). The principal purpose of including this component in the assessment framework is to determine whether learning disabled children's knowledge base is confounded by their language competence. A thorough assessment of language competence includes socialized speech, language regu-

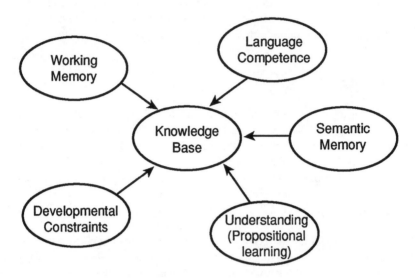

Figure 9-3. Components related to the knowledge base plane.

lation, language function, metalinguistic variables, pragmatics, and semantic output. These variables, as well as their appropriate testing instruments, are discussed elsewhere in this text.

Working memory. According to models of information processing (e.g., see Chapter 5), the human as a processor is assumed to have both a short-term memory and a long-term memory. Unfortunately, previous studies of learning disabled children's short-term memory operations, such as rehearsal (Torgesen & Goodman, 1977), have not explained how constraints in long-term memory contribute to academic performance (see Chapter 6). Furthermore, measures (e.g., digit span) commonly used in assessing differences between learning disabled and nondisabled children's memory are weakly correlated with academic ability (Daneman & Carpenter, 1980), suggesting that such short-term memory tasks may not capture the essence of academic performance, namely the combination of processing and long-term memory storage functions. The combination of processing and storage functions is referred to as "working memory" and reflects a system for temporary storage and information manipulation (see Chapter 5 for further discussion). In working memory, structural (also called capacity) limits are generally imposed on the complexity of information that may be recalled. Butterfield (1981) operationalized structural limits as an experimental variable that cannot be manipulated or improved upon. Based on this assumption, the focus of assessment is on the extent to which working memory performance separates learning disabled subjects from their nondisabled counterparts *after* control processes have been trained and effectively used. Long-term memory reflects the production of symbols or content and may be assessed in tests of general information or associational events.

Previous studies of the assessment of knowledge base components focused on accessing accurate information from long-term memory. Several investigators (see Worden, 1986, for a review) have suggested that learning disabled children's long-term memory is intact, but that the strategies necessary to gain access to this information are impaired. This notion has been recently challenged (Baker et al., 1987), and there is evidence to suggest that learning disabled children's long-term memory on tasks that require semantic processing is clearly deficient when compared with their nondisabled peers (Swanson, 1986).

Some experimental evidence suggests that children with learning disabilities may have problems in the structural component of information processing (e.g., Baker et al., 1987; Brainerd, Kingman, & Howe, 1986; Swanson, 1987b; Torgesen & Houck, 1980). For example, Torgesen and Houck (1980) completed a series of eight experiments in which subgroups of learning disabled and nondisabled children were compared on a digit span task. Treatment variations across the eight experimental conditions included manipulations of rehearsal, incentives, and related mnemonic activities. Not all learning disabled subjects benefited from strategy intervention, suggesting that structural or capacity difficulty may exist in some children with learning disabilities.

Developmental constraints. An initial step toward understanding learning disabled children's knowledge base is to determine what cognitive constraints underlie performance. Piagetian analysis provides perhaps the most elaborate attempt at describing and assessing constraints that underlie thought processes. Although Piagetian research on children with learning disabilities is meager, existing studies appear to suggest that learning disabled children perform much like younger children (e.g., Reid & Knight-Arest, 1981; Speece, McKinney, & Appelbaum, 1986). Speece et al. (1986) demonstrated in a 3-year longitudinal investigation with five measures of conservation (space, number, substance, weight, continuous and discontinuous quantity), that learning disabled children demonstrated a developmental delay in attaining the stage of concrete operations. When this stage was achieved, however, children with learning disabilities acquired specific concepts at rates similar to those of nondisabled children. Thus, it appears that the developmentally delayed transition between preoperational and concrete operational stages may provide important information related to the developmental constraints under which learning disabled children operate.

According to Piaget's developmental theory of intelligence, stages in processing are related to concept and perceptual attainment. Specific tests can be developed to ascertain developmental milestones (see Piaget & Inhelder, 1969). The examiner may assess the child by using observation and task manipulation to get the child to answer several questions. Sample questions about a child's cognitive development may include the following:

1. Can the child consider the point of view of others (socialized speech)?

2. Does the child have a mental representation of a sequential series of actions (e.g., can the child explain how to get from one place to another or draw it on paper)?

3. Does the child know that liquids or solids are not transformed without changing their mass or volume?

4. Is the child capable of mentally returning to a point to overcome perceptual contradiction (reversibility)?

5. Can the child see that objects with common features form a class of objects (class inclusion)?

6. Does the child have a language of quantity (e.g., "more than," "less than")?

7. Does the child understand relational terms (e.g., "darker," "larger," "weaker")?

8. Does the child have the ability to arrange objects according to some quantified dimension, such as weight or size, on an ordinal scale?

9. Can the child change his or her mode of thinking from inductive to deductive thinking?

Understanding ability.   Before children can attempt to process information effectively, they must understand the problem at hand. Understanding ability refers to the capacity to extrapolate inductive patterns, that is, to know how to combine pieces of information into an internally connected whole (see discussion in Chapter 5 on Bruner, Goodnow, & Austin, 1956). Swanson (1981, 1982) found that students with learning disabilities were deficient in their ability to extrapolate rules and concepts from tasks requiring inductive reasoning (e.g., conjunctive, disjunctive, condition rules; see Chapter 5). The results suggest that understanding ability becomes differentiated among ability groups during encoding. Thus, assessment should focus on the ability to combine information inductively into a complex pattern at the earlier stages of processing.

Several studies have assessed a child's ability to extrapolate inductive patterns on various reasoning tasks (see Sternberg, 1984, for a review), for example, analogies, classifications, series, and completions. Six information processing components on these reasoning tasks have been identified: encoding, inference, mapping, application, justification, and response preparation. Children's differences are revealed to the extent that individuals use strategies on each component. Strategies become differentiated by the relative amount of time devoted to each component. For example, consider the following analogy: teacher : classroom : doctor (a) hospital, (b) courtroom. The child might receive no precuing terms (a blank field), one term (teacher), two terms (teacher : classroom), three terms (teacher : classroom : doctor), four terms (teacher : classroom : doctor : (a) hospital), or five terms (teacher : classroom : doctor : (a) hospital, (b) courtroom). The child's difficulty in solving this analogy may involve encoding (knowledge of each term of the analogy), inference (relationship of the first two terms), mapping (relationship of the first and third terms), application (relationship of the third term to the answer options), and/or response (correct answer or justification process).

Semantic memory.   Assessment of a child's knowledge base must also include information on semantic memory. Semantic memory, which has been found to be deficient in learning disabled children (Swanson, 1986), represents a repository of word knowledge. Such a repository consists of associative links between words as well as word features—orthographic, phonemic, and semantic. Semantic memory is facilitated by the kind and amount of verbal knowledge available in the individual's memory. Adequate assessment of semantic memory would include an assessment of both *declarative* and *procedural* knowledge. Declarative knowledge is related to an individual's recall of facts, concepts, symbols, and so forth, whereas procedural knowledge is related to the information retained on processes, strategies, plans, and/or operations.

Assessment of semantic memory also focuses on the *reconstruction* of information, which may be conceptualized as a memory for gist or the sense of a situation (Neisser, 1981; see also Chapter 5). The assumption is that all humans actively rework or reconstruct information in accordance with their cognitive structures and verbal abilities. What children provide at the output stage or what they recall does not accurately represent input. An important question is "How discrepant are the learning disabled child's output responses from the original input?" In answer to this question, Worden (Worden, Malgren, & Gabourie, 1982; Worden & Nakamura, 1983) tested students with learning disabilities on their recall of prose material. The results suggested that the learning disabled students had difficulty remembering the main ideas of a story to the same extent as nondisabled students (also see Wong & Sawatsky, 1984).

Strategy

An assessment of the strategy plane involves determining the explicit action a student is going to carry out to provide an answer to a problem (Brown

& Palincsar, 1988). As shown in Figure 9–4, a strategy is composed of several components interrelated within decision making. These components may include, for example, a means–end analysis (Simon, 1981), definition of subgoals (Pitt, 1983), and various forms of logic (Bransford, Stein, Arbitman-Smith, & Vye, 1985). Consistent with Anderson (1983), it is assumed that strategies are a form of knowledge (procedural knowledge), and therefore a distinction must be made between the statement of what one can do and what is procedurally required. An example of a plan of action from the previous think-aloud protocol is shown in Statement 4 (see Table 9–1). Further attempts to uncover strategic knowledge have generally focused on five component levels for assessment (Belmont, Butterfield, & Ferretti, 1982; Brown & Palincsar, 1982; Campione et al., 1982; Meichenbaum, 1982; Pressley & Levin, 1987; Wong, 1987):

1. *Explanation:* The child's ability to provide a description of the procedures, plans, or strategies he or she will use to perform the task successfully. Hopefully, the strategy is general enough to explain a series of related task demands.

2. *Prediction:* The child's expectation related to a hypothetical plan or strategy that could be carried out. The ability to generate a series of plans, as well as to predict their expected outcomes, is important because it is the only way by which the appropriateness of a strategy can be intuitively assessed (e.g., Brown & Palincsar, 1988).

3. *Integration:* The ability to link and organize substrategies into one general coherent strategy. The assessment focus is on determining whether the strategy encompasses logically related routines of lower problem solving strategies.

4. *Classification:* The ability to identify the relevant attributes for problem solution. Verbalization of attribute dimensions, attribute discrimination, attribute labeling, and other aspects of attribute learning has clear and natural implications for the ability to develop a strategy for problem solution.

5. *Summarization:* The ability to state succinctly the principal relationship between attributes and strategy. Strategies should represent a succinct statement of how the problem or question is to be answered.

In short, an assessment of these components determines the learning disabled child's ability to verbally generate a theory of learning or, more specifically, determines what the learning disabled child knows about the composition of learning strategies.

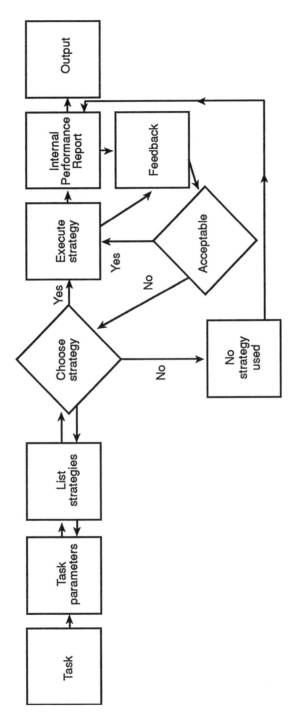

Figure 9–4. Components of the strategy plane.

WHAT IS PRACTICAL?

Let us look at this cognitive plane in a practical sense. One assumption of the strategy model is that the child will be able to articulate his or her own thought processes, exercise control over those processes, see the relevant features of a problem, generate an hypothesis, and so on. Furthermore, one seeks to determine the relationship between the child's hypothesis and overall level of performance. The most direct means to assess this cognitive plane is to ask the child to think aloud. Therefore, an assessment of the child's plan, or a particular way of approaching a problem, would include an analysis of a set of verbal statements. Any set of verbal statements on the child's part related to how he or she plans to perform the task, regardless of the sophistication of the content, can be indicative of a strategy. Also, whether the set of verbal statements is actually followed to generate a behavior is not important. The potentiality of strategy generation, on the other hand, is how children generate a strategy that is interpreted within the context of the task they are doing. Their set of verbal statements should specify what the outcomes of their behavior will be, how they will achieve these outcomes, how they indicate specific sequences of actions, and what procedures or routes they will use to reach the correct response.

Following are some diagnostic questions that can be used to probe children to provide a verbal explanation of the strategies they will use to perform a task.

General questions
What do you think would be the best way to answer this question (problem, task)?
How do these items relate?
What do you think you need to do first? Second? . . .
Are there different ways to solve this problem?
Can you restate the question in your own words? And provide an answer?
How did you define the problem?

Specific probing questions
Explanation
Have you tried to solve this type of problem before? How did you solve it?
Can you explain the strategy you used to another student?
Prediction
Can you make up a simple way of solving this problem?
What would happen if you used this strategy?
Even if you can't answer the question, how would you begin to answer it? Is that a beginning point that will help you answer the question?
What is the simplest (hardest, funniest, craziest) answer you (could have answered) can provide for this question?
What do you think the outcome of your response would be?

Classification
What do you need to know to solve this problem?
What is the question specifically asking?
How many things are talked about? Describe each.

Integration
How do the steps you told me about relate to one another?
What's the first thing you'll do? Is that going to help you in the overall problem solution?

Summarization
Can you tell me quickly the steps you would use to solve this problem?
Tell me the first, second, third, and so on.
Can you tell me in one sentence how you plan to answer this question (could have answered this question)?

WHAT ARE THE PROBLEMS OF THE STRATEGY ASSESSMENT PLANE?

Besides problems related to the other planes (e.g., the knowledge base plane), several practical issues occur when an assessment of strategic awareness is implemented. These problems are generally related to the motivation and cognitive style of the child.

Maintaining child interest and motivation are certainly issues to be contended with in cognitive assessment. Wagner and Kistner (1989) stressed that the motivational factors that learning disabled persons actually use cause them to perform at a level below their actual intellectual potential. Therefore, the attainment of strategic development and training must have an incentive quality. The use of contingent incentive has been successful for compensating for a child's cognitive style and task behavior.

Cognitive style has been used to describe individual differences in behavior responding. Children who show a preferred cognitive style may also show further differences in motivation, attention, or cognitive organization. For example, in the Matching Familiar Figures Test (Kagen, Pearson, & Welch, 1966), the child is asked to match a common figure (e.g., teddy bear) with the identical stimulus of an array of six pictures in which small details vary from the standard. Two styles are assessed. *Reflective* children evaluate their responses before answering, and *impulsive* children check the standard less often and use fewer analytical scanning strategies. Reflective children perform better than impulsive children on tasks of discrimination learning, reasoning, memory, and Piagetian measures. It is inferred that impulsivity is related to less efficient or lower level problem solving strategies. Experimenters have been successful in altering cognitive styles through direct instructions of appropriate response tactics, reinforcing or modeling a different response style, reinforcing for slow responding, and demonstrating scanning strategies (Witkin et al., 1977).

Likewise, the distinction between *field dependence–independence* is regarded as relating both to cognition and personality and to learning (Witkin et al., 1977). Field-dependent and field-independent children are considered comparable in learning and memory abilities, but different in the strategies used in the material they learn. Field-independent children tend to make greater use of their language as mediator for processing information, whereas field-dependent children often cannot impose structure on material and need an external source (e.g., teacher-generated cue or hints).

SUMMARY

This chapter has delineated some of the assumptions and mental components that contribute to a comprehensive model of cognitive assessment. Discussion of further components is provided in the next chapter, as well as a summary related to both chapters.

REFERENCES

Anderson, J. R. (1983). *The architecture of cognition.* Cambridge, MA: Harvard University Press.

Baker, J. G., Ceci, S. J., & Herrmann, N. D. (1987). Semantic structure and processing: Implications for the learning disabled child. In H. L. Swanson (Ed.), *Memory and learning disabilities* (pp. 83–110). Greenwich, CT: JAI Press.

Belmont, S., Butterfield, E., & Ferretti, R. P. (1982). To secure transfer of training instruct self-management skills. In D. K. Detterman & R. J. Sternberg (Eds.), *How and how much can intelligence be increased* (pp. 147–154). Norwood, NJ: Ablex.

Borkowski, J. G., Carr, M., & Pressley, M. (1987). "Spontaneous" strategy use: Perspectives from metacognitive theory. *Intelligence, 11,* 61–75.

Borkowski, J. G., Johnston, M. B., & Reid, M. K. (1987). Metacognition, motivation, and controlled performance. In S. J. Ceci (Ed.), *Handbook of cognitive, social and neuropsychological aspects of learning disabilities* (pp. 147–174). Hillsdale, NJ: Erlbaum.

Brainerd, C. J., Kingman, J., & Howe, M. L. (1986). Long-term memory development and learning disability: Storage and retrieval loci of disabled/nondisabled differences. In S. Ceci (Ed.), *Handbook of cognitive, social, and neuropsychological aspects of learning disabilities* (pp. 161–184). Hillsdale, NJ: Erlbaum.

Bransford, J. D., Stein, B. S., Arbitman-Smith, R., & Vye, N. J. (1985). Three approaches to improving thinking and learning skills. In J. W. Segal, S. F. Chipman, & R. Glaser (Eds.), *Thinking and learning skills: Relating instruction to basic research* (Vol. 1, pp. 133–200). Hillsdale, NJ: Erlbaum.

Brown, A. L., Armbruster, B. B., & Baker, L. (1985). The role of metacognition in reading and studying. In J. Ornasanu (Ed.), *Reading comprehension: From research to practice* (pp. 49–75). Hillsdale, NJ: Erlbaum.

Brown, A., & Campione, J. C. (1981). Inducing flexible thinking: The problem of access. In M. Friedman, J. P. Das, & N. O'Connor (Eds.), *Intelligence and learning* (pp. 515–530). New York: Plenum Press.

Brown, A. L., & Campione, J. C. (1986). Psychological theory and the study of learning disabilities. *American Psychologist, 41,* 1059–1068.

Brown, A., & Palincsar, A. (1982). Inducing strategic learning from texts by means of informed, self-control training. *Topics in Learning and Learning Disabilities, 2,* 1–18.

Brown, A. L., & Palincsar, A. S. (1988). Reciprocal teaching of comprehension strategies: A natural history of one program for enhancing learning. In J. Borkowski & J. P. Das (Eds.), *Intelligence and cognition in special children: Comparative studies of giftedness, mental retardation, and learning disabilities.* New York: Ablex.

Bruner, J. S., Goodnow, J., & Austin, G. (1956). *A study of thinking.* New York: Wiley.

Bryan, T., Donahue, M., Pearl, R., & Herzog, A. (1984). Conversational interactions between mothers and learning-disabled or nondisabled children during a problem-solving task. *Journal of Speech and Hearing Disorders, 49,* 64–71.

Butterfield, E. (1981). Testing process theories of intelligence. In M. Friedman, J. Das, & N. O'Connor (Eds.), *Intelligence and learning* (pp. 277–296). New York: Plenum Press.

Campione, J. C., Brown, A. L., & Ferrara, R. A. (1982). Mental retardation and intelligence. In R. J. Sternberg (Ed.), *Handbook of human intelligence* (pp. 392–473). New York: Cambridge University Press.

Chi, M. T. H. (1978). Knowledge structures and memory development. In R. Siegler (Ed.), *Children's thinking: What develops?* (pp. 73–96). Hillsdale, NJ: Erlbaum.

Chi, M. T. H., & Koeske, R. D. (1984). Network presentation of a child's dinosaur knowledge. *Developmental Psychology, 19,* 29–39.

Daneman, M., & Carpenter, P. A. (1980). Individual differences in working memory and reading. *Journal of Verbal Learning and Verbal Behavior, 19,* 450–466.

Donahue, M. (1986). Linguistic and communicative development in learning disabled children. In S. J. Ceci (Ed.), *Handbook of cognitive, social, and neuropsychological aspects of learning disabilities* (pp. 263–289). Hillsdale, NJ: Erlbaum.

Ericsson, K. A., & Simon, H. A. (1984). *Protocol analysis: Verbal reports as data.* Cambridge, MA: MIT Press.

Hayes-Roth, B., & Thorndyke, P. (1979). *Decision-making during the planning process.* Santa Monica, CA: Rand Corporation.

Kagen, J., Pearson, W., & Welch, L. (1966). Modifiability of an impulsive tempo. *Journal of Educational Psychology, 57,* 359–365.

Meichenbaum, D. (1982). *Teaching thinking: A cognitive behavioral approach.* Austin, TX: Society for Learning Disabilities and Remedial Education.

Neisser, U. (1967). *Cognitive psychology.* New York: Appleton-Century-Crofts.

Neisser, U. (1981). John Dean's memory: A case study. *Cognition, 9,* 1–22.

Palincsar, A. S., & Brown, A. L. (1984). Reciprocal teaching of comprehension-fostering and comprehension-monitoring activities. *Cognition and Instruction, 1*, 117–175.

Palincsar, A. S., & Brown, A. (1987). Enhancing instructional time through attention to metacognition. *Journal of Learning Disabilities, 20*, 66–76.

Piaget, J., & Inhelder, B. (1969). *The psychology of the child*. New York: Basic Books.

Pressley, M., Johnson, C. J., & Symons, S. (1987). Elaborating to learn and learning to elaborate. *Journal of Learning Disabilities, 20*, 76–91.

Pressley, M., & Levin, J. R. (1987). Elaborative learning strategies for the inefficient learner. In S. J. Ceci (Ed.), *Handbook of cognitive, social and neuropsychological aspects of learning disabilities* (pp. 175–212). Hillsdale, NJ: Erlbaum.

Reid, D. K., & Knight-Arest, I. (1981). Cognitive processing in learning disabled and normally achieving boys in a goal-oriented task. In M. Friedman, J. Das, & N. O'Connor (Eds.), *Intelligence and learning* (pp. 503–508). New York: Plenum Press.

Rumelhart, D. (1978). *Toward an interactive model of reading* (Tech. Rep. No. 56). La Jolla, CA: University of California at San Diego, Center for Human Information Processing.

Scott, M., Greenfield, D., & Sterental, E. (1986). Abstract categorization ability as a predictor of learning disability classification. *Intelligence, 10*, 377–387.

Simon, H. A. (1981). Information processing model of cognition. *Journal of the American Society for Information Science, 32*, 364–375.

Speece, D. L., McKinney, J. D., & Appelbaum, M. E. (1986). Longitudinal development of conversation skills in learning disabled children. *Journal of Learning Disabilities, 19*, 302–307.

Sternberg, R. J. (1984). Toward a triarchic theory of human intelligence. *Behavioral and Brain Sciences, 2*, 269–315.

Sternberg, R. J. (1987). A unified theory of intellectual exceptionality. In J. D. Day & J. G. Borkowski (Eds.), *Intelligence and exceptionality: New directions for theory, assessment, and instructional practices* (pp. 135–172). Norwood, NJ: Ablex.

Swanson, H. L. (1981). Encoding of logical connective rules in learning disabled children. *Journal of Abnormal Child Psychology, 9*, 507–516.

Swanson, H. L. (1982). Conceptual processes as a function of age and enforced attention in learning disabled children: Evidence for deficient rule learning. *Contemporary Educational Psychology, 7*, 152–160.

Swanson, H. L. (1983). Relations among metamemory, rehearsal activity and word recall in learning disabled and nondisabled readers. *British Journal of Educational Psychology, 53*, 186–194.

Swanson, H. L. (1984). Process assessment of intelligence in learning disabled and mentally retarded children: A multidirectional model. *Educational Psychologist, 19*, 149–162.

Swanson, H. L. (1985). Assessing learning disabled children's intellectual performance: An information processing perspective. In K. Gadow (Ed.), *Advances in learning and behavior disabilities* (Vol. 4, pp. 225–272). Greenwich, CT: JAI Press.

Swanson, H. L. (1986). Do semantic memory deficiencies underlie learning disabled readers' encoding processes? *Journal of Experimental Child Psychology, 41*, 461–488.

Swanson, H. L. (1987a). Information processing theory and learning disabilities:

An overview. *Journal of Learning Disabilities, 20,* 3–7.

Swanson, H. L. (1987b). Verbal-coding deficits in the recall of pictorial information by learning disabled children: The influence of a lexical system for input operations. *American Educational Research Journal, 24,* 143–170.

Torgensen, J., & Goodman, I. (1977). Verbal rehearsal and short-term memory in reading disabled children. *Child Development, 48,* 56–60.

Torgensen, J., & Houck, G. (1980). Processing deficiencies of learning disabled children who perform poorly on the digit span test. *Journal of Educational Psychology, 72,* 141–160.

Torgesen, J. K., Murphy, H. A., & Ivey, C. (1979). The effects of an orienting task on the memory performance of reading disabled children. *Journal of Learning Disabilities, 12,* 396–401.

Vellutino, F. (1979). *Dyslexia: Theory and research.* Cambridge, MA: MIT Press.

Vellutino, F., Steger, J., DeSetto, L., & Phillips, F. (1975). Immediate and delayed recognition of visual stimuli in poor and normal readers. *Journal of Experimental Child Psychology, 19,* 223–232.

Wagner, R. K., & Kistner, J. (1989). Implications of the distinction between academic and practical intelligence for learning disabled children. In H. L. Swanson & B. Keogh (Eds.), *Learning disabilities: Theoretical and research issues* (pp. 75–92). Hillsdale, NJ: Erlbaum.

Waldrop, M. M. (1984). The necessity of knowledge. *Science, 223,* 1279–1282.

Witkin, H., and others (1977). Field-dependent and field-independent cognitive styles and their educational implications. *Review of Educational Research, 47,* 1–64.

Wong, B. Y. L. (1978). The effects of directive cues on the organization of memory and recall in good and poor readers. *Journal of Educational Research, 72,* 32–38.

Wong, B. Y. L. (1987). Directions of future research in metacognition and learning disabilities. In H. L. Swanson (Ed.), *Memory and learning disabilities* (pp. 335–356). Greenwich, CT: JAI Press.

Wong, B. Y. L., & Sawatsky, D. (1984). Sentence elaboration and retention of good, average and poor readers. *Learning Disability Quarterly, 6,* 229–236.

Worden, P. E. (1986). Comprehension and memory for prose in the learning disabled. In S. J. Ceci (Ed.), *Handbook of cognitive, social and neuropsychological aspects of learning disabilities* (Vol. 1, pp. 241–263). Hillsdale, NJ: Erlbaum.

Worden, P. E., Malgren, I., & Gabourie, P. (1982). Memory for stories in learning disabled adults. *Journal of Learning Disabilities, 15,* 145–152.

Worden, P. E., & Nakamura, G. V. (1983). Story comprehension and recall in learning-disabled vs. normal college students. *Journal of Educational Psychology, 74,* 633–641.

10

A Cognitive Assessment Approach II

H. LEE SWANSON

We continue our discussion of the cognitive assessment model introduced in Chapter 9 by focusing on two additional components: strategy abstraction and metacognition. Discussion related to both chapters is integrated by examining some think-aloud protocols, as well as by illustrating how the model can be adapted to current assessment practice.

WHAT ARE THE FINAL TWO COMPONENTS OF A COGNITIVE MODEL?

Strategy Abstraction

Most children with learning disabilities fail to apply previously learned strategies to different contexts in an effective manner (e.g., Borkowski, Johnston, & Reid, 1987). This failure suggests that the inability to transfer strategies may be related to splintered (i.e. task-specific) strategies or isolated procedural knowledge (Palincsar & Brown, 1987). Whereas the strategy plane of our model focuses on a child's knowing-how abilities, the strategy abstraction plane focuses on the depth and breadth of the child's plan of action for learning. These concepts are consistent with the proposal that children with learning disabilities fail to revise and to expand their procedural or strategic knowledge (Wong, 1987). As shown in Figure 10–1, the strategy abstraction plane consists of assessing children's cognition in relation to components related to potential and strategy transformation.

Potential. To assess a learning disabled student's potential, progressive prompts or cues are used to bring about a satisfactory response to task items (Ferrara, Brown, & Campione, 1986). Strategy abstraction ability is determined by the student's ability to benefit from prompts that have been presented in an earlier situation. The use of this assessment method, called *dynamic assessment,* has only recently appeared in the learning disabilities literature (Brown & Campione, 1986). Dynamic assessment methods rely on the expert guidance of a teacher and the use of prompts (hints) to reveal the current state of a child's understanding. The child is prompted with a series

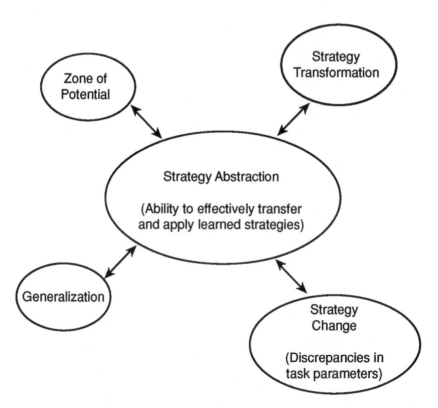

Figure 10–1. Components related to the strategy abstraction plane.

of questions. The number of hints needed for problem solution is considered the child's *zone of potential* (the degree of competence that can be achieved with aid). Children with a wide zone of potential are those who show a reduction in the number of prompts or cues needed across similar problems (see Swanson & Watson, 1982, for review). Supportive prompts can be utilized with some computerized programs (Campione, Brown, Ferrara, Jones, & Steinberg, 1985) so that dynamic assistance is provided on problems that a child can solve independently.

Suppose a child is presented with a classical Piagetian task in which conservation of volume is assessed (represented mathematically as height × width × length). Two beakers are filled with water. The child sees that the amounts are equal. The liquid in one container is poured into a rectangular container or flat dish; the liquid in the other container is poured into a square container or test tube. The child is asked if each container has the same volume of water. An important concept being assessed is whether the child can recognize that an increase in height may compensate for a decrease in length or width. In this situation, intellectual development will, of course, reflect reversibility, compensation, and seriation. Cuing or prompting a response may reflect child-directed questions in terms of a downward progression:

1. If height is increased with width and length remaining constant, will volume increase?

2. Will the amount of space occupied by the liquid change if changes are made in the length and height of a container when the width is the same as the original container?

3. Will the amount of space occupied by the liquid change if length remains constant and height and width change?

4. Do the liquids assume the shape of the container?

5. Are the sizes of the containers different?

6. Is anything lost in the liquid when I move it from one container to another?

7. Can you compare the sizes of the rectangles?

8. Are the areas of the rectangles the same?

9. What do we call these shapes? Which direction (dimension) is this on the shape?

10. Are these lengths equal?

These questions provide an assessment of the number of cues as well as the concepts the child will need to correctly perform the task.

Generalization.   An important subcomponent of strategy abstraction is the ability to generalize processing skills to a comparable problem. For example, can a learning disabled child generalize an acquired rule or strategy to a comparable task without being prompted? When learning disabled children are taught to use new learning strategies, they often do not use these new strategies on transfer tasks (see Borkowski et al., 1987, for a review). An important study by Gelzheiser (1984) illustrates this point.

Gelzheiser developed an intervention program to teach learning disabled children (a) to employ study strategies to aid recall of categorizable pictures (the training task), (b) to transfer strategies to a prose task, and (c) to understand that recall would be more effective as a result of the transfer of skills. All learning disabled students in the experimental condition were presented rules to use in studying information and were provided instruction to discriminate which strategies would be applicable to various tasks. Although the students' performance improved during the training phase, their recall on the transfer task was poor. These results were consistent with other studies which indicated that learning disabled students do not readily generalize strategies.

Transfer performance also may be affected by other areas of difficulty, such as planning a series of actions, monitoring effectiveness of strategies, and evaluating strategies (Palincsar & Brown, 1987; Pressley, Johnson, & Symons, 1987). It appears that explicit training is necessary to ensure transfer of previous training effects (see Borkowski et al., 1987, for a review). As an example, assume that the learning disabled child has been prompted to provide the responses through directive questions. Can the child next transfer his or her acquired rule, hypothesis, or strategy to a comparable task? The generalizability of a strategy determines whether the skill is specific or can be transferred to a comparable problem. Some principles to ensure strategy generalization follow:

1. Training should occur in a wide range of settings and by several individuals.

2. Stimuli in the training setting should be present in the assessment setting.

3. Transfer of skills should include natural contingencies that occur in various settings.

4. Transfer behavior should be reinforced.

5. Distraction or irrelevant cues should be systematically presented in the training periods.

Strategy change.   Once strategy generalization has been assessed, a focus is placed on the child's ability to disregard or reimplement a strategy as tasks demand. In other words, a strategic behavior can be appreciated only by examining the entire sequence of responses when a variation in task, questions, or operations occurs. It is assumed that representational thought (transformation of experience into mental events) evolves when a discrepancy exists, the strategic status quo is maintained, and there is no internal need to change a strategy. A discrepancy in task parameters and demands creates a potential for change in representational thought. For example, it is of little value if children have a reading strategy to determine word meaning if they cannot react to a change in the task demands (e.g., word meaning during conversation, see Statements 37–40 in Table 9–1). Consequently, strategic behavior is assessed by examining an entire sequence of responses with variations in tasks, questions, and operations. Previous research suggested that proficient learners feel that changes in learning approach and strategy selection come about through increased effort in response to task failure, whereas inefficient learners often attribute task failure to their abilities. Thus, children with learning disabilities are more likely to stop trying (Wagner & Kistner, 1989) and are less likely to use strategy modifications (e.g., Borkowski, Weyhing, & Carr, 1988; Garner & Reis, 1981).

Strategy transformation.   A final subcomponent of strategy abstraction focuses on the learning disabled child's ability to modify existing and useful strategies into more efficient and powerful procedures. Although learning disabled children tend to exhibit strategies that can be modified through direct instruction (Dallago & Moeley, 1980), nondisabled children tend to transform those simple strategies into "expert strategies" (Swanson & Cooney, 1985; Swanson & Rhine, 1985). Some strategy transformation difficulties found in learning disabled students include their inability to (a) rely on memory retrieval processes that access results (e.g., recall answers to simple addition problems); (b) reduce information to a rule or function with constant relationships (decode information to a rule and simplify the procedure); (c) replace one procedure with a simpler one that achieves the same goals; (d) combine several strategies or operations into a single unit (efficient processing relies on superordinate as opposed to subordinate organization procedures); and (e) delete unnecessary parts for problem solution.

Two studies (Swanson & Cooney, 1985; Swanson & Rhine, 1985) illustrate this point. These studies assumed that a possible mechanism that permits superior performance on arithmetic tasks, related to a feature of the functional components of information processing, is strategy transformation. Consider the information "handling rate" of junior-high learning disabled and nondisabled students in correctly answering simple addition problems. In these studies, it was assumed that nondisabled children become proficient on certain tasks because they have learned simple strategies and, through practice, discovered ways to modify them into more efficient and powerful procedures. In particular, the proficient learner uses rules to eliminate unnecessary or redundant steps in order to hold increasing amounts of information. Such transformations include the extent to which children rely on memory rather than computation (reduction to results), identify steps that provide an answer with minimal calculation (reduction to rule), replace any procedure with another that more efficiently accomplishes the same result (alternate method), group mental operations into a single set to save processing capacity (unit building), avoid unnecessary computations (process elimination), and change previously learned strategies to reduce task difficulty (reordering). As can be seen in Figure 10–2, when arithmetic tasks were presented to reveal such transformations, learning disabled children were inferior to their normal counterparts in processing information. When learning disabled readers' information processing scores were further analyzed, they were found to have spent less time than nondisabled children in scanning math problem sets (encoding) in order to simplify computation procedures. Thus, although the learning disabled children in this study were able to correctly do math problems, an information processing analysis suggested that a number of important components needed to be mastered before their processing efficiency would be comparable to that of nondisabled children.

In summary, the strategy abstraction plane assesses a child's ability to use fewer promptings from a previous presentation of information, the extent to which a child's strategy can be generalized to a new problem calling for the same conceptual plan, and the extent to which a child can reject that plan and develop another strategy or refine a strategy as task demands and response requirements change.

Metacognition

The metacognitive plane focuses on children's knowledge about their own cognitive resources and the compatibility between perceptions of self as learner and the learning situation (e.g., Brown, Armbruster, & Baker, 1985). Whether metacognition is regarded as a higher level activity than strategic behavior is debatable; however, it is generally agreed that metacognition identifies some of the parameters of learning and performance (Brown & Palincsar, 1988). The metacognitive difficulties of learning disabled students and the implications for assessment have been documented (Baker & Brown, 1984; Palincsar & Brown, 1987; Swanson, 1983; Wong & Jones, 1982). Assessment of learning disabled children's metacognition involves interviewing the children. Unfortunately, metacognitive interviews suffer from reliability and validity difficulties and, as discussed earlier, are limited by the subject's language skill (e.g., Cavanaugh & Perlmutter, 1982; Pressley, Borkowski, & O'Sullivan, 1984; Swanson, 1987). Most criticism of metacognitive interviewing has been directed toward the practice of interviewing children prior to or after task performance. Children tend to verbalize what they ought to do or should do during task performance, not what they will do. One means of control for this problem has been to use several types of probe questions

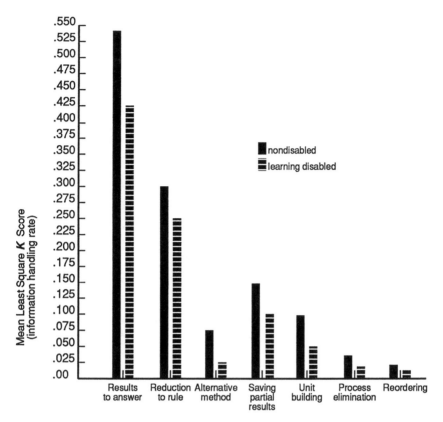

Figure 10-2. Comparison between disabled and nondisabled children in the amount of correctly processed information for arithmetic facts as a function of type of transformation rules. From "Strategy Transformations in Learning Disabled Children" by H. L. Swanson and J. Cooney, 1985, *Learning Disability Quarterly, 8*, p. 226. Copyright by the Council for Learning Disabilities. Reprinted by permission.

during actual task performance. This procedure has been used successfully with adults to assess interim decision making (Hayes-Roth & Thorndyke, 1979). Such probe questions do not require the child to verbalize all thoughts during task performance, which may interfere with performance, but require them to verbalize only intermittently.

In the proposed assessment model, the metacognitive plane has four components (see Figure 10-3): Level 1—assessing the child's perception of the characteristics or ability of someone who can do a particular task (assessment of this concept is found in the protocol Statements 9–12 in Table 9–1); Level 2—assessing the child's awareness of task parameters (see Statements 13–16 in Table 9–1); Level 3—assessing the child's perception of a strategic model

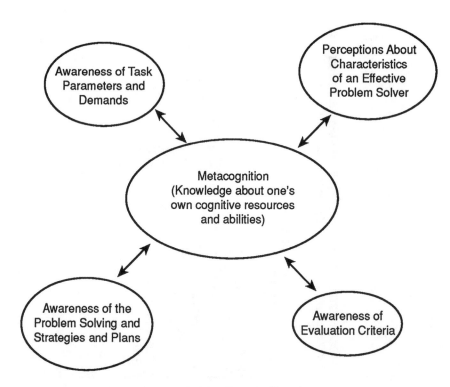

Figure 10-3. Components related to the metacognitive plane.

(although Statements 28–30 in Table 9–1 allude to this notion, a more appropriate "probe" would ask general questions that incorporate several academic areas); and Level 4—assessing how the child plans to evaluate his or her knowledge about strategies. For practical purposes, this area of assessment relates to the kinds of "feedback" the child uses to evaluate existing knowledge (see Statements 50–53 in Table 9–1).

Assessment questions can be modeled after Kreutzer, Leonard, and Flavell's (1975) investigation of children's metamemorial knowledge on each level. Level 1 serves as a guiding concept of the child's personal limitations and goals in a general task. In the area of categorization (e.g., "In what way are a fly and a tree alike?"), questions might include the following:

1. What makes someone really good in knowing how things are alike? (Focus on child's specialization of abilities.)

2. The other day someone answered this question very quickly, and I asked him how he did that. What do you think he said? (Focus on specific skills possessed.)

3. Suppose two girls came from different homes. One girl was wealthy and had a lot of puzzles and naming games. The other girl was poor and didn't learn how to do name games until she was in school for a couple of years. Do you think one of the girls would do better than the other? Why?

Level 2 focuses on task variables or, more specifically, the child's awareness of task parameters. Sample questions might include the following:

1. One day I asked Jane to tell me how a cat and a mouse are alike, and I asked Harold how a shovel and a cloud are alike. Which person had the hardest question? Who do you think did the best? (Focus on recognizing relationships.)

2. Harold's dad is a musician, and Lee's dad is a plumber. Do you think the question "Which way are a violin and a piano related?" would be easier for Harold to understand? Why?

3. Is there anything special about the two words in the question (structural cues of the question)?

4. Tell me how learning and this test are related (form a completion of a relationship)?

Level 3, perception of a strategic model, suggests how the child intends to represent the problems and generate some potential solutions. The child chooses a problem solving strategy in response to specific problem solving characteristics. The strategy, in turn, is related directly to the executive decisions. Sample questions of the child's understanding of this level may include the following:

1. If you had to understand the relationship of 7 and 144, or how those two numbers are alike, to have an A for today, what would you do first, second, and so on to solve the problem?

2. What do you do if you want to know how they are related?

3. Where would you look for information if you did not know the answer?

Level 4 focuses on the child's evaluation criteria and relates to how the child plans to evaluate prospective strategies. For example, the child might simply decide to guess on a question or say "I don't know" for each ambiguous or unknown question. Level 4 relates to the child's perceived criteria (a) during the task performance, (b) during the early strategies of the hypothesis testing, and (c) during the feedback provided by the examiner or teacher. Sample questions to assess this level may include the following:

1. If your answer to a question is wrong, how will you know that? How will you know your alternative plan is correct?

2. How will you relate the teacher's feedback on the test to what you think the answer is? (Ideally, the child's criteria for his or her performance is made at the same time that he or she is performing the task. This increases the likelihood that perceived criteria will be more clearly assessed before feedback is given.)

WHAT ADDITIONAL EXAMPLES CAN BE PRODUCED?

Two protocols in addition to Table 9–1 are provided as brief examples of each plane (except the knowledge base plane). Assessment of the knowledge base plane was not included because it is characteristic of many diagnostic orientations that assess language, long-term memory, and problem solving ability. The child in the first protocol is functioning within the preoperational range, and the child in the second protocol is functioning within the concrete operational range. The think-aloud protocol illustrates the kind of probing that is necessary by the teacher or diagnostician to determine a child's cognitive abilities.

Child 1—Preoperational (Transition to Concrete)

For the first protocol, the teacher and child were working on comparisons and analogies. The 7-year-old child was asked the question, "When you mix oil and water, why does the oil stay on top?"

1. **S:** Do you mean when the oil is in the jar?
2. **T:** I mean when the oil and water are mixed together in the same jar.
3. **S:** Oh, you mean when they are all mixed together?
4. **T:** Yes.
5. **S:** I don't think I know why the oil gets on top. I think because it's sorta like smoke.
6. **T:** You mean the oil is like smoke.
7. **S:** Yeah.
8. **T:** How is it like smoke?
9. **S:** Well, you know how it sorta floats up to the sky and it moves around. Well, I don't know, maybe that's not right.
10. **T:** Tyler, who do you think might be able to answer this question?
11. **S:** Oh, probably Jay (his 20-year-old cousin).
12. **T:** Why would Jay know the answer?
13. **S:** Because he has science and is smart. Um—my teacher might know cause she does experiments.

14. **T:** Can you ask me a question that is like the one I asked you?
15. **S:** Um—I have to think for awhile. Oh, I know one. How come a boat in the lake would sink if you filled it with water?
16. **T:** That's a good question; you know that from riding in your canoe, don't you?
17. **S:** Yeah, because we like to dump it over but Pop told us never to sink it.
18. **T:** What could you do to find out the answer?
19. **S:** Well, I don't know. I could ask Jay.
20. **T:** Have you ever done a problem before like this one?
21. **S:** No, I've never heard of it before. Maybe I could mix 'em together and see what happens.
22. **T:** Would that help you get the answer?
23. **S:** Wait. I think I know. It's because the oil isn't as heavy as the water. Is that why it squishes up to the top?
24. **T:** Yes, that's right. How did you know? What made you think of the answer?
25. **S:** Well, I was just thinking about the canoe and everything, and then I was sorta thinking about my toys in the bathtub, and I just guessed.
26. **T:** Can you think of anything else like we were just talking about?
27. **S:** I bet oil would go to the top if you mixed it with milk.
28. **T:** Why do you think it would?
29. **S:** 'Cause it would be like water and be lighter and squish to the top. I think I'll ask Baker (his friend) to see if he knows this. I bet he doesn't.

In Statements 1–5, the child defines the goal and characterizes the task. Information is not given on the child's organization of subroutines (executive control). Statements 6–9 represent the child's explanation of an already understood concept (aspect of strategy plane), and Statements 10–13 characterize the child's perception of someone who can do a particular task (metacognition). Statements 14–25 represent an assessment of the child's plan for problem solution. Specifically, Statements 15 and 17 are explanation, 19 is ability (metacognition) and executive function, 21 and 23 are prediction, and 24–25 represent summation and executive function. Statements 27–29 provide some basis for strategy abstraction. The concept has been generalized or transferred to a comparable problem. A primary weakness of these questions is a lack of clear delineation of problem solving strategies.

Child 2—Concrete Operational

Child 2 was asked questions focusing on the child's ability to recognize and describe essential relations between objects or ideas. The 9-year-old child was asked, "How are butter and lard the same?"

1. **T:** What steps are you going to take to answer this question?
2. **S:** First, I would ask what words mean, then try and figure it out, and once I figured it out, I'd write it down.
3. **T:** If the answer you get isn't right, how will you find the right answer?
4. **S:** I'd ask the teacher, if she'd tell me. Look it up in the dictionary.
5. **T:** If your answer is correct, is there another way of going about getting the same answer?
6. **S:** Not that I know of.
7. **T:** What does a person have to be able to do to answer the question?
8. **S:** Have to think, has to listen to the question.
9. **T:** What parts of the question tell you what is being asked?
10. **S:** Butter, and lard, same.
11. **T:** What are you going to do to answer this question?
12. **S:** Listen and think about what you're doing . . . ask what lard means . . . look it up in dictionary . . . answer it.
13. **T:** How will you know if you're right or not?
14. **S:** Dictionaries don't lie.
15. **T:** Have you ever answered a question like this before? How did you figure out the answer?
16. **S:** No.
17. **T:** Do you think that your "method" will give you the right answer? Why?
18. **S:** Yes, that's all you need.
19. **T:** Before you can tell me how they are the same, what do you need to do?
20. **S:** Look up the words in the dictionary, know how to read, nothing else.
21. **T:** Can you tell me what parts of the problem (state it) are important to have so that you can answer it?
22. **S:** Butter, lard, and same.
23. **T:** Can you tell me exactly what it is you are going to do to answer the question?
24. **S:** Listen, then you're gonna think and then you're gonna look up words in the dictionary and then you're going to answer the question.
25. **T:** How are butter and lard alike?
26. **S:** No response.
27. **T:** What is butter?
28. **S:** It's yellow and smooth.
29. **T:** What is lard?
30. **S:** I don't know. (Given chance to look it up.) It's greasy pig fat.
31. **T:** What are they used for?
32. **S:** Butter's used for taste.
33. **T:** What do they feel like?
34. **S:** They're both greasy. That's how they are alike.
35. **T:** How are butter and shortening alike?

36. S: Um . . . I guess like butter and lard—they're both greasy.
37. T: The teacher showed pictures of butter and shortening and asked how they're the same.
38. S: I told you, they're both greasy.
39. T: If I had 40 cents and went to the store to buy candy worth 20 cents, how much would I have left?
40. S: 40 cents minus 20 cents is 20 cents. (continued sequence)

Statements 1–6 clearly delineate the child's coordinating, directing, and organizing search strategies (executive control). Also indicated are the child's perceived criteria (metacognition). Statements 8–14 reflect metacognition, but more specifically perceived ability (8), task parameters and/or classification (10), strategy (12), and criteria (14). Statements 15–24 reflect the child's specific plan for answering the question. Components assessed include explanation (16), prediction (18), integration (20), classification (22), and summarization (24). Strategy abstraction is reflected in Statements 25–40, in which a series of prompts or cues is provided to the child. Then a separate, different task (but conceptually related) is provided (39) to determine transfer. Statements 39 and 40 are provided to assess whether the child can leave the hypothesis when it is no longer appropriate.

WHAT ARE THE ASSESSMENT ISSUES?

In our research, we have collected numerous protocols that reveal difficulties in learning disabled children's ability to "smoothly" integrate the various cognitive planes. Three methodological problems must be considered, however, before one assesses learning disabled children's cognitive ability within the framework of a multidirectional model. First, since the think-aloud protocols are expressed in the child's natural language, it is necessary to develop coding procedures that have high interrater reliability. A sample coding procedure that has high interrater agreement (about 85%) is provided by Swanson (1984a). Furthermore, these codes have been tested in a naturalistic setting (e.g., verbal protocols obtained from classroom interactions).

Second, the efficacy of our assessment model is contingent on the ability of the examiner to ask the child questions that have clear theoretical reference to information processing. These theoretical references are needed to direct children's verbal responding. The use of these questions is not programmed, but rather their use depends on the context. Different questions are triggered by specific situations, but explicit direction is given to assess all previously mentioned cognitive planes. It might be said that the examiner needs to be a "strategist" in posing the problem, as well as in asking an explicit question that focuses the child's attention on a particular set of events. In short, the examiner needs to do mental work along with the child.

Third, although the interrogative approach uncovers components of children's thinking (see Bovet, 1982), such an approach may direct the child to produce specific kinds of information that do not direct their task performance. These discrepancies provide an important beginning step for intervention.

SUMMARY

In this chapter and Chapter 9, we reviewed cognitive components considered relevant in learning disabled children's functioning. Five cognitive planes need to be assessed: (a) the relationship between strategy and overall performance (strategy); (b) the knowledge base that influences strategy usage (knowledge base); (c) the ability to coordinate, direct, and organize search strategies (executive control); (d) the metacognitive parameters of learning and performance (metacognition); and (e) the abstracting of problem solving strategies (strategy abstraction). Within each plane, different components of cognitive skills were presented. The multidirectional model suggests that learning disabled children's intelligent behavior may represent a poor coordination of the various cognitive planes into a complex act (e.g., math or reading). Although it is proposed that learning disabled children's cognitive functioning, like that of their normal counterparts, is opportunistic (multidirectional), the cognitive activity of the former does not adequately guide them to a correct final response.

We hope that the proposed theoretical model of cognitive functioning can be used to generate educational interventions for underlying mental processes believed to influence learning disabled children's performance. Nevertheless, this model is obviously not without limitations. First, the cognitive planes, especially the executive function plane, are in need of more detailed specification; that is, how do the components of the executive function plane act independently of and dependently on the metacognitive and strategy planes. Second, the uniqueness of how the cognitive planes become discordant and thus affect learning, needs a more detailed treatment. To merely state that learning disabled children suffer from poor interim decisions related to poor synchronization of the various cognitive planes merely restates the phenomenon. An explanation of the mechanisms coordinating these planes is required. Third, although the various cognitive planes and components have been tested in some detail with adult and mentally retarded populations, only a few of their respective components have received extensive study in learning disabled populations, and those have been isolated mainly to the areas of memory or reading. Finally, the think-aloud procedure has not been subjected to the same kinds of empirical validation that the psychometric approach has. The proposed multidirectional model may also be challenged in terms of its practicality, two aspects of which are addressed here.

Is the Model Usable?

Table 10-1 provides an overview of procedures for applying the proposed model to assessing cognitive abilities in learning disabled children. Most public schools evaluate learning disabled children with psychological tests administered in some sequential fashion. The proposed assessment model does not argue against the merits of this practice, and even recognizes that certain subtests may provide useful information about information processing. However, a complement to the psychometric approach is to identify the "how" of cognitive performance. Results of questioning children on weak subtest areas sometimes suggest that they use diverse information across and within various cognitive planes to guide their responding. Some of their responses may arise from strategy abstraction, whereas others stem from a low level of problem solving (e.g., classification). The think-aloud protocol discussed in this chapter illustrates such diverse problem solving.

The notion of multidirectional assessment can be illustrated with the administration of a particular subtest (e.g., the Similarities subtest of the Wechsler Intelligence Scale for Children–Revised) to a child whose performance is below average. The diagnostician begins to assess the student's lack of skill(s) by asking questions from various planes. The planes may initially be probed in a hierarchical fashion (Step 1—strategic plane, Step 2—knowledge base, etc.); however, the diagnostician soon discovers that the child's thinking aloud rarely produces a strategic approach in a systematic or hierarchical fashion within a particular plane. Furthermore, the child makes tentative decisions about his or her responses without the requirement that all thinking fit completely into a hierarchical (step-by-step) strategy. That is, the child may develop an independent or idiosyncratic problem solving approach within or between planes. The important implication of this assessment procedure is to determine how well the child incorporates planes and component levels into a correct final response by asking questions across and within assessment planes.

Is the Theoretical Model Practical?

At first glance, the multidirectional model seems rather complex and cumbersome by postulating five assessment planes and several levels of component analysis. The apparent difficulty in applying this assessment has been lessened to a certain extent with the development of sample probe questions across and within planes. In many cases, however, questions that are generated by the examiner involve a new set of questions for each child. The diverse verbal behaviors of children in the process of thinking aloud guide further questioning of their performance.

TABLE 10-1
Cognitive Planes and Components to be Assessed in Learning Disabled Children

Cognitive Plane	Suggested Dependent Measures	Purpose of Assessment
1. Knowledge base	Academic intelligence	Determine amount of available information from long-term memory.
a. Language	Component analysis of verbal "thinking aloud" protocols	Determine language (e.g., language regulation).
b. Structural	Response to instructed strategy training	Determine if performance difference between ability group still resides after optimal training.
c. Cognitive process	Response to selected Piagetian measures (e.g., conservation)	Determine developmental level of problem solving ability.
d. Understanding	Response to rule learning task (see Swanson, 1982).	Determine ability to relate isolated pieces of information into a logical connection.
e. Semantic memory	Recall of prose material	Determine ability to remember gist or main idea of information presented.
2. Executive function	Response to probe question of high and low processing difficulty (e.g., Similarities, Block Design)	Determine ability to order, prioritize, and coordinate strategies.
3. Metacognition a. Person b. Task c. Strategy d. Feedback	Response to probe questions about academic tasks (e.g., reading and math—see Kreutzer, Leonard, & Flavell, 1975) for adapting questions	Determines child's self-knowledge on the parameters of learning.

TABLE 10–1 (continued)

Cognitive Plane	Suggested Dependent Measures	Purpose of Assessment
4. Strategy a. Explanation b. Prediction c. Integration d. Classification	Response to probe question on a task (e.g., reading comprehension problem) of high and low difficulty	Determine child's ability to generate a series of verbal statements that are succinct and that include relevant attributes of the problem; as well as the child's self-diagnosis of success.
5. Strategy Abstraction a. Zone of potential	Response to presentation prompts to problems previously failed	Determine child's ability to benefit from instruction on failed tasks.
b. Generalization	Response to above problem presented in different form and a determination is made of additional need for prompts	Apply what has been learned to a similar task but with fewer cues.
c. Abandonment	Response to different problems when above strategy (algorithm) is inappropriate for solution	
d. Transformation	Response to tasks (e.g., arithmetic) in which a refinement of strategies occurs after repeated practice	Discriminate when to use and not use algorithm, and refine existing algorithms into more time-efficient procedures.

REFERENCES

Baker, L., & Brown, A. L. (1984). Metacognitive skills of reading. In D. Pearson (Ed.), Handbook of reading research (pp. 353–394). New York: Longman.

Borkowski, J. G., Johnston, M. B., & Reid, M. K. (1987). Metacognition, motivation, and controlled performance. In S. J. Ceci (Ed.), Handbook of cognitive, social and neuropsychological aspects of learning disabilities (pp. 147–174). Hillsdale, NJ: Erlbaum.

Borkowski, J. G., Weyhing, R. S., & Carr, M. (1988). Effects of attributional retraining on strategy-based reading comprehension in learning-disabled students. Journal of Educational Psychology, 80, 46–53.

Bovet, M. (1982). Learning research within Piagetian lines. Topics in Learning and Learning Disabilities, 1, 11–20.

Brown, A. L., Armbruster, B. B., & Baker, L. (1985). The role of metacognition in reading and studying. In J. Ornasanu (Ed.), Reading comprehension: From research to practice (pp. 49–75). Hillsdale, NJ: Erlbaum.

Brown, A. L., & Palincsar, A. S. (1988). Reciprocal teaching of comprehension strategies: A natural history of one program for enhancing learning. In J. Borkowski & J. P. Das (Eds.), Intelligence and cognition in special children: Comparative studies of giftedness, mental retardation, and learning disabilities. New York: Ablex.

Campione, J. C., Brown, A. L., Ferrara, R. A., Jones, R. S., & Steinberg, E. (1985). Breakdown in flexible use of information: Intelligence-related differences in transfer following equivalent learning performance. Intelligence, 9, 297–315.

Cavanaugh, J., & Perlmutter, M. (1982). Metamemory: A critical examination. Child Development, 53, 11–28.

Dallago, M. L. P., & Moeley, B. E. (1980). Free recall in boys of normal and poor reading levels as a function of task manipulation. Journal of Experimental Child Psychology, 30, 62–78.

Ferrara, R. A., Brown, A. L., & Campione, J. C. (1987). The continuous performance test in learning disabled and nondisabled children. Journal of Learning Disabilities, 20, 614–619.

Garner, R., & Reis, R. (1981). Monitoring and resolving comprehension obstacles: An investigation of spontaneous look backs among upper grade good and poor comprehenders. Reading Research Quarterly, 16, 569–582.

Gelzheiser, L. M. (1984). Generalization from categorical memory tasks to prose by learning disabled adolescents. Journal of Educational Psychology, 76, 1128–1138.

Hayes-Roth, B., & Thorndyke, P. (1979). Decision-making during the planning process. Santa Monica, CA: Rand Corp.

Kreutzer, M., Leonard, C., & Flavell, J. (1975). An interview study of children's knowledge about memory. Monographs of the Society for Research in Child Development, 40(1, Serial No. 159).

Palincsar, A. S., & Brown, A. (1987). Enhancing instructional time through attention to metacognition. Journal of Learning Disabilities, 20, 66–76.

Pressley, M., Borkowski, J. G., & O'Sullivan, J. T. (1984). Memory strategy instruction is made of this: Metamemory and durable strategy use. Educational Psychologist, 10, 94–107.

Pressley, M., Johnson, C. J., & Symons, S. (1987). Elaborating to learn and learning to elaborate. Journal of Learning Disabilities, 20, 76–91.

Swanson, H. L. (1983). Relations among metamemory, rehearsal activity and word recall in learning disabled and nondisabled readers. *British Journal of Educational Psychology, 53,* 186–194.

Swanson, H. L. (1984). Does theory guide teaching practice? Naturalistic observations in classrooms. *Remedial and Special Education, 5,* 7–15.

Swanson, H. L. (1987). The validity of metamemory—Memory links with children of high and low verbal ability. *British Journal of Educational Psychology, 57,* 179–190.

Swanson, H. L., & Cooney, J. (1985). Strategy transformations in learning disabled children. *Learning Disability Quarterly, 8,* 221–231.

Swanson, H. L., & Rhine, B. (1985). Strategy transformations in learning disabled children's math performance: Clues to the development of expertise. *Journal of Learning Disabilities, 18,* 596–603.

Swanson, H. L., & Watson, B. (1982). *Educational and psychological assessment of exceptional children.* St. Louis, MO: Mosby.

Wagner, R. K., & Kistner, J. (1989). Implications of the distinction between academic and practical intelligence for learning disabled children. In H. L. Swanson & B. Keogh (Eds.), *Learning disabilities: Theoretical and research issues* (pp. 75–92). Hillsdale, NJ: Erlbaum.

Wong, B. Y. L. (1987). Directions of future research in metacognition and learning disabilities. In H. L. Swanson (Ed.), *Memory and learning disabilities* (pp. 335–356). Greenwich, CT: JAI Press.

Wong, B. Y. L., & Jones, W. (1982). Increasing metacomprehension in learning-disabled and normally-achieving students through self-questioning training. *Learning Disability Quarterly, 5,* 228–240.

PART IV

LEARNING DISABILITIES IN AN EDUCATIONAL CONTEXT

The most important outgrowth of the research and assessment practices that help us understand the nature of learning disabilities and the particular problems of a given individual is our ability to intervene. We have learned that the optimistic stance adopted by the early professionals in learning disabilities—that we could cure learning problems in the early grades—does not hold: We cannot cure learning disabilities. We can, however, teach students to become aware of their difficulties and to utilize techniques and strategies that enable them to improve their performances.

Although our knowledge of separate aspects of learning difficulties is often quite precise, a perusal of the data comparing the power of various intervention approaches suggests that the most effective instructional interventions do not assume that each difficulty needs to be addressed separately. Rather, instructional procedures need to be functionally meaningful, contingent on the student's immediate attempts, and interpersonally interactive.

In Part IV, some of the most prominent difficulties described in each of the various research literatures related to language, literacy, and mathematics are noted. The intervention research is also reviewed, with an eye toward determining the direction current pedagogy is taking. Whenever possible, concrete suggestions for empirically validated intervention approaches are provided.

11

The Cognitive Curriculum

D. KIM REID

Part IV of this text is concerned with learning disabilities in an educational context. The chapters in this section address the cognitive curriculum, oral language, literacy, and mathematics. Chapter 15 describes the current trend away from reductionism and toward a more holistic approach to the study of learning and learning disabilities, a view largely compatible with the constructivist and ecological approaches described in Chapter 4. Evidence of the impact of antireductionist theories and frameworks (constructivist as well as ecological approaches) can be observed throughout these educationally oriented chapters. In this chapter, we review briefly what we have learned about the nature of learning disabilities and address some of the major concerns in educating these persons.

WHAT HAVE WE LEARNED ABOUT STUDENTS WITH LEARNING DISABILITIES?

The 3% to 7% of school-aged children who are assigned to classes and other services for students with learning disabilities do not constitute a homogeneous group of learners. Intervention with these children is typically directed toward remediation or the use of bypass strategies, because there is no expectation that learning disabilities can be cured. Even the most widely used behavioral and medical interventions have had equivocal results and may, in the worst scenario, mask other treatable conditions. Gibbs and Cooper (1989), for example, found that 96% of 242 9- to 11-year-old students receiving academic services for learning disabilities had fundamental language disorders, but only 6% were receiving language intervention.

The earlier the attempt to diagnose learning disabilities, the more clinical ambiguity accompanies the diagnosis, especially with respect to attention deficit disorders. Not unexpectedly, therefore, few services designed specifically for preschool children with learning disabilities exist. Furthermore, like the population in general, the group of persons experiencing learning disabilities is aging. Although some attempts have been made to design and implement programs to support transition to adulthood, higher education, and/or employment, relatively few opportunities for assistance are currently available.

The information processing perspective, which frames the majority of research studies being done in the field, has illuminated the nature of many of the component cognitive problems that persons with learning disabilities bring to the classroom. These processing difficulties include encoding, organizing, storing, retrieving, comparing, and generating information. Unlike the principles of education derived from behaviorism, those deduced from the findings of information processing research indicate that *students* are in control of the learning process, not teachers, materials, or established curricula. Learning occurs (or fails to occur) as the result of interactions among students' executive routines, strategic processes, and background knowledge, all of which may be impoverished in persons with learning disabilities. In addition, information processing studies have demonstrated that memory processes among learning disabled persons function more like those of younger people than those of their peers. Processing tends to be more effortful (less automatic), but the use of strategic behaviors tends to be immature, inappropriate, inflexible, and less well tuned to specific task demands.

This line of research has had minimal impact on instructional practices. Even when teachers have been taught to teach strategic behaviors, they frequently fail to do so (Swanson, 1984), and the results of attempted interventions have been consistently disappointing (Ellis, 1986; Wong, 1985), especially with respect to maintenance and generalization. Perhaps the difficulties with the transfer and generalizability of teaching strategic behaviors listed in Chapter 6 account, in part at least, for this lack of application to educational practice. Interventions derived from constructivist and ecological approaches have met with far greater success.

WHAT ARE THE CURRENT MAJOR CONCERNS OF EDUCATING THE LEARNING DISABLED?

Many current educational concerns have been addressed throughout the previous chapters of this book (e.g., service extension and delivery programs, diagnosis and assessment, strategic behaviors). Here, the discussion is limited to a few additional, central issues that have been emerging along with the rise of the cognitive curriculum. Whether any particular issue has a causal or resultant relationship to the cognitive curriculum is difficult to say. Both the issues and the associated curriculum changes are outgrowths of the shift away from associationism and toward views of human learning that credit the learner with the ability to select, interpret, and thereby control information and cognitive processes (see Chapter 4 for an overview). Foremost among these issues are (a) reevaluation of the dynamics of the teaching–learning interchange; (b) redefinition of the role and designation of teachers; (c) emergence of early, spontaneous knowledge; and (d) impact that fear, stress, and dependency have on motivation to learn.

Reevaluation of the Teaching–Learning Interchange

In conformance with the principles of behaviorism, teaching in American education has come to mean presenting decontextualized, simplified components of a task one at a time until each component has been mastered. The implicit assumption that students will be able to use those components in a flexible, coordinated manner, however, has not held (A. L. Brown & Campione, 1981, 1984; Gagné, 1965). Although educational procedures for average and gifted achievers have undergone significant changes in the last few years, special education has remained entrenched in behaviorism. Arguing that learning disabled students need more structure than their peers, most resource room teachers present traditional, behavioral lessons to students individually, at a slower pace, often in smaller increments, and nearly entirely in the form of drill and practice of each component in isolation: Behavioral objectives remain the driving force behind special education. The results have not been impressive.

Throughout their years of schooling, many students with learning disabilities continuously fail. Some are still practicing isolated basic skills (or strategies, if the instructors are more enlightened) in teacher-designed exercises during their high school resource room classes. The essential nature of their schooling differs from that of their peers who are reading, writing reports, and otherwise engaging in context-embedded activities that enhance their knowledge-acquisition abilities as well as their knowledge per se. Large numbers of the "exercise" students drop out. Nearly all are unprepared for advanced academic and/or employment training, despite their average or nearly average IQs. Most will tell you that they hate school. What they do know, they have learned outside of school and yet, ironically, few are capable of high levels of independent learning.

Educators and legislators alike seem befuddled. They know that education is not working as well as it must if the United States is to compete successfully in the emerging global economy. They realize that additional funding alone will not solve the problems. What is exciting and positive about this turn of events is that a climate of change is afoot in educational circles. New conceptualizations of the teaching–learning process are emerging, and administrative support is falling behind the winds of change. The new, experimental attitude is likely to smooth the way for widespread applications of the highly effective practices now being demonstrated in the research literature.

A renewed interest in learning among scientists in a wide array of disciplines has revitalized both classroom and laboratory-based instructional research. Perhaps the major impact has been the pervasive, fundamental recognition that students are actively in control of what is learned. It is the students who give meaning to the activities in which they engage; they select, interpret, and make sense out of information. Resnick (1989) has referred to this activity as "cognitive bootstrapping."

But students' self-regulation depends on interactions with the physical and social world. A nurturant social environment can promote and provoke learning. Students learn by participating in events and activities with others, from comparing their own thoughts and solutions with those of others, from hearing arguments and perspectives of which they would not have thought, from having to explain or defend their own thinking, and from gradually adopting the ideas and strategies to which they are exposed.

Many behaviors required for learning are impaired among persons with learning disabilities. Even when they begin with equivalent achievement levels, learning disabled students have comparative difficulty applying their knowledge to novel, but related situations (A. L. Brown, Campione, Reeve, Ferrara, & Palincsar, in press). With more exposure and greater levels of assistance, however, these students do acquire knowledge and knowledge-acquisition strategies without teacher-directed drill and practice (Wansart, 1990). Furthermore, they are internally motivated, they persist and experiment when trying to solve problems, and they construct meaning from experience without being directed to do so (Wansart, 1990). Contrary to the deficit-oriented research of the information processing tradition, much of the recent constructivist and ecological research has given us a new appreciation for the resources and abilities that disabled learners have available.

Elements of the immediate instructional environment.   Because it has become clear that students with learning disabilities are as inherently active as their peers, special educators are beginning to shift their emphasis away from lessons and materials toward the dynamics of the teacher–student interchange, toward practices that carefully monitor changes in students' thinking and understanding throughout the instructional session. This interest in the microgenetic elements of instruction has been building for some time, especially within the constructivist traditions.

Dialogue.   Gallagher and Reid (1983), for example, chose as the most educationally relevant legacies of Piaget's work, (a) the interactive, interdependent nature of intense, personalized dialogue between experimenter and child in the clinical method, and (b) the use of social interaction as a means to elevate levels of understanding (see especially Inhelder, Sinclair, & Bovet's, 1974, studies on learning). Even with the most careful dialogic support, the authors caution, it is imperative to remember that the student must still play an active role in selecting, interpreting, organizing, and reorganizing what is assimilated into background knowledge (i.e., bootstrapping). Neither teachers spouting lessons to groups of children nor individual worksheets completed at each student's pace foster the active construction that is isomorphic to learning.

Palincsar (1986) highlighted the importance of dialogue in scaffolded instruction. The metaphor of scaffolding suggests that temporary supports are put in place until the student is able to stand (perform) alone. Wood, Bruner, and Ross (1976) described it as a process of enabling students to solve a problem, achieve a goal, or carry out a task that would be beyond their ability if they were not given help. By scaffolding instruction, teachers enable students to operate within the *zone of proximal development,* defined as "the distance between the actual developmental level as determined by independent problem solving and the level of potential development as determined through problem solving under adult guidance, or in collaboration with more capable peers" (Vygotsky, 1978, p. 86). Using several examples of classroom discussions that were collected during a study using the reciprocal teaching format (see Table 11–1), Palincsar showed how the most effective teachers (a) are responsive to the students' contributions and comments, (b) keep the discussion focused, (c) build meaning by extending the students' current level of knowledge, (d) conduct ongoing diagnoses of the students' understanding, (e) adjust task difficulty in accordance with the students' momentary needs, and (f) give feedback and support for correct productions.

Duffy et al. (1987) conducted a naturalistic study in which classroom teachers were asked to teach the *reasoning* associated with reading strategies. They, too, found that the most successful teachers did more than provide the explanations, modeling, and demonstrations characteristic of direct instruction. These teachers "generated spontaneous explanations throughout the lesson, elaborating in response to students' restructured understandings of the teacher's model or demonstrations" (p. 364). These qualitative differences in verbal interactions were important to creating an instructional environment that fostered achievement. Missiuna and Samuels (1989) also found this contingent, mediated learning more effective with preschoolers who had language, learning, and behavioral difficulties.

Stone (1989; Stone & Conca, in press; Wertsch & Stone, 1979) argued that *prolepsis* is an integral component of scaffolding, one that helps make sense of the dynamics occurring within the zone of proximal development. The term refers to an utterance that presupposes that the listener has some information that, thus, is not made explicit during the communication. What

---

TABLE 11-1
Example of Effective Dialogue

READING:
There are many different creatures in the sea. Many of the fish you see will be swimming in schools. They are looking for food. Most of them are friendly.

But you might see some unusual fish. You might see a big, flat fish. It looks as if it has wings. You might see a sea horse. It swims with its head up and its tail down. It carries baby sea horses in a pocket on its front.

1. T: I need someone to ask a question about the new information I just shared with you.
2. S2: How does the sea horses . . . carry their babies in their pouch?
3. T: Okay. Does someone remember the answer?
4. S5: Um, that's the only way they can carry them. They don't have any hands or anything.
5. T: Now, was he doing a little bit of predicting or figuring out how that sea horse is able to do that? Did the story really tell why they carry them in their pouches?
6. S5: Or they might drowned. They might not be able to swim and they might drowned.
7. T: You are right in all of your answers and thinking. Your question was a good question in that it got us thinking about why they did have pouches and why they carry their babies there, but, you were going a bit further than the written word. You were pretty smart to figure that out. Can anyone think of a question that they did give us the answer in the story?
8. S4: Um, what kind of animals are they?
9. S6: Um . . . sea horses.
10. T: What else did they see besides the sea horses?
11. S6: Um . . . crawfish.
12. T: See, what you might have wanted to ask, and C____ might have wanted to ask "Why were they called unusual fish or animals?" Why do they call a sea horse unusual? . . . Because they carry babies in a pouch. Most fish don't do that, right? That you could have asked using information here.
13. S3: Why do the fish go to school?
14. T: Great question. I did say that. Who could answer his question?
15. S2: Um . . . [pause] Maybe to keep safe, away . . .
16. S1: I know another way. A big pile, a school, a big pile of fish is called a school of fish.

TABLE 11–1 (continued)

17. T: Do you think maybe R____ wasn't quite sure what school meant in this story? Is it the kind of school that we are in? We come to school to learn, don't we? But in this story it does mean a big gathering of fish. But, I bet that they do learn how to get food, and it's also for . . .
18. S1: To protect them.
19. T: Very good. Okay, can someone summarize what we've learned in this part? What was the most important information that we've learned from this story already, M____?
20. S4: Them going to school.
21. T: Who's them?
22. S4: The fish.
23. T: Do they go to school or are they living in schools? Do you think they have rooms like we do?
24. S2: Yeah.
25. T: They just gather together and that's how they make a school. And, that might seem a little unusual. Now, let's see what other unusual creatures there might be. Do you know what I mean by creatures?

From "The Role of Dialogue in Providing Scaffolded Instruction" by A. S. Palincsar, 1986, *Educational Psychologist, 21*, pp. 87–89. Copyright 1986 by Lawrence Erlbaum Associates. Reprinted with permission.

is unspoken creates a challenge for the hearer, who must construct a set of assumptions in his or her mind that re-creates the essence of the knowledge the speaker takes for granted. Consequently, the hearer is led to construct the speaker's perspective on the topic being discussed. "Context-creation is an inevitable component of all comprehension" (Stone, 1989, p. 36). By studying dialogue, educators are examining the ongoing and ever-shifting understandings of both parties' immediate contexts. If there is mutual trust, the listener is likely to adopt the speaker's perspective as his or her own. If the speaker is more knowledgeable than the hearer, the construction is very likely to lead to cognitive growth.

Cooperative learning. Schunk (1989) in his work on self-efficacy and Doise, Mugny, and Perret-Clermont (1975) in their work on the causal role of social interaction in intellectual development have demonstrated that a superior model is facilitative, but not necessary, to the achievement of progress. In cooperative learning settings in which students share responsibility for task completion, Schunk found that models who are similar or only slightly better in competence provide the best information for increasing achievement to students with learning disabilities. Furthermore, multiple models are only as effective as a single model who is also coping with the task, but are more effective than a model who has already mastered the task, even if the expert is the teacher. In addition to Schunk's assumption that other coping models have a more powerful impact because learning disabled students do not think that they can attain a teacher's level of competence, Reid (1989) speculated that the facilitative effect is related to similar, and therefore comprehensible, levels and strategies for information processing.

Doise et al. (1975) also found that individuals learn better in social settings. Furthermore, groups achieve levels of performance that are superior to and cannot be accounted for by the performance of even the most advanced member. These sociologists explained that in group efforts, one student's interfering actions force the others to integrate aspects of the problem that might have gone unnoticed. Consequently, group work requires the coordination of disparate points of view. They also argued that growth is produced by "the conflict of communication," a mechanism that resembles prolepsis and comprises one aspect of Piaget's (1977) more robust description of the effects of contradiction. Therefore, learning is promoted by the social interaction itself, not, as some have suggested, by the copying of a model's performance.

As Piaget (1957) noted, however, even imitation requires a process of construction. Reid and Knight-Arest (1981), for example, found that although learning disabled students could (and did) copy useful task explanations that they heard from their peers, their apparently advanced responses were empty verbalisms. They parroted the explanations without constructing a mental representation of the task that approximated that of their peers and thus forgot their newfound responses in a matter of weeks. Not only did their average peers maintain their new level of understanding, but they provided additional correct explanations several weeks later, indicating that they had used their new insights to build enhanced understandings. Taken together, many of the studies in this chapter (on both the topic of dialogue and other aspects of the cognitive curriculum) suggest that this difficulty with constructing and reconstructing the immediate environment can be focused on and supported by dialogue and other nonverbal communications that are carefully calibrated to students' needs.

Holism, exposed reasoning, contextualization, and other holy cows.   In their overview of the results of their decade-long research program on interactive learning, A. L. Brown et al. (in press) highlighted other important aspects of the cognitive curriculum. In their reciprocal teaching procedures, strategies that are both domain-specific and necessary to task completion become the focus of a *metascript* (Gallimore & Tharp, 1983), a verbal instructional format that provides general guidelines, but leaves room for responsive teaching. The research related to the use of reciprocal teaching in reading instruction is discussed at length in Chapter 13. Their extension of the procedure to mathematics instruction is illustrated here.

In reciprocal teaching, participants (usually the students and the adult teacher) are jointly responsible for task solution. They take turns leading the discussion that makes the strategies for task solution observable, that monitors progress, and that attempts to impose meaning. The nonleaders play the role of supportive critics. These very general guidelines constitute the *domain-independent* aspects of the intervention. Characteristic monitoring errors observed among sixth to eighth graders in solving algebraic word problems served as the *domain-specific* activities that structured the dialogue: (a) estimating the answer, (b) extracting relevant facts, (c) keeping track of the quantities that the algebraic expressions stood for, (d) drawing visual representations, (e) checking the accuracy of calculations, and (f) making sense. Preliminary data suggest that the extension of this metascript to mathematics will yield results comparable to those generated with respect to reading achievement.

The reciprocal teaching procedure derives much of its power from the dynamics of cooperative learning, including prolepsis and the carefully focused, carefully calibrated nature of the dialogue. It also illustrates other important characteristics of the cognitive curriculum listed in Table 11-2. Rather than reduce the task to the mastery of its component parts, the process of meaning construction or problem solving is addressed *holistically* in all its complexity, with the skills and strategies necessary to task completion practiced in context. The integrity of the goal—making sense of text or solving a problem—is always maintained and is always clear.

Activities and strategies that are necessary for task completion are used flexibly to structure the social dialogue with the assumption that the processes will be internalized more easily since they will be made *observable and accessible* (Vygotsky, 1978), another important feature of the cognitive curriculum. Data reveal that students who learn reciprocal teaching do internalize the procedures: They apply them independently and also extend their use beyond the content and setting in which they were taught.

In the cognitive curriculum, *transfer and generalization* become the criteria for judging instructional effectiveness, because they are signs that the knowledge accrued is likely to be used independently in appropriate situations. Piaget (1979), for example, argued that one could not assume that learners have acquired a knowledge structure, unless they could use it as a basis for making deductions. A child who understands that number is independent of order, for example, can deduce that the sum of the objects he or she has counted from left to right will be the same if he or she counts them from right to left; the child does not have to count them a second time. Perhaps one of the most important failures of our current special education practices is that we have let task performance per se serve as a demonstration of competence.

TABLE 11–2
Elements of the Cognitive Curriculum

---

1. Interactive, carefully calibrated dialogue.
2. Negotiation of the zone of proximal development.
3. Exposure of usually covert reasoning processes.
4. Intentional use of prolepsis and the "conflict of communication."
5. Encouragement of "cognitive bootstrapping," personally meaningful mental constructions.
6. Joint (expert–novice) responsibility for task solution.
7. Holistic, contextualized presentation of content and skills.
8. Emphasis on domain-specific knowledge.
9. Transfer and generalization as mastery criteria.
10. Consensus as the arbiter of accuracy.
11. Ongoing diagnosis of responses to instruction.
12. Teacher interaction as coaching and scaffolding.
13. Extension of early, spontaneous learning.
14. Behavior interpreted from the students' point of view.
15. Fostering a sense of autonomy and risk taking.

In three consecutive summer reading programs for readers of all ability levels, I noticed that the use of the reciprocal teaching strategy leads to *consensus seeking* (see also A. L. Brown et al., in press). This important aspect of cooperative learning is often overlooked in discussions of its benefits. Learning disabled students are notorious for their inability to judge whether their assumptions and answers are accurate (perhaps due to their comparatively low levels of knowledge [Berger & Reid, 1989]) and useful to reach the desired goal. Sharing responsibility for task completion allows students who are less competent to make these metacognitive judgments to observe and appreciate the elements of decision making in which more successful students engage.

Finally, *ongoing diagnosis* is not limited to daily or even occasional assessment of student products. It is a moment-to-moment activity that provides the basis for subsequent instructional responses and responsiveness. Its microgenetic quality allows the instructor to observe not only what the learner can do, but how he or she *responds* to assistance and instruction (Campione & Brown, 1984, 1987). The latter information is far more informative to teachers than is a student's level of performance.

Reciprocal teaching is not the only approach to instruction currently gaining acceptance in special education (see also, e.g., situated learning: J. S. Brown, Collins, & Duguid, 1989; Collins, 1990), but it is the best researched and the most efficient and powerful for learning disabled students. Resnick's

(1989) review of a broad array of successful instructional programs designed to teach thinking, learning, or other higher order cognitive abilities sums up the important characteristics of the cognitive curriculum that have just been discussed: (a) the intellectual work is shared, (b) tasks are accomplished jointly, (c) skills are taught within the context of the task for which they are appropriate and necessary, (d) usually hidden processes are made overt, (e) student observation and commentary is encouraged, (f) students participate in the whole task while they build up their skills bit by bit, (g) programs are organized around subject matter rather than general abilities, and (h) instruction focuses on meaning construction and interpretations that link symbols to their referents (p. 13).

Redefinition of the Role and Designation of Teachers

Clearly, the essential character of teaching is changing. Teachers are no longer all-knowing dispensers of knowledge. They are instead "respected authorities" (Palincsar, 1986) who help their students "exercise cognitive activities that are just emerging" (A. L. Brown et al., in press). To the extent that they are needed, teachers participate in the joint construction of meaning and in joint problem solving activities, scaffolding student behaviors with the goal of improving students' levels of participation until they can perform without assistance. Teachers ask leading questions, provide explanations, challenge responses, provide examples, and stir up opposing viewpoints (Gallagher & Reid, 1983).

Many teachers would argue that they already engage in such activities, and many of the most effective do. Few special education teachers, however, adopt such practices. Instead, they tend to devise lessons, explain them, and have students practice the target behaviors, hopefully to some level of mastery. Armed by their knowledge that learning disabled students often need more structure and nurturance than their average peers, special educators emphasize the use of reinforcements and skill practice in programs designed to control student behavior. Research has demonstrated repeatedly, however, that shared learning experiences, such as reciprocal teaching, are more effective by nearly every standard. The most delayed students, in fact, tend to make the greatest gains (Palincsar & Brown, 1984; Reid, 1989).

Special education teachers will be asked, in their emerging role, to design activities that respect the learner's integrity and his or her constructions and reconstructions as they emerge as the teaching–learning dialogue proceeds. Worksheets will probably be used only incidentally, because they are decontextualized and, therefore, do not promote meaningful learning that is likely to generalize and transfer. Furthermore, independent seat work fails to foster thinking, problem solving, and so forth. Although teachers will continue to decide goals and manage classrooms, students will have more opportunities to decide what they read, to study content of their own choosing, and to function somewhat more independently in a learning environment that nurtures risk taking.

The research on dialogue tells us that teachers need to listen more carefully to what students say, to welcome their participation, and to use attempts at making sense and solving problems to diagnose students' shifting mental representations of the task. Teachers' verbalizations need to be responsive to the students' needs at each point in time. Students, therefore, need to talk as much as or perhaps even more than teachers. The concept of prolepsis alerts us to the need for teachers to try to help students create a mental model that fosters shared understandings. Both verbal and nonverbal communications can be used to build bridges from what students know to what they do not yet know.

Inherent in the idea of scaffolding is the concept that teachers must enable students to participate in complex tasks that they cannot perform independently. Students will make errors that must be gradually corrected through redirection and feedback. Our experience has been that inviting students to participate at a level at which mistakes are inevitable is the aspect of scaffolding to which special education teachers are most resistant: They are accustomed to giving instructions that so tightly control student responses that few errors are expected. In our summer programs, teachers frequently lamented that they had taught (in a direct instruction sense) questioning (summarizing, predicting, clarifying) skills and yet students were still having difficulties. Teachers will have to become used to the impact of teaching toward the gradual acquisition of complex tasks.

Not only the nature of the activities in which teachers engage will change, but also the timing and origin of those activities. Lessons will act like metascripts in which general guidelines are immersed in interactions that are dependent on students' participation, even when the students assume the role of teachers.

The cooperative learning research reveals that teacher–student interactions may be far less important than we have assumed: Student–student interactions have a greater impact on social development and academic achievement (Johnson, 1980). The most common of these instructional arrangements include peer tutoring, traditional cooperative learning (students working together to attain a common goal, often by taking responsibility for different aspects of the task), and methods of interactive teaching (students and teachers participate as group members who perform instructional tasks jointly, e.g., reciprocal teaching). The teacher's role is to foster collaboration (rather than to make comparative judgments concerning students' progress and abilities), to scaffold, and to manage the establishment and operations of the groups. The collaborative learning environments, "through a nexus of social support, shared goals, modeling and incidental instruction, awaken new levels of competence in the young" (A. L. Brown & Palincsar, in press).

Teaching is becoming more interactive, whether the teacher, other students, or computers and other instructional media are carrying out the instruction. Buggy and apprenticeship models are tailoring programs to respond to students' individual responses, just as teachers are being asked to do. No change is ever easy, but a more positive prognosis for persons with learning disabilities is worth the effort.

Emergence of Early, Spontaneous Knowledge

One outgrowth of the recognition that students construct their own knowledge has been a focus on the genesis (or development) of knowledge. Instead of viewing the child's preschool behaviors through the film of adult understandings, scientists are now examining them from the child's point of view (see Heath, 1980). Children who arrive at kindergartens (and even preschools) are now invested with a learning history, rather than viewed as coming to school to begin to learn. The cognitive curriculum capitalizes on that knowledge base.

Previous frameworks for examining children's attainments have included developmental and readiness models. The developmental model (see Gesell, 1940) was an essentially maturational one in which age-appropriate benchmarks were used to determine whether a child's progress was satisfactory in motor development, communication, social skills, and/or adaptive behavior.

Readiness models, on the other hand, assumed that underlying processes, such as concept development, perception, acuity, and so forth, had to develop to a certain point *before* instruction in such complex processes as reading and arithmetic would "take." A mental age of 6, for example, was once thought to be prerequisite to reading, and conservation ability was considered prerequisite to the understanding of number. Examining children's spontaneous behaviors from their perspective, however, has revealed that they begin reading, writing, and counting at a very young age.

Between approximately 18 months and 2 years of age, children gradually develop the ability to think about events that occurred in the past and objects that are no longer in view (Piaget, 1970, 1977). As a consequence of this ability to use mental symbols (known as the *symbolic function),* children begin to engage in language usage, imitation, symbolic play, mental imagery, drawing, and gestures.

These early, spontaneous behaviors gradually evolve from primitive, idiosyncratic approximations to sophisticated, culturally shared attainments. Children's writing, for example, begins with scribbles and progresses through a series of transformations that eventually become recognizable as the English alphabet (Teale & Sulzby, 1986). As children begin to understand that letters relate to sounds, they invent spelling patterns that ultimately take on the arbitrary characteristics of English words (Read, 1975). Reading begins with the attachment of meaning to familiar environmental symbols, such as the writing on cookie boxes or the golden arches, and goes through several shifts from meaning attribution (e.g., pretend reading), to attempts to map oral language onto the orthographic presentation (e.g., word decoding), to coordination of the meaning with the graphophonemic stimuli, and finally to automatic word recognition that leaves the mind free to concentrate on meaning alone. The earliest behaviors are no longer considered precursors that lead to literacy, but rather as literacy behaviors in rudimentary form.

A more profound insight that has been gained from the study of early, spontaneous behaviors is that they are meant to serve communicative, social functions (see Saxe, Guberman, & Gearhart, 1987, for an overview of the impact on early number development). The decontextualized nature of much early instruction is a significant departure from the bootstrapping that precedes schooling and fails to utilize significant learning abilities, such as how to learn from examples (A. L. Brown & Kane, 1988), that children develop prior to school entrance. The cognitive curriculum attempts to correct that mismatch. A recent survey of preschool programs for children with learning disabilities, however, indicated that they are random, confusing, and eclectic (Esterly & Griffin, 1987) and do not as yet uniformly and intentionally nurture the early development of literacy and mathematical behaviors.

Motivation to Learn

Research directed at understanding motivation and self-regulation in educational settings suggests that these may be implicated in the failure of learning disabled children to show generalization and maintenance of social skills learning (Adelman & Taylor, 1982) and behavioral and academic performance in classrooms (Switzky & Schultz, 1988). A recent study of over 450 9- to 19-year-old students classified either as learning disabled or emotionally handicapped (Deci, Hodges, Pierson, & Tomassone, in preparation) illustrates important and characteristic types of findings.

In previous studies with normally achieving students, researchers had determined that behavior could be called *internally motivated* when the individual initiates and regulates behavior without the need for externally imposed demands, control, or rewards. The regulators and rewards are the person's thoughts, feelings, and actions. Children are better able to self-regulate when they (a) know what behaviors lead to success and feel competent to execute them and (b) feel autonomous rather than pressured and controlled by significant adults (Grolnick, Ryan, & Deci, 1989). The combination of autonomy and competence leads to enhanced conceptual understanding, greater creativity, higher self-esteem, and lower anxiety (Deci et al., in preparation).

In their study with learning disabled students, Deci et al. (in preparation) found that a sense of competence is a strong psychological dynamic affecting both documented achievement and self-rated adjustment. A second significant predictor of achievement and adjustment was maternal support for autonomy among the younger student and teacher warmth among the high school group.

The findings that internal motivational variables are related to achievement and adjustment for learning disabled students and that control has negative effects on internal motivation make a strong case against behavior modification programs. As Deci et al. (in preparation) explain, external controls dispensed by teachers and parents might have the short-term benefits of reducing confusion and ensuring that more time is spent on task, but the long-term costs might be substantial: Such controls interfere with learning disabled students' assumption of responsibility for the initiation and regulation of their behavior, academic achievement, and school adjustment. Although it is important to provide students experiencing learning disabilities with structure (i.e., information about expected outcomes and the relations between outcomes and behavior), it may be disastrous to exert control (i.e., pressure to behave, think, or feel particular ways).

For teachers and parents to be assured that the structures they provide are not perceived as controlling, they must review them from the child's point of view. For example, adults can provide clear rationales for structures and limits. They can allow the child as much choice as possible, including the choice to accept the consequences rather than follow the structures. Finally, they can acknowledge the child's perspective and reflect his or her feelings (e.g., "I know that you are unhappy about . . .").

This new line of research is important because it supports the arguments for changing the nature of teaching that were advanced above in the description of the cognitive curriculum. Adults need to encourage students with learning disabilities to take initiative, to explore, and to experiment during learning, rather than to behave in carefully prescribed ways (Cohen, 1986). When learning disabled students are unprepared to accept more responsibility for participation and decision making, tactics must be found to enhance motivational readiness (Adelman, MacDonald, Nelson, Smith, & Taylor, 1990).

SUMMARY AND CONCLUSIONS

Four major concerns that have accompanied the rise of the cognitive curriculum have been discussed. First, interest in the dynamics of the teaching–learning interchange has begun to focus on the role of dialogue and the effects of cooperative learning arrangements. Instruction that has been demonstrated effective with learning disabled students has also been holistic, contextualized, and designed to make the usually covert processes of reasoning observable. Although such instructional designs are still sparse and experimental, the research results are so promising that it is difficult to imagine that they do not foreshadow future widespread practices.

Second, if the nature of teaching is to change, so must the role of the teacher. Rather than acting as dispensers of knowledge, teachers will act as coaches who enable students to engage in activities that they could not negotiate alone. Teachers will listen more, talk less, and tailor instruction to the moment-to-moment needs expressed by highly participatory students. Furthermore, a broader spectrum of persons and technology will assume some traditional teaching roles.

Third, the cognitive curriculum is also being shaped by our recognition that students learn a good deal on their own before they come to school. We will see in subsequent chapters that early education is being restructured to build on this early learning.

The final topic discussed was the importance of autonomy and competence on internally motivated behavior, which in turn affects both achievement and adjustment. Even nonintellective behaviors support the child-centered, risk-taking character of the cognitive curriculum.

REFERENCES

Adelman, H. S., MacDonald, V. M., Nelson, P., Smith, D. C., & Taylor, L. (1990). Motivational readiness and the participation of children with learning and behavior problems in psychoeducational decision making. *Journal of Learning Disabilities, 23,* 171–176.

Adelman, H. S., & Taylor, L. (1982). Enhancing the motivation and skill needed to overcome interpersonal problems. *Journal of Learning Disabilities, 5,* 438–446.

Berger, R. S., & Reid, D. K. (1989). Differences that make a difference: Comparisons of metacomponential functioning and knowledge base among groups of high and low IQ learning disabled, mildly mentally retarded and normally achieving adults. *Journal of Learning Disabilities, 22,* 422–429.

Brown, A. L., & Campione, J. C. (1981). Inducing flexible thinking: A problem of access. In M. Friedman, J. P. Das, & N. O'Connor (Eds.), *Intelligence and learning* (pp. 515–530). New York: Plenum Press.

Brown, A. L., & Campione, J. C. (1984). Three faces of transfer: Implications for early competence, individual differences, and instruction. In M. Lamb, A. Brown, & B. Rogoff (Eds.), *Advances in developmental psychology* (Vol. 3, pp. 143–192). Hillsdale, NJ: Erlbaum.

Brown, A. L., Campione, J. C., Reeve, R. A., Ferrara, R. A., & Palincsar, A. S. (in press). Interactive learning, individual understanding: The case of reading and mathematics. In L. T. Landsman (Ed.), *Culture, schooling, and psychological development.* Hillsdale, NJ: Erlbaum.

Brown, A. L., & Palincsar, A. S. (1989). Guided cooperative learning and individual knowledge acquisition. In L. B. Resnick (Ed.), *Knowing and learning: Issues for a cognitive psychology and instruction.* Hillsdale, NJ: Erlbaum.

Brown, A. L., & Kane, M. J. (1988). Preschool children can learn to transfer: Learning to learn and learning from example. *Cognitive Psychology, 20,* 493–523.

Brown, J. S., Collins, A., & Duguid, P. (1989). Situated cognition and the culture of learning. *Educational Researcher, 18,* 32–42.

Campione, J. C., & Brown, A. L. (1984). Learning ability and transfer propensity as sources of individual differences in intelligence. In P. H. Brooks, R. Sperber, & C. McCauley (Eds.), *Learning and cognition in the mentally retarded* (pp. 265–293). Baltimore: University Park Press.

Campione, J. C., & Brown, A. L. (1987). Linking dynamic assessment with school achievement. In C. Lidz (Ed.), *Dynamic assessment* (pp. 82–115). New York: Guilford.

Cohen, M. W. (1986). Intrinsic motivation in the special education classroom. *Journal of Learning Disabilities, 19,* 258–261.

Collins, A. (1990). Cognitive apprenticeship and instructional technology. In B. F. Jones & L. Idol (Eds.), *Dimensions of thinking and cognitive instruction.* Hillsdale, NJ: Erlbaum.

Deci, E. L., Hodges, R., Pierson, L., & Tomassone, J. (in preparation). *Motivationally relevant predictors of achievement and adjustment in learning disabled emotionally handicapped students.*

Doise, W., Mugny, G., & Perret-Clermont, A. N. (1975). Social interaction and the development of cognitive operations. *European Journal of Social Psychology, 5,* 367–383.

Duffy, G. G., Roehler, L. R., Sivan, E., Rackliffe, G., Book, C., Meloth, M. S., Vavrus, L. G., Wesselman, R., Putman, J., & Bassiri, D. (1987). The effects of explaining the reasoning associated with using reading strategies. *Reading Research Quarterly, 22,* 347–368.

Ellis, E. S. (1986). The role of motivation and pedagogy on the generalization of cognitive training by the mildly handicapped. *Journal of Learning Disabilities, 19,* 66–70.

Esterly, D. L., & Griffin, H. C. (1987). Preschool programs for children with learning disabilities. *Journal of Learning Disabilities, 20,* 571–573.

Gagné, R. M. (1965). *The conditions of learning.* New York: Holt, Rinehart and Winston.

Gallagher, J. M., & Reid, D. K. (1983). *The learning theory of Piaget and Inhelder.* Austin, TX: PRO-ED.

Gallimore, R., & Tharp, R. G. (1983). *The regulatory functions of teacher questions: A microanalysis of reading comprehension lessons* (Tech. Rep. No. 109). Honolulu: Kanehameha Educational Research Institute, The Kanehameha Schools.

Gesell, A. (1940). *The first 5 years of life.* New York: Harper and Brothers.

Gibbs, D. P., & Cooper, E. (1989). Prevalence of communication disorders in students with learning disabilities. *Journal of Learning Disabilities, 22,* 60–63.

Grolnick, W. S., Ryan, R. M., & Deci, E. L. (1989). *The inner resources for school achievement: Motivational mediators of children's perceptions of their parents.* Unpublished manuscript, University of Rochester.

Heath, S. B. (1980). Preschool and the future of print: The functions and uses of literacy. *Journal of Communication, 30,* 123–133.

Inhelder, B., Sinclair, M., & Bovet, M. (1974). *Learning and the development of cognition.* Cambridge, MA: Harvard University Press.

Johnson, D. W. (1980). Group processes: Influences of student–student interaction on school outcomes. In J. H.

McMillan (Ed.), *The social psychology of school learning* (pp. 123–168). New York: Academic Press.

Missiuna, C., & Samuels, M. T. (1989). Dynamic assessment of preschool children with special needs: Comparison of mediation and instruction. *Remedial and Special Education, 10,* 53–62.

Palincsar, A. S. (1986). The role of dialogue in providing scaffolded instruction. *Educational Psychologist, 21,* 73–98.

Palincsar, A. S., & Brown, A. L. (1984). Reciprocal teaching of comprehension-fostering and comprehension monitoring activities. *Cognition and Instruction, 1,* 117–175.

Piaget, J. (1957). *Plays, dreams, and imitation in childhood.* New York: Norton (Original French edition published 1927)

Piaget, J. (1970). *Structuralism.* New York: Basic Books.

Piaget, J. (1977). *The development of thought: Equilibration of cognitive structures.* New York: Viking Penguin. (Original French edition published 1975)

Piaget, J. (1979). *Piaget on Piaget.* New Haven, CT: Yale University Film Board.

Read, C. (1975). Lessons to be learned from the preschool orthographer. In E. H. Lenneberg & E. Lenneberg (Eds.), *Foundations of language development: A multidisciplinary approach* (Vol 2). New York: Academic Press.

Reid, D. K. (1989). The role of cooperative learning in comprehensive instruction. *Journal of Reading, Writing, and Learning Disabilities—International, 4,* 229–242.

Reid, D. K., & Knight-Arest, I. (1981). Cognitive processing in learning disabled and normally achieving boys in a goal-oriented task. In M. Freidman, J. Das, & N. O'Connor (Eds.), *Intelli-gence and learning* (pp. 503–508). New York: Plenum Press.

Resnick, L. B. (1989). Introductions. In L. B. Resnick (Ed.), *Knowing learning and instruction* (pp. 1–24). Hillsdale, NJ: Erlbaum.

Saxe, G. B., Guberman, S. R., & Gearhart, M. (1987). Social processes in early number development. *Monographs of the Society for Research in Child Development.* Chicago: University of Chicago Press.

Schunk, D. H. (1989). Self-efficacy and cognitive achievement: Implications for students with learning problems. *Journal of Learning Disabilities, 23,* 14–22.

Stone, C. A. (1989). Improving the effectiveness of strategy instruction for the learning disabled: The role of communicational dynamics. *Remedial and Special Education, 12,* 35–42.

Stone, C. A., & Conca, L. (in press). A social constructivist perspective on the nature and origins of strategy deficiencies in learning-disabled children. In L. Meltzer (Ed.), *Cognitive, linguistic and developmental perspectives on learning disorders.* Austin, TX: PRO-ED.

Swanson, H. L. (1984). Does theory guide teaching practice? Naturalistic observations in classrooms. *Remedial and Special Education, 5,* 7–15.

Switzky, H. N., & Schultz, G. F. (1988). Intrinsic motivation and learning performance: Implications for individual educational programming for learners with mild handicaps. *Remedial and Special Education, 9,* 7–14.

Teale, W. H., & Sulzby, E. (Eds.). (1986). *Emergent literacy.* Norwood, NJ: Ablex.

Vygotsky, L. S. (1978). *Mind in society: The development of higher psychological processes* (M. Cole, V. John-Steiner, S. Siribner, & E. Soulserman, Eds. and Trans.). Cambridge, MA: Harvard University Press.

Wansart, W. L. (1990). Developing metacognition through collaborative problem solving in a writing process classroom. *Journal of Learning Disabilities, 23,* 164–170.

Wertsch, J. V., & Stone, C. A. (1979, October). *A social interactional analysis of learning disabilities remediation.* Paper presented at the International Conference of the Association for Children with Learning Disabilities, San Francisco.

Wong, B. Y. L. (1985). Issues in cognitive-behavioral interventions in academic skill areas. *Journal of Abnormal Child Psychology, 13,* 425–442.

Wood, P., Bruner, J., & Ross, G. (1976). The role of tutoring in problem solving. *Journal of Child Psychology and Psychiatry, 17,* 89–100.

12

Oral Language

WAYNE P. HRESKO

Oral language is a major area of emphasis in understanding learning disabilities. Concern for the communication abilities of the learning disabled is not a new phenomenon. As early as 1967, Myklebust and Johnson were convinced that language impairments were widespread among the learning disabled. In fact, in the definition offered in Chapter 1 of this book, learning disabilities *are defined* as problems in oral and written language. Preoccupation with perceptual–motor deficits during the formative years of the field, however, eclipsed the importance of communication.

WHAT WAS THE ORIENTATION TO LANGUAGE IN THE EARLY STAGES OF THE LEARNING DISABILITY FIELD?

During the formative years of the learning disabilities field, the predominant view of language was behavioral. Early in the associationists' attempts to explain language acquisition and functioning (Skinner, 1957), questions arose concerning the viability of the model (Chomsky, 1959) with such ferocity that the Skinnerian explanation of language was dropped from serious consideration. Other associationist explanations of language, however, gained acceptance. Osgood (1953), working from a Hullian orientation, proposed a model for the communication process. This model, as discussed below, also came under fire.

Associationism is best described as a strong reductionist theory. From this perspective, language is a behavior and is placed in the same context as other observable behaviors. Language behavior was thought of as either one-stage (S → R) or two-stage mediated (Sr → sR) learning (where S = external stimulus, R = external response, r = internal response, and s = internal stimulus). Focusing on the individual word and the meaning attached to that word, the associationists all but ignored the developmental aspects of language. The presence of a given verbal behavior, in the presence of an appropriate stimulus, was thought sufficient to ensure the continued use of that utterance. Several assumptions were absent from the associationist view. First, any type of innate mechanism for the acquisition of language was ignored. Associationism did not acknowledge internal, genetically transmitted devices for language acquisition. Language acquisition corresponded to the established rules of behavioral learning theory. Second, the effects of neurological impairment were not directly addressed. Either neurological impairment deterred necessary physical responses, or related performance variables were impaired. Furthermore, maturational lag was interpreted as indicative of inadequately formed associations. Third, critical periods of language acquisition (see Lenneberg, 1967) were not acknowledged. When an individual's language is seen as defective, the behaviorist interprets the problem in terms of the specific difficulty impairing the language learning rather than as delayed maturation.

WHAT WAS OSGOOD'S MODEL AND WHAT WAS ITS INFLUENCE?

Osgood's (1953) model had tremendous influence in the field of learning disabilities. Osgood, who intended to apply mediated stimulus–response theory to communicative behavior, generated a three-stage, two-dimensional model of the process of communication. This model was refined through the collaborative work of Osgood and Miron. The model attempted to incorporate the understanding of meaning, a task omitted in other behavioral models.

Osgood's model is termed a mediated model, because it employs an intervening (mediating) step between the stimulus and the response. The development of meaning is explained as the development of associations between various internal stages and observable behavior. The model supposes a sequence of events that relates S to r. A resultant s leads, in turn, to R: Sr → sR. This model is commonly referred to as an underlying abilities model, because "it indicates the several sensory, cognitive, and motor systems necessary for normal linguistic performance. . . . These prerequisite systems can be called "subsymbolic" in that they are required for normal symbolic behavior though, in and of themselves, they are not symbolic" (Taylor & Swinney, 1972, p. 49).

The model explains behavior on three levels of neurological organization: the projective level, the integrational level, and the representational level. Each level is concerned with different functions. At the projective level, the child, for example, withdraws from pain or has a startled reaction to a loud noise. At the integrational level, the child's responses are automatic in nature, but the response is the result of some type of association rather than a reflexive reaction. Predictive mechanisms direct the child's responses to certain sequential grammatical structures. Most children respond to a given noun phrase such as "Jack and Jill . . ." with an associated verb phrase. At the representational level, conscious consideration of meaning occurs. Associations between representations are the outcome of actions at this level. Mediation is stressed and becomes the essential element in the development of meaning.

Osgood also postulated three levels of language functioning: decoding, association, and encoding. Decoding is synonymous with reception, encoding with expression, and association with the mediating process.

Wepman and his colleagues (e.g., Wepman, 1960) developed a similar model of communication. Wepman's model contributed to the understanding of communication through the inclusion of a feedback mechanism, a memory component, and the defining of modalities of transmission (auditory and visual modes of input and vocal and motor modes of output). Wepman's and Osgood's models, however, remained essentially similar.

HOW WAS THE OSGOOD MODEL OPERATIONALIZED?

Building upon the early work of Seiver, who attempted to synthesize the Osgood and Wepman models of communication, Kirk, McCarthy, and Kirk (1963) developed a test that dominated both language assessment and intervention programs in the schools, especially in learning disabilities. The test was called The Illinois Test of Psycholinguistic Abilities (ITPA). The representational subtests of the ITPA are based on the representational and integrational (automatic) levels of Osgood's model (see Table 12–1). At the automatic level, six additional subtests are included that assess functions thought to be automatic in nature, although highly organized and integrated (see Table 12–2). The ITPA was extensively used in the formative years of the field and, for a number of years, was the major tool of the trade. Numerous techniques and teaching devices have been based on the ITPA.

TABLE 12-1
The Representational Subtests of the Illinois Test of Psycholinguistic Abilities

---

1. *Auditory Reception:* The child's ability to differentiate meaningful from nonmeaningful sentences is measured. The child is required to answer "yes" or "no" to questions such as "Do porpoises precipitate?"

2. *Visual Reception:* The child is presented with a visual stimulus and is then required to choose (by pointing) a conceptually similar one from among four alternatives.

3. *Auditory Association:* This subtest is designed to evaluate the development of semiautonomic systems in the child. The child is required to respond to a series of verbal analogies by completing the second half of an analogy, such as "Sugar is white; grass is _____."

4. *Visual Association:* Children are asked to associate concepts. The stimulus consists of a picture to which the children respond by pointing to one of four choices. They are asked, "What goes with this?"

5. *Verbal Expression:* The child is asked to describe a series of objects presented one by one. The child is evaluated with respect to ability to verbalize about the color, size, shape, function, etc., of the object in question.

6. *Manual Expression:* A series of pictures is shown to the child, who pantomimes the use to which the object is put.

Assumptions Underlying the ITPA

The ITPA is based on a number of assumptions. First, the model assumes that an appropriate frame of reference for analyzing the language of children is that of adult communication. Variations in language use between adult and child, therefore, are viewed from a quantitative perspective. Second, the model assumes that language acquisition can be understood in terms of the principles of learning theory, and therefore does not attempt to elucidate sequences of language acquisition. Third, the model regards the factors identified as discrete and isolable. Functioning, for example, at the auditory representational level is viewed as separate and distinct from functioning at the auditory associational level. Fourth, each discrete element described by the model is assumed to be essential for adequate language functioning. Should any be at deficit, school achievement and language functioning would be expected to be adversely affected. Fifth, the model assumes that once a problem has been identified, intervention can be instituted that will improve not only the underlying abilities, but also language and academic functioning.

TABLE 12-2
The Associational Subtests of the Illinois Test of Psycholinguistic Abilities

1. *Grammatic Closure:* This subtest attempts to assess the child's understanding of English syntax. The child is presented with pictures and a stimulus sentence with part omitted. For example, the child may be shown pictures, one with a dog and one with two dogs. The examiner would say, "Here is a dog. Here are two _____."

2. *Auditory Closure* (optional): This subtest assesses the child's ability to generate a whole word when only parts of the word are presented. An example would be the oral presentation of "-ovie -tar," to which the child is expected to reply "movie star."

3. *Visual Closure:* This subtest assesses the child's ability to identify an object when only part is shown, for example, to identify a shoe when only a heel is visible in the drawing.

4. *Sound Blending* (optional): This subtest requires the child to synthesize a series of separate phonemes presented orally into a word.

5. *Auditory Sequential Memory:* Essentially a test of digit span, the goal of this test is to ascertain the child's short-term memory ability.

6. *Visual Sequential Memory:* A visual test of short-term memory, this test asks the child to reconstruct from memory a sequence of nonmeaningful geometric designs.

Two assumptions underlying the specific abilities model—that is, those dealing with adult-based concepts of language processing and the lack of interest regarding the sequence of acquisition in the development of language—are more philosophical in nature than the other four. Some of the most compelling reasons for questioning these assumptions are found in the literature dealing with the acquisition of language and emerging cognitive abilities. Research from the fields of cognitive and developmental psychology leaves little doubt that a child's cognitive abilities indicate differential abilities at different developmental periods. Each level is qualitatively distinct from the preceding and succeeding ones (Bloom & Lahey, 1978; Gallagher & Reid, 1981; Sinclair-de-Zwart, 1973). Language has a strong symbiotic relationship to cognitive development (Bloom & Lahey, 1978; Verhave, 1972). "It is, for example, possible to assume that there are inherent schema (principles of organization or cognitive structures) and that these structures are crucial in determining the form of output" (Verhave, 1972, p. 192). This interactionist position argues that since adult and individual cognitive structures differ, adult and individual languages differ. J.F. Miller and Yoder (1974) cogently argued that a developmental approach to the assessment and intervention of individual language difficulties must be utilized, regardless of the theoretical framework in which the intervention or assessment takes place.

The third assumption regards the discrete nature of the abilities measured by the ITPA. This assumption consists of two parts: (a) the specific subtests are discrete, and (b) the dimensions of the model (levels, processes, and channels) are discrete. A number of excellent reviews have addressed these issues (e.g., Newcomer & Hammill, 1976; Proger, Cross, & Burger, 1973; Sedlak & Weener, 1973) and failed to substantiate this assumption.

The question to be asked is whether the ITPA has *construct* validity. One method of establishing the construct validity of a device is to factor analyze it, expecting that the emergent factor structure will replicate the theoretical model. If the model hypothesizing the existence of a visual channel and an auditory channel were true, the factor structure would emerge with one factor representing the visual tasks, and one representing the auditory tasks. The studies that have employed only the subtests of the ITPA in the factor analyses (without any criterion tests) offer scant support for the channel–level–process model on which the ITPA is based (Sedlak & Weener, 1973, p. 124).

Other researchers have concluded that some consistent results are evidenced: A general psycholinguistic factor and channel abilities often emerge (Proger et al., 1973). The main criticisms of the factor analytic studies are that any given factor structure can change with the population being studied, and that the use of subtests to define emerging structures is questionable. Sedlak and Weener (1973), however, raised the most critical question: What would be the appropriate factor structure to hypothesize, since the emergence of one dimension would of necessity violate another? They wrote, "Factors which would honor channel distinctions would violate level and process distinctions; factors which would honor process distinctions would cut across channels and levels, and so forth" (p. 125).

Newcomer and Hammill (1976) dismissed the importance of these studies for lack of appropriate criterion tests. When criterion tests are left out, the result is "a treatment which maximized their intercorrelations and resulted in multiple subtest loadings on large general factors" (p. 36).

If factor studies that used criterion measures are reviewed, the situation becomes more clear. Two studies (Hare, Hammill, & Bartel, 1973; Newcomer, Hare, Hammill, & McGettigan, 1975) in which the ITPA was factor analyzed, along with criterion measures designed to tap each of the ITPA subtest areas, confirmed the structure of the ITPA at least for the dimensions of organization and process. "Any weakness regarding the construct validity of the ITPA subtest appears primarily due to the modality dimension" (Newcomer & Hammill, 1976, p. 37).

The differences between the results of studies using criterion measures and those not employing such measures are significant. Studies using only the subtests of the ITPA indicated that the channels of communication often emerged, whereas those using the criterion measures found no evidence for the existence of such channels. This finding is important, because one very extensive use to which the ITPA has been put is determining the modality preferences of children. Newcomer and Hammill (1976) suggested, "While certain groups of individuals may produce characteristic patterns of modality strengths and weaknesses, this information has no empirically demonstrated relevance for academic instruction" (p. 62). Similarly, Proger et al. (1973) concluded, "While one would like to believe that individualizing instruction on the basis of modality strengths leads to more efficient progress, the research reviewed . . . does not support this view" (p. 175).

The fourth assumption of the ITPA is that the abilities identified are related to language, and language functioning will be adversely affected if any or all of these abilities are at deficit. The assumption is that the abilities measure language. From current thinking regarding language, the ITPA is, at best, a model of communication. Even as a measure of communication, however, the model is inadequate as judged by its developer (Osgood, 1975). Language can be viewed as communication, or as a simplistic code, or as information processing, but not as a composite of discrete abilities. Newcomer and Hammill (1976) noted that little research has attempted to relate the ITPA to recognized measures of language. The belief that the ITPA is a measure of language rests more on faith than on evidence.

The assumption regarding the ability to improve deficit functions and their relation to academic achievement is extremely important. This assumption underlies the use to which the ITPA has been put. The research on the "trainability" of the ITPA abilities has been negative. Numerous methods of intervention have been employed in attempts to "train" the abilities identified by the ITPA as deficient. These methods include (but are not restricted to) activities and programs developed by Bush and Giles (1969), Karnes (1972), Kirk and Kirk (1971), and Minskoff, Wiseman, and Minskoff (1972). In addition, others have attempted to analyze the training programs with reference to the length of time in training, the types of subjects, the materials used, the number of subjects, and the measures used in assessing performance (Hammill & Larsen, 1974; Newcomer & Hammill, 1976; Proger et al., 1973; Sedlak & Weener, 1973). The most significant finding of these reviews is the lack of consistent, replicable results. A simple reporting of the number of studies involved in attempts at training psycholinguistic processes is astounding. Newcomer and Hammill (1976) reported that over 281 studies were conducted between 1962 and 1973. Despite the vast number of studies, the results are unclear.

Newcomer and Hammill (1976) reviewed the training studies by discussing the findings according to the populations studies. For example, with the retarded population, they concluded that "there was not a single subtest for which a majority of the researchers reported that training was beneficial" (p. 73). Considering the disadvantaged, they found evidence of positive effects of training only for those subtests related to association skills and verbal expression. At the preschool level, positive effects of training were noted at the associational level. For the child of elementary school age, the verbal expression area and subtests of general language ability appear to be open to remediation. When all studies are reviewed, only two subtests appear consistently amenable to intervention, Auditory Association and Verbal Expression. The subtests least likely to respond to intervention are Visual Sequential Memory and Visual Closure. Comparable results were found by Logan and Colarusso (1978). The major conclusion to be drawn is that the efficacy of training psycholinguistic functioning has not been demonstrated.

Effects on Academic Gains

Referring to the relation of the abilities to academic achievement, Newcomer (1975) stated that, for all intents and purposes, there exists an "insignificant and partially useless relationship between most ITPA subtests and measures of academic achievement" (p. 403). Sedlak and Weener (1973) concluded,

> The crucial question, therefore, appears to be to what extent remediation programs directed at psycholinguistic deficits will affect measures of school achievement. The results thus far indicate that programs directed solely at psycholinguistic deficits have little, if any, effect on school achievement. (p. 142)

Despite the research findings and the major changes in theoretically accepted positions in the fields of psychology and psycholinguistics, the controversy over the ITPA and related training programs continues. In the absence of new data to support the position, defenders (Lund, Foster, & McCall-Perez, 1978) continue to challenge the conclusions reached by opponents (Hammill & Larsen, 1974, 1978). Unfortunately, the continued defense of what appears to be a highly untenable position neither clarifies the issues nor furthers the state of the art.

The assumption that abilities measured by the ITPA are necessary for academic success also fairs poorly. The reviews of Hammill and Larsen (1974), Newcomer and Hammill (1976), and Sedlak and Weener (1973) are exceedingly consistent in their findings for the areas of reading, spelling, and arithmetic: When IQ is controlled, no subtest is significantly correlated. Inability to confirm the model's assumptions, as well as the knowledge that the test itself is not valid, reliable, or adequately formed, leads to the conclusion that use of the ITPA for educational diagnosis and/or intervention can be neither recommended nor supported.

HOW DOES THE COGNITIVE-DEVELOPMENTAL APPROACH VIEW LANGUAGE DEVELOPMENT?

"Language" can refer to many things. First, it is a code of communication (Bloom & Lahey, 1978). Second, it can refer to communication and interactions between or among people (Halliday, 1978). Third, it is the basis of much of the information people acquire and is itself information (Bever, 1970). Language is inextricably bound to the cognitive development of the child.

The most influential individual addressing a cognitive approach to language was Noam Chomsky, whose theory of transformational generative grammar (1959, 1965) was the impetus for developmental psycholinguistics. During the 1960s, linguists and information processing psychologists were becoming more and more closely aligned. Psycholinguists were beginning to consider the study of cognition a field within psycholinguistics, one that G.A. Miller (1965) referred to as *cognitive psycholinguistics.* This new strain of psycholinguistics would, in Miller's words,

> be forced to accept a more cognitive approach . . . , to talk about hypothesis testing instead of discrimination learning, about the evaluation of hypotheses instead of the reinforcement of responses, about rules instead of habits, about productivity instead of generalizations, about innate and universal human capabilities instead of special methods of teaching vocal responses, about symbols instead of conditioned stimuli, about sentences instead of words or vocal noises, about linguistic structure instead of chains of responses—in short, about language instead of learning theory. (p. 20)

Cognitive psycholinguists viewed language as acquired by the *active* child. Language became perceived as an actively constructed system developed by each individual from his or her personal experience with objects and persons:

> That is, language is not learned in the sense of the direct acquisition of knowledge from experience but rather as the induction of rules and categories across many instances. Meaning, for example, derives not from associations, but from a dynamic creative process of the individual as he or she interacts with and draws from the environment. (Hresko & Reid, 1979, p. 6)

For those adhering to a cognitive approach, (a) language is acquired without direct instruction, (b) there are differences in the structure of adult and individual language, (c) research should focus on the child, and (d) the poor use of language in social contexts may place limits on the individual by affecting how others view the individual.

The Cognitive Perspective of Language Acquisition

From a cognitive perspective, two different yet complementary views of language acquisition and learning appeared in the 1960s and 1970s. The earlier position suggested that the individual is endowed with universal language structures, that is, a natural ability or propensity to acquire language (Chomsky, 1965; McNeill, 1966). This model proposed the existence of a language acquisition device (LAD). Although useful in explaining the occurrence of linguistic universals, the LAD explains little of the nature of language acquisition, or of the relation of the emergence of language to other emerging systems. The later view of language acquisition (Bloom, 1970; Bloom & Lahey, 1978; Sinclair-de-Zwart, 1973) suggested that general cognitive structures guide the acquisition of language, and that the cognitive and linguistic systems are inextricably bound in development (Lewis & Cherry, 1977). The individual extracts from interactions with the environment (e.g., objects, people, actions) the information necessary to determine how to construct exemplars of the linguistic system (or code), how to function with the code, and how to express various meanings (to others) with the code. The individual actively sorts and chooses the information to attend to, tries various combinations to see their effect, and thus actively constructs language (Kuczaj, 1982). "Children are thus active participants in the learning process and bring to it a set of behaviors and organizational strategies that allow them to benefit from the adult's facilitating behaviors" (Friel-Patti & Conti-Ramsden, 1988).

At present, the view that language and cognition are intertwined and codeveloping has been widely accepted. A cognitive approach adheres to this tenet. Furthermore, no research suggests that a student classified as learning disabled acquires language in a manner different from other, normally achieving students.

A Cognitive Basis for Language Development

The cognitive approach does not subscribe to the position that language can be taught through traditional behavioral techniques (de Villiers & de Villiers, 1978). For instance, if language were learned through methods of association, the number of sentences and words to which one would have to be exposed would be astronomical. Second, children learn correct usage even when the models to which they are exposed are inadequate. Third, children during language acquisition are observed to make errors in usage, as if attempting to develop a rule by generalizing an instance. For example, children say "goed" or "comed" when first learning the rule for forming the past tense of irregular words, even though they had been observed previously to use "went" and "came." In addition, cognitive psycholinguists recognize that, although operant techniques appear useful in teaching some specific language structures, the programs are less than successful when generalization to novel situations is necessary.

Early diary studies and, more recently, studies by Bloom (1970), Bloom, Lightbown, and Hood (1975), and Brown (1973) regarding adult–child language differences have supported evidence that language structures appear across children in a given sequence, and that this sequence is relatively invariant (Bloom & Lahey, 1978). Differences in the well-formedness of the language have been noted, along with differences in apparent processing ability. Even when the utterances between individual and adult appear the same, Bloom and Lahey maintained that "although adult and individual utterances may be identical in their surface form, there are almost certainly important differences between their underlying cognitive and linguistic representations" (p. 253).

The difference between the associationists and the cognitive psycholinguists rests on their beliefs of what language is and how one intervenes. Language, when viewed as a communication code, can be seen to have little use for postulated underlying abilities or labels and sentence patterns. Therefore, the proper focus of research is on the form of language, the content expressed, and the use to which the individual puts language.

The focus of the associationist model is on performance variables that affect the ability to attend to information in the environment. Several points must be noted. First, the psychological variables that affect information processing are not, in and of themselves, language. Second, most individuals with underlying ability deficits learn language in spite of their deficits and, after language is attained, still have their specific deficits. Bloom and Lahey (1978) reviewed the work on social abilities of the learning disabled, and concluded that they perform less adequately than their peers in social settings requiring language. Similarly, Bloom (1977) found that one aspect of the learning disabled child's language problem is in the communicative aspect of language. The learning disabled fail to respond adequately to listeners' reactions to what has been said. The abilities to monitor and to modify language in order to meet the demands of the situation are often impaired.

The cognitive psycholinguists are at variance with several positions taken by the proponents of the specific abilities and behavioral orientations. Perhaps the most important is what constitutes the basis for studying language. For cognitive psycholinguists (and for us), the proper study of language is language, not processing variables related to language, especially if the goal of the program is to intervene in the child's language development. Intervention, however, must recognize, in a way the behaviorists fail to do, that it is the individual who must construct language. The learning of particular content, therefore, is viewed as an inappropriate instructional goal. Language learning is instead viewed as having to be flexible and creative, both syntactically and semantically.

A comparison of the Osgoodian and cognitive psycholinguistic approaches indicates disagreement at the most fundamental level—the theories simply do not interact. Perhaps the only point of agreement of the conventional and alternative approaches is that both believe that adequate function of the components of their respective theories is necessary for school success. Fundamental differences, however, as to what constitutes language, whether language can be taught, and what methods of intervention should be used, provide significant obstacles to any synthesis of the models.

WHAT HAVE COGNITIVE RESEARCHERS LEARNED ABOUT THE LANGUAGE OF THE LEARNING DISABLED?

Because the learning disabled constitute a population whose characteristics include neurological involvement, the question of how the theory handles neurological impairment is important. The literature has shown that neurological impairment might affect a child's acquisition of language (1) by limiting the child's ability to extract information from the environment and hence to structure linguistic material, and (2) by limiting the child's ability during certain critical stages of language development. Researchers have only begun to investigate questions of how neurological impairment might affect language acquisition. Most of the efforts by the psycholinguists have centered on determining the sequence and strategies employed in language acquisition.

With more of the biological nature of the individual being recognized in the cognitive psycholinguistic approach, the theory is able to absorb ideas of critical periods of language development. In Lenneberg's (1967) now classic work, he presented the idea that during the child's neurobiological growth, certain time spans are critical for the acquisition of language. Among the evidence cited is the finding that, depending on the age at onset, the condition known as aphasia (problems with oral language ability) has differential prognoses. The younger the child, the better the chances are for the remission of symptoms. Others have analyzed the myelination of the nervous system, relating that phenomenon to language acquisition. The cognitive psycholinguistic model has no difficulty in incorporating these findings. They reflect an understanding of the interaction of the organism with the environment, an interaction that is, to a large extent, a function of the intactness of the organism.

Of critical importance is the manner in which the concept of maturational lag is handled. The psycholinguists recognize that individuals acquire language (and other abilities) at differing rates. For some children, the process appears to move at an average rate; for others, the sequence is more rapid; and for some, the sequence is normal but the rate is delayed. If the individual is maturing neurologically at a delayed pace, the development of structures dependent on neurological functioning would also be expected to be delayed. Regarding the question of defective language (in that the language is inferior or intrinsically disturbed), the cognitive psycholinguists recognize that distortions may occur in the child's acquisition of language (Bloom & Lahey, 1978).

Model to Evaluate the Language Abilities of the Learning Disabled

One of the most important models for delineating language abilities and disabilities is that of Bloom and Lahey (1978). Although operationalized over a decade ago, this model is still very useful in examining the components of language functioning. This model delineates three aspects of oral language: form, content, and use. Although the model does not contain an evaluation of language processing (Cupples & Lewis, 1984), it does provide for a multifaceted description of oral language. Language form refers to the structure of language, including grammar, syntax, and morphology (see Figure 12–1). Language content refers to the meanings, concepts, and lexical entries that the individual possesses (see Figure 12–2). Language use refers to how individuals combine language content and form to effectively communicate (see Figure 12–3). Research has provided evidence that learning disabled children have difficulties with any and all aspects of the Bloom and Lahey model: form (see Wiig & Semel, 1980; Wren, 1983), content (see Harris-Schmidt, 1983; Hoskins, 1983; Wiig & Semel, 1980), and use (see T.H. Bryan, Donahue, Pearl, & Sturm, 1981). Others have suggested that "metavariables" must be included in any discussion of language (Cornett & Chabon, 1986), because these variables affect the ability to organize, apply, or generalize knowledge (Swanson, 1982; Torgesen & Greenstein, 1982; Wren, 1983).

The Syntactic Abilities of the Learning Disabled

Research is fairly clear in substantiating a relation between language ability and academic abilities. Therefore, the syntax of the learning disabled has been studied by a number of researchers, employing both experimental tasks and established language assessment devices. Cumulative research suggests that the overall and expressive syntactic development of learning disabled students is delayed (e.g., Idol-Maestas, 1980; Morice & Slaghuis, 1985; Wiig, Becker-Redding, & Semel, 1983; Wiig, Semel, & Abele, 1981), increases with age (e.g., Idol-Maestas, 1980; Wiig, 1984), and plateaus at levels expected of younger students (e.g., Wiig et al., 1983). Furthermore, these difficulties may be significant enough to interfere with informal and elliptical conversations (Donahue, Pearl, & Bryan, 1982). "It appears that the characterization

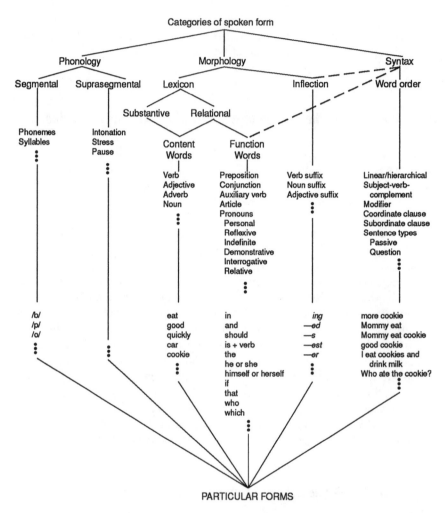

Figure 12-1. The categories of spoken form and particular forms. From *Language Development and Language Disorders* (p. 16) by L. Bloom and M. Lahey, 1978, New York: Wiley. Copyright 1978 by Macmillan Publishing Co. Reprinted with permission.

of learning disabled children as 'subtly dysphasic' (Denckla & Rudel, 1976) may be understated" (Donahue et al., 1982).

Recently, research using shadowing techniques examined the language processing and reading abilities in children. "Speech shadowing [analogous to oral reading] requires listeners to repeat continuous spoken language, with their oral reproductions being as close to simultaneous as possible with the incoming speech signals" (Jordan, 1988, p. 358). This research affirmed that good readers were better able to exploit the syntactic features of the text

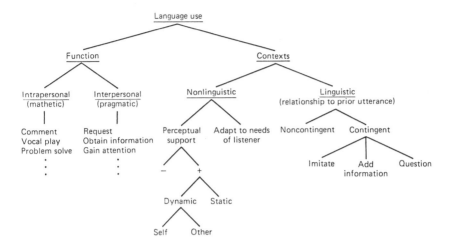

Figure 12-2. The uses of language. From *Language Development and Language Disorders* (p. 19) by L. Bloom and M. Lahey, 1978, New York: Wiley. Copyright 1978 by Macmillan Publishing Co. Reprinted with permission.

than were poor readers: "children who read aloud poorly were less proficient than skilled readers in their ability to process spoken language rapidly and to exploit syntactic cues" (Jordan, 1988, p. 373).

Hresko (1979), employing an experimental sentence repetition task based on the work of Clay (1971), found that 5- and 6-year-old learning disabled children were much poorer in the development of syntactic ability than were normally achieving children of the same age group. They evidenced difficulty with sentences exemplifying unfamiliar declarative constructions, proposed clauses and phrases, and relative clauses. In addition, the use of function words was inferior. Similar sentence repetition studies of the learning disabled have revealed difficulties with other constructions: contractions, conjunctions, noun–pronoun reference, number agreement, and the use of the verb "to be" (McCoulskey, 1971; Rosenthal, 1970; Young, 1971).

Wiig, Semel, and Crouse (1973) and Hresko, Rosenberg, and Buchanan (1978) found differences in morphological ability between normal and learning disabled children. Their results led them to conclude that the learning disabled children were delayed in the acquisition and development of morphological rules.

Using the Northwestern Syntax Screening Test (NSST), Wiig and Semel (1975) found differences between learning disabled children and normal children in both the expressive and receptive domains. On the expressive portion of the test, 62% of the learning disabled scored below the 25th percentile. Concerned with the abilities of the learning disabled individual through adolescence, Wiig and Semel (1975) assessed productive capabilities in a task

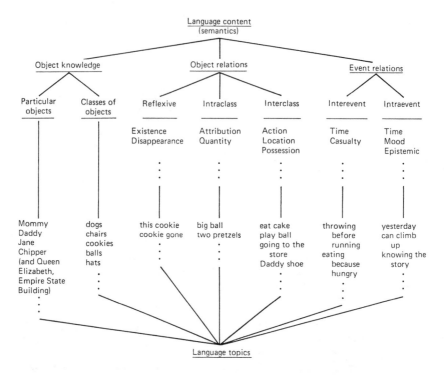

Figure 12–3. The content and topics of language. From *Language Development and Language Disorders* (p. 12) by L. Bloom and M. Lahey, New York: Wiley. Copyright 1978 by Macmillan Publishing Co. Reprinted with permission.

requiring the adolescent to include a stimulus word in a self-produced sentence. Wiig and Semel indicated that learning disabled adolescents were more likely than normal children to produce either an ungrammatical sentence or an incomplete sentence.

As can be seen, the cognitive psycholinguistic approach has been successful in establishing some syntactic characteristics of the learning disabled, at both elementary school age and adolescence. The small number of studies reviewed here are illustrative of an increasingly large body of literature. For a more comprehensive treatment, the reader is referred to reviews by T. H. Bryan (1978) and Wiig and Semel (1980).

Some researchers have failed to evidence significant syntactic deficits among the learning disabled population. Roth and Spekman (1989), for example, analyzed the syntactic complexity of normally achieving and learning disabled students (aged 8 years through 14 years) and found few substantive differences. The authors, however, pointed to a number of potential reasons. First, the assessed IQs of the learning disabled students for the most part exceeded 110. Thus, the IQs for this sample exceeded the average for the general learning disabled population (Kavale & Forness, 1984). Second, several authors have noted the existence of subgroups of learning disabled individuals. Since only one language measure was used in this study, perhaps a specific subset of the learning disabled population was identified. Third, the potential exists that the syntactic structures measured in this analysis were within the linguistic competence of this group. As the authors noted, perhaps it is the quantity and not the quality of the linguistic output that distinguishes learning disabled from normally achieving children. In the words of Griffith, Ripich, and Dastoli (1986), "They generally spoke less, but their pattern of propositional use followed that of nondisabled children." This is consistent with the findings of Graybeal (1981) and Hansen (1982). Additionally, Simms and Crump (1983) found syntactic difficulties when using measures of the total number of T-units ("basic unit of expression consisting of a single main clause and the subordinate clause joined to it"; Hunt, 1965, p. 20) produced and the syntactic density score (a weighted measure designed to include T-units, clause length, embedded clauses, etc.). They were unable to find differences, however, when they employed a more recognized (and sophisticated) measure, average T-unit length.

Semantic Problems Displayed by the Learning Disabled

As the general field of cognitive psycholinguistics has moved from an isolated consideration of syntax to interest in the semantic aspects of language, those interested in the learning disabled have included in their research evaluations of the semantic capabilities of the learning disabled. In the study of Hresko, Rosenberg, and Buchanan (1978), learning disabled children were found to have vocabulary deficits, evidenced by lack of facility with nouns, adjectives, verbs, and adverbs. This finding is at variance with that of Wiig and Semel (1976), who reported no difficulty on the part of the learning disabled with respect to vocabulary. Their finding, however, is restricted to nouns and not the other classes noted by Hresko et al. (1978). Wiig and Semel (1975) assessed the abilities of learning disabled adolescents to picture name (Visual Confrontation subtest of the Boston VA Aphasia Test; Goodglass & Kaplan, 1972) and to retrieve and name antonyms (Verbal Opposites subtest of the Detroit Tests of Learning Aptitude; Baker & Leland, 1959). In the results of both tasks, the learning disabled adolescents made more errors and took longer to respond than did normal adolescents. Hresko's (1979) sentence repetition study indicated that learning disabled children had a greater tendency than normal children to change the semantic elements of the sentence when imitating. In analyzing the results of studies dealing with learning disabled children and adolescents with regard to semantics, Wiig and Semel (1976) concluded, "The consistent observation across age levels of anomia and verbal paraphasia as an aspect of dyslexia and learning disabilities . . . strengthens the positions that the convergent language production deficits in learning disabilities reflect subtle aphasia" (p. 216).

Related to semantic abilities is the ability to both comprehend and use figurative language (e.g., "kick the bucket," "spill the beans"), including sarcasm, idioms, similes and metaphors, and proverbs. Several authors have identified problems with figurative language as a characteristic of learning disabled individuals (Blue, 1981; Donahue & Bryan, 1984; Stimson, 1983; Wiig & Semel, 1984). Some (e.g., Nippold & Fey, 1983) have suggested that use of figurative language may be a useful assessment tool. The ability to interpret and use figurative language is important since it occurs with frequency in both conversational language (Hoffman & Honeck, 1980) and written language (Arter, 1976; Lockhart, 1972). As learning disabled individuals move into the realm of adolescence, their ability to interpret and use figurative language becomes more important (Nippold, 1985). Unfortunately, few studies have looked at the figurative language abilities of learning disabled individuals. Representative studies include those of Stimson (1983) and Strand (1982). Stimson's study suggests that learning disabled students within the middle school age range have significant difficulties with the understanding of both predictive metaphors (one topic and one vehicle) and proportional metaphors (two topics and two vehicles with an underlying analogical relationship). Strand, using a similar age range, noted that figurative language development in learning disabled individuals showed a similar but delayed pattern of development compared with that of normal subjects.

Other studies (Wiig, Semel, & Nystrom, 1982) suggest that the problems of language production of learning disabled individuals may be more pronounced than previously thought and that standardized assessment devices may not be sensitive to the difficulties of learning disabled children. The above studies appear to justify the conclusion that learning disabled children evidence language difficulties.

Phonological Problems Displayed by the Learning Disabled

The area of phonological development of learning disabled children is sorely neglected. Although some information exists regarding the discrimination of speech sounds by these children, descriptions of their articulation ability is lacking. As Turton (1975) pointed out, the relation between auditory discrimination ability and articulation disorders has been advanced by numerous authors (Carrell & Pendergast, 1954; Cohen & Diehl, 1963; Kronvall & Diehl, 1954; Reid, 1947a, 1947b; Templin, 1957). More recent research suggests that any relation between articulation disorders and auditory discrimination problems must be viewed cautiously. Marquardt and Saxman (1972) suggested that any relation is, at best, tenuous. Aram and Nation (1975) indicated that language deficits appear hierarchically ordered in that problems in semantics subsume problems in syntax and phonology, whereas problems in syntax subsume only phonology, and problems in phonology stand alone.

Communication Abilities of the Learning Disabled

Since the original edition of this text, emphasis on the conversational abilities of learning disabled individuals has increased. Specifically, this interest has been in the area of pragmatics, the use of language in context. Thus, the investigation of pragmatics includes the examination of the individual's competence in interpersonal communication (Hopper & Naremore, 1973). The study of pragmatics also includes the study of code switching, or the ability to change roles according to the perceived needs of those involved in the communicative interaction.

Several researchers have found differences in narrative abilities among learning disabled and nondisabled students. Generally, learning disabled individuals transmit less information during language interactions. For example, in narrative production (spontaneous storytelling), learning disabled individuals included fewer words and idea units, and had a higher proportion of pronouns without specified antecedents (Feagans & Applebaum, 1986; Feagans & Short, 1984). Generally, language-based difficulties persist into adolescence. Also, several authors have found that learning disabled adolescents continued to exhibit language deficits in narrative production, including a lack of cohesion and less adaptation to the needs of the listener (Caro & Schneider, 1983; Roth, 1986; Roth & Spekman, 1986; Tuch, 1977). Roth and Spekman (1985) analyzed the narrative productions of learning disabled individuals 8 to 13 years of age using Stein and Glenn's (1979) story grammar. The authors noted that the learning disabled clearly used the underlying story grammar to construct their narratives in the same general order as their normal counterparts; however, the learning disabled students created stories that were significantly shorter, had fewer episodes and fewer supporting details, and, as above, failed to adequately address the need for cohesion. Others (Boucher, 1984, 1986; Griffith et al., 1986) suggest that narrative deficits are pronounced only with complex stories and propositions, and that learning disabled adolescents perform as well as their peers with very simple stories, perhaps because learning disabled individuals have deficits in knowledge of story grammar and thus are unable to apply this knowledge to retrieving and presenting story information.

Conversation (discourse) is also an area in which deficits have been noted. Knight-Arest (1984) studied the communicative effectiveness of learning disabled individuals aged 10 to 13. In her study, learning disabled and normally achieving students were required to "teach" other students how to play checkers. The results suggested that learning disabled individuals did not transmit as much information as normal individuals, although they talked more. Furthermore, they failed to describe their actions (preferring to engage in demonstrations) and repeated rather than reformulated instructions. Similar findings have been evidenced by others studying dyadic verbal abilities (Spekman, 1981).

Another variable of communication that has been studied is perception of linguistic stress, which involves interactions of suprasegmental elements such as vocal pitch, intensity, and duration. Linguistic stress provides emphasis to the listener and indicates heavy information load or important information (Baltaxe, 1984). Linguistic stress is probably the most important way in which emphasis is denoted since it occurs either alone or in combination with other techniques such as word order, clefting, and use of noun phrases. Several researchers have found that learning disabled individuals have difficulties determining the meaning of vocal cues in conversation (T. H. Bryan, 1977; Courtwright & Courtwright, 1983; Wiig & Semel, 1984). One representative study by Highnam and Morris (1987) investigated the perception of linguistic stress and semantic appropriateness. Their learning disabled and normal students were required to judge several pairs of sentences with regard to semantic and stress correctness. Statistical analysis revealed significant differences between the groups, indicating that the learning disabled group had more difficulty in determining both the correctness of stress and the semantic appropriateness of the stimuli. The authors concluded that the difficulties represent a symbolic deficit in interpreting meaning.

Referential communication skills, that is, the ability to assume designated communicative roles, play a vital role in person-to-person interactions. A limited number of studies are available on the referential communication skills of learning disabled individuals. The studies are differentiated according to whether the subject was the speaker (T. H. Bryan, Donahue, Pearl, & Sturm, 1981; Donahue, Pearl, & Bryan, 1982; Meline, 1978; Noel, 1980; Spekman, 1981) or the listener (T. H. Bryan, Donahue, Pearl, & Sturm, 1981; Donahue, 1981; Donahue et al., 1980; Meline & Meline, 1983; Winkler, Brinton, Fujiki, & Frome, 1984). Regardless of the role assumed, the studies indicate that learning disabled individuals generally have difficulties with referential communication skills. For example, using a TV talk show format, T. H. Bryan, Donahue, Pearl, and Sturm (1981) investigated the ability of learning disabled second and fourth graders to perform as a talk show host during an interview. They did not, in the words of Mishler (1975a, 1975b), perform as "powerful speakers" who took control and maintained that control through questions and responses. Their findings indicate that the learning disabled were less likely to use advanced strategies for initiating interviews and were unable to sustain interactions (i.e., they asked fewer questions and did not use open-ended questions). Unfortunately, as T. H. Bryan, Donahue, Pearl, and Sturm (1981) noted, it is not possible at this juncture to differentiate among the deficits associated with linguistics, strategies, and social deficits. Olsen, Wong, and Marx (1983) found similar results. Their interpretation of results suggests that the learning disabled individuals' lack of organizational abilities and planfulness indicate a lack of ability to regulate their communicative process, thus suggesting a passive cognitive style. In the end, the learning disabled individual may have definite deficits in metacognitive linguistic strategies and pragmatic abilities. This view is consistent with the inactive learner conceptualization of Wong (1982) and Wong and Jones (1982).

A study by Meline (1986), however, cast some doubt regarding the assumption of referential deficits in learning disabled students. Meline suggested that learning disabled/language impaired individuals are as capable as their age-mates in referential abilities (in the role of the speaker), despite immature lexicons. Furthermore, the learning disabled students in this study produced significantly less verbal output than their counterparts. Also with regard to referential skills, the results of some studies indicate that learning disabled individuals have a tendency to use an unassertive conversational style (T. H. Bryan, Donahue, & Pearl, 1981; Donahue, 1981; Fey, Leonard, Fey, & O'Connor, 1978; Watson, 1977). Others indicate that the learning disabled are able to modify their presentation according to the needs of the listener (e.g., Boucher, 1984).

Nonverbal communication has also been studied in learning disabled students. Much of the research in nonverbal communication stems from the work on social abilities of learning disabled students. Several investigators have suggested that both expressive and receptive nonverbal communication abilities are affected. It appears that learning disabled individuals are relatively insensitive to the nonverbal communication of their normal peers (T. H. Bryan, 1974, 1976, 1978; T. H. Bryan, Wheeler, Felcan, & Henek, 1976). For example, learning disabled individuals appear to be less able to interpret nonverbal indications of affirmations and negations (Brook, 1977). Similarly, Puckett (1980) indicated that academically talented students were better able than learning disabled individuals at interpreting the nonverbal gestures of teachers. Cermak, Coster, and Drake (1980) suggested that the ability to use appropriate gestures is impaired in learning disabled students. With regard to nonverbal communication in interactions with other students and adults, learning disabled students use less ingratiating behavior, invade private space, elicit negative impressions, and are generally viewed as offensive (J. H. Bryan & Perlmutter, 1979; J. H. Bryan & Sherman, 1980; J. H. Bryan, Sherman, & Fisher, 1980). Some researchers, however, have noted that nonverbal communication abilities (and disabilities) appear situation specific and usually appear in more artificial settings.

The Effects of Language Difficulties on Academic Achievement

Most academic tasks require the use of language or language-related abilities. The interest in the relation between language deficits and academic deficits has a long history. That the language disabilities of the learning disabled might impinge upon other academic abilities has been recognized by many. For example, Stanovich (1986) proposed that the high correlation between listening comprehension ability (i.e., receptive language) and reading ability suggests that comprehension problems are probably implicated in reading disorders. In fact, he suggested that "The pervasive comprehension deficits could result from a very generalized lack of linguistic awareness that is characteristic of learning-disabled children (Downing, 1980; Menyuk & Flood, 1981).

Language Intervention with the Learning Disabled

Many research studies exist regarding intervention techniques with language disabled/learning disabled individuals. Few cumulative reports, however, are available. One such cumulative report, by Ny, Foster, and Seaman (1987), suggested a number of trends in language intervention. First, language intervention, overall, appears to be quite effective. This means that, overall, language intervention techniques allowed language disordered students to move approximately 35 percentile points in ability as opposed to those without intervention. Second, language intervention was most pronounced for young, clinical populations. Third, the longer the treatment session, the more the gain. Fourth, syntax oriented interventions achieved the most gains. Fifth, pragmatic interventions appeared to achieve the least gains. Finally, interventions that required modeling were more effective than those requiring general stimulation. Apparently, the most advantageous techniques are those that require adherence to a model, are long term, deal with young students, are oriented toward syntax, and are specific to the deficit.

With regard to the form of language intervention, evidence suggests that, in the same manner of Bloom and Lahey (1978), use of the normal developmental sequence is appropriate for intervention with both young learning disabled children and older learning disabled adolescents (Dyer, Santarcangelo, & Luce, 1987).

SUMMARY

Oral language is a major area of emphasis in understanding learning disabilities. Early theories about the acquisition and functioning of oral language abilities centered around behavioral and, later, associational points of view. These beliefs were soon questioned, however, due to the absence of several important assumptions, such as an innate mechanism for language, the effects of neurological impairments, and the issue of delayed maturation in language acquisition.

Osgood (1953) developed a model that sought to incorporate the understanding of meaning into language, which had been omitted from other behavioral models. The model details three levels of neurological organization and three levels of language functioning. Wepman (1960) developed a similar model of communication, which incorporated a feedback mechanism, a memory component, and the defining of modalities of transmission.

Osgood's model was operationalized through the development of the ITPA. This instrument focused on the representational and automatic levels of the model, and six subtests were designed for each component. Six basic assumptions underlie the ITPA, and these assumptions have been highly questioned and extensively researched by professionals in the field. An analysis of this data leads to the conclusion that use of the ITPA for educational diagnosis and/or intervention is unwise.

The cognitive–developmental approach to language development holds no parallels to the behavioral model. Those subscribing to this theory hold that language is acquired without direct instruction, differences exist between the structure of adult and child language, research should focus on the child, and poor use of language in social contexts may place limits on a child. Chomsky (1959, 1965) was the most influential individual during the formative years of cognitive psycholinguistics, laying the groundwork for future theoretical development.

According to cognitive psycholinguists, language is acquired through general cognitive structures, and the cognitive and linguistic systems are closely intertwined. In no way do those subscribing to the cognitive approach believe that language is learned through traditional behavioral techniques. Research has supported this idea, along with the notion that language structures appear across children in a sequence that is relatively invariant. Many important differences also exist between the associationistic and cognitive viewpoints.

With regard to the learning disabled, it is important to focus on the neurological aspects of language acquisition, an area that researchers have only begun to investigate. Most efforts to date have centered on determining the sequence and strategies used when acquiring language. With more focus on the biological and neurological nature of the child, the cognitive viewpoint can address the notion of critical periods of language development, as well as the idea that individuals acquire language at differing rates.

Bloom and Lahey (1978) developed one of the most important models for detailing language abilities and disabilities. The model focuses on three aspects of oral language, form, content, and use, and includes a multifaceted description of oral language.

Research is fairly clear in substantiating a relationship between language ability and academic aptitude, resulting in the extensive study of the syntactic abilities of the learning disabled, which has been shown to be delayed. Further research has indicated delays in the acquisition and development of morphological rules, as well as differences between learning disabled children and normal children in both expressive and receptive domains. Some research has failed to support these results; however, several extenuating factors have been noted that may have contributed to these findings.

The field of cognitive psycholinguistics has broadened to encompass the semantic capabilities of the learning disabled. Most research has supported the theory that these capabilities are indeed at deficit. Few studies exist, however, that focus on the phonological abilities of learning disabled individuals. Some authors have advanced the notion of a relationship between auditory discrimination ability and articulation disorders. These interpretations should be viewed with caution, however.

When evaluating the research concerning the characteristics of the learning disabled from a framework of syntax, semantics, and phonology, one finds that cognitive psycholinguistics has provided a useful model for studying the language problems of learning disabled individuals.

The study of the language abilities of the learning disabled has extended to include conversational capabilities, particularly in the area of pragmatics. Areas of study include competence in interpersonal communication, code switching, differences in narrative abilities, discourse, perception of linguistic stress, referential communication skills, and nonverbal communication skills. Generally, these abilities have been shown to fall short of what would be expected. Additionally, research has shown that the academic abilities of individuals with language difficulties are also at deficit.

Currently, many research studies exist targeting intervention techniques with language and learning disabled persons. Generally, language intervention techniques have been shown to be effective, particularly those dealing with young children, adherence to a model, long-term techniques, an orientation toward syntax, and specificity to the particular deficit.

REFERENCES

Aram, S. M., & Nation, J. E. (1975). Patterns of language behavior in children with developmental language disorders. *Journal of Speech and Hearing Research, 18,* 229–241.

Arter, J. L. (1976). *The effects of metaphor on reading comprehension.* Unpublished doctoral dissertation, University of Illinois at Urbana-Champaign.

Baker, H. J., & Leland, B. (1959). *Detroit Tests of Learning Aptitude.* Indianapolis: Bobbs-Merrill.

Baltaxe, C. A. (1984). Use of contrastive stress in normal, aphasic, and autistic children. *Journal of Speech and Hearing Research, 27,* 97–105.

Bever, T. G. (1970). The cognitive basis for linguistic structures. In J. Hayes (Ed.), *Cognition and the development of language* (pp. 279–362). New York: Wiley.

Bloom, L. (1970). *Language development: Form and function in emerging grammars.* Cambridge, MA: MIT Press.

Bloom, L. (1977). *LD3*. Paper presented at the New York Child Language Association, New York.

Bloom, L., & Lahey, M. (1978). *Language development and language disorders.* New York: Wiley.

Bloom, L., Lightbown, P., & Hood, L. (1975). Structure and variation in child language. *Monographs of the Society for Research in Child Development, 40.*

Blue, C. M. (1981). Types of utterances to avoid when speaking to language impaired children. *Language, Speech, and Hearing Services in School, 12*(2), 120–124.

Boucher, C. R. (1984). Pragmatics: The verbal language of learning disabled and nondisabled boys. *Learning Disability Quarterly, 7*, 271–286.

Boucher, C. R. (1986). Pragmatics: The meaning of verbal language in learning disabled and nondisabled boys. *Learning Disability Quarterly, 9*, 285–294.

Brook, R. M. (1977). *Ability to recognize nonverbal affirmation and negation amongst learning disabled children.* (University Microfilms International No. 77-28-841).

Brown, A. L. (1973). Judgments of recency for long sequences of pictures: The absence of a developmental thread. *Journal of Experimental Child Psychology, 15*, 473–480.

Bryan, J. H. & Perlmutter, B. (1979). Immediate expressions of LD children by female adults. *Learning Disability Quarterly, 1*, 80–88.

Bryan, J. H., & Sherman, R. (1980). Immediate impressions of nonverbal ingratiation attempts by learning disabled boys. *Learning Disability Quarterly, 3*, 19–28.

Bryan, J. H., Sherman, R., & Fisher, A. (1980). Learning disabled boys' nonverbal behaviors within a dyadic interview. *Learning Disability Quarterly, 3*, 65–72.

Bryan, T. H. (1974). An observational analysis of classroom behaviors of children with learning disabilities. *Journal of Learning Disabilities, 7*, 26–34.

Bryan, T. H. (1976). Peer popularity of learning disability children: A replication. *Journal of Learning Disabilities, 9*(5), 49–53.

Bryan, T. H. (1977). Learning disabled children's comprehension of nonverbal communication. *Journal of Learning Disabilities, 10*, 501–506.

Bryan, T. H. (1978). Social relationships and verbal interactions of learning disabled children. *Journal of Learning Disabilities, 11*, 107–115.

Bryan, T. H., Donahue, M., & Pearl, R. (1981). Learning disabled children's peer interactions during a small group problem solving task. *Learning Disability Quarterly, 4*, 13–22.

Bryan, T. H., Donahue, M., Pearl, R., & Sturm, C. (1981). Learning disabled children's conversational skills—The "TV Talk Show." *Learning Disability Quarterly, 4*, 250–259.

Bryan, T. H., Wheeler, R., Felcan, J., & Henek, T. (1976). Come on, dummy: An observational study of children's communications. *Journal of Learning Disabilities, 9*(10), 53–61.

Bush, W. J., & Giles, M. T. (1969). *Aids to psycholinguistic teaching.* Columbus, OH: Merrill.

Caro, D., & Schneider, P. (1983). Creating referents in text: A comparison of learning disabled and normal adolescents' text. *Proceedings of the Wisconsin Symposium for Research in Child Language Disorders.* Madison, WI: University of Wisconsin.

Carrell, J., & Pendergast, K. (1954). An experimental study of the possible relation between errors of speech and spelling. *Journal of Speech and Hearing Disorders, 19*, 327–334.

Cermak, S. A., Coster, W., & Drake, C. (1980). Representational and nonrepresentational gestures in boys with learning disabilities. *American Journal of Occupational Therapy, 34*, 1–19.

Chomsky, N. (1959). A review of B. F. Skinner's *Verbal Behavior. Language, 35,* 26–58.

Chomsky, N. (1965). *Aspects of the theory of syntax.* Cambridge, MA: MIT Press.

Clay, M. M. (1971). Sentence repetition: Elicited imitation of a controlled set of syntactic structures by four language groups. *Monograph of the Society for Research in Child Development, 36.*

Cohen, J. H., & Diehl, C. F. (1963). Relation of speech sound discrimination ability to articulation-type speech defects. *Journal of Speech and Hearing Disorders, 28,* 187–190.

Cornett, B. S., & Chabon, S. S. (1986). Speech–language pathologists as language-learning disabilities specialists: Rites of passages. *American Speech–Language–Hearing Association, 29*(3), 29–31.

Courtwright, J., & Courtwright, I. (1983). The perception of nonvocal cues of emotional meaning by language-disordered and normal children. *Journal of Speech and Hearing Research, 26,* 412–417.

Cupples, W. P., & Lewis, M. E. B. (1984). Language-based learning disabilities: Differential diagnosis and implementation. *Learning Disabilities, 3*(11), 129–140.

Denckla, M., & Rudel, R. (1976). Naming of object drawings by dyslexic and other learning disabled children. *Brain and Language, 3,* 1–16.

de Villiers, J. G., & de Villiers, P. A. (1978). *Language acquisition.* Cambridge, MA: Harvard University Press.

Donahue, M. L. (1981). Learning disabled children's conversational competence: An attempt to activate the inactive listener. *Proceedings from the Second Wisconsin Symposium on Research in Child Language Disorders, 2,* 39–55.

Donahue, M. L., & Bryan, T. (1984). Communicative skills and peer relations of learning-disabled adolescents. *Topics in Language Disorders, 4*(2), 10–21.

Donahue, M. L., Pearl, R., & Bryan, T. (1980). Learning disabled children's conversational competence: Responses to inadequate messages. *Applied Psycholinguistics, 1,* 387–403.

Donahue, M. L., Pearl, R., & Bryan, T. (1982). Learning disabled children's syntactic proficiency on a communicative task. *Journal of Speech and Hearing Disorders, 47,* 397–403.

Downing, J. (1980). Learning to read with understanding. In M. McCullough (Ed.), *Persisting problems in reading education* (pp. 163–178). Newark, DE: International Reading Association.

Dyer, K., Santarcangelo, S., & Luce, S. C. (1987). Developmental influences in teaching language forms to individuals with developmental disabilities. *Journal of Speech and Hearing Disorders, 52,* 335–347.

Feagans, L., & Applebaum, M. I. (1986). Validation of language subtypes in learning disabled children. *Journal of Educational Psychology, 78,* 358–364.

Feagans, L., & Short, E. (1984). Developmental differences in the comprehension and production of narratives by reading disabled and normally achieving children. *Child Development, 55,* 1727–1736.

Fey, M. E., Leonard, L. B., Fey, S. H., & O'Connor, C. A. (1978, October). *The intent to communicate in language-impaired children.* Paper presented at the Third Annual Boston University Conference on Language Development, Boston, MA.

Friel-Patti, S., & Conti-Ramsden, G. (1988). Intervention tactics for learning disabled children with oral language impairments. In D. K. Reid, *Teaching the learning disabled* (pp. 140–161). Boston: Allyn and Bacon.

Gallagher, J. M., & Reid, D. K. (1981). *The learning theory of Piaget and Inhelder*. Austin, TX: PRO-ED.

Goodglass, H., & Kaplan, E. (1972). *The assessment of aphasia and related disorders*. Philadelphia: Lea and Febiger.

Graybeal, C. (1981). Memory for stories in language-impaired children. *Applied Psycholinguistics, 2,* 269–283.

Griffith, P. L., Ripich, D. N., & Dastoli, S. L. (1986). Story structure, cohesion, and propositions in story recalls by learning-disabled and nondisabled children. *Journal of Psycholinguistic Research, 15,* 539–555.

Hammill, D. D., & Larsen, S. C. (1974). The relationship of selected auditory perceptual skills to reading ability. *Journal of Learning Disabilities, 7,* 429–436.

Hammill, D. D., & Larsen, S. C. (1978). *The Test of Written Language*. Austin, TX: PRO-ED.

Hansen, C. (1982). Story retelling used with average and learning disabled readers as a measure of reading comprehension. *Learning Disability Quarterly, 1,* 62–69.

Hare, B., Hammill, D. D., & Bartel, N. R. (1973). Construct validity of selected ITPA subtests. *Exceptional Children, 40,* 13–20.

Harris-Schmidt, G. (1983). In C. T. Wren (Ed.), *Language learning disabilities*. Rockville, MD: Aspen Systems.

Highnam, C., & Morris, V. (1987). Linguistic stress judgments of language learning disabled students. *Journal of Communication Disorders, 20,* 93–103.

Hoffman, R. R., & Honeck, R. P. (1980). A peacock looks at its legs: Cognitive science and figurative language. In R. P. Honeck & R. R. Hoffman (Eds.), *Cognition and figurative language* (pp. 3–24). Hillsdale, NJ: Erlbaum.

Hopper, R., & Naremore, R. C. (1973). *Children's speech: A practical introduction to communication development*. New York: Harper and Row.

Hoskins, R. (1983). In C. T. Wren (Ed.), *Language learning disabilities*. Rockville, MD: Aspen Systems.

Hresko, W. P. (1979). Elicited imitation ability of children from learning disabled and regular classes. *Journal of Learning Disabilities, 12,* 456–461.

Hresko, W. P., & Reid, D. K. (1979). Language and the learning disabled: Models, research, and intervention. *Learning disabilities: An audio journal for continuing education, 3* (audio cassette, transcript). New York: Grune & Stratton.

Hresko, W. P., Rosenberg, S., & Buchanan, L. (1978). *Use of the Carrow Test of Auditory Comprehension of Language with learning disabled children*. Paper presented at the Council for Exceptional Children, Kansas City, KS.

Hunt, K. W. (1965). Grammatical structures written at three grade levels. *National Council of Teachers of English Research Reports*, No. 3.

Idol-Maestas, L. (1980). Oral language responses of children with reading difficulties. *Journal of Speech Education, 14,* 336–404.

Jordan, N. C. (1988). Language processing and reading ability in children: A study based on speech-shadowing techniques. *Journal of Psycholinguistic Research, 17,* 357–377.

Karnes, M. B. (1972). *Goal program: Language development*. Springfield, MA: Milton Bradley.

Kavale, K. A., & Forness, S. R. (1984). A meta-analysis of the validity of *Wechsler Scale* profiles and recategorizations:

Patterns or parodies? *Learning Disability Quarterly, 7,* 136–156.

Kirk, S. A., & Kirk, W. D. (1971). *Psycholinguistic learning disabilities: Diagnosis and remediation.* Urbana, IL: University of Illinois Press.

Kirk, S. A., McCarthy, J., & Kirk, W. (1963). *The Illinois Test of Psycholinguistic Abilities.* Urbana, IL: University of Illinois Press.

Knight-Arest, I. (1984). Communicative effectiveness of learning disabled and normally achieving 10- to 13-year-old boys. *Learning Disability Quarterly, 7,* 237–245.

Kronvall, E. L., & Diehl, C. F. (1954). The relationship of auditory discrimination of articulatory defects of children with no known organic impairment. *Journal of Speech and Hearing Disorders, 19,* 115–119.

Kuczaj, S. (1982). On the nature of syntactic development. In S. Kuczaj (Ed.), *Language development: Syntax and semantics* (pp. 37–71). Hillsdale, NJ: Erlbaum.

Lenneberg, E. H. (1967). *Biological foundations of language.* New York: Wiley.

Lewis, M., & Cherry, L. (1977). Social behavior and language acquisition. In M. Lewis & L. Rosenblum (Eds.), *Interaction, conversation and development of language* (pp. 227–245). New York: Wiley.

Lockhart, M. (1972). *A description of similes from children's fiction.* Unpublished master's thesis, University of Alberta, Edmonton.

Logan, R., & Colarusso, R. (1978). The effectiveness of the MWM & GOAL programs in developing general language abilities. *Learning Disability Quarterly, 1,* 32–38.

Lund, K. A., Foster, G. E., & McCall-Perez, F. C. (1978). The effectiveness of psycholinguistic training: A reevaluation. *Exceptional Children, 44,* 310–319.

Marquardt, T. P., & Saxman, J. H. (1972). Language comprehension and auditory discrimination in articulation deficient children. *Journal of Speech and Hearing Research, 15,* 382–389.

McCoulskey, M. (1971). *Sentence repetition ability of children with language and/or learning disabilities.* Unpublished doctoral dissertation, University of Texas, Austin.

McNeill, D. (1966). Developmental psycholinguistics. In F. Smith & G. A. Miller (Eds.), *The genesis of language: A psycholinguistic approach* (pp. 15–84). Cambridge, MA: MIT Press.

Meline, T. J. (1978). Referential communication skills of learning disabled/language impaired children. *Applied Psycholinguistics, 7,* 129–140.

Meline, T., & Meline, N. (1983). Facing a communicative obstacle: Pragmatics of language-impaired children. *Perceptual and Motor Skills, 56,* 469–470.

Menyuk, P., & Flood, J. (1981). Linguistic competence, reading, writing problems and remediation. *Bulletin of the Orton Society, 31,* 13–28.

Miller, G. A. (1965). Some preliminaries to psycholinguistics. *American Psychologist, 20,* 15–20.

Miller, J. F., & Yoder, D. E. (1974). An ontogenetic language teaching strategy for retarded children. In R. L. Schiefelbusch & L. L. Lloyd (Eds.), *Language perspectives: Acquisition, retardation, and intervention.* Austin, TX: PRO-ED.

Minskoff, E. H., Wiseman, D. E., & Minskoff, J. G. (1972). *The MWN program for developing language abilities.* Ridgefield, NJ: Educational Performance Associates.

Mishler, E. (1975a). Studies in dialogue and discourse: An exponential law of successive questioning. *Language in Society, 4,* 31–52.

Mishler, E. (1975b). Studies in dialogue and discourse: II. Types of discourse initiated by and sustained through questioning. *Journal of Psycholinguistic Research, 4,* 99–121.

Morice, R., & Slaghuis, W. (1985). Language performance and reading ability at 8 years of age. *Applied Psycholinguistics, 6,* 141–160.

Myklebust, H. R., & Johnson, D. J. (1967). *Learning disabilities: Educational principles and practices.* New York: Grune and Stratton.

Newcomer, P. L. (1975). The ITPA and academic achievement: *Academic Therapy, 10,* 401–406.

Newcomer, P. L., & Hammill, D. D. (1976). *Psycholinguistics in the schools.* Columbus, OH: Merrill.

Newcomer, P. L., Hare, B., Hammill, D. D., & McGettigan, J. (1975). Construct validity of the Illinois Test of Psycholinguistic Abilities. *Journal of Learning Disabilities, 8,* 220–231.

Nippold, M. A. (1985). Comprehension of figurative language in youth. *Topics in Language Disorders,* 5(3), 1–20.

Nippold, M. A., & Fey, S. H. (1983). Metaphoric understanding in preadolescents having a history of language acquisition difficulties. *Language, Speech, and Hearing Services in the Schools, 14,* 171–180.

Noel, M. M. (1980). Referential communication abilities of learning disabled children. *Learning Disability Quarterly,* 2, 70–75.

Ny, C., Foster, S. H., & Seaman, D. (1987). Effectiveness of language intervention with the language/learning disabled. *Journal of Speech and Hearing Disorders, 52,* 348–357.

Olsen, J. L., Wong, B. Y. L., & Marx, R. W. (1983). Linguistic and metacognitive aspects of normally achieving and learning disabled children's communication process. *Learning Disability Quarterly, 6,* 289–304.

Osgood, C. E. (1953). *Method and theory in experimental psychology.* New York: Oxford University Press.

Osgood, C. E. (1975). A dinosaur caper: Psycholinguistics past, present, and future. In D. Aaronson & R. W. Rieber (Eds.), Developmental psycholinguistics and communication disorders. *Annals of the New York Academy of Sciences, 263,* 16–26.

Proger, B. B., Cross, L. H., & Burger, R. M. (1973). Construct validation of standardized tests in special education: A framework of reference and application to ITPA research. In L. Mann & D. A. Sabatino (Eds.), *The first review of special education* (Vol. 1) (pp. 165–199). Philadelphia: JSE Press.

Puckett, D. (1980). An investigation of nonverbal sensitivity of academically talented, average, and learning disabled male students. *University Microfilms International* No. 8020387.

Reid, G. (1947a). The efficacy of speech reeducation of functional articulatory defects in the elementary school. *Journal of Speech Disorders, 12,* 301–313.

Reid, G. (1947b). The etiology and nature of functional articulatory defects in elementary school children. *Journal of Speech and Hearing Disorders, 12,* 143–150.

Rosenthal, J. H. (1970). A preliminary psycholinguistic study of children with learning disabilities. *Journal of Learning Disabilities, 3,* 11–15.

Roth, F. P. (1986). Oral narrative abilities of learning-disabled students. *Topics in Language Development,* 7(1), 21–30.

Roth, F. P., & Spekman, N. J. (1985, June). *Story grammar analysis of narratives produced by learning disabled and normally achieving students.* Paper presented at the Symposium on

Research in Child Language Disorders, Madison, WI.

Roth, F. P., & Spekman, N. J. (1986). Narrative discourse: Spontaneously-generated stories of learning disabled and normally achieving students. *Journal of Speech and Hearing Research, 51,* 8–23.

Roth, F. P., & Spekman, N. J. (1989). The oral syntactic proficiency of learning disabled students: A spontaneous story sampling analysis. *Journal of Speech and Hearing Research, 32,* 62–77.

Sedlak, R. A., & Weener, P. (1973). Review of research on the Illinois Test of Psycholinguistic Abilities. In L. Mann & D. A. Sabatino (Eds.), *The first review of special education* (Vol. 1, pp. 113–163). Philadelphia: JSE Press.

Simms, R. B., & Crump, W. D. (1983). Syntactic development in the oral language of learning disabled and normal students at the intermediate and secondary level. *Learning Disability Quarterly, 6,* 155–165.

Sinclair deZwart, H., (1973). Language acquisition and cognitive development. In T. E. Moore (Ed.), *Cognitive development and the acquisition of language* (pp. 9–26). New York: Academic Press.

Skinner, B. F. (1957). *Verbal behavior.* New York: Appleton-Century-Crofts.

Spekman, N. (1981). A study of the dyadic verbal communication abilities of learning disabled and normally achieving 4th and 5th grade boys. *Learning Disability Quarterly, 4,* 139–151.

Stanovich, K. E. (1986). Cognitive processes and the reading problems of learning-disabled children: Evaluating the assumption of specificity. In J. K. Torgesen & B. Y. L. Wong (Eds.), *Psychological and educational perspectives on learning disabilities* (pp. 87–131). New York: Academic Press.

Stein, N., & Glenn, C. (1979). An analysis of story comprehension in elementary school children. In R. O. Freedle (Ed.), *New directions in discourse processing* (Vol. 2). Norwood, NJ: Ablex.

Stimson, W. (1983). *Metaphoric competence of learning disabled and normally achieving children.* Unpublished doctoral dissertation, University of North Texas, Denton.

Strand, K. E. (1982). *The development of idiom comprehension in language disordered children.* Paper presented at the Symposium on Research in Child Language Disorders, Madison, WI.

Swanson, H. L. (1982). Strategies and constraints—A commentary. *Topics in Learning and Learning Disabilities, 2,* 79–81.

Taylor, O., & Swinney, D. (1972). The onset of language. In J. V. Marge & M. Marge (Eds.), *Principles of childhood language disabilities.* New York: Appleton-Century-Crofts.

Templin, M. C. (1957). *Certain language skills in children.* Minneapolis, University of Minnesota Press.

Torgesen, J., & Greenstein, J. (1982). Why do some learning disabled children have problems remembering? Does it make a difference? *Topics in Learning and Learning Disabilities, 2,* 54–61.

Tuch, S. (1977). The production of coherent narrative text by older language impaired children. *South African Journal of Communicative Disorders, 24,* 42–59.

Turton, L. J. (1975). Developmental and linguistic aspects of learning disabilities. In W. M. Cruickshank & D. P. Hallahan (Eds.), *Perceptual and learning disabilities in children* (Vol. 1), *Psychoeducational practices.* Syracuse, NY: Syracuse University Press.

Verhave, T. A. (1972). A review of Chomsky's "Language and mind." *Journal of Psycholinguistic Research, 2,* 183–195.

Watson, L. (1977, November). *Conversational participation by language deficient and normal children.* Paper presented at the meeting of the American Speech and Hearing Association, Chicago.

Wepman, J. M. (1960). Auditory discrimination, speech, & reading. *Elementary School Journal, 60,* 325-333.

Wiig, E. (1984). Language abilities in adolescents: A question of cognitive strategies. *Topics in Language Disorders, 4,* 41-58.

Wiig, E. H., Becker-Redding, U., & Semel, E. M. (1983). A cross-cultural, cross-linguistic comparison of language abilities of 7- to 8- and 12- to 13-year old children with learning disabilities. *Journal of Learning Disabilities, 16,* 576-585.

Wiig, E. H., & Semel, E. M. (1975). Productive language abilities in learning disabled adolescents. *Journal of Learning Disabilities, 8,* 578-586.

Wiig, E. H., & Semel, E. M. (1976). *Language disabilities in children and adolescents.* Columbus, OH: Merrill.

Wiig, E. H., & Semel, E. M. (1980). *Language assessment and intervention for the learning disabled.* Columbus, OH: Merrill.

Wiig, E. H., & Semel, E. M. (1984). *Language assessment and intervention for the learning disabled.* Columbus, OH: Merrill.

Wiig, E. H., Semel, E. M., & Abele, E. (1981). Perception and interpretation of ambiguous sentences by learning disabled twelve-year-olds. *Journal of Learning Disabilities, 6,* 457-465.

Wiig, E. H., Semel, E. M., & Crouse, M. A. B. (1973). The use of morphology by high-risk and learning disabled children. *Journal of Learning Disabilities, 6,* 457-465.

Wiig, E. H., Semel, E. M., & Nystrom, L. A. (1982). Comparison of rapid naming abilities in language-learning-disabled and academically achieving eight-year-olds. *Language, Speech, and Hearing in Schools, 13,* 11-23.

Winkler, E., Brinton, B., Fujiki, D., & Frome, D. (1984, November). *Conversational repair strategies in normal and language-disordered children.* Paper presented at the meeting of the American Speech-Language-Hearing Association, San Francisco.

Wong, B. Y. L. (1982). Understanding the learning disabled student's reading problems: Contributions from cognitive psychology. *Topics in Learning and Learning Disabilities, 1*(4), 43-50.

Wong, B. Y. L., & Jones, W. (1982). Increasing metacomprehension in learning disabled and normally achieving students through self-questioning training. *Learning Disability Quarterly, 5,* 228-240.

Wren, C. T. (Ed.). (1983). *Language learning disabilities.* Rockville, MD: Aspen Systems.

Young, S. (1971). *Preliminary investigation of sentence repetition ability in children with language and learning disabilities.* Unpublished master's thesis, University of Texas, Austin.

13

Literacy: New Directions

D. KIM REID

Reading, perhaps more than any other domain of interest to professionals in the learning disabilities field, has benefited from the explosion of research in the new cognitive science tradition. Thanks to scientists' interests in the complexity of reading, nearly all traditions that operate within cognitive science have contributed to our understanding of the reading process: Because fluent reading requires both high-level comprehension abilities and lower level word decoding skills, adherents from the information processing, constructivist, and ecological perspectives have found niches for their particular approaches. Our knowledge of both reading disability and effective reading instruction has expanded considerably as a result of this burgeoning research effort. Not long ago, when we published the first edition of this text, the field was in turmoil regarding whether reading occurred from the bottom up (distinctive features, orthography, etc.) or the top down (semantic, syntactic, and lexical knowledge). Today, the relationships among these types of processing have been elucidated, their implications for instruction determined, and causal elements in reading disability illuminated.

Investigations of the writing process are relatively recent in the learning disabilities literature. Hardly more than a decade ago, the vast majority of research was confined to handwriting, spelling, and grammar (see the first edition of this text). Most analyses were at the word level, but, a few, more enlightened analyses were at the sentence level. The current preoccupation with discourse and composing is an outgrowth of the ascendency of constructivist, holistic frameworks and theories and what Perfetti (1989) referred to as "intellectual breezes": "The approach to cognition that sought discreet components of information processing is being replaced by one that sees cognitive life determined by complex interactions among those components" (p. 307).

This chapter begins with a discussion of reading disability. A complete review of the literature is beyond the scope of this book, but its essence has been captured by Stanovich's (1988) elegant model synthesizing (and accounting for) a large majority of the important findings. Because many intervention studies have been done in reading comprehension, the focus here is limited to effective educational interventions, rather than on the nature of comprehension difficulties. (Such a discussion would, to a large extent, rehash many of the findings reported in Part II of this book.) The research designed to improve reading performance (i.e., learning to read) is addressed separately from the research designed to improve content mastery (i.e., reading to learn, which nearly always includes some attention to writing). Finally, the characteristic problems that learning disabled persons experience with composing are surveyed. The reader who is not acquainted with psycholinguistics may want to read Chapter 12 to become familiar with the terminology before proceeding.

WHAT KINDS OF PROBLEMS ARE EXPERIENCED BY DISABLED READERS?

Poor readers are classified into two major types: dyslexic (sometimes called specific reading/learning disabled) and garden variety. Dyslexics are assumed to have a neurologically based cognitive deficit that is specific to the requirements of reading. Normally, the higher one's measured intelligence, the higher one's reading achievement is expected to be. By definition, this relationship does not hold for dyslexic students. Although their reading performance is poor, intelligence lies within or close to the average range. The assumption of specificity suggests that only their reading performance is affected.

Scientists (for reviews of the evidence, see Perfetti, 1985; Siegel & Heaven, 1986) have shown that all poor readers experience difficulties decoding words, especially pseudowords (e.g., *rane*). The cause of these problems is a lack of sensitivity to phonological processing, which makes learning grapheme–phoneme (letter–sound) correspondences difficult.

Poor readers have problems retaining phonological information in memory, making explicit reports about sound segments at the phoneme level, and naming words (Brady, Shankweiler, & Mann, 1983; Jorm, 1983; Liberman,

1983; Mann, 1984; Mann & Liberman, 1984; Perfetti, Beck, & Hughes, 1981). Consequently, measures of spoken language tend to be more highly associated with reading disability than with visual processing skills, intelligence, or other general cognitive abilities (Mann, 1984; Mann, Cowin, & Schoenheimer, 1988). Although poor readers perceive oral language cues as well as their peers do, they differ in their ability to *use* those cues: They are impaired in their ability to recall word strings and to recover the structure of spoken language. The vast majority of dyslexics, who have sustained decoding problems, experience *severe* difficulties with phonological processing. (There may be a group of dyslexics with visual processing deficits, but their numbers appear to be few, and little is known about the nature of their disorder.)

Garden variety poor readers also experience difficulties with phonological processing, but their problems are considerably less severe. Their cognitive status can best be described as a *developmental lag:* When compared with performance of younger, nondisabled students matched for reading level, their performance does not differ on cognitive tasks related to reading— vocabulary, word naming, pseudoword naming, strategic and nonstrategic memory tasks, and rhyming (Stanovich, 1988). Because garden variety poor readers learn more slowly, a younger skilled reader would be expected to make greater progress than an older unskilled reader in a given period of time. The rate rather than the kind of development differentiates this group from normal achievers.

Stanovich (1988) synthesized the research findings: He agreed with Ellis (1985) that the appropriate metaphor for dyslexia is obesity, not measles. Like fat and skinny people, reading disorders lie along a continuum (rather than cluster into subtypes) (see Figures 13–1 and 13–2). The point on the continuum that determines a deviation sufficiently significant that it should be labeled, in the case of obesity, as a disease entity or, in the case of reading disorder, as dyslexia is arbitrary.

At one end of the continuum are those students who are good readers, and at the other end are those with severe phonological deficits, the dyslexics. Between them lie the garden variety poor readers with mild phonological problems. Stanovich pointed out that there is a continuous gradation between the two types of poor readers that can be defined by where they are with respect to measured intelligence and reading. By current *definitional* standards,

> the concept of dyslexia requires that the deficits displayed by such children not extend too much into other domains of cognitive functioning. If they did, this would depress the constellation of abilities we call intelligence, reduce the reading/intelligence discrepancy, and the child would no longer be dyslexic! Indeed, he/she would have become a garden variety! (Stanovich, 1988, p. 601)

Although the dyslexic has the more severe phonological processing problem, it is localized and is not accompanied by other cognitive limitations. The more

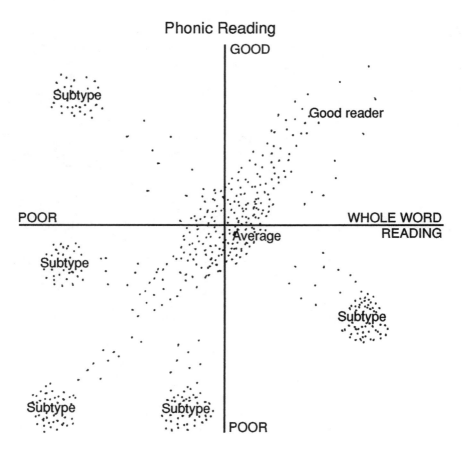

Figure 13–1. A cluster view of reading disabilities subtypes. Adapted from "Explaining the Difference Between the Dyslexic and the Garden-Variety Poor Reader: The Phonological-Core Variable-Difference Model" by K. E. Stanovich, 1988, *Journal of Learning Disabilities, 21,* p. 590. Copyright 1988 by PRO-ED. Adapted with permission.

global deficit of the garden variety poor reader, on the other hand, extends into a variety of domains, some of which (e.g., vocabulary, short-term memory, language comprehension) may also interfere with reading achievement.

This model has been very widely accepted, but it has several complications, the most serious of which was also defined by Stanovich (1986). He coined the term *Mathew effect* to denote a process in which early deficits metamorphose into pervasive, nonlocalized cognitive, behavioral, and motivational disturbances. Reading begins very early and facilitates the development of other cognitive abilities which, in turn, lay the foundation for successful reading achievement at more advanced levels—in a rich-get-richer, poor-get-

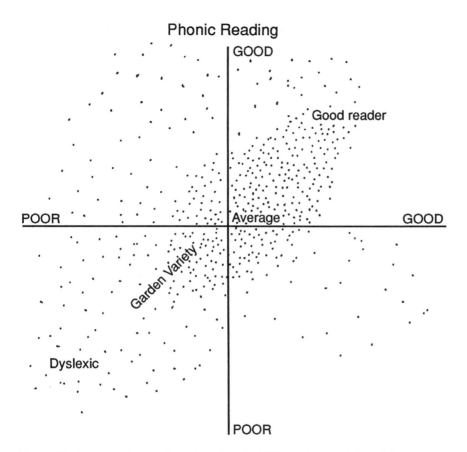

Figure 13–2. A continuum view of reading disabilities subtypes. Adapted from "Explaining the Difference Between the Dyslexic and the Garden-Variety Poor Reader: The Phonological-Core Variable-Difference Model" by K. E. Stanovich, 1988, *Journal of Learning Disabilities, 21*, p. 590. Copyright 1988 by PRO-ED. Adapted with permission.

poorer fashion. Consequently, poor readers display increasingly more global cognitive deficits as they grow older. Using the model described above, an early dyslexic might very well grow up to be a garden variety poor reader, definitional artifacts aside.

WHAT METHODS PROMOTE LEARNING TO READ?

Reading is neither a top–down nor a bottom–up process. It is instead an interactive process (Rumelhart, 1977) in which information abstracted from the distinctive features of letters, orthography, lexicon, syntax, and semantics is available virtually simultaneously. The phonics approaches to early reading instruction that dominated special education practice during the last decade are being replaced with more holistic instructional procedures that do not divorce decoding from meaning, but attend to both in meaningful ways (Bateson & Bateson, 1987).

Although they are still carefully engineered to reveal the regularities of the sound–symbol system, even beginning reading materials focus on the ultimate and social goal of reading—construction of meaning from print. Not only are individual readings more representative of a variety of literary forms (e.g., poetry, stories, expository passages), they are more reminiscent of trade books and often are reprinted selections from children's literature. Some reading series even group selections by topic to underscore one's ability to learn from text, to contrast the form of literary structures, to allow elaboration from heightened background knowledge, and so forth. Phonics are not neglected: Classroom readers are still accompanied by the ubiquitous workbook, and children at risk for reading disability are receiving extra instruction in decoding skills. (For a summary of research-supported direct-instructional techniques for teaching decoding skills to learning disabled students, see Simmons & Kameenui, 1989.) What is both significantly different from past practice and in keeping with the tenets of the cognitive curriculum, however, is that the code is being learned in the context in which it needs to be used.

Contextualization is also apparent in a larger sense. Of the three foundational requirements of reading—word identification, parsing, and proposition encoding—the latter two, and to a lesser extent even the first (see the section on the emergence of early spontaneous behaviors in the previous chapter), depend on linguistic skills (Kintsch, 1989) acquired outside of and prior to schooling. Although it is designed to take advantage of the grammatical and pragmatic competence that is achieved during the preschool years when literacy is essentially embedded, both physically and socially, in the environmental context, reading instruction in school gradually shifts meaning construction to symbols.

Furthermore, breaking the code, amassing a sight vocabulary, and constructing meaning from symbols are three important outcomes of initial reading instruction that continue to develop with practice at reading connected text. Perfetti (1989) noted, for example, that word recognition never becomes automatic. Words accrue in sight vocabulary one at a time, so students always have some words that are processed automatically and others that require effortful analysis. Because there is no clear line of demarcation between decoding and comprehension processes (i.e., a threshold at which the child has learned enough basic skills to enable him or her to read text), there is no reason to limit experience with discourse in favor of basic skills—a practice rather common in special education.

Reciprocal Teaching

The reciprocal teaching procedure (Palincsar & Brown, 1986) provides a powerful example of how a smooth transition can be effected between the acquired literacy behaviors children bring with them to school and the demands of school learning. It simultaneously provides a detailed example of how progress in learning to read can be promoted through extended practice with discourse. The teaching was done by real teachers in real classrooms. Because these were first-grade students identified as being at risk for academic problems, teachers read the text to the students as a format for providing early lessons in text comprehension. Groups were composed of 4 at-risk and 2 "catalyst" students who were progressing satisfactorily.

The teacher explained and modeled (using direct instruction) four strategic activities: self-questioning (related to the main idea), summarizing, predicting, and evaluating (identifying and clarifying difficult sections of text). A comprehensive review of the reading and reading instruction research revealed that these activities were inherent, in an implicit sense, in successful comprehension (Brown, Palincsar, & Armbruster, 1984). Reciprocal teaching makes these behaviors both observable and accessible.

Once the four behaviors had been introduced, teacher and children used them as a metascript to guide discussions of the text to which they listened. The script called for the children's taking turns "playing teacher" and leading their peers through the set of structuring activities, with guidance from the adult teacher and helpful criticism from the other children. The four strategies were demonstrated and elucidated as the students cooperatively attempted to make sense of the passage. The students were not only practicing reading strategies within the context of the passage, they were learning when and where such strategies are functional. "Students" answered the "teacher's" questions, commented on the effectiveness of the summary, discussed the clues that enabled them to make predictions, and offered their own strategies and interpretations for the clarification of difficult passages. The intervention continued for 20 consecutive school days for 30 minutes a day.

It would be helpful to return to the sample dialogue from this study that was presented in Table 11–1. Notice that there are neither right nor wrong answers, only those that conform more or less closely to the contours of the text and to the information and abilities the children have and think, or are encouraged by the teacher, to apply. There is no needless drill and no attempt to reduce comprehension to a series of component skills. (In summer reading programs in which I used this technique with primary school at-risk learners reading both their own and published stories, pupils were as likely to raise and discuss issues related to decoding when they were important as they were to raise issues related to text meaning and interpretation.)

The reciprocal teaching procedure is of particular interest because it has met great success in both listening and reading comprehension with learning disabled students who, when the procedure was initiated, answered text comprehension questions with about 30% accuracy. Using a minimum of 80% accuracy on 5 successive days as their criterion, Brown, Campione, Reeve, Ferrara, and Palincsar (in press) estimated that 80% of the 287 junior high school students and 366 first- to third-grade students who took part in their experiments were successful. The students have also maintained their independent mastery for 6 months to 1 year after instruction, and they spontaneously generalized use of the technique to other classroom activities. Standardized test scores revealed gains of approximately 2 years.

Mediated Learning

In a naturalistic research program on instructional mediation being carried out by Duffy, Roehler, and colleagues (Duffy et al., 1986; Duffy et al., 1987), third-grade teachers of garden variety poor readers have been learning to make explicit the reasoning associated with reading strategies. Teachers were taught to recast basal reading skills as problem-solving strategies and to model the cognitive and metacognitive acts involved in the recommended drill and practice exercises. Teaching students to *search* their repertoires of strategies for one that would be appropriate to identifying a particular unknown compound word, for example, and to *reason* aloud about "how to look for recognizable word parts, how to combine mentally the meaning of two words, and how to think about the combined meaning to see if it makes sense in the text" (Duffy et al, 1987, p. 351) was the essence of the intervention process. The results indicated that the teachers in the treatment groups were more explicit than were control teachers. The poor readers in the treatment groups were more aware of lesson content and the need to be strategic. They also scored better on nontraditional, standardized, and maintenance measures of reading achievement.

The transcript in Table 13–1 illustrates the type of instruction that occurs and provides an ongoing interpretation of events. It is important to note that both the teacher's talk and the task demands shape students' understanding. Furthermore, students and teachers engage in *mutual mediation* through an interactive cycle of elaboration and restructuring that occurs over time.

Cognitive Apprenticeship

A synthesis of new directions in intervention research in reading is embodied in Collins, Brown, and Newman's (1990) concept of cognitive apprenticeship. The methods of cognitive apprenticeship are observation, coaching, and successive approximation. In apprenticeship, skills are continually used by expert practitioners in the accomplishment of meaningful tasks: Knowledge

TABLE 13–1
Mediated Learning:
Interpreting Instructional Interaction

The Instructional Interaction	Interpretation
T: This time I want you to choose the main idea by yourself and see if you agree with the person whom I will ask to do it aloud.	The teacher provides directions for using the skill in a paragraph. The paragraph to be read is part of an article in a language arts text.
S: (Students silently read a paragraph about groups of people bringing words to the English language.)	
T: All right. Have you done all the steps and chosen the main idea? John, what did you choose?	The teacher asks for a response.
S: People came to America.	Student provides an answer. Teacher notes the answer and determines that he misunderstood how to figure out the main idea. The teacher decides on what additional information to present.
T: I'm going to give all of you a clue. In this particular paragraph, it (the main idea) is not stated. There is no single sentence that really tells you the main idea so you are going to have to sit back and say to yourself, "What one thing is this paragraph mostly about?" Remember I did that on the one I showed you? All of you do that, if you haven't already.	Having decided that the students were looking for stated main ideas, the teacher reminds them of the model she provided for how to figure out implied main ideas.
S: (Students are silent.)	Students try to apply the cue provided by the teacher.

TABLE 13-1 (continued)

The Instructional Interaction	Interpretation
T: Now, John, do you have the main idea? S: Yes. People brought language.	The teacher asks for a response. Student provides an answer.
T: Would you tell us what you did so we will know how you came up with that answer? S: I read the whole paragraph.	The teacher asks for the process John used to see how he arrived at his answer. John tries to articulate what he did. The teacher assesses and decides what to say next.
T: All right. You read the whole paragraph. Then what did you do? S: I thought about what it was all about and that was my main idea.	The teacher prompts John to see if he can tell her more about how he got his answer. The student provides additional description. The teacher assesses his answer and decides that he is not attending to one important thing. She then decides what to say next.
T: That's good thinking, John. He gave us a main idea. But I think one important piece is missing.	The teacher reinforces John for what he did well but states that one more thing needs to be attended to. She is cueing the students to an elaboration that she is about to provide.

TABLE 13-1 (continued)

The Instructional Interaction	Interpretation
T: Remember earlier in the lesson when I said that I take all the important ideas, think about how they go together, and tie them together with the one idea they all seem to have in common? That's what is needed here. Do like I did. Think about what the ideas describe for you and how those all go together. Tie all the important ideas together.	The teacher provides an elaboration on her original explanation, reminding them of previously provided information and emphasizing how to "tie ideas together."
S: (shouting out) I just got one.	Student responds.
T: All right. What did you think, Mary?	Teacher asks for answer.
S: Each group of people brought their own set of words.	Mary provides an answer and the teacher assesses, deciding what to say next.
T: That's pretty close to it. I could accept that. I would not argue with that. Scott?	The teacher reinforces the answer and asks for another response in order to have more data before elaborating.
S: After a while, these words became part of our language.	Scott answers. The teacher assesses and decides what to say next.
T: Let's look at Scott's answer. We've read the whole paragraph. We've sat back and thought, "What one thing is this all about?" We know it's talking about groups of people, their language, and how some of ours became theirs. Scott's main idea doesn't quite tie all those ideas together. The key is the tie between all those ideas.	The teacher, having assessed both answers, decides that they do not yet understand how to tie the ideas together. She elaborates by reemphasizing the need for a tie across all ideas.

TABLE 13–1 (continued)

The Instructional Interaction	Interpretation
T: You have a changed one, Scott?	The teacher asks for an answer.
S: We borrowed words from other places, and they borrowed words from us.	The student provides a re-stated main idea. The teacher assesses Scott's restructured main ideas.
T: Okay. I think Scott gave a good one. He tied all the ideas together. The tie was the borrowing of words.	The teacher reinforces Scott's combining of ideas into a main idea.
T: Notice, we don't always say what the main idea is in the same way. But we should come close to each other.	The teacher states the individual nature of cognitive processing.
T: The main idea needs to tie together all the important ideas.	
T: Let's look at page 4, the last paragraph.	The teacher moves to another example to provide other opportunities for guided practice.

From "The Subtleties of Instructional Mediation" by G. G. Duffy and L. R. Roehler, 1986, *Educational Leadership, 43*, 23–27. Copyright 1986 by the Association for Supervision and Curriculum Development. Reprinted with permission.

is acquired by the apprentices in social and meaningful contexts. As illustrations of successful apprenticeship programs, Collins et al. listed reciprocal teaching, Scardamalia and Bereiter's procedural facilitation of writing, and Schoenfeld's method for teaching mathematical problem solving. More recently, Collins et al. (1990) explored how technology can support such interventions. The specific characteristics of instruction that technology is well suited to address are listed in Table 13–2. The computer allows learning to be situated in real life contexts through simulation of both real world (e.g., how information is coded in DNA) and expert performance (e.g., medical diagnosis) processes.

In summary, the distinctions between learning to read and reading to learn are blurring, as are those between decoding and the construction of meaning, and those between learning to read and learning to write. Basal reading series are introducing children to expository text from the outset, with selections more and more frequently grouped around topics. Because reading is defined as the construction of meaning from print, "reading" for any other purpose (e.g., to practice decoding) is not reading at all. Furthermore, since we continually learn how to read better as a function of practice, reading to learn helps us learn to read as well. Recent attempts to improve content area reading reflect our belated awareness of this synthesis.

WHAT METHODS PROMOTE READING (AND WRITING) TO LEARN?

Schooling directed at the mastery of a body of knowledge has been made obsolete by the information explosion. Instead of content specialists, schools

---

TABLE 13–2
Benefits from Technology in Cognitive Apprenticeship

---

1. Students learn by applying their knowledge under conditions that simulate those of the actual task.
2. Exposure to expert solutions enables students to observe typically covert processes which can clarify what is happening and why.
3. Coaching both provides help on a need-to-know basis and suggests new ways of responding.
4. Simulations preserve the student's performance as an object for study.
5. Abstractions about rules and procedures can be articulated and compared to alternatives and/or to the solutions of others.
6. Experimentation fosters invention and discovery, goal setting and achievement, and hypothesis formation and testing.

TABLE 13-3
Metacognitive Skills Needed To Read Critically

The reader must:
1. Clarify text demands.
2. Attend to the most important content.
3. Test new information against background knowledge.
4. Test content for consistency across paragraphs.
5. Monitor activity to ensure comprehension.
6. Make and evaluate inferences.
7. Extend and refine what was learned.

---

need to develop *intelligent novices* (Brown, Bransford, Ferrara, & Campione, 1983), students who know how to acquire the knowledge they need. The strategies these intelligent novices need to develop (Brown, 1980) are presented in Table 13-3. Educators are discovering, however, that writing is also a powerful avenue to learning to read and to acquiring content knowledge. Indeed, much of the new research in reading to learn that has been conducted with learning disabled children integrates reading and writing.

Communities of Learning in Content-Area Instruction

Brown and Campione (in press) recently completed a study of reading to learn in science. The instructional group included 90 fifth and sixth graders, who were instructed for 3 hours a week for the entire school year. Nearly 25% of the students had been diagnosed as learning disabled. Students were divided into research groups, one for each of five subtopics in a biology unit on independence in nature. The experimenters provided learning materials: books, articles, magazines, videotapes, access to a library, and adult guidance upon request. The object of the research effort was to prepare a book used to teach other children from the class in small learning groups, which consisted of a member from each research group. The learners were schooled in the original reciprocal teaching format. Unlike the previous studies, however, the expert in each learning group conducted the reciprocal teaching interchange. An example of a protocol from an early point in the discussions is presented in Table 13-4. As the children became increasingly involved in argument and explanation, the reciprocal teaching metascript took on less and less importance, while techniques taught to the research groups— analogical reasoning, causal explanation, types of evidence, argumentation, and predictions—gained in frequency. To complete the long-term assignment,

TABLE 13–4
The Meaning of Camouflage

S₁: (*Question*) What does camouflage mean?
S₂: It means you invisible like G. I. Joe. (*spontaneous analogy*)
S₁: (*Question*) What color can it (the chameleon) go?
S₃: Brown.
S₁: No.
S₂: Green?
S₁: No.
All: (*Clarification*) What? [confusion]
S₁: (*Question. Clarification. Thought Experiment*) What color would it be if it was on a fire engine—red, right? And if it's on a car—black, right? And on a cab—yellow, right?
All: No! No!
S₄: It can only be greenish or brownish, like in nature.
S₁: [indignant] It says (reading text), "A chameleon can take on the color of its background"—so it can be any color, right? (*Clarification*)
S₄: No, No! It can only be colors like brown earth and green trees and yucky color like mud—like G. I. Joe.
S₆: So he matches.
S₁: (*Question. Clarification. Thought Experiment.*) But what if he's not in the grass, what if he's in a whitish kinda color?
S₆: He would turn white?
All: No
S₁: (*Question. Clarification*—still confused) But what if he doesn't have that color? What if he can't turn that color?
S₅: He just moves on down to another spot that has his color.
S₄: No, only green and brown and yucky.
S₁: (*Question*, persistent) Can it be blue like water in the forest?
S₃: Water in the forest isn't blue; it's yucky colored, so chameleons can be yucky colored too.
S₁: (*Summary*) Ok. Ok. I summarize it change color.
 T: What does?
S₁: (sigh) Chameleon change color to hide from its enemies. It can be green—umh brown—yucky color [pause] so it has to stay in the forest 'cause those colors are there.
S₁: (*Question*) I have another question. How does it change color?
 T: Good question. Anyone know?
S₆: It doesn't say.
 T: Do we really know how it changes?
S₁: No.
 T: Any predictions? No?

TABLE 13-4 (continued)

T: (*Prediction*) I think it might be a chemical in its body. Let's read to find out.

S$_1$: [Six days later, discussing the walkingstick insect that disguises itself by changing shape]

Ok, it goes invisible because it looks like a twig. It's frozen and twiglike on the tree and on the ground. Some things change color, to nature colors, green and brown; some things hold still, some things pretend to be twigs, I get it.

From "Communities of Learning and Thinking: Or a Context by Any Other Name" by A. L. Brown & J. C. Campione, in press, *Human development*. Reprinted with permission of S. Karger AG, Basel.

the students were involved in extensive reading, writing and revising, publishing, and computer usage.

Brown and Campione have not yet analyzed all of their data, but they have already reported "dramatic qualitative improvement in thinking processes" that were revealed in verbal exchanges and in writing. These improvements included use of deep analogies (using structural similarities to explain the mechanisms of systematic relationships), causal explanations, use of evidence, plausible reasoning, highly developed argumentation formats, and prediction that extended beyond the texts to the world and into thought experiments (what if . . .). Improvements in writing included increasingly sophisticated argumentation, compare-and-contrast structures, and hierarchical ordering of content.

Brown and Campione suggested that the students served as apprentice learners in this experiment: They learned how to find out, how to write using a computer, and how to explain. Because the teachers were not biology teachers, they served as expert models of learning, learning along with the students. Children, however, also served as expert models to other children: Some acquired expertise in the subject matter, others became graphics experts, and some concentrated on publishing. Instead of a teacher–learner structure, a community of learners developed.

There are significant contrasts between traditional content area and/or reading instruction groups and this experiment with research teams. In traditional settings, students read assigned pieces from a text on a schedule dictated by a teacher, who knows the material the students are trying to learn. The purpose for reading is to prove that they have read and to demonstrate the knowledge they acquired through reading. They are held individually accountable by the teacher, the only one with access to their written products. In contrast, students working in research teams share a common database. They write their own text using information they have secured on a need-to-know basis. They set their own agendas and schedules to meet the date when the books they are producing must be available. They raise and answer their own questions, read and write for the purposes of learning and sharing information with others, and continually discuss their ideas and written products with other members of the team. Teachers become models for learning, not arbiters of accuracy.

Reid (1989) described a similar interactive teaching intervention (Gallagher & Reid, 1983) during a 6-week summer reading program. Students were of mixed ability levels, ranging from just having finished the first through the sixth grades. Approximately 8 to 12 students were in each age-level group, with irregular numbers of disabled readers. Two to three teachers, enrolled in a master's level internship in teaching reading, taught each group. Using Brown and Campione's (in press) terminology, these groups constituted "mini" learning communities.

Each group studied a topic selected from those recommended by their teachers. The topics they chose—sleep, monsters, rocketry, cartoons, and newspapers—served as the content domain to be learned. The teachers provided a classroom library with a variety of literary structures (e.g., books with stories, expository text, cartoons, and poetry; magazines; newspapers; videotapes), took the children on field trips (e.g., to the local city newspaper offices, the local university hospital sleep laboratory), and created environments (e.g., a parachute-domed dreamland, a monster village). Each group had the responsibility for producing a book (or a cartoon book or the summer program's newspaper) on the topic they studied, with each child contributing a passage. Older students wrote essays; younger ones wrote paragraphs or stories. The rocketry group also actually built and launched model rockets.

The instructional model (Reid, 1988) included direct instruction for declarative and procedural knowledge, followed by cooperative, scaffolded instruction to practice procedural and conditional learning. As students became more proficient and self-directed, they worked more frequently with their peers, and teachers assisted as requested. Because the teachers were accustomed to monopolizing, we implemented a 1-minute gag rule, in which no teacher was permitted to talk longer than that in any conversational turn.

Our interest in this program, and in previous, shorter summer programs of a similar nature, was in the performances of the 5 most distressed readers (in each case, all of whom had been identified and labeled as learning disabled). Before and after the program, measures were taken with a standardized test of reading. Each summer, we found that only the reading disordered students made significant gains—in the neighborhood of 6 months' progress, which is quite impressive considering the intervention lasted only a few weeks. We made no attempt to measure writing progress. For all of the students with reading disorders, the summer experience of reading for information was a significant departure from the reading exercises they completed during the school year. Although some had had paragraph writing instruction, none had collaborated on the writing of a book. The high levels of excitement and the sense of ownership were easily observed.

Cooperative Integrated Reading and Composition

Slavin, Stevens, and Madden (1988) used a cooperative learning framework as the basis for designing Cooperative Integrated Reading and Composition (CIRC), an intervention program for reading and writing that was conducted in the mainstream setting. To address the needs of individual readers using a basal series, reading pairs were assigned homogeneously and included in larger groups with heterogeneously grouped pairs. Teachers used direct instruction techniques to introduce the stories for 20 minutes each day. The students then cooperatively completed a set of prescribed tasks: partner reading, story structure and story related writing, words out loud, word meaning, story retelling, and spelling. The same groups were used for writing. The weekly curriculum included a 1-hour writer's workshop, including a 10-minute teacher-led instructional session at the beginning of the hour and a 10-minute sharing time at the end. Direct instruction on writing required another two 1-hour sessions. Special education resource room teachers and remedial reading teachers continued to see their students outside the mainstream classroom setting.

The results of a series of studies demonstrated that (a) all students in the CIRC program, including those with learning disabilities, made significant progress beyond that of the traditional-instruction control groups; (b) the greatest gains were in reading comprehension; and (c) the handicapped students did not progress as well as their normally achieving peers in writing.

In terms of the difficulties described above that characterize both dyslexic and garden variety poor readers, we would expect that both groups would have difficulties writing, but that, given equivalent knowledge, dyslexics would be less hampered in composing than garden variety poor readers whose difficulties extend beyond those involved in reading per se. Since so little emphasis on writing is given in special education settings, however, it would make sense to assume that learning to compose would be delayed in both groups. A recent study supports this assumption (Wansart, 1990).

Writing to Read

Two learning disabled readers in a fourth-grade classroom that used writing process (Graves, 1983) and writing-based reading (Hansen, 1987) programs were observed throughout the school year by an adult participant–observer. As the students wrote drafts, revised them, shared them, received feedback from their peers, and edited and redrafted them, the learning disabled students, like their peers, began to internalize the rules and strategies of writing and evaluating writing. They engaged increasingly in active self-regulation. Although it took them somewhat longer than their peers, the learning disabled children learned and adopted the problem solving strategies of the community. Collaboration with peers scaffolded the learning of the disabled students, while they learned from instruction and both teacher and peer modeling. Although the students also received special education services, the supportive context of the collaborative setting had a greater impact on the learning disabled youngsters' academic ability and problem solving skills (Wansart, 1990).

To summarize, the new directions in research evaluating educational methods to promote reading and writing as content learning tools and as bootstrapping activities (experience in reading and writing improves the ability to read and write) focus on the use of context and opportunities for collaboration. Direct instructional techniques are utilized: Children are not expected to invent writing structures, study skills, and/or content knowledge for themselves. The *contingent* nature of the intervention method differs from other methods. Not only do teachers use direct instruction to make elements of the instructional process clear, they also interact continuously with students to make certain that student behavior related to the application and utilization of the processes is practiced effectively in the solution of problems and completion of tasks. When students work together, they serve as models for each other. By discussing task demands, they make their reasoning explicit and observable, so that other students can benefit from their thinking. When children work in groups, teachers provide information on a request or contingency basis (i.e., when either the children recognize that they need guidance or the teacher recognizes the need and scaffolds their performances).

Whole Language Approaches to Reading and Writing Instruction

As the fascination with skills hierarchies wanes and research indicates that learning is best promoted in environments that emphasize domain-specific knowledge (Glaser, 1984), those who teach students with learning disabilities to read are increasingly using methods that foster the simultaneous acquisition of reading and content knowledge. Context is probably the single most pervasive emphasis emerging in the instructional literature that relates to poor readers. Strategies are being taught in context, decoding is being taught in context, and now reading itself is being addressed in context, as a form of language related to other language forms (speaking, listening, and writing) and in the context of meaningful information.

It is not surprising that most of this work addresses cooperative learning groups in mainstream settings, because the service delivery structure of special education (e.g., individual educational plans based on behavioral objectives and resource-room pullouts for brief periods of time) militates against integrated instruction where time usage is flexible and students cooperate rather than remain individually accountable (McGill-Franzen & Allington, in press). Although research projects are being reported in the literature about both the reading comprehension and writing deficits of learning disabled readers and the methods of intervention that have been demonstrated to be successful when used to teach them (see Graham & Johnson, 1989, for an overview), these have been conducted on a technique-by-technique basis. Aside from articles recognizing the importance of collaboration between regular education and resource room teachers (cf. Idol, West, & Lloyd, 1988), virtually no work has been done to find ways to improve and restructure resource room education per se. Although the assumption upon which most resource room instruction has been based—that teaching skills in isolation is effective—has been and continues to be seriously challenged by the vast majority of research findings across the major theoretical traditions, special educators are hemmed in.

In response to the increasing pressure for holistic instructional procedures, Rhodes and Dudley-Marling (1988) wrote a text to guide teachers in tailoring whole language methods to the specific needs of learning disabled children. DuCharme, Earl, and Poplin (1989) also generated a list of "do's" specifically intended for the instruction of the learning disabled. Among these are (a) always combine reading and writing instruction, (b) encourage collaborative writing to foster discussion and directed debates, and (c) emphasize content and gradually impose restrictions on form.

WHAT IS KNOWN ABOUT WRITING PROBLEMS EXPERIENCED BY LEARNING DISABLED STUDENTS?

Despite Nodine's (1983) call for studies investigating learning disabled students' writing process (rather than products), such research is still quite rare. In a recent review that examined both composition (product as well as process studies) and the transcription skills of spelling and handwriting, Lynch and Jones (1989) found only 17 studies that investigated writing in students determined to be learning disabled by school district, state, and federal guidelines.

Whether difficulties with the mechanics of writing impede progress for learning disabled children is still unclear. MacArthur and Graham (1987) found that they do, whereas Newcomer, Barenbaum, and Nodine's (1988) data suggested that learning disabled students perform equally poorly when dictating or writing stories.

It is indisputably clear, however, that students with learning disabilities lack the ability to control and manage text structure. In a series of studies, the Barenbaum–Newcomer–Nodine triumvirate (Barenbaum, Newcomer, & Nodine, 1987; Newcomer, Barenbaum, & Nodine, 1988; Nodine, Barenbaum, & Newcomer, 1985) demonstrated that students with learning disabilities have inadequate knowledge of story structure. Although many children may abstract the regular elements of stories as a function of reading, learning disabled students do not.

Regarding expository text, Englert and her colleagues (Englert, Raphael, Fear, & Anderson, 1988; Englert & Thomas, 1987; Thomas, Englert, & Gregg, 1987) found that learning disabled students know little about expository text and how it is composed. This lack of metacognitive awareness, a sense of when a paper was complete, and the ability to organize information according to categories all predicted holistic scores on compositions. Students with learning disabilities made more early terminations, irrelevancies, mechanical errors, and redundancies than their normally achieving peers. Wong, Wong, and Blenkinsop's (1989) comparison of normally achieving and learning disabled adolescents' composing problems across developmental levels indicated that writing problems of the learning disabled could be characterized as developmentally delayed. Interestingly, this finding is in keeping with expectations from Stanovich's (1988) model of reading disorders.

Both research groups concluded that students with learning disabilities need explicit instruction in writing strategies, including emphasis on how text is structured. The research reviewed in the sections above suggests, however, that this instruction need not and should not be taught as an exercise. Stories as well as exposition should serve social, communicative functions. Furthermore, learning disabled children can learn to write when they share the responsibility for writing with their peers in collaborative and/or scaffolded learning environments. In such a case, mutual mediation is promoted as important and useful information is provided on a contingent basis.

Finally, the studies that have focused on the mechanics of writing are also of interest to this discussion. Those studies that implemented a behavioral intervention, such as a self-instructional procedure, by and large failed to produce improvements that transferred, generalized, or were maintained over time (see Lynch & Jones, 1989). On the other hand, when Nulman and Gerber (1984) used a contingent imitation and modeling procedure that encouraged students to engage in problem solving (showing the correct spelling when a word was misspelled and modeling the correct spelling) and Gerber (1986) extended the modeling to include analogical reasoning (looking for similarities to words previously spelled), the students' gains transferred to other spelling lists, with each successive list requiring fewer trials to criterion. As Kronick (1990) argued, bottom–up information taught in a rational (rather than rote) manner can become as meaningful as top–down information. Like any strategy instruction, spelling interventions benefit from mutual, contingent mediation.

SUMMARY AND CONCLUSIONS

Reading disorders are of two types: dyslexic and garden variety. Dyslexics experience reading difficulties that would not be expected given their IQs. Indeed, in a special series in the *Journal of Learning Disabilities* (Wong, 1989), several researchers debated the possible elimination of IQ as a defining characteristic of learning disabilities, arguing that variables such as phonological encoding would be better discriminators. Garden variety poor readers, on the other hand, have difficulties in addition to phonological processing problems that are correlated with IQ, for example, vocabulary, short-term memory, and language comprehension problems. Reading ability, however, appears to fall along a continuum, with phonological encoding problems attenuating as the line approaches normal achievement.

Learning to read is a process that begins prior to schooling and shifts gradually from generating meaning from context to the nearly exclusive reliance on symbols. Techniques that have been demonstrated effective for use with learning disabled students have the following characteristics: They utilize direct and collaborative instruction, mutual contingent mediation, and holistic presentation of material in meaningful contexts.

Only the emphases shift when instruction is directed at reading and writing to learn. Because of the information explosion, the object of schooling has shifted from the production of content masters to that of intelligent novices, that is, students who know how to acquire knowledge. Metascripts to guide the pursuit of domain-specific knowledge enable learners to collaborate in ways that make learning contingent on the need to know, impose purpose, and foster a sense of autonomy.

Although little is known about the problems learning disabled students experience with writing, it is clear that their problems extend beyond the mechanics of spelling and handwriting. Learning disabled students seem to be metacognitively unaware of the structure of both narrative and expository text.

REFERENCES

Barenbaum, E., Newcomer, P., & Nodine, B. (1987). Children's ability to write stories as a function of variation in task, age, and developmental level. *Learning Disability Quarterly, 10,* 175–188.

Bateson, G., & Bateson, M. C. (1987). *Angels fear: Toward an epistemology of the sacred.* New York: Macmillan.

Brady, S., Shankweiler, D., & Mann, V. (1983). Speech perception and memory coding in relation to reading ability. *Journal of Experimental Child Psychology, 35,* 345–367.

Brown, A. L. (1980). Metacognitive development and reading. In R. J. Spiro, B. C. Bruce, & W. F. Brewer (Eds.), *Theoretical issues in reading compre-*

hension (pp. 453–481). Hillsdale, NJ: Erlbaum.

Brown, A. L., Bransford, J. D., Ferrara, R. A., & Campione, J. C. (1983). Learning, remembering, and understanding. In J. H. Flavell & E. M. Markman (Eds.), *Handbook of child psychology* (Vol. 3, pp. 77–166). New York: Wiley.

Brown, A. L., & Campione, J. C. (in press). Communities of learning and thinking: Or a context by any other name. *Human Development.*

Brown, A. L., Campione, J. C., Reeve, R. A., Ferrara, R. A., & Palincsar, A. S. (in press). Interactive learning and individual understanding: The case of reading and mathematics. In L. T. Landsmann (Ed.), *Culture, schooling and psychological development.* Hillsdale, NJ: Erlbaum.

Brown, A. L., Palincsar, A. S., & Armbruster, B. B. (1984). Instructing comprehension-fostering activities in interactive learning situations. In H. Mandl, N. Stein, & T. Trabasso (Eds.), *Learning and comprehension of text* (pp. 255–286). Hillsdale, NJ: Erlbaum.

Collins, A. (in press). Cognitive apprenticeship and instructional technology. In B. F. Jones & L. Idol (Eds.), *Dimensions of thinking and cognitive instruction.* Hillsdale, NJ: Erlbaum.

Collins, A., Brown, J. S., & Newman, S. E. (1990). Cognitive apprenticeship: Teaching the crafts of reading, writing, and mathematics. In L. B. Resnick (Ed.), *Knowing, learning, and instruction* (pp. 453–494). Hillsdale, NJ: Erlbaum.

DuCharme, C., Earl, J., & Poplin, M. S. (1989). The author model: The constructivist view of the writing process. *Learning Disability Quarterly, 12,* 237–247.

Duffy, G. G., & Roehler, L. R. (1986). The subtleties of instructional mediation. *Educational Leadership, 43,* 23–27.

Duffy, G. G., Roehler, L. R., Meloth, M. S., Vavrus, L. G., Book, C., Putnam, J., & Wesselman, R. (1986). The relationship between explicit verbal explanations during reading skill instruction and student awareness and achievement: A study of reading teacher effects. *Reading Research Quarterly, 21,* 237–252.

Duffy, G. G., Roehler, L. R., Sivan, E., Rackliffe, G., Book, C., Meloth, M. S., Vavrus, L. G., Wesselman, R., Putnam, J., & Bassiri, D. (1987). *Reading Research Quarterly, 22,* 347–368.

Ellis, A. W. (1985). The cognitive neuropsychology of developmental (and acquired) dyslexia: A critical survey. *Cognitive Neuropsychology, 2,* 169–205.

Englert, C. S., Raphael, T. E., Fear, K. L., & Anderson, L. M. (1988). Students' metacognitive knowledge about how to write informational texts. *Learning Disability Quarterly, 11,* 18–46.

Englert, C. S., & Thomas, C. C. (1987). Sensitivity to text structure in reading and writing: A comparison between learning disabled and non-learning disabled students. *Learning Disability Quarterly, 10,* 93–105.

Gallagher, J. M., & Reid, D. K. (1983). *The learning theory of Piaget and Inhelder.* Austin, TX: PRO-ED.

Gerber, M. M. (1986). Generalization of spelling strategies as a result of contingent imitation/modeling and mastery criteria. *Journal of Learning Disabilities, 19,* 530–537.

Glaser, R. (1984). Education and thinking: The role of knowledge. *American Psychologist, 39,* 93–104.

Graham, S., & Johnson, L. A. (1989). Research-supported teacher activities that influence the text reading of students with learning disabilities. *LD Forum, 15,* 27–30.

Graves, D. H. (1983). *Writing: Teachers and children at work.* Exeter, NH: Heinemann.

Hansen, J. (1987). *When writers read.* Portsmouth, NH: Heinemann.

Idol, L., West, J. F., & Lloyd, S. R. (1988). Organizing and implementing specialized reading programs: A collaborative approach involving classroom, remedial, and special education teachers. *Remedial and Special Education, 9,* 54–61.

Jorm, I. Y. (1983). Specific reading retardation and working memory: A review. *British Journal of Psychology, 74,* 311–342.

Kintsch, W. (1989). Learning from text. In L. B. Resnick (Ed.), *Knowing, learning, and instruction* (pp. 25–46). Hillsdale, NJ: Erlbaum.

Kronick, D. (1990). Holism and empiricism as complementary paradigms. *Journal of Learning Disabilities, 23,* 5–8.

Liberman, I. Y. (1983). A language-oriented view of reading and its disabilities. In H. Mykelbust (Ed.), *Progress in learning disabilities* (Vol. 5., pp. 81–102). New York: Grune and Stratton.

Lynch, E. M., & Jones, S. D. (1989). Process and product: A review of the research on LD children's writing skills. *Learning Disability Quarterly, 12,* 74–86.

MacArthur, C. A., & Graham, S. (1987). Learning disabled students' composing under three methods of text production: Handwriting, word processing, and dictation. *Journal of Special Education, 21,* 22–42.

Mann, V. A. (1984). Reading skill and language skill. *Developmental Review, 4,* 1–15.

Mann, V. A., Cowin, E., & Schoenheimer, J. (1988, March). *Phonological processing, language comprehension, and read-* ing ability. Paper presented at the Austin Invitational Research Symposium on Learning Disabilities.

Mann, V. A., & Liberman, I. Y. (1984). Phonological awareness and verbal short-term memory. *Journal of Learning Disabilities, 17,* 592–599.

McGill-Franzen, A., & Allington, R. L. (In press). The gridlock of low reading achievement: Perspectives on practice and policy. *Remedial and Special Education.*

Newcomer, P. L., Barenbaum, E. M., & Nodine, B. F. (1988). Comparison of the story production of LD, normal-achieving, and low-achieving children under two modes of production. *Learning Disability Quarterly, 11,* 82–96.

Nodine, B. F. (1983). Foreward: Process not product. *Topics in Learning and Learning Disabilities, 3,* ix–xii.

Nodine, B. F., Barenbaum, E., & Newcomer, P. (1985). Story composition by learning disabled, reading disabled, and normal children. *Learning Disability Quarterly, 8,* 167–179.

Nulman, J. A. H., & Gerber, M. M. (1984). Improving spelling performance by imitating a child's errors. *Journal of Learning Disabilities, 17,* 328–333.

Palincsar, A. S., & Brown, A. L. (1986). Interactive teaching to promote independent learning from text. *Reading Teacher, 39,* 771–777.

Perfetti, C. A. (1985). *Reading ability.* New York: Oxford University Press.

Perfetti, C. A. (1989). There are generalized abilities and one of them is reading. In L. B. Resnick (Ed.), *Knowing, learning, and instruction* (pp. 307–335). Hillsdale, NJ: Erlbaum.

Perfetti, C. A., Beck, I., & Hughes, C. (1981, April). *Phonemic knowledge and learning to read: A longitudinal study of first graders.* Paper presented at the Society for Research in Child Development, Boston.

Reid, D. K. (1988). *Teaching the learning disabled: A cognitive developmental approach.* Boston: Allyn and Bacon.

Reid, D. K. (1989). The role of cooperative learning in comprehensive instruction. *Journal of Reading, Writing, and Learning Disabilities—International, 4,* 229–242.

Rhodes, L. K., & Dudley-Marling, C. (1988). *Readers and writers with a difference: A holistic approach to teaching learning disabled and remedial students.* Portsmouth, NH: Heinemann.

Rumelhart, D. E. (1977). *Toward an interactive model of reading.* (Tech. Rep. No. 56). La Jolla, CA: Center for Human Information Processing.

Siegel, L. S., & Heaven, R. (1986). Defining and categorizing learning disabilities. In S. Ceci (Ed.), *Handbook of cognitive, social and neuropsychological aspects of learning disabilities* (Vol. 1, pp. 95–121). Hillsdale, NJ: Erlbaum.

Simmons, D. C., & Kameenui, E. J. (1989). Direct instruction of decoding skills and strategies. *LD Forum, 15,* 35–38.

Slavin, R. E., Stevens, R. J., & Madden, N. A. (1988). Accommodating student diversity in reading and writing instruction: A cooperative learning approach. *Remedial and Special Education, 9,* 60–66.

Stanovich, K. E. (1986). Mathew effects in reading: Some consequences of individual differences in the acquisition of literacy. *Reading Research Quarterly, 21,* 360–407.

Stanovich, K. E. (1988). Explaining the differences between the dyslexic and the garden-variety poor reader: The phonological-core variable-difference model. *Journal of Learning Disabilities, 21,* 590–604.

Thomas, C. C., Englert, C. S., & Gregg, S. (1987). An analysis of errors and strategies in the expository writing of learning disabled students. *Remedial and Special Education, 8,* 21–30.

Wansart, W. L. (1990). *Learning disabled or learning enabled? Writing in a collaborative classroom context.* Manuscript submitted for publication.

Wong, B. Y. L. (1989). Is IQ necessary in the definition of learning disabilities? Introduction to the special series. *Journal of Learning Disabilities, 22,* 468.

Wong, B. Y. L., Wong, R., & Blenkinsop, J. (1989). Cognitive and metacognitive aspects of learning disabled adolescents' composing problems. *Learning Disability Quarterly, 12,* 300–322.

14

Teaching Mathematics Developmentally to Children Classified as Learning Disabled

ARTHUR J. BAROODY

To help children avoid or overcome learning difficulties in mathematics, educators must understand how children learn mathematics and why they encounter difficulties. An educator's view of the cause of learning disabilities explicitly or implicitly determines the conduct of instruction or remediation. This chapter examines the mathematical instruction of children classified as learning disabled from the perspective of cognitive theory (e.g., see R. B. Davis, 1984; Nesher, 1986; Shuell, 1986).

The chapter begins by discussing different views of learning disabilities and what view is most practical from an educator's point of view. It then provides an overview of (a) the way children learn mathematics, (b) the reasons why they often encounter learning difficulties, (c) some general guidelines for teaching and remedying mathematical difficulties, and (d) a sample of common difficulties and instructional suggestions. The chapter concludes with a case study that illustrates the difficulties commonly faced by children classified as learning disabled.

The term mathematical learning disability often is not used precisely or carefully (e.g., Allardice & Ginsburg, 1983; Blankenship, 1988; Cawley, 1984b; Coles, 1978; Farnham-Diggory, 1978). Learning disabilities have been attributed to an organic brain dysfunction, perhaps so minimal as to be difficult

Preparation of this chapter was supported, in part, by Grant No. MDR-8470191 from the National Science Foundation awarded to H. P. Ginsburg and A. J. Baroody and a grant from the University of Illinois Research Board awarded to A. J. Baroody.

or impossible to detect by current diagnostic methods (e.g., DeRuiter & Wansart, 1982; Kaliski, 1962; Kosc, 1974; Rourke & Strang, 1983; Strauss & Kephart, 1955). Certainly, some children experience difficulty learning mathematics as a result of neurological impairments (see, e.g., Deloche & Seron, 1987; Luria, 1969; Strauss & Lehtinen, 1947), and meeting the learning needs of children with real handicaps may well require special instructional methods. However, such students comprise a very small proportion of the children classified as learning disabled (e.g., Tucker, 1985), and including in this classification children without clear signs of an organic dysfunction is a questionable practice at best (e.g., Algozzine & Ysseldyke, 1986; Blankenship, 1988; Cawley, 1985a; Ysseldyke & Algozzine, 1983).

In his classification scheme, Kosc (1974) distinguished between organically based impairments and learning deficits (Kidron, 1985). He called specific impairments in learning mathematical concepts or computations associated with an organic dysfunction *dyscalculia*. *Developmental dyscalculia* implies a genetic or congenital disorder (e.g., Kosc, 1970), and *acquired dyscalculia* is the result of brain damage or dysfunction occurring after birth (e.g., Sears, 1986). *Acalculia* refers to a general and severe deficiency in mathematical learning, and *oligocalculia* refers to a general depression of mathematical ability. On the other hand, Kosc called learning deficits, which are attributed to inadequate instruction, illness, emotional problems, and so forth, *pseudo-dyscalculia*, *pseudo-acalculia*, or *pseudo-oligocalculia*.

Like others who have proposed minimal brain damage as an explanation for learning difficulties, Kosc (1974) classified as impaired children with "soft signs" of neurological dysfunction (developmental abnormalities such as fine and gross motor-coordination deficiencies, mixed or confused laterality, strabismus, defective or slow speech development, short attention span, and general awkwardness). In contrast to "hard signs" (e.g., an abnormal EEG or brain-wave pattern), soft signs are not clear indications of brain damage (Coles, 1978). Indeed, reviews of the literature (e.g., Coles, 1978) fail to find a convincing link between soft signs ("evidence" of minimal brain damage) and learning problems. In brief, many children are labeled as impaired on the basis of questionable evidence.

Perhaps most children labeled learning disabled are, in David Elkind's words, "curriculum disabled," not organically impaired (cited in Hendrickson, 1983). In other words, such children have learning difficulties because mathematics is not taught in a psychologically appropriate manner. Moreover, ineffective instruction most likely compounds the learning difficulties of those children with genuine neurological involvement (e.g., Fitzmaurice-Hayes, 1985a; Kosc, 1974). Given that the neurological concept of learning disability is often misapplied, this chapter focuses on the instruction of learning difficulties in a general sense, especially those difficulties resulting from inappropriate instruction.

WHAT IS THE COGNITIVE VIEW OF LEARNING AND COGNITION?

Mental Structures

In a cognitive view, genuine learning is not simply a matter of absorbing information, and knowledge is not merely a copy of reality (e.g., Baroody, 1987a). Instead, a child actively constructs a representation of reality (a mental structure). Initially, the representation will be incomplete or inaccurate from an expert's perspective but, with the appropriate experiences, it can become progressively more complete and accurate. Sophisticated representations permit more flexible reasoning and more effective problem solving than do unsophisticated representations (e.g., R. B. Davis, 1983). Indeed, with development, thinking can change qualitatively (e.g., an insight can provide a fresh and more powerful perspective). Furthermore, the effective use of knowledge depends on the development of structures that serve an executive function (e.g., the monitoring of performance) and personality structures (e.g., interests that energize performance).

Conceptual knowledge.   Like other "consequential knowledge" (Sternberg, 1984a, 1984b), mathematical knowledge is not simply a collection of facts and procedures to be memorized through repeated practice. It includes a highly structured body of information replete with relationships. According to cognitive theory, children construct mental structures (schemata) to represent important regularities in their experiences. R. C. Anderson (1984) defines a schema as a representation of relationships, which can summarize information about many particular cases. It provides a system "for recognizing recurring sets of features" (J. R. Anderson, 1980, p. 254) and a framework for assimilating new facts or relationships (Shuell, 1986).

Strategies.   Mathematical knowledge also includes strategies for applying existing knowledge and making sense of new situations (problem solving skills). According to cognitive theory, children construct mental structures to deal effectively with their environment and learn more about it. Indeed, Piaget defined a schema as an organized pattern of actions (Ginsburg & Opper, 1988). Strategies can be task specific (e.g., a counting-on routine used to compute sums) or broadly applied (e.g., a mnemonic to learn factual information) (e.g., Pressley, Goodchild, Fleet, Zajchowski, & Evans, 1989). Cognitive learning strategies (e.g., labeling and rehearsing information to foster memorization) are general techniques for facilitating learning. Heuristics (e.g., drawing a picture to help understand a problem) are general strategies for facilitating problem solving.

Metacognition. Conceptual knowledge and strategies are not sufficient to ensure their effective use in completing assignments, learning new material, solving problems, and so forth (see Palincsar, 1986). Children also must have awareness of the resources a task requires and oversight or regulation of resource use (e.g., Baker & Brown, 1984; Reeve & Brown, 1985). Knowledge about one's own knowledge (concepts, learning strategies, or thinking processes) and the active monitoring and regulation of learning and cognitive processes is called *metacognition* (e.g., A. L. Brown, 1978; Flavell, 1976; Flavell & Wellman, 1977). In brief, metacognitive knowledge permits self-regulated learning and problem solving.

Affect. According to Piaget and Inhelder (1969), cognition and affect are complementary aspects of behavior. The affective elements (needs, feelings, and interests) energize or motivate action and thus exert a tremendous influence upon learning (Reyes, 1984). Beliefs link cognition and affect in that they are assumptions about the self or world that prompt certain actions (Baroody, 1987a). In brief, affective factors and belief structures shape an individual's disposition to learn and to use knowledge.

Processes of Change

Understanding and strategies are actively constructed by relating new experiences to what is already known or by combining existing pieces of knowledge. Both processes involve making a connection (insight), and both are mechanisms for making schemata more complete and accurate.

Assimilation and accommodation. Learners filter new information in terms of what they already know. The process of interpreting and incorporating new information in terms of existing knowledge is called *assimilation* (e.g., Piaget, 1964). During the process of assimilation, a child may encounter aspects of the new experiences that do not exactly fit existing structures. This creates a disequilibrium, which requires an adjustment. Adjusting existing concepts or strategies to meet the demands of a new experience is called *accommodation.* Through the complementary processes of assimilation and accommodation, then, knowledge structures become enriched and more responsive to the environment. That is, they provide a more complete and accurate understanding of reality or way of responding to it. In this view, learning is not merely a process of adding information; it is a process that transforms mental structures (DeRuiter & Wansart, 1982).

Integration. By reflecting on experiences, a child may relate or integrate existing but previously isolated aspects of knowledge. This can occur when an experience causes two schemata to come into a conflict (e.g., see Figure

14–1). The resulting disequilibrium induces the schemata to reorganize into a single new schema that is more complete and accurate.

Informal Mathematical Knowledge.

Preschool development.   Research (e.g., Baroody, 1987a; Court, 1920; Fuson & Hall, 1983; Gelman & Gallistel, 1978; Ginsburg, 1989; Starkey & Gelman, 1982) shows that the development of mathematical knowledge begins well before children enter school. This *informal* knowledge is based, in large part, on counting experiences and provides an important basis for learning formal (school-taught, largely written or symbolic) mathematics. Rule-governed errors, such as counting "eighteen, nineteen, *tenteen,*" suggest that pre-schoolers do not merely absorb information or imitate solutions passively, but actively construct their mathematical knowledge (Ginsburg, 1989).

Personal mathematics of school children.   Even after children begin school, they often continue to rely on their informal mathematics instead of doing

Rule 1 (learned as a result of earlier shape-recognition training): "A parallelogram and a rectangle are *different* shapes"

← CONFLICT →
caused by a request to analyze the characteristics of a rectangle ("A rectangle is a *four-sided shape with parallel* and equal *opposite sides*") and the resulting disequilibrium induces reorganization

Rule 2 (learned in a recent geometry lesson): "A parallelogram is a four-sided shape with parallel opposite sides"

↓

New (more complete and accurate) rule:
A *rectangle* is a special kind of *parallelogram;* it is *different* from the broader category of parallelograms in that it has equal sides

Figure 14–1.   Integration of conflicting geometry schemata.

mathematics the way it is taught (e.g., Resnick & Ford, 1981); that is, children do not simply imitate and quickly adopt adult strategies or patterns of thought (Brownell, 1935). For example, despite the emphasis in many schools on memorizing the number facts, children persist in computing (e.g., Baroody, 1985; Carpenter & Moser, 1984). In fact, regardless of the teacher, mathematics curriculum, community, or country, children, at least initially, rely on counting to compute sums, differences, and products (see, e.g., Ginsburg, Posner, & Russell, 1981; Ginsburg & Russell, 1981; Kouba, 1986). School children invent and rely on informal arithmetic procedures because these methods allow them to cope with their environment in a meaningful manner.

Strengths and limitations.   Informal mathematics enables children to exhibit surprising strengths. For example, cognitive research (e.g., Carpenter, 1986; Carpenter & Moser, 1983; Riley, Greeno, & Heller, 1983) indicates that young children have previously unsuspected problem solving skill. Even kindergartners and first graders can solve simple addition and subtraction word problems by using counting strategies that model the meaning of a problem. On the other hand, informal mathematical knowledge may not be complete, coherent, or logical (see, e.g., Baroody & Ginsburg, 1986; Piaget, 1965). A significant inconsistency, for example, is that even when young children can deal effectively with quantitative questions involving small numbers, they cannot always do so with large numbers (e.g., Gelman, 1972).

Formal Mathematics

School-taught mathematics.   Formal mathematics, which is taught in school and which uses written symbols, can greatly extend children's ability to deal with quantitative issues. Indeed, the mathematical skills and concepts taught in the primary grades are not only the foundation for learning more advanced mathematics later in school, but are basic "survival skills" in our technologically oriented society. This formal mathematics is powerful in various ways. It is a highly precise and logical body of knowledge. Written algorithms (step-by-step procedures) greatly increase calculation efficiency, especially with larger quantities, and provide a long-lasting record. However, the extent to which children benefit from formal instruction depends on how well it meshes with their thinking.

Informal mathematics: A foundation for formal mathematics.   Although formal mathematics can greatly extend their capabilities, children cannot immediately comprehend abstract instruction. In a cognitive view, the meaningful learning of school mathematics involves the assimilation of information, not merely its absorption. A basis for assimilating school-taught mathematical knowledge is children's informal mathematical knowledge. Mathematical symbols, computational algorithms, and formulas can make sense to children if this formal mathematics can be connected to their existing, personal, counting-based knowledge of mathematics.

Schema Development

Weak versus strong schemata. R. C. Anderson (1984) differentiated between weak and strong schemata. A weak schema contains a collection of facts that are largely unconnected or unrelated. This greatly limits a child's ability to use existing knowledge to learn new material or to solve problems. For example, with isolated pieces of knowledge, the child cannot reason out an answer, but must rely on looking up a precedent: a similar, previous experience. If a looked-up response is incorrect, the child has no other avenues (connections) to explore and may simply give up or resort to guessing. If a problem is changed even superficially from what was learned, the child—if simply not stumped—may relate the "novel" problem to a different (and inappropriate) precedent. In other words, because weak schemata include knowledge narrow in scope, they provide an uncertain basis for reasoning and may yield inconsistent responses.

On the other hand, a strong schema involves well connected knowledge. This enables a child to coordinate a wide range of information to comprehend new material and to solve problems. A strong schema implies that comprehension is principle driven (general in scope) and that predictions can be derived (reasoned out) in a logical and consistent fashion.

Developmental trends. Applied to the development of mathematical thinking, the weak versus strong schema distinction should be thought of as a continuum rather than a dichotomy (Baroody & Ginsburg, 1986). Indeed, cognitive research indicates that with any mathematical content, learners progress, relatively speaking, from concrete to abstract conceptions, from incomplete to complete knowledge, and from unsystematic to systematic thinking (e.g., Baroody, 1987a; Crowley, 1987; Lunkenbein, 1985; van Erp & Heshusius, 1986); that is, for a first grader learning to add or a college student learning calculus, understanding begins imprecisely with the apparent. Initial cognitive structures, which emerge from concrete activities and are based on global perceptions, can be characterized as intuitive or infralogical (e.g., Lunkenbein, 1985). Because this intuitive, unanalyzed, impressionistic knowledge is context bound, spotty, and unsystematic (e.g., Ginsburg, 1989; Lunkenbein, 1985), reasoning is idiosyncratic and prototypical. In brief, initial knowledge may be characterized as a weak schema.

Knowledge in a particular domain only gradually becomes relatively abstract, complete, and systematic. In time, a student begins to abstract and formulate the properties and relations of a domain. Initially, such knowledge may not be organized into a coherent system and may be of limited generality and logically inconsistent. Reasoning still remains more descriptive or precedent driven than truly deductive. Further advances in development entail recognizing and defining precise properties and logical relations and organizing this information into an axiomatic system. A student is then capable of seeing logical implications and reasoning deductively. For a few, mathematical knowledge is taken a step further. Properties and relations are formally defined in terms of abstract symbols, which can be used to build a self-contained system of deductions of increasing complexity (P. J. Davis & Hersh, 1981). Thus, schemata can range from weak (intuitive or infralogical) to relatively weak (principled but unsystematic) to relatively strong (principled and systematic) to strong (principles formally defined).

Even when instruction is highly effective, students cannot construct entirely complete and accurate structures all at once (Resnick & Ford, 1981). Therefore, incomplete structures and the systematic errors that result are the natural products of instruction (Resnick et al., 1989). In general, then, errors should be viewed as *incomplete* responses rather than wrong responses (e.g., DeRuiter & Wansart, 1982).

The case of number-combination knowledge. Like other consequential mathematical knowledge, the essence of number-combination knowledge is structure (Baroody, 1988c). It would make sense, then, that the evolution of this knowledge and its proficient use would depend upon the elaboration of schemata. Initially, children may assimilate arithmetic problems (e.g., 5 + 3) to existing but inadequate structures and respond ineffectively. For example, some children with little or no understanding of addition appear to assimilate or interpret an unfamiliar arithmetic question such as "5 + 2 = ?" as a number-comparison query, which results in the systematic error of responding with the larger addend: "Five."

At some point, children "see" the connection between mental addition and their informal arithmetic knowledge (i.e., assimilate the formal addition terminology to their informal incrementing concept) and realize that an addend must be increased. Children commonly exploit their well-learned number-after knowledge for this purpose (e.g., "Five plus one is just the number after five: six") (e.g., Baroody, 1985). Initially, such a strategy may not be used discriminately. The result is a systematic error, such as responding to 5 + 0, 5 + 1, and 5 + 3 with the same answer, "six."

With experience and feedback, children construct more adequate (complete and integrated) schemata. The discovery of a relationship or the integration of knowledge can produce sudden qualitative changes in performance (e.g., the mastery of a whole set of related combinations). Thus, children need not practice each combination to make a "copy" of individual facts. For example, by assimilating expressions involving 0 to their informal knowledge that adding nothing to a collection leaves it unchanged, children can suddenly make sense of symbolic problems such as 5 + 0. Now a child can distinguish between, say, 5 + 0 and 5 + 1 and respond appropriately to each (see, e.g., Baroody, 1988a). Moreoover, taking into account their informal knowledge that adding 1 and more than 1 to a number cannot have the same sum may compel children to distinguish between combinations involving 1 (e.g., 5 + 1) and those involving larger numbers (e.g., 5 + 3) (Baroody, 1989c). For problems involving the addition of more than 1, they may devise a more genuine estimation strategy such as choosing a number (2 to 6) more than the larger addend (Baroody, 1983).

With further insights and practice, schemata become more elaborate, interconnected, and automatic and, hence, provide a basis for more effective problem solving (see R. C. Anderson, 1984; Greeno, 1978; Kaye, 1986; Norman & Rumelhart, 1975; Resnick & Ford, 1981). For example, children first view addition as adding something to an initial set to make it larger (Weaver, 1982). Because of this informal incrementing concept of addition, children do not realize that addition is commutative: Addend order is irrelevant to the outcome (e.g., Baroody & Gannon, 1984). As a result, they view 6 + 2 and 2 + 6 as different problems (6 and 2 more and 2 and 6 more) with *different* sums (see, e.g., Siegel, 1957). Once they discover that addition is commutative, children may learn an unknown combination such as 2 + 6 = 8 with little or no practice because they know it is equivalent to a known fact (6 + 2 = 8).

Children use known addition facts in various other ways to do mental arithmetic. For example, children typically learn the doubles like 5 + 5 = 10 quickly, and many discover that they can use this knowledge to reason out the sums of near doubles like 5 + 6 that they do not know. More specifically, they use existing knowledge to construct a "doubles-plus-one" thinking strategy: Retrieve the sum of the double and then use the number-after rule to increment the retrieved sum by one. Extant knowledge of addition combinations can also serve as data for subtraction (e.g., 5 + 3 = 8, therefore, 8 − 5 is 3) and multiplication (e.g., knowledge of the addition doubles such as 6 + 6 = 12 can serve as the data for the times-two combinations such as 6 × 2 = ?) (Baroody, 1988c).

WHAT CAUSES CHILDREN TO HAVE MATHEMATICAL LEARNING DIFFICULTIES?

Psychologically Inappropriate Instruction

Children have difficulty learning or using mathematics because, all too frequently, formal instruction does not suit them.

The absorption model. Formal mathematical instruction, even at the elementary level, is too often based on the assumption that children simply absorb information and make a mental copy of it. Too frequently, this simplistic view of learning is also the basis of special education (e.g., Reid & Hresko, 1981). Thus, school mathematics, even for children with learning difficulties, is all too often based on a tell–show–drill approach (Suydam & Osborne, 1977, cited in Blankenship, 1984):

1. Instruction begins with the class being told what they need to know. Often, the teacher verbally explains the lesson. Sometimes, the students are expected to get the new information by reading their textbook.

2. The lesson is illustrated with examples. For example, the teacher may show how to do a procedure on the chalkboard, or the concept or procedure may be illustrated further by examples and pictures in the textbook.

3. The children then imitate the teacher and practice the fact or skill until it is automatic. Predicated on the assumption that "practice makes perfect," students are regularly given extensive written assignments (e.g., Moyer & Moyer, 1985). For the most part, then, doing mathematics is reduced to manipulating written symbols to obtain correct answers (R. B. Davis, 1984).

Gaps. An absorption-model approach, even when done well, fails to take adequate account of the nature of children's mathematical learning. Such an approach overlooks the crucial developmental process of assimilation and the key developmental issue of readiness. All too often, the result is a gap between formal instruction and children's existing (informal) knowledge.

Gaps occur because instruction is too abstract. If objects and counting are not discouraged entirely, they are usually allowed only briefly to introduce topics such as arithmetic or place value (e.g., Carpenter & Moser, 1984). Unfortunately, a highly verbal approach to instruction frequently is not meaningful to children, even when accompanied by pictures and demonstrations. For example, the reliance on textbook pictures of groups of 10 items and single items to foster an understanding of grouping and positional notation (base-10 place-value concepts) is typically inadequate (e.g., Baroody, 1987a; Hendrickson, 1983). Moreover, too often, the written symbols and the manipulations involving these symbols make little or no sense to children (e.g, R. B. Davis, 1984).

A gap can occur when formal instruction overlooks individual readiness and moves too quickly. Mathematics instruction is frequently done in a large group and practiced alone without direct feedback. Because children do not have the same readiness to learn a mathematical concept or skill, a lesson or exercise may not be appropriate for everyone in class (e.g., Blankenship, 1984). Thus, new instruction that is introduced to a group of students will probably not be assimilated by all.

The Results of Psychologically Inappropriate Instruction

Because it does not adequately take into account the psychology of the child, instruction based on an absorption model often fails to foster meaningful learning, a desire to learn, mastery of basic skills, strategic behaviors and metacognitive skills, and constructive beliefs. Such an approach frequently undermines independent learning and problem solving ability.

Rote learning. A gap between formal instruction and a child's existing informal knowledge prevents assimilation. According to Piaget's *moderate novelty principle*, a child (or adult) cannot assimilate information that is unrelated to past experiences; that is, an individual cannot connect highly novel or unfamiliar information to existing knowledge and, thus, cannot interpret it. Simply put, understanding cannot be imposed. When training is conducted in an abstract and lockstep manner, the information presented is frequently too unfamiliar to be assimilated. As a result, children are forced to memorize mathematics by rote, as isolated bits of meaningless information.

In other words, a tell–show–drill regimen often fosters the development and maintenance of weak or relatively weak schemata. For most of the formal mathematics to which they are exposed, children are not given the means, the opportunity, the incentive, or the time to develop stronger schemata (Baroody & Ginsburg, 1986); that is, they are not encouraged to look for a relationship between new information and their existing knowledge or between pieces of acquired knowledge. The result is that students do not develop the sophisticated representations that permit the assimilation of more advanced mathematics, flexible reasoning, or nontrivial mathematical problem solving.

Disinterest. A gap between formal instruction and children's existing knowledge can have serious affective consequences: It can undercut children's interest in mathematics, their motivation to learn it, and their willingness to engage in mathematical problem solving. Piaget's moderate novelty principle describes a key link between cognition and affect. Children are naturally interested in "moderately novel" information; that is, somewhat unfamiliar situations excite natural curiosity. On the other hand, when presented with new, unfamiliar information that they cannot assimilate, children (and adults) quickly lose interest in the incomprehensible information and tune it out. Indeed, many children feel frustrated and helpless when confronted with a torrent of meaningless words and written symbols. Heavy doses of practice with exercises that seem to children to be pointless can further deaden interest.

Inaccurate or incomplete learning. Gaps between children's relatively concrete informal mathematics and their relatively abstract formal instruction are a key reason for learning difficulties (Allardice & Ginsburg, 1983; Ginsburg, 1989; Hiebert, 1984). Some children fail to memorize meaningless information correctly or at all and, as a result, learn concepts or procedures in an incomplete or incorrect fashion. Systematic errors or "bugs" are symptoms of this partially correct or incorrect knowledge (e.g., J. S. Brown & Burton, 1978; Buswell & Judd, 1925; Cox, 1975; Ginsburg, 1989; Van Lehn, 1983). For instance, presented with an unfamiliar operation, children sometimes resort to using a familiar operation (Bug 1 in Table 14–1). A common error among children with little or no knowledge of the remaining algorithm is the incorrect procedure of subtracting the smaller term from the larger, even when the smaller term is the top number (Bug 2). Because children do not understand the underlying place-value rationale for the algorithm, many learn the procedure incompletely. Note that Bug 3 indicates less procedural knowledge than Bugs 4 and 5, which entail some effort to reduce. Subtraction involving 0 frequently prompts other invented procedures, such as in Bugs 6 and 7. Bug 8, consisting of a partially correct procedure and an incorrect procedure, illustrates the common case of multiple bugs.

Learning problems are compounded when new topics are introduced before a child has had a chance to assimilate more basic lessons. Because new topics often build upon previous lessons, the child gets caught in a downward spiral of failure; that is, when learning difficulties occur, a child has little opportunity to catch up, old problems create new learning difficulties, and the child falls further and further behind. As the gap between instruction and a child's existing knowledge increases, the chances of the child's making sense of the mathematics decreases. Moreover, an inadequate or incomplete knowledge base is a serious barrier to problem solving (e.g., Davis, 1984).

Passivity.   A gap between formal instruction and informal knowledge forces children into the role of passive recipients of knowledge and discourages independent thinking. Because understanding, exploring, questioning, and reflecting are not encouraged, a tell–show–drill approach to instruction frequently fails to foster the learning and use of task-specific strategies, cognitive learning strategies, or heuristics. Because of a focus on memorizing *the* correct written procedure, schooling often discourages children from inventing or using their own informal strategies. When mathematics is merely a basket of facts and procedures to be memorized (see Anderson, 1984), some children may discover that rehearsal is a useful strategy for acquiring information, but most may learn few other strategies necessary for self-regulated learning. Moreover, they may not develop strategies for facilitating problem solving, such as the heuristic of evaluating new problems in terms of familiar ones.

A tell–show–drill approach too often fails to foster the learning of metacognitive skills or provide an opportunity to practice them. A steady diet

TABLE 14–1
Some Common Subtraction Bugs

1.	53 − 27 34	37 − 16 53	5.	203 − 27 86	206 − 58 58
2.	53 − 27 34	164 − 89 125	6.	128 − 107 1	245 − 108 107
3.	53 − 27 36	206 − 58 258	7.	208 − 127 101	340 − 176 170
4.	203 − 27 276	206 − 58 248	8.	103 − 27 26	206 − 58 158

Explanations:

1. Adds instead of subtracts.
2. Subtracts large from the small.
3. Borrows without reducing.
4. Borrows from 0, changes it to 9, but does not reduce.
5. Skips over 0 to borrow.
6. Subtracts $N - 0 = 0$.
7. Subtracts $0 - N = 0$.
8. Skips over 0 to borrow and subtracts $0 - N = N$.

of rote learning and meaningless drill fosters blind rule-following (e.g., Brown, 1978; Holt, 1964). As a result, even "successful" students, who have faithfully memorized their lessons, often fail to use their knowledge effectively when learning new material or solving problems (e.g., Allardice & Ginsburg, 1983). Information learned by rote frequently does not transfer, because children do not see how it is applicable to a new task. For example, because they do not understand the underlying rationale for the algorithm, many students master a carrying procedure for two-digit addition, but then cannot apply this knowledge to three-digit addition. Even many successful students are unable to solve problems that differ at all from what they have been taught (see, e.g., Carpenter, Mathews, Lindquist, & Silver, 1984; Wertheimer, 1945). Moreover, because they do not practice self-regulatory skills such as self-monitoring, many children get into the habit of depending on an authority, such as the teacher, to determine the correctness of their answers.

Debilitating beliefs. A gap between formal instruction and children's informal knowledge can make mathematics seem incomprehensible, foreign, and arbitrary. Indeed, the way in which mathematics is taught can profoundly affect how children view mathematics, their learning of the topic, and themselves (Baroody, 1987a). When mathematics is taught in an abstract and lock-step manner, children "hear" such unspoken "messages" as

- Only geniuses can understand mathematics. Just do as you're told. You're not smart enough to understand it.

- Mathematics is a bunch of facts and procedures. Normal children memorize it quickly. You're dumb if you can't.

- In mathematics, there is one correct method for doing things. Good children follow directions. You're bad if you use an unacceptable procedure such as counting.

Such beliefs can have a powerful impact on how children go about learning and using mathematics (Cobb, 1985a, 1985b; Pressley et al., 1989; Reyes, 1984; Schoenfeld, 1985). The destructive beliefs fostered by a tell–show–drill approach can discourage independent thinking and problem solving ability. For example, an emphasis on memorizing written procedures teaches children that mathematics does not involve thinking and that their own ideas and strategies are not relevant or, at best, are inferior substitutes for real math. Because they conclude that mathematics does not make sense, many children stop monitoring their work thoughtfully and dispense with assigned work as quickly as possible (e.g., Holt, 1964). As a result, they may not be the least bit troubled by an unreasonable answer, even when it is incompatible with what they do know (e.g., Hiebert & Wearne, 1984; Schoenfeld, 1985). For instance, children who use the small-from-large bug frequently overlook the fact that subtraction cannot yield a difference that is larger than the starting amount:

$$\begin{array}{r} 22 \\ -\ 5 \\ \hline 23 \end{array}$$

The Case of Number-Fact Deficiencies: A Common Learning Difficulty

A weakness in basic number-combination knowledge is characteristic of children having difficulty with mathematics (e.g., Ackerman, Anhalt, & Dykman, 1986; Allardice & Ginsburg, 1983; Baroody, 1987a; Fleischner, Garnett, & Shepard, 1982; Goldman, Pellegrino, & Mertz, 1988; Hasselbring, Goin, & Bransford, 1987; Russell & Ginsburg, 1984; Svenson & Broquist, 1975; Torgesen & Young, 1983). Larger basic combinations (e.g., single-digit combinations with sums over 10) are especially difficult for children labeled learning disabled (e.g., Kraner, 1980; Smith, 1921). A related deficiency is an inability to mentally add multidigit combinations efficiently, including relatively simple facts involving 10 (e.g., 40 + 10 = ?) and multiples of 10 (e.g., 400 + 100 = ?) (Baroody, 1987a). Such children typically count on rather than efficiently recall sums for both single-digit problems (e.g., 9 + 5: "9; 10, 11, 12, 13, *14*") and multidigit problems (e.g., 40 + 10: 40; 41, 42, 43, 44, 45, 46, 47, 48, 49, *50*").

Such deficiencies are commonly attributed to insufficient practice (e.g., Pellegrino & Goldman, 1987; Torgesen & Young, 1983). This may well contribute to the problem, but it may not be the primary source of the difficulty for many. Number-fact deficiencies have also been attributed to a memory deficit (Ackerman et al., 1986; Bley & Thornton, 1981; Webster, 1979, 1980). Although it is unclear whether this is the primary cause in some cases, it may not be the underlying difficulty for many children labeled learning disabled.

The fundamental problem for many such children may be that they fail to learn effective strategies for memorizing consequential knowledge (Allardice & Ginsburg, 1983), and thus fail to develop a rich network of relationships (Baroody, 1985, 1987a; Myers & Thornton, 1977). Such children may not realize that they should look for patterns or relationships. For example, asked how he could help a first grader learn the addition combinations, Tommy, an 8-year-old labeled learning disabled (Baroody, 1989a), responded: "Yeah, just by telling them the answers. Make them study it." Ironically, he recommended a strategy that had not proved entirely effective for himself. His beliefs about teaching and learning the basic number combinations reflected his own tell–show–drill schooling.

Faced with the burden of memorizing many apparently isolated facts, children such as Tommy may feel overwhelmed with the chore and simply give up. For example, it may have been helpful in mastering the subtraction facts if Tommy had learned to relate them to known addition combinations (e.g., 9 − 4 = ?: What do I have to add to 4 to make 9?) (e.g., Baroody, Ginsburg, & Waxman, 1983; Siegler, 1987). The same holds true for multidigit mental arithmetic. For example, Tommy may have been able to master adding 10 to a decade if he were helped to connect this to his existing counting (decade-after) knowledge (e.g., 40 + 10 is the decade after 40: 50) or his existing N + 1 knowledge (e.g., 40 + 10 parallels 4 + 1 = 5).

WHAT ARE THE INSTRUCTIONAL IMPLICATIONS OF COGNITIVE PSYCHOLOGY?

An Ecological Approach

When a child has difficulty learning mathematics, educators must examine the nature of his or her mathematics program and gauge whether it is psychologically appropriate for the pupil. This is especially important for students with whom mathematical achievement is not consistent with ability. Educators frequently attribute learning difficulties solely or primarily to internal causes: characteristics of the child such as laziness, perceptual problems, or thinking disorders. Distractibility, confusion, poor memory for facts, inability to generalize, hyperactivity, and perseveration are often cited as characteristics of learning disabled children (e.g., Kosc, 1974; Lerner, 1971; Sears, 1986) and as organically based causes of learning difficulties (e.g., Homan, 1970; Strauss & Kephart, 1955).

In many cases, however, such behaviors may result from meaningless, uninteresting, or psychologically punishing instruction. "It seems that nothing is more likely to produce . . . inattentive behavior than work that the child perceives as being beyond his comprehension" (Allardice & Ginsburg, 1983, p. 341). When instruction does not make sense to children, it should not be surprising that they become muddled or forgetful, or fail to apply their knowledge. When instruction is not engaging or when it is painful (e.g., humiliating or frustrating), some children, quite understandably, rebel or engage in avoidance behaviors. When assigned work makes little or no sense or is personally irrelevant to students, it encourages thoughtless and hasty completion of assignments. Perseveration is further encouraged when worksheets typically focus on a single skill. Indeed, it makes some sense to figure out what is involved in the first few problems and then mindlessly use the same procedure to complete the rest of the page. In effect, such characteristics as poor memory, inattentiveness, and mechanical responding are often *symptoms* of learning difficulties rather than their causes. Clearly, however, such behaviors can contribute to and further complicate a learning difficulty (e.g., Kirk & Chalfant, 1984).

In many cases, the nature of instruction must be changed. Instruction has focused too long on memorizing arithmetic knowledge: on mastering facts rather than on understanding relationships; on *how* to perform algorithms rather than on *why* they work (e.g., Fitzmaurice-Hayes, 1985b). Unfortunately, remedial efforts for children classified as learning disabled (see, e.g., Blankenship, 1978, 1985) too frequently have the same narrow objectives and merely entail amplified efforts to foster absorption. More specifically, remediation often attempts to ensure memorization of facts and procedures through repeatedly reviewing unlearned information, profusely rewarding progress, and/or fostering overlearning via huge amounts of practice (Moyer & Moyer, 1985). Like the instruction that fostered learning difficulties in the first place, remedial strategies are frequently too abstract and fail to actively engage a child's thinking and interest (van Erp & Heshusius, 1986). Too often, then, a tell–show–drill approach to remediation does not work and may even make matters worse (Moyer & Moyer, 1985). Sometimes, efforts are made to make special adaptations or adjustments in techniques for fostering absorption. Although introducing special tricks or Band-Aids to help students master facts or procedures (e.g., mnemonics or "low-stress algorithms") may be helpful in the short term, they are not long-term solutions (Hendrickson, 1983).

Some General Instructional Guidelines

Educators, including those in the field of special education, should focus on preventing learning difficulties rather than simply curing them (Hendrickson, 1983). Instruction for *all* children should focus on fostering understanding, problem solving ability, and the propensity to use mathematical knowledge thoughtfully (Commission on Standards for School Mathematics, 1989). Until effective instructional techniques to achieve these aims have been developed and tested, developing special techniques of instruction for children classified as learning disabled should not be a priority (cf. Blankenship, 1988; Epstein & Cullinan, 1983; Scruggs & Mastropieri, 1986). Eight general guidelines for developing effective instruction are described below.

1. *Instruction should take into account a child's individual pattern of strengths and weaknesses.* In practice, the category of learning disabled includes children with diverse characteristics, difficulties, and etiologies (e.g., Blankenship, 1988; Cawley, 1984a, 1985a). Therefore, it is essential to treat each child as an individual and to focus on his or her particular strengths and weaknesses (e.g., Cawley, 1984b). Furthermore, because no one instructional technique will be effective with every individual, it is important to try various methods until an effective approach is found.

Indeed, research (e.g., Baroody, 1987b) suggests that there are important individual differences in informal mathematical knowledge, even among those just entering school (Baroody & Ginsburg, 1982). For example, children vary greatly in their ability to solve simple arithmetic problems, even with objects present (e.g., Carpenter & Moser, 1983; Ginsburg & Russell, 1981; Lindvall & Ibarra, 1979). Those with weak informal arithmetic skills will find it especially difficult to master formal skills such as the basic addition facts. With schooling, the range of individual differences in mathematical performance often becomes even more pronounced. Individual differences become especially apparent when number-fact training and place-value–related instruction is introduced. Weaknesses in basic formal skills and concepts will make it more difficult to understand and master more advanced work in mathematics, such as the addition of fractions and decimals. It is essential, then, to identify and remedy deficiencies in informal and basic formal knowledge quickly, before the child is entangled in a spiral of failure.

Special educators differ on how to best meet individual needs. Advocates of the basic-ability approach assume that learning disabled children have a deficiency in one or more general abilities that underlie learning, such as auditory, visual, tactual-kinesthetic, imagery, or language processing (Blankenship, 1984). Remediation can take the form of correcting the underlying processing deficit or gearing academic instruction to a child's processing strengths. The first approach (see, e.g., Bley & Thornton, 1981) identifies a general processing deficit as the source of an academic difficulty. For instance, a visual-memory disability might be identified as a cause of a numeral-reversing problem. Remediation initially focuses on visual-memory exercises. Only after general visual-memory skills are strengthened do remedial efforts focus on numeral writing. The second approach (see, e.g., Flinter, 1979; Mann & Suiter, 1974; Meyers & Burton, 1989) begins by identifying a child's processing strengths and weaknesses or learning style. Remedial efforts then compensate for deficient processes by utilizing a child's intact processes or preferred modality. For example, for a "visual learner" with an "auditory deficit," a teacher is supposed to minimize verbal instruction and use more demonstrations, pictures, and the like.

Unfortunately, little evidence supports either basic-ability approach (e.g., Cawley, 1985c; Gibson & Levin, 1975; Vellutino, Steger, Moyer, Harding, & Niles, 1977). Efforts to train general processes or match instruction to a preferred modality have not produced improvements in academic performance (e.g., Arter & Jenkins, 1979; Blankenship, 1984; Gibson & Levin, 1975). Moreover, an ability to process information may have more to do with a child's conceptual readiness than with learning style, and the learning style of a child may itself vary with a variety of factors including readiness. Furthermore, instead of narrowing the kind of representations presented a child, using a wide variety of representations—concrete, pictorial, verbal, and symbolic (Cawley, 1985a; Commission on Standards for School Mathematics, 1989; Dienes, 1960; Lesh, Landau, & Hamilton, 1980; van Erp & Heshusius, 1986)—may help to develop a deeper understanding of mathematical concepts.

"While it was assumed for many years that 'basic psychological processes' referred to such constructs as perception and perceptual–motor integration, it is now generally acknowledged that a disturbance in *cognitive* processes, such as thinking, conceptualizing, abstracting, reasoning, and evaluating, is an underlying cause of learning disabilities (Hall, 1980)" (Fleischner & O'Loughlin, 1985, p. 169). This more recent information processing approach focuses on deficits or delays in basic underlying abilities involved with acquiring, retrieving, or using information (see, e.g., Cherkes-Julkowski, 1985a; DeRuiter & Wansart, 1982; Swanson, 1982). For example, Case (1982) proposed that the amount of mental space (M-Space) or capacity (M-Capacity) to deal with a task increases with age. Although there is not unequivocal empirical support for the model, it is possible that delays in development of this processing capacity might interfere with learning school mathematics. Research needs to disentangle the effects of maturation and experiential (task-specific) factors, such as readiness for a task, previous exposure to a task, or previous practice of component skills. Indeed, research (e.g., Cermak, 1983; Siegel & Linder, 1984; Webster, 1979, 1980) is only beginning to expand our understanding of learning disabilities as an information-processing difficulty (Reid & Hresko, 1981). We as yet do not have the empirical data to delineate confidently the perceptual or cognitive attributes of children with learning disabilities (Cawley, 1985a).

Although key general processes may yet be identified (Cawley, 1984b), it now appears that a direct-skills approach is more useful; that is, a teacher should focus on what specific skills and concepts a child knows and does not know. Knowledge of specific strengths and weaknesses permits a teacher to more effectively (a) focus efforts on what needs attention, (b) gauge readiness for instruction (see Vygotsky, 1978), and (c) exploit strengths to remedy weaknesses. For example, by assessing specific families of combinations (relationships, rules, or patterns), a teacher might discover that a child has essentially mastered sums to 10 but not sums over 10, including the large doubles (6 + 6 to 9 + 9). Instruction can now concentrate on learning the easiest large sums: the large doubles. Mastery of the small doubles (1 + 1 to 5 + 5) indicates that the child is ready for this challenge. The teacher might use exercises designed to help the child see that sums of the large doubles are all even and a continuation of the count-by-two pattern of the small doubles (e.g., see Figure 14–2). Once mastered, the large addition doubles can be used to help master near doubles like 6 + 7.

2. *Instruction should foster children's informal mathematical knowledge.* Instruction must cultivate children's informal concepts to establish a firm foundation for formal instruction. In general, to foster the construction of new concepts, it is important to begin with relatively concrete and familiar experiences (e.g., Engelhardt, Ashlock, & Wiebe, 1984; Flinter, 1979; Ginsburg, 1989; van Erp & Heshusius, 1986). For example, instead of introducing an arithmetic operation such as addition at a symbolic level and requiring children to memorize facts quickly, operations should be introduced in terms of familiar counting experiences. Especially at the first, children should be encouraged to compute with their fingers, blocks, marks, and so forth, *not* discouraged from using informal methods.

Name _____   Date _____

9.21 Math Detective

James was given the following list of addition problems to do for homework. He knew some of the problems right away and wrote those answers in. The rest he had to figure out, and it seemed like an awful lot to do by counting. Can you help James out? Do these combinations form a pattern that James can use to think out the answer without counting out each sum? Discuss your ideas with your group and then finish the worksheet.

$0 + 0 =$ $\boxed{0}$

$1 + 1 =$ $\boxed{2}$

$2 + 2 =$ $\boxed{4}$

$3 + 3 =$ $\boxed{6}$

$4 + 4 =$ $\boxed{}$

$5 + 5 =$ $\boxed{10}$

$6 + 6 =$ $\boxed{}$

$7 + 7 =$ $\boxed{}$

$8 + 8 =$ $\boxed{}$

$9 + 9 =$ $\boxed{}$

Figure 14–2. Exercise that highlights the count-by-two pattern of the doubles' sums. From *Elementary Mathematics Activities: A Teacher's Guidebook* (p. 241) by A. J. Baroody and M. Hank, 1990, Boston: Allyn and Bacon. Copyright 1990 by Allyn and Bacon. Reprinted with permission.

Moreover, it is important to foster children's spontaneously invented strategies. This is a key sign that children are actively monitoring their performance and not merely responding in a mechanical fashion. Under favorable conditions, even children with severe learning difficulties can monitor their performance and invent more sophisticated computing strategies (Baroody, 1987a). Unfortunately, children classified as learning disabled often fail to transform existing strategies into more efficient procedures, which would reduce the demands placed on working memory and free their attention to deal with other, higher level tasks (e.g., Swanson & Rhine, 1985). In many cases, such problems may be traced to the nature and pace of instruction.

To foster informal notions and strategies, a teacher should encourage children to discuss and share their thoughts and methods. Invented procedures, for example, should be recognized and praised. In unstructured and structured settings, children should be given many opportunities to explore informal ideas and to use informal methods. For instance, even after formal arithmetic symbols are introduced, children should be given ample opportunity to compute arithmetic solutions in ways that are meaningful to them. Informal calculation can provide an important basis for discovering numerical relationships, such as the commutativity principle or the number-after rule for adding 1.

If informal concepts or strategy transformations do not occur spontaneously in a reasonable amount of time, a teacher should first evaluate whether (a) the instruction is meaningful, and (b) the child is ready for the instruction. Some children may need and benefit from more direct or explicit instruction. For example, many children classified as learning disabled fail to invent thinking strategies to reason out basic number facts (e.g., Allardice & Ginsburg, 1983; Baroody, 1987a; Myers & Thornton, 1977; Swanson & Rhine, 1985). Many, but not all (e.g., see Allardice & Ginsburg, 1983), apparently can effectively be taught such strategies (e.g., see Thornton, 1978; Thornton, Jones, & Toohey, 1983; Thornton & Toohey, 1985).

3. *Formal instruction should build on children's informal knowledge.* Understanding and intrinsic motivation are fostered by moderately novel instruction. Therefore, exploiting children's informal mathematics can make formal instruction more meaningful and interesting. Once children have sound informal knowledge, formal symbols and procedures can be introduced in terms of this familiar knowledge. For example, the symbolic fact $5 + 5 = 10$ can be related to the total number of fingers on both hands or the sum of 5 cents and 5 cents. Research (e.g., Baroody, 1987a; Ginsburg, 1989) suggests that even children considered to have severe learning difficulties have important informal knowledge upon which formal instruction can build.

A key role for teachers is to help children see the *connections* between their informal knowledge and formal symbols or procedures. Many times children fail to link concrete (or pictorial) models to formal representations. Thus, simply using manipulatives before written work is introduced may not help children to understand the formal mathematics. Through questions and discussions, a teacher should explicitly link concrete (or pictorial) and symbolic representations (e.g., Bell, Fuson, & Lesh, 1976; Resnick & Ford, 1981). For example, a teacher may use dice with 0 to 5 dots to help introduce addition informally. Then a teacher may need to relate formal expression such as 5 + 0 to it by asking children to show the problem with dot dice or reminding them "five plus zero" is like a dice roll of "five dots and no dots."

4. *It is important to develop skill efficiency.* Because school mathematics routinely builds on more basic skills, it is important that a child use basic skills accurately and automatically. Automatic subskills reduce the load on working memory and free attention to focus on more complex tasks (e.g., Hasselbring et al., 1987; Resnick & Ford, 1981). For example, learning the multidigit multiplication algorithm is easier if two component skills (recall of basic multiplication combinations and application of the written addition algorithm including renaming) are automatic (e.g., Baroody, 1987a; Goldman et al., 1988; Kaye, 1986).

Clearly, practice is important for developing efficiency with basic skills such as number-fact recall; however, it should be administered wisely and not at the expense of other important objectives, such as fostering thinking skills and interest in mathematics. It is essential that practice come after the development of understanding or the opportunity to learn relationships (e.g., Baroody, 1987a; Brownell, 1935; Goldman et al., 1988). Moreover, it can usually be done in an entertaining manner that promotes interests in learning. For instance, a wide variety of games can be used to provide practice for a range of skills including the basic number facts (e.g., Baroody, 1987a, 1989b).

5. *Instruction should focus on concepts and problem solving skill.* In addition to the mastery of basic skills, society increasingly expects and many jobs now require the attainment of comprehension and problem solving skills (Commission on Standards for School Mathematics, 1989; R. B. Davis, 1984; Glaser, 1981). Because conceptualizing and solving problems depends upon a well-connected knowledge, it is essential that children understand mathematics and develop a rich body of relational knowledge as well as factual knowledge. Unfortunately, many children, especially those classified as learning disabled, lack such knowledge (e.g., Baroody, 1987a; Kaliski, 1962). Moreover, even when they have adequate reading skills, children labeled learning disabled have difficulty solving all but the simplest arithmetic word problems (e.g., Blankenship & Lovitt, 1976; Englert, Culatta, & Horn, 1987; Fleischner & Garnett, 1983; Ginsburg & Russell, 1981; Russell & Ginsburg, 1984).

Nevertheless, some evidence (e.g., Baroody, 1987a; Lloyd, Saltzman, & Kauffman, 1981, cited in Cawley, 1984b) indicates that a meaningful approach can promote transfer of academic skills among children labeled learning disabled, belying the belief that such children must master all competencies by rote (Cawley, 1984b). Although more research needs to be done (e.g., Blankenship, 1984; Cawley, 1985a; Cawley, Fitzmaurice, Shaw, Kahn, & Bates, 1979), a few studies (e.g., see Fleischner & Garnett, 1983; Fleischner, Nuzum, & Marzola, 1987) suggest that learning disabled children can benefit from problem solving instruction. To ensure that all children achieve their potential (see Commission on Standards for School Mathematics, 1989), instruction for children labeled learning disabled should be oriented toward fostering understanding and problem solving (e.g., Cawley, 1984a, 1985a; Fitzmaurice-Hayes, 1984a, 1985b; Fleischner & O'Loughlin, 1985).

Instruction should focus on discovering and describing relationships and patterns (Commission on Standards for School Mathematics, 1989). Patterns and relationships provide the underlying structure for the logical organization of mathematical knowledge, and their recognition provides a basis for forming mathematical concepts, formulating hypotheses, and making predictions (Fitzmaurice-Hayes, 1985b). Mathematics affords numerous opportunities to observe, describe, and use patterns or relationships (e.g., Fitzmaurice-Hayes, 1985b). The basic number facts, for example, are an ideal topic for structured discovery learning, fostering analytic skills, and encouraging a propensity to look for and apply relationships and patterns (e.g., Baroody, 1987a). Indeed, basic number-fact instruction should concentrate on helping children to discover and describe how counting (number-after) knowledge can be used to answer $N + 1$ combinations, how knowledge of one fact can be used to answer commuted combinations, how knowledge of addition can be used to answer subtraction combinations, and so forth. Fact mastery should help children discover and learn combination patterns such as subtracting 0 leaves a number unchanged, subtracting a number from itself leaves 0, subtracting two adjacent numbers in the count sequence (e.g., $6 - 5$ or $8 - 7$) leaves 1 (the difference-of-one rule). Moreover, children can be encouraged to *extend* these arithmetic patterns to larger numbers. For example, to foster generalization of the difference-of-one rule, a teacher can pose the question, "What do you think the answer will be if we subtract 46 and 45?"

Problem solving should be an integral aspect of instruction from the beginning (e.g., Carpenter & Moser, 1984; Cawley, 1984a; Cawley et al., 1979). For example, simple arithmetic word problems should be used to introduce operations such as addition, not deferred until formal skills have been mastered (e.g., Carpenter, 1986). Children should be encouraged to model word problems using objects, fingers, blocks, or tallies. Later, formal representations can be related to word problems and children's informal procedures for solving them. In this way, word problems can help make formal representations—even atypical expressions such as $7 + ? = 10$—more concrete and understandable (e.g., Bebout, 1986).

Problems should be used to encourage thoughtful analysis, not merely as a means for practicing computation (e.g., Cawley et al., 1979). Toward this end, it is better to give students a few, interesting problems rather than many, uninteresting ones. To foster the habit of carefully analyzing problems, use nonroutine word problems (e.g., problems containing extraneous information and more than one operation) or mixed problems (e.g., some problems involving addition, some involving subtraction) (e.g., Englert et al., 1987). In brief, it is essential to develop an analytic and critical frame of mind or approach to problems.

Superficial tricks such as the keyword approach do not encourage thoughtful analyses and should be avoided. Although looking for a word that signals a particular operation (e.g., "Whenever you see 'left,' it means subtract") may work in some cases, a keyword approach can lead a child astray, particularly when confronted with nonroutine or real-world problems. For example, blindly using a left-means-subtract rule will not work with the following problem: "When Mrs. Jones's class went out for recess, the boys left five jackets and the girls left three. How many jackets were left?" (Kilpatrick, 1985).

With any topic, the focus should be on understanding and the thoughtful use of knowledge (e.g., Flinter, 1979). This can be fostered by asking children to justify their responses (e.g., see Lampert, 1986), asking pupils if there is another way a problem can be solved (e.g., Lankford, 1974), introducing new materials or new tasks that require knowledge transfer (e.g., Cawley, 1985b), pointing out contradictory results (e.g., Baroody, 1987a; Cherkes-Julkowski, 1985b), or presenting situations that create cognitive conflict (e.g., Hendrickson, 1983), such as the one illustrated in Figure 14–1. Using examples *and* nonexamples is especially important in helping children to construct an accurate concept (see Figure 14–3). It is important to connect different representations of a concept. For example, many students do not realize and need help seeing that fractions, ratios, proportions, probability, and division are all related (e.g., 1/3, 1:3, 1 for every 3, 1 in 3 chances, 1 ÷ 3). Asking children to create their own word problems for their peers can be an interesting activity that requires thoughtful application and further ensures meaningful learning.

6. *Instruction should foster strategic skills for acquiring and using knowledge.* Education should help students develop cognitive learning strategies, that is, learn how to learn. Without instruction, effective learners frequently develop an array of techniques for acquiring and storing information more efficiently (Scheid, 1989); that is, with experience, many children seem to infer techniques that make them more effective learners (A. L. Brown, Bransford, Ferrara, & Campione, 1983). The same is not true of many children with learning problems (Scheid, 1989). Indeed, children with learning disabilities are often characterized as passive learners, who do not feel they have control over their learning (e.g., Cherkes-Julkowski, 1985b; Ryan, Short, & Weed, 1986).

Given the central importance of metacognitive skills in learning new material, strategy transfer, and successful problem solving, it is important

A. Concept of equivalent parts using one-half as an example.

Circle examples of one-half. Cross out those figures that do not show one-half.

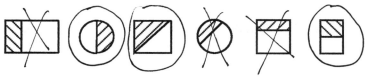

B. Concept of one-half.
Circle examples of one-half. Cross out those figures that do not show one-half.

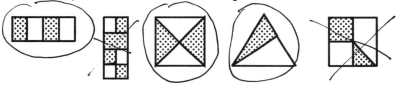

Figure 14–3.   Using examples and nonexamples to illustrate fraction concepts.

to encourage their development (Glaser, 1981; Pressley et al., 1989). Moreover, instruction should cultivate an inclination to monitor and reflect on their own thinking and performance (Commission on Standards for School Mathematics, 1989). Children classified as learning disabled are often described as deficient in metacognitive skills, such as applying an appropriate strategy to learn new material, recognizing what knowledge they have at their disposal to solve problems, or checking the reasonableness of answers (e.g., Allardice & Ginsburg, 1983; A. L. Brown, 1978; Cherkes-Julkowski, 1985b; Slife, Weiss, & Bell, 1985). Indeed, in many cases, the fundamental problem is not the lack of factual, procedural, or strategic knowledge per se, but the process of *selecting* appropriate knowledge and *using* it effectively (e.g., A. L. Brown, 1978).

A number of studies suggest that children classified as learning disabled can learn cognitive-learning or metacognitive strategies, and a few studies indicate that they can generalize this learning (Scheid, 1989). Effective strategy instruction involves explicitly describing and modeling strategies, informing students about the purpose and usefulness of strategies, practicing the strategy with a variety of materials and meaningful tasks, and providing opportunities for transfer (Scheid, 1989). For example, if a child mechanically responds "five" to the problem 5 + 3 on a mental-addition task, it might help to encourage the pupil to analyze the response in terms of his or her existing knowledge about addition. A teacher might ask to be given a problem such as 5 + 4, quickly respond with "five," and then think aloud: "Wait, does an answer of five make sense? What do you think?" After discussing the implausibility of the answer, the teacher might explicitly state, "It's a good idea to think about your answer to see if it makes sense." The child could then be encouraged to monitor and correct additional responses.

Children should also be taught heuristics or strategies for analyzing and solving problems, such as defining the knowns and the unknowns, determining what information is needed, or drawing a picture (e.g., Cawley et al., 1979; Cook & Slife, 1985; Fleischner et al., 1987; Flinter, 1979; Thornton & Bley, 1982). Most children need to learn such strategies to engage in independent problem solving. However, it is important to emphasize that heuristics should be used to understand the problem, so that the heuristic is not simply applied mechanically.

7. *Instruction should take into account affective factors.* Personality factors (e.g., interests, motivation, and feelings) have a tremendous impact on performance (e.g., DeRuiter & Wansart, 1982). Many children, particularly those labeled learning disabled, develop a fear of failure and employ protective mechanisms such as avoidance behaviors (e.g., procrastination or an unwillingness to try), which make learning even less likely (Allardice & Ginsburg, 1983; Holt, 1964). Such difficulties frequently stem from the way mathematics is taught—an overemphasis on responding quickly, knowing *the* correct answer, collecting rewards, avoiding punishment, and so forth (see, e.g., Tobias, 1978). For example, children frequently are expected to memorize number facts quickly and to respond efficiently on timed tests, and they often are accordingly rewarded (through praise, star charts, etc.) or punished (through some form of humiliation).

Instruction needs to encourage a curiosity about mathematics and a disposition to learn it, confident and flexible use of mathematical knowledge, and a willingness to persevere at difficult mathematical tasks (Commission on Standards for School Mathematics, 1989). These aims can be furthered by regularly posing problems to children (for which they are ready) and encouraging them to invent their own solutions. Whether solving problems or learning new material, children should be encouraged to use what they already know to understand a new task and deal with it. Moreover, relating instruction to children's personal lives can make mathematical instruction more meaningful and interesting. For example, by relating a fact such as $7 \times 4 = 28$ to a familiar experience such as scoring four touchdowns in a football game, a child is more inclined to view such information as personally useful and may more readily master the fact. It may even prompt some football enthusiasts to explore and master other related combinations on their own: What if a team scored five touchdowns? Six? Seven?

8. *Instruction should foster constructive beliefs.* Implicitly and explicitly, schooling too often fosters beliefs that prompt passivity (e.g., "No matter what

I do, math isn't going to make sense"), undercut intrinsic motivation (e.g., "Learning is simply a means of getting what is really important: rewards"), or otherwise hinder thoughtful learning and problem solving (e.g., "Since I can't think how to do the problem quickly, it can't be solved"). Destructive beliefs underlie debilitating fears (e.g., "Only smart people are lovable and smart people always respond quickly; if I don't always respond quickly, then I'm not lovable") and, in extreme cases, math anxiety (Baroody, 1987a). Furthermore, labeling children learning disabled too often validates and reinforces destructive beliefs.

Fostering constructive beliefs should be a basic aspect of any mathematical instruction. For example, instruction needs to cultivate an appreciation of mathematics as a tool for making sense of the world and a meaningful sense that mathematics can be learned (Commission on Standards for School Mathematics, 1989). Moreover, many children may need help recognizing that it is intelligent to ask questions when something is not understood; informal knowledge is relevant to understanding mathematics; mathematics is, at heart, thinking and problem solving; or a key aspect of mathematics is the search for patterns or relationships. Teachers must help children construct such beliefs by explicitly stating them and then confirming these statements by how they teach.

Particularly with children who have had a history of learning difficulties, it is essential to dispel beliefs that block their learning. Otherwise, a pupil may well resist and foredoom remedial efforts. In particular, it is important to point out the inaccuracy of perfectionistic beliefs and help children develop perspective. It is not necessary or even possible to be right all the time. Indeed, errors are a natural part of learning and something from which we can learn. It is also particularly important to encourage positive beliefs about children's informal mathematics. This can be done by presenting an accepting attitude toward children's informal mathematics, noting informal strengths and their value, and developing perspective about informal mathematics (e.g., finger counting played an important role in the development of our number system; finger counting strategies are common among children).

WHAT ARE COMMON LEARNING DIFFICULTIES AND SOME INSTRUCTIONAL RECOMMENDATIONS?

Mathematics programs for children classified as learning disabled should not be limited to computation, but should be comprehensive, including such topics as geometry, fractions, and decimals (e.g., Cawley, 1985a). Common difficulties and some suggestions for the meaningful teaching of these and other topics are described below.

Oral Counting

Difficulties.   To count to 100, a child needs to know (a) the single-digit sequence 1 to 9; (b) a 9 signals a transition (e.g., 19 signals the end of the teens and the beginning of a new series); (c) the transition terms for the new series (e.g., 20 follows 19); (d) the rules for generating the new series (e.g., the 20s and all subsequent series are generated by combining the transition term with, in turn, each term in the single-digit sequence; and (e) the exceptions to the rules (Baroody, 1989b). Among kindergartners entering school, the first component is typically intact and automatic. Many will not have the second component and, as a result, they overextend their counting rules (i.e., make rule-governed errors such as ". . . nineteen, ten-teen, eleven-teen . . ." or ". . . twenty-nine, twenty-ten, twenty-eleven . . ."). Some may recognize the need for a transition but have not learned the decade term to begin the next series (e.g., they count to 29 and stop cold because they do not know that 30 is next). Indeed, it is not until first grade that many children recognize that the decade series parallels the single-digit sequence (e.g., six + ty, seven + ty, eight + ty) and master the decade (transition) terms ("ten, twenty, thirty . . . ninety"). Some children may stop at 20 or 30 because they have not discovered the pattern of repeating the single-digit sequence with each successive decade (e.g., "twenty" is followed by "twenty + one, twenty + two . . . twenty + nine"). Finally, the exceptions often cause difficulties. For example, 15 is the most commonly missed teen (e.g., Fuson, 1988). Children often overgeneralize the teen pattern ("five-teen"), skip the difficult term, or substitute something for it (e.g., ". . . thirteen, fourteen, fourteen, sixteen . . .").

Instruction.   Stories and rhymes are entertaining ways of cultivating a familiarity with the count sequence to 10 or 12 (Baroody & Hank, 1990). Many children find that counting with objects is more interesting than oral counting alone (e.g., Fuson & Hall, 1983). Games that involve counting objects, then, can provide counting practice that is meaningful and interesting.

For the number sequence beyond 10 or 12, instruction should focus on encouraging children to discern *patterns*: 9 ends a series, the decade sequence parallels the 1 to 9 sequence, and new series, by and large, consist of the decade combined with the 1 to 9 sequence. A number chart in which the 0 and the decades begin each row can be used to highlight such patterns (Spitzer, 1954). Children can, for example, color all the squares in which a 9 appears in the 1s place and then discuss the location of these colored squares: They always appear at the end of series, right before the next decade.

Exceptions to the rules, such as 15, may require special attention. One interesting and useful way to work on patterns and exceptions is an error-detection activity in which children have to find someone else's mistakes (e.g., "Cookie Monster is just learning how to count and sometimes makes mistakes; tell him if he counts incorrectly"). Note that this activity can also be used with those children who need to master the rote sequence to 12.

Object Counting

Difficulties. To enumerate sets of objects correctly, a child must know (a) that each object in a set is labeled with one counting word (one-for-one tagging), and (b) how to keep track of counted and uncounted objects so that each object is tagged only once. Kindergartners typically have mastered the first component, but many have not devised effective keeping-track strategies (e.g., Fuson, 1988), which may result in their skipping an item or items or counting an item or items more than once, particularly when the set is large and/or haphazardly arranged.

Instruction. The nature of instruction depends upon a child's type of error. If a child is having difficultly with one-for-one tagging, emphasize the importance of accuracy and encourage the pupil to count slowly and carefully (e.g., Strauss & Lehtinen, 1947). If a child basically uses one-for-one tagging, teach the child keeping-track strategies such as putting counted items in a separate pile. Again, error-detection activities and a wide variety of games that involve using a die or counting spaces can be interesting vehicles for enumeration instruction and practice.

Numerical Relationships

Difficulties. By the time they enter kindergarten, children typically have learned to use their mental representation of the number sequence in some elaborate and flexible ways (e.g., Fuson, Richards, & Briars, 1982). Asked what comes after a number 1 to 9, most children no longer have to count from 1 to determine the successor but can automatically cite it. Citing the number before a given number is more difficult, because children have to operate on the number-sequence representation in the "opposite" direction. Moreover, the term "before" may be relatively unfamiliar to children and assimilated (interpreted) as "after" (see Donaldson & Balfour, 1968). Because it may serve as a prerequisite for counting backward, a deficiency in number-before knowledge can impede the development of this counting skill. Difficulty in counting backward can, in turn, hinder the development of counting down, an informal subtraction strategy (see "Informal Arithmetic" below).

Most children entering school can use their representation of the number sequence to determine which of two adjacent numbers indicates the larger quantity (e.g., "Which is more, seven or eight?"). From their experiences with small sets and numbers, they construct a magnitude-comparison rule: A number that comes after another in the number sequence is more than its predecessor (Schaeffer, Eggleston, & Scott, 1974). As children master the number-after relationships for more and more of the number sequence, they can apply the comparison rule to larger and larger numbers. However, children with relatively little informal mathematical experience or those with learning difficulties may not develop this number-comparison ability (see Baroody, 1988b, 1989c). Unfortunately, this important skill is often overlooked in the evaluation and the teaching of kindergartners. Gauging which term is "less" is even more difficult because, in part, children rarely hear or apply the term (e.g., Donaldson & Balfour, 1968; Kaliski, 1962; Weiner, 1974).

Instruction. For children who have not yet mastered the number-after skill, provide a "running start from one" (e.g., "When we count, we say, one, two, three, four, five, and then comes?"). Next, practice with abbreviated running starts (e.g., "Three, four, five, and then comes?"), and, finally, eliminate the running start altogether (e.g., "Five and then comes?"). For children who have not mastered the number-before skill, use a pictorial representation of the number sequence (e.g., a number list) to show that a number has two neighbors: one that comes before and one that comes after. The game of dominoes can be adapted to practice either number-after or number-before skills.

For children who cannot tell which of two adjacent numbers is more, highlight the idea that a number further along in the counting sequence is more. This can be done concretely by using interlocking blocks to build a staircase model of the number sequence and noting, for example, that the 6 step comes after and is bigger than the 5 step (Baroody, 1987a). In a similar vein, Stern (1949) suggested using a counting board into which proportionally sized blocks are fitted. Then use activities or games, such as Wynroth's (1986) Cards More Than (War using cards picturing object arrays), to foster reasoning out answers by counting or using number-after knowledge. Similar activities and games can be used to teach less than. Initially, it may be helpful to substitute "not so many as" for the relatively unfamiliar term "less" (Kaliski, 1962).

Reading and Writing Single-Digit Numerals

Difficulties. Reading numerals entails distinguishing among these symbols. This requires constructing a mental image of each numeral: knowing its component parts and how the parts fit together to form the whole (see Gibson & Levin, 1975). Children frequently confuse numerals that share similar characteristics (2 and 5, or 6 and 9) (Baroody, 1987a). For example, 6 and 9 are difficult to discriminate because both numerals have the same parts (a curve and a loop), share a part–whole relationship (the curve joins the loop), and differ only in where the curve joins the loop.

Writing difficulties, such as writing a numeral in reverse, are frequently cited as common characteristics of children labeled as learning disabled (see, e.g., Mann & Suiter, 1974; Sears, 1986). Numeral writing entails constructing a plan for translating this mental image into motor actions. A motor plan then consists of a set of rules that specify where to start, how to proceed, when to change direction, and when to stop (Goodnow & Levine, 1973). Without a correct or complete motor plan (a preplanned strategy), a child may, for example, repeatedly start in the wrong place and head in the wrong direction, and, as a result, reverse the numeral (Baroody, 1987a).

Instruction.   Instruction on numeral reading should focus on helping construct an accurate mental image of each numeral; that is, it should help children analyze a numeral into its component parts, recognize how these parts fit together, and, most importantly, see how these parts and part–whole relationships *distinguish* it from other numerals. Similar-looking numerals (e.g., 6 and 9) should be taught simultaneously to underscore their difference. Point out that orientation (the way something faces) is important to identifying numerals, unlike identifying many other objects (e.g., a person is the same person regardless of the angle of view).

Instruction on numeral writing should focus on helping children construct an accurate and a complete motor plan. After describing and demonstrating a motor plan, it may help some children to define the starting point with a dot. As children practice tracing, copying, or writing a numeral, talk them through the motor plan and, if necessary, have them verbally rehearse their plan of action (see Stern, 1949).

Informal Arithmetic

Difficulties.   Successfully solving a word problem depends upon a child's ability to represent it: determine what is given, what is unknown, and how to use the given to determine the unknown. Some kindergartners and most first graders can, without formal training, assimilate and model with objects the meaning of simple addition word problems, such as "Joey had five marbles and he won three more. How many marbles does he have altogether?" (Carpenter & Moser, 1983, 1984). A common strategy is concrete counting-all (e.g., for 5 + 3: solution is put up 5 fingers and then 3 fingers and count all the fingers). A child who does not understand the problem or who has not constructed an addition strategy may count each set of fingers separately, represent only one set, or act confused.

With experience, children spontaneously abandon concrete procedures and invent verbal-counting procedures for calculating sums (e.g., Groen & Resnick, 1977). Self-monitoring also leads children to invent increasingly sophisticated verbal strategies (Baroody, 1987a). For example, many children abandon a counting-from-one procedure (e.g., 3 + 6: "1, 2, 3; 4 [is one more], 5 [is two more], 6 [is three more], 7 [is four more], 8 [is five more], 9 [is six more]") in favor of a strategy that disregards addend order (e.g., 3 + 6: "1, 2, 3, 4, 5, 6: 7 [is one more], 8 [is two more], 9 [is three more]"), which in turn is replaced by a counting-on strategy (e.g., 3 + 6: "6; 7 [is one more], 8 [is two more], 9 [is three more]") (e.g., Baroody, 1987b; Baroody & Gannon, 1984). Although such development can be explained in terms of a cognitive drive for economy (see Baroody & Ginsburg, 1986), some researchers (e.g., Secada, Fuson, & Hall, 1983; Steffe, von Glasersfeld, Richards, & Cobb, 1983) have argued that the development of counting-on is indicative of a conceptual leap in understanding number. In any case, some children, particularly those without adequate informal experience, do not make such progress in a timely fashion or, perhaps, at all (e.g., Baroody, Berent, & Packman, 1982; Bley & Thornton, 1981; Lerner, 1971).

Subtraction is often problematic for children partly because of their informal strategies for determining differences (Baroody, 1984). A concrete take-away or a counting-down procedure models their informal concept of subtraction as take away. For 5 − 3, for example, a concrete take-away procedure entails representing the 5 with fingers, blocks, or tally marks and then folding down 3 fingers, removing 3 blocks, or crossing out 3 tallies, respectively. Counting down is a verbal procedure that for 5 − 3, say, entails beginning with 5 and counts 4 (1 taken away), 3 (2 taken away), 2 (3 taken away). Such a strategy can be used with ease as long as the numbers involved are small. If the minuend (starting amount) is large, as in 16 − 9, the child has to start counting backward in relatively unfamiliar territory. If the subtrahend (number taken away) is relatively large, the child is faced with a formidable keeping-track process. With 16 − 9, for example, the child has to keep track of counting back nine times. Many children then encounter difficulty with larger subtraction problems and grow to dislike subtraction, unless they invent or learn more efficient ways of determining differences in their informal (counting-down) strategy for solving for differences (Baroody, 1984).

Instruction.   Arithmetic operations such as addition and subtraction should be introduced with simple word problems (e.g., Carpenter, 1986) and other situations meaningful to children (e.g., dice games). If a child does not spontaneously use an informal strategy, try modeling a concrete counting-all (or take-away) procedure. Begin with problems involving the addition or subtraction of 1. Using games or other meaningful and interesting activities, give children ample opportunities to invent more sophisticated strategies. If a child does not invent a more advanced procedure after many months of practice, more direct measures may be needed. For example, to foster the invention of counting on, give a child 5 pennies and 3 pennies and ask how much 5 and 3 are altogether. Before the child counts the first set, cover the 5 pennies and ask how many are there. Then encourage the child to continue from 5 and count the set of 3 ("six, seven, eight"). For subtraction, encourage children to develop alternative strategies to concrete take away or counting down. For example, encourage them to relate subtraction problems to their knowledge of addition (e.g., "For 10 − 7, think: what must I add to 7 to make 10?") or to invent a counting-up strategy (e.g., 10 − 7: "7; 8 [differs by one], 9 [differs by two], 10 [differs by three]—three").

Part-Part-Whole Skills and Concepts

Difficulties.   The elaboration of a part-part–whole concept is one of the most important developments during the elementary years (Resnick, 1983). Children need to discover that a number such as 7 can be thought of in many different ways. They do not realize that a whole can be constructed from different parts (e.g., 7 can be composed from 6 and 1, 5 and 2, etc.). Because their addition knowledge is disconnected, many children do not see 6 + 1, 5 + 2, 4 + 3, and so forth, as related and would predict that they have different sums. Moreover, because of their incrementing view of addition, many children even view 5 + 2 and 2 + 5 as different problems (as 5 and 2 more, and 2 and 5 more, respectively) and assume that they have *different* sums (e.g., Baroody & Gannon, 1984). Therefore, children have to discover that different-looking problems, such as 6 + 1 = ? and 5 + 2 = ? can actually have the same sum and that order is irrelevant to the outcome of addition (e.g., both 5 + 2 and 2 + 5 have the same sum).

Children also need to see that a number such as 7 can, in turn, be a part of a larger whole (e.g., 7 + 2 = 9). An important discovery is that part-part–whole relationships connect addition and subtraction. For example, 9 − 7 = ? can be figured out by knowing what must be added to 7 to make 9 (e.g., Baroody et al., 1983). The answer can be determined by counting up (e.g., "7, 8 [is one more], 9 [is two more]: two") or by recalling that 7 plus 2 is 9. Children who have not made this connection may continue to compute differences by using a concrete take-away or counting-down strategy.

The elaboration of a part-part–whole concept may enable children to solve more difficult missing–second-part problems (A + ? = C), such as "Joey had 5 marbles and won some more. Now he has 8. How many did he win?" (e.g., Riley et al., 1983). Even more difficult for children are missing–first-part problems (? + B = C), such as "Joey had some marbles, and he won 3 more. Now he has 8. How many did he start with?" This type of problem may be especially difficult to assimilate because of children's informal incrementing concept.

Instruction.   The same-sum-as and commutativity concepts can be fostered by guided discovery learning with children of various ability levels (Baroody, 1987a). These regularities can be modeled concretely by "number sticks" constructed from interlocking blocks (see Figure 14–4).

Children should be capable of successfully solving missing-addend word problems with objects or pictorial expression (see Figure 14–5) by counting

numbered
interlocking
blocks ➡

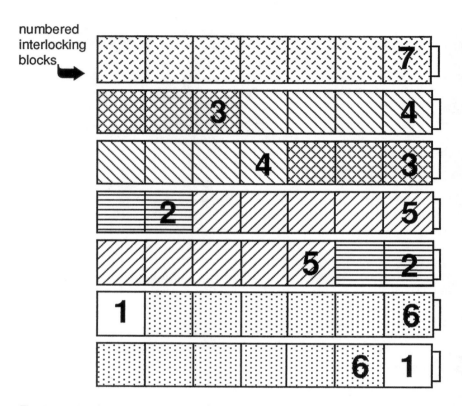

Figure 14-4. Concrete representations of same-sum-as and commutativity concepts. Adapted from *A Guide to Teaching Mathematics in the Primary Grades* (p. 215) by A. J. Baroody, 1989, Boston: Allyn and Bacon. Copyright 1989 by Allyn and Bacon. Used with permission.

before they are asked to solve formal expressions such as 7 + ? = 9. Note that for Problem 1 of Frame B, the child would be encouraged to read the problem as, "Three and what are the same number as four?" If necessary, have the child start by adding 1 dot in the empty box, then 2, and so forth until both sides of the equation have the same number of dots. This type of missing-addend training is a good preparation for relating subtraction to addition and solving subtraction expressions such as 9 − 7 = ? in terms of addition.

Base-10 Place-Value Skills and Concepts

Difficulties. Because of their counting-based concept of number, children interpret a multidigit numeral such as 16 as 16 units and, perhaps, as 15 and

Name_____   Date_____

8.28 Fill In

Directions: For each expression below, figure out how many dots
should go in the empty box. Draw in the dots or write a number to
show how many dots belong in the box.

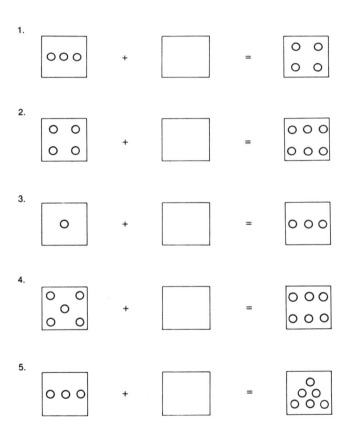

Figure 14–5. Semiconcrete representation of a missing-addend problem. From
Elementary Mathematics Activities: A Teacher's Guidebook (p. 183) by A. J. Baroody
and M. Hank, 1990, Boston: Allyn and Bacon. Copyright 1990 by Allyn and Bacon.
Reprinted with permission.

1 more. They do not think of multidigit numbers in terms of 1s, 10s, 100s, and so forth. The convention of using position to denote value (e.g., the 1 in 16 represents a 10 and the 6 represents six 1s) is foreign to their thinking and difficult to assimilate. Children need to learn that (a) items can be grouped, and grouped items are treated differently from ungrouped items; (b) the group size (10 in base 10) is used repeatedly to group smaller groups (e.g., ten 10s are grouped to make 100, ten 100s make 1,000, etc.); and (c) successively larger groups are arranged from left to right and the number in each group is denoted by a single-digit numeral (Hendrickson, 1983).

Because children typically begin to read and write multidigit numerals before they understand the underlying place-value rationale, they frequently make errors. For example, some kindergartners may fail to relate written numbers to their knowledge of the counting sequence and read the digits of a multidigit numeral separately (e.g., read 27 as "two, seven"). They may not recognize that the order of the digits is important and read, for instance, both 17 and 71 as "seventeen." Many first graders have not learned that 0 acts as a placeholder and read, for example, 103 as "thirteen" (the 0 means nothing) or "ten-three" (assimilate the unfamiliar symbolism in terms of the known numbers). Common writing errors include writing numerals as they are heard (e.g., writing "seventeen" as 71 because "seven" is heard first or writing "forty-two" as 402 because the decade term is heard) (e.g., Ginsburg, 1989; Luria, 1969).

Children learn relatively quickly to recognize the 1s, 10s, 100s, and 1,000s places. Unfortunately, this can be learned rotely and, hence, may represent a rather superficial understanding of place value (Resnick, 1982). Even noting place value (e.g., the 2 in 243 represents two 100s; the 4, four 10s; and the 3, three 1s) or representing a numeral with manipulatives such as Dienes blocks (e.g., setting out 2 flats, 4 longs, and 3 small cubes to show 243) can be learned by rote and not guarantee an understanding of place value (e.g., Ross, 1989a). Ross (e.g., 1989b) argued that some children who correctly label, for instance, 2 longs and 6 units as 26 are simply making a "face-value error": noting 2 of something, not necessarily 10s, and 6 of something else, not necessarily 1s. She found that when 26 objects were rearranged into 6 groups of 4 items each with 2 left over, such children thought the 2 in 26 represented the ungrouped items and the 6 represented the 6 groups!

To execute the (vertical) multidigit addition and subtraction algorithm, terms should be lined up from the right side so that the 1s-place digits form a single column, the 10s-place digits line up vertically, and so forth. Children who do not understand the underlying place-value rationale for the procedure may make one of several errors (e.g., Baroody, 1989b). Some may make no effort to align terms correctly. Some may be confused and align on the left at times and on the right at other times. Perhaps because they are influenced by left-to-right reading procedures, some may consistently align on the left. Alignment difficulties may appear when children have to solve problems presented in a horizontal line (Luria, 1969), copy problems from a text, record verbally presented problems, or set up word problems. Alignment-related errors are especially likely to occur when a child is required to write or copy problems vertically or do worksheet exercises in which the problems are printed vertically.

Children usually have little difficulty mastering a two-, three-, or even four-digit written addition procedure that does not involve renaming (carrying or borrowing). These step-by-step procedures are rather straightforward and entail minimal knowledge of place value. Although many children rotely master the two-digit renaming algorithms, often such learning does not transfer to problems involving three digits or more (Ginsburg, 1989). Because they do not comprehend the underlying rationale of such algorithms, many children fail to learn all (or any) of the steps (Engelhardt et al., 1984). Quite often, the results are systematic errors such as those listed in Table 14–1 (e.g., Ashlock, 1982; J. S. Brown & Burton, 1978).

Instruction.   Base-10 place-value instruction should use concrete experiences to build on children's informal conception of number. This instruction should begin by helping children with the idea of grouping, particularly by 10. Interlocking blocks may be an especially good manipulative for initial training, because a child can put 10 blocks together to form a "10-stick." Both base-10 and place-value concepts can be fostered by having children keep score of any game that goes beyond 10 points. It may be helpful to introduce an increasingly abstract scoring process illustrated in Figure 14–6. It may also be useful to introduce semiconcrete or pictorial representations before children graduate to symbolic work (see Figure 14–6).

Note that the scoring procedure in Figure 14–6 not only embodies base-10 ideas (e.g., ten 1s can be collected to form one group of 10) and place-value concepts (e.g., 0 indicates an empty column and serves as a placeholder), it provides a concrete basis for learning to read and write multidigit numerals. Moreover, it provides a concrete model for the written carrying procedure. (A model for the written borrowing procedure can be created by having players or teams begin with a preset score and eliminating a block for each point scored. The winner is the first to reach 0.) Fuson (e.g., 1986) suggested that a teacher should point out how *each* step in the written procedure parallels aspects of the concrete model.

Geometry

Difficulties.   The van Hiele model suggests that knowledge of geometry proceeds gradually through a series of stages (Crowley, 1987). At the intuitive level (Level 0), children learn to recognize geometric figures such as squares and circles by their physical appearance. At Level 1, children begin to learn

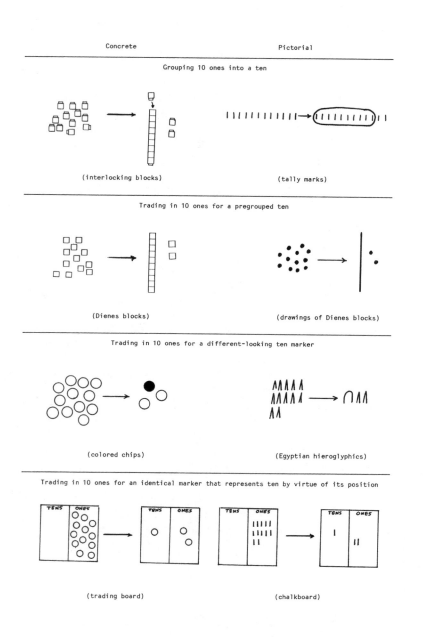

Figure 14-6. Increasingly abstract models of multidigit numbers using objects and pictures.

the characteristics or attributes of the forms in isolation. At Level 2, they establish *relationships* among the attributes of a form (e.g., in a quadrilateral, parallel opposite sides necessitates equal opposite angles) and among figures (e.g., a square is a rectangle because it has all the properties of this figure). At more advanced levels, a person can construct geometric proofs and see geometry in the abstract (e.g., compare different axiomatic systems).

Elementary instruction typically focuses on the first two levels (memorizing the names and the attributes of forms). As a result, children develop partial and even correct concepts. For example, many children fail to identify a square as a rectangle because instruction does not help them understand that a form is defined by its critical attributes (e.g., a square has all the critical attributes of a rectangle) and how the critical attributes are related (e.g., a square is a special class of rectangles, because it is a rectangle with an additional critical attribute: four equal sides).

Instruction.   Initial instruction in geometry should focus on exploring patterns. With interlocking blocks, colored paper, beads, sticks, pattern blocks, or geoboards, children might first copy patterns, then analyze patterns and deduce the next or a missing element, and, finally, create their own patterns (DeGuire, 1987). Such instruction can foster pattern-searching strategies, constructive beliefs (e.g., mathematics is at heart a search for patterns), and a propensity to look for patterns.

The focus of later instruction should be on defining the critical attributes of figures and the relationships among figures and attributes (e.g., Baroody, 1989b). In defining the critical attributes of a form (concept), it is important to use a variety of examples (e.g., both ▭ and □ to illustrate rectangles) and nonexamples (e.g., ◇ and △ are not rectangles). This will help children see relationships among figures (e.g., a square is a rectangle with a special feature: all sides equal). Using, for example, attribute blocks and small hoops, concrete models of Venn diagrams can be constructed that highlight relationships among figures (e.g., the hoop containing squares would be set inside that for rectangles to show that squares are a subclass of rectangles).

Fractions

Difficulties.   Children must understand that a fraction is a part of so many *equal-sized* parts. They must learn that the more parts a whole is divided into, the smaller each part. To solve fraction problems, it is essential to define or identify the whole (R. B. Davis, 1986). (Consider the problem, The Jones Boys Gang ordered 2 pizzas each divided into 8 pieces, but only ate 9 pieces. If the question is what fraction of the 2 pizzas were eaten, the whole is the total number of pieces, and the correct answer is $\frac{9}{16}$. If the question is what fraction of a pizza was eaten, the whole is 1 pizza and the correct answer is 1⅛.) To add and subtract fractions, children need to understand that the fractions must have a common denominator—a common unit.

Children frequently have an incomplete concept of fractions as a part of so many (depicted but not equivalent) parts and, hence, make the kind of error shown in Frame A of Figure 14–7. Because they are often introduced to fractions using only one type of representation (i.e., pie diagrams in which *a* whole is divided into parts), children commonly fail to differentiate between a fraction of one whole and a fraction of a set of things (R. B. Davis, 1986; Silver, 1983). As a result, they become confused when given fraction problems that involve more than one thing and make errors like that shown in Frame B. Another common error is choosing as the larger fraction the one with the larger denominator. For example, children conclude that ⅓ must be bigger than ½ because they incorrectly apply their magnitutde comparison rules for whole numbers (e.g., Post, Wachsmuth, Lesh, & Behr, 1985). Because they do not really understand the rationale underlying the procedure, children invent various procedures for performing arithmetic operations with fractions. A common systematic error is illustrated in Frame C.

Instruction.   Sharing activities are a useful way of introducing fractions in an informal manner. Such activities allow children to see concretely a whole divided *equally* into parts. Begin with sharing something between 2 children and labeling each share "one-half." Later introduce one-fourth, then one-third, and then other fraction terms. These activities should be done with multiple representations of both discrete quantities (sharing objects such as cookies, crayons, interlocking blocks, several pies) and continuous quantities (e.g., a candy bar, pattern blocks, Cuisenaire rods, a pie). To avoid confusing a fraction of a whole and a fraction of a collection, children should be taught the heuristic of defining the whole (see Figure 14–8). Fair-sharing activities can also be used to help children learn about the relative magnitude of fractions: the more people that share something, the smaller the shares. In time, formal symbols can be introduced and related to these concrete situations. Likewise, arithmetic operations should first be introduced with concrete materials. For example, Cuisenaire rods can be used to model finding a common basis (denominator) in which to add two unlike fractions (see, e.g., Van de Walle & Thompson, 1984).

Decimals

Difficulties.   Children must learn that decimals, like fractions, represent parts of wholes as well as wholes but have their own system of notation. As with fractions, they must learn that the more parts a whole is divided into, the

A.   Common fraction error due to not understanding that a fraction represents a part of so many
equivalent parts.

Write a fraction to show what part of the pie is shaded:___¹/₃___.

B.   Fraction error due to a failure to define the whole correctly.

For each diagram, color in 1/4.

C.   Fraction Bug: Add across top, add across the bottom.

7/8 + 7/8 = ¹⁴/₁₆

Figure 14-7. Some common errors with fractions.

smaller each part. They must also learn that the value of the digits is specified by their position.

Because they have no understanding of decimal representation, many
children assimilate the symbols in terms of existing knowledge and make such
errors as blindly using their rules for comparing the magnitude of whole numbers (e.g., consider .135 to be larger than .48 or .2) (e.g., Hiebert, 1987).
Children who do not appreciate the place-value notation system but at least
understand that more subdivisions imply smaller parts choose the decimal
with the fewest digits (e.g., consider .2 to be larger than .367 or .48) (Resnick et al., 1989). The systematic error of overlooking the decimal point when
operating on decimals (e.g., 5 + .2 = .7) is also the result of overlooking

1. Zeta Omega Omega fraternity took a bus trip to the zoo to visit some of its new pledges. They piled into two buses, filling 22 of the 24 seats on each bus. Write what fraction of the seats was filled.

2. Zeta Omega Omega ordered 6 pizzas from Putrid Pizzas for their Pledge Banquet. The pizzas were each divided into 6 pieces. Having somewhat more sense than the fraternity brothers, the pledges ate only 7 pieces. Write what fraction of a pizza was eaten.

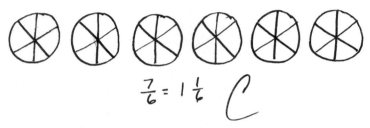

Figure 14–8. Fraction problems that entail defining the whole.

the place value of the digits and is encouraging teaching practice of asking students to add same-sized decimals such as .5 + .2 (Hiebert, 1987).

Instruction. Dienes blocks can be a particularly useful concrete model for introducing decimals and arithmetic operations with decimals (Hiebert, 1987). By using cubes to represent 1s, flats to represent 10ths, longs to represent 100ths, and units to represent 1,000ths, and relating these concrete models to written representations of decimals, children can learn to write and compare decimals in a meaningful fashion. Such an approach also fosters an understanding of the place value of each digit. Likewise, by modeling addition and subtraction with Dienes blocks first, children should have a firmer basis for operating on decimal symbols.

THE CASE OF MARK

I conclude the chapter with the case of Mark (Baroody, 1986, 1987a), because it illustrates and combines a number of important points. I agreed to see the 12-year-old because his mother seemed desperate. Convinced that there was something wrong with his brain because he was learning disabled, she wanted him examined to see if there was anything that could be done for him.

Shy about entering my office, Mark's first words revealed his fear: "So you're going to find out how dumb I am!" I explained that the purpose of the meeting was to find out what he did know about math and what he did not know so that his parents and teachers would be in a better position to help him learn. To help him feel more comfortable and to evaluate basic number fact and arithmetic skills, we then played several math games. Mark was perceptive: "These games—they're really tests, aren't they?" I explained the rationale for each test, pointed out that clearly he had learned much math already, and noted that doing math and having fun are not mutually exclusive. Satisfied, Mark began to relax and open up.

Mark outlined his math program and difficulties. The boy noted with despair that he could not remember the formulas for computing area. Further questioning revealed that he did not understand the concept of area. To see if he was capable of learning this aspect of formal mathematics, the topic was introduced in a way that built upon his informal knowledge. I gave Mark a 4 × 3 inch cardboard rectangle, helped him mark off 1-inch lengths on the sides, and connected the marks to divide the rectangle into 1-inch squares. After Mark measured how big a square was (1 inch on each side or "1 square inch"), I asked him to figure out how many square inches the 4 × 3 figure had. Mark counted the squares and found 12. This process was repeated a number of times with rectangles of different dimensions. Asked if he noticed anything about how the dimensions of the sides and the area might be related, he thought for a while. Then suddenly he exclaimed with excitement, "You just have to multiply the numbers!" I summarized the discovery: "You multiply the length and the width." (See Steps 1–4, Figure 14-9.)

Mark was then shown a cardboard parallelogram with a base of 4 inches and a height of 3 inches. Mark's enthusiasm for determining areas evaporated immediately. I empathized, "It looks impossible, doesn't it? But let's try looking at the problem in a more familiar way." I then cut off one of the protruding ends, placed it on the other end, and created a rectangle (see Step 5, Figure 14-9). Mark's response was immediate: "Oh, it's just base times height—12!" When topics such as area of base systems were introduced in a meaningful manner (i.e., using an informal approach and building on previous knowledge), Mark appeared to be an alert and quick learner (e.g., see Baroody, 1986).

The case of Mark is typical of altogether too many children labeled learning disabled (see Baroody, 1987a; Ginsburg, 1989). The label, in effect, blames learning difficulties on the child: an inability to absorb information and keep apace with classmates is due to a mental defect (Allardice & Ginsburg, 1983; Coles, 1978). In Mark's case, however, learning problems did not stem from a learning disability or a brain dysfunction, but from psychologically inappropriate (meaningless and uninteresting) instruction. His instruction did not encourage searching for patterns or relationships, reflecting or thinking about

Step 1:   Rectangle marked off in units of 1-square inch.

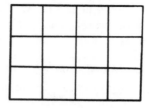

Step 2:   Total number of 1"-squares determined (by counting): 12.

Step 3:   Discovery of Area = Length x Width encouraged by the suggestion to find a relationship
           between the informally computed area and the dimensions of the sides.

Step 4:   Discovery formalized as a formula: A = L x W.

Step 5:   The area of a parallelogram is reformulated in terms of a familiar problem.

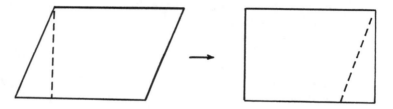

Step 6:   Discovery of the connection between the area of a rectangle and parallelogram,
           formalized as the formula A = L x W.

Step 7:   Repeat the process with different units (e.g., square centimeters) and different
           forms (e.g., squares and half a square or triangle).

Figure 14-9. Meaningful instruction regarding the area of a parallelogram. Reprinted by permission of the publisher from A. J. Baroody, *Children's Mathematical Thinking: A Developmental Framework for Preschool, Primary, and Special Education Teachers.* (New York: Teachers College Press, copyright 1987 by Teachers College, Columbia University. All rights reserved). Figure 5.1 on page 67.

problems, developing strategies for solving problems, or actively applying existing knowledge. It did encourage rote memorization and passivity. It did foster beliefs that undermined his desire and capacity to learn. He believed that school mathematics was merely a basket of facts that all "normal" children memorize quickly. He believed that mathematics had little to do with his own experience and was something he could not possibly understand. Unlike some of his more successful classmates, Mark was not inclined to memorize by rote material that he did not understand or that he did not see as useful. Like many children, he blamed his failure on himself: "I can't do math because I'm stupid." Mark had given up on learning school mathematics, which was less punishing—in the short term.

Accepting Mark's informal strengths and building on them to teach formal mathematics allowed Mark to feel competent and to understand mathematics. He began to enjoy searching for patterns and solving problems. He began to risk asking questions and making mistakes. Perhaps as important to its success, the intervention provided Mark perspective by debunking his destructive beliefs and fostering constructive beliefs. With this child and many children labeled learning disabled, effective remediation primarily depends on designing psychologically appropriate instruction. Indeed, a developmental approach in the first place would probably have eliminated the need for remedial instruction.

REFERENCES

Ackerman, P. T., Anhalt, J. M., & Dykman, R. A. (1986). Arithmetic automatization failure in children with attention and reading disorders: Association and sequela. *Journal of Learning Disabilities, 19,* 222–232.

Algozzine, B., & Ysseldyke, J. E. (1986). The future of the LD field: Screening and diagnosis. *Journal of Learning Disabilities, 19,* 394–398.

Allardice, B. S., & Ginsburg, H. P. (1983). Children's learning problems in mathematics. In H. P. Ginsburg (Ed.), *The development of mathematical thinking* (pp. 319–349). New York: Academic Press.

Anderson, J. R. (1980). *Cognitive psychology and its implications.* San Francisco: W. H. Freeman.

Anderson, R. C. (1984). Some reflections on the acquisition of knowledge. *Educational Researcher, 13*(9), 5–10.

Arter, J. A., & Jenkins, J. R. (1979). Differential diagnosis—prescriptive teaching: A critical appraisal. *Review of Educational Research, 49,* 517–555.

Ashlock, R. B. (1982). *Error patterns in computation.* Columbus, OH: Merrill.

Baker, L., & Brown, A. L. (1984). Cognitive monitoring in reading. In J. Flood (Ed.), *Understanding reading comprehension* (pp. 21–44). Newark, DE: International Reading Association.

Baroody, A. J. (1983). The development of children's informal addition. In J. C. Bergeron & N. Herscovics (Eds.), *Proceedings of the Fifth Annual Meeting of the North American Chapter of the International Group for the Psychology of Mathematics Education* (Vol. 1, pp. 222–229). Montreal: University of Montreal.

Baroody, A. J. (1984). Children's difficulties in subtraction: Some causes and questions. *Journal for Research in Mathematics Education, 15,* 203–213.

Baroody, A. J. (1985). Mastery of basic number combinations: Internalization of relationships or facts? *Journal for Research in Mathematics Education, 16,* 83–98.

Baroody, A. J. (1986). The value of informal approaches to mathematics instruction and remediation. *Arithmetic Teacher, 33*(5), 14–18.

Baroody, A. J. (1987a). *Children's mathematical thinking: A developmental framework for preschool, primary, and special education teachers.* New York: Teachers College Press.

Baroody, A. J. (1987b). The development of counting strategies for single-digit addition. *Journal for Research in Mathematics Education, 18,* 141–157.

Baroody, A. J. (1988a). Mental addition development of children classified as mentally handicapped. *Educational Studies in Mathematics, 19,* 369–388.

Baroody, A. J. (1988b). Number-comparison learning by children classified as mentally handicapped. *American Journal of Mental Deficiency, 92,* 461–471.

Baroody, A. J. (1988c). A schema model of mental-arithmetic development. In M. J. Behr, C. B. Lacampagne, & M. M. Wheeler (Eds.), *Proceedings of the Tenth Annual Meeting of the North American Chapter of the International Group for the Psychology of Mathematics Education* (pp. 36–43). De Kalb, IL: Northern Illinois University.

Baroody, A. J. (1989a). *The case of Tommy: A child labeled learning disabled.* Unpublished manuscript. University of Illinois at Urbana-Champaign.

Baroody, A. J. (1989b). *A guide to teaching mathematics in the primary grades.* Boston: Allyn and Bacon.

Baroody, A. J. (1989c). Kindergartners' mental addition with single-digit combinations. *Journal for Research in Mathematics Education, 20,* 159–172.

Baroody, A. J., Berent, R., & Packman, D. (1982). The use of mathematical structure by inner city children. *Focus on Learning Problems in Mathematics, 4*(2), 5–13.

Baroody, A. J., & Gannon, K. E. (1984). The development of the commutativity principle and economical addition strategies. *Cognition and Instruction, 1,* 321–329.

Baroody, A. J., & Ginsburg, H. P. (1982). Preschoolers' informal mathematical skills: Research and diagnosis. *American Journal of Diseases of Children, 136,* 195–197.

Baroody, A. J., & Ginsburg, H. P. (1986). The relationship between initial meaningful and mechanical knowledge of arithmetic. In J. Hiebert (Ed.), *Conceptual and procedural knowledge: The case of mathematics* (pp. 75–112). Hillsdale, NJ: Erlbaum.

Baroody, A. J., Ginsburg, H. P., & Waxman, B. (1983). Children's use of mathematical structure. *Journal for Research in Mathematics Education, 14,* 156–168.

Baroody, A. J., & Hank, M. (1990). *Elementary mathematics activities: Teachers' guidebook.* Boston: Allyn and Bacon.

Bebout, H. C. (1986, April). *Children's symbolic representation of addition and subtraction verbal problems.* Paper presented at the annual meeting of the American Education Research Association, San Francisco.

Bell, M. S., Fuson, K. C., & Lesh, R. A. (1976). *Algebraic and arithmetic structures: A concrete approach for elementary school teachers.* New York: Free Press.

Blankenship, C. S. (1978). Remediating systematic inversion errors in subtraction through the use of demonstration and feedback. *Learning Disability Quarterly, 1,* 12–22.

Blankenship, C. S. (1984). Curriculum and instruction: An examination of models in special and regular education. In J. F. Cawley (Ed.), *Developmental teaching of mathematics for the learning disabled* (pp. 29–53). Rockville, MD: Aspen.

Blankenship, C. S. (1985). A behavioral view of mathematical learning problems. In J. F. Cawley (Ed.), *Cognitive strategies and mathematics for the learning disabled* (pp. 49–74). Rockville, MD: Aspen.

Blankenship, C. S. (1988, October). *Learning disabilities: Toward the year*

2000. Paper presented at the Bicentennial Conference of the Australian Association of Special Education, Sydney, Australia.

Blankenship, C. S., & Lovitt, T. C. (1976). Story problems: Merely confusing or downright befuddling? *Journal of Research in Mathematics Education, 7,* 290–298.

Bley, N. S., & Thornton, C. A. (1981). *Teaching mathematics to the learning disabled.* Rockville, MD: Aspen.

Brown, A. L. (1978). Knowing when, where, and how to remember: A problem of metacognition. In R. Glaser (Ed.), *Advances in instructional psychology* (pp. 77–163). Hillsdale, NJ: Erlbaum.

Brown, A. L., Bransford, J., Ferrara, R., & Campione, J. (1983). Learning, remembering, and understanding. In J. Flavell & E. Markman (Eds.), *Handbook of child psychology: Vol. 3. Cognitive Development* (pp. 77–166). New York: Wiley.

Brown, J. S., & Burton, R. R. (1978). Diagnostic models for procedural bugs in basic mathematical skills. *Cognitive Science, 2,* 155–192.

Brownell, W. A. (1935). Psychological considerations in the learning and teaching of arithmetic. In *The teaching of arithmetic* (10th Yearbook of the National Council of Teachers of Mathematics, pp. 1–31). New York: Bureau of Publications, Teachers College, Columbia University.

Buswell, G. T., & Judd, C. H. (1925). Summary of educational investigations relating to arithmetic. *Supplementary Educational Monographs,* No. 27. Chicago: University of Chicago Press.

Carpenter, T. P. (1986). Conceptual knowledge as a foundation for procedural knowledge: Implications from research on the initial learning of arithmetic. In J. Hiebert (Ed.), *Conceptual and procedural knowledge: The case of mathematics* (pp. 113–132). Hillsdale, NJ: Erlbaum.

Carpenter, T. P., Mathews, W., Lindquist, M. M., & Silver, E. A. (1984). Achievement in mathematics: Results from the National Assessment. *Elementary School Journal, 84,* 485–495.

Carpenter, T. P., & Moser, M. M. (1983). The acquisition of addition and subtraction concepts. In R. Lesh & M. Landau (Eds.), *Acquisition of mathematical concepts and processes* (pp. 7–44). New York: Academic Press.

Carpenter, T. P., & Moser, M. M. (1984). The acquisition of addition and subtraction concepts in grades one through three. *Journal for Research in Mathematics Education, 15,* 179–202.

Case, R. (1982). General developmental influences on the acquisition of elementary concepts and algorithms in arithmetic. In T. Carpenter, J. Moser, & T. Romberg (Eds.), *Addition and subtraction: A cognitive perspective* (pp. 156–170). Hillsdale, NJ: Erlbaum.

Cawley, J. F. (1984a). An integrative approach to needs of learning disabled children: Expanded use of mathematics. In J. F. Cawley (Ed.), *Developmental teaching of mathematics for the learning disabled* (pp. 55–80). Rockville, MD: Aspen.

Cawley, J. F. (1984b). Learning disabilities: Issues and alternatives. In J. F. Cawley (Ed.), *Developmental teaching of mathematics for the learning disabled* (pp. 1–28). Rockville, MD: Aspen.

Cawley, J. F. (1985a). Cognition and the learning disabled. In J. F. Cawley (Ed.), *Cognitive strategies and mathematics for the learning disabled* (pp. 1–32). Rockville, MD: Aspen.

Cawley, J. F. (1985b). Learning disability and mathematics appraisal. In J. F. Cawley (Ed.), *Practical mathematics:*

Appraisal of the learning disabled (pp. 1–40). Rockville, MD: Aspen.

Cawley, J. F. (1985c). Nonmathematics appraisal. In J. F. Cawley (Ed.), *Practical mathematics: Appraisal of the learning disabled* (pp. 147–175). Rockville, MD: Aspen.

Cawley, J. F., Fitzmaurice, A. M., Shaw, R. A., Kahn, H., & Bates, H., III (1979). Math word problems: Suggestions for LD students. *Learning Disability Quarterly, 2*(2), 25–41.

Cermak, L. S. (1983). Information processing deficits in children with learning disabilities. *Journal of Learning Disabilities, 16,* 599–605.

Cherkes-Julkowski, M. (1985a). Information-processing: A cognitive view. In J. F. Cawley (Ed.), *Cognitive strategies and mathematics for the learning disabled* (pp. 117–138). Rockville, MD: Aspen.

Cherkes-Julkowski, M. (1985b). Metacognitive considerations in mathematics instruction for the learning disabled. In J. F. Cawley (Ed.), *Cognitive strategies and mathematics for the learning disabled* (pp. 99–116). Rockville, MD: Aspen.

Cobb, P. (1985a). A reaction to three early number papers. *Journal for Research in Mathematics Education, 16,* 141–145.

Cobb, P. (1985b). Two children's anticipations, beliefs, and motivations. *Educational Studies in Mathematics, 16,* 111–126.

Coles, G. S. (1978). The learning disability test battery: Empirical and social issues. *Harvard Educational Review, 48,* 313–340.

Commission on Standards for School Mathematics. (1989). *Curriculum and evaluation standards for school mathematics.* Reston, VA: National Council of Teachers of Mathematics.

Cook, R. E., & Slife, B. D. (1985). Developing problem-solving skills. *Academic Therapy, 21,* 5–13.

Court, S. R. A. (1920). Numbers, time, and space in the first five years of a child's life. *Pedagogical Seminary, 27,* 71–89.

Cox, L. S. (1975). Systematic errors in the four vertical algorithms in normal and handicapped populations. *Journal for Research in Mathematics Education, 6,* 202–220.

Crowley, M. L. (1987). The van Hiele model of the development of geometric thought. In M. M. Lindquist & A. P. Shulte (Eds.), *Learning and teaching geometry, K–12* (pp. 1–16). Reston, VA: National Council of Teachers of Mathematics.

Davis, P. J., & Hersh, R. (1981). *The mathematical experience.* Boston: Houghton-Mifflin.

Davis, R. B. (1983). Complex mathematical cognition. In H. P. Ginsburg (Ed.), *The development of mathematical thinking* (pp. 253–290). New York: Academic Press.

Davis, R. B. (1984). *Learning mathematics: The cognitive science approach to mathematics education.* Norwood, NJ: Ablex.

Davis, R. B. (1986). *The learning of mathematics by elementary school children.* Unpublished manuscript, University of Illinois.

DeGuire, L. J. (1987). Geometry: An avenue for teaching problem solving in grades K–9. In M. M. Lindquist & A. P. Shulte (Eds.), *Learning and teaching geometry, K–12* (pp. 59–68). Reston, VA: National Council of Teachers of Mathematics.

Deloche, G., & Seron, X. (Eds.). (1987). *Mathematical disabilities: A cognitive neuropsychological perspective.* Hillsdale, NJ: Erlbaum.

DeRuiter, J. A., & Wansart, W. L. (1982). *Psychology of learning disabilities.* Rockville, MD: Aspen.

Dienes, Z. P. (1960). *Building up mathematics.* New York: Hutchinson.

Donaldson, M., & Balfour, G. (1968). Less is more. *British Journal of Psychology, 59,* 461–471.

Engelhardt, J. M., Ashlock, R. B., & Wiebe, J. H. (1984). *Helping children understand and use numerals.* Boston: Allyn and Bacon.

Englert, C. S., Culatta, B. E., & Horn, D. G. (1987). Influence of irrelevant information in addition word problems on problem solving. *Learning Disabilities Quarterly, 10*(1), 29–36.

Epstein, M. H., & Cullinan, D. (1983). Academic performance of behaviorally disordered and learning-disabled pupils. *Journal of Special Education, 17,* 303–307.

Farnham-Diggory, S. (1978). *Learning disabilities: A psychological perspective.* Cambridge, MA: Harvard University Press.

Fitzmaurice-Hayes, A. M. (1984a). Curriculum and instructional activities Grade 2 through Grade 4. In J. F. Cawley (Ed.), *Developmental teaching of mathematics for the learning disabled* (pp. 115–144). Rockville, MD: Aspen.

Fitzmaurice-Hayes, A. M. (1984b). Curriculum and instructional activities Pre-K through Grade 2. In J. F. Cawley (Ed.), *Developmental teaching of mathematics for the learning disabled* (pp. 95–114). Rockville, MD: Aspen.

Fitzmaurice-Hayes, A. M. (1985a). Assessment of the severely impaired mathematics student. In J. F. Cawley (Ed.), *Practical mathematics: Appraisal of the learning disabled* (pp. 249–277). Rockville, MD: Aspen.

Fitzmaurice-Hayes, A. M. (1985b). Classroom implications. In J. F. Cawley (Ed.), *Cognitive strategies and mathematics for the learning disabled* (pp. 209–236). Rockville, MD: Aspen.

Flavell, J. H. (1976). Metacognitive aspects of problem solving. In L. B. Resnick (Ed.), *The nature of intelligence.* Hillsdale, NJ: Erlbaum.

Flavell, J. H., & Wellman, H. M. (1977). Metamemory. In R. V. Kail & J. W. Hagen (Eds.), *Perspectives on the development of memory and cognition* (pp. 3–33). Hillsdale, NJ: Erlbaum.

Fleischner, J. E., & Garnett, K. (1983). Arithmetic difficulties among learning disabled children: Background and current directions [Special issue]. *Learning Disabilities, 2*(9).

Fleischner, J. E., Garnett, K., & Shepard, M. (1982). Proficiency in arithmetic basic fact computation by learning disabled and nondisabled children. *Focus on Learning Problems in Mathematics, 4*(2), 47–55.

Fleischner, J. E., Nuzum, M. B., & Marzola, E. S. (1987). Devising an instructional program to teach arithmetic problem-solving skills to students with learning disabilities. *Journal of Learning Disabilities, 20,* 214–217.

Fleischner, J. E., & O'Loughlin, M. (1985). Solving story problems: Implications of research for teaching the learning disabled. In J. F. Cawley (Ed.), *Cognitive strategies and mathematics for the learning disabled* (pp. 163–181). Rockville, MD: Aspen.

Flinter, P. (1979). Educational implications of dyscalculia. *Arithmetic Teacher, 26*(7), 42–46.

Fuson, K. C. (1986). Roles of representation and verbalization in the teaching of multi-digit addition and subtraction. *European Journal of Psychology of Education, 1*(2), 35–36.

Fuson, K. C. (1988). *Children's counting and concepts of number.* New York: Springer-Verlag.

Fuson, K. C., & Hall, J. W. (1983). The acquisition of early number word meanings: A conceptual analysis and review. In H. P. Ginsburg (Ed.), *The development of mathematical thinking* (pp. 49–107). New York: Academic Press.

Fuson, K. C., Richards, J., & Briars, D. J. (1982). The acquisition and elaboration of the number word sequence. In C. Brainerd (Ed.), *Children's logical and mathematical cognition: Progress in cognitive development* (pp. 33–92). New York: Springer-Verlag.

Gelman, R. (1972). The nature and development of early number concepts. In H. W. Reese (Ed.), *Advances in child development and behavior* (Vol. 7, pp. 115–167). New York: Academic Press.

Gelman, R., & Gallistel, C. (1978). *Young children's understanding of number.* Cambridge: Harvard University Press.

Gibson, E. J., & Levin, H. (1975). *The psychology of reading.* Cambridge: MIT Press.

Ginsburg, H. P. (1989). *Children's arithmetic* (2nd ed.). Austin, TX: PRO-ED.

Ginsburg, H., & Opper, S. (1988). *Piaget's theory of intellectual development: An introduction* (3rd ed.). Englewood Cliffs, NJ: Prentice-Hall.

Ginsburg, H. P., Posner, J. K., & Russell, R. L. (1981). The development of mental addition as a function of schooling. *Journal of Cross-Cultural Psychology, 12,* 163–178.

Ginsburg, H. P., & Russell, R. L. (1981). Social class and racial influences on early mathematical thinking. *Monographs of the Society for Research in Child Development, 46,* 16 (Serial No. 193).

Glaser, R. (1981). The future of testing: A research agenda for cognitive psychology and psychometrics. *American Psychologist, 36,* 923–936.

Goldman, S. R., Pellegrino, J. W., & Mertz, D. L. (1988). Extended practice of basic addition facts: Strategy changes in learning disabled students. *Cognition and Instruction, 5,* 223–265.

Goodnow, J., & Levine, R. A. (1973). "The grammar of action": Sequence and syntax in children's copying. *Cognitive Psychology, 4,* 82–98.

Greeno, J. G. (1978). Understanding and procedural knowledge in mathematics education. *Educational Psychologist, 12,* 262–283.

Groen, G. J., & Resnick, L. B. (1977). Can preschool children invent addition algorithms? *Journal of Educational Psychology, 69,* 645–652.

Hall, R. J. (1980). Cognitive behavior modification and information-processing skill: Of exceptional children. *Exceptional Education Quarterly, 1,* 9–15.

Hasselbring, T. S., Goin, L. I., & Bransford, J. D. (1987). Effective mathematics instruction: Developing automaticity. *Teaching Exceptional Children, 19*(3), 30–33.

Hendrickson, A. D. (1983). Prevention or cure? Another look at mathematics learning problems. In D. Carnine, D. Elkind, A. D. Hendrickson, D. Meichenbaum, R. L. Sieben, & F. Smith (Eds.), *Interdisciplinary voices in learning disabilities and remedial education* (pp. 93–107). Austin, TX: PRO-ED.

Hiebert, J. (1984). Children's mathematics learning: The struggle to link form and understanding. *The Elementary School Journal, 84,* 497–513.

Hiebert, J. (1987, April). *Transition to the formal languages of mathematics.* Paper presented at the biennial meeting of the Society for Research in Child Development, Baltimore, MD.

Hiebert, J., & Wearne, D. (1984, April). *A model of students' decimal computation procedures.* Paper presented at the annual meeting of the National Council of Teachers of Mathematics, San Francisco.

Holt, J. (1964). *How children fail.* New York: Delta.

Homan, D. R. (1970). The child with a learning disability in arithmetic. *Arithmetic Teacher, 17,* 199–203.

Kaliski, L. (1962). Arithmetic and the brain-injured child. *Arithmetic Teacher, 9,* 245–251.

Kaye, D. B. (1986). The development of mathematical cognition. *Cognitive Development, 1,* 157–170.

Kidron, R. (1985). *Arithmetic disabilities: Characterization, diagnosis and treatment.* Tel Aviv, Israel: Otzar Hamoreh.

Kilpatrick, J. (1985). Doing mathematics without understanding it: A commentary on Higbee and Kunihira. *Educational Psychologists, 20,* 65–68.

Kirk, S. A., & Chalfant, J. L. (1984). *Academic and developmental learning disabilities.* Denver: Love Publishing.

Kosc, L. (1970). A contribution to the nomenclature and classification of disorders in mathematical abilities. *Studia Psychologica, 12,* 12–28.

Kosc, L. (1974). Developmental dyscalculia. *Journal of Learning Disabilities, 7,* 164–177.

Kouba, V. (1986, April). *How young children solve multiplication and division word problems.* Paper presented at the National Council of Teachers of Mathematics research presession, Washington, DC.

Kraner, R. E. (1980). Math deficits of learning disabled first graders with mathematics as a primary and secondary disorder. *Focus on Learning Problems in Mathematics, 2*(3), 7–27.

Lampert, M. (1986). Knowing, doing, and teaching multiplication. *Cognition and Instruction, 3,* 305–342.

Lankford, F. G. (1974). What can a teacher learn about a pupil's thinking, through oral interviews. *Arithmetic Teacher, 21,* 26–32.

Lerner, J. (1971). *Children with learning disabilities.* Boston: Houghton Mifflin.

Lesh, R., Landau, M., & Hamilton, E. (1980). Rational number ideas and the role of representational systems. In R. Karplus (Ed.), *Proceedings of the Fourth International Conference for the Psychology of Mathematics Education* (pp. 50–59). Berkeley, CA: Lawrence Hall of Science.

Lindvall, C. M., & Ibarra, C. G. (1979, April). *The relationship of mode of presentation and of school/community differences to the ability of kindergarten children to comprehend simple story problems.* Paper presented at the annual meeting of the American Educational Research Association, Boston.

Lloyd, J., Saltzman, N., & Kauffman, J. (1981). Predictable generalization in academic learning as a result of preskills and strategy training. *Learning Disability Quarterly, 4,* 203–216.

Lunkenbein, D. (1985, April). *Cognitive structures underlying processes and conceptions in geometry.* Paper presented at the research presession of the annual meeting of the National Council of Teachers of Mathematics, San Antonio, TX.

Luria, A. R. (1969). On the pathology of computational observation. In J. Kilpatrick & I. Wirszup (Eds.), *Soviet studies in the psychology of learning and teaching mathematics* (Vol. 1, pp. 37–74). Chicago: University of Chicago Press.

Mann, P. H., & Suiter, P. (1974). *Handbook in diagnostic teaching: A learning disabilities approach.* Boston: Allyn and Bacon.

Meyers, M. J., & Burton, G. M. (1989). Yes you can ... Plan appropriate instruction for learning disabled students. *Arithmetic Teacher, 36*(7), 46–50.

Moyer, M. B., & Moyer, J. C. (1985). Ensuring that practice makes perfect: Implications for children with learning difficulties. *Arithmetic Teacher, 33*(1), 40–42.

Myers, A. C., & Thornton, C. A. (1977). The learning disabled child—Learning the basic facts. *Arithmetic Teacher, 25*(3), 46–50.

Nesher, P. (1986). Learning mathematics: A cognitive perspective. *American Psychologist, 41,* 1114–1122.

Norman, D. D., & Rumelhart, D. E. (1975). *Explorations in cognition.* San Francisco: W. H. Freeman.

Palincsar, A. S. (1986). Metacognitive strategy instruction. *Exceptional Children, 53,* 118–124.

Pellegrino, J. W., & Goldman, S. R. (1987). Information processing and elementary mathematics. *Journal of Learning Disabilities, 20,* 23–32, 57.

Piaget, J. (1964). Development and learning. In R. E. Ripple & V. N. Rockcastle (Eds.), *Piaget rediscovered* (pp. 7–20). Ithaca, NY: Cornell University.

Piaget, J. (1965). *The child's conception of number.* New York: Norton.

Piaget, J., & Inhelder, B. (1969). *The psychology of the child.* New York: Basic Books.

Post, T. R., Wachsmuth, I., Lesh, R., & Behr, M. J. (1985). Order and equivalence of rationale numbers: A cognitive analysis. *Journal for Research in Mathematics Education, 16,* 18–36.

Pressley, M., Goodchild, F., Fleet, J., Zajchowski, R., & Evans, E. D. (1989). The challenges of classroom strategy instruction. *Elementary School Journal, 89,* 301–342.

Reeve, R. A., & Brown, A. L. (1985). Metacognition reconsidered. Implications for intervention research. *Abnormal Child Psychology, 13,* 343–356.

Reid, D. K., & Hresko, W. P. (1981). *A cognitive approach to learning disabilities.* New York: McGraw-Hill.

Resnick, L. B. (1982). Syntax and semantics in learning to subtract. In T. P. Carpenter, J. M. Moser, & T. A. Romberg (Eds.), *Addition and subtraction: A cognitive perspective* (pp. 136–155). Hillsdale, NJ: Erlbaum.

Resnick, L. B. (1983). A developmental theory of numbers understanding. In H. P. Ginsburg (Ed.), *The development of mathematical thinking* (pp. 109–151). New York: Academic Press.

Resnick, L. B., & Ford, W. W. (1981). *The psychology of mathematics for instruction.* Hillsdale, NJ: Erlbaum.

Resnick, L. B., Nesher, P., Leonard, F., Magone, M., Omanson, S., & Peled, I. (1989). Conceptual bases for arithmetic errors: The case of decimal fractions. *Journal for Research in Mathematics Education, 20,* 8–27.

Reyes, L. H. (1984). Affective variables and mathematics education. *Elementary School Journal, 84,* 558–581.

Riley, M. S., Greeno, J. G., & Heller, J. I. (1983). Development of children's problem-solving ability in arithmetic. In H. P. Ginsburg (Ed.), *The development of mathematical thinking* (pp. 153–200). New York: Academic Press.

Ross, S. (1989a, April). *Children's interpretations of two-digit numerals: Face value or place value?* Paper presented at the annual meeting of the American Educational Research Association, San Francisco.

Ross, S. H. (1989b). Parts, wholes, and place value: A developmental view. *Arithmetic Teacher, 36*(6), 47–51.

Rourke, B. P., & Strang, J. D. (1983). Subtypes of reading and arithmetic disabilities: A neuropsychological analysis. In M. Rutter (Ed.), *Developmental neuropsychiatry* (pp. 473–488). New York: Guilford Press.

Russell, R., & Ginsburg, H. P. (1984). Cognitive analysis of children's mathematics difficulties. *Cognition and Instruction, 1*, 217–244.

Ryan, E. B., Short, E., & Weed, K. A. (1986). The role of cognitive strategy training in improving academic performance of learning disabled children. *Journal of Learning Disabilities, 9*, 521–529.

Schaeffer, B., Eggleston, V., & Scott, J. (1974). Number development in young children. *Cognitive Psychology, 6*, 357–379.

Scheid, K. (1989). *Cognitive and metacognitive learning strategies: Their role in the instruction of special education students.* Columbus, OH: LINC Resources.

Schoenfeld, A. H. (1985). *Mathematical problem solving.* New York: Academic Press.

Scruggs, T. E., & Mastropieri, M. A. (1986). Academic characteristics of behaviorally disordered and learning disabled students. *Behavioral Disorders, 11*, 184–190.

Sears, C. J. (1986). Mathematics for the learning disabled child in the regular classroom. *Arithmetic Teacher, 33*(5), 5–11.

Secada, W. G., Fuson, K. C., & Hall, J. (1983). The transition from counting-all to counting-on in addition. *Journal for Research in Mathematics Education, 14*, 47–57.

Schuell, T. J. (1986). Cognitive conceptions of learning. *Review of Educational Research, 56*, 411–436.

Siegel, L. S., & Linder, B. A. (1984). Short-term memory processes in children with reading and arithmetic learning disabilities. *Developmental Psychology, 20*, 200–207.

Siegel, S. (1957). Discrimination among mental defective, normal, schizophrenic and brain-damaged subjects on the visual verbal concept formation test. *American Journal of Mental Deficiency, 62*, 338–343.

Siegler, R. S. (1987). Strategy choices in subtraction. In J. Sloboda & D. Rogers (Eds.), *Cognitive process in mathematics* (pp. 81–106). Oxford, England: Oxford University Press.

Silver, E. A. (1983). Probing young adults' thinking about rational numbers. *Focus on Learning Problems in Mathematics, 5*, 105–117.

Slife, B. D., Weiss, J., & Bell, T. (1985). Separability of metacognition and cognition: Problem-solving in learning disabled and regular students. *Journal of Educational Psychology, 77*, 437–444.

Smith, J. H. (1921). Arithmetical combinations. *Elementary School Journal, 10*, 762–770.

Spitzer, H. F. (1954). *The teaching of arithmetic* (2nd ed.). Boston: Houghton Mifflin.

Starkey, P., & Gelman, R. (1982). The development of addition and subtraction abilities prior to formal schooling in arithmetic. In T. P. Carpenter, J. M. Moser, & T. A. Romberg (Eds.), *Addition and subtraction: A cognitive perspective* (pp. 99–106). Hillsdale, NJ: Erlbaum.

Steffe, L. P., von Glasersfeld, E., Richards, J., & Cobb, P. (1983). *Children's counting types.* New York: Praeger.

Stern, C. (1949). *Children discover arithmetic.* New York: Harpers.

Sternberg, R. J. (Ed.). (1984a). *Mechanisms of cognitive development.* New York: W. H. Freeman.

Sternberg, R. J. (Ed.), (1984b). *Human abilities: An information processing approach.* New York: W. H. Freeman.

Strauss, A. A., & Kephart, N. C. (1955). *Psychopathology and education of the brain-injured child. Vol. II. Progress in theory and clinic.* New York: Grune and Stratton.

Strauss, A. A., & Lehtinen, L. E. (1947). *Psychopathology and education of the brain-injured child.* New York: Grune and Stratton.

Suydam, M. N., & Osborne, A. (1977). *The status of pre-college science, mathematics, and social science education: 1955–1975. Vol. II: Mathematics education.* Columbus, OH: The Ohio State University Center for Science and Mathematics Education.

Svenson, O., & Broquist, S. (1975). Strategies for solving simple addition problems: A comparison of normal and subnormal children. *Scandinavian Journal of Psychology, 16,* 143–151.

Swanson, H. L. (1982). A multidirectional model for assessing learning disabled students' intelligence: An information processing framework. *Learning Disability Quarterly, 5,* 312–326.

Swanson, H. L., & Rhine, B. (1985). Strategy transformations in learning disabled children's math performance: Clues to the development of expertise. *Journal of Learning Disabilities, 18,* 596–603.

Thornton, C. A. (1978). Emphasizing thinking strategies in basic fact instruction. *Journal for Research in Mathematics Education, 9,* 214–227.

Thornton, C. A., & Bley, N. S. (1982). Problem solving: Help in the right direction for LD students. *Arithmetic Teacher, 29*(6), 26–41.

Thornton, C. A., Jones, G. A., & Toohey, M. A. (1983). A multisensory approach to thinking strategies for remedial instruction in basic addition facts. *Journal for Research in Mathematics Education, 14,* 198–203.

Thornton, C. A., & Toohey, M. A. (1985). Basic math facts: Guidelines for teaching and learning. *Learning Disabilities Focus, 1*(1), 44–57.

Tobias, S. (1978). *Overcoming math anxiety.* New York: Norton.

Torgesen, J. K., & Young, K. A. (1983). Priorities for the use of microcomputers with learning disabled children. *Journal of Learning Disabilities, 16,* 234–237.

Tucker, J. A. (1985). Curriculum-based assessment: An introduction. *Exceptional Children, 52,* 199–204.

Van de Walle, J., & Thompson, C. S. (1984). Fractions with fraction strips. *Arithmetic Teacher, 32*(4), 4–9.

van Erp, J. W. M., & Heshusius, L. (1986). Action psychology: Learning as the interiorization of action in early instruction of mathematically disabled learners. *Journal of Learning Disabilities, 19,* 274–279.

Van Lehn, K. (1983). On the representation of procedures in repair theory. In H. P. Ginsburg (Ed.), *The development of mathematical thinking* (pp. 197–252). New York: Academic Press.

Vellutino, F. R., Steger, B. M., Moyer, S. C., Harding, C. J., & Niles, J. A. (1977). Has the perceptual deficit hypothesis led us astray? *Journal of Learning Disabilities, 10,* 375–385.

Vygotsky, L. S. (1978). *Mind in society: The development of higher psychological processes.* Cambridge, MA: Harvard University Press.

Weaver, J. F. (1982). Interpretation of number operations and symbolic representations of addition and subtraction. In T. P. Carpenter, J. M. Moser, & T. A. Romberg (Eds.), *Addition and subtraction: A cognitive perspective* (pp. 60–66). Hillsdale, NJ: Erlbaum.

Webster, R. E. (1979). Visual and aural short-term memory capacity deficits in mathematically disabled students. *Journal of Educational Research, 72,* 277–283.

Webster, R. E. (1980). Short-term memory in mathematics-proficient and mathematics-disabled students as a function of input-modality/output-modality pairings. *Journal of Special Education, 14,* 67–78.

Weiner, S. L. (1974). On the development of more and less. *Journal of Experimental Child Psychology, 17,* 271–287.

Wertheimer, M. (1945). *Productive thinking.* New York: Harper and Row.

Wynroth, L. (1986). *Wynroth math program—The natural numbers sequence.* Ithaca, NY: Wynroth Math Program.

Ysseldyke, J. E., & Algozzine, B. (1983). LD or not LD: That's not the question! *Annual Review of Learning Disabilities, 1,* 26–28.

15

Future Perspectives

LOUS HESHUSIUS

This chapter explores implications of what is involved in the current major paradigm shift occurring across the sciences and social sciences. This shift is away from mechanistic explanations of our understandings of what counts as real and how we may know and toward a holistic one. Holism is not a new theory, but a new way of seeing within which existing theories are *transformed* so that their most basic assumptions are no longer the same. Paradigm shifts of this magnitude rarely occur and are never merely intellectual, cognitive shifts, but are related with one's entire outlook on life.

This chapter provides an introduction to the current paradigm shift and its relation to the field of learning disabilities. It also provides a selective bibliography that categorizes some key readings. This bibliography is by no means exhaustive: The literature related to this paradigm shift is mushrooming. I have chosen sources that have been critical in the development of my own understandings. I hope that this chapter and its references inspire the reader not familiar with this literature to pursue the study of this fascinating and important shift.

The author would like to thank Neita Israelite of York University for her helpful comments on an earlier draft of this paper.

The chapter addresses two major questions: (a) What constitutes the shift away from a mechanistic paradigm to a holistic one? (b) How does the paradigm shift relate to the field of learning disabilities?

HOW DO PEOPLE DECIDE WHAT COUNTS AS REAL FOR THEM?

> I spent that first day picking holes in paper, then went home in a smoldering temper.
> "What's the matter, Love? Didn't he like it at school, then?"
> "They never gave me the present."
> "Present? What present?"
> "They said they'd give me a present."
> "Well, now, I'm sure they didn't."
> "They did! They said 'You're Laurie Lee, aren't you? Well you just sit there for the present.' I sat there all day but I never got it.
> I ain't going back there again." (Laurie Lee)

This vignette, recorded by Donaldson (1978, p. 9), vividly illustrates some central points of holistic thought: What counts as real and how we know about it are human constructions, constructions of which we ourselves are an inextricable part. What is real is a construction shaped by each person's unique personal, social, cultural, and political place in the world and by his or her immediate needs, motivations, and *purposes*. What Laurie Lee, the teacher, and the parent each "knows" is guided by his or her own sense-making abilities. (Although this example relates to the individual, the same, as we will see, holds for communal knowing, including scientific knowing.) Donaldson commented that the obvious way to explain this episode is to say that the child did not understand the adult. Yet, on very little reflection, it becomes clear that the adult also failed to understand the child. The adult did not place himself or herself imaginatively at the child's point of view. Donaldson proceeded to illustrate how Piaget (whose work she nevertheless highly respects) ignored the contextual ways in which children make sense, or rather cannot always make sense, out of tasks presented to them. If Piagetian tasks are recast in contexts that are familiar to children so that they can use *their* understandings of the motivations and intentions of the characters involved in the tasks and of the experimenter's intention and use of language, and can act in ways congruent with *their* personal purposes, they can perform important cognitive functions at much younger ages than Piaget thought possible (see also Gardner, 1983, pp. 21, 84).

Another illustration of how human beings act in ways congruent with their personal perceptions of meaning when they engage in learning can be seen in a qualitative study by Polakov (1986). Polakov was interested in the child's experience of literary acquisition. She talked at length with children about their reading at home and at school, and also obtained their views on the basal reader series they were using in their kindergarten program. The following is a page from the children's basal reader (Polakov, 1986, p. 41) in which reading is reduced to word recognition and is disembedded and separated from story engagement and from the real lives of children. This format is fairly common to remedial materials used in many programs for students with learning disabilities.

Little ant
Big ant
Walk, little ant, walk
Little ant hill
Big ant hill
Walk to little ant hill
Walk to big ant hill
Funny little ant
Funny big ant

This is how the children in Polakov's study viewed these materials:

Liz: The stories are too boring . . . they're so dumb and boring . . . and I hate those dopey books and the worksheets. . . . We have to sit there and do this and that and worksheets all the time.
Val: What do you think kids could tell the people who write those books?
Liz: Tell the teachers not to get those books anymore.
Val: What books should the teachers get?
Liz: Get the books that are more interesting so kids will like to read the stories.
Val: Sasha, if you were the boss of the class what would you change?
Sasha: I'd get the *Ant and Bee* books—'cos the story is fun and the kid reads the red words and the big person reads the black words and you both read the story *together*. And it has much more pages. In kindergarten the books are dumb and there are little papers with the words on and you have to write them and it's so boring—I sit there and try to make up my own story out of the words so it's more interesting.

When Polakov asked how Liz knows how to read a story with rather difficult words in it, Liz said,

Well, I read this book a lot of times and also I see the picture in my head, and how it sounds in my ears—and also 'cos it's *my favorite book*. I always know the words in my *favorite* books. (Polakov, 1986, pp. 40–42)

Poplin recalled a similar interchange when she asked a child how he knew how to spell the word "horse." He said, "in utter disgust at my naivete, 'Because I love them'" (Poplin, 1988a, p. 410).

Personal values, emotions, and goals (all shaped by one's place in the world) constitute the most basic impulse to learning, and these are recognized and capitalized upon within the emerging science of wholeness. Theory building in the field of learning disabilities has moved through several phases of attempting to isolate one aspect of human learning as *the* single cause for hypothesized learning disabilities. We first put the blame on neurology and poor memory and attention, moved on to faultily learned behaviors, and more recently shifted to ineffective cognitive and information processing strategies. The emerging science of wholeness, however, points to the futility of this search for independent causes: What we have considered independent factors are not independent. They do not have an existence of their own. Neurology, behavior, and cognition—however important they all are—are now seen to be molded by and subservient to the holistic nature of inherent meaning-making activity. Emotions, values, and goals, long severed from scientific inquiry because of their nonmaterial nature, have been restored to their central place in the emerging science of wholeness (Bohm & Peat, 1987; Briggs & Peat, 1984; Cousins, 1985; LeShan & Margenau, 1982; Prigogine & Stengers, 1984).

To welcome holistic principles for the study of how people learn, we do not have to rely exclusively on what people (including ourselves) can tell about their learning. With regard to research on brain function, Nobel laureates Roger Sperry (biology) and Sir John Eccles (neuroscience) (in Cousins, 1985, pp. 45, 174) concluded that current scientific evidence compellingly shows that brain activities are *not* in first instance directly caused by neurological activity (which has been the standard position). The brain functions holistically: Intentions, values, and goals exert top–down "causal control" over brain activities. Emotional aspects of human behavior appear to be "an eminently conscious property": "The key development here is a new causal interpretation that ascribes to inner experience an integral causal control role in brain function and behavior" (Sperry, in Cousins, 1985, p. 45).

Cousins (1985, p. 45) commented that our customary attitude toward the emotional components of brain processing has been irritation or bemusement since we believed in "pure cognition." Today's understanding of the brain, however, clearly suggests that emotions, in all their finely graded shadings, contribute to cognitive processes across both hemispheres of the brain. This means, in fact, that emotions are an intrinsic part of what we have always called "thinking." Bohm and Peat (1987) wrote, "Intellect, emotion, and will cannot actually be separated, and the connection is so intimate . . . that there is no point at which one of them ends and the others begin" (pp. 218–219).

For educators, this holistic turn in our understanding of brain function and the fundamental relationship between brain function and consciousness (of which intentions, feelings, and values are both eminent and immanent parts) necessitates a fundamental reorientation of how we think about teaching children who do not learn well in school. The force of such reorientation needs to steer us away from considering isolated factors (neurology, behavior, cognition) as primarily and fundamentally responsible for learning and not learning, and therefore as dictating the essence of assessment and instruction. We can no longer avoid emotions, passions, interests, and values as fundamental to all aspects of learning and knowing (although these are viewed as "dirty words" in mainstream social science and professional journals; Poplin, 1988a, p. 409). Instead, they must be accorded a central place within a holistic conception of what it means to do science, not only with regard to understanding human behavior, but also with regard to the formal endeavor of science itself (see Bohm & Peat, 1987; Briggs & Peat, 1984; Cousins, 1985; Prigogine & Stengers, 1984).

Before starting the more systematic overview of issues, I would like to illustrate the power of emotions, needs, and perceptions on learning. Gil, now a successful industrial arts high school teacher, who had major problems learning to read (and who, at a later age, taught himself to read sufficiently well to make it through college), recalled,

> I still can hear my parents say, he was so smart when he was in kindergarten and in first grade . . . When I went to third grade, I just went right down the tube . . . But I was still the cool guy in the class, and I had an image to live up to. I didn't want anybody taking that image away from me . . . when it came time to read in class, I would be a real pain so I wouldn't have to read. I'd do anything to get out of it. Like things that I don't want to say because they are not too cool.
>
> And then she [teacher] called on me and I would be so hyped that I would say: "I'm not reading . . . I'm not reading this junk," and then I would just walk out of the class . . . They had no way of testing me how I really was, because you know something, any test that I took I just checked off. I just wanted to get out of there you know. (Heshusius, 1984a, p. 473)

Emotions, resistance, the personal/political act to do whatever is necessary to "save face," all permeated Gil's experiences and definitions of "learning" in school.

WHAT CONSTITUTES THE SHIFT AWAY FROM A MECHANISTIC PARADIGM TO A HOLISTIC ONE?

The Functions of a Paradigm and a Paradigm Shift

A paradigm has been described as a worldview; a way of seeing that is also a way of not seeing; a set of "ultimate benchmarks"; those most fundamental sets of beliefs by which we think, feel, and act, but of which we may not be aware. Paradigms represent "a distillation of what we think about the world, but cannot prove" (Lincoln & Guba, 1985, p. 115). Through paradigms, we construct answers to the following questions: (a) What counts as real (and, by implication, what does not count as real)? (b) How do we allow each other (and how not) to construct knowledge about what counts as real? (c) How do we account for change and stability? (Battista, 1982, p. 209). Paradigms, when made conscious, make explicit how we think about how we think about the phenomena of our interests. A paradigm, as a set of fundamental beliefs, includes reference to values, practices, symbols, methods, models, theories, and the actual criteria employed for problem selection and criteria for evaluation. A paradigm provides a "total" way of seeing and of knowing. Therefore, a paradigm shift fundamentally changes a total way of seeing and of knowing.

As Briggs and Peat (1984) stated, what scientists in the Middle Ages, or in the 17th century, knew about the universe, today's scientists no longer know: "Instead, we 'know' a different universe" (p. 32). For instance, the 17th century scientist knew a universe in which all matter ultimately consisted of solid particles that moved around only when acted upon by external forces. Now, with quantum mechanics, we no longer know such a universe. We now know a universe in which no solid particles are found, but only ever-changing electromagnetic fields. The 17th century universe was known independently of the human observer: It looked the same to everyone. Since Einstein, we do not know a universe that looks the same to everyone. We know a different universe, one that looks different to different observers, depending on their places and velocities.

I would like to jump ahead for a moment and relate this shift concept to the field of learning disabilities. In the 1960s, what the field knew about Jenny who was "learning disabled" was her neurological disorder. Behaviorists a decade later no longer knew this; they "knew" a different Jenny, a Jenny in whom faulty learning had been reinforced. They "knew" that faulty responses could be subtracted from her repertoire of behavior, as others could be added, by the correct programmatic control of stimuli and reinforcement techniques. When the field moved into information processing, Jenny was no longer "known" by her neurology or by her learned behaviors, but by her particular set of cognitive strategies, or lack thereof. For the purpose of this chapter, however, what these models have *in common*, regardless of their major theoretical differences, is a mechanistic–reductionistic way of "thinking about thinking" about the phenomena of interest. These commonalities are many and are profound (see Tables 15–1 and 15–3). The second part of this chapter describes how Jenny may be "known" differently again through a holistic construction of reality.

Briggs and Peat (1984) provided an illustration of what it means to "shift" (see Figure 15–1). The shift in Briggs and Peat's example is illustrated at the visual–perceptual level, but it nevertheless clearly shows how one can see totally different things in the "same" phenomenon. It shows that there

Figure 15-1.   To believe it is to see it. From *The Looking Glass Universe: The Emerging Science of Wholeness* (p. 25) by John P. Briggs and F. David Peat, 1984. New York: Simon and Schuster. Reprinted with permission.

are, in fact, no phenomena independent of what we think we are going to see. In more scholarly terms, there are no data, no facts, independent of theory and of values. Do you see the rabbit? What about the duck? You can make yourself shift, literally, from one meaning to the other, while looking at exactly the same imprints on paper. You can consciously tell your mind what to see. There are real, conscious choices to be made. This duck–rabbit shift also nicely illustrates that one cannot see the two meanings *simultaneously:* They are incompatible.

The paradigm shift discussed in this chapter is between two ways of constructing our understanding of what counts as real and how we may know. More complicated than a simple visual–perceptual shift of imprints on paper, the paradigm shift deals, as we will see, with fundamentally different assumptions about how we understand and can know the world and ourselves.

During most of a paradigm's life, its fundamental beliefs are taken for granted as if no others could exist, and we are unaware of the most basic assumptions by which we function. We are unaware that there are other ways of seeing. When the assumptions no longer provide adequate answers to important questions of the time, and when events occur for which the paradigm cannot account, and questions are raised that the paradigm cannot answer, the process of becoming self-conscious about the paradigm's boundaries occur. (For further discussion on the concept of paradigm and paradigm shifts, see Battista, 1982; Briggs & Peat, 1984; Capra, 1982; Heshusius, 1989; LeShan & Margenau, 1982; Lincoln & Guba, 1985.)

Major Assumptions of Mechanistic Thought

Many accounts have traced the dominant paradigm of the last three centuries to the rise of the natural sciences during the 17th century when such giants as Descartes, Newton, Locke, and Bacon lifted us out of the authority of the church and the aristocracy of the Middle Ages and into the authority of their own particular constructions of science and the philosophy of science. Their mechanistic assumptions about what counts as real and how we are allowed to know about it has guided intellectual and practical life since that time.

Although I am using the term "mechanistic," the labels "Newtonian," "atomistic," "rational–technical," and "reductionistic" also refer to the same set of beliefs and assumptions. The use of different terms is often related to the particular discipline or field of inquiry used as point of departure, or to the particular assumption an author stresses. Poplin (1988b), for instance, analyzes the field of learning disabilities in the light of the assumption of reductionism, a basic belief about the nature of reality and of knowing inherent in the 17th century paradigm. The use of different labels for the same set of principles should not confuse the reader once the assumptions of the paradigm are grasped and the synchronicity of all assumptions within the paradigm are understood.

The major fundamental beliefs underlying the mechanistic paradigm are listed in the left column of Table 15–1. These are the belief in the possibility of separating fact from value and the knower from the known by the use of a method; the belief in a reality as objective, atomistic, reductionistic, potentially predictable, and certain; and the belief in a reality that can be understood only by breaking it into components and mastering it through mathematical formulations. The nature of the processes involved in progress is seen as causal, additive, sequential, continuous, and the same for all organisms and systems. Table 15–1 further summarizes how these paradigmatic assumptions in general have been translated into special education theory and practice.

Although the mechanistic paradigm has been with us for some 300 years, accounts of its inadequacies and, in fact, of its demise are mushrooming. Ironically, physics, the field in which the mechanistic paradigm was constructed, was the first area of study to call it into question. Other areas of inquiry that have debunked mechanistic assumptions include ecology, holistic medicine, feminist thought on the impact of gender on definitions of what it means to be scientific, the sociology of knowledge, and qualitative approaches to inquiry in the social sciences. LeShan and Margenau (1982), Capra (1982), and Polkinghorne (1983) observed that, for the first time in 300 years, we are asking fundamental questions again.

TABLE 15-1
Key Assumptions of the Mechanistic Paradigm

Key Assumptions	Translations into Special Education Theory and Practice
The Nature of Reality	
• Is objective. Fact can be separated from value, the observer from the observed, the knower from the known.	• Attempts to objectify knowledge and knowing; only that which can be reliably measured gains the status of formal knowledge; categorization of exceptionalities by objective diagnoses; right–wrong answers, errorless learning.
• Is understood through a mathematical symbol system.	• Quantification and ranking (statistically significant findings, frequency counts, test scores) as indices of children's real abilities; diagnostic testing.
• Is reductionistic. The dynamics of the whole can be understood from the properties of the parts.	• Learning equates mastery of lengthy sequences of processes, behaviors, and learning strategies; focus on deficits within the student.
• Consists of components. Knowledge of pieces adds up to knowledge of the whole. Order is brought about by exerting external control.	• Isolated skill training, worksheets, bottom–up approaches to literacy; task analysis; learning equates mastery of predetermined, known curriculum outcomes.
• Can be known with certainty with the gathering of sufficient data.	• Predictive instruments, search for causality in diagnosis; answers to problems lie in "more research" and "more data."

TABLE 15-1 (continued)

Key Assumptions	Translations into Special Education Theory and Practice
The Nature of Progress	
• Is deterministic. All events have direct causes and consequences.	• Causal linkages between diagnoses and instruction; task analysis, mastery learning; precision teaching; programmed and sequentialized materials; controlled vocabulary; daily charting; curriculum-based assessment; "individualized" education (meaning the same for all students but at their own pace).
• Is additive, incremental, sequential, and continuous, which leads to prediction and control. Progress is brought about under conditions of external control through the use of "method."	
• Is the same regardless of personal meaning and context.	
The Nature of the Organism/System	
• Is reactive.	• Behaviorism, stimulus control, reinforcement, input–output models; unidirectional control of curriculum by teacher.

Based on Doll, 1986a, 1986b; Fischer & Rizzo, 1974; Heshusius, 1982, 1984b, 1986a, 1986b; Iano, 1986, 1987; Mitchell, 1980; Poplin, 1984a, 1984b, 1985, 1987.

Adapted from "The Newtonian–Mechanistic Paradigm, Special Education, and Contours of Alternatives" by L. Heshusius, 1989, *Journal of Learning Disabilities, 22*(7), p. 405. Copyright 1989 by PRO-ED. Reprinted with permission.

Major Assumptions of Holistic Thought

Assumptions about what counts as real and how we can know about it have undergone a drastic and most fundamental change in the move from a mechanistic to a holistic paradigm. Again, terminology in naming the paradigm is not always consistent. The terms "emergent," "alternative," "new," and "holistic–constructivist" (see Poplin, 1988a) are also used.

Ecology and modern physics have led us to recognize the complex *interconnectedness* and *interdependency* of *all* events. Today's physics shows that observer and observed are inextricably connected: The observer or the knower creates in a profound way the observed or the known. The very act of observing or of measuring shapes what is observed. Heisenberg's often-quoted dictum states that what we observe is not nature itself, but nature exposed to our ways of questioning. Our ways of observing, measuring, and asking questions decide what we get; that is *we* create our knowledge ourselves. Our knowing *is us*. Therefore, our consciousness about the way we know needs to be explicitly included in the description of what we know. This is what is meant in the statement that science is now understood to be epistemic, or systemic. "Science" (and "research" and "method") are no less but no more than human constructs themselves. They are human agreements, the nature of which has and will change across time, across settings, and across particular ideologies, needs, and interests.

The belief in the possibility of objectivity has been a grand illusion, or, according to Bohm and Peat (1987, p. 51), it has constituted "false play," a pretense that there is no pretense. No method leads to "truth," "proof," or "objective data" that are independent of our own human construction of them. Every method, including what has been called the scientific method, is a value, a choice, a preference, a subjective motive. As Gergen (1987) wrote, "To speak of data is to construct the world in a particular way" (p. 50). This does not mean that we may as well forget about science, method, and research, because we "can't have objective data anyway." Indeed, we cannot have objective data, but that is no problem within contemporary thought. What is meant is that we are in a period of history in which the very definitions of what it means to be scientific and to do research are being reconstructed in a fundamental way. Science and research are no longer seen as primarily methodological endeavors (which is what technology would continue to be), but as centrally human and moral enterprises. Thus, not only what we do with what we come to know engenders human and moral consequences, but *science itself* is seen as an intensely human and moral act. Many issues are of course involved in this reconceptualization of what it means to be scientifically engaged, a discussion of which is beyond the scope of this chapter. Elsewhere (Heshusius, 1989), I briefly discussed some of these issues in relation to the study of exceptionality. For elaborate discussion, see the references noted in Table 15–5.

Another major axiom of the holistic paradigm is that the whole is both *more than* and *different from* the sum of its parts. At the same time, the whole as whole dynamically interacts with its parts, which do not have an independent life of their own. In other words, when we speak of "parts," we are actually trying to talk about something we cannot properly talk about because they do not really exist in themselves. As Briggs and Peat (1984, p. 147) stated, parts are in reality only our abstractions. Therefore, when we talk, in our case, about neurology, memory, attention, behavior, and cognition, we must remain aware that we are trying to isolate something that in reality cannot be isolated, as it comes into being only by virtue of the intricate web of connections involved in human sense-making activity. The emerging science of wholeness is indeed properly referred to by many as "the science of complexity."

Holism, then, reverses the mechanistic–reductionistic position: The dynamics of the whole cannot be understood from the properties of the parts, but rather the properties of the parts can be understood only from the dynamics of the whole. Knowledge of the parts does not lead to knowing the whole. Dynamic and ever-changing *relations,* then, not pieces and parts, form the fundamental "stuff" of which reality is made.

Holism tells us that self-regulation and self-organization of all organisms and systems prevent the existence of fixed and reliable linkages among the whole and its relations. Interrelationships are dynamic and nonlinear. Final stages are unpredictable from initial conditions, because in-between stages occur, not through linear, fixed, sequential processes which we think are under our control (as the mechanistic paradigm believes), but through processes of self-organization and self-regulation in each organism and in each system which are not under our control. Many have argued, for example, that our planet is in its current mess because we have created chaos and disorder through our mechanistic beliefs, which have made us ignore, deny, and thwart the inherent purposiveness and order in all that is. Likewise, as we will see later, holistic assumptions attribute reasons for not learning to the thwarting of self-organization, self-regulation, and inherent purposiveness of the learner.

The basic impulse for growth and progress thus emerges from inherent purpose and inherent order, not from external causal forces. Growth is characterized by the emergence of higher forms of complexity which cannot be explained by mechanistic and reductionistic principles, but are explained by inherent purposiveness and self-organization and self-regulation. Within holistic assumptions, then, *change, progress, or growth does not make reference to a lower order force or part, as does mechanistic–reductionistic thought, but to characteristics of organisms and systems themselves.* Thus, within holistic thought, as we will see later, learning disabilities cannot be attributed to one or even a few isolated factors (which would be the lower order force, or the isolated part, such as behavior, neurology, or information processing), but to characteristics of the very organism–system itself, which, in this case, is the whole learner in a particular context.

I am aware of the cursory nature of this overview of general holistic principles, but I believe that they will become more clear as we proceed. Also, by carefully comparing this general discussion with Table 15–4, the underlying importance of holism for special education should become more transparent. Readers who understand whole language, or are familiar with other forms of holistic education, may already see its relationship to these general holistic principles.

HOW DOES THE PARADIGM SHIFT RELATE TO THE FIELD OF LEARNING DISABILITIES

Mechanistic Assumptions and Learning Disabilities

Table 15–2, based on Poplin (1988b), provides an overview of the mainstream theories in the field of learning disabilities. Table 15–3, based on the same reference, shows how the beliefs inherent in these theories constitute manifestations of reductionism. To *reduce* comes from the Latin verb *reducere,* which means "to pull back," and which connotes that if one thing is reduced to another, it is implied by it. *Reducere* also means "to save": If one idea seems strange, complex, or unacceptable, its meaning can be saved by reducing it to a more familiar or more acceptable one (see LeShan & Margenau, 1982, p. 93). The belief that one could account for complex systems in terms of less complex components has been a fundamental belief in the history of Western science. In recent decades, however, reductionism has been abandoned by modern philosophy of science as an inappropriate way to define what it means to be scientific (for discussions on reductionism, see Briggs & Peat, 1984; Koch, 1981; Poplin, 1988b; Prigogine & Stengers, 1984, pp. 173, 174).

Comparing Tables 15–1, 15–2, and 15–3 should help the reader to see the *synchronization* of all assumptions within the paradigm. Synchronization means that by believing in one assumption, all others are instantly implied. All assumptions are interdependent and parasitic upon each other: They call each other into being. One cannot, for instance, plan instruction according to short-term behavioral objectives without engaging in component analysis, sequencing tasks, objectifying knowledge by stipulating known and fixed outcomes, seeing learning as mastery over these components and sequences, seeing measurement as equivalent to knowing, controlling context, limiting student's initiative, limiting the place of novelty and unpredictability, and placing unidirectional control on assessment and instruction.

We can now refer back to the kindergarten basal reader presenting "Little Ant" and to the many remedial, programmed materials used in learning

TABLE 15–2
Overview of Theoretical Models of Learning Disabilities 1950 to Present

	Medical model (1950s)	Psychological process model (1960s)	Behavioral model (1970s)	Cognitive/learning strategies (1980s)
Emphasis	Neurological pathways	Prerequisite skills for academic success	Academic product or consequent behavior	Information processing and metacognition necessary for academic success
Etiology	Brain damage or dysfunction	Minimal neurological dysfunction	Lack of learned behaviors or learned nonadaptive behaviors	Insufficient strategies or study skills with which to process information necessary for school success
Diagnosis	Largely neurological	Soft neurological signs, psychological process testing; some intelligence and academic tests, or modality frame of reference	Discrepancy between IQ and academic achievement, criterion-referenced tests, and observation of specific academic and social school tasks	Discrepancy between IQ and academic achievement, with cognitive skills tests and/or observation of specific strategies

TABLE 15-2 (continued)

Assessment	Academic assessment, largely anecdotal case studies	Psychological process; some basic academic skills	Testing of student behavior against task analysis of skills, examination of reinforcement contingencies	Testing of student behavior and processing against known cognitive and/or learning strategies used by successful learners, often task analyzed
Instruction/ treatment	Extremely structured, clutter-free environment; motoric and other neurological training; some basic skills emphasis; some medication	Psychological or psycholinguistic training with less emphasis on actual academic skills; medication, sensory integration, and/or modality training	Direct instruction using task analysis of skills (behaviors) and application of reinforcement principles	Direct instruction in strategies used by successful school learners; also use of principles of reinforcement, particularly self-management and self-talk
Goals	Function in community	Function in school; less community emphasis	Almost exclusively school-related goals, some social but primarily academic mainstream	Almost exclusively school-related goals; some social but primarily academic mainstream
Some major figures	Werner, Strauss, Lehtinen, Cruickshank	Kirk, Frostig, Minskoff, Kephart, Barsch, Wepman	Lovitt, Carnine, Jenkins, Haring, Bateman	Torgesen, Hallahan, Deshler, Schumaker, Alley, Meichenbaum, Feuerstein, Wong

From "The Reductionistic Fallacy in Learning Disabilities: Replicating the Past by Reducing the Present" by M. S. Poplin, 1988, *Journal of Learning Disabilities, 21*(7), p. 391. Copyright 1988 by PRO-ED. Reprinted with permission.

TABLE 15-3
**The Reductionistic Fallacy Underlying the Psychological Processing Model,
the Behavioral Model, and the Cognitive/Strategies Model**

---

1. View learning disabilities as discrete, real phenomenon rather than as a possible and still hypothetical explanation of certain phenomena.

2. Place the onus of responsibility for cause and/or cure for learning disabilities directly on the student.

3. Propose a diagnosis of the goal of which is to document specific deficits in the learner.

4. Attempt to segment learning into parts.

5. Propose instructional procedures that reflect the mechanistic belief that instruction is most effective when it is most tightly controlled, leaving the learner predominantly passive. Learning comes into existence only under externally controlled conditions.

6. Prescribe that the diagnosis of the deficit must be also the essence of intervention which makes all intervention deficit driven.

7. Teaching becomes unidirectional controlled intervention.

8. Assume a right and wrong posture about the teaching and learning process.

9. Assume almost exclusively school goals rather than life goals.

10. Support the segregation of students into different categories.

Adapted from "The Reductionistic Fallacy in Learning Disabilities: Replicating the Past by Reducing the Present" by M. S. Poplin, 1988, *Journal of Learning Disabilities, 21*(7), pp. 394–396. Copyright 1988 by PRO-ED. Adapted with permission.

disabilities classrooms and see how they are manifestations of mechanistic–reductionistic assumptions. The following underlie the construction of reading exercises, such as that promoted by the "Little Ant" story: controlled progress through fragmentation; additiveness and sequentiality; objectification of knowledge; controlled context which leads to disembeddedness, to disengagement from storyline, to learning as mastery over components; and so forth. The "Little Ant" story illustrates the reductionistic fallacy, the belief that somehow, miraculously, the whole (reading as the construction of meaning from print) is "saved" in the parts and evolves out of the sum of the parts.

Poplin (1985, 1988b) and Heshusius (1989) probably have provided the most detailed analyses of the inadequacies and untenability of the mechanistic–reductionistic grounding of mainstream theories in learning disabilities;

however, others have provided similar discussions of other aspects of the field of special education (Fischer & Rizzo, 1974; Heshusius, 1982, 1986a, 1986b; Iano, 1986, 1987; Poplin, 1984a, 1984b, 1987; Skrtic, 1986, 1988; Wood & Shears, 1986). Iano (1986, 1987), for instance, focused on teaching, and Skrtic (1988) provided an analysis of the organizational–service delivery aspects of special education. Others have critiqued mechanistic thought in the form of behavioral models with regard to severe disabilities (Ballard, 1987; D. L. Ferguson, 1989; Guess & Siegel, 1988). Still others have acknowledged their sympathy and agreement with these critiques (Forness, 1988; Reid, 1988; Skrtic, 1986).

Holistic Assumptions and What They May Mean to the Field of Learning Disabilities

Table 15–4 draws connections between holistic principles and implications for an understanding of learning (and therefore of not learning). Synchronization among all principles is also a characteristic of the holistic paradigm. For instance, when a child works out a math problem about buying a toy in a store or selling candy at a fair, all holistic principles come into play: personal purpose, self-regulation and self-organization, and relations with symbols and persons for real-life meanings. The beliefs underlying the whole language approach to literacy acquisition likewise involve all holistic educational manifestations.

Table 15–4, at this point, is a pedagogical device, listing what can be gathered from the slowly increasing, but still limited, references that have addressed holistic education. The table is not exhaustive, and I am certain it will need to be refined, extended, and reorganized in the future as we come to understand more thoroughly holism in general and the ways in which it affects the study of human behavior and human learning.

As mainstream theories in the field of learning disabilities share the fundamental mechanistic–reductionistic beliefs (notwithstanding their important theoretical differences), we can see them on a continuum based on what they share. The shift to holistic principles, however, demands a shift in the paradigmatic beliefs themselves. Therefore, holism is a transformation of basic assumptions, rather than a continuation or modification of them. A holistic educator (in an ideal situation, that is, where there would be no mechanistic constraints, a situation of course that is still very rare) would no longer adhere to the basic beliefs of existing models: not in systematic fragmentation and quantification as inherently worthwhile activities; not in the pretense (however well intended) to render "objective data"; not in the superimposition of additive and sequential ordering; and not in the need to endlessly search for variables that are hypothesized to cause learning disabilities and that are then taken to be the real causes according to which instruction, assessment, and

TABLE 15-4
The Emerging Science of Wholeness and Learning

Key Principles	Implications for Understanding Learning
The Nature of Reality	
• Is epistemic: Reality is dependent on our construction of it. Fact cannot be separated from value. The observer cannot be separated from the observed. "Method" itself is a human agreement. There are potentially infinite ways of knowing.	• Learning is the personal–social construction of meaning, which occurs on many levels (intuitive, emotional, rational, kinesthetic, physical, artistic) and is propelled by a person's values and interests. Traditionally hypothesized "causes" for learning (and for not learning) do not have an existence independent from the human need to make sense.
• Is holistic. The whole is more than and different from the sum of the parts. "Parts" are properly relations which can be understood only from the dynamics of the whole.	• Learning starts from the whole, moves to "parts," and back to the whole at a higher level of complexity.
• Is inherently orderly and complex. This order of organized complexity may be discovered. Order cannot be externally forced.	• Understanding the interdependency of relations is central: within oneself (emotional, intellectual, spiritual, artistic, physical), between self and other (community, global, and planetary life), and between subject matter.

TABLE 15–4 (continued)

Key Principles	Implications for Understanding Learning
The Nature of Progress	
• Occurs through dynamic and nonlinear interrelationships. Progress is transformative, integrative, and purposeful.	• Visible progress is not steady and linear, but zigzags. Authentic learning occurs only when learning is connected by the learner to his or her personal uses and purposes. Literacy is acquired for the purpose of authentic communication. What becomes new knowledge is regulated by existing knowledge which the learner reconstructs and transforms.
• Is nondeterministic. The whole reorganizes itself through self-organization and self-regulations. Results of transformation cannot be predicted or controlled from knowledge of initial condition. The whole cannot be explained by knowledge of parts.	• The learner expresses his or her new knowledge in many varied, but equally valid ways, which may well include novel and unpredictable ways. Assessment consists of documenting expressions of learning from multiple (potentially unlimited number) authentic learning situations.

TABLE 15-4 (continued)

Key Principles	Implications for Understanding Learning
The Nature of the Organism/System	
• Is immanently active, inherently goal directed, self-organizing and self-regulating.	• The learner is always learning. He or she always has a purpose for what he or she decides to learn according to the impulse to self-regulate and self-organize. "Errors" are ways of making meaning. There is no "one best way" to learn, and the process of learning can be fostered but not programmed or controlled.
• Is of an open system, always exchanging information with its environment.	• Learning occurs within social, cultural, and political systems of symbols and social exchanges.

remediation should be based. The holistic educator is not obsessed with "variables" because learning, within holism, cannot be explained in terms of one or a few variables. Variables conceived of as isolated causes are a figment of the reductionistic imagination.

Again, the shift to holism does not imply that there are not children who have problems learning what needs to be learned, or that learning has nothing to do with neurology, behavior, or cognition and information processing. Within holistic thought, learning and knowing have neurological, behavioral, and information processing facets to them, but not in their isolated forms causally connected to learning. Rather, they are shaped by and are interdependent and interacting in dynamic, nonlinear ways with other facets of human behavior, and are guided by the intentions of the child as a meaning-needing and meaning-creating human being. Thus, for the holistic educator, although neurological, behavioral, and information processing facets are involved, they do not "cause" learning. This is indeed turning the reductionistic position on its head by stating that a higher from of complexity is not directly brought about by the lower components, and is not contained or "saved" in them. Holism states that a higher form of complexity exercises downward influence on the lower. This holistic position has emerged from the study of subatomic phenomena, chemistry, medicine, ecology, and brain research and is starting to influence an array of other fields.

This position, I believe, is exactly what Poplin (1988a) meant by her discussion of the person's "spiral" as the determiner of what will be and what will not be learned. Poplin borrowed the concept of spiral from Piaget, but in Poplin's version the spiral constitutes all a person's experiences and life circumstances, including the social, cultural, ethnic, and political; the many transformations of past learnings; and his or her present and immediate understandings, interests, motives, reasons, and needs. It is the spiral as a whole, not its pieces (and not what *we* think the child is about or should be about), that determines the interrelated functioning of cognition, emotions, behavior, information processing, and so forth, and, therefore, what will or will not be learned. This means that if one wants to say something valuable about the role of information processing, cognition, neurology, or behavior in learning, or, for that matter, of motivation, purpose, meaning, and so forth, it cannot be validly said in isolation of a person's spiral. It is also to say that, from a holistic perspective, instruction geared primarily toward the abstraction of such isolated variables is doomed in terms of authentic learning outcomes. Of course, one can manage to teach children behaviors, correct responses, or cognitive strategies. None of this is to say that existing models have not, at least to some degree, accomplished, within controlled settings, what they set out to accomplish according to their particular framework. From a holistic perspective, however, it is to say that they can do no more. Their reductionistic design excludes the child as a living organism, ignoring many of the very impulses for authentic learning and thus for generalization. From a holistic perspective, the immense problems of maintenance and generalization that characterize all mainstream models are not surprising. I have always thought that mainstream theories in learning disabilities had it backwards: If one wants learning to be for real-life purposes (which is what all models in their search for generalization wish for), why would one want to start with artificial, synthetic exercises and then worry about "programming" for generalization (Kimball & Heron, 1988, p. 427) or "engineering" for generalization (Meichenbaum, 1983, p. 135)? Why not *start* with real-life purposes? The reductionistic belief that real life can be "saved" when reducing it has engaged us in artificial, synthetic endeavors.

It has been said that if we were to teach 1-year-olds to walk in the fragmented, reductionistic manner that we typically use when following the dictates of mainstream teaching theories, many children would become crippled. Montessori used to say that children learn their native language so well because no one teaches them. I feel sure what she meant was that no one teaches them in artificially structured ways. We do, of course, "teach" our children to talk by interacting with them in real-life, purposeful situations for authentic communication reasons. The current teaching situation illustrates the unbelievable influence the last four centuries of the mechanistic–reductionistic construction have had on our understanding of what counts as real and what does not, and how we may and may not know.

Laurie Lee, Liz, Sasha, and Gil, along with all other human beings, show the holistic educator something more than and different from neurology, cognition, information processing, and/or behavior when they engage in learning, or from the school's perspective, in not learning. Holistic assumptions offer a framework for both addressing other facets involved in learning while conceptualizing learning as more than and different from the sum of facets. If that sounds like a paradox within a mechanistic construction of what counts as real, it is. From a holistic understanding of how reality fits together, however, "facets" are understood to be constituted by the whole, which is an entity in itself and different from the sum of the relations it constitutes.

Once the meanings of self-organization, self-regulation, and dynamic interaction are grasped, it becomes clear that externally controlled, programmed ordering of progress contradicts these crucial holistic principles (indeed contradicts natural learning) and can, in fact, thwart authentic progress. I hope the reader does not, at this point, infer from the self-organization/self-regulation principle a "hands-off" implication for teaching which results in the nice kind of "chaos" not infrequently found in the 1960's laissez faire approach to education. On the contrary, knowledge, guidance, and mentoring are of utter importance. Meaningful progress can be fostered, but not forced or programmatically controlled. Also, such guidance and fostering are not an easier route for teachers to take. I believe that for successful holistic education, a far more thorough understanding of human behavior, of oneself and self-development, of subject matter and its relationship to other subjects, and of the worlds of children (as well as a deep attentiveness and vigilance to all that occurs in one's classroom), is needed than for mechanistically informed teaching.

Documenting Authentic Learning Outcomes (for Assessment)

The holistic principles of self-organization, self-regulation, inherent order, and inherent purpose are beautifully expressed by Ralph Waldo Emerson (in Gilman, 1965, p. 51):

> What can we see or acquire but what we are? You have observed a man reading Virgil. Well, that author is a thousand books to a thousand persons. Take the book into your two hands and read your eyes out, you will never find what I find.

Holistic educators would agree. Learning is a personal–social construction of meaning. With regard to our approaches to assessment (or what I prefer to call documenting authentic learning outcomes), the holistic conception of learning necessitates a fundamental shift. Holistic thought defies the validity of data or evidence in the form of results of standardized testing, or as counting correct responses to predetermined tasks with known outcomes, the key process in the now-popular special education curriculum and data based movements to assessment (see, e.g., Bursuck & Lessen, 1987; Deno, 1985, 1987; Gickling & Thompson, 1985; Tucker, 1985). What holistic thought objects to is not the need for data and evidence, which are important, but the mechanistic construction of the form data and evidence should take.

For the remainder of this section, I have relied primarily on Dudley-Marling (1986), Heshusius (1989), Poplin (1988a), Valencia and Pearson (1988), and Weaver (1982), and will not repeat these particular references throughout.

Holistic thought, then, gives meaning to the terms data and evidence in the form of a record, *a documentation* of what children actually (a) do, not only on their own, but also, and very importantly, in interaction with both teacher and peers; (b) think and feel about what they are doing; and (c) accomplish, when engaged in authentic activities involving reading, writing, math, or any other learning adventure.

Authenticity of that which is used as an indicator of learning is central to any concrete act of assessment. Indicators need to reflect real reading, real writing, and learning for real purposes, rather than exercises in learning. They need to reflect the awareness that different social interchanges with contexts and persons require different learning abilities. They should reflect the *dynamic processes* of the student's actual engagements in thought, feeling, and behavior. Assessment should reflect learning as a *social engagement:* Knowing what a student can do "with some slight assistance" (Donaldson,

1978, p. 104) is as important (and some say more important) as knowing what he or she can do on his or her own. Being helped along a little is the natural way people learn within authentic learning situations. This Vygotskian understanding of learning, with its related concepts of scaffolding and the zone of proximal development, bridges the gap between instruction and assessment by intertwining them. (For a warning of the ease with which these concepts can be translated back into mechanistic forms, if one does not thoroughly grasp the deeper underlying assumptions, see Searle, 1984.)

Holistic assessment understands *variability* to be a key characteristic of all learning. People do not learn in a stable, steadily progressing manner, as mechanistic thought believes. Their progress, instead, zigzags, necessitating time to reflect on and to approach the same concepts from many different perspectives. Learners often fall back somewhat in observable progress when new concepts are introduced or after hard work has been accomplished (see also Gardner, 1983; Graves, 1983). Errors are ways of making meaning, and should never be punished, even if only by counting and recording them as "wrong." Errors are not "wrong" pieces of understanding or of performance; rather, they provide great insights into how the person thinks and are intrinsic, natural, expected, and valued activities in learning. In fact, it has become clear that growth and error naturally "go hand in hand" (Weaver, 1982, p. 439) and that we can stunt growth by penalizing students for making errors. Weaver (1982, p. 443) suggested that we "take delight" in new kinds of errors that often appear when students learn new concepts and see them for what they are: signs of progress. To see errors as meaning-making is also important because young children, in particular, interpret *situations*, not words out of context (see Donaldson, 1978; Erickson, 1984). Thus, it becomes important for the teacher–assessor to inquire into the learner's perception of the entire context when "errors" occur, to understand how the learner has interpreted the task contextually in the first place. This is not to say, however, as Weaver (1982) also stressed, that what the adult mindset calls errors should go unnoticed or ignored. Rather, they should be dealt with nonpunitively within the larger purpose of contextual meaning-making.

Concretely, holistic assessment relies on "kid-watching" (Y. M. Goodman, 1978), on close and continuing observation *and* interaction with children as they engage in authentic learning activities, and on documenting such observation and interaction. Multiplicity of assessment data and assessment sources, from various contexts, is the goal of holistic assessment, not single measures, because holism tries not to fall into the reductionistic fallacy in which learning is reduced to a simplistic entity so that it can be measured by a single or a few measures. It conceives of learning in all its complexity and understands learning to express itself in many, varied, and equally valid ways.

Among possible indicators of authentic learning and possible sources and ways to gather data for assessment are the following: students' thoughts about what they read, their dialogues with peers as they talk about their interpretations of text, their thoughts about what they see as the most important ideas and their decisions how to summarize readings, their generated questions about the material learned, their oral retelling of stories for meaningful purposes (e.g., retelling to young children), their dialogue during writing conferences, their reluctance to stop reading when the period is over, the increased difficulty level in material selected, students' greater concentration during silent reading and greater impatience with disturbances, the quality of their oral reading miscues (see Y. M. Goodman & Burke, 1972), students' recall of past experiences in the construction of new meanings, their dialectic journal-writing approaches, the generation of their own math story problems, the sharing with peers of their favorite parts of readings and of favorite characters, and evidence that they see the relationship of what is learned to other subject areas and to novel situations.

Of course, evidence of accomplishments also comes from settings other than the classroom. Ability to read restaurant menus and TV guides, correct money exchange when buying things, parents' reports about the frequency of and interest in reading, notes students write each other, and letters written to relatives of friends are all valid indicators of learning. Also, and not least important, assessment needs to focus on individual student's needs, concerns, interests, past experiences, and hobbies so that what needs to be learned can be generated through the child's "spiral." These data should be kept in cumulative files, open to both students and parents. Finally, assessment needs to consider the particular teacher–child match (see also Messick, 1984, p. 5) and the mutual trust that is critical to authentic learning processes (see particularly Erickson, 1987; J. Miller, 1988; and Poplin, 1988a for the importance of trust in learning).

Different Levels of Knowing

Within holistic understanding, learning and knowing occur at many different but equally valid and interrelated levels. They occur not only at the rational level, but also at the intuitive, inner, and aesthetic levels, and through fantasy and imagination. It makes no sense to attach a higher level of "reality" or "truth" to one over the other (LeShan & Margenau, 1982; Prigogine & Stengers, 1984). Forms of education that are based on holistic principles— such as the Waldorff schools (including the Waldorff schools for special education, see J. Miller, 1988; Richards, 1980); Ashton-Warner's work (1964; see also J. Miller, 1988; Poplin, 1988a); Ann Sullivan's teaching of Helen Keller; "Snoezelen," a way of being, conceived of originally for severely retarded persons, that frees the person to dwell in a world of their senses as a way to know (see Hulsegge & Verheul, 1986); and whole language approaches to literacy acquisition—all take as their starting point the natural integration and the equal validity of many levels of knowing.

Learning as the Social-Cultural Construction of Meaning

In this section, I discuss in greater detail the framework that holistic thought provides for considering the social–cultural forces that influence a person's construction of meaning, that is, of learning and of knowing. Expanding on earlier work (Heshusius, 1989), I would like to highlight this dimension because it is so glaringly absent from the mainstream theories of learning disabilities, from Piagetian theory (Banks, 1988; Gardner, 1983), and from information processing approaches to learning (Gardner, 1985; Poplin, 1988b).

Erickson (1984, p. 529), in his review of ethnographic studies in cognitive anthropology and anthropological psychology, showed how learning ability, once thought to be innate and relatively context independent, is far more than previously understood to be reflexively constituted in the context of personal and social use and purpose. These studies show that by changing settings, tools, meanings, and symbols, and by changing the social forms of relations among people, one has profoundly changed the nature of the situation, the learning task, and the demands on the ability of the learner. This is so because self-regulation and self-organization are in constant relation to one's environment. Erickson (1984) wrote,

> It is not surprising that a child can display arithmetic competence while dealing with change at the grocery store and yet seem to lack that performance when doing what seems to be the "same" arithmetic problem on a worksheet or at the blackboard, even if the problem were displayed using pictures of coins with which the child is familiar rather than using numerals with which the child might be less familiar. Still, a picture of a coin is not a coin, and relations with the teacher and fellow students are not the same as relations with a store clerk . . . The nature of the task in the store and in the classroom is very different and so is the nature of the abilities required to accomplish it. (p. 529)

Saxe (1988), in a fascinating report on accumulating research on children's out-of-school mathematics, and in his study on Brazilian child candy sellers, showed how real-life versus classroom activities contrast remarkably. Life processes "appeared tightly interwoven with socio-cultural artifacts and supports" (p. 15).

> As an inherent part of candy selling, children must construct fairly complex mathematical goals, goals that take form in a web of such socio-cultural processing as inflating monetary system, practice-linked conventions, and patterns of social interaction. (p. 15)

The key finding of Saxe's study was that sellers, when in school, used their street mathematics to work school math problems, but the influence of schooling on sellers' out-of-school math was not very strong. Saxe concluded that a "worthy objective" is for children to have some "ownership" of classroom mathematics, which is "a possibility only if classroom mathematics becomes transparent and functional to them" (p. 20).

Sarason (cited in McKean, 1985, p. 25) recalled how the light went on for him when he arrived one morning at the institution for mentally retarded persons and heard that several residents whom he had tested and found wanting in intelligence had escaped from the institution. Residents who had not been able to trace their way out of a maze on paper had plotted their way out of a 24-hour supervised institution!

We have tended to assume that differential performance between controlled versus real-life settings on tasks that seem the same occurs because of the concrete–abstract nature of the difference, but the present perspective attributes the difference to far more complex dimensions: those of problem definition by self versus other and of self-regulation and organization in context. When a person has ownership over the formation of a problem, his or her needs, experiences, and interests are intimately involved. The person goes through a series of decision making points, each one engaging both abilities and processes of social interchange with both symbols and people (neither come into play when tracing mazes or doing math problems on worksheets). In school learning, it is not that tasks are "out of context," but that they are in a context in which the power relations and processes of social interchange with people and with symbols are such that the learner has no influence or ownership over problem formation. Typically, the tasks offer little or no context for personal–social use and purpose (see Erickson, 1984, p. 533).

From this perspective, then, different situations and contexts demand different learning abilities. Therefore, different contexts both define and evaluate learning differently. This view can inform the field of learning disabilities, particularly with regard to the different social, cultural, ethnic, gender, and socioeconomic constructions of meaning, and thus of the different ways of learning that children bring to school. Learning processes and learning outcomes that differ from the norm may, in many cases, be neither less nor more than different social, cultural, ethnic, gender, and socioeconomic patterns of interaction and different constructions of what it means to know, what matters and what does not, and how one goes about learning.

Holzman and LaCerva (1986) described how they reached students in a New York, multiracial, inner-city high school class for learning disabilities by situating the use of thought processes directly in the students' social, cultural, and socioeconomic contexts. These were students who "could not" and "would not" write or read and who wanted to "burn all textbooks." Holzman and LaCerva engaged students in discussions about the racism and poverty in their lives as a backdrop for comparing various social studies texts, including one written for students with learning disabilities containing simple vocabulary and few concepts, centering around the history of great (Anglo) men. Students came to see how accounts of history are not objective, but are constructed under constraints of the time, as well as the authors' particular interests. They decided they needed a history book that came out of *their* experiences and started to rewrite their text collectively from their own personal–political perspectives. Students who had refused to read or write for years engaged in the construction of meaning through reading and writing, but only because *their* needs, concerns, interests, and experiences— which deviated considerably from Anglo middle-class symbols, experiences, and social relations—were acknowledged and respected and taken as the point of departure.

Other research has documented how cultural and ethnic backgrounds shape the understanding of what it means to learn and how to go about learning. For non-Anglo students, for instance, learning typically means engaging in cooperation, not in individual competition (against self or against others), as is more often the case for Anglo middle-class children (see Delgado-Gaitan & Trueba, 1985; Trueba, Guthrie, & Au, 1981). With regard to gender, Gilligan (1982) showed that girls learn about moral behavior within the framework of caring and nurturing relationships, whereas boys in our culture more typically develop ideas about moral behavior according to abstract rules. Heath (1982) documented the striking differences in types of cognitive styles and patterns of language use among a middle-class, Anglo, school-oriented community; a Black, mill, rural community; and an Anglo, mill, Appalachian community. She illustrated how "culture" is, in fact, "ways of taking meaning" from the environment. It shapes how children learn to read or to "take meaning" from books. For additional research that addresses the crucial role of culture in learning, see overviews by Erickson (1984), Gardner (1983, 1985), Trueba and Delgado-Gaitan (1988), and a special issue of the *Anthropology and Education Quarterly* on the education of minority students (Jacob & Jordan, 1987).

It is important to stress that cultural shaping does not start later in life, but is present from the start (Gardner, 1983, p. 325). This is not to suggest, however, that the causes of school failure are in the cultural differences in minority children's cognitive styles, their cultural definitions of learning, their different languages, their different styles of nonverbal and verbal interaction, or their different patterns of socialization. We have left behind the derogatory concept of "cultural deprivation" or "cultural disadvantage" of the 1960s and 1970s (and into the early 1980s). We are now behaving a bit more "nicely" by shifting the blame for failure from deprivation and disadvantage to difference. Such a shift, however, is not what is advocated here. Reexamination of the ways in which we construct knowledge, including the phenomenon of "failure" is what is needed. Socio-cultural differences are real enough, but, as McDermott (1987) noted, these differences should not serve to justify the continuation of *our* explaining *their* failure, and then attributing *their failure* to our explanation of their differences:

Perhaps we could find something better to do with our social science. We must be wary of our powers of articulation and explanation when they can keep us systematically dumb about ourselves. . . . The breakthrough comes when we realize that their situation is not theirs alone; it is ours as well. We help to make failure possible by our presence, by our explanations, and by our successes; similarly, those who fail in school, by their presence, by their being explained, by their failures, make our successes possible. This being the case, what would an account of minority school failure look like, but an account of ourselves? (p. 362)

We have not even begun to scratch the surface of what this anthropologically oriented line of research on the school failure of minority students may possibly tell us both about the many minority students we now diagnose as learning disabled and about ourselves as educators and as researchers and theoreticians.

Research on learning as the social–cultural construction of meaning has also led to the development of resistance theory. Learners, when the context in which they find themselves is irrelevant, boring, alienating, or threatening, engage in active resistance according to self-organizing and self-regulating principles. In the beginning of this chapter, we saw how Gil needed to "save face" at all costs. Liz and Sasha resisted the meaningless "Little Ant" story by dreaming away and doing their own thing. Laurie Lee never wanted to go back to school. Researchers (see Erickson, 1984, 1987; McDermott, 1974, 1977; Meek, Armstrong, Austerfield, Graham, & Plackett, 1983; C. M. M. Miller, 1985), using ethnographic methodology, which involves carefully observing and recording what actually goes on in classrooms, have found that children consciously and actively resist what they find boring, alienating, or threatening by engaging in various forms of creative responses in the form of personal–political activities that include acting out, daydreaming, manipulating assignments, and actively working at not working.

Boredom and alienation, I fear, are not uncommon in many classes for students labeled learning disabled. Elsewhere (Heshusius, 1984b), I ventured to record some of my own and my students' struggles with boredom and resistance in the face of mechanistically informed prescriptions for teaching and learning. Adelman and Taylor (1986), Deardorff (1982), Deci and Chandler (1986), Poplin (1988b), F. Smith (1987), J.K. Smith (1983), van Manen (1984), and Wood and Shears (1986), all wrote of the problems of boredom, tediousness, or "amotivation" resulting from skill-based instruction.

Reasons for Not Learning

From an holistic perspective, learning is regarded as the result of many interrelated aspects within holistic human meaning-making, and thus is not learning. Behavior learned in the past, as well as neurological, cognitive, and information processing aspects of human functioning, can all play parts in not learning, but within holistic understanding, none can "cause" learning disabilities "on its own" because the existence of each depends on the inter-relationship to the whole of human sense-making. From our current perspective then, not learning can occur for many complex and interrelated reasons, which include, but may not be limited to, the following: (a) lack of trust and lack of authentic relationship between teacher and student; (b) the "piecemeal philosophy" of mechanistic thought to instruction in which, as someone recently said, the real reason for learning is a "secret that only the teacher knows"; (c) the emphasis on "precision" (see Poplin, 1988b) in which form is valued over purpose and function; (d) the tightly controlled curriculum, which lacks personal purpose and use and lacks the possibility of personal ownership by the student over problem formation and over the learning process, thereby thwarting self-organization and self-regulation; (e) the lack of clarity regarding the relations between subject matters; (f) insufficient previous experience; (g) the cultural–ethnic, gender, and socioeconomic mismatches between teacher and student and between student and the school's or teacher's definition of learning and learning tasks; and (h) any one or any combination of the above, the resulting lack of interest in what the school has to offer, and the resulting diversion of the students' inherent meaning-making needs into other "undesirable" directions (see particularly Poplin, 1988a, for elaboration of several of these reasons involved in not learning; see also J. Miller, 1988).

Learning Disability Theory in Transition

Movements within the field of learning disabilities transform certain aspects of the mechanistic grounding of mainstream theories. Recent sociological and critical theory analyses of the field (see Carrier, 1983, 1987; Coles, 1978, 1987; Franklin, 1987; Sleeter, 1986) have provided explanations for the emergence of the construct of learning disabilities in terms of society's structure and values, rather than in terms of deficits within children. Although this perspective does not challenge mechanistically informed assessment and instruction and does not provide alternative instructional constructs, it contributes to the field's critical self-examination, which is crucial to any process of change.

A second movement that directly addresses instructional principles comes from scholars who bring Piagetian constructs to the field (see, e.g., Reid & Hresko, 1981). These scholars acknowledge, to a far greater extent than do mainstream theories, the complexity of human learning and the centrality of inner activity through the constructs of assimilation and accommodation in constructing a cognitive sense of one's world. These facets of Piagetian theory are certainly compatible with holistic principles. For a holistic educator, Piagetian thought would be far more preferable than mainstream theories of learning disabilities. As was touched upon in the introduction to this chapter, however, Piaget's work is too exclusively cognitive (see also Donaldson, 1978; Gardner, 1985; Poplin, 1988b) and does not deal sufficiently with the inextricable relation between the cognitive, the personal, the emotional, and the social and cultural constructions of meaning by the learner.

Another major influence has been the work by Adelman and Taylor (summarized in Adelman & Taylor, 1986), whose work has focused on the immense importance of motivation and "motivational readiness." I believe their work also contributes greatly to the needed transformation by focusing on the central role of affect and motivation in learning. From a holistic perspective, motivational theories do not yet sufficiently counter the entire web of mechanistic assumptions in assessment and instruction and may perhaps be better interpreted as humanistic education.

CONCLUSION

Holistic assumptions are not new; they have been affecting the disciplines for centuries as an "understream" of mechanistic construction of the world. Holistic principles in education also are not new and can be found in various aspects of the educational philosophy of Steiner (Waldorff schools), Warner, and Pestalozzi (see overview by J. Miller, 1988); in whole language theory; and in forms of qualitative/ethnographic research that are congruent with holistic assumptions (among many others see, e.g., Bogdan & Biklen, 1982; Lincoln & Guba, 1985; Poplin, 1987; J. K. Smith, 1983). (Also see Table 15–5.) What *is* new is that holism has become a major force in nearly all areas of life and study and is no longer an understream, easy to be ignored. Of course, holism too is a paradigm, constrained by the limits of who we currently are and of our present needs, and, in time, it will also show its limitations. It is undeniable, however, that holism currently provides a set of paradigmatic lenses through which we may construct a more adequate representation of what counts as real and how we may know about it. This overview has presented the contours of the importance of holism for constructing conceptions of what "learning" and "not learning" means, while acknowledging that much remains to be refined, documented, and extended.

I am grateful to this book's editors for inviting me to write this chapter and for taking what some may see as a risk. The risk, however, is only a risk within a mechanistic–reductionistic perspective: For many, anxiety is involved in letting go of the belief in the possibility of objectivity and in the realization that we ourselves are constructing what we come to know. What the future of learning disabilities will look like will depend on how we wish to shape it, what we wish to value for the youngsters with whom we interact,

---

TABLE 15–5
Toward a Holistic Paradigm: Selected References

---

a. *Science and Philosophy of Science:*
   Berman, 1984   Cousins, 1985
   Bernstein, 1983   Gould, 1981
   Bohm and Peat, 1987   LeShan and Margenau, 1982
   Briggs and Peat, 1984   Prigogine and Stengers, 1984
   Capra, 1982

b. *Gender and Science:*
   Bordo, 1987   Gilligan, 1982
   Dodson-Gray, 1982   Keller, 1985
   French, 1985

c. *Social Science, Education, Educational Inquiry:*
   Bogdan and Biklen, 1982   Lincoln and Guba, 1985
   Doll, 1986c, 1986b   J. Miller, 1988
   Donmoyer, 1985   Polkinghorne, 1983
   K. S. Goodman, 1982, 1986   J. K. Smith, 1983, 1988
   LeShan and Margenau, 1982   Valle, 1981

d. *Special Education:*
   Fischer and Rizzo, 1974   Iano, 1986, 1987
   Heshusius, 1982, 1989   Poplin, 1988a, 1988b

e. *Culture:*
   Gould, 1981   Takiki, 1979
   Highwater, 1981

f. *Economy and Politics*
   Ferguson, 1980

g. *Religion:*
   Fox, 1983

h. *Special Journal Issues on the Paradigm Shift Toward Holism:*

   Journal of Counseling and Development. Paradigm Shifts: Considerations for Practice. Special Issue, 1985, 64(3).

   Learning Disability Quarterly. Holism. Special Issue, 1984, 7(4).

   Revision. The Journal of Consciousness and Change. Critical Questions About New Paradigm Thinking, 1986, 9(1).

---

and whether we wish to continue to focus on the deficits we have hypothesized for them or on their personal purposes and shared learning characteristics. The most positive message inherent in the emerging science of wholeness is that the choice is up to us.

REFERENCES

Adelman, H. S., & Taylor, L. (1986). *An introduction to learning disabilities.* Glenview, IL: Scott, Foresman.

Ashton-Warner, S. (1964). *Teacher.* New York: Bantam.

Ballard, K. D. (1987). The limitations of behavioural approaches to teaching: Some implications for special education. *The Exceptional Child, 34,* 197–212.

Banks, T. A. (1988). *Multi-ethnic education: Theory and practice.* Boston: Allyn and Bacon.

Battista, J. R. (1982). The holistic paradigm and general system theory. In W. Gray, J. Fidler, & J. Battista (Eds.), *General systems theory and the psychological sciences* (Vol. I, pp. 209–210). Seaside, CA: Intersystems Publications.

Berman, M. (1984). *The reenchantment of the world.* New York: Bantam.

Bernstein, R. J. (1983). *Beyond objectivity and relativity: Science, hermeneutics, and praxis.* Philadelphia: University of Pennsylvania Press.

Bogdan, R. C., & Biklen, S. K. (1982). *Qualitative research for education: An introduction to theory and methods.* Boston: Allyn and Bacon.

Bohm, D., & Peat, F. D. (1987). *Science, order, and creativity.* New York: Bantam.

Bordo, S. R. (1987). *The flight to objectivity: Essays on Cartesianism and culture.* Albany, NY: State University of New York Press.

Briggs, D. P., & Peat, F. D. (1984). *Looking glass universe: The emerging science of wholeness.* New York: Simon and Schuster.

Bursuck, W. D., & Lessen, E. (1987). A classroom-based model for assessing students with learning disabilities. *Learning Disabilities Focus, 3*(1), 17–29.

Capra, F. (1982). *The turning point: Science, society and the rising culture.* New York: Simon and Schuster.

Carrier, J. G. (1983). Explaining educability: An investigation of political support for the Children with Learning Disabilities Act of 1969. *British Journal of Sociology of Education, 4*(2), 125–140.

Carrier, J. G. (1987). The politics of early learning disability theory. In B. M. Franklin (Ed.), *Learning disabilities: Dissenting essays* (pp. 47–66). Philadelphia: Falmer.

Coles, G. C. (1978). The learning disabilities test battery: Empirical and social issues. *Harvard Educational Review, 48,* 313–340.

Coles, G. C. (1987). *The learning mystique. A critical look at "learning disabilities.* New York: Pantheon.

Cousins, N. (1985). *Nobel Prize conversations by Sir John Eccles, Roger Sperry, Ilya Prigogine, Brian Josephson.* Dallas: Saybrook.

Deardorff, B. (1982). Confessions of a former skills teacher. *Learning, 11*(4), 42–43.

Deci, E. L., & Chandler, C. L. (1986). The importance of motivation for the future of the LD field. *Journal of Learning Disabilities, 19*(10), 587–594.

Delgado-Gaitan, C., & Trueba, H. (1985). Ethnographic study of participant structures in task completion: Reinterpretation of "handicaps" in Mexican Children. *Learning Disability Quarterly, 8,* 67–75.

Deno, S. L. (1985). Curriculum-based measurement: The emergent alternative. *Exceptional Children, 52,* 219–232.

Deno, S. L. (1987). Curriculum-based measurement. *Teaching Exceptional Children, 20*(1), 41–42.

Dodson-Gray, E. (1982). *Patriarchy as a conceptual trap.* Wellesley, MA: Roundtable Press.

Doll, W. E. (1986a, October). *Curriculum beyond stability: Schon, Prigogine, Piaget.* Paper presented at Bergamo Curriculum Conference, Bergamo, OH.

Doll, W. E. (1986b). Prigogine: A new sense of order, a new curriculum. *Theory Into Practice, 25*(1), 10–16.

Donaldson, M. (1978). *Children's minds.* New York: Norton.

Donmoyer, R. (1985). The rescue from relativism: Two failed attempts and an alternative strategy. *Educational Researcher, 14*(10), 13–20.

Dudley-Marling, C. (1986). Assessing the written language development of learning disabled children: An holistic perspective. *Canadian Journal of Special Education, 2*(1), 33–43.

Erickson, F. (1984). School literacy, reasoning, and civility: An anthropologist's perspective. *Review of Educational Research, 54,* 525–546.

Erickson, F. (1987). Transformation and school success: The politics and culture of educational achievement. *Anthropology and Education Quarterly, 18,* 335–356.

Ferguson, D. L. (1989). Severity of need and educational excellence: Public school reform and students with disabilities. In D. Biklen, D. Ferguson, & A. Ford (Eds.), *Schooling and Disability* (pp. 25–58). Eighty–eighth Yearbook, National Society for the Study of Education, Part II. Distributed by The University of Chicago Press.

Ferguson, M. (1980). *The Acquarian conspiracy: Personal and social transformation in the 1980s.* Los Angeles: Houghton Mifflin.

Fischer, C. T., & Rizzo, A. A. (1974). A paradigm for humanizing special education. *The Journal of Special Education, 8,* 321–329.

Forness, S. R. (1988). Reductionism, paradigm shifts, and learning disabilities. *Journal of Learning Disabilities, 21*(7), 421–424.

Fox, M. (1983). *Original blessing: A primer in creation spirituality.* Santa Fe, NM: Bear and Co.

Franklin, B. M. (1987). *Learning disabilities: Dissenting essays.* New York: Falmer.

French, M. (1985). *Beyond power: On woman, men, and morals.* New York: Ballantine.

Gardner, H. (1983). *Frames of mind: The theory of multiple intelligences.* New York: Basic Books.

Gardner, H. (1985). *The mind's new science: A history of the cognitive revolution.* New York: Basic Books.

Gergen, K. (1987). On the social construction of knowledge. In K. Westhues (Ed.), *Basic principles for social science in our time* (pp. 38–52). Waterloo, Ontario: University of St. Jerome's College Press.

Gickling, E. E., & Thompson, V. P. (1985). A personal view of curriculum based assessment. *Exceptional Children, 52,* 205–218.

Gilligan, C. (1982). *In a different voice.* Cambridge, MA: Harvard University Press.

Gilman, W. H. (Ed.). (1965). *Selected writing of Ralph Waldo Emerson.* New York: New American Library.

Goodman, K. S. (1982). Revaluing readers and reading. *Topics in Learning and Learning Disabilities, 1*(4), 87–93.

Goodman, K. S. (1986). *What's whole in whole language?* Richmond Hill, Ontario: Scholastic.

Goodman, Y. M. (1978, June). Kid watching: An alternative to testing. *National Principal* (pp. 41–45).

Goodman, Y. M., & Burke, C. L. (1972). *Reading miscue inventory manual: Procedures for diagnosis and evaluation.* New York: Macmillan.

Gould, J. S. (1981). *The mismeasure of man.* New York: Norton.

Graves, D. H. (1983). *Writing: Teachers and children at work.* Portsmouth, NH: Heinemann.

Guess, D., & Siegel, E. (1988). Students with severe and multiple disabilities. In E. L. Meyer & T. M. Skrtic (Eds.), *Exceptional children and youth* (pp. 293–320). Denver: Love.

Heath, S. B. (1982). What no bedtime story means: Narrative skills at home and school. *Language in Society, 11,* 49–76.

Heshusius, L. (1982). At the heart of the advocacy dilemma: A mechanistic world view. *Exceptional Children, 49,* 6–11.

Heshusius, L. (1984a). The survival story of a non-reader: An interview. *Journal of Learning Disabilities, 7*(8), 472–476.

Heshusius, L. (1984b). Why would they and I want to do it? A phenomeno-logical–theoretical view of special education. *Learning Disability Quarterly, 7,* 363–368.

Heshusius, L. (1986a). Paradigm shifts and special education: A response to Ulman and Rosenberg. *Exceptional Children, 52,* 461–465.

Heshusius, L. (1986b). Pedagogy, special education, and the lives of young children: A critical and futuristic perspective. *Journal of Education, 168*(3), 25–38.

Heshusius, L. (1989). The Newtonian-mechanistic paradigm, special education, and contours of alternatives. An overview. *Journal of Learning Disabilities, 22*(7), 403–415.

Highwater, T. (1981). *The primal mind. Vision and reality in Indian America.* New York: New American Library.

Holzman, L., & LaCerva, C. (1986, October). *Development, learning and learning disabilities.* Paper presented at the 8th International Conference on Learning Disabilities, Kansas City, MO.

Hulsegge, J., & Verheul, A. (1986). *Snoezelen: Another world.* Chesterfield, England: Rompa.

Iano, R. P. (1986). The study and development of teaching: With implications for the advancement of special education. *Remedial and Special Education, 7*(5), 50–61.

Iano, R. P. (1987). Rebuttal: Neither the absolute certainty of prescriptive law nor a surrender to mysticism. *Remedial and Special Education, 8*(1), 52–61.

Jacob, E., & Jordan, C. (Guest Eds.). (1987). Explaining the school performance of minority students [Special issue]. *Anthropology and Education Quarterly, 8*(4).

Keller, E. F. (1985). *Reflections on gender and science.* New Haven, CT: Yale University Press.

Kimball, W. H., & Heron, T. E. (1988). A behavioral commentary on Poplin's discussion of reductionistic fallacy and holistic/constructivist principles. *Journal of Learning Disabilities, 21*(7), 425–428.

Koch, S. (1981). The nature and limits of psychological knowledge. *American Psychologist, 36,* 257–269.

LeShan, L., & Margenau, H. (1982). *Einstein's space and van Gogh's sky. Physical reality and beyond.* New York: Macmillan.

Lincoln, Y. S., & Guba, E. G. (1985). *Naturalistic inquiry.* Beverly Hills, CA: Sage.

McDermott, R. P. (1977). The ethnography of speaking and reading. In R. Shuy (Ed.), *Linguistics* (pp. 153–185). Newark, DE: International Reading Association.

McDermott, R. P. (1987). The explanation of minority school failure, again. *Anthropology and Education Quarterly, 18*, 361–375.

McKean, K. (1985). Intelligence: New ways to measure the wisdom of man. *Discover, 6*(10), 25–41.

Meek, M., Armstrong, S., Austerfield, V., Graham, J., & Plackett, E. (1983). *Achieving literacy: Longitudinal studies of adolescents learning to read.* Boston: Routledge and Kegan Paul.

Meichenbaum, D. (1983). Teaching thinking: A cognitive–behavioral approach. In D. Carnine, D. Elkind, A. D. Hendrickson, D. Meichenbaum, R. L. Sieben, & F. Smith (Eds.), *Interdisciplinary voices in learning disabilities and remedial education* (pp. 127–142). Austin, TX: PRO-ED.

Messick, S. (1984). Assessment in context: Appraising student performance in relation to instructional quality. *Educational Researcher, 13*(13), 3–8.

Miller, C. M. M. (1985). *The viability of students with special learning needs remaining in regular classrooms: Perceptions of students, teachers, parents and administrators, and observations of teachers' responses to student diversity.* Unpublished master's thesis, York University, Toronto.

Miller, J. (1988). *The holistic curriculum.* Toronto: OISE Press.

Mitchell, R. M. (1980). Is professionalism succumbing to a push-button mentality? *Counterpoint, 1*(2), 14.

Polakov, V. (1986). On meaningmaking and stories: Young children's experience with texts. *Phenomenology and Pedagogy, 4*(3), 37–47.

Polkinghorne, D. (1983). *Methodology for the human sciences.* Albany: State University of New York Press.

Poplin, M. S. (1984a). Research practices in learning disabilities. *Learning Disability Quarterly, 7*, 2–5.

Poplin, M. S. (1984b). Toward an holistic view of persons with learning disabilities. *Learning Disability Quarterly, 7*, 290–294.

Poplin, M. S. (1985). Reductionism from the medical model to the classroom: The past, present and future of learning disabilities. *Research Communications in Psychology, Psychiatry and Behavior, 10*(1&2), 37–70.

Poplin, M. S. (1987). Self-imposed blindness: The scientific method in education. *Remedial and Special Education, 8*(6), 31–37.

Poplin, M. S. (1988a). Holistic/constructivist principles of the teaching/learning process: Implications for the field of learning disabilities. *Journal of Learning Disabilities, 21*(7), 401–416.

Poplin, M. S. (1988b). The reductionistic fallacy in learning disabilities: Replicating the past by reducing the present. *Journal of Learning Disabilities, 21*(7), 389–400.

Prigogine, I., & Stengers, I. (1984). *Order out of chaos: Man's new dialogue with nature.* New York: Bantam Books.

Reid, D. K. (1988). Reflections on the pragmatics of a paradigm shift. *Journal of Learning Disabilities, 21*(7), 417–420.

Reid, D. K., & Hresko, W. P. (Guest eds.). (1981). Piaget learning and learning disabilities [Special issue]. *Topics in Learning and Learning Disabilities, 1*(1).

Richards, M. V. (1980). *Toward wholeness: Rudolf Steiner education in America.* Middletown, CT: Wesleyan University Press.

Saxe, G. B. (1988). Candy selling and math learning. *Educational Researcher, 17*(6), 14–20.

Searle, D. (1984). Scaffolding: Who's building whose building? *Language Arts, 61*(5), 480–483.

Skrtic, T. M. (1986). The crisis in special education knowledge: A perspective on perspective. *Focus on Exceptional Children, 18*(7), 1–16.

Skrtic, T. M. (1988). The organizational context of special education. In E. L. Meyers & T. M. Skrtic (Eds.), *Exceptional children and youth* (pp. 479–518). Denver: Love.

Sleeter, C. E. (1986). Learning disabilities: The social construction of a special education category. *Exceptional Children, 53*(1), 46–54.

Smith, F. (1987). *Insult to intelligence.* New York: Arbor House.

Smith, J. K. (1983). Quantitative versus qualitative research: An attempt to clarify the issue. *Educational Researcher, 12,* 6–13.

Smith, J. K. (1988). The evaluator/researcher as person vs. the person as evaluator/researcher. *Educational Researcher, 17,* 118–123.

Takiki, R. T. (1979). Iron cages. *Race and culture in 19th century America.* New York: Alfred A. Knopf.

Trueba, H. T., & Delgado-Gaitan, C. (1988). *School and society: Learning content through culture.* New York: Praeger.

Trueba, H. T., Guthrie, G., & Au, K. (Eds.). (1981). *Culture and the bilingual classroom.* Rowley, MA: Newbury House.

Tucker, J. A. (1985). Curriculum-based assessment: An introduction. *Exceptional Children, 52,* 199–204.

Valencia, S. W., & Pearson, P. D. (1988). Principles for classroom comprehension assessment. *Remedial and Special Education, 9*(1), 26–35.

Valle, R. S. (1981). Relativistic quantum psychology. In R. S. Valle & R. von Eckarteberg (Eds.), *The metaphors of consciousness* (pp. 417–434). New York: Plenum Press.

van Manen, M. (1984). "Doing" phenomenological research and writing: An introduction. *Curriculum Practice Monograph Series, 7.* Department of Secondary Education, University of Alberta, Edmonton.

Weaver, C. (1982). Welcoming errors as signs of growth. *Language Arts, 59,* 438–444.

Wood, S., & Shears, B. (1986). *Teaching children with severe learning difficulties: A radical reappraisal.* London: Croom Helm.

Author Index

Subject Index

and standard error of measurement, 231
task analysis, 235
and validity, 231–232
Assimilation, 110, 378
Associationist model of language
development, 327
Associations, 105
Asthma, 77, 80
Attention, 31, 32–35
Attention deficit disorders (ADD)
compared with learning disabilities, 87
definition of, 71–74
diagnostic criteria in DSM-III-R, 35, 36,
85
and diet, 95
and Feingold diet, 95
importance of, 30–35, 36
medications for, 89–93
megavitamin therapy for, 94–95
and neurotransmitters, 75–76
prevalence of, 88
screening and diagnostic tools available
to health professionals, 83, 85
and sugar, 95
typical course of, 87–88
Attention deficit hyperactivity disorder
(ADHD), 35, 36
Attribute assessment model, 223–226, 234
Authenticity, 453
Autoimmune disorders, 77
Automaticity, 145–146
Availability, 254

Base-10 place-value skills and concepts,
408–412
Bayesian estimation, 241
BEAM, 19, 82
Behavioral approach to assessment
conceptual aspects of, 233
differences between attribute and
behavioral model, 234
establishment of content validity,
234–235
limitations of, 236
task analysis, 235
Behavioral model of learning disabilities,
19, 444–446
Behaviorism, 19, 105
Biochemical theories of learning disabilities,
94–96
Biological constructivism, 108–112,
116–119

Boston VA Aphasia Test, 333
Brain electrical activity mapping (BEAM),
19, 75
Brain injury, 162–163
Brain mapping, 19, 75
Brain, study of, 74–76
Buddy system, 50
Bypass techniques, 30

Cancer, 79
Carbarmazepine, 78
Central nervous system dysfunction, 18
Child abuse, 79
Chlorpromazine, 92
Classification, 266, 269, 291
Cleft lip and palate, 20
*Clinical Modification of World Health
Organization's International Classification
of Diseases* (ICD-9-CM), 73
CMV. *See* Cytomegalovirus (CMV)
Cocaine, 78
Coding, 23
Cognition, process of, 105–106
Cognitive apprenticeship, 356, 361
Cognitive approach to learning disabilities
and active learning, 22
and coding, 23
and educational treatment, 25
and knowledge systems, 23–24
overview of, 444–446
principles of learning based on, 25–26
rationale for, 22–25
and utilization of knowledge, 23
Cognitive approach to mathematics instruction, 377–383, 390–401
Cognitive assessment. *See also* Assessment
assumptions of, 252–255
availability versus accessibility, 253–254
components of, 258–267, 290–291
concrete operational range, 285–287
critique of, 288
developmental constraints, 263–264
executive function, 258–261, 290
generalization, 278, 291
issues of, 287–288
knowledge base, 261–265
language competence, 261–262, 290
metacognition, 280–284, 290
model to evaluate language abilities of
learning disabled, 329, 330, 331
ongoing diagnosis and cognitive
curriculum, 306